APPLIED MATHEMATICS FOR TODAY:

SENIOR

SI METRIC EDITION

APPLIED MATHEMATICS FOR TODAY:
SENIOR
SI METRIC EDITION

"The Metric Commission has granted use
of the National Symbol for Metric Conversion"

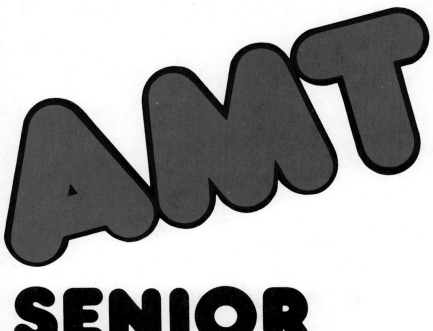

SENIOR

SI METRIC EDITION

Dino Dottori B.Sc.
Head, Mathematics Department
Glendale Secondary School
Hamilton, Ontario

George Knill B.Sc.
Head, Mathematics Department
Sir Allan MacNab Secondary School
Hamilton, Ontario

John Seymour B.A., M.Ed.
Vice Principal
Stuart Scott Public School
Newmarket, Ontario

McGRAW-HILL RYERSON LIMITED

Toronto   Montreal   New York   London   Sydney
Johannesburg   Mexico   Panama   Auckland   Düsseldorf
Singapore   São Paulo   New Delhi
Tokyo   Bogotá   St. Louis   San Francisco   Madrid   Paris

Canadian Cataloguing in Publication Data

DOTTORI, DINO, 1937—
  AMT

ISBN 0-07-082232-8

1. MATHEMATICS — 1961—   I. KNILL, GEORGE, 1938—
II. SEYMOUR, JOHN, 1931—   III. TITLE.   IV. TITLE:
APPLIED MATHEMATICS FOR TODAY.

QA39.2.D68   510   C76-017213-7

APPLIED MATHEMATICS FOR TODAY: SENIOR
BOOK I SECOND EDITION (METRIC)

7 8 9 0 D 6 5 4 3

Illustrations by Samuel Daniel

Printed and bound in Canada

THE RYERSON MATHEMATICS PROGRAM

CORE TEXTS

MATHEMATICS FOR TODAY AND TOMORROW
APPLIED MATHEMATICS FOR TODAY: AN INTRODUCTION
APPLIED MATHEMATICS FOR TODAY: INTERMEDIATE
APPLIED MATHEMATICS FOR TODAY: SENIOR
FOUNDATIONS OF MATHEMATICS FOR TOMORROW: AN INTRODUCTION
FOUNDATIONS OF MATHEMATICS FOR TOMORROW: INTERMEDIATE
FOUNDATIONS OF MATHEMATICS FOR TOMORROW: SENIOR

COMPANION BOOKLETS

MATHEMATICS SKILLBUILDING
MATHEMATICS FOR ENRICHMENT
BUSINESS MATH EXERCISES
TECHNICAL MATH EXERCISES
PERIMETER, AREA AND VOLUME
TRIGONOMETRY
STATICS
MATHEMATICS OF BUSINESS

Applied Mathematics for Today: Senior

This is not a revision, but a new edition of Applied Mathematics for Today Book 2 by Kierstead et al (1970) in the Ryerson Mathematics Program. Pertinent material from the original companion booklets *Statics* and *Mathematics of Business* has been incorporated into this second edition.

Contents

REVIEW AND PREVIEW TO CHAPTER 1

EXERCISE 1

1. Find the grand total by adding both horizontal and vertical totals. Can you add two-digit numbers in one pass?

(a)

2.5	5.8	3.4	0.7	2.3
4.7	9.0	9.6	5.1	1.7
3.8	3.6	4.8	2.8	6.2
5.2	5.1	1.5	3.4	5.3
7.3	1.3	2.6	1.7	9.7

(b)

3.4	4.6	0.4	2.3	3.9
5.2	7.9	5.2	0.0	5.4
7.6	1.4	0.7	5.4	7.6
1.3	3.7	1.3	1.6	2.8
2.5	5.8	4.7	2.8	1.1

"Thanks a million."
If you make $5/h, work an 8 h d, a 5 d week, a 50 week a, how long will it take to make $1 000 000?

(c)

4.2	7.1	6.2	3.2	3.1
3.7	4.8	3.9	1.7	5.2
1.6	5.7	5.8	2.5	4.6
5.8	3.2	4.6	8.1	8.1
2.1	1.5	1.4	6.2	7.4

(d)

5.1	6.1	2.1	6.4	2.2
3.7	2.4	8.7	8.6	4.2
2.8	2.3	6.1	2.2	3.8
8.0	3.3	3.7	6.9	1.7
3.0	9.4	5.6	2.3	1.8

(e)

3.9	4.4	0.1	5.2	3.1
4.5	0.1	5.6	9.1	7.1
4.3	5.0	2.5	6.4	0.5
1.8	7.9	7.6	8.0	8.3
5.9	1.4	2.3	8.6	9.8

(f) Find the grand grand-total.

The Romans expressed all fractions in terms of 12 parts. How would we express their equivalent of $\frac{3+4/12}{12}$? The Latin word for 1/12 is *unciae*. What English word is derived from it?

2. Add:

(a) $\frac{5}{8}+\frac{3}{4}$ (b) $\frac{5}{6}+\frac{1}{3}$ (c) $\frac{4}{9}+\frac{2}{3}$

(d) $\frac{3}{7}+\frac{5}{8}$ (e) $\frac{4}{11}+\frac{2}{3}$ (f) $\frac{4}{7}+\frac{3}{5}$

(g) $\frac{1}{3}+\frac{5}{8}$ (h) $\frac{4}{9}+\frac{2}{5}$ (i) $\frac{3}{8}+\frac{1}{2}$

(j) $\frac{5}{7}+\frac{3}{4}$ (k) $\frac{1}{8}+\frac{1}{3}$ (l) $\frac{5}{13}+\frac{2}{3}$

3. Multiply:

(a) $\frac{2}{3}\times\frac{1}{5}$ (b) $\frac{7}{8}\times\frac{5}{9}$ (c) $\frac{1}{6}\times\frac{5}{8}$

(d) $\frac{3}{4}\times\frac{8}{9}$ (e) $\frac{1}{7}\times\frac{21}{25}$ (f) $\frac{4}{7}\times\frac{21}{44}$

(g) $\frac{4}{9}\times\frac{3}{5}$ (h) $\frac{5}{12}\times\frac{6}{11}$ (i) $\frac{8}{15}\times\frac{12}{13}$

(j) $\frac{15}{28}\times\frac{7}{10}$ (k) $\frac{5}{9}\times\frac{3}{8}$ (l) $\frac{4}{17}\times\frac{17}{20}$

4. Simplify the following:

(a) $\frac{1}{4}\times\frac{4}{7}+\frac{3}{7}\times\frac{2}{3}$ (b) $\frac{2}{5}\times\frac{10}{11}+\frac{6}{11}\times\frac{5}{6}$

(c) $\frac{9}{10}\times\frac{5}{8}+\frac{3}{4}\times\frac{8}{9}$ (d) $\frac{4}{9}\times\frac{3}{8}+\frac{4}{3}\times\frac{1}{2}$

(e) $\frac{5}{6}+\frac{4}{15}\times\frac{5}{8}+\frac{2}{3}$ (f) $\frac{3}{5}+\frac{5}{6}\times\frac{2}{25}-\frac{1}{3}$

(g) $\frac{5}{12}+\frac{2}{3}\times\frac{3}{4}-\frac{7}{12}$ (h) $\frac{4}{7}+\frac{3}{5}\times\frac{10}{21}+\frac{1}{2}$

(i) $\frac{3}{4}(\frac{1}{3}+\frac{1}{2})$ (j) $\frac{5}{6}(\frac{2}{5}+\frac{3}{4})$

(k) $\frac{4}{5}(\frac{1}{3}+3)$ (l) $\frac{3}{4}(\frac{2}{5}+\frac{1}{3})$

5. Simplify to 3 significant figures:

(a) $25.46\times13.2\div5.71$ (b) $73.96\div4.21\times31.5$

(c) $0.0134\times568\div47.1$ (d) $1.784\div15.1\times17.4$

(e) $5.86(47.3+29.6)$ (f) $92.3(14.6-9.8)$

(g) $9.75(43.2+75.8)$ (h) $0.083(784.6+215.4)$

(i) $(5.346+28.654)(0.0593+0.0407)$

(j) $(3.874-1.374)(47.6+52.4)$

Perform the following calculations:

1. $3.675+21.635-15.219$ **2.** $5.675\times21.31\times8.475$

3. $6.875\times8.375\div21.65$ **4.** $84.75\div21.84\times5.395$

5. $51.35+21.6\times53.7$ **6.** $55.37-85.65\div21.65$

7. $83.5\times21.9-152.65$ **8.** $3.585(21.75-18.39)$

9. $(64.75+28.73)\div84.65$ **10.** $(42.65)^2\div85.73$

applied mathematics for today: senior

Probability

1.1 EXPERIMENTS IN PROBABILITY

The following investigations are designed to help develop an intuitive idea of probability. Work together in groups doing the investigations simultaneously if possible. Reproduce the tables shown in the text and fill in the data for your group. When all groups have completed the investigation total the results from all groups, enter them in the table and answer the questions.

INVESTIGATION 1.1

1. Each member of the group will toss 2 coins 25 times. Record the results as in Table 1-1.

Student	Frequency of		
	0 heads	1 head	2 heads
1 2 3 4 5 6			
Group total			
Class total			

Table 1-1

(a) Examine the ratio $\dfrac{\text{frequency of ''2 heads''}}{\text{number of tosses}}$ for the 25 tosses, for your group total and for the class total.

(b) As the number of tosses increases, what value does the ratio $\dfrac{\text{frequency of ''2 heads''}}{\text{number of tosses}}$ approach?

2. Each member of the group will throw a pair of dice 10 times. Record the results as in Table 1-2.

Student	Number of sevens	$\dfrac{\text{Number of sevens}}{\text{total number of throws}}$
1 2 3 4 5 6		
Group total		
Class total		

Table 1-2

(a) Examine the ratio $\dfrac{\text{number of sevens}}{\text{total number of throws}}$ for your 10 throws, for the group total and for the class total.

(b) As the number of throws increases, what value does the ratio $\dfrac{\text{number of sevens}}{\text{total number of throws}}$ approach?

3. Each member of the group will spread a deck of cards face down and select 10 cards. Tabulate results according to Table 1-3.

Student	Number of black cards	$\dfrac{\text{Black}}{\text{total selections}}$	Number of spades	$\dfrac{\text{Spades}}{\text{total selections}}$	Number of aces of spades	$\dfrac{\text{Aces spades}}{\text{total selections}}$
1 2 3 4 5 6						
Group total						
Class total						

Table 1-3

(a) Examine each of the ratios for your 10 selections, group totals, class totals.

(b) As the number of selections increases, what value does each ratio approach?

(c) Which of the three outcomes is most likely? Least likely?

1.2 CALCULATING PROBABILITIES

If a coin is tossed, what is the probability that it will land heads? If a pair of dice are thrown, what are the chances of seven turning up? If a single card is drawn from a deck, what is the probability it is black? a spade? an ace? the ace of spades?

To answer these questions we must first determine the *sample*

applied mathematics for today: senior

space we are dealing with in each case. When a coin is tossed it will normally land either heads or tails, therefore the sample space is {*H*, *T*}. When throwing a single die the sample space is {1, 2, 3, 4, 5, 6}.

The number of elements in the sample space will be referred to as the "total number of possible outcomes," and we shall represent it by *N*. In the problems we will consider in this section, we shall assume that each element in the sample space is equally likely to be an outcome.

We shall consider the probability (*P*) of an event happening to be the number of ways it can happen, which we shall call successes (*S*), divided by the total number of possible outcomes (*N*).

$$\frac{\text{Probability}}{\text{of an event}} = \frac{\text{Number of possible successful outcomes}}{\text{Total number of equally possible outcomes}}$$

$$P = \frac{S}{N}$$

This gives the theoretical probability of an event. Now let us discuss the kind of problems which introduced this section.

EXAMPLE 1. *If 3 coins are tossed, what is the probability that 3 heads will turn up?*

Solution

(H) (H) (H) (H) (T) (T) (T) (T)

(H) (H) (T) (T) (H) (H) (T) (T)

(H) (T) (H) (T) (H) (T) (H) (T)

Figure 1-4

Possible successful outcomes $S = 1$

Total possible outcomes $N = 8$

∴ probability of three heads $P = \frac{1}{8}$

EXAMPLE 2. *If a pair of dice are thrown, what is the probability of seven turning up?*

Solution

Figure 1-5

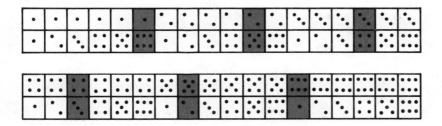

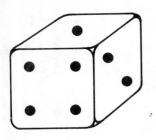

Do all dice have the same opposite faces?

As Figure 1-5 illustrates:

Possible successful outcomes $S = 6$

Total possible outcomes $N = 36$

∴ probability of seven $P = \frac{6}{36} = \frac{1}{6}$

EXAMPLE 3.   *If a single card is drawn from a deck of cards, what are the chances it is* (a) *black?* (b) *a spade?* (c) *an ace?* (d) *the ace of spades?*

Solution
(a) Possible successful outcomes

$$S = 26 \quad (13 \text{ clubs and } 13 \text{ spades})$$

Total possible outcomes

$$N = 52 \quad (52 \text{ cards in a deck})$$

∴ probability of a black card

$$P = \frac{26}{52} = \frac{1}{2}$$

(b) Possible successful outcomes

$$S = 13 \quad (13 \text{ spades})$$

Total possible outcomes

$$N = 52 \quad (52 \text{ cards})$$

∴ probability of a spade

$$P = \frac{13}{52} = \frac{1}{4}$$

(c) To abbreviate the solution we shall use only symbols.

$$S = 4 \quad \begin{array}{l}(\text{aces of spades, hearts,} \\ \text{diamonds and clubs})\end{array}$$

$$N = 52$$

∴ probability of an ace

$$P = \frac{4}{52} = \frac{1}{13}$$

(d) The chances it is the ace of spades:

$$S = 1$$

$$N = 52$$

∴ probability of the ace of spades

$$P = \frac{1}{52}$$

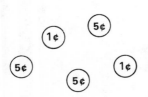

EXAMPLE 4.   *On a table there are five coins: two pennies and three nickels.*
(a) *What is the probability of randomly selecting a dime?*

applied mathematics for today: senior

(b) If the table has only five pennies on it, what is the probability of picking a penny?

Solution

(a)
$$S = 0$$
$$N = 5$$
$$\therefore \quad P = \tfrac{0}{5} = 0$$

If an event is impossible, the probability $P = 0$.

(b)
$$S = 5$$
$$N = 5$$
$$\therefore \quad P = \tfrac{5}{5} = 1$$

If an event is certain, the probability $P = 1$.

EXAMPLE 5. *If two coins are tossed on a table, what is the probability that they will both land heads?*

Coin A	H	H	T	T
Coin B	H	T	H	T

Table 1-6

Solution: We can list the possibilities as in Table 1-6, from which we see that

$$S = 1$$
$$N = 4$$
$$\therefore \quad P = \tfrac{1}{4}$$

$\therefore$ the probability of two heads is $\tfrac{1}{4}$.

EXERCISE 1-2

A **1.** A single die is thrown.
(a) How many possible outcomes are there?
(b) If a success is throwing an even number, how many outcomes are successes?
(c) What is the probability of throwing an even number?
2. (a) A box contains three black marbles and four white marbles. If your task is to pick one marble at random, what value has N?
(b) If we wish to calculate the probability of selecting a black marble what value has S?
(c) Calculate P.

3. (a) A drawer contains four black socks and five white socks. If you have a white sock in your hand, what is the probability of your reaching in the dark and selecting one sock to make a matching pair?

What image would be seen by someone
(a) looking into mirror #1?
(b) looking into mirror #2?

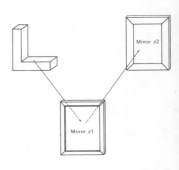

N = Total number of possible outcomes.

(b) How many socks would you have to pick to be sure of getting a matching pair if you had none in your hand to start?

(c) If the drawer contained four black socks and six white socks and you had none in your hand, how many would you have to select to be certain of getting a pair of white socks?

B **4.** In a single throw of one die, what is the probability of throwing (a) a 1? (b) a 5? (c) a 9?

5. (a) In a single throw of two dice, what are the probabilities of throwing each of the 11 possible outcomes?
(b) What pattern do you notice in the results?

6. In a single throw of three dice, what is the probability of the throw totalling (a) 3? (b) 5?

7. In a random draw from a deck of cards what is the probability of drawing (a) a red queen? (b) a face card? (c) the 6 of spades? (d) an ace?

8. A box contains 12 green marbles, 6 red marbles and 2 white marbles. Calculate the probability of choosing at random (a) a green marble, (b) a red marble, (c) a white marble, (d) not a green marble, (e) not a red marble, (f) not a white marble.

9. In a throw of a single die, what is the probability of getting 4 or greater?

10. In a throw of two dice, what is the probability of getting 8 or greater?

11. 5000 people each hold one ticket in a lottery, and there are five prizes drawn.
(a) What is the probability of winning a prize?
(b) What is the probability of winning 1st prize?
(c) What is the probability of winning 1st or 2nd prize?

12. In a medical experiment 10 people are given two cold pills "A", 10 people are given two cold pills "B", 10 people are given one cold pill "A" and one cold pill "B", and 10 people are given two sugar pills. No one is told what they receive. What is the probability of a subject receiving:

(a) two cold pills "A"   (b) one or more cold pills "B"
(c) no medication

13. A set of cards numbered from 1 to 100 is shuffled and a card drawn at random. What is the probability that the number on the card (a) is even? (b) ends in a 6? (c) is divisible by 5?

14. Three coins are thrown on a table. What is the probability of (a) three tails? (b) one head and two tails?

15. A quarter, a dime and a nickel are tossed on a table. What is the probability that the quarter is heads and the dime and nickel are both tails?

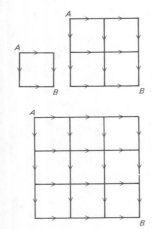

In each case how many paths are there from A to B if you can travel to the right and/or down only?

1.3 LAW OF LARGE NUMBERS

A coin is flipped 50 times and a record of the results is kept as shown in Table 1-7. We shall consider a head as being a success. A cumulative frequency of successes (S) is recorded. The cumulative total column contains the total of all successes up to that point in the investigation. The ratio of successes to the total number of tosses $\left(\dfrac{S}{N}\right)$ is expressed as a decimal.

Number of toss N	Heads or tails H, T	Cumulative total—heads S	Ratio $\dfrac{S}{N}$
1	H	1	1
2	H	2	1
3	T	2	0.66
4	H	3	0.75
5	H	4	0.80
.	.	.	.
.	.	.	.
.	.	.	.
49	T	23	0.47
50	H	24	0.48

Table 1-7

A graph is constructed (Figure 1-8) with $\dfrac{S}{N}$ shown on the vertical scale from 0 to 1 and N shown on a horizontal scale from 0 to 50. Since the probability P for a head is $\frac{1}{2}$ or 0.5, a P is marked on the $\dfrac{S}{N}$ axis at 0.5 and a horizontal line is drawn across the graph at this point.

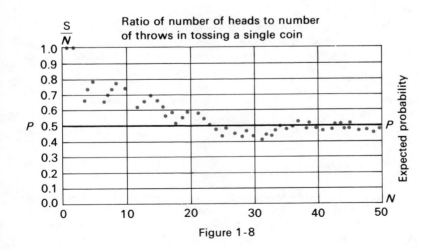

Figure 1-8

Notice that when N was small, the ratio $\frac{S}{N}$ varied widely from the expected value for P. However, as N increased, the value came closer to 0.5. This is an example of the phenomenon described by The Law of Large Numbers.

> The Law of Large Numbers: As the value of N increases, the value of $\frac{S}{N}$ approaches P.

This law is frequently misinterpreted. It does NOT suggest that if heads has not turned up for several tosses it is more likely to turn up on the next toss. A coin has no memory.

INVESTIGATION 1.3

Perform the following experiments to illustrate the law of large numbers. On each graph draw a line at the expected probability and compare your experimental results to the theoretical value.

1. Make a table and graph for 100 throws of a single die. Consider a one or a two as a success. Keep a record of every throw and a cumulative frequency of successes, but calculate and plot $\frac{S}{N}$ for every fifth throw only.

2. In a box or bag place four pieces of chalk, one of which is distinguishable by sight but not touch. This may be accomplished by using a marking pen. Repeat as for question 1, counting a success as picking the marked chalk by chance (without looking) from the container.

3. Make up a set of seven cards and mark two of them. A success is selecting a marked card at random. Make one hundred selections, shuffling the cards after each; table and graph the results as in question 1.

4. Throw three coins on the desk 50 times, and note the number of heads turning up at each throw.
(a) Consider a success to be two or more heads, calculate and graph $\frac{S}{N}$ at five-throw intervals.

(b) Use the same data but consider a success to be exactly two heads. Graph as for (a).

1.4 EMPIRICAL PROBABILITIES

In all cases discussed previously, it has been possible to forecast the total number of successful outcomes and to calculate P theoretically. But in fact some of the most useful applications of probability concern events where this is not possible. The work of actuaries in calculating life insurance premiums, for example, centres around determining the probability of an individual living to a certain age.

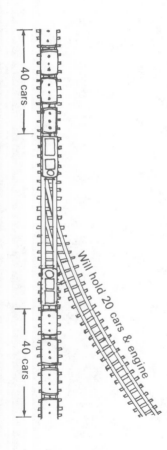

40 cars

Will hold 20 cars & engine

40 cars

Two trains of 40 cars each meet on a single line at a spur which will hold 20 cars and a locomotive. How can the trains pass?

applied mathematics for today: senior

In Section 1.3 we observed how the value of $\frac{S}{N}$ approached P for large values of N. We can now use this fact to help us approximate P by experiment.

INVESTIGATION 1.4

1. If a thumb tack is thrown on a desk, what is the probability that it will land point up? Make up a table similar to the tables in Investigation 1.3 with columns N, S and $\frac{S}{N}$. Calculate and graph $\frac{S}{N}$ for every tenth throw of 200 throws. (The process may be speeded up by throwing 10 tacks at once, add 10 to the N and add the number that land point up to S.)

2. On visits to fair grounds or carnivals you may have seen a game where a coin is rolled onto a board which is covered with squares similar to graph paper. If the coin lands in a square without touching a line then the thrower wins.

Select a coin and on a sheet of paper draw squares with lengths of sides twice the diameter of the coin. Using a table with columns for N, S and $\frac{S}{N}$, and a graph, make 100 throws plotting $\left(N, \frac{S}{N}\right)$ for every fifth throw. Estimate the probability of winning your game. (At the carnival the squares are usually just larger than the coin, which of course reduces even further the probability of winning.)

3. Select a matchstick, toothpick, needle or pin. On a piece of paper construct a set of several parallel lines with distance between the lines equal to the length of the object chosen. If the object is dropped at random on the paper within the parallel lines, what is the probability that it will come to rest touching one of the lines? Set up a table and graph for 100 throws as directed in Investigation 1.3. Estimate the probability of the needle touching a line. (Figure 1-9.)

In the 1700's a mathematician named Buffon suggested that this predicts the value for P to be $\frac{2}{\pi}$. Does your investigation confirm this value?

4. (a) Determine empirically the probability of tossing a coin into a dish from behind a desk 1.5 m away. Use 25 tosses as a basis for your calculation.

(b) If you pay back the coin plus double the amount for a success how much would you win or lose, according to your calculation in (a), if a total of $10 in coins was tossed?

5. Ask 30 people to select a number "From one to twelve." Determine the probability that they will select a number from the middle half. (4, 5, 6, 7, 8 or 9).

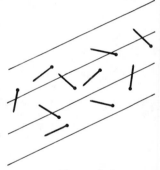

Figure 1-9

Tom and Harry toss coins. Tom wins when it's tails, Harry wins when it's heads. Harry has $h, Tom has $t. The probability than Harry wins all Tom's money is $\frac{h}{h+t}$. What is the probability that Tom wins all Harry's money?

1.5 COMPOUND PROBABILITIES: *Either of Two Mutually Exclusive Events*

EXAMPLE 1. *What is the probability of throwing either a 2 or a 3 on a single throw of a die?*

Solution
(i) By possible successful outcomes:

$$S = 2, \qquad N = 6$$
$$\therefore \quad P = \tfrac{2}{6} = \tfrac{1}{3}$$

(i) By compound probabilities:
Probability of throwing a two:

$$S_1 = 1, \qquad N = 6$$
$$\therefore \quad P_1 = \tfrac{1}{6}$$

Probability of throwing a three:

$$S_2 = 1, \qquad N = 6$$
$$\therefore \quad P_2 = \tfrac{1}{6}$$

Probability for either outcome;
From solution (i) $P = \tfrac{1}{3}$

$$= \tfrac{1}{6} + \tfrac{1}{6}$$
$$= P_1 + P_2$$

The expression "mutually exclusive" means that the events cannot both occur at once. For example, in drawing a card from a deck of playing cards, the events of drawing a face card or a spade are not mutually exclusive since it is possible to do both at one draw (the king of spades, for instance). We could not use the formula in this case.

To illustrate this fact, let us consider four cards numbered 1 to 4; 1 and 2 are coloured, 3 and 4 are white. What is the probability of drawing at random either a coloured card or an even-numbered card?

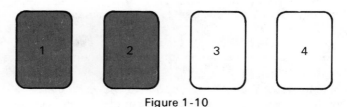

Figure 1-10

From Figure 1-10 we see that
$$S = 3 \quad \text{(cards 1, 2, 4)}$$
$$N = 4$$
$$\therefore \quad P = \tfrac{3}{4}$$

applied mathematics for today: senior

The probability of a coloured card, $P_1 = \frac{1}{2}$.
The probability of an even-numbered card, $P_2 = \frac{1}{2}$.

Note that $P \neq P_1 + P_2$. If it were, this would indicate certain success. But you are not certain of drawing even or coloured—you might draw card 3. The discrepancy is due to the fact that card 2 is both coloured and even.

> If an event can happen in N equally likely ways in which two *mutually exclusive* results are considered successful, with probabilities of success P_1 and P_2, then the probability of either happening is
>
> $$P = P_1 + P_2$$

EXAMPLE 2. *A bag contains two black, five white and eight red marbles. What is the probability of drawing a black or a red marble on one draw?*

Solution

Probability of drawing a black marble:

$$P_1 = \frac{S_1}{N}$$

$$= \frac{2}{15}$$

Probability of drawing a red marble:

$$P_2 = \frac{S_2}{N}$$

$$= \frac{8}{15}$$

$$\therefore \quad P = \frac{2}{15} + \frac{8}{15}$$

$$= \frac{10}{15} = \frac{2}{3}$$

Check this result by using possible successful outcomes.

A traveler drives 150 km at 50 km/h and flies 150 km at 100 km/h. What is the average speed?

EXERCISE 1-5

A   **1.** Which of the following events are mutually exclusive?
(a) Being 180 cm tall and being under 160 cm tall.
(b) Having brown eyes and black hair.
(c) Living in Toronto and living in Ontario.
(d) Living in Winnipeg and living in Alberta.
(e) Drawing a black card and drawing a queen.
(f) Having a three and a five turn up on a pair of dice.
(g) Having a figure that is a triangle and the interior angles add up to 360°.

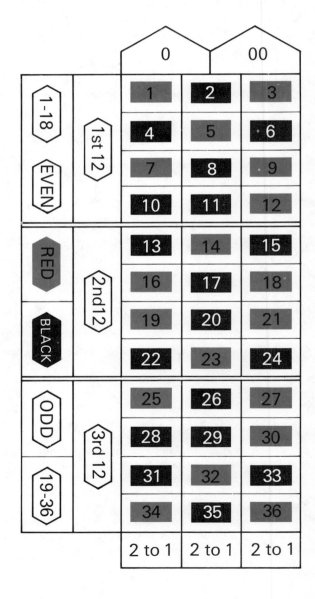

In the game of roulette a small ivory ball is thrown into a spinning wheel with numbers 00 and 0 to 36 on the rim. All the numbers except 00 and 0 are black or red (the zeros are green). A player may bet on a particular number; on red or black; on the sequences 1 to 12, 13 to 24, or 25 to 36; on even or on odd; on high (19 to 36) or low (1 to 18).

Various combinations of numbers may also be wagered on. If 0 or 00 comes up, only bets on these alone or in combination are winners.

What is the probability of winning by betting on red? on even? on high? on 1 to 12? on a single number?

(h) Having a figure that has two obtuse angles and the figure is a parallelogram.

(i) From a deck of cards draw a spade and a one-eyed jack.

2. If P_1, P_2 and P_3 are the probabilities of mutually exclusive outcomes from a particular event, what is the probability P of any of P_1, P_2 or P_3 happening?

(a) $P_1 = \frac{1}{5}$ $P_2 = \frac{3}{5}$

(b) $P_1 = \frac{1}{6}$ $P_2 = \frac{1}{3}$

(c) $P_1 = \frac{2}{7}$ $P_2 = \frac{1}{7}$ $P_3 = \frac{2}{7}$

(d) $P_1 = \frac{1}{6}$ $P_2 = \frac{5}{12}$ $P_3 = \frac{1}{4}$

(e) $P_1 = \frac{4}{9}$ $P_2 = \frac{1}{6}$

(f) $P_1 = \frac{1}{8}$ $P_2 = \frac{1}{4}$

(g) $P_1 = \frac{3}{25}$ $P_2 = \frac{1}{5}$ $P_3 = \frac{3}{10}$

(h) $P_1 = \frac{2}{5}$ $P_2 = \frac{1}{5}$ $P_3 = \frac{2}{5}$

B

3. A student is asked to pick a number from 1 to 10. What is the probability he will pick (a) an even number? (b) number 5?

4. In drawing from a deck of playing cards what is the probability of drawing a black ace or a red face card?

5. In the game of craps, the thrower wins if on the first throw of a pair of dice he throws 7 or 11. Calculate P_1, the probability of throwing 7, and P_2, the probability of throwing 11, and the probability P of winning on the first throw.

6. In craps, if the player throws 2, 3 or 12 with a pair of dice on the first throw, he loses. What is the probability of his losing on the first throw?

7. A bag contains three black, four white and five red marbles.
(a) What is the probability of drawing a red or a white marble?
(b) What is the probability of drawing a black marble? This question could be rephrased to read: What is the probability of not drawing a red or a white marble?

> If an event must be either a success or a failure, and the probability of success is P, then the probability of failure is $1 - P$

8. A bag of 100 marbles contains 30 black marbles. Calculate in two ways the probability of not drawing a black marble from the bag when selecting one marble at random.

9. An owner enters two horses in a race. The probability that one of them will win is $\frac{1}{6}$, the probability that the other will win is $\frac{1}{9}$. What is the probability that either will win? What is the probability that both will lose?

10. Rolling a pair of dice what is the probability of rolling (a) over seven? (b) under seven? (c) Not rolling seven?

"Heads I win. Tails you lose." What is the probability of winning?

11. In a medical test 25 people receive pill *A*, 25 people receive pill *B*, and 25 people receive pill *C*, a placebo. What is the probability that an individual in the experiment receives a medical treatment?

12. Sixty-four ball bearings dropped onto a probability board bounce off nails and fill the pockets as shown in Figure 1-11. What is the probability of a bearing landing in (a) pocket *A*? (b) pocket *B*? (c) pocket *A* or *B*? (d) not pocket *D*? (e) to the right of *D*?

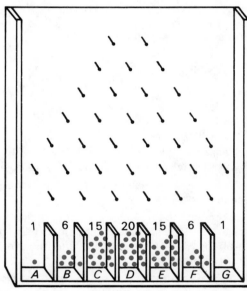

Figure 1-11

1.6 COMPOUND PROBABILITIES: *Both of Two Independent Events*

Events are *independent* if the success of one does not depend on the success of the other. If a coin is tossed and a die is thrown, the events of the coin landing heads and the die coming up a 3 are independent.

applied mathematics for today: senior

EXAMPLE 1. *A player throws a pair of dice, one red and the other green. What is the probability of throwing a 4 on the red die and a 5 on the green die?*

Solution
(i) By possible successful outcomes:
From the work we have studied we know that

$$S = 1 \quad \text{(red 4 and green 5)}$$
$$N = 36$$
$$P = \tfrac{1}{36}$$

(ii) By compound probabilities:
Probability of throwing a red 4:

$$S_1 = 1$$
$$N_1 = 6$$
$$P_1 = \tfrac{1}{6}$$

Probability of throwing a green 5:

$$S_2 = 1$$
$$N_2 = 6$$
$$P_2 = \tfrac{1}{6}$$

Probability of both:
From solution (i)

$$P = \tfrac{1}{36}$$
$$= \tfrac{1}{6} \times \tfrac{1}{6}$$
$$= P_1 \times P_2$$

If the probabilities of two independent events are P_1 and P_2, then the probability of both happening is

$$P = P_1 \times P_2$$

EXAMPLE 2. *What is the probability of tossing two heads in a row?*

Solution

For the first toss, $\quad P_1 = \tfrac{1}{2}$
For the second toss, $\quad P_2 = \tfrac{1}{2}$
For both heads, $\quad P = P_1 \times P_2$
$$= \tfrac{1}{2} \times \tfrac{1}{2}$$
$$= \tfrac{1}{4}$$

More complicated problems may be illustrated by means of tree diagrams showing all the possible outcomes, as in the next example.

EXAMPLE 3. *Draw a tree diagram to illustrate the number of possible outcomes of a contest to be settled by winning three out of five tosses of a coin. Find the probability of winning two, then losing two, then winning the last toss.*

Solution The vertices of the tree diagram (Figure 1-12) can be called decision points since these represent tosses of the coin which decide wins or losses. At each decision point the probability of the desired outcome is 0.5 (since the probability of heads or tails is $\frac{1}{2}$). The probability of win, win, loss, loss, win is $(\frac{1}{2}) \times (\frac{1}{2}) \times (\frac{1}{2}) \times (\frac{1}{2}) \times (\frac{1}{2})$ or $\frac{1}{32}$.

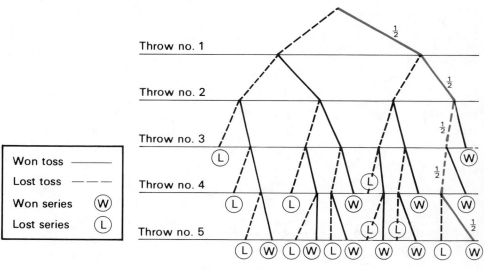

Figure 1-12

Flip 2 coins. If they are not both heads what is the probability that they are both tails?

EXERCISE 1-6

1. Which of the following events are independent?
(a) Throwing a 4 with one die and a 6 with another.
(b) A cloudy sky and rainy weather.
(c) Wearing a black hat and winning the sweepstakes.
(d) Eating rich foods and gaining in mass.
(e) Drawing a spade and drawing a heart from the same deck without replacing the card first drawn.
(f) Picking the winner of the Grey Cup and the Stanley Cup.

applied mathematics for today: senior

(g) Picking the winner of the first race at a track meet and picking the winners of the first two races.

(h) Studying for a test and passing the test.

2. If P_1, P_2 and P_3 are the probabilities of independent events happening, what is the probability of all happening where:

(a) $P_1 = \frac{1}{3}$ $P_2 = \frac{1}{4}$
(b) $P_1 = \frac{1}{4}$ $P_2 = \frac{2}{5}$
(c) $P_1 = \frac{1}{2}$ $P_2 = \frac{1}{4}$
(d) $P_1 = \frac{1}{5}$ $P_2 = \frac{1}{7}$ $P_3 = \frac{35}{90}$
(e) $P_1 = \frac{2}{5}$ $P_2 = \frac{4}{7}$ $P_3 = \frac{5}{8}$
(f) $P_1 = \frac{4}{7}$ $P_2 = \frac{1}{3}$
(g) $P_1 = \frac{5}{7}$ $P_2 = \frac{1}{5}$ $P_3 = \frac{7}{12}$
(h) $P_1 = \frac{99}{1000}$ $P_2 = \frac{7}{99}$ $P_3 = \frac{1}{7}$

3. (a) Can independent events be mutually exclusive?
(b) Can mutually exclusive events be independent?

B **4.** What is the probability of throwing two 7's in a row with a pair of dice?

5. What is the probability of drawing a spade twice in a row from a deck of cards, if the card is replaced after the first draw?

6. Find the probability of tossing three tails in a row.

7. A bag contains four black marbles, three green marbles and two white marbles. What is the probability of drawing a black marble on the first draw and a white marble on the second draw if the marbles are replaced after each draw?

8. In a game of roulette, a player who places $1 on a winning number will get $36. A player hopes to win $46 656 by placing $1 on his lucky number and leaving all his winnings on the number for three consecutive wins. What is the probability of his winning this amount? (the wheel is numbered 0, 00, 1, . . . , 36)

9. A player rolls a pair of dice and then picks a card from a deck of playing cards. What is the probability of throwing a 10 and picking a club?

10. Make a tree diagram to show the possible outcomes of a "two wins out of three" coin-tossing contest. In how many different ways may a player win the series?

11. Make a tree diagram for a best three out of five play-off between two teams. In how many series does the victorious team (a) win three straight? (b) win the first two then lose two? (c) lose the first two games?

12. A particular design of parachute has a record of failure of once in 2000 jumps. The reserve chute has a record of failure once in 1200 jumps. What is the probability of both chutes failing?

13. Choosing paths at random what is the probability of going directly from A to B? (Figure 1-13).

C **14.** As agent 002 you have been chosen to smuggle the Countess De Toures out of the country. You may select either route. What is your best chance of success? (Figure 1-14).

Flip a nickel and a penny. If the nickel is a head what is the probability they are both heads?

Figure 1-13

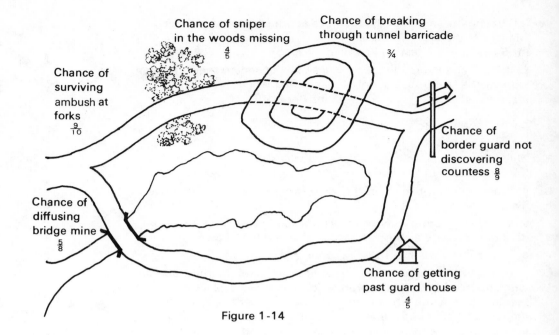

Chance of sniper in the woods missing $\frac{4}{5}$

Chance of breaking through tunnel barricade $\frac{3}{4}$

Chance of surviving ambush at forks $\frac{9}{10}$

Chance of border guard not discovering countess $\frac{8}{9}$

Chance of diffusing bridge mine $\frac{5}{8}$

Chance of getting past guard house $\frac{4}{5}$

Figure 1-14

15.

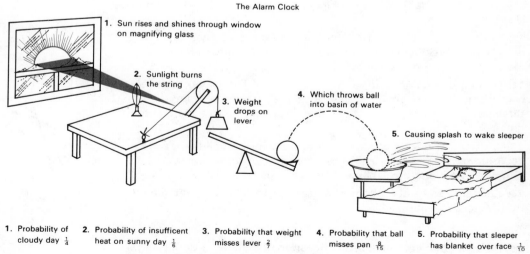

The Alarm Clock

1. Sun rises and shines through window on magnifying glass

2. Sunlight burns the string

3. Weight drops on lever

4. Which throws ball into basin of water

5. Causing splash to wake sleeper

1. Probability of cloudy day $\frac{1}{4}$

2. Probability of insufficent heat on sunny day $\frac{1}{6}$

3. Probability that weight misses lever $\frac{2}{7}$

4. Probability that ball misses pan $\frac{8}{15}$

5. Probability that sleeper has blanket over face $\frac{1}{10}$

What is the probability that the alarm clock will work?

REVIEW EXERCISE

A
1. Give the mathematical probability of the following events:
(a) Throwing a "two" with one die.
(b) Throwing a "two" with two dice.
(c) Selecting a "heart" at random from a deck of cards.
(d) Picking a black marble from a bag containing 4 black and 7 green.

2. What is the probability of (a) a certain event? (b) an impossible event?

3. Tossing a fair coin four times the results have been head, head, head, head. What is the probability of a tail on the next flip?

4. (a) Describe *mutually exclusive* events.
(b) If A and B are mutually exclusive events and the probability of A is $\frac{1}{2}$ and the probability of B is $\frac{1}{4}$, what is the probability of A or B?

5. (a) Describe *independent* events.
(b) If A and B are independent events and the probability of A is $\frac{1}{3}$ and the probability of B is $\frac{1}{4}$, what is the probability of A and B?

B
6. A bag contains three red marbles, five green marbles and four blue marbles. Find the following probabilities:
(a) Pick a blue on one pick.
(b) Not pick a red on one pick.
(c) Pick a red or a blue on one pick.
(d) Pick first a red and then a blue on two picks without replacing the first pick.
(e) Pick first a blue and then a red on two picks without replacing the first pick.
(f) Pick a blue and a red in either order on two picks without replacing after the first pick.

7. (a) Are "Throwing a seven with two dice" and "Both dice the same" mutually exclusive events?
(b) What is the probability of each?
(c) What is the probability of either one or the other?
(d) What is the probability of both on one throw?

8. (a) Are "Smokey Joe" winning in the first race and "Sloe Sam" winning in the second race independent events?
(b) If the probability of "Smokey Joe" winning is $\frac{1}{5}$ and the probability of "Sloe Sam" winning is $\frac{1}{8}$, what is the probability of both winning?

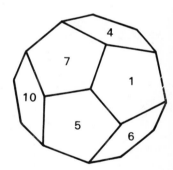

9. A regular dodecahedron has 12 faces, numbered "1" to "12." If the dodecahedron is rolled, what is the probability of:
(a) An even number turning up?
(b) A number divisible by three turning up?
(c) A "15" turning up?

10. Of a pair of regular tetrahedrons, one is red and the other is blue. If they are rolled, what is the probability of:
(a) A "4" turning up on the blue tetrahedron and a "3" on the red?
(b) A "2" turning up on both tetrahedrons?
(c) A "1" on one and a "3" on the other?

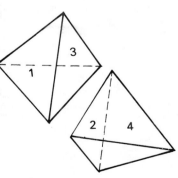

(d) A sum of six on the turned-up faces?

(e) A sum of five on the turned-up faces?

11. (a) What is the probability of moving directly from *A* to *E* if choices of route at each vertex are made at random. Backtracking is not considered.

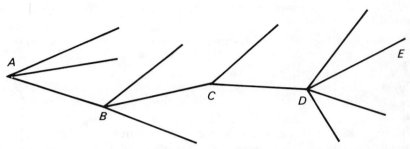

(b) What is the probability of moving from *A* to *D* without backtracking?

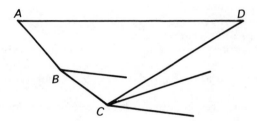

12. *Complete as many as possible of the following questions in five minutes.*

What is the probability of each of the following occurrences?

(a) Throwing a 5 with one die.

(b) Throwing a 2 or a 3 with one die.

(c) Throwing 12 with one die.

(d) Throwing 7 with a pair of dice.

(e) Tossing a coin and getting heads.

(f) Tossing a coin twice and getting heads twice.

(g) Picking a spade from a deck of 52 cards.

(h) Picking an ace from a deck of 52 cards.

(i) Picking the ace of spades from a deck of 52 cards.

(j) Throwing two coins and getting at least one head.

(k) Being born in June.

(l) Picking a red marble from a bag containing no red marbles.

(m) Picking a red or a white marble from a bag containing three red, two white, one green.

(n) Picking a red then a white marble from a bag containing three red, two white, one green if the first marble is replaced after it is drawn.

(o) Tossing three heads in a row.

HAPPY BIRTHDAY

What is the probability of two people in your class having the same birthday? At first thought it may seem unlikely if you have less than 180 people in the class and highly improbable with a class of, say, 24. Let us examine the problem using our knowledge of probabilities. We can do this best by first examining the probability of all birthdays being on different days.

The first student we consider in the class can have any birthday so the probability of no common birthday is $\frac{365}{365}$. The second student can have any other birthday so the probability of no coincidence is $\frac{364}{365}$. The third student can have any birthday except the previous two, so the probability of no coincidence is $\frac{363}{365}$. If there are 24 students in the class the probability of the last student having a unique birthday is $\frac{365-23}{365}=\frac{342}{365}$.

From the work in this chapter on compound probabilities, the probability of all these events happening (that is, no one having the same birthday as anyone else) is given by the expression

$$1 \times \frac{364}{365} \times \frac{363}{365} \times \frac{362}{365} \times \ldots \times \frac{342}{365} \doteq 0.46.$$

Since the probability of no one having the same birthday is 0.46, the probability of at least two people having the same birthday is

$$1-0.46 \quad \text{or} \quad 0.54$$

which means it is more likely to happen than not happen.

STATISTICS

The study of statistics involves the gathering and organizing of numerical data, its display and its interpretation.

Do statistics prove? To the extent that they will show the probability of a hypothesis being true, it might be said that they prove.

Do statistics lie? Statistics can be made to *seem* to prove almost anything.

In determining probabilities deductively, the validity of our work depends on *equally likely outcomes*. With statistics we must work with a whole population or a *random sample* of that population. The best way to prove that most people buy Brand A is to sample shoppers in a store where Brand A is on sale at half price! Statistics don't lie but statisticians may, for instance by withholding information (such as where a survey was taken), and this can be as misleading as giving false information.

In a society where we are continually subjected to persuaders—commercial, political and social—it is important that every citizen be able to apply a critical judgement whenever anyone implies that 'statistics prove'.

REVIEW AND PREVIEW TO CHAPTER 2

A slide rule will give the square root of a number to two or three significant figures depending on where the number lies on the scale and the skill of the user. The accuracy of the answer can be increased by dividing the square root as found on the slide rule into the original number and averaging the divisor and quotient. This is really just using Newton's method in conjunction with a slide rule first estimate. An electronic calculator will give even greater accuracy.

EXAMPLE 1

$$\sqrt{41.20} \doteq 6.42$$

$$\frac{41.20}{6.42} \doteq 6.417$$

$$\frac{6.420 + 6.417}{2} \doteq 6.419$$

EXAMPLE 2.

$$\sqrt{14\,938} \doteq 122$$

$$\frac{14\,938}{122} \doteq 122.4$$

$$\frac{122.0 + 122.4}{2} \doteq 122.2$$

Further divisions may be used to get greater accuracy.

Find the square root of the following numbers to four significant figures.

1. 5.634	**2.** 84.31	**3.** 75.81
4. 129.6	**5.** 342.7	**6.** 758.3
7. 89.20	**8.** 47.32	**9.** 1.365
10. 4.391	**11.** 0.0145	**12.** 0.5871
13. 0.008 739	**14.** 0.000 841	**15.** 0.3421
16. 0.000 187 2	**17.** 4.713×10^4	**18.** 5.934×10^6
19. 1.142×10^7	**20.** 3.817×10^9	**21.** 5.723×10^{-2}
22. 7.105×10^{-3}	**23.** 8.893×10^{-5}	**24.** 2.346×10^{-8}

Perform the following calculations:

1. $\dfrac{6.275 + 5.325}{9.415 - 7.625}$

2. $\dfrac{3.125 \times 5.375}{8.985 + 6.215}$

3. $\dfrac{0.4255 - 0.2145}{1.375 \times 4.125}$

4. $\dfrac{65.55 \times 6.375}{8.635 \times 41.65}$

5. $\dfrac{42.65 - 21.27}{88.25 \div 3.754}$

6. $\dfrac{35.65 \div 5.375}{28.75 - 4.265}$

7. $\dfrac{675.5 - 882.7}{452.6 - 327.5}$

8. $\dfrac{0.4251 \div 0.7835}{2.615 \times 0.2175}$

9. $\dfrac{3.125 \times 6.375}{6.375 + 3.125}$

10. $\dfrac{0.7185 - 0.9227}{6.315 + 2.127}$

Statistics

2.1 FREQUENCY DISTRIBUTIONS

A. *With Discrete Data.*

If data is obtained by counting, it belongs to a discrete set of numbers. There will be no fractions, and each value will be exact.

EXAMPLE 1. *Toss four coins 50 times and record the number of heads which turn up on each toss. Tabulate the results in a frequency table and construct a frequency polygon.*

Solution Construct a table showing the possible numbers of heads, perform the experiment and tally the results.

Frequency Table for the Number of Heads in
Tossing Four Coins

Number of heads	Tallies	Frequency
0	I	1
1	JHT JHT JHT III	18
2	JHT JHT JHT JHT	20
3	JHT II	7
4	JHT	4

Table 2-1

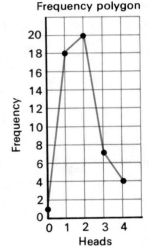

Frequency polygon

Figure 2-2

A frequency polygon is constructed by graphing the frequencies and joining the points with straight lines. (Figure 2-2)

If the number of cases is large, it is wise to group the data into classes. The class intervals should be easy to work with and should give about 12 classes.

EXAMPLE 2. *A book is opened at random and the page is recorded. Construct a frequency table and a histogram.*

Solution The book selected had 500 pages so it is advisable to group the data to get meaningful information.

$500 \div 12 \doteq 42$

Fifty is a number near 42 and easy to work with

∴we shall use 50 as our class interval.

Random Book Opening

Page number	Frequency
0–49	1
50–99	5
100–149	13
150–199	23
200–249	32
250–299	33
300–349	21
350–399	14
400–449	6
450–500	1

Table 2-3

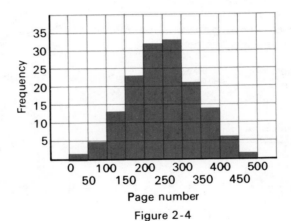

Figure 2-4

A histogram is a vertical bar graph on which the class intervals are marked along the horizontal axis and the frequency on the vertical axis. Each bar represents the number of cases in the class interval.

B. With Continuous Data.

If data is obtained by measuring, the value obtained will be approximate, the precision being limited by the measuring instrument we use. In placing the values in a frequency table we must set class intervals to group the data. If our measures are to the nearest unit, then the class boundaries will be the half unit. For example, if we measure the heights of students to the nearest centimetre and the class interval of 3 cm is from 160 cm to 163 cm, then students with heights between 159.5 cm and 163.5 cm would fall in this class; therefore the class boundaries are 159.5 cm and 163.5 cm.

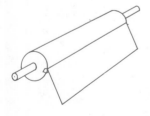

How many metres of veneer 2.0 mm thick can be peeled from a log 500 mm in diameter if a central core 50 mm in diameter is wasted?

26   applied mathematics for today: senior

EXAMPLE 3. *The hand-spans for a class are measured to the nearest centimetre. Make a frequency table and show the data on a histogram. Convert the histogram to a frequency polygon by joining the mid-points of the tops of the bars.*

Solution

Hand-spans in centimetres of Grade 9
High School Students

Class values	Class boundaries	Frequency
17	16.5–17.5	1
18	17.5–18.5	3
19	18.5–19.5	8
20	19.5–20.5	12
21	20.5–21.5	12
22	21.5–22.5	8
23	22.5–23.5	4
24	23.5–24.5	2
25	24.5–25.5	1

Table 2-5

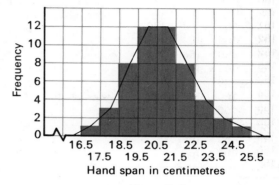

Figure 2-6

The midpoints of the tops of the bars occur halfway through each class interval and are at the class midvalue. In the example above, the class includes values from 60 to 63 cm and has a class midvalue of 61.5 cm. Notice that $\dfrac{60+63}{2} = 61.5$.

In trying to draw conclusions about a whole population from a given sample, it is often of assistance to graph the frequency curve corresponding to the given data. A frequency curve is constructed by plotting the frequencies against the class midvalues and joining the points with a smooth curve. To construct a frequency curve from the data in Example 3, see Table 2-7 and Figure 2-8.

Midvalues	Frequency
17	1
18	3
19	8
20	12
21	12
22	8
23	4
24	2
25	1

Table 2-7

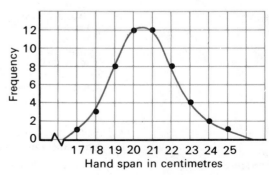

Figure 2-8

statistics   27

Table 2-9

Heights of 50 students to nearest centimetre			
150	157	162	168
150	157	162	168
151	157	163	169
152	158	164	170
152	158	164	172
153	159	164	172
153	159	165	175
154	160	165	176
155	160	166	179
155	160	166	180
155	161	167	184
156	161	167	
156	161	167	

EXERCISE 2-1

B **1.** Construct a frequency table using the data in the margin on the heights of students. Illustrate the data by means of a frequency polygon. Group the data with 3 cm class intervals.

2. The masses in kilograms of 100 students are given in table 2-10. Group the data into suitable classes and construct a frequency table and histogram.

Masses of 100 students in kilograms									
58	62	52	56	50	60	60	54	68	50
58	60	55	43	55	54	46	56	49	55
56	56	51	55	49	52	55	60	56	62
51	54	59	53	61	53	67	56	55	54
65	59	63	55	55	46	53	52	71	59
68	59	44	45	49	59	51	57	51	65
61	70	59	62	64	64	52	54	77	57
72	49	51	57	61	53	64	51	53	87
48	55	59	69	69	57	40	46	55	59
59	63	55	56	71	90	62	44	66	67

Table 2-10

3. Construct a histogram from the frequency table 2-11. Where the class interval is $5000 make the bar five times wider than where the class interval is $1000 *and divide the frequency by* 5. Consider a suitable method of indicating the "over $25 000" group.

Canadian Taxpayers by Income
1971

Income	Frequency
$1 000–$2 000	280 000
2 000– 3 000	770 000
3 000– 4 000	870 000
4 000– 5 000	870 000
5 000– 6 000	800 000
6 000– 7 000	720 000
7 000– 8 000	670 000
8 000– 9 000	560 000
9 000–10 000	460 000
10 000–15 000	980 000
15 000–20 000	220 000
20 000–25 000	70 000
over 25 000	94 000

Source: Information Canada
Table 2-11

C **4.** Measure the hand-spans of the students in your class. Group the data and construct a frequency table and frequency polygon.

5. Have at least 30 subjects use an unmarked straight edge, such as a book, to construct a line estimated to be 15 cm in length. Measure the

Find the centre of the circle using a drafting triangle and pencil.

applied mathematics for today: senior

segments to the nearest millimetre. Group the data and construct a frequency table and histogram.

2.2 MEASURES OF CENTRAL TENDENCY

When we are looking for a single number to represent a whole set of data, it is usually a suitable measure of central tendency that is chosen. It must be remembered, however, that much information cannot be contained in a single number, it must be used in conjunction with other statistics.

A. The Mean

The mean is the statistic usually meant when people say, "The average number is..."

> The mean of a set of values is the sum of the values divided by the number of values in the set, and is usually represented by $\bar{x}$ (x bar). For a set of values $x_1, x_2, x_3, \ldots, x_n$:
>
> $$\bar{x} = \frac{x_1 + x_2 + x_3 + \ldots + x_n}{n}$$

If a large number of values is involved with many repetitions, the calculation can be shortened by using an expanded frequency table. (See Table 2-12.)

Sample Test Data

Test mark	Frequency	Frequency times test mark
x	f	$f \cdot x$
0	0	0
1	0	0
2	0	0
3	0	0
4	1	4
5	2	10
6	2	12
7	4	28
8	5	40
9	6	54
10	3	30
11	4	44
12	1	12
13	0	0
14	1	14
15	0	0
	$\sum f = 29$	$\sum fx = 248$

Table 2-12

Sample Test Data

Test mark	Frequency	Cumulative frequency
0	0	0
1	0	0
2	0	0
3	0	0
4	1	1
5	2	3
6	2	5
7	4	9
8	5	14
9	6	20
10	3	23
11	4	27
12	1	28
13	0	28
14	1	29
15	0	29
	$n = 29$	

Table 2-13

The "frequency times test mark" column allows us to multiply 5×8 instead of adding $8+8+8+8+8$.

Σ is the Greek capital letter "sigma" which is used to indicate "the sum of." Therefore Σf is the sum of the frequencies $(\Sigma f = n)$. For a frequency distribution:

$$\bar{x} = \frac{\Sigma f \cdot x}{n}$$

For the sample data.

$$\bar{x} = \frac{248}{29} \doteq 8.6$$

B. The Median

The examination marks of five students were 32, 64, 68, 70, and 72. The mean mark is 61.2 which is lower than all but one of the students' marks; the mean has been lowered by the one very low mark. A better measure of the average performance of the class would be the middle mark. This mark is called the median. The median of the five marks is 68.

To find the median of a set of values, order the values in a frequency table. If there are n values, the median value is the $\frac{n+1}{2}$ value. Where $\frac{n+1}{2}$ comes out a fraction, calculate the mean of the two nearest values.

> The median of a set of n ordered values $x_1, x_2, x_3 \ldots x_n$ is
>
> i) $M = x_{\frac{n+1}{2}}$ if n is odd.   ii) $M = \frac{x_{\frac{n}{2}} + x_{\frac{n+2}{2}}}{2}$ if n is even.

In Table 2-13 $n = 29$, $\therefore \frac{n+1}{2} = \frac{30}{2} = 15$. The median mark is the 15th mark.

From the cumulative frequency column, it is found that the 15th mark is a 9. Therefore the median mark is 9.

C. The Mode

> The mode of a set of values is the value which occurs most frequently or at least more frequently than those values about it.

In two hypothetical measures of students' foot-lengths, the data might result in the following frequency curves.

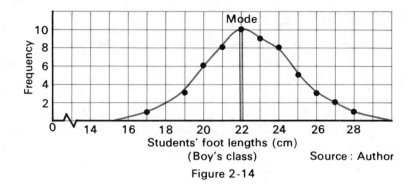

Students' foot lengths (cm)
(Boy's class)   Source : Author

Figure 2-14

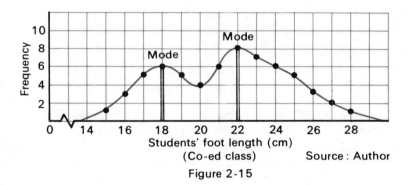

Students' foot length (cm)
(Co-ed class)   Source : Author

Figure 2-15

In the boys' class, the data gave us a **normal distribution** with a mode of 22 cm. This is called a normal distribution because it follows the usual pattern of a chance distribution over a large number of cases. The graph of a normal distribution is usually referred to as a **bell curve**.

In the co-ed class, the fact that girls tend to have smaller feet gave us one modal value of 18 cm and another of 22 cm. In spite of the fact that the 22 cm value has a greater frequency than the 18 cm value, we would refer to this curve as being **bi-modal** or as having two modes. **This statistic is of particular value to manufacturers, who, for produc-tion planning, are interested in which sizes or styles are selling best.

The three **measures of central tendency** are the **mean**, the **median**, and the **mode**:

12
13
14——— **Median**: halfway value: $\frac{14+17}{2} = 15.5$
17
17——— **Mode**: most frequently occurring value = 17.
18

Mean $= \frac{\text{sum}}{n} = \frac{91}{6} \doteq 15.2$

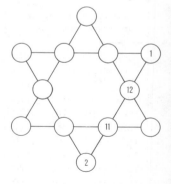

Place the numbers from 1 to 12 in the circles so that the sum along each row is 26.

EXERCISE 2-2

A **1.** Find the mean of each of the following sets of numbers.
(a) 3, 5, 5, 7, 4, 8, 6, 2, 5, 9
(b) 8, 3, 2, 4, 6, 7, 9, 3, 4, 0
(c) 1, 8, 7, 5, 6, 3, 7, 4, 8, 3
(d) 4, −2, −5, 3, −9, 5, 4, −3, 0, 5
(e) −8, 6, 4, 5, −2, −4, 3, 5, 1, −7

2. Find the median of each of the following sets of numbers.
(a) 4, 7, 7, 8, 12
(b) 1, 3, 4, 7, 9, 11
(c) 7, 8, 12, 15, 15, 21, 25
(d) −5, −3, 0, 2, 4, 8, 12, 15
(e) −8, −6, −3, 4, 4, 6, 9, 9, 9

3. Find the mode(s) of each of the following sets of numbers.
(a) 31, 34, 34, 36, 36, 36, 37, 37, 39
(b) 8, 12, 12, 14, 15, 15, 21, 21, 21, 21, 25
(c) 4, 4, 6, 9, 9, 9, 12
(d) 18, 19, 20, 20, 23, 23, 27, 27, 27, 28
(e) −7, −6, −5, −5, 0, 0, 2, 4
(f) 8, 12, 14, 16, 23, 25, 34

B **4.** Find the mean, median, and mode of the set of numbers 21, 22, 23, 23, 24, 24, 24, 25, 25, 26, 29, 30.

5. Find the mean and mode for the data from Table 2-5 (Hand-spans in centimetres of Grade 9....) If you were a glove manufacturer, which statistic would interest you most? Why?

6. Find the mean mass for the student data given in Table 2-10.

7. (a) Order by rank the following data and find the median value.

Number of manufacturing establishments by province (1970)		
Newfoundland—	245	Ontario— 12 740
Prince Edward Island—	153	Manitoba— 1 356
Nova Scotia—	795	Saskatchewan— 723
New Brunswick—	609	Alberta— 1 821
Quebec—	10 136	British Columbia—3 303

b) Calculate the median value for the above data if we include the territorial districts:

Yukon—15	Northwest Territories—14

Source: Information Canada

8. Find the mean height of the students from the data in the margin. Use a 3 cm class interval. (See question 1, exercise 2-1.)

Heights of 50 students to nearest centimetre			
150	157	162	168
150	157	162	168
151	157	163	169
152	158	164	170
152	158	164	172
153	159	164	172
153	159	165	175
154	160	165	176
155	160	166	179
155	160	166	180
155	161	167	184
156	161	167	
156	161	167	

applied mathematics for today: senior

2.3 PERCENTILES

It is often desirable to compare a person's performance to the performance of others in the same group. For example, in a fitness test, all of the first-year students ran 100 m. It would be unreasonable to compare their times against the track records for the 100 m dash, since this group includes both athletes and nonathletes. It might help the students to be able to rate their performance against a standard derived from testing a large number of year one students on the same task. A suitable instrument for doing this is a percentile scale. A runner's time might be classified as being in the 72 nd percentile of those of all year one students tested in the 100 m run.

> A score in the nth percentile is as high or higher than $n\%$ of the scores.

> The median is the 50th percentile score.

Can you write the numbers from 1 to 10 using four 4's, basic operations and powers?

$$1 = (4 \div 4) \div (4 \div 4)$$
$$2 =$$
$$3 =$$
$$4 =$$

EXAMPLE 1. *George ran the 100 m dash in 14.5 s. Out of a test group of 275 students, 46 ran better times. In what percentile was George's time?*

Solution

$$275 - 46 = 229$$

George's time was as good or better than 229 out of 275.
∴ percentile

$$= \frac{229}{275} \times 100$$

$$\doteq 83.3$$

His time is in the 83.3 percentile.

EXAMPLE 2. *Mary is in the 56th percentile in standing long jump. If there are 148 students in her group, find her rank.*

Solution 56th percentile indicates her distance is as good as or better than the distances achieved by 56% of the students in the group.

$$\frac{56}{100} \times 148 \doteq 82.9$$

$$\doteq 83$$

$$148 - 83 = 65$$

There are 65 students with better distances.
∴ Mary's rank is 66 out of 148.

Class values	Frequency
0–15	9
16–30	16
31–45	25
46–60	22
61–75	18
76–90	6

EXAMPLE 3. *The frequency distribution table for a set of contest scores is given in the margin.*

(a) Construct a table showing the class boundaries and cumulative frequencies.

(b) Construct a cumulative frequency polygon.

(c) Find the 29th percentile score.

(d) Find the percentile ranking of a score of 70.

Boundary: the number halfway between the highest class value in one class and lowest class value in the next.

Solution (a)

Class values	Frequency	Boundaries	Cumulative frequency
		0*	0
0–15	9		
		15.5	9
16–30	16		
		30.5	25
31–45	25		
		45.5	50
46–60	22		
		60.5	72
61–75	18		
		75.5	90
76–90	6		
		90*	96

Cumulative frequency: the total number of cases with values less than the given boundary value.

* If it were possible to get less than zero or more than 90, these values would be −0.5 and 90.5 respectively.

Solution (b) A cumulative frequency polygon graphs the cumulative frequencies against the boundary values.

Solution (c)
Find the 29th percentile score.

applied mathematics for today: senior

This score is equal to or higher than 29% of the 96 scores.

$$\therefore n = \frac{29}{100} \times 96$$

$$= 27.8$$

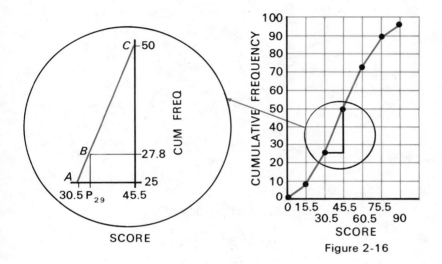

Figure 2-16

We calculate the score as though the values within each class were evenly distributed. Since Slope AB = Slope AC

$$\frac{27.8 - 25}{P_{29} - 30.5} = \frac{50 - 25}{45.5 - 30.5}$$

$$\frac{2.8}{P_{29} - 30.5} = \frac{5}{3}$$

$$3(2.8) = 5(P_{29} - 30.5)$$

$$8.4 = 5P_{29} - 152.5$$

$$P_{29} = 32.2$$

The 29th percentile score is 32.2.

Solution (d)
Find the percentile ranking of a score of 70.
Since a score of 70 is in the interval from 60.5 − 75.5 we shall use this area on the graph.

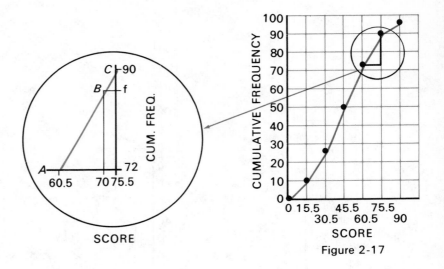

Figure 2-17

$$\text{Slope } AB = \text{Slope } AC$$

$$\frac{f-72}{70-60.5} = \frac{90-72}{75.5-60.5}$$

$$\frac{f-72}{9.5} = \frac{18}{15}$$

$$15f - 1080 = 171$$

$$f = 83.4$$

To change the frequency to a percentile

$$\frac{83.4}{96} \times 100 = 86.9$$

The score is in the 86.9th percentile.

EXAMPLE 4. *Given the following distribution of scores, find the median score.*

Boundary values	Cumulative frequency
0	0
5.5	3
10.5	12
15.5	24
20.5	31
25	35

applied mathematics for today: senior

Solution The median score is the 50th percentile score.

$$f = \frac{50}{100} \times 35$$

$$= 17.5$$

17.5 is in the cumulative frequency interval between 12 and 24.

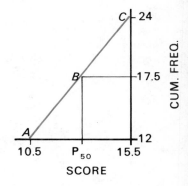

When calculating the median from boundary values we do not add 1 to n.

$$\text{Slope } AB = \text{Slope } AC$$

$$\frac{17.5 - 12}{P_{50} - 10.5} = \frac{24 - 12}{15.5 - 10.5}$$

$$\frac{5.5}{P_{50} - 10.5} = \frac{12}{5}$$

$$5(5.5) = 12(P_{50} - 10.5)$$

$$27.5 = 12P_{50} - 126$$

$$P_{50} = 12.8$$

The median value is 12.8.

EXERCISE 2-3

A **1.** A student receives 69% on a mathematics examination and is in the 56th percentile. Explain the meaning of each score.

2. In a group of 200 scores, find the percentile score in each case.
(a) Equal to or better than (i) 100 scores
                           (ii) 180 scores
                           (iii) 65 scores
(b) A rank of   (i) 41st
                           (ii) 151st
                           (iii) 97th

3. In a group of 50 scores:
(a) Find the number of scores the following are equal to or better than:

        (i) 40th percentile
        (ii) 74th percentile
        (iii) 12th percentile

(b) Find the rank of the following scores

        (i) 64th percentile
        (ii) 90th percentile
        (iii) 24th percentile

B **4.** Find each of the following scores as a percentage and as a percentile.

	Score	Rank
(a)	$\dfrac{47}{50}$	$\dfrac{7}{30}$
(b)	$\dfrac{65}{70}$	$\dfrac{3}{22}$
(c)	$\dfrac{7}{15}$	$\dfrac{13}{20}$
(d)	$\dfrac{29}{50}$	$\dfrac{25}{30}$
(e)	$\dfrac{132}{150}$	$\dfrac{8}{75}$
(f)	$\dfrac{66}{75}$	$\dfrac{4}{25}$

Can you find 3 natural numbers whose sum is equal to their product?

$$a + b + c = abc$$

5. Find the rank corresponding to each of the following percentile scores.

(a) 80th percentile out of 50
(b) 45th percentile out of 120
(c) 75th percentile out of 159
(d) 18th percentile out of 140
(e) 50th percentile out of 87
(f) 24th percentile out of 58

6. Given the following frequency distribution:

Scores	Frequency	Boundary values	Cumulative frequency
0–10	4		
11–20	20		
21–30	52		
31–40	17		
41–50	7		

(a) Complete the table.
(b) Construct a cumulative frequency polygon.
(c) Determine the median score.
(d) Determine scores corresponding to the 15th and 95th percentile.

7. (a) Complete a frequency distribution table, as in question 6, for the data in the margin. Use a 3 cm class interval.
b) Calculate the median height.
c) Calculate the scores corresponding to the 60th and 80th percentiles.

8. Three frequently referred to percentiles are the quartiles. These are: *the first quartile*, corresponding to the 25th percentile; *the second quartile*, corresponding to the 50th percentile (the median); *the third*

Heights of 50 students to nearest centimetre

150	157	162	168
150	157	162	168
151	157	163	169
152	158	164	170
152	158	164	172
153	159	164	172
153	159	165	175
154	160	165	176
155	160	166	179
155	160	166	180
155	161	167	184
156	161	167	
156	161	167	

$P_{25} = Q_1$ first quartile
$P_{50} = M$, median
$P_{75} = Q_3$ third quartile

applied mathematics for today: senior

quartile corresponding to the 75th percentile.
Find the three quartile values for the following data.

Masses of 100 students in kilograms									
58	62	52	56	50	60	60	54	68	50
58	60	55	43	55	54	46	56	49	55
56	56	51	55	49	52	55	60	56	62
51	54	59	53	61	53	67	56	55	54
65	59	63	55	55	46	53	52	71	59
68	59	44	45	49	59	51	57	51	65
61	70	59	62	64	64	52	54	77	57
72	49	51	57	61	53	64	51	53	87
48	55	59	69	69	57	40	46	55	59
59	63	55	56	71	90	62	44	66	67

9. Find the Q_1 and Q_3 for the data given in question 7.

2.4 MEASURES OF DISPERSION

When using statistics to describe data, in addition to showing what value the data is centred about, it is useful to have some measure of how the data is spread.
Consider the following set of test marks

Class Mark Distribution

Class values	Class midvalues x	Frequency f	x · f
15–19	17	1	17
20–24	22	3	66
25–29	27	4	108
30–34	32	8	256
35–39	37	6	222
40–44	42	2	84
45–49	47	1	47
		25	800
$\bar{x} = \dfrac{800}{25} = 32.$			

Table 2-18

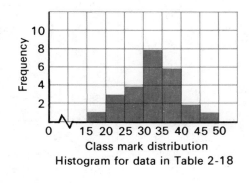

Class mark distribution
Histogram for data in Table 2-18

From the table we see that the mean mark is 32. We shall consider two statistics which will describe the dispersion of this data.

A. *The Range*

The range of a set of values is the difference between the largest and smallest value.
   We shall use the following convention:

I. Where the actual values are given:

> For a set of n ordered values $x_1, x_2, \ldots, x_n$
>
> Range $R = x_n - x_1$

II. Where a frequency distribution is given:

> Range $=$ (Upper boundary value of distribution) $-$ (Lower boundary value of distribution)

EXAMPLE 1. *Find the range of the values* 5, 14, 16, 17, 18

Solution

$$R = 18 - 5$$
$$= 13$$

EXAMPLE 2. *Find the range of the class mark distribution given in Table 2-18.*

Class values	Class boundaries
	14.5
15–19	
	19.5
20–24	
	24.5
25–29	
	29.5
30–34	
	34.5
35–39	
	39.5
40–44	
	44.5
45–49	
	49.5

Figure 2-19

Class Mark Distribution

Class values	Class midvalues x	Frequency f	$x \cdot f$
15–19	17	1	17
20–24	22	3	66
25–29	27	4	108
30–34	32	8	256
35–39	37	6	222
40–44	42	2	84
45–49	47	1	47
		$\overline{25}$	$\overline{800}$

$$\bar{x} = \frac{800}{25} = 32.$$

Table 2-18

Solution

$$R = 49.5 - 14.5$$
$$= 35$$

The range suffers from the same defect as the mean. It is overly affected by extreme values. For the values 5, 14, 16, 17, 18:

$$R = 18 - 5$$
$$= 13$$

Yet most of the values are within a range of 3.

applied mathematics for today: senior

B. Standard Deviation

The term standard deviation refers to *the standard deviation from the mean.*

$$S.D. = \sqrt{\frac{\sum (x - \bar{x})^2}{n}}$$

I. Where the number of cases is small and actual values are used:

EXAMPLE 3. *Find the standard deviation of the values 5, 14, 16, 17, 18.*

Solution
(i) Find the mean.

(i) x	(ii) $x - \bar{x}$	(iii) $(x - \bar{x})^2$
5	−9	81
14	0	0
16	2	4
17	3	9
18	4	16
$\sum x = 70$ $\bar{x} = \dfrac{70}{5}$ $= 14$	$\sum (x - \bar{x}) = 0$	$\sum (x - \bar{x})^2 = 110$ $\sqrt{\dfrac{\sum (x - \bar{x})^2}{n}} = 4.7$

Table 2-20

ii) We might consider taking the mean of these differences as a measure of dispersion, but when we add them we find that the sum is zero. Since this is true for all cases, it makes a poor statistic.

iii) In order to overcome this difficulty we can turn the differences into positive values by squaring them first and then finding the mean. Squaring the differences increases sensitivity to extreme values.

$$\frac{\sum (x - \bar{x})^2}{n} = \frac{110}{5} = 22$$

Since we squared the differences to make them positive, we shall now take the square root:

$$\sqrt{\frac{\sum (x - \bar{x})^2}{n}} = \sqrt{22}$$

$$\doteq 4.7$$

II. Where a frequency distribution is used, the class midvalues are used to represent each value in the class.

Example 4. *Find the standard deviation of the class mark distribution given in Table* 2-18.

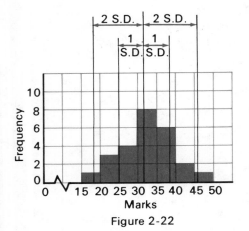

Figure 2-22

Class values	Class midvalues x	Frequency f	x · f	x − x̄	(x − x̄)²	f(x − x̄)²
15–19	17	1	17	−15	225	225
20–24	22	3	66	−10	100	300
25–29	27	4	108	−5	25	100
30–34	32	8	256	0	0	0
35–39	37	6	222	5	25	150
40–44	42	2	84	10	100	200
45–49	47	1	47	15	225	225
		25	800			1200

$$\bar{x} = \frac{\sum x \cdot f}{n}$$

$$= \frac{800}{25}$$

$$= 32$$

$$S.D. = \sqrt{\frac{\sum f(x - \bar{x})^2}{n}}$$

$$= \sqrt{\frac{1200}{25}}$$

$$= \sqrt{48}$$

$$\doteq 6.9$$

The standard deviation is 6.9

Table 2-21

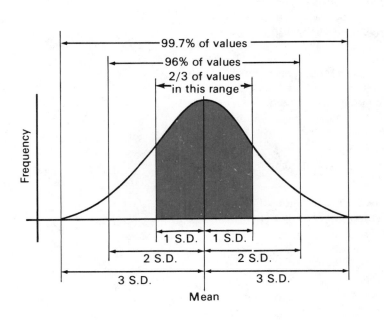

applied mathematics for today: senior

In the case of a normal distribution, the standard deviation has the following important characteristics:

1. Approximately two thirds of the values lie within one standard deviation of the mean.

2. Approximately 96% of the values lie within two standard deviations of the mean.

3. Practically all of the values will be within three standard deviations of the mean (99.7%).

EXERCISE 2-4

A **1.** Find the range for the following sets of numbers.

(a) 5, 7, 3, 4, 8, 2, 3   (b) 6.4, 5.2, 3.8, 9.7

(c) 6, −4, 1, 0, 5, −1, 2   (d) 3.2, 4.6, 1.3, −2.4

(e) 58.4, 73.2, 61.5, 87.4   (f) 126, 489, 205, 783

2. Find the range for the following distributions:

(a)

Boundary values	Cumulative frequency
14.5 cm	0
19.5	4
24.5	10
29.5	16
34.5	18
39.5	19

(b)

Class values	Frequency
1–9 kg	2
10–19	4
20–29	7
30–39	3
40–49	1

(c)

Boundary values	Cumulative frequency
−5.95°C	0
−4.95	8
−3.95	13
−2.95	20
−1.95	25
−0.95	27
0.00	27

(d)

Class values	Frequency
50–79 m	15
80–99	13
100–119	9
120–139	6
140–159	1
160–179	4

Find a right triangle with integral sides whose perimeter in metres is equal to its area in square metres. Can you find another?
$a + b + c = \frac{1}{2}ab$

B **3.** A soft drink machine is designed to dispense 250 cm^3 for each measure. The actual measures in cubic centimetres for a sample of 10 cups were 246, 252, 251, 248, 249, 250, 246, 253, 250, 249. Find the standard deviation of the amounts.

4. Find the standard deviation of the number of tacks landing point up in throwing six tacks 100 times.

Number of tacks point up	Frequency
0	1
1	2
2	16
3	28
4	32
5	18
6	3

Source: Students

Table 2-23

5. A class of students received the listed marks on a mathematics test. Find the range and standard deviation.

8	11	12	14	15	16	16	18	22
9	11	13	14	15	16	17	18	23
9	12	13	14	15	16	17	19	23
10	12	14	15	15	16	17	20	24

Table 2-24

6. One hundred test scores have a mean of 63 with a standard deviation of 4.6. The scores are normally distributed.
a) Between what two values would you expect two thirds of the values to lie?
b) Between what two values would you expect almost all of the values (99.7%) to lie?

7. Find the standard deviation of the heights of the students listed in the margin. Group data in 3 cm class intervals.

8. The mean mass of 1000 students is 62.0 kg with a standard deviation of 5.8 kg. If the masses are normally distributed, how many students should be in each range illustrated below?

Heights of 50 students to nearest centimetre			
150	157	162	168
150	157	162	168
151	157	163	169
152	158	164	170
152	158	164	172
153	159	164	172
153	159	165	175
154	160	165	176
155	160	166	179
155	160	166	180
155	161	167	184
156	161	167	
156	161	167	

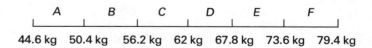

A   B   C   D   E   F
44.6 kg   50.4 kg   56.2 kg   62 kg   67.8 kg   73.6 kg   79.4 kg

2.5 PRACTICAL STATISTICS

In our normal daily routine we are constantly being subjected to statistical reports. For instance, are you overweight or underweight? The criteria will probably be a height-mass table which gives average masses for men and women of a given height. Since there is a close relationship between overweight and heart disease, life insurance companies are greatly interested in this statistic. For height-mass tables to be of value, it is necessary to know the measure of variability. Since the average person is not familiar with standard deviation, the tables frequently give a range of "healthy" masses for a given height.

When insurance companies calculate the premium to be charged for a policy, they must know the mean number of premiums they can expect to collect from people of a given age taking out the insurance.

To do this, the complete life expectancy of the individual must be calculated. This figure represents the average number of years of life remaining to individuals of this age. It is the result of calculations done on mortality figures gathered from past experience of the insurance companies. Life expectancy figures are shown in column 3 of the male and female sections of the Canadian life table (Table 2-26), which is a form of mortality table. Column 1 of the table gives the number living per 100 000 live births at age x. We can use this to calculate the median age expectancy for various ages. For 100 000 births, about 44 000 males are still alive at age 75, therefore the median age expectancy at birth for a male is between 70 and 75 a. Comparable calculations indicate female life expectancy to be slightly higher; what is it? More complete tables would allow calculation of the median age expectancy to the nearest year.

To determine your present median age expectancy, find the number out of 100 000 alive at your age for your gender. For example, if you are 20 and male the number alive is 95 915. Take one-half of this, 47 958. This number lies between the number living at ages 70 and 75. Therefore your median age expectancy is between 70 and 75 a. Notice that the older you get, the greater your age expectancy but the shorter your complete expectation of life.

As medical science conquers disease our life expectancy increases. This figure can be found for various subsets of the population as well. We would expect men engaged in hazardous occupations to have shorter life expectancies, hence there is risk pay in some industries. The life expectancy is also affected by where you live and what sex you are, as Table 2-27 illustrates.

a

This is the symbol for year and is derived from *annum*, the Latin word for year.

Canadian Life Table

<table>
<tr><th rowspan="3">Age</th><th colspan="3">Male</th><th colspan="3">Female</th></tr>
<tr><th rowspan="2">Number living at each age</th><th rowspan="2">Number dying between each age and the next</th><th rowspan="2">Expectation of life (a)</th><th rowspan="2">Number living at each age</th><th rowspan="2">Number dying between each age and the next</th><th rowspan="2">Expectation of life (a)</th></tr>
<tr></tr>
<tr><td>At birth</td><td>100 000</td><td>2 525</td><td>68.75</td><td>100 000</td><td>2 008</td><td>75.18</td></tr>
<tr><td>1 a</td><td>97 475</td><td>156</td><td>69.53</td><td>97 992</td><td>130</td><td>75.71</td></tr>
<tr><td>2 a</td><td>97 319</td><td>102</td><td>68.64</td><td>97 862</td><td>86</td><td>74.81</td></tr>
<tr><td>3 a</td><td>97 217</td><td>88</td><td>67.71</td><td>97 776</td><td>68</td><td>73.88</td></tr>
<tr><td>4 a</td><td>97 129</td><td>74</td><td>66.77</td><td>97 708</td><td>61</td><td>72.93</td></tr>
<tr><td>5 a</td><td>97 055</td><td>268</td><td>65.82</td><td>97 647</td><td>202</td><td>71.79</td></tr>
<tr><td>10 a</td><td>96 787</td><td>271</td><td>61.00</td><td>97 445</td><td>154</td><td>67.12</td></tr>
<tr><td>15 a</td><td>96 516</td><td>601</td><td>56.16</td><td>97 291</td><td>235</td><td>62.22</td></tr>
<tr><td>20 a</td><td>95 915</td><td>855</td><td>51.50</td><td>97 056</td><td>271</td><td>57.37</td></tr>
<tr><td>25 a</td><td>95 060</td><td>753</td><td>46.94</td><td>96 785</td><td>311</td><td>52.52</td></tr>
<tr><td>30 a</td><td>94 307</td><td>767</td><td>42.29</td><td>96 474</td><td>428</td><td>47.68</td></tr>
<tr><td>35 a</td><td>93 540</td><td>1 032</td><td>37.62</td><td>96 046</td><td>630</td><td>42.88</td></tr>
<tr><td>40 a</td><td>92 508</td><td>1 615</td><td>33.01</td><td>95 416</td><td>979</td><td>38.15</td></tr>
<tr><td>45 a</td><td>90 893</td><td>2 594</td><td>28.55</td><td>94 437</td><td>1 536</td><td>33.51</td></tr>
<tr><td>50 a</td><td>88 299</td><td>4 180</td><td>24.31</td><td>92 901</td><td>2 333</td><td>29.02</td></tr>
<tr><td>55 a</td><td>84 119</td><td>6 258</td><td>20.38</td><td>90 568</td><td>3 467</td><td>24.70</td></tr>
<tr><td>60 a</td><td>77 861</td><td>8 877</td><td>16.81</td><td>87 101</td><td>5 160</td><td>20.58</td></tr>
<tr><td>65 a</td><td>68 984</td><td>11 436</td><td>13.63</td><td>81 941</td><td>7 568</td><td>16.71</td></tr>
<tr><td>70 a</td><td>57 548</td><td>13 544</td><td>10.83</td><td>74 373</td><td>10 892</td><td>13.14</td></tr>
<tr><td>75 a</td><td>44 004</td><td>14 859</td><td>8.37</td><td>63 481</td><td>15 273</td><td>9.94</td></tr>
<tr><td>80 a</td><td>29 145</td><td>13 552</td><td>6.36</td><td>48 208</td><td>18 321</td><td>7.26</td></tr>
<tr><td>85 a</td><td>15 593</td><td>9 401</td><td>4.79</td><td>29 887</td><td>16 534</td><td>5.16</td></tr>
<tr><td>90 a</td><td>6 192</td><td>4 551</td><td>3.60</td><td>13 353</td><td>9 767</td><td>3.60</td></tr>
<tr><td>95 a</td><td>1 641</td><td>1 389</td><td>2.71</td><td>3 586</td><td>3 148</td><td>2.48</td></tr>
<tr><td>100 a</td><td>252</td><td></td><td>2.04</td><td>438</td><td></td><td>1.69</td></tr>
</table>

From: *Canadian Life Table*, 1966, *Canada Year Book*, 1973

Table 2-26

Average masses (ages 16–17)		
Height (cm)	Mass (kg)	
	Boys	Girls
150		47
152		49
154		51
156	49	52
158	51	53
160	54	54
162	55	55
164	56	56
166	59	57
168	61	59
170	62	60
172	63	62
174	65	63
176	66	64
178	67	65
180	69	65
182	70	
184	72	
186	74	
188	76	

Table 2-25

Life Expectancy at Birth by Sex and Province

Province	Male	Female	Province	Male	Female
Newfoundland	68.9	74.4	Ontario	68.7	75.3
Prince Edward Island	68.3	75.5	Manitoba	69.8	76.1
Nova Scotia	68.3	74.8	Saskatchewan	70.4	76.4
New Brunswick	68.5	75.2	Alberta	70.1	76.2
Quebec	67.9	73.9	British Columbia	69.2	75.8

Source: Information Canada

Table 2-27

EXAMPLE 1. *If you are 30 a old and male, what is the probability that you will live to be 85?*

Solution From Table 2-26 for males aged 30, $\quad N = 94\,307$
Since living to age 85 may
be considered a success, $\quad\quad\quad\quad\quad\quad\quad S = 15\,593$

$$P = \frac{S}{N}$$

$$= \frac{15\,593}{94\,307} = 0.16$$

EXAMPLE 2. *An insurance company sells whole life insurance for an annual premium of $15.25/$1000 to women at age 25. What is the average return in premiums the company would expect to receive?*

Solution From the mortality table, at age 25 the complete expectation of life for females is 52.52 a. Therefore the average return on premiums will be
$$52.52 \times \$15.52 = \$800.93$$

It may seem unlikely that the insurance company can pay out $1000 with the expectation of $801; however the premiums are in effect an annuity (see Chapter 7) and earn interest from the date they are paid.

Sports produce a great many statistics. Every hockey game adds to the list of "shots on goal," "goals for," "goals against," "goals per game average," "20-goal players," etc. Every baseball game provides "hits," "runs," "errors," "batting averages," "earned runs," etc., and many players have contracts setting out how these statistics affect their income.

School administration planners for new housing areas are very interested in the average number of children per family, and it does not bother them if the number turns out to be 2.3 instead of a whole number.

EXERCISE 2-5

B **1.** An insurance company charges a premium of $13.50/$1000 whole life insurance at age 25 for men. Use Table 2-26 to calculate how much in total premiums the company would expect to receive from a policy of $20 000.

2. If you live to be 35 in good health, what is the probability that you will live to be 75?

3. If you won a contest at age 20 which promised to pay you $100 a week for life, how much would you expect to receive in your lifetime according to your complete expectation of life as indicated in Table 2-26?

C **4.** If in Canada the average number of people per dwelling is 3.7, estimate the number of people living in your block (or apartment building). Suggest factors which might affect the accuracy of your estimate. (A dwelling is a single apartment unit rather than the whole building).

A train travelling at 60 km/h passes a point in 45 s. How long is the train?

1 a = 52.143 weeks

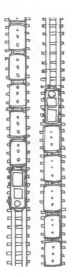

2.6 QUALITY CONTROL IN INDUSTRY

With the advent of mass production, quality control has become a specialized function in the manufacturing process. When a single craftsman or guild was responsible for making a product by hand, each item was subjected to careful scrutiny and testing throughout its production. When items are being produced by the thousands, with very little of the process under direct human control, it is necessary to rely on statistics and probability to test the quality of the product.

An electronics firm may produce millions of components in a year. It would be uneconomical to test every one and a purchaser would rather chance a few defective parts than pay the higher price that would result from such extensive testing. In situations such as this, samples of the product are regularly selected and tested, the samples being selected at random by an employee in the quality control department. In some cases items are selected for testing from a production line at regular time intervals.

Some products, such as fuels, must be tested by sampling since they are consumed in the testing process.

Two trains of equal length each travelling at 60 km/h but in opposite directions, pass each other from engine passing engine to caboose passing caboose in 45 s. How long are the trains? How far is the point where the engines passed from the point where the cabooses passed?

EXAMPLE 1. *A factory produces small electric motors for toys. The company accepts a risk of 2% defects. The quality control department selects 10 motors per batch of 100 for testing. If any are defective the batch is rejected and sent back for further testing and analysis.*
(*a*) *What is the probability of rejecting a batch with exactly two defective?*
(*b*) *What is the probability of accepting a batch with five defective?*

Solution (a) To find the probability of rejecting a batch with two defective, we shall first consider the probability of not selecting a defective one from a batch with two defectives.

On the first draw there are 98 good out of 100, $\therefore P_1 = \dfrac{98}{100}$

On the second draw there are 97 good out of 99, $\therefore P_2 = \dfrac{97}{99}$

. . . .

On the tenth draw there are 89 good out of 91, $\therefore P_{10} = \dfrac{89}{91}$

Since these events are independent,

$$P = \frac{98}{100} \times \frac{97}{99} \times \frac{96}{98} \cdots \frac{91}{93} \times \frac{90}{92} \times \frac{89}{91}$$

$$= \frac{90 \times 89}{100 \times 99} \doteq 0.8$$

$$1 - 0.8 = 0.2$$

Therefore the probability of rejecting a batch with two defective is 0.2.

applied mathematics for today: senior

A batch with two defective will be rejected on an average of once in five occurrences.

(b) To consider the probability of accepting a batch with five defective, we shall consider the probability of drawing 10 good motors from a batch of 100 with five defective.

On the first draw there are 95 good out of 100, $\therefore P_1 = \dfrac{95}{100}$

On the second draw there are 94 good out of 99, $\therefore P_2 = \dfrac{94}{99}$

. . . .

On the tenth draw there are 86 good out of 91, $\therefore P_{10} = \dfrac{86}{91}$

$$P = \frac{95}{100} \times \frac{94}{99} \times \frac{93}{98} \times \frac{92}{97} \times \frac{91}{96} \times \frac{90}{95} \times \frac{89}{94} \times \frac{88}{93} \times \frac{87}{92} \times \frac{86}{91}$$

$$\doteq 0.59$$

Approximately six times out of 10 a batch with five defectives would be passed.

In order to reduce this probability a more intensive testing program or more sophisticated statistical methods would have to be used.

Some products must be manufactured within certain tolerances. It is not simply a matter of whether or not they work.

Let us suppose Acme Metal Products produces washers to fit on bolts. The product specification limits on the hole in one size of washer are 5.1 mm minimum to 5.2 mm maximum. The machine turning out washers of this size produces washers with a mean hole diameter of 5.15 mm and a standard deviation of 0.01 mm. In a normal distribution, 99.74% of the values will be within three standard deviations of the mean (see Figure 2-28), therefore only 0.13% will be beyond three standard deviations on either side of the mean. The company is willing to accept this as a maximum percentage of defects.

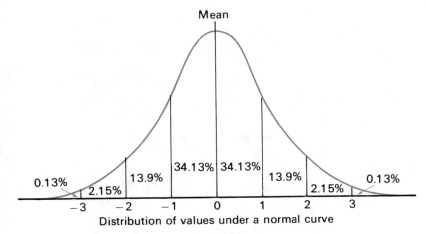

Distribution of values under a normal curve

Figure 2-28

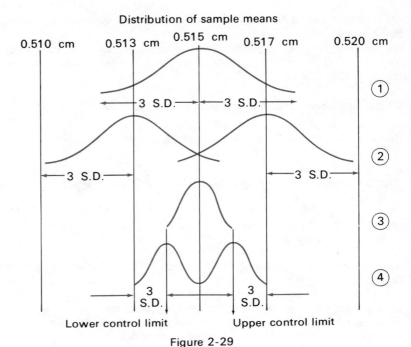

Distribution of sample means

Figure 2-29

In Figure 2-29, curve ① shows the distribution of hole diameters about the mean. The mean hole diameter can vary from 5.13 to 5.17 mm (curve ②) and 99.7% of the washers will still have hole diameters within the production specification limits.

$$\frac{0.5128 + 0.5137 + 0.5154 + 0,5167}{4} = 0.515$$

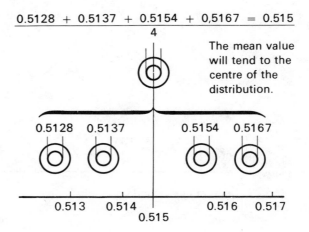

The mean value will tend to the centre of the distribution.

To increase the reliability of the tests, at regular intervals samples of nine washers are taken and the mean hole diameter is calculated. The means of the hole diameter for samples of size n will form a distribution with standard deviation $\dfrac{\text{S.D.}}{\sqrt{n}}$ (curve ③). If one item selected has a hole diameter near the limit, it will tend to be offset by the averaging of the other diameters. The standard deviation of samples of nine washers will be $\dfrac{0.001}{\sqrt{9}} = \dfrac{0.001}{3}$ cm. The 3 S.D. limit for the sample means will be 0.01 mm.

In order to keep the mean hole diameters between 5.13 and 5.17 mm, it will be necessary to accept only sample means between 5.14 and 5.16 mm (curve ④). These are called the lower and upper control limits.

In the quality control department a graph showing the mean hole diameter and the upper and lower control limits would be drawn (Figure 2-30). If the graph approaches or exceeds the control limits, investigations will be made to determine the cause.

Quality control chart for washer hole size

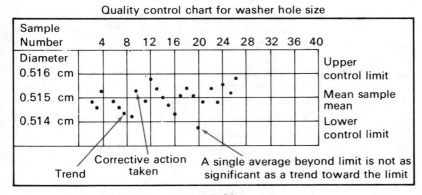

Figure 2-30

Other statistical tests beyond the range of this text would be used to ensure that the standard deviation of the hole diameter was kept within acceptable limits. Figure 2-31 shows why averages are used in sampling.

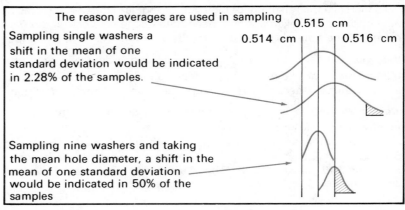

The reason averages are used in sampling

Sampling single washers a shift in the mean of one standard deviation would be indicated in 2.28% of the samples.

0.515 cm

0.514 cm | 0.516 cm

Sampling nine washers and taking the mean hole diameter, a shift in the mean of one standard deviation would be indicated in 50% of the samples

Figure 2-31

EXERCISE 2-6

B **1.** In a batch of four items one is defective. What is the probability of catching the defect if a sample of two is tested?

2. On a production line of locks every 20th lock is tested in a run of 100. If one or more defective locks are found, the run is rejected and returned for further testing. If no defects are found, the run is accepted.
(a) What is the probability of rejecting a run with two defective locks?
(b) What is the probability of accepting a run with two defective locks?
(c) What is the probability of accepting a run with five defective locks?

3. (a) In a batch of 10 items how many must be tested to give a 0.5 probability that there are no defects?
(b) What is the probability of passing batches under the above inspection system i) with one defect? ii) with two defects? iii) with four defects? iv) with five defects?

4. Sheet metal is rolled to a thickness of 2.50 mm with upper and lower control limits of 2.48 mm and 2.52 mm respectively. Samples of four measures of thickness are taken at regular intervals, and the mean thickness is plotted on a quality control chart. Construct the chart and plot values for the samples indicated in Table 2-32. Indicate where action may be required.

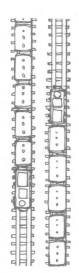

Two trains each travelling at 60 km/h but in opposite directions, pass each other in 45 s. If one train is twice as long as the other how long is each train? How far is the point where the engines pass from the point where the cabooses pass?

Sample	1	2	3	4	5	6	7	8
Item 1	2.54 mm	2.50 mm	2.48 mm	2.48 mm	2.50 mm	2.51 mm	2.49 mm	2.52 mm
2	2.51	2.49	2.46	2.47	2.51	2.53	2.50	2.50
3	2.48	2.48	2.45	2.46	2.49	2.52	2.51	2.50
4	2.49	2.49	2.54	2.47	2.50	2.47	2.51	2,51

Table 2-32

5. A thread manufacturer produces thread designed to have a mean breaking strength of 7.0 N. Random samples of nine pieces are tested. The lower control limit for mean breaking strength is 6.1 N. If this represents a 3 S.D. limit, what is the standard deviation of the sample means? What is the standard deviation of the breaking strength of the thread?

REVIEW EXERCISE

A **1.** For the set of numbers 2, 7, 8, 9, 9 give:
(a) mean   (b) median   (c) mode   (d) range

2. (a) In a field of 20 competitors Jane throws the javelin as far as or further than 16 of them. What is her percentile rank?
(b) Out of 250 field day competitors Wayne has 14 points, which is in the 90th percentile. How many competitors has Wayne equalled or exceeded?

B **3.**

Enrolment by Grade in Canadian Publicly Controlled Schools.
1969–1970

Grade	Enrolment $\times 10^5$	Grade	Enrolment $\times 10^5$
Kindergarten	3.59	Grade 7	4.58
Grade 1	4.99	8	4.47
2	4.45	9	4.33
3	4.91	10	3.92
4	4.85	11	3.39
5	4.77	12	2.02
6	4.67	13	0.50

Source: Information Canada

Table 2-33

(a) Select a suitable graph form and illustrate the above data.
(b) Give two reasons to account for the rapid decline in enrolment from grade 12 to grade 13.

4. The mass of 75 pennies was determined on laboratory scales.

Mass (g)	Frequency
3.00–3.04	3
3.05–3.09	5
3.10–3.14	14
3.15–3.19	22
3.20–3.24	18
3.25–3.29	9
3.30–3.34	4

Table 2-34

Find the mean, range and standard deviation.

5. An aptitude test given to 100 students gave the following results.

Class values	Boundary values	Frequency	Cumulative frequency
	39.5		
40–49		4	
	49.5		
50–59		17	
	59.5		
60–69		30	
	69.5		
70–79		27	
	79.5		
80–89		15	
	89.5		
90–99		7	
	99.5		

(a) Complete the table and find the median score.

(b) Find the 75th percentile score.

6. A sample of 10 light bulbs has one defective. If two are sampled:

(a) What is the probability of not finding the defect?

(b) What is the probability of finding the defect?

7. A batch of 25 motor parts has two defective and five are tested. Find the following probabilities:

(a) Finding no defective parts.

(b) Finding at least one defective part.

8. A stamping machine is turning out washers with a mean hole diameter of 5.10 mm. The standard deviation of hole diameters is 0.04 mm. On a production run of 100 000 washers how many would you expect to have a diameter greater than 5.18 mm or less than 5.02 mm?

applied mathematics for today: senior

REVIEW AND PREVIEW TO CHAPTER 3

EXERCISE 1 *DISTRIBUTIVE PROPERTY*

1. Expand.
(a) $2(x-3)$
(b) $4(2a-3b+2c)$
(c) $-3(x-3y)$
(d) $-5(2a-3b-1)$
(e) $2x(x+3)$
(f) $-2m(3m-2n)$
(g) $-3x(x^2-2x+1)$
(h) $-3x^2y(2xy-3-2y)$

2. Expand and simplify.
(a) $(x-3)(x-2)$
(b) $(a+3)(a+7)$
(c) $(2m-1)(2m-1)$
(d) $(3x+4)(x+5)$
(e) $(3x-2)(3x+2)$
(f) $(2a-3b)(a+2b)$
(g) $(4x-2y)(3x-5y)$
(h) $(3a+2c)(2a-7c)$
(i) $(x-7)^2$
(j) $(2x+5)^2$

> If it is 10:00 now, what time will it be 121 036 842 h later?

3. Expand and simplify.
(a) $2(x+7)(x+6)$
(b) $3(x-4)(x+3)$
(c) $-2(a-3)(2a+1)$
(d) $4(x+3y)(x-y)$
(e) $2(x+3)^2$
(f) $-3(x-4)^2$
(g) $-2(x+2y)^2$
(h) $4(2a-5b)(3a-b)$

EXERCISE 2 *FORMULA SOLVING AND SUBSTITUTION*

1. (a) If $V=lwh$, find V when $l=10$, $w=6$, $h=4$.
(b) If $A=\frac{1}{2}bh$, find A when $b=20$, $h=16$.
(c) If $P=2(l+w)$, find l when $P=146$, $w=13$.
(d) If $S=\frac{n}{2}(a+l)$, find l when $S=590$, $n=20$, $a=1$.
(e) If $A=p+prt$, find t when $A=3500$, $p=500$, $r=3$.
(f) If $V=lwh$, find w when $V=500$, $h=5$, $l=50$.

2. Solve each of the following formulas for the variable indicated.
(a) $V=lwh$, for l
(b) $D=ST$, for T
(c) $E=IR$, for I
(d) $P=2(l+w)$, for l
(e) $S=\frac{n}{2}(a+l)$, for a
(f) $A=p+prt$, for t
(g) $s=ut+\frac{1}{2}at^2$, for a
(h) $A=\frac{h}{2}(x+y)$, for x

Solve the following equations:

1. $3.675x=42.65$
2. $68.45x+3.175=9.389$

3. $0.2657x-1.255=4.375$
4. $1.675-24.75x=8.924$

5. $(8.361+21.375)x=163.75$
6. $\dfrac{3.284}{5.693}x-1.259=\dfrac{34.29}{12.67}$

7. $6.375x+21.45=(118.5)^2$
8. $42.75x+\dfrac{2.375}{4.689}=\dfrac{52.65}{21.75}$

9. $5.275(1.077-21.65x)=82.63$
10. $\dfrac{54.35}{x}+21.75=6.525$

polynomials and rational expressions   55

CHAPTER 3

Polynomials and Rational Expressions

3.1 PRODUCTS OF POLYNOMIALS

monomials
$2x^2$
$3mnt$
7
binomials
$2x-7$
$3a^2+7$
$3x^4-6a^2$
trinomials
$a+b-c$
$2x^2-3x+2$
$4x^2+6a-1$

A *polynomial* is an algebraic expression of the form $7x^2+4x-5$ or $2m-7$ or $a^2-2ab+b^2$. In the polynomial $7x^2+4x-5$ the quantities $7x^2$, $4x$, and -5 are called terms.

EXAMPLE 1. *Expand and simplify:* $2(x-3a)-4(3x+2a)-(x-a)$

Solution

$$2(x-3a)-4(3x+2a)-(x-a)=2(x-3a)-4(3x+2a)-1(x-a)$$
$$=2x-6a-12x-8a-x+a$$
$$=-11x-13a$$

EXAMPLE 2. *Expand and simplify:*
$3(x-2)(x+3)-2(x+1)^2-(2x-1)(x+3)$

Solution

These steps may be done mentally

$$3(x-2)(x+3)-2(x+1)^2-(2x-1)(x+3)$$
$$=3(x-2)(x+3)-2(x+1)(x+1)-(2x-1)(x+3)$$
$$=3(x^2+3x-2x-6)-2(x^2+x+x+1)-(2x^2+6x-x-3)$$
$$=3(x^2+x-6)-2(x^2+2x+1)-(2x^2+5x-3)$$
$$=3x^2+3x-18-2x^2-4x-2-2x^2-5x+3$$
$$=-x^2-6x-17$$

EXAMPLE 3. *Expand* $(2x-1)(3x^2-2x+4)$

Solution

$$(2x-1)(3x^2-2x+4)$$
$$=(2x-1)(3x^2-2x+4)$$
$$=6x^3-4x^2+8x-3x^2+2x-4$$
$$=6x^3-7x^2+10x-4$$

EXERCISE 3-1

B **1.** Expand and simplify.

(a) $2(x-3)-4(x+5)$ (b) $3(2a-4b)-4(3a+2b)$

(c) $3(a-2b+4c)-4(2a+b-3c)+3(3a-2b-c)$

(d) $2(x-y-7)-(3x-2y+4)+5(x+y)$

(e) $3(2t^2-4t+3)-2(t^2+3t-1)-(3t^2+5)$

(f) $3x(2x-7)-x(x+4)-5x(x-5)$

(g) $m(2m-n)-3m(3m-4n)+2m(5m-n)$

2. Expand and collect like terms.

(a) $(x-1)(x+3)+(x+4)(x+3)$

(b) $(2x-1)(x+2)+(x+2)^2$

(c) $2(a-1)(a-2)+3(a+4)(a-3)$

(d) $3(4b+1)(b-2)-2(2b+4)(b-1)$

(e) $2(x-3)^2-(2x-1)(x-2)$

(f) $3(2m-1)(2m+1)-(2m+3)^2$

(g) $(x-y)(x+2y)-3(x^2-y^2)$

(h) $(x+3)(1-x)-3+4(x+2)^2$

(i) $2(a-3b)(a-b)-(a-b)^2+6b^2$

3. Expand and simplify.

(a) $(x+1)(x^2+x+1)$ (b) $(2x-3)(3x^2-2x+5)$

(c) $(3a-1)(2a^2-2a-3)$ (d) $(x^2-7x+3)(2x+1)$

(e) $(2b+1)(3b^3-2b^2+2b-4)$ (f) $(x^2+2x-1)(x^2-3x-2)$

C **4.** Expand and collect like terms.

(a) $(x+\frac{1}{2})(x-\frac{1}{2})+(x+\frac{1}{2})^2$ (b) $(a+\frac{1}{2})^2-(a-\frac{1}{4})^2$

(c) $5(x-\frac{1}{2})(x-\frac{1}{2})-3(x+\frac{1}{4})^2$ (d) $(x+2)(x-\frac{1}{2})-2(x+4)(x-\frac{1}{4})$

3.2 THE COMMON FACTOR

In Section 3.1 the distributive law was used to expand:

$$a(b+c)=ab+ac$$

We will now use the distributive law to reverse the process—which we call factoring:

$$ab+ac=a(b+c)$$

EXAMPLE 1. *Factor* (a) $5x+15$ (b) $ab-ac-a$

Solution The common factor is found by inspection. The other factor is found by division.

(a) $5x+15=5(x+3)$ (b) $ab-ac-a=a(b-c-1)$

Do these steps mentally.

EXAMPLE 2. *Factor (a)* $x(x+3)-2(x+3)$ *(b)* $2x(x-1)-(x-1)$

Solution

(a) $x(x+3)-2(x+3) = (x+3)(x-2)$

(b) $2x(x-1)-(x-1) = (x-1)(2x-1)$

Group to get common factors.

EXAMPLE 3. *Factor* $2x^2+4x+3xy+6y$

Solution

$$2x^2+4x+3xy+6y$$
$$= (2x^2+4x)+(3xy+6y)$$
$$= 2x(x+2)+3y(x+2)$$
$$= (x+2)(2x+3y)$$

EXERCISE 3-2

HINT
See Example 3.

B   **1.** Factor.
(a) $3x+6$
(c) x^3+7x
(e) p^2m^2-pmn
(g) $24a^2b-6ab^2$

(b) $3x^2+5x$
(d) $x^4+7x^3+5x^2$
(f) $6y^2-3y$
(h) $5mnt+10m^2nt-30m^2n^2t^2$

2. Factor.
(a) $3x(x+3)+4(x+3)$
(c) $3x^2(x-1)-4(x-1)$
(e) $5(t+7)+6t(t+7)$

(b) $2a(a-7)-3(a-7)$
(d) $5a(a+3)+(a+3)$
(f) $2x(x+5)-(x+5)$

3. Factor.
(a) $x^2+2x+xy+2y$
(c) $2x^2-5x+2xy-5y$
(e) $x^2+3x-xy-3y$
(g) $2ab-3b-2ax+3x$

(b) $x^2+5x+xt+5t$
(d) $5at+4t+5a+4$
(f) $3xy-2x-3y+2$
(h) $4mx^2-2mx+2x-1$

BINOMIALS
$$\overset{\displaystyle \diagup \quad \diagdown}{(x+1)(x-3)}$$
$$= \underline{x^2-2x-3}$$
TRINOMIAL

3.3 FACTORING TRINOMIALS: x^2+bx+c

The product of two binomials is often a trinomial. It follows that the factors of a trinomial (which is factorable) are often in the form of two binomials.

EXAMPLE 1.   *Expand* $(x+m)(x+n)$

Solution

$$(x+m)(x+n) = x^2 + nx + mx + mn$$
$$= x^2 + mx + nx + mn$$
$$= x^2 + (m+n)x + mn$$

$$
\begin{array}{c}
\xrightarrow{\text{EXPANDING}} \\
(x+m)(x+n) = x^2 + (m+n)x + mn \\
\xleftarrow{\text{FACTORING}}
\end{array}
$$

EXAMPLE 2.   *Factor* $x^2 + 9x + 20$

Solution
$$y^2 + 2y - 15$$
$$x^2 + 9x + 20$$
$$x^2 + (m+n)x + mn$$

We see that $m + n = 9$ and $mn = 20$.
The two numbers whose sum is 9 and whose product is 20 are 5 and 4.

$$\therefore \quad x^2 + 9x + 20 = (x+5)(x+4).$$

EXAMPLE 3.   *Factor* $y^2 + 2y - 15$

Solution
$$y^2 + 2y - 15$$

$$m + n = 2 \quad \text{and} \quad mn = -15$$

$\therefore$ the values of m and n are 5 and -3.
$\therefore y^2 + 2y - 15 = (y+5)(y-3).$

Addition
ZERO
ONE
TWO
THREE

EXERCISE 3-3

B   **1.** Factor.
(a) $x^2 + 7x + 12$ (b) $x^2 + 6x + 8$
(c) $x^2 - 5x + 6$ (d) $x^2 + 2x - 8$
(e) $x^2 - 3x - 10$ (f) $x^2 + 12x + 36$
(g) $x^2 - x - 2$ (h) $x^2 - x - 12$
(i) $x^2 + x - 12$ (j) $x^2 + 12x + 20$

2. Factor and check by expanding your answer.
(a) $x^2 + 8x + 12$ (b) $x^2 - 13x + 36$
(c) $x^2 + 5x - 36$ (d) $x^2 + 10x + 16$
(e) $x^2 - x - 30$ (f) $x^2 + 6x - 27$
(g) $x^2 - 16$ (h) $x^2 - 9$
(i) $x^2 - 14x + 49$ (j) $x^2 - 25$

3. Factor.
(a) $x^2 + 7xy + 12y^2$ (b) $x^2 - xy - 12y^2$

Write an expression for
100 using four nines.

(c) $a^2-3ab-4b^2$ (d) $p^2-8pq-9q^2$
(e) $s^2+3st+2t^2$ (f) $c^2+cd-12d^2$
(g) m^2-9n^2 (h) $a^2b^2-2ab+1$
(i) $x^2+9xy+18y^2$ (j) $a^2-2ab-15b^2$

4. Find three factors of each of the following by first finding a common factor.

(a) $4a^2-8a-60$ (b) $3b^2+15b-42$
(c) $6c^2-12c+6$ (d) $5d^2-50d+125$
(e) $2e^2+10e-48$ (f) $x-5x^2+6x^3$
(g) $4a^2-100$ (h) $2x^2+24x+72$
(i) $7a^2-63$ (j) $ax^2+ax-30a$

C   **5.** Factor.

(a) $x^2+x+\frac{1}{4}$ (b) $x^2-x+\frac{1}{4}$
(c) $x^2+\frac{1}{2}x+\frac{1}{16}$ (d) $x^2-\frac{1}{4}x-\frac{1}{8}$
(e) $x^2-\frac{1}{4}$ (f) $x^2-\frac{5}{6}x-\frac{1}{6}$

3.4   FACTORING TRINOMIALS: ax^2+bx+c

To factor a trinomial ax^2+bx+c, where a, b, $c \in I$ and $a \neq 1$, a method similar to that of Section 3.3 is used.

EXAMPLE 1.   *Factor $x^2-12x+35$*

Solution We want to find two numbers whose sum is -12 and whose product is 35. The numbers are -5 and -7.

$$\therefore \quad x^2-12x+35=(x-5)(x-7).$$

Insert signs of operation to make

$$3\blacksquare5\blacksquare4\blacksquare2\blacksquare=13$$

a true statement.

EXAMPLE 2.   (a) *Expand* $(2x+5)(x+2)$ (b) *Factor* $2x^2+9x+10$

Solution

(a) $(2x+5)(x+2)$
     $=2x^2+4x+5x+10$
     $=2x^2+9x+10$

(b) $2x^2+9x+10$
     $=2x^2+4x+5x+10$
     $=(2x^2+4x)+(5x+10)$
     $=2x(x+2)+5(x+2)$
     $=(x+2)(2x+5)$

The problem of factoring $2x^2+9x+10$ is simple enough once we replace $9x$ by $4x+5x$. But how do we know to decompose $9x$ into $4x+5x$? Notice that $(4x)(5x)=(2x^2)(10)$. Here, although we are still looking for two numbers whose sum is 9, we now require their product to be $2 \times 10 = 20$. Suppose the two numbers are p and q. Then $p+q=9$ and $pq=20$, so the values of p and q are 4 and 5.

EXAMPLE 3.   *Factor* (a) $2x^2-5x+3$ (b) $12x^2-8x-15$

Solution

$p+q=-5, \quad p \times q = 3 \times 2 = 6$
The values of p and q are -2 and -3
$\therefore \quad 2x^2-5x+3$
$= 2x^2-3x-2x+3$
$= (2x^2-3x)-(2x-3)$
$= x(2x-3)-(2x-3)$
$= (2x-3)(x-1)$

(b) $12x^2-8x-15$
$p+q=-8 \quad$ and $\quad p \times q = -180$
$\therefore \quad p=-18 \quad$ and $\quad q=10$
$12x^2-8x-15$
$= 12x^2-18x+10x-15$
$= (12x^2-18x)+(10x-15)$
$= 6x(2x-3)+5(2x-3)$
$= (2x-3)(6x+5).$

Put the numbers 1 to 9 in
the spaces to make the
statements true:

$$\blacksquare - \blacksquare \div \blacksquare = 1$$
$$\blacksquare - \blacksquare \times \blacksquare = 1$$
$$\blacksquare + \blacksquare - \blacksquare = 1$$

EXERCISE 3-4

B **1.** Factor by decomposing the middle term.
(a) $2x^2+7x+5$ (b) $3x^2+7x+2$
(c) $6x^2+19x+10$ (d) $2x^2+5x-3$
(e) $5x^2-17x+6$ (f) $2x^2-3x-14$
(g) $6x^2+19x+15$ (h) $6x^2+13x+6$
(i) $8x^2+x-9$ (j) $10x^2-21x-10$

2. Factor.
(a) $2x^2+5x-3$ (b) $5m^2-17m+6$
(c) $6x^2-13x-5$ (d) $9a^2-18ab+8b^2$
(e) $15r^2-31r+14$ (f) $4x^2+8xy+3y^2$
(g) $28y^2-39xy+8x^2$ (h) $12x^2-5xy-2y^2$
(i) $3m^2-19mn-14n^2$ (j) $10a^2-13ab-30b^2$

3.5 DIVISION AND SPECIAL FACTORING

When one factor is known the second can be found by division. We can divide polynomials by a method similar to long division in arithmetic.

EXAMPLE 1. *Divide (x^2+5x+7) by $(x+2)$*

Solution

$$\begin{array}{r}
x+3 \\
x+2{\overline{\smash{\big)}\,x^2+5x+7}} \\
\underline{x^2+2x} \\
3x+7 \\
\underline{3x+6} \\
1
\end{array}$$
— Subtract
— Remainder

$(x+2)$ is *not* a factor of x^2+5x+7 since division yields a remainder which is not zero.

EXAMPLE 2. *Divide* $(14x^4-29x^2+12-x^3)$ *by* $(3x-6+7x^2)$

Solution Rearrange both polynomials in descending powers of x. Leave a space for any power of x that is missing.

3 is a factor of 12 because 3 divides 12 evenly (remainder $= 0$)

$$\begin{array}{r}
2x^2-\ x-2 \\
7x^2+3x-6{\overline{\smash{\big)}\,14x^4-\ x^3-29x^2\ \ \ \ \ \ +12}} \\
\underline{14x^4+6x^3-12x^2} \\
-7x^3-17x^2 \\
\underline{-7x^3-\ 3x^2+6x} \\
-14x^2-6x+12 \\
\underline{-14x^2-6x+12} \\
0
\end{array}$$

$(7x^2+3x-6)$ is a factor of $14x^4-x^3-29x^2+12$ since division yields a remainder of 0.

D
I
V
I
S
I
O
N

EXERCISE 3-5

A **1.** Simplify.

(a) $\dfrac{x^5}{x^2}$ (b) $\dfrac{x^3}{x}$ (c) $\dfrac{x^7}{x^6}$ (d) $\dfrac{x^3}{x^3}$

(e) $\dfrac{6x^4}{2x^2}$ (f) $\dfrac{18x^6}{3x^3}$ (g) $\dfrac{-12x^4}{2x^3}$ (h) $\dfrac{24x^6}{-6x^4}$

(i) $\dfrac{-18x^7}{-9x^5}$ (j) $\dfrac{21x^3}{-7x^3}$ (k) $\dfrac{-3x^4}{-3x^2}$ (l) $\dfrac{-22x^8}{11x^8}$

F
A
C
T
O
R
I
N
G

B **2.** Divide.

(a) $(x^2+7x+12)\div(x+4)$ (b) $(x^2-4x-12)\div(x+2)$
(c) $(x^2-6x+9)\div(x-3)$ (d) $(x^2-x-12)\div(x-4)$
(e) $(x^2+3x-11)\div(x+5)$ (f) $(x^2-11x+25)\div(x-7)$

3. Divide
(a) $(3x^2-7x+3)\div(x+1)$
(b) $(x^3-7x+6)\div(x+2)$
(c) $(9a^2-27a+14)\div(3a-7)$
(d) $(p^4+p^3+7p^2-6p+9)\div(p^2+2p+8)$
(e) $(6c^3-13c^2-4c+15)\div(2c-3)$

4. Divide and check by multiplying.
(a) $(7y^3-96y^2-28y)\div(7y+2)$ (b) $(p^3+3p-1-3p^2)\div(p-1)$
(c) $(x^3-38x-10)\div(x-5)$ (d) $(a^2-4)\div(a-2)$

applied mathematics for today: senior

5. Refer to 4(d) and state the factors of $a^2 - 4$.

6. (a) Divide $x^3 + 27$ by $x + 3$.
(b) What is the remainder?
(c) State the factors of $x^3 + 27$.

7. Divide $y^3 - 64$ by $y - 4$ and state the factors of $y^3 - 64$.

8. Use the method of questions 6 and 7 to factor the following:
(a) $a^3 + 8$ (b) $a^3 - 8$ (c) $x^3 + 1$
(d) $x^3 - 1$ (e) $b^3 - 125$ (f) $b^3 + 125$

9. Determine by division whether $(a + 2)$ is a factor of
(a) $a^2 + 6a + 8$ (b) $a^3 + 2a^2 + a + 4$
(c) $2a^3 + 2a^2 - 3a + 2$ (d) $3a^3 + 7a^2 + 4a$

3.6 REDUCING RATIONAL EXPRESSIONS

Thus far in Chapter 3 we have been performing operations to help study the properties of polynomial expressions. We will now consider the set of *rational expressions* that includes the set of all polynomials. Polynomials are manufactured using the operations addition, subtraction, and multiplication. If division is included we may obtain rational expressions.

A rational number is of the form $\frac{a}{b}$ where a, $b \in I$ and $b \neq 0$, such as

$\frac{5}{x}$, $\frac{2x+3}{x}$, $\frac{x+3}{(x-3)(x-4)}$, which are rational expressions for every real value of x (except those which make the denominator zero).

Remembering that 1 is the identity element of multiplication in our real number system allows us to perform some interesting manipulations with rational expressions.

The number 1 may be written as $\frac{1}{1}$ or $\frac{2}{2}$ or $\frac{8}{8}$. Therefore

$$\frac{3}{4} = \frac{3 \times 2}{4 \times 2} = \frac{6}{8} \quad \text{and} \quad \frac{16}{24} = \frac{16 \div 8}{24 \div 8} = \frac{2}{3}.$$

Multiplying or dividing by any of the equivalent numerals for 1 gives an equivalent rational expression.

> **Principle of Equivalent Rational Expressions:**
>
> $$\frac{a}{b} = \frac{ka}{kb} = \frac{a \div m}{b \div m} = \frac{a \times \frac{1}{n}}{b \times \frac{1}{n}} \quad b, k, m, n \neq 0$$

EXERCISE 3-6

A **1.** State the value of x for which each of the following is *not* a rational expression.

(a) $\frac{5}{x}$ (b) $\frac{x+4}{x+5}$ (c) $\frac{x+1}{x^2}$

(d) $\dfrac{x^2}{x+1}$ (e) $\dfrac{x}{(x-3)(x-4)}$ (f) $\dfrac{2x}{(x+1)(x+2)}$

(g) $\dfrac{3x}{2x-1}$ (h) $\dfrac{2x}{3-x}$ (i) $\dfrac{x+2}{(4-x)(1+x)}$

(j) $\dfrac{2x+3}{(x+7)^2}$

2. Complete the following:

Write an expression for 19 using four eights.

(a) $\dfrac{2}{3}=\dfrac{\blacksquare}{18}$ (b) $\dfrac{4}{20}=\dfrac{\blacksquare}{5}$

(c) $\dfrac{5}{6}=\dfrac{20}{\blacksquare}$ (d) $\dfrac{3}{7}=\dfrac{18}{\blacksquare}$

(e) $\dfrac{4}{5}=\dfrac{\blacksquare}{5a}$ (f) $\dfrac{4x}{5y}=\dfrac{\blacksquare}{5xy}$

(g) $\dfrac{2}{3}=\dfrac{\blacksquare}{3(x+1)}$ (h) $\dfrac{2}{5}=\dfrac{2(x-3)}{\blacksquare}$

(i) $\dfrac{x+3}{x-7}=\dfrac{\blacksquare}{(x-7)(x-9)}$

3. Reduce the following rational expressions to lowest terms by first factoring the numerator and denominator and then dividing.

(a) $\dfrac{2a}{6a^2}$ (b) $\dfrac{-12xy}{-6x}$ (c) $\dfrac{36a^2b^2}{9ab}$

(d) $\dfrac{4x+6y}{2}$ (e) $\dfrac{6ab-9ac}{3a}$ (f) $\dfrac{2x}{2y-8t}$

(g) $\dfrac{5ax}{10ay+15at}$ (h) $\dfrac{3x+6}{x+2}$ (i) $\dfrac{2ab-ac}{6b-3c}$

(j) $\dfrac{x^2+2x}{x^3-3x}$ (k) $\dfrac{x+2}{x^2-4}$ (l) $\dfrac{a^2+7a}{a^2-49}$

4. Reduce to lowest terms.

(a) $\dfrac{x^2+7x+12}{x^2+6x+8}$ (b) $\dfrac{x^2-x-12}{x^2+x-20}$

(c) $\dfrac{y^2+3y+2}{y^2+5y+6}$ (d) $\dfrac{x^2-4}{x^2-4x+4}$

(e) $\dfrac{m^2-2m-15}{m^2-5m}$ (f) $\dfrac{6k^2-k-12}{6k^2-17k+12}$

(g) $\dfrac{6x^2+11x+3}{4x^2-9}$ (h) $\dfrac{6m^2+5m-4}{3m^2-8m-16}$

Put the numbers 1 to 9 in the spaces to make the statements true:

$\blacksquare-\blacksquare\div\blacksquare=2$

$\blacksquare-\blacksquare+\blacksquare=2$

$\blacksquare\times\blacksquare-\blacksquare=2$

3.7 MULTIPLICATION AND DIVISION OF RATIONAL EXPRESSIONS

To find the product of two rational numbers

$$\frac{a}{b}\times\frac{c}{d}=\frac{ac}{bd}$$

64   applied mathematics for today: senior

To divide by a rational number, multiply by its reciprocal.

$$\frac{a}{b} \div \frac{c}{d} = \frac{a}{b} \times \frac{d}{c} = \frac{ad}{bc}$$

EXAMPLE 1. *Simplify*

(a) $\dfrac{7a^2b}{3a} \times \dfrac{9a^3}{28b^2}$

(b) $\dfrac{x^2 - y^2}{6} \times \dfrac{3}{x+y}$

Solution

(a) $\dfrac{7a^2b}{3a} \times \dfrac{9a^3}{28b^2}$

$\quad = \dfrac{7 \times 9 \times a^2b \times a^3}{3 \times 28 \times a \times b^2}$

$\quad = \dfrac{3a^4}{4b}$

(b) $\dfrac{x^2 - y^2}{6} \times \dfrac{3}{x+y}$ $\qquad\qquad x+y \neq 0$

$\quad = \dfrac{(x-y)(x+y) \times 3}{6 \times (x+y)}$

$\quad = \dfrac{x-y}{2}$

EXAMPLE 2. *Simplify*

(a) $\dfrac{5a^2b^2}{9abc^2} \div \dfrac{10a^2}{3c}$

(b) $\dfrac{x^2 - y^2}{2x - 3y} \div \dfrac{x+y}{4x - 6y}$

Solution

(a) $\dfrac{5a^2b^2}{9abc^2} \div \dfrac{10a^2}{3c}$

$\quad = \dfrac{5a^2b^2}{9abc^2} \times \dfrac{3c}{10a^2}$

$\quad = \dfrac{5 \times 3 \times a^2b^2c}{9 \times 10 \times a^3bc^2}$

$\quad = \dfrac{b}{6ac}$

(b) $\dfrac{x^2 - y^2}{2x - 3y} \div \dfrac{x+y}{4x - 6y}$ $\qquad x+y \neq 0,$
$\qquad\qquad\qquad\qquad\qquad\qquad 2x - 3y \neq 0$

$\quad = \dfrac{x^2 - y^2}{2x - 3y} \times \dfrac{4x - 6y}{x+y}$

$\quad = \dfrac{(x-y)(x+y)2(2x - 3y)}{(2x - 3y)(x+y)}$

$\quad = 2(x - y)$

EXERCISE 3-7

A **1.** Simplify.

(a) $\frac{2}{3} \times \frac{3}{5}$

(b) $\frac{1}{4} \times \frac{5}{7}$

(c) $5 \times \frac{3}{7}$

(d) $(-\frac{1}{2})(\frac{3}{4})$

(e) $-\frac{4}{5} \times -\frac{2}{3}$

(f) $\frac{3}{4} \div \frac{1}{2}$

(g) $\frac{5}{6} \div \frac{2}{3}$

(h) $-\frac{2}{3} \div -\frac{3}{4}$

2. Simplify.

(a) $\dfrac{2a}{3} \times \dfrac{b}{a}$

(b) $\dfrac{2x}{3y} \times \dfrac{5y}{x}$

(c) $\dfrac{-3a}{2b} \times \dfrac{2b}{3a}$

(d) $\dfrac{-4x}{m} \times \dfrac{-m}{2x}$

(e) $\dfrac{2a}{3} \div \dfrac{a}{b}$

(f) $\dfrac{-2m}{3t} \div \dfrac{2m}{3t}$

B **3.** Simplify.

(a) $\dfrac{5x}{24y} \times \dfrac{12y}{35x}$

(b) $\dfrac{x+y}{-10} \times \dfrac{2}{x+y}$

(c) $\dfrac{6x^2y}{35xy^2} \times \dfrac{14x^3y}{9xy^2}$

(d) $\dfrac{(a+b)^2}{x-7y} \times \dfrac{x-7y}{a+b}$

polynomials and rational expressions   65

(e) $\dfrac{x^2+4x-12}{x^2+9x+18} \div \dfrac{3x+12}{6x+18}$ (f) $\dfrac{a^2-6a+8}{a^2+3a+2} \div \dfrac{a^2-4a}{a^2-4}$

(g) $\dfrac{a^2-11a+30}{a^2-6a+9} \div \dfrac{a^2-5a}{a^2-3a}$ (h) $\dfrac{x^2-y^2}{a^2-ab} \div \dfrac{x^2+xy}{ab-b^2}$

5. Simplify.

(a) $\dfrac{x^2-x-20}{x^2-25} \times \dfrac{x^2-x-2}{x^2+2x-8} \div \dfrac{x^2-1}{x^2+5x}$

(b) $\dfrac{x^2-4x+4}{x^2+6x+9} \times \dfrac{x^2-x-12}{x^2-8x+16} \div \dfrac{x^2-3x+2}{x^2-9}$

(c) $\dfrac{2a^2+a-1}{a^2-4a+3} \div \dfrac{6a^2+a-2}{2a^2-5a+3} \times \dfrac{3a^2-7a-6}{2a^2-7a+6}$

(d) $\dfrac{4x^2-1}{2x^2+7x+3} \times \dfrac{3x^2+5x-2}{2x^2-x-10} \div \dfrac{6x^2-5x+1}{2x^2+x-15}$

(e) $\dfrac{2x+6}{4x+4} \times \dfrac{2x^2-3x-5}{3x^2+5x-12} \div \dfrac{2x^2-19x+35}{3x^2-25x+28}$

3.8 ADDITION AND SUBTRACTION OF RATIONAL EXPRESSIONS

$\dfrac{3}{7}+\dfrac{2}{7}=\dfrac{3+2}{7}$

$=\dfrac{5}{7}$

To add or subtract rational expressions with the same denominator, add or subtract the numerators and use the same denominator.

$$\boxed{\dfrac{a}{b}+\dfrac{c}{b}=\dfrac{a+c}{b} \quad \text{or} \quad \dfrac{a}{b}-\dfrac{c}{b}=\dfrac{a-c}{b}}$$

$\dfrac{2}{7}+\dfrac{1}{3}=\dfrac{6}{21}+\dfrac{7}{21}$

$=\dfrac{6+7}{21}$

$=\dfrac{13}{21}$

In order to add or subtract rational expressions with different denominators, change each expression to an equivalent fraction with a common denominator.

$$\boxed{\dfrac{a}{b}+\dfrac{c}{d}=\dfrac{ad}{bd}+\dfrac{cb}{bd}=\dfrac{ad+cb}{bd} \quad \text{or} \quad \dfrac{a}{b}-\dfrac{c}{d}=\dfrac{ad}{bd}-\dfrac{cb}{bd}=\dfrac{ad-cb}{bd}}$$

EXAMPLE 1. Simplify $\dfrac{2}{3ab}+\dfrac{5}{6bc}+\dfrac{3}{4ac}$

Solution

common denominator is 12*abc*.

$\dfrac{2}{3ab}+\dfrac{5}{6bc}+\dfrac{3}{4ac}$

$=\dfrac{2(4c)}{12abc}+\dfrac{5(2a)}{12abc}+\dfrac{3(3b)}{12abc}$

$=\dfrac{8c+10a+9b}{12abc}$

EXAMPLE 2. *Simplify*

(a) $\dfrac{a+5}{a+6}-\dfrac{a-1}{a+3}$ (b) $\dfrac{3}{x^2+x-12}+\dfrac{2}{x^2+6x+8}$

Solution

(a) $\dfrac{a+5}{a+6}-\dfrac{a-1}{a+3}$

$=\dfrac{(a+5)(a+3)}{(a+6)(a+3)}-\dfrac{(a-1)(a+6)}{(a+6)(a+3)}$

$=\dfrac{(a^2+8a+15)-(a^2+5a-6)}{(a+6)(a+3)}$

$=\dfrac{a^2+8a+15-a^2-5a+6}{(a+6)(a+3)}$

$=\dfrac{3a+21}{(a+6)(a+3)}$

(b) $\dfrac{3}{x^2+x-12}+\dfrac{2}{x^2+6x+8}$

$=\dfrac{3}{(x+4)(x-3)}+\dfrac{2}{(x+4)(x+2)}$

$=\dfrac{3(x+2)}{(x+4)(x-3)(x+2)}+\dfrac{2(x-3)}{(x+4)(x-3)(x+2)}$

$=\dfrac{3x+6+2x-6}{(x+4)(x-3)(x+2)}$

$=\dfrac{5x}{(x+4)(x-3)(x+2)}$

Write an expression for 5 using four sevens.

EXERCISE 3-8

A **1.** Simplify.

(a) $\dfrac{3}{7}+\dfrac{2}{7}$ (b) $\dfrac{7}{13}-\dfrac{4}{13}$ (c) $\dfrac{5x}{2}-\dfrac{x}{2}$

(d) $\dfrac{5}{x}-\dfrac{1}{x}$ (e) $\dfrac{9}{2a}-\dfrac{4}{2a}$ (f) $\dfrac{7m}{3}+\dfrac{3m}{3}$

(g) $\dfrac{8a}{5}-\dfrac{2a}{5}$ (h) $\dfrac{2}{y-1}+\dfrac{4}{y-1}$ (i) $\dfrac{9}{x+1}-\dfrac{5}{x+1}$

(j) $\dfrac{6}{a+3}+\dfrac{4}{a+3}$ (k) $\dfrac{11}{a+b}-\dfrac{7}{a+b}$ (l) $\dfrac{a}{x+y}-\dfrac{b}{x+y}$

B **2.** Simplify.

(a) $\dfrac{3x}{7}+\dfrac{2x}{3}$ (b) $\dfrac{5a}{2}-\dfrac{3a}{5}$ (c) $\dfrac{3m}{6}+\dfrac{2m}{4}$

(d) $\dfrac{x}{8}-\dfrac{2x}{3}$ (e) $\dfrac{5x}{6}-\dfrac{2x}{5}$ (f) $\dfrac{2a}{11}-\dfrac{3b}{2}$

(g) $\dfrac{5d}{2}+\dfrac{3c}{7}$ (h) $\dfrac{3a}{4}+\dfrac{2b}{3}-\dfrac{5c}{6}$

3. Simplify.

(a) $\dfrac{3}{x}+\dfrac{4}{y}$ (b) $\dfrac{5}{a}+\dfrac{2}{b}$ (c) $\dfrac{7}{m}-\dfrac{3}{n}$

Find the dimensions of a

rectangle

whose area and perimeter are the same number.

(d) $\dfrac{2}{3m}+\dfrac{5}{2n}$ (e) $\dfrac{3}{4a}-\dfrac{5}{3b}$ (f) $\dfrac{x}{y}+\dfrac{y}{x}$

(g) $\dfrac{a}{xy}+\dfrac{b}{yz}$ (h) $\dfrac{x}{a}+\dfrac{y}{b}-\dfrac{z}{c}$

4. Simplify.

(a) $\dfrac{x+3}{4}+\dfrac{x+5}{3}$ (b) $\dfrac{x-1}{2}+\dfrac{x+7}{5}$ (c) $\dfrac{a-3}{3}-\dfrac{a+4}{5}$

(d) $\dfrac{m+1}{6}-\dfrac{m-7}{5}$ (e) $\dfrac{b+4}{6}-\dfrac{b+2}{3}$ (f) $\dfrac{2a-1}{4}+\dfrac{3a+2}{5}$

(g) $\dfrac{2x+3y}{9}-\dfrac{x+4y}{2}$ (h) $\dfrac{2b+3c}{6}-\dfrac{b-2c}{2}$

5. Simplify.

(a) $\dfrac{5}{x+3}+\dfrac{2}{x+2}$ (b) $\dfrac{3}{a-1}+\dfrac{5}{a+2}$ (c) $\dfrac{4}{m+3}-\dfrac{3}{m-1}$

(d) $\dfrac{5}{b+4}-\dfrac{2}{b-3}$ (e) $\dfrac{x+3}{x+1}+\dfrac{x-2}{x-1}$ (f) $\dfrac{m-5}{m+1}+\dfrac{m-3}{m-2}$

(g) $\dfrac{x-4}{x-2}-\dfrac{x-7}{x-5}$ (h) $\dfrac{a+2}{a-3}-\dfrac{a-4}{a+3}$

6. Simplify.

(a) $\dfrac{2}{x^2-x-12}+\dfrac{3}{x^2-6x+8}$ (b) $\dfrac{4}{x^2+7x+10}-\dfrac{3}{x^2-x-6}$

(c) $\dfrac{5}{a^2+7a+12}-\dfrac{2}{a^2+6a+9}$ (d) $\dfrac{2a}{a^2-4}-\dfrac{a}{a+2}$

(e) $\dfrac{2x^2}{x^2-y^2}-\dfrac{2x}{x+y}$ (f) $\dfrac{a^2+3a+2}{a^2-1}-\dfrac{2a}{a+1}$

(g) $\dfrac{3}{x-y}-\dfrac{2}{x+y}+\dfrac{7}{x^2-y^2}$ (h) $\dfrac{2a^2}{a^2-b^2}-\dfrac{2a^2}{a^2+ab}$

C **7.** If $\dfrac{I}{R}=\dfrac{I}{R_1}+\dfrac{I}{R_2}$, find R.

8. If $\dfrac{I}{R}=\dfrac{I}{R_1}+\dfrac{I}{R_2}+\dfrac{I}{R_3}$, find R.

9. If $PV=\dfrac{R}{(1+i)}+\dfrac{R}{(1+i)^2}+\dfrac{R}{(1+i)^3}$, then $PV=\dfrac{\blacksquare}{(1+i)^3}$

REVIEW EXERCISE

B **1. Expand and simplify.**
(a) $2(x+7)-3(x-2)+6$
(b) $(a-3)(a+2)-2(a+4)(a+1)$
(c) $(x+3)^2-2(x-1)(x+2)$
(d) $2(2a-1)(a-3)-(a+4)^2-2(1-3a)$
(e) $2(x+1)(x-2)-3(x+4)(x-2)+6$
(f) $(2x-1)(x^2+3x-4)$
(g) $\left(x+\dfrac{2}{x}\right)^2-\left(x-\dfrac{2}{x}\right)^2$
(h) $5(x-\tfrac{1}{2})(x+\tfrac{1}{2})-3(x-\tfrac{1}{3})(x-\tfrac{1}{4})$

2. Factor the following.

(a) $3x + 15$ (b) $ax + ay - a$ (c) $x^2 - 2x + x - 2$

(d) $x^2 - y^2$ (e) $a^2 - 7a + 12$ (f) $a^2 - a - 12$

(g) $x^2 + 5x - 36$ (h) $x^2 - 64$ (i) $16p^2 - 25q^2$

(j) $2x^2 + 16x + 24$ (k) $x^3 - 15x^2 + 56x$ (l) $p^3 - 1$

(m) $a^3 - 27$ (n) $2x^2 + 9x + 10$ (o) $m^3 + n^3$

(p) $a^3 + 64$ (q) $4a^2 + 8ab + 3b^2$ (r) $15x^2 - 31x + 14$

(s) $5x^2 + 22xy - 48y^2$ (t) $9m^2 - 27m + 14$

3. Reduce to lowest terms.

(a) $\dfrac{36x^2y^2}{6x^2y}$ (b) $\dfrac{-40a^2b^3c}{-10abc}$ (c) $\dfrac{3a^2 - 6a}{3a}$

(d) $\dfrac{4x - 8y}{3x - 6y}$ (e) $\dfrac{x^2 + 6x + 8}{x^2 + 7x + 12}$ (f) $\dfrac{x^2 - 9}{x^2 - 6x + 9}$

(g) $\dfrac{x^2 - 5x}{x^2 - 2x - 15}$ (h) $\dfrac{6x^2 - x - 12}{6x^2 - 17x + 12}$ (i) $\dfrac{8x^2 - 10x - 3}{4x^2 - 4x - 3}$

4. Simplify.

(a) $\dfrac{3a^2}{4b^3} \times \dfrac{8b^2}{6a}$ (b) $\dfrac{36x^2y^3}{12xy} \times \dfrac{x^3y^3}{2xy^6}$

(c) $\dfrac{4a^2b}{3ab^2} \div \dfrac{2ab}{3b^2}$ (d) $\dfrac{x^2 - 8x + 16}{x^2 + 3x - 10} \times \dfrac{x^2 + 2x - 8}{x^2 - 16}$

(e) $\dfrac{x^2 + 11x + 30}{x^2 + x - 20} \div \dfrac{x^2 + 8x + 12}{x^2 - 8x + 16}$ (f) $\dfrac{2x^2 - x - 3}{x^2 + 2x + 1} \times \dfrac{2x^2 + 5x + 3}{4x^2 - 9}$

(g) $\dfrac{x^2 - 25}{x^2 + 3x + 2} \div \dfrac{x^2 - 7x + 10}{5x + 10}$

5. Simplify.

(a) $\dfrac{3x}{2} + \dfrac{4y}{3}$ (b) $\dfrac{5a}{3} - \dfrac{2b}{4}$

(c) $\dfrac{3}{m} - \dfrac{2}{n}$ (d) $\dfrac{2}{a} + \dfrac{3}{b} - \dfrac{2}{c}$

(e) $\dfrac{3x + 1}{2} + \dfrac{5x - 1}{3}$ (f) $\dfrac{2a + 3b}{4} - \dfrac{3a - 2b}{6}$

(g) $\dfrac{1}{x + 1} + \dfrac{2}{x + 2} + \dfrac{3}{x + 3}$ (h) $\dfrac{3}{x - 1} - \dfrac{2}{x - 2}$

(i) $\dfrac{x + 2}{x + 3} + \dfrac{x + 1}{x + 2}$ (j) $\dfrac{3}{x^2 - x - 12} - \dfrac{2}{x^2 - 6x + 8}$

(k) $\dfrac{5}{(x - 5)^2} - \dfrac{x + 5}{x - 5}$ (l) $\dfrac{2x^2 + 7}{x^2 + x - 2} - \dfrac{x - 3}{x + 2}$

Put the numbers from 1 to 9 in the spaces to make the statement true:

$$\blacksquare - \blacksquare \div \blacksquare = 3$$

$$\blacksquare + \blacksquare \div \blacksquare = 3$$

$$\blacksquare - \blacksquare - \blacksquare = 3$$

REVIEW AND PREVIEW TO CHAPTER 4

EXERCISE 1 *Solving Linear Equations*

1. Solve.

(a) $2x+3+8x=23$

(b) $11x+5=9x-7$

(c) $3x+4=6x-11$

(d) $5x+4-2x=7+4x-5$

(e) $5a-3a+7=7a-23$

(f) $3b+13-5b+8=0$

(g) $-3x+14=2x+7-3x+2$

(h) $3m-7-8+2m=15$

2. Solve.

(a) $2(x-3)+3=-15$

(b) $3(x-2)-2(x+3)=0$

(c) $2(2a-1)-(3a+2)=8$

(d) $5(2b-3)-7=4-(b+7)$

(e) $4=3m-4(m-2)+6(2m+3)$

(f) $4y+7-(3y-4)=2(1-2y)+6(y-1)$

(g) $-2-(x-7)-3(4x-2)=17$

(h) $2(1-3a)-(2a-3)+5(a-1)=7$

(i) $2(3t-4)+2t-5=5t$

(j) $4(2m-4)-3(1-3m)-(1-m)=7$

3. Solve.

(a) $2[1-2(x+1)]+3=4$

(b) $3[2x-(x+4)-2]=6$

(c) $5-[3x+2(1-2x)]-(x-1)=6x$

(d) $4x-3=2[1-3(1-2x)+4]-2$

How long will it take to cut a 10 m board into 10 pieces if it takes 30 s per cut?

EXERCISE 2 *Solving Linear Equations*

1. Solve.

(a) $\dfrac{x}{3}=7$

(b) $\dfrac{x+1}{2}=5$

(c) $\dfrac{x}{2}+\dfrac{x}{3}=4$

(d) $\dfrac{2x}{5}-\dfrac{3x}{2}=7$

(e) $\dfrac{x+1}{3}-\dfrac{x-2}{4}=1$

(f) $\dfrac{1-2x}{5}-\dfrac{3x+2}{6}=\dfrac{1}{2}$

(g) $\dfrac{3x-1}{4}-\dfrac{2x+1}{3}=-2$

(h) $\dfrac{2x+1}{5}=\dfrac{1-x}{2}+2$

(i) $3x-\dfrac{2x-1}{2}=\dfrac{3x}{4}$

(j) $\dfrac{5}{3}-2x-\dfrac{1-x}{2}=\dfrac{2x-1}{3}$

2. Solve.

(a) $(x-2)(x+3)=(x+4)(x+1)$

(b) $(2x-1)(x-3)=(2x+1)(x+4)$

(c) $(x+2)(x+3)-(x-7)(x+1)=2$

(d) $3x^2-(1+3x)(1+x)-6=2(x-1)$

(e) $2x(x-1)-(x+1)(x+2)=x^2$

(f) $2(x-1)^2-(x-3)^2=x^2+7$

(g) $2(1-2x)(x+1)-2(x+1)(x-1)=6x(1-x)$

(h) $2(2x-1)(x+3)-3-4x^2=2(x-1)$

applied mathematics for today: senior

$$m = \frac{\Delta y}{\Delta x} = \frac{y_2 - y_1}{x_2 - x_1}$$

Determine the slope of the line passing through:

1. (1.764, 2.831) and (4.817, 1.819)
2. (16.45, 18.71) and (13.22, 11.86)
3. (5.281, 6.813) and (−4.815, −8.432)
4. (−12.43, −16.81) and (22.58, −11.78)
5. (0.0716, −0.0153) and (0.1076, −0.0324)
6. (166.4, 583.2) and (243.8, −686.7)
7. (0.5813, −0.7614) and (0.8176, −0.7883)
8. (−24.81, −66.82) and (−83.76, −243.71)
9. (−8.413, −9.754) and (0.689, −4.777)
10. (5784, 9763) and (7555, 8648)

CHAPTER 4

Quadratic Equations

4.1 SOLVING QUADRATIC EQUATIONS BY FACTORING

When a polynomial of the second degree is equated to zero we have a quadratic equation. Examples of quadratic equations are:

$$x^2 - 3x + 2 = 0$$
$$x^2 - 25 = 0$$
$$x^2 - 7x = 0$$
$$3x^2 + 5x + 4 = 0$$

In general:

> an equation of the form $ax^2 + bx + c = 0$, $a \neq 0$, where a, b, c represent real numbers, is called a quadratic equation.

We now must investigate methods of solving quadratic equations so that we will be able to solve problems which involve them.

The first method is by *factoring the polynomial*. If a quadratic polynomial can be factored, a solution to the corresponding quadratic equation can easily be obtained. After factoring we make use of the fact that we have the product of two real numbers equal to zero.

> If $ab = 0$, then $a = 0$ or $b = 0$ or $a = b = 0$.

The domain of all the variables in this chapter is R, the set of real numbers.

The root of an equation is a value of the variable which makes the sentence true.

EXAMPLE 1. *Solve (a)* $(x-2)(x-3) = 0$ *(b)* $x(x-5) = 0$

Solution

(a) $(x-2)(x-3) = 0$
   $x - 2 = 0$ or $x - 3 = 0$
   $x = 2$ or $x = 3$

(b) $x(x-5) = 0$
   $x = 0$ or $x - 5 = 0$
   $x = 0$ or $x = 5$

EXAMPLE 2. *Solve and check* $x^2 + 5x + 6 = 0$

Solution

$$x^2 + 5x + 6 = 0$$
$$(x + 2)(x + 3) = 0$$
$$x + 2 = 0 \quad \text{or} \quad x + 3 = 0$$
$$x = -2 \quad \text{or} \quad x = -3$$

Check: If $x = -2$

$LS = x^2 + 5x + 6$
$\quad = (-2)^2 + 5(-2) + 6$
$\quad = 4 - 10 + 6$
$\quad = 0$
$RS = 0$

If $x = -3$

$LS = x^2 + 5x + 6$
$\quad = (-3)^2 + 5(-3) + 6$
$\quad = 9 - 15 + 6$
$\quad = 0$
$RS = 0$

$\therefore$ -2 and -3 are the correct roots.

EXAMPLE 3. *Solve* $2x^2 + 5x - 3 = 0$

Solution

$$2x^2 + 5x - 3 = 0$$
$$2x^2 + 6x - x - 3 = 0$$
$$2x(x + 3) - (x + 3) = 0$$
$$(x + 3)(2x - 1) = 0$$
$$x + 3 = 0 \quad \text{or} \quad 2x - 1 = 0$$
$$x = -3 \quad \text{or} \quad x = \tfrac{1}{2}$$

$p + q = 5$
$p \times q = -6$
$p = 6, \quad q = -1$

EXERCISE 4-1

B **1.** Solve.

(a) $(x - 2)(x + 3) = 0$
(b) $(x + 1)(x + 2) = 0$
(c) $(x - 3)(x - 4) = 0$
(d) $(x + 5)(x - 4) = 0$
(e) $x(x + 4) = 0$
(f) $2x(x - 3) = 0$

2. Solve by first factoring.

Watch for common factors.

(a) $x^2 - 7x + 12 = 0$
(b) $x^2 - x - 6 = 0$
(c) $x^2 + 4x + 3 = 0$
(d) $x^2 + 3x - 10 = 0$
(e) $x^2 - 2x - 15 = 0$
(f) $x^2 + 6x + 9 = 0$
(g) $x^2 - 9x + 20 = 0$
(h) $x^2 - 8x + 16 = 0$
(i) $x^2 + 4x - 21 = 0$
(j) $x^2 + x - 30 = 0$
(k) $2x^2 + 8x + 6 = 0$
(l) $3x^2 + 6x - 24 = 0$

3. Solve by first factoring.

(a) $x^2 - 4 = 0$
(b) $x^2 - 49 = 0$
(c) $x^2 - 25 = 0$
(d) $x^2 - 64 = 0$
(e) $x^2 - 100 = 0$
(f) $x^2 - 81 = 0$
(g) $2x^2 - 72 = 0$
(h) $4x^2 - 36 = 0$

4. Solve.

(a) $x^2 - 10x + 21 = 0$
(b) $x^2 - 2x - 8 = 0$
(c) $3x^2 - 4x - 7 = 0$
(d) $6x^2 + 7x + 2 = 0$
(e) $9x^2 - 1 = 0$
(f) $3x^2 - 5x = 0$

(g) $7x^2 - 28 = 0$ (h) $x^2 - 7x = 0$
(i) $4x^2 - 9 = 0$ (j) $3x^2 - 11x - 14 = 0$
(k) $2x^2 + 7x + 5 = 0$ (l) $5x^2 - 17x + 6 = 0$
(m) $2x^2 - 3x - 14 = 0$ (n) $6x^2 + 13x + 6 = 0$
(o) $10x^2 - 21x - 10 = 0$ (p) $15x^2 - 31x + 14 = 0$

C

Put the numbers from 1 to 9 in the spaces to make the statements true:

$$\blacksquare + \blacksquare \div \blacksquare = 4$$
$$\blacksquare \times \blacksquare \div \blacksquare = 4$$
$$\blacksquare - \blacksquare + \blacksquare = 4$$

5. What is the radius of a circle whose area is 154 cm²? (Use $A = \pi r^2$ and $\pi \doteq \frac{22}{7}$.)

6. What is the radius of a right circular cone whose volume is 264 cm³ and whose height is 14 cm? (Use $V = \frac{1}{3}\pi r^2 h$ and $\pi \doteq \frac{22}{7}$.)

4.2 SOLVING QUADRATIC EQUATIONS BY COMPLETING THE SQUARE

In Section 4.1 we solved the quadratic equation $ax^2 + bx + c = 0$ by factoring the polynomial $ax^2 + bx + c$. If the polynomial cannot be factored we may *complete the square* to solve the equation.

INVESTIGATION 4.2

1. Add a number to each of the following to make a perfect square.
(a) $x^2 + 6x + \blacksquare$ (b) $x^2 + 10x + \blacksquare$
(c) $x^2 - 8x + \blacksquare$ (d) $x^2 - 12x + \blacksquare$
(e) $x^2 + 4x + \blacksquare$ (f) $x^2 - 14x + \blacksquare$
(g) $x^2 + 5x + \blacksquare$ (h) $x^2 - 3x + \blacksquare$

(i) $x^2 + bx + \blacksquare$ (j) $x^2 + \frac{b}{a}x + \blacksquare$

2. We wish to solve $x^2 - 6x - 1 = 0$.
(a) Can $x^2 - 6x - 1$ be factored?
(b) Add 1 to each side of the given equation.
(c) What must be added to $x^2 - 6x$ to make it a perfect square?
(d) Since we are dealing with an equation, what must now be added to the other side of the equation?
(e) Write the factors of the perfect square as the square of a binomial.
(f) By taking the square roots of each side of the equation, find the two values of $x - 3$.
(g) What are the two values of x?

If $m^2 = 25$ then $m = 5$ or -5

3. Solve the following by completing the square.
(a) $x^2 - 4x - 1 = 0$ (b) $x^2 + 8x - 3 = 0$
(c) $x^2 - 10x + 4 = 0$ (d) $x^2 + 6x + 2 = 0$
(e) $x^2 + 2x - 5 = 0$ (f) $x^2 - 12x + 3 = 0$

4. Complete the following solution for $3x^2 - 4x - 6 = 0$ in your notebook.

$$3x^2 - 4x - 6 = 0$$

$$x^2 - \tfrac{4}{3}x - 2 = 0 \qquad \text{Dividing by 3, the coefficient of } x^2$$

$$x^2 - \tfrac{4}{3}x = \blacksquare \qquad \text{Adding 2 to each side}$$

$$x^2 - \tfrac{4}{3}x + \blacksquare = 2 + \blacksquare \qquad \text{Adding } \blacksquare \text{ to make } x^2 - \tfrac{4}{3}x$$
a perfect square

$$(x - \blacksquare)^2 = \blacksquare \qquad \text{Rewriting as the square}$$
of a binomial

$$x - \blacksquare = +\blacksquare \quad \text{or} \quad x - \blacksquare = -\blacksquare \qquad \text{Taking the square root}$$
of both sides

$$x = \blacksquare \quad \text{or} \quad x = \blacksquare.$$

5. Solve the following by completing the square.

(a) $2x^2 + 12x - 3 = 0$ (b) $3x^2 - 12x - 1 = 0$

(c) $3x^2 + 5x - 7 = 0$ (d) $2x^2 - 3x - 2 = 0$

(e) $4x^2 - 5x - 6 = 0$ (f) $2x^2 + 5x - 12 = 0$

6. Complete the solution for $ax^2 + bx + c = 0$ in your notebook.

Find the fifth root of 7776.

$$ax^2 + bx + c = 0$$

$$x^2 + \frac{b}{a}x + \blacksquare = 0$$

$$x^2 + \frac{b}{a}x = \blacksquare$$

$$x^2 + \frac{b}{a}x + \blacksquare = \blacksquare - \frac{c}{a}$$

$$(x + \blacksquare)^2 = \blacksquare$$

$$x + \blacksquare = +\blacksquare \quad \text{or} \quad x + \blacksquare = -\blacksquare$$

$$x = \blacksquare \quad \text{or} \quad x = \blacksquare$$

4.3 SOLVING QUADRATIC EQUATIONS BY THE FORMULAS

By completing the square we can derive the formulas to solve the general quadratic equation. These formulas enable us to solve any quadratic equation.

> The solution of $ax^2 + bx + c = 0$, $a \neq 0$ is
> $$x = \frac{-b + \sqrt{b^2 - 4ac}}{2a} \quad \text{or} \quad x = \frac{-b - \sqrt{b^2 - 4ac}}{2a}$$

EXAMPLE 1. *Solve* $2x^2 - 7x + 6 = 0$

Solution By comparison with $ax^2 + bx + c = 0$, $a = 2$, $b = -7$, $c = 6$. Substituting into the formulas,

$$x = \frac{-b + \sqrt{b^2 - 4ac}}{2a} \qquad \text{or} \quad x = \frac{-b - \sqrt{b^2 - 4ac}}{2a}$$

$$= \frac{-(-7) + \sqrt{(-7)^2 - 4(2)(6)}}{2(2)} \qquad = \frac{-(-7) - \sqrt{(-7)^2 - 4(2)(6)}}{2(2)}$$

$$=\frac{7+\sqrt{49-48}}{4} \qquad =\frac{7-\sqrt{49-48}}{4}$$

$$=\frac{7+1}{4} \qquad\qquad =\frac{7-1}{4}$$

$$=2 \qquad\qquad\qquad =\frac{3}{2}$$

∴ the roots are 2, $\frac{3}{2}$.

This example could have been solved by factoring, but it was chosen to illustrate that the formulas will enable you to solve any quadratic equation. The next example is not factorable.

EXAMPLE 2. *Solve* $4x^2-7x+2=0$

Solution Here $a=4$, $b=-7$, and $c=2$.

Write an expression for 36 using four sixes.

$$x=\frac{-b+\sqrt{b^2-4ac}}{2a} \quad \text{or} \quad x=\frac{-b-\sqrt{b^2-4ac}}{2a}$$

$$=\frac{7+\sqrt{49-32}}{8} \qquad =\frac{7-\sqrt{49-32}}{8}$$

$$=\frac{7+\sqrt{17}}{8} \qquad\qquad =\frac{7-\sqrt{17}}{8}$$

∴ the roots are $\dfrac{7+\sqrt{17}}{8}$ and $\dfrac{7-\sqrt{17}}{8}$

It should be noted that $\dfrac{7+\sqrt{17}}{8}$ and $\dfrac{7-\sqrt{17}}{8}$ are the exact roots of $4x^2-7x+2=0$. Once they have been found, $4x^2-7x+2=0$ has been solved. In practice, decimal approximations for the roots may be required.

EXAMPLE 3. *Find the roots of* $3x^2+5x+1=0$ *correct to two decimal places.*

Solution $a=3$, $b=5$, $c=1$

$$x=\frac{-b+\sqrt{b^2-4ac}}{2a} \quad \text{or} \quad x=\frac{-b-\sqrt{b^2-4ac}}{2a}$$

$$=\frac{-5+\sqrt{25-12}}{6} \qquad =\frac{-5-\sqrt{25-12}}{6}$$

From tables $\sqrt{13}\doteq3.606$

$$=\frac{-5+\sqrt{13}}{6} \qquad\qquad =\frac{-5-\sqrt{13}}{6}$$

$$\doteq\frac{-5+3.606}{6} \qquad\qquad \doteq\frac{-5-3.606}{6}$$

applied mathematics for today: senior

$$=\frac{-1.39}{6}\qquad\qquad\qquad=\frac{-8.606}{6}$$

$$=-0.232\qquad\qquad\qquad=-1.434$$

∴ the roots are −0.23 and −1.43 correct to two decimal places.

When a quadratic equation is expressed in the form $ax^2+bx+c=0$, it may be solved by using the factoring method if the factors of ax^2+bx+c are apparent or readily obtainable. If not, use the general formulas, which always produce an answer.

The largest of T consecutive integers is Q. What is the smallest?

EXERCISE 4-3

A   **1.** Determine the values of a, b, and c for each of the following.
(a) $2x^2+3x+4=0$ (b) $3x^2-5x+2=0$
(c) $x^2+7x-1=0$ (d) $4x^2-x-3=0$
(e) $5x^2-3x=0$ (f) $x^2-25=0$
(g) $x^2+5x=16$ (h) $2x^2=3x+4$
(i) $2x^2+3=5x$ (j) $3x^2+17=0$

B   **2.** Solve each of the following by using the general formula.
(a) $x^2-7x+12=0$ (b) $3x^2-6x+1=0$
(c) $x^2-6x-7=0$ (d) $x^2-3x-88=0$
(e) $3x^2-5x+2=0$ (f) $2x^2-6x=1$
(g) $3x^2+6x-2=0$ (h) $7x^2-2x-1=0$
(i) $2x^2+5x+1=0$ (j) $x^2=2x-1$
(k) $3x^2+2x-7=0$ (l) $2x^2-25x+77=0$
(m) $x^2-9=0$ (n) $x^2-5x=0$

3. Find the roots of the following correct to two decimal places.
(a) $x^2+3x+1=0$ (b) $x^2-3x-5=0$
(c) $x^2-5x+1=0$ (d) $2x^2-3x-4=0$
(e) $2x^2-5=0$ (f) $3x^2-5x=3$
(g) $5x^2+3=11x$ (h) $6x^2-7x+1=0$

4. Solve the following using any method.
(a) $x^2-5x+6=0$ (b) $x^2-2x-3=0$
(c) $x^2-2x-2=0$ (d) $20x^2+x-15=0$
(e) $2x^2-7x-15=0$ (f) $x^2-11x+28=0$
(g) $3x^2+6x-10=0$ (h) $4x^2-4x-1=0$
(i) $2x^2-4x-5=0$ (j) $5x^2-15x+9=0$
(k) $2x^2+7x=0$ (l) $x^2-5=0$
(m) $2x^2+6x-20=0$ (n) $2x^2+8x+2=0$

Watch for common factors.

C   **5.** Solve the following.
(a) $2(x^2-1)=3x$ (b) $4x(x+3)+5=0$

(c) $(x-1)(x+3)-6=0$ (d) $\dfrac{1}{x}=2x+1$

4.4 NATURE OF THE ROOTS

The quadratic equation $ax^2+bx+c=0$, where $a \neq 0$ and a, b, c are real numbers, has the two roots $\dfrac{-b+\sqrt{b^2-4ac}}{2a}$ and $\dfrac{-b-\sqrt{b^2-4ac}}{2a}$, but you will recall from your study of radicals that $\sqrt{x}$ is only defined as a **real number** when x is a nonnegative number. So $ax^2+bx+c=0$ has real roots only when $b^2-4ac \geqq 0$.

The two formulas are similar except $\sqrt{b^2-4ac}$ is added in one case and subtracted in the other. If $b^2-4ac=0$ (and hence $\sqrt{b^2-4ac}=0$) the two real roots will be equal.

If $b^2-4ac>0$, there will be two distinct real roots.

If $b^2-4ac<0$, $\sqrt{b^2-4ac}$ is not a real number. We call such a number an **imaginary number.** The set of real numbers together with the set of imaginary numbers make up the set of complex numbers. However for the purposes of this book the set of real numbers is sufficient.

$\dfrac{-b+\sqrt{b^2-4ac}}{2a}$

$\dfrac{-b-\sqrt{b^2-4ac}}{2a}$

$\sqrt{-4}$ is an imaginary number

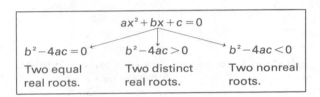

	$ax^2+bx+c=0$	
$b^2-4ac=0$	$b^2-4ac>0$	$b^2-4ac<0$
Two equal real roots.	Two distinct real roots.	Two nonreal roots.

The value of b^2-4ac enables us to determine the nature of the roots of a quadratic equation without actually solving the equation. b^2-4ac is called the **discriminant** of $ax^2+bx+c=0$.

EXAMPLE 1. *Without solving, state the nature of the roots of*
(a) $x^2+4x+4=0$ (b) $x^2+4x-5=0$ (c) $x^2+4x+5=0$

Solution
(a, $x^2+4x+4=0$
    $a=1, b=4, c=4$

$$b^2-4ac=4^2-4(1)(4)$$
$$=16-16$$
$$=0$$

∴ there are two equal real roots.

(b) $x^2+4x-5=0$
    $a=1, b=4, c=-5$

$$b^2-4ac=4^2-4(1)(-5)$$
$$=16+20$$
$$=36$$

∴ there are two distinct real roots.

c) $x^2 + 4x + 5 = 0$

$a = 1$, $b = 4$, $c = 5$

$$b^2 - 4ac = 4^2 - 4(1)(5)$$
$$= 16 - 20$$
$$= -4$$

$\therefore$ there are two nonreal roots.

EXERCISE 4-4

A **1.** Complete the following table.

	Equation $ax^2 + bx + c = 0$	Discriminant $b^2 - 4ac$	Nature of Roots
(a)	$x^2 + 6x + 9 = 0$		
(b)	$x^2 - 4x + 1 = 0$		
(c)	$x^2 - 2x + 3 = 0$		
(d)	$x^2 - x - 3 = 0$		
(e)	$x^2 + x + 7 = 0$		
(f)	$x^2 - 4x + 4 = 0$		

B **2.** Calculate the discriminant of each of the following quadratic equations and then state the nature of the roots.

(a) $3x^2 - 6x + 2 = 0$ (b) $4x^2 + 5x + 3 = 0$
(c) $9x^2 - 12x + 4 = 0$ (d) $x^2 + 4x + 5 = 0$
(e) $x^2 - 49 = 0$ (f) $25x^2 - 40x + 16 = 0$
(g) $3x^2 - 2x - 5 = 0$ (h) $2x^2 + 5x = 0$
(i) $2x^2 + x + 16 = 0$ (j) $x^2 + 7 = 2x$
(k) $2(x^2 + 1) - 3 = 2x$ (l) $2x^2 = 0$

3. Solve the following quadratic equations. State which have nonreal roots.

(a) $3x^2 - 7x + 5 = 0$ (b) $16x^2 + 8x + 1 = 0$
(c) $2x^2 - 7x + 4 = 0$ (d) $2x^2 - 5x + 6 = 0$
(e) $4x^2 - 25 = 0$ (f) $3x^2 - 4x = 0$

How would you measure 4ℓ of fluid using a 3ℓ and a 5ℓ container?

4.5 PROBLEMS INVOLVING QUADRATICS

In this section we shall consider some problems that involve quadratic equations. It should be noted that if a problem is solved by means of a quadratic equation it does not follow that both roots of the equation will be admissible as solutions to the problem. For instance, a length cannot be negative, nor can the number of seats in a room be fractional. A root of an equation which is excluded by the conditions of the problem is called an **inadmissible solution**.

EXERCISE 4-5

A **1.** State the algebraic expressions for:
(a) the sum of three consecutive integers.
(b) a number plus its square.
(c) the square of a number less twice the number.
(d) the sum of the squares of two consecutive numbers.
(e) the area of a rectangle if the length is twice the width.
(f) the area of a square with sides $x+3$.
(g) the time, if the distance is 100 km and the speed is x km/h.
(h) the distance if the speed is x km/h and the time is 3 h.

Put the numbers from 1 to 9 in the spaces to make the statements true:

$$\blacksquare \times \blacksquare - \blacksquare = 5$$
$$\blacksquare \div \blacksquare + \blacksquare = 5$$
$$\blacksquare + \blacksquare - \blacksquare = 5$$

NUMBER PROBLEMS

EXAMPLE 1. *The sum of the squares of three consecutive integers is 77. Find the integers.*

Solution Let x, $x+1$, $x+2$ represent the three integers.

$$\therefore \quad x^2 + (x+1)^2 + (x+2)^2 = 77$$

$$x^2 + (x^2 + 2x + 1) + (x^2 + 4x + 4) = 77$$

$$x^2 + x^2 + 2x + 1 + x^2 + 4x + 4 = 77 \quad \text{remove brackets}$$

$$3x^2 + 6x + 5 = 77 \quad \text{collect like terms}$$

$$3x^2 + 6x - 72 = 0$$

$$x^2 + 2x - 24 = 0 \quad \text{divide by 3}$$

$$(x+6)(x-4) = 0 \quad \text{factoring}$$

$$\therefore \quad x = -6 \quad \text{or} \quad x = 4$$

and $\quad x+1 = -5 \quad$ or $\quad x+1 = 5$

and $\quad x+2 = -4 \quad$ or $\quad x+2 = 6$

$\therefore$ the three integers are $-6, -5, -4$ or 4, 5, 6.

B **2.** The sum of the squares of two consecutive integers is 113. Find the integers.

3. The sum of the squares of three consecutive integers is 302. Find the integers.

4. The sum of the squares of four consecutive integers is 966. Find the integers.

5. Two integers differ by 8 and the sum of their squares is 130. Find the integers.

6. The sum of two numbers is 13 and their product is 42. Find the numbers.

7. The sum of two numbers is 17 and their product is 52. Find the numbers.

applied mathematics for today: senior

AREA PROBLEMS

EXAMPLE 2. *The side of one square is 2 m longer than the side of another square. The sum of their areas is 52 m². Find the dimensions of each square.*

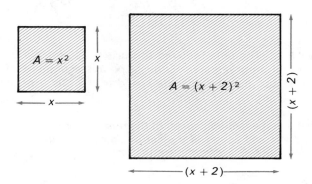

Solution Let x and $x+2$ represent the lengths of the sides of the squares in metres.

∴ the areas of the squares
are x^2 and $(x+2)^2$ respectively.

$$x^2+(x+2)^2=52$$
$$x^2+x^2+4x+4=52$$
$$2x^2+4x-48=0 \quad \text{Divide by 2}$$
$$x^2+2x-24=0$$
$$(x+6)(x-4)=0$$
$$x=-6 \quad \text{or} \quad x=4$$

The solution -6 is inadmissible since a length must be positive. Therefore the lengths of the sides of the squares are 4 m and 6 m.

8. The side of one square is 3 cm longer than the side of another square. Their combined area is 117 cm². Find the dimensions of each square.

9. A rectangle is 4 cm longer than it is wide. If its area is 192 cm², find its dimensions.

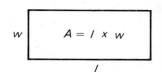

10. The length and width of a rectangle differ by 4 cm. If its area is 96 cm² find its dimensions.

11. The base of a triangle is 6 cm longer than its height. The area of the triangle is 56 cm². Find the length of the base.

12. A rectangular label on a book has an area of 44 cm² and a perimeter of 27 cm. Calculate the dimensions.

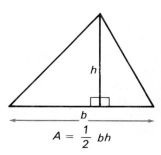

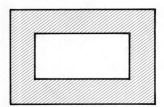

13. A rectangular sheet of tin is 15 cm long and 9 cm wide. A uniform strip is to be cut off all around the sheet. If the remaining area is to be 112 cm², calculate the width of the strip.

DISTANCE, SPEED, TIME PROBLEMS

EXAMPLE 3. *The time required to make a 240 km trip by car is 2 h less than the time required by bus. The average speed of the car is 20 km/h faster than the average speed of the bus. Find the average speed of each.*

Solution Let the average speed of the bus in kilometres per hour be x. Then the average speed of the car in kilometres per hour is $x + 20$.

	D	S	T
BUS	240	x	$\dfrac{240}{x}$
CAR	240	$x+20$	$\dfrac{240}{x+20}$

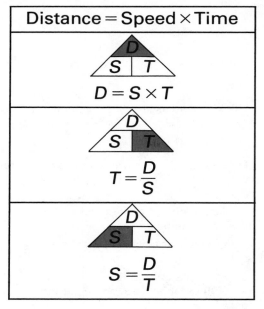

Distance = Speed × Time
$D = S \times T$
$T = \dfrac{D}{S}$
$S = \dfrac{D}{T}$

$\dfrac{240}{x} - \dfrac{240}{(x+20)} = 2$ The difference in the times is 2.

applied mathematics for today: senior

Multiply both sides by $x(x+20)$

$$240(x+20)-240x=2x(x+20)$$
$$240x+4800-240x=2x^2+40x$$
$$2x^2+40x-4800=0$$
$$x^2+20x-2400=0$$
$$(x+60)(x-40)=0$$
$$x+60=0 \quad \text{or} \quad x-40=0$$
$$x=-60 \quad \text{or} \quad x=40$$

The solution -60 is inadmissible for the speed of the bus, therefore the average speed of the bus is 40 km/h and the average speed of the car is 60 km/h.

14. The time required to make a 120 km trip by motorboat is 2 h less than the time required by sailboat. The average speed of the motor-boat is 5 km/h faster than that of the sailboat. Find the average speed of each.

15. On a cross country trip of 360 km, one motorcycle averaged 10 km/h faster than another. The difference in their times was 3 h. Find the average speed of each bike.

16. The time required for a train to make a 175 km trip is 1.5 h less than the time required by car. The average rate of the car is 15 km/h less than the average speed of the train for the same trip. Find the average speed of each.

17. An engine hauls a train 125 km. It is then replaced by a second engine which averages 5 km/h faster than the first. The second engine pulls the train 165 km. If the time for the 290 km is 5.5 h, find the average speed with each engine.

REVIEW EXERCISE

B **1.** Solve by factoring.
(a) $x^2+7x+12=0$
(b) $x^2-4x-21=0$
(c) $x^2-6x+9=0$
(d) $2x^2-14x-36=0$
(e) $x^2-36=0$
(f) $x^2-x-42=0$
(g) $2x^2-3x-2=0$
(h) $2x^2+11x+12=0$
(i) $3x^2-5x+2=0$
(j) $6x^2+5x-4=0$
(k) $10x^2+13x-3=0$
(l) $6x^2+37x+6=0$

2. Solve.
(a) $x^2+x-1=0$
(b) $16x^2-15x-1=0$
(c) $x^2-x-2=0$
(d) $2x^2-x=1$
(e) $x^2=5x-1$
(f) $5x^2-6x-12=0$
(g) $10x^2+2x-1=0$
(h) $27x^2-24x-16=0$
(i) $15x^2+7x-2=0$
(j) $3x^2-7=0$
(k) $5x^2-20x=0$
(l) $3x-x^2+7=0$

3. Calculate the discriminant of each of the following quadratic equations and then state the nature of the roots.

Put the numbers from 1 to 9 in the spaces to make the statements true:

$$\blacksquare - \blacksquare + \blacksquare = 6$$
$$\blacksquare \div \blacksquare \times \blacksquare = 6$$
$$\blacksquare - \blacksquare - \blacksquare = 6$$

(a) $3x^2 + x + 7 = 0$
(c) $4x^2 - 25 = 0$
(e) $2x^2 + 7x - 2 = 0$

(b) $4x^2 - 12x + 9 = 0$
(d) $9x^2 + 6x = -1$
(f) $x^2 = 7x + 1$

4. The sum of the squares of three consecutive integers is 245. Find the integers.

5. Two integers differ by 5 and the sum of their squares is 193. Find the integers.

6. A rectangle is 5 cm longer than it is wide. If its area is 176 cm², find its dimensions.

7. The side of one square is 1 cm longer than the side of another square. If their combined area is 145 cm², find the dimensions of each square.

8. On a trip of 300 km, one car averaged 10 km/h faster than another car. The difference in their times was 1 h. Find the average speed of each car.

9. It takes a motorboat 2 h longer to travel 40 km up river than it does on the return trip. The average speed up river is 10 km/h slower than the speed on the return trip. What is the speed of the boat travelling up the river?

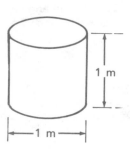

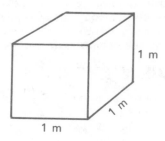

Which has the greater volume?

How much greater?

REVIEW AND PREVIEW TO CHAPTER 5

EXERCISE 1   *Relations*

1. Determine whether the given point lies on the given line.

(a) $y = 3x + 4$; $(1, 7)$

(b) $y = 2x - 4$; $(-3, -9)$

(c) $y = \frac{1}{2}x + 2$; $(2, 4)$

(d) $y = -4x + 3$; $(-2, 11)$

(e) $2x + y = 5$; $(1, 4)$

(f) $2x - 3y = 7$; $(10, 2)$

(g) $3y - 2x + 5 = 0$; $(1, -1)$

(h) $2x + 3y = 0$; $(1, 1)$

2. Determine whether the given ordered pair satisfies the given relation.

(a) $y = x^2$; $(-1, 1)$

(b) $y = -3x^2$; $(2, 12)$

(c) $y = 2x^2 - 3$; $(3, 14)$

(d) $x = 2y^2$; $(8, -2)$

(e) $x^2 + y^2 = 25$; $(-4, 3)$

(f) $y = 2x^2 + 3x - 1$; $(-2, -1)$

(g) $x^2 + y^2 = 10$; $(-1, -3)$

(h) $y = -2x^2 - 4x + 5$; $(-1, 7)$

EXERCISE 2   *Graphing Linear Equations*

1. Sketch the graph of each of the following.

(a) $y = 2x + 1$

(b) $y = -x + 3$

(c) $y = \frac{x + 1}{2}$

(d) $y = \frac{1}{2}x - 2$

(e) $2x + y = 7$

(f) $3x + 2y = 6$

(g) $5x - y = 4$

(h) $5x - 2y = 5$

$$ax^2 + bx + c = 0 \qquad x = \frac{-b \pm \sqrt{b^2 - 4ac}}{2a}$$

Solve the following equations:

1. $3.25x^2 - 7.12x + 1.25 = 0$

2. $485.7x^2 + 21.65x - 247.3 = 0$

3. $21.25x^2 + 32.65x - 47.35 = 0$

4. $6.125x^2 + 24.35x + 3.675 = 0$

5. $0.025\,75x^2 + 0.135\,7x - 0.042\,70 = 0$

CHAPTER 5

Quadratic Functions

5.1 THE GENERAL QUADRATIC FUNCTION

The Titan Missile Club has built a missile capable of being fired in a vertical direction with an initial speed of 100 m/s. Let us suppose for a moment that there is no gravitational force pulling the missile back to earth and no resistance due to the air. The height h of the missile in metres, in time t seconds, is given by the equation

$$h = 100t.$$

A table of values could be drawn up as in Table 5-1 and the relation graphed as in Figure 5-2.

t	h
0	0
1	100
3	300
5	500
7	700
9	900

Table 5-1

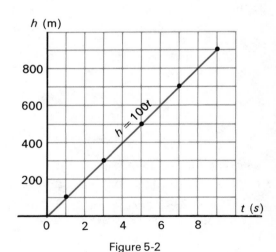

Figure 5-2

We see that the graph of the relation defined by $h = 100t$ is a straight line. By comparing $h = 100t$ with the form of the general linear function, $y = mx + b$, it is clear that $h = 100t$ represents a **linear function** whose graph has slope 100 and which meets the vertical axis at 0.

Whereas air resistance might be negligible on the missile, the pull of gravity is not. Taking gravity into account, the height h of the rocket in metres, in time t seconds, is given by the following equation

applied mathematics for today: senior

$$h = 100t - 4.9t^2$$

Once again a table of values could be drawn up (Table 5-3) and the relation graphed (Figure 5-4).

Find the axis of symmetry of each figure.

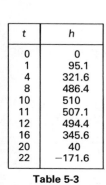

t	h
0	0
1	95.1
4	321.6
8	486.4
10	510
11	507.1
12	494.4
16	345.6
20	40
22	−171.6

Table 5-3

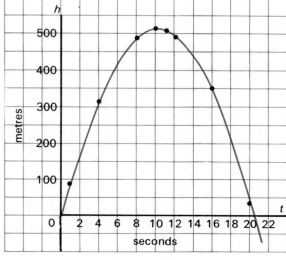

Figure 5-4

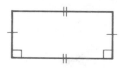

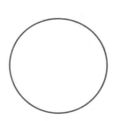

The graph of the relation defined by $h = 100t - 4.9t^2$ is a **parabola**. The degree of the defining equation $h = 100t - 4.9t^2$ is second degree, so this relation is said to be quadratic. You will recall that a **function** is a set of ordered pairs (x, y) such that for each value of x there is only one corresponding value of y.

Just as the general linear function is defined by $y = mx + b$, so the general quadratic function is defined by

$$y = ax^2 + bx + c, \quad a \neq 0$$

In this chapter we will study quadratic functions.

EXERCISE 5-1

A **1.** Which of the following define linear functions?
(a) $y = 2x - 4$
(b) $y = 3x^2 + 22$
(c) $2x - 3y = 11$
(d) $3x^2 = 2y - 11$
(e) $\dfrac{x+1}{2} = y$
(f) $y = 3x^3 + 2x - 1$
(g) $2x^2 + x^4 = y$
(h) $y = (x-1)^2 + 4$

2. Which of the following define quadratic functions?
(a) $y = 3x^3 - 2x + 4$
(b) $y = 3x - 2x^2$
(c) $y = 3x + 6$
(d) $y = 2x(x + 1)$

(e) $y = 3x(x^2 - 4)$

(f) $y = (2x - 1)(x + 3)$

(g) $y = 4(x^2 - x) + x$

(h) $y = x^4 - x^2$

3. State the values of a, b, and c in each of the following quadratic functions.

(a) $y = 2x^2 + 3x + 7$

(b) $y = -3x^2 - 4x + 3$

(c) $y = x^2 + 5$

(d) $y = -2x^2 + 6x$

(e) $y = (x - 1)(x + 4)$

(f) $y = 2x(x + 5)$

(g) $y + 3 = 2x^2 + 6x$

(h) $y + 2x - 3 = x^2$

Put the numbers from 1 to 9 in the spaces to make the statements true:

$\blacksquare \times \blacksquare + \blacksquare = 7$

$\blacksquare \div \blacksquare + \blacksquare = 7$

$\blacksquare + \blacksquare - \blacksquare = 7$

4. State the value(s) of k for which the following define quadratic functions.

(a) $y = kx^2 - 7x + 6$

(b) $y = 2x^2 - kx$

(c) $y = x^k + 6x - 4$

(d) $y = 3x^2 + 2x^k - 2$

(e) $y = (k - 3)x^2 + 6x$

(f) $y = -3x^2 + (k + 2)x - 1$

5.2 QUADRATIC FUNCTION DEFINED BY $y = ax^2$

One method of studying quadratic functions is through their graphs. We now look at the graph of $y = ax^2 + bx + c$ in stages. First let us look at $y = ax^2$, where $b = c = 0$ in the general quadratic function,

$$y = ax^2 + bx + c, \ a \neq 0.$$

INVESTIGATION 5.2

1. (a) Complete Table 5-5 in your notebook and then use the values from the table to graph on the same axes:

(i) $y = x^2$

(ii) $y = 2x^2$

(iii) $y = 3x^2$

(iv) $y = \frac{1}{2}x^2$

(v) $y = \frac{1}{3}x^2$

x	$y = x^2$	$y = 2x^2$	$y = 3x^2$	$y = \frac{1}{2}x^2$	$y = \frac{1}{3}x^2$
-3	9	18	27	$\frac{9}{2}$	3
-2	4		12	2	
-1		2			
0					
1					
2					
3					

Table 5-5

(b) We say each of these curves opens upward or is **concave upwards**. Is a positive, zero, or negative in each case?

(c) Are there any points on the curves below the x-axis?

(d) Does each curve have a minimum point? If so, what is it?

(e) Fold the graph along the y-axis. What do you observe?

applied mathematics for today: senior

(f) Notice that for every point (a, b) that satisfies $y = x^2$, there is a corresponding point $(-a, b)$ also satisfying $y = x^2$. This is because the curve is symmetric about a line, in this case the y-axis. Are the other four curves symmetric about the y-axis?

(g) The point of intersection of a parabola with its **axis of symmetry** is called its **vertex**. What are the co-ordinates of the vertex of each of these parabolas?

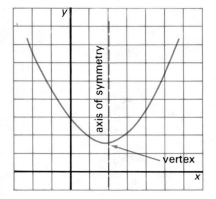
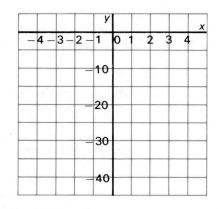

(h) Which parabola is flattest?

(i) Which parabola is sharpest?

(j) What happens to the graph of a parabola as a increases in value?

(k) What happens to the graph of a parabola as a decreases in value?

2. (a) Using the same axes, draw a table similar to Table 5-5 and graph the functions defined by each of the following for the interval $-3 \leq x \leq 3$.

(i) $y = -x^2$ (ii) $y = -2x^2$ (iii) $y = -4x^2$

(iv) $y = -\frac{1}{2}x^2$ (v) $y = -\frac{1}{4}x^2$

(b) We say each of these curves opens downward or is **concave downward**. Is a positive, zero, or negative in each case?

(c) Are there any points on the curves above the x-axis?

(d) Does each curve have a maximum point? If so, what is it?

(e) What is the axis of symmetry of these curves?

(f) What is the vertex of each curve?

(g) Which parabola is flattest?

(h) Which parabola is sharpest?

3. Without making a table of values, sketch the following on the same set of axes.

(a) $y = 2x^2$ (b) $y = -3x^2$ (c) $y = \frac{2}{3}x^2$

(d) $y = -\frac{1}{5}x^2$ (e) $y = \frac{1}{4}x^2$ (f) $y = -6x^2$

5.3 QUADRATIC FUNCTION DEFINED BY $y = ax^2 + c$

Section 5.2 dealt with the role of a in $y = ax^2$. Let us now see what effect the constant term c, when it is not zero, has on the graph of a quadratic function defined by $y = ax^2 + bx + c$, $a \neq 0$, $b = 0$.

INVESTIGATION 5.3

1. (a) Using the same axes graph the functions defined by each of the following for the interval $-3 \leq x \leq 3$.

(i) $y = x^2 - 3$ (ii) $y = x^2$ (iii) $y = x^2 + 3$

(b) What is the direction of opening of each parabola?

Write an expression for 10 using four fives.

(c) What is the axis of symmetry of each parabola?
(d) What are the coordinates of the vertex of each parabola?
(e) Is the vertex a maximum point or a minimum point?
(f) How do the three graphs seem to be related?

2. (a) Using the same set of axes graph the functions defined by each of the following for the interval $-3 \leq x \leq 3$.

(i) $y = -x^2 - 2$ (ii) $y = -x^2$ (iii) $y = -x^2 + 2$

(b) What is the direction of opening of each parabola?
(c) What is the equation of the axis of symmetry of each parabola?
(d) What are the coordinates of the vertex of each parabola?
(e) Is the vertex a maximum point or a minimum point?
(f) How do these graphs seem to be related?

3. (a) Using the same set of axes, graph the functions defined by $y = 3x^2 + 2$ and $y = 3x^2 - 1$ for the interval $-2 \leq x \leq 2$.

(b) What is the direction of opening of each parabola?
(c) What is the equation of the axis of symmetry of each parabola?
(d) What are the coordinates of the vertex of each parabola?
(e) Is the vertex a maximum point or a minimum point?
(f) How do these graphs seem to be related?

4. Without making a table of values, sketch on the same set of axes $y = x^2$, $y = x^2 + 2$, $y = x^2 - 3$, $y = x^2 + 6$, $y = x^2 - 5$.

5. Sketch the following on the same set of axes.

(a) $y = -2x^2$ (b) $y = -2x^2 - 3$
(c) $y = 2x^2 - 2$ (d) $y = 2x^2 + 4$

6. Complete the following table in your notebook

Quadratic function	Direction of opening	Equation of axis of symmetry	Vertex	Max. or min.	Value of max. or min.
$y = x^2$	upward	$x = 0$		min.	
$y = -2x^2$				max.	
$y = x^2 + 4$			$(0, 4)$		4
$y = -x^2 + 5$	downward				
$y = 5x^2 + 100$					
$y = -\frac{1}{2}x^2 - 2$					
$y = ax^2 + c,\ a > 0$					
$y = ax^2 + c,\ a < 0$					

5.4 QUADRATIC FUNCTION DEFINED BY $y = a(x - s)^2 + t$

Before moving on to consider $y = ax^2 + bx + c$, it will be helpful to look at the graphs of $y = a(x - s)^2 + t$. Note that if $s = 0$ we have $y = ax^2 + t$, which represents a parabola as considered in the previous section. If $s = t = 0$ we have $y = ax^2$, which we discussed in Section 5.2.

INVESTIGATION 5.4

1. (a) Using the same set of axes graph the quadratic functions defined by $y = \frac{1}{2}(x - 0)^2$ and $y = \frac{1}{2}(x - 3)^2$, for the interval $-2 \leq x \leq 5$.
(b) What is the direction of opening of each parabola?
(c) What is the equation of the axis of symmetry of each parabola?
(d) What are the coordinates of the vertex of each parabola?
(e) Is the vertex a maximum point or a minimum point?
(f) How are the graphs related?

2. (a) Using the same set of axes, graph the quadratic functions defined by $y = \frac{1}{2}(x - 3)^2 + 0$ and $y = \frac{1}{2}(x - 3)^2 + 4$ for the interval $0 \leq x \leq 5$.
(b) What is the direction of opening of each parabola?
(c) What is the axis of symmetry of each parabola?
(d) What are the coordinates of the vertex of each parabola?
(e) Is the vertex a maximum point or a minimum point?
(f) How are the graphs related?

3. (a) Using the same axes, sketch graphs of each of the following.
(i) $y = -(x - 0)^2 + 0$ (ii) $y = -(x - 0)^2 + 2$
(iii) $y = -(x - 3)^2 + 0$ (iv) $y = -(x - 3)^2 + 2$
(b) What is the direction of opening of each parabola?
(c) What is the equation of the axis of symmetry of each parabola?
(d) What are the coordinates of the vertex of each parabola?
(e) Is the vertex a maximum point or a minimum point?

4. Complete the following table in your notebook.

Quadratic function	Direction of opening	Equation of axis of symmetry	Vertex	Max. or min.	Value of max. or min.
$y = x^2 + 5$					5
$y = (x-1)^2 + 3$		$x - 1 = 0$	$(1, 3)$	min.	
$y = (x+2)^2 - 4$					
$y = 2(x-3)^2 + 5$					
$y = -3(x+2)^2 + 1$	downward				
$y = -\frac{1}{2}(x-3)^2 - 7$					
$y = a(x-s)^2 + t,\ a > 0$					
$y = a(x-s)^2 + t,\ a < 0$					

5.5 QUADRATIC FUNCTION DEFINED BY $y = ax^2 + bx + c$

In question 2 of Investigation 5.4 we graphed $y = \frac{1}{2}(x-3)^2 + 4$. But we can rewrite $y = \frac{1}{2}(x-3)^2 + 4$ as follows:

$$y = \frac{1}{2}(x-3)^2 + 4 = \frac{1}{2}(x^2 - 6x + 9) + 4$$
$$= \frac{1}{2}x^2 - 3x + \frac{9}{2} + 4$$
$$= \frac{1}{2}x^2 - 3x + \frac{17}{2}$$

The diagonal of a square is $4x$ m. What is the area of the square in terms of x.

Thus $y = \frac{1}{2}(x-3)^2 + 4$ defines a quadratic function of the form
$$y = ax^2 + bx + c$$

Similarly $y = -(x-3)^2 + 2$ (see question 3, Investigation 5.4) could be rewritten as:

$$y = -(x-3)^2 + 2$$
$$= -(x^2 - 6x + 9) + 2$$
$$= -x^2 + 6x - 7$$

Again, $y = -(x-3)^2 + 2$ defines a quadratic function of the form
$$y = ax^2 + bx + c$$

In general, $a(x-s)^2 + t$ can be expressed in the form $y = ax^2 + bx + c$. However, $y = a(x-s)^2 + t$ is the more useful form of the equation of a quadratic because the coordinates of the vertex and the equation of the axis of symmetry are readily obtained. If we convert $y = ax^2 + bx + c$ to the form $y = a(x-s)^2 + t$ we can study the general quadratic function. To do this we must be able to "**complete the square**" (see Chapter 4, Section 2). Recall that to complete the square you add the square of half the coefficient of x:

$$y = ax^2 + bx + c = a\left[x^2 + \frac{b}{a}x \qquad\qquad + \frac{c}{a} \right]$$
$$= a\left[x^2 + \frac{b}{a}x + \left(\frac{b}{2a}\right)^2 - \left(\frac{b}{2a}\right)^2 + \frac{c}{a} \right]$$
$$= a\left[\left(x + \frac{b}{2a}\right)^2 + \frac{-b^2 + 4ac}{4a^2} \right]$$

applied mathematics for today: senior

$$= a\left(x + \frac{b}{2a}\right)^2 + \frac{-b^2 + 4ac}{4a}$$

EXAMPLE 1. *Express* $y = x^2 - 4x + 5$ *in the form* $y = a(x - s)^2 + t$ *by completing the square.*

Solution

$$y = x^2 - 4x + 5 = x^2 - 4x + 4 - 4 + 5$$
$$= (x - 2)^2 + 1$$

EXAMPLE 2. *Express* $y = 2x^2 - 12x + 22$ *in the form* $y = a(x - s)^2 + t$.

Solution

$$
\begin{aligned}
y = 2x^2 - 12x + 22 &= [2x^2 - 12x] + 22 && \text{grouping} \\
&= 2[x^2 - 6x] + 22 && \text{factoring 2} \\
&= 2[x^2 - 6x + 9 - 9] + 22 && \text{completing the square} \\
&= 2[(x - 3)^2 - 9] + 22 && \text{writing the perfect square} \\
&= 2(x - 3)^2 - 18 + 22 && \text{removing square brackets} \\
&= 2(x - 3)^2 + 4 && \text{simplifying}
\end{aligned}
$$

EXAMPLE 3. *Express* $y = -3x^2 + 12x - 7$ *in the form* $y = a(x - s)^2 + t$.

Solution

$$
\begin{aligned}
y = -3x^2 + 12x - 7 &= [-3x^2 + 12x] - 7 && \text{grouping} \\
&= -3[x^2 - 4x] - 7 && \text{factoring } -3 \\
&= -3[x^2 - 4x + 4 - 4] - 7 && \text{completing the square} \\
&= -3[(x - 2)^2 - 4] - 7 && \text{writing the perfect square} \\
&= -3(x - 2)^2 + 12 - 7 && \text{removing square brackets} \\
&= -3(x - 2)^2 + 5 && \text{simplifying}
\end{aligned}
$$

EXERCISE 5-5

A **1.** Express the following as perfect squares.
(a) $x^2 + 6x + 9$ (b) $x^2 + 4x + 4$ (c) $x^2 + 8x + 16$
(d) $x^2 - 4x + 4$ (e) $x^2 - 10x + 25$ (f) $x^2 + 14x + 49$
(g) $x^2 - 6x + 9$ (h) $x^2 - 2x + 1$ (i) $x^2 + x + \frac{1}{4}$

2. What number must be added to each of the following in order to make the sum a perfect square?
(a) $x^2 + 6x$ (b) $x^2 + 4x$ (c) $x^2 + 2x$
(d) $x^2 - 8x$ (e) $x^2 + 12x$ (f) $x^2 - 10x$
(g) $x^2 + 20x$ (h) $x^2 - 18x$ (i) $x^2 + 16x$

3. What number must be added to each of the following in order to make the sum a perfect square?
(a) $x^2 + 5x$ (b) $x^2 + 7x$ (c) $x^2 - 3x$
(d) $x^2 - 11x$ (e) $x^2 + x$ (f) $x^2 - x$
(g) $x^2 + \frac{4}{5}x$ (h) $x^2 - \frac{1}{3}x$ (i) $x^2 + \frac{1}{2}x$

(j) $x^2 - \frac{3}{4}x$ (k) $x^2 + \frac{2}{7}x$ (l) $x^2 - \frac{5}{6}x$

B **4.** Express each of the following in the form $y = a(x - s)^2 + t$.
(a) $y = x^2 + 6x + 7$ (b) $y = x^2 - 4x + 3$
(c) $y = x^2 + 8x - 13$ (d) $y = x^2 - 10x + 21$
(e) $y = x^2 + 2x + 3$ (f) $y = x^2 - 12x - 4$
(g) $y = x^2 - 14x - 3$ (h) $y = x^2 + 20x$

5. Express each of the following in the form $y = a(x - s)^2 + t$.
(a) $y = 2x^2 + 4x + 7$ (b) $y = 3x^2 - 12x - 2$
(c) $y = 2x^2 + 16x + 8$ (d) $y = -2x^2 - 8x - 5$
(e) $y = -3x^2 + 6x - 1$ (f) $y = -4x^2 - 16x + 1$

6. Express each of the following in the form $y = a(x - s)^2 + t$.
(a) $y = 2x^2 + 6x + 7$ (b) $y = 3x^2 - 15x + 4$
(c) $y = -3x^2 - 2x + 7$ (d) $y = 6x^2 - 5x + 2$
(e) $y = -4x^2 + 5x - 1$ (f) $y = 4x^2 - 10x + 3$

7. (a) Express $y = 2x^2 - 14x + 12$ in the form $y = a(x - s)^2 + t$.
(b) What is the equation of the axis of symmetry of the parabola defined by $y = 2x^2 - 14x + 12$?
(c) What are the coordinates of the vertex of $y = 2x^2 - 14x + 12$?
(d) Does the vertex represent a maximum or minimum point?

8. (a) Express $y = -2x^2 + 5x - 4$ in the form $y = a(x - s)^2 + t$.
(b) State the equation of the axis of symmetry and the coordinates of the vertex of the parabola defined by $y = -2x^2 + 5x - 4$.
(c) Does the vertex represent a maximum or minimum point?

9. (a) State the vertex and the equation of the axis of symmetry of the function defined by $y = -5x^2 - 10x - 8$.
(b) Does the vertex represent a maximum or minimum point?

5.6 INTERCEPTS

In the general linear function, $y = mx + b$, b represents the value of the y-intercept. The **y-intercept** of a relation is the y-coordinate of the point of intersection of the graph of the relation and the y-axis. Similarly, the **x-intercept** of a relation is the x-coordinate of the point of intersection of the graph of the relation and the x-axis.

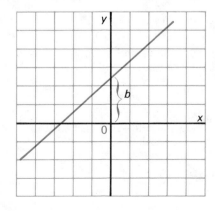

You will recall from earlier work that to find a y-intercept you substitute $x = 0$ into the equation (since the x-coordinate of points on the y-axis is zero) and solve for y. To find an x-intercept, you substitute $y = 0$ into the equation (since the y-coordinate of points on the x-axis is zero) and solve for x. For this reason the x-intercepts are sometimes called the **zeros of the relation.**

EXAMPLE 1. *Find the x- and y-intercepts of the quadratic function defined by $y = x^2 - 5x - 6$.*

Solution
If $x = 0$, $y = 0 - 0 - 6$, $\therefore$ the y-intercept is -6.

$$\text{If } y = 0, \qquad 0 = x^2 - 5x - 6$$
$$0 = (x - 6)(x + 1)$$
$$x - 6 = 0 \quad \text{or} \quad x + 1 = 0$$
$$\therefore \quad x = 6 \quad \text{or} \quad x = -1.$$

$\therefore$ the x-intercepts are 6 and -1.

Put the numbers from 1 to 9 in the spaces to make the statements true:

$$\boxtimes \times \boxtimes + \boxtimes = 8$$
$$\boxtimes \div \boxtimes + \boxtimes = 8$$
$$\boxtimes - \boxtimes + \boxtimes = 8$$

Note that the problem of determining the x-intercepts of the graph of a quadratic function is the same as that of finding the roots of the corresponding quadratic equation. To solve a quadratic equation we first try to factor the polynomial. If the factors are not obvious, we use the general quadratic formulas:

$$x = \frac{-b + \sqrt{b^2 - 4ac}}{2a} \quad \text{and} \quad x = \frac{-b - \sqrt{b^2 - 4ac}}{2a}$$

EXAMPLE 2. *Find the x- and y-intercepts of $y = 3x^2 + 5x - 7$.*

Solution
If $x = 0$, $y = -7$
$\therefore$ the y-intercept is -7.
If $y = 0$, $3x^2 + 5x - 7 = 0$.
$\therefore \quad a = 3$, $b = 5$, $c = -7$, and

$$x = \frac{-b + \sqrt{b^2 - 4ac}}{2a} \quad \text{or} \quad x = \frac{-b - \sqrt{b^2 - 4ac}}{2a}$$

$$\therefore \quad x = \frac{-5 + \sqrt{25 + 84}}{6} \quad \text{or} \quad x = \frac{-5 - \sqrt{25 + 84}}{6}$$

$$\therefore \quad x = \frac{-5 + \sqrt{109}}{6} \quad \text{or} \quad x = \frac{-5 - \sqrt{109}}{6}$$

$\therefore$ the x-intercepts are $\dfrac{-5 + \sqrt{109}}{6}$ and $\dfrac{-5 - \sqrt{109}}{6}$

To plot the intercepts we take the value $\sqrt{109} \doteq 10.4$

quadratic functions   95

EXERCISE 5-6

A **1.** Find the x- and y-intercepts of the following.

(a) $2x + 3y = 6$ (b) $4x - 3y = 12$

(c) $y = 2x - 6$ (d) $y = -3x + 12$

(e) $2y + 5x = 10$ (f) $3x + 5y - 15 = 0$

B **2.** Find the x- and y-intercepts of each of the following.

(a) $y = x^2 + 7x + 12$ (b) $y = x^2 + 5x + 6$

(c) $y = x^2 - x - 12$ (d) $y = x^2 + 2x - 15$

(e) $y = -x^2 - 7x - 10$ (f) $y = -x^2 + 4x + 12$

(g) $y = -x^2 + 8x - 12$ (h) $y = 4x^2 - 28x$

(i) $y = 2x^2 + 5x - 12$ (j) $y = 2x^2 - 3x - 2$

(k) $y = x^2 + 8x + 9$ (l) $y = 4x^2 - 5x - 6$

3. (a) How many y-intercepts does a quadratic function have?

(b) What is the maximum number of x-intercepts a quadratic function may have?

4. (a) Find the x-intercepts of:

(i) $y = x^2 + 2x + 1$ (ii) $y = 4x^2 - 12x + 9$

(b) How many x-intercepts are there?

5. (a) Find the x-intercepts of:

(i) $y = x^2 + x + 1$ (ii) $y = 4x^2 + 5x + 3$

(b) How many x-intercepts are there?

6. (a) Using the same set of axes, sketch the graphs of each of the following clearly indicating the vertex, y-intercept, and x-intercepts.

(i) $y = x^2 + 4x + 4$ (ii) $y = x^2 + 4x - 5$ (iii) $y = x^2 + 4x + 7$

(b) Does the vertex represent a maximum point or a minimum point in each case?

(c) What is the maximum or minimum value?

7. Sketch the graphs of each of the following. Indicate the vertex, y-intercept, and x-intercepts in each case.

(a) $y = x^2 + x - 6$ (b) $y = x^2 + 2x - 8$

(c) $y = -x^2 + 6x - 5$ (d) $y = -x^2 + 8x - 12$

(e) $y = 2x^2 + 5x - 3$ (f) $y = x^2 + 2x + 5$

(g) $y = -x^2 - 4x - 6$ (h) $y = 2x^2 + 5x - 1$

5.7 MAXIMUM AND MINIMUM VALUES

EXAMPLE 1. *Sketch the graph of $y = 2x^2 + 3$ and determine whether the function has a maximum or minimum value. State the value of x at which the maximum or minimum occurs.*

Solution

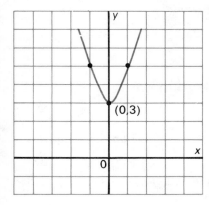

(0,3)

minimum of 3 when $x = 0$

EXAMPLE 2. *Sketch the graph of* $y = -2x^2 + 12x - 13$. *Determine the maximum or minimum value of the function and state the value of x at which it occurs.*

Solution

$y = -2x^2 + 12x - 13$
$= [-2x^2 + 12x] - 13$
$= -2[x^2 - 6x] - 13$
$= -2[x^2 - 6x + 9 - 9] - 13$
$= -2[(x - 3)^2 - 9] - 13$
$= -2(x - 3)^2 + 18 - 13$
$= -2(x - 3)^2 + 5$

maximum of 5 when $x = 3$

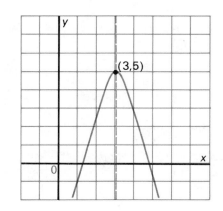

(3,5)

EXERCISE 5-7

A **1.** State the maximum or minimum value of each of the following. Also state the value of x where the maximum or minimum occurs.

(a) $y = 3x^2$ (b) $y = -2x^2$ (c) $y = x^2 + 2$

(d) $y = 3x^2 - 4$ (e) $y = -4x^2 + 7$ (f) $y = -3x^2 - 6$

(g) $y = \frac{1}{2}x^2 + 11$ (h) $y = -\frac{1}{3}x^2 - 5$

2. Find the maximum or minimum values of each of the following quadratic functions and state the corresponding value of x.

(a) $y = (x - 2)^2 + 3$ (b) $y = 2(x + 3)^2 - 4$

(c) $y = -(x - 3)^2 - 4$ (d) $y = -7(x + 1)^2 + 10$

(e) $y = 19(x + 3)^2 - 18$ (f) $y = -3(x - 5)^2 - 2$

(g) $y = 4 + 2(x - 1)^2$ (h) $y = -5 + 3(x + 2)^2$

Draw three straight lines to separate the dots.

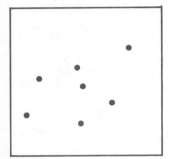

B **3.** By first completing the square, determine the maximum or minimum value of each of the following. State the corresponding value of x.

(a) $y = x^2 + 6x + 7$
(b) $y = x^2 - 4x + 1$
(c) $y = -x^2 - 2x - 3$
(d) $y = 2x^2 + 12x + 5$
(e) $y = -3x^2 + 6x - 4$
(f) $y = 2x^2 + 3x - 2$
(g) $y = -4x^2 + 20x - 7$
(h) $y = 3x^2 + 4x$

5.8 MAXIMUM AND MINIMUM PROBLEMS

EXAMPLE 1. *Find two positive numbers whose sum is 12 and whose product is a maximum.*

Solution Let the numbers be x and $(12 - x)$. The product of the numbers is

$$P = x(12 - x)$$
$$= 12x - x^2$$
$$= -x^2 + 12x$$

We now complete the square to find the maximum value of the function.

$$P = -x^2 + 12x$$
$$= -[x^2 - 12x]$$
$$= -[x^2 - 12x + 36 - 36]$$
$$= -[(x - 6)^2 - 36]$$
$$= -(x - 6)^2 + 36$$

The product is a maximum of 36 when $x = 6$.
The two numbers are 6 and 6.

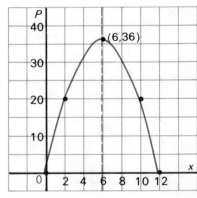

EXAMPLE 2. *A rectangular field is to be enclosed with 600 m of fencing. What dimensions will produce a maximum area?*

Solution Let the width in metres be x.
Then the length is $300 - x$.
The area enclosed by the fence is

$$A = x(300 - x)$$
$$= 300x - x^2$$
$$= -x^2 + 300$$

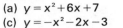

$300 - x$

applied mathematics for today: senior

To find the maximum area we complete the square:

$A = -x^2 + 300x$

$\quad = -[x^2 - 300x]$

$\quad = -[x^2 - 300x + 22\,500 - 22\,500]$

$\quad = -[(x - 150)^2 - 22\,500]$

$\quad = -(x - 150)^2 + 22\,500$

The value of A is maximum (22 500) when $x = 150$.
A width of 150 m and a length of 150 m will produce a maximum area.

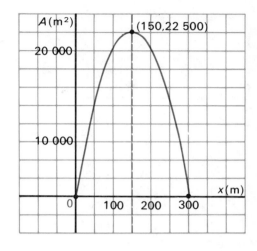

EXERCISE 5-8

A **1.** Complete the following statements (only use one variable: x).
(a) The sum of two numbers is 20.
Let one number be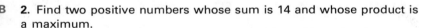
Then the other number is ▨
(b) The sum of two numbers is 33.
Let one number be ▨
Then the other number is ▨
(c) The perimeter of a rectangle is 200 cm.
Let the width be ▨
Then the length is ▨
(d) The perimeter of a rectangle is 400 m.
Let the width be ▨
Then the length is ▨
(e) A rectangular field, bounded on one side by a river, is to be fenced on 3 sides with 600 m of fence.
Let the width be ▨
Then the length is ▨

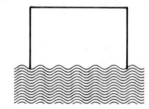

B **2.** Find two positive numbers whose sum is 14 and whose product is a maximum.

3. Find two positive real numbers whose sum is 14 if the sum of their squares is a minimum.

4. A rectangular field is to be enclosed with 400 m of fencing. What dimensions will produce a maximum area?

5. A rectangular parking lot is to be fenced with 80 m of fencing on three sides, leaving the fourth side open to the street. If the area is to be a maximum, what should the width be?

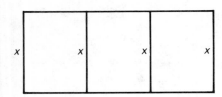

6. A rectangular field is to be enclosed by a fence and then divided into three smaller plots by two fences parallel to one side of the field. If there are 1600 m of fence available, find the dimensions of the field giving maximum area.

7. Forty centimetres of picture frame moulding are purchased to frame a small rectangular mosaic. What is the maximum area which can be enclosed?

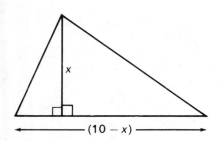

8. If the sum of the base and height of a triangle must be 10 cm, how long should you make the base to give a maximum area?

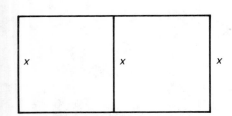

9. A rectangular field is to be enclosed by a fence and then divided into two smaller plots by a fence parallel to one side of the field. If 400 m of fence are available, find the dimensions of the field giving maximum area.

5.9 GRAPHS OF POLYNOMIAL FUNCTIONS

EXERCISE 5-9

A **1.** (a) Graph the linear function defined by $y = 3x + 2$.
(b) Find the x- and y-intercepts.
(c) Does $y = 3x + 2$ have a maximum or minimum value?

2. (a) Graph the quadratic function defined by $y = 3x^2 - 12$.
(b) Find the x- and y-intercepts.
(c) Does $y = 3x^2 - 12$ have a maximum or minimum value?

3. (a) Graph the **cubic function** defined by $y = x^3 - 3x^2 - x + 3$.
(b) Find the x- and y-intercepts.
(c) How many x-intercepts are there?
(d) What are the roots of $x^3 - 3x^2 - x + 3 = 0$?
(e) Does $y = x^3 - 3x^2 - x + 3$ have a maximum or minimum value?

4. Graph the following cubic functions.
(a) $y = x^3 - 3x$ \qquad\qquad (b) $y = x^3 - 13x - 12$

5. (a) Graph the **quartic function** defined by $y = x^4 - 4x^3 - 4x^2 + 16x$.
(b) Find the x- and y-intercepts.
(c) How many x-intercepts are there?
(d) What are the roots of $x^4 - 4x^3 - 4x^2 + 16x = 0$?
(e) Does $y = x^4 - 4x^3 - 4x^2 + 16x$ have a maximum or minimum value?

6. Graph the quartic function defined by $y = x^4 - 5x^2 + 3$.

7. Graph the **quintic function** defined by $y = x^5 - 5x^3 - 4x$.

REVIEW EXERCISE

1. (a) Graph the parabola represented by $y = \frac{1}{4}x^2$.
(b) Name the vertex and axis of symmetry of $y = \frac{1}{4}x^2$.
(c) Using the result of (a) sketch graphs of the following parabolas on one set of axes.
(i) $y = -\frac{1}{4}x^2$
(ii) $y = \frac{1}{4}x^2 + 2$
(iii) $y = \frac{1}{4}(x + 3)^2$
(iv) $y = \frac{1}{4}(x - 1)^2 + 5$
(d) Name the vertex and axis of symmetry of each parabola in (c).

2. Find the coordinates of the vertex of each of the following parabolas and state whether the vertex represents a maximum point or a minimum point.
(a) $y = x^2 + 2$
(b) $y = 2(x + 3)^2 - 4$
(c) $y = -(x - 2)^2 + 5$
(d) $y = -\frac{1}{3}(x + 5)^2 - 7$

3. Express each of the following in the form $y = a(x - s)^2 + t$.
(a) $y = 2x^2 - 6x + 9$
(b) $y = -3x^2 + 9x - 7$
(c) $y = x^2 + 2x + 8$
(d) $y = 2x^2 + 4x + 4$
(e) $y = x^2 + 2x - 6$
(f) $y = -\frac{1}{2}x^2 - 2x + \frac{1}{3}$

4. State the maximum or minimum value of each function represented in question 3 and state when the maximum or minimum occurs.

5. Sketch the graphs of each of the following. Indicate the vertex, y-intercept, and x-intercepts in each case.
(a) $y = x^2 + 3x - 10$
(b) $y = 2x^2 + 8x$
(c) $y = -2x^2 + 8$
(d) $y = x^2 + 6x + 9$
(e) $y = -2x^2 - 5x + 3$
(f) $y = x^2 + 2x + 6$

6. Find the dimensions of the rectangular lot having maximum area that can be enclosed by a fence 600 m long.

7. Find the maximum or minimum value of:
(a) $y = 2x^2 + 6x - 3$
(b) $y = -2x^2 + 3x + 6$
(c) $y = -4x^2 + 8x + 5$
(d) $y = 3x^2 + 10x$

Find the next term.

NAMES AND NUMBERS

Pythagoras is best known for his work with right angle triangles, but he also founded a school of thought that believed the apparently bewildering chaos of nature could be reduced to mathematical order, and that the universe itself conforms to an understandable numerical pattern.

This branch of Pythagorean thought is the basis of numerology, the magical theory of numbers, which assumes the additional belief that the name of a thing contains the essence of its being. According to this belief there is no difference, for instance, between the name 'frog' and the animal itself. Similarly, your name not only distinguishes you from other people, it also defines the person that is you.

But how to analyse the meanings of millions of different names? The task is hopeless unless they are reduced to a reasonably small number of types. Numerologists do this by turning all names into numbers.

To find the number of your name you start by giving each letter a number. There are different systems of doing this, but in the one most widely used the numbers from 1 to 9 are written down and the letters of the alphabet are written underneath in their normal order:

```
1  2  3  4  5  6  7  8  9
A  B  C  D  E  F  G  H  I
J  K  L  M  N  O  P  Q  R
S  T  U  V  W  X  Y  Z
```

Now write down you name and the number equivalents for each letter. Then add the numbers. If the total has two figures or more, add these figures together and repeat the process until you reach a single number. This is called the 'digital root'. For example:

```
L   I   N   D   A      C   O   V   E   L   Y
3 + 9 + 5 + 4 + 1  +  3 + 6 + 4 + 5 + 3 + 7
```

The numbers total 50. Add 5 and 0 to give 5. Then 5 is the digital root of 50, and the number of the name Linda Covely.

The number of your name found by this method is believed by numerologists to show your basic character and personality, and the type of life you will lead. Each number has a different interpretation, roughly as follows.

People whose names add up to *one* are supposed to be positive, self-assertive, ambitious, and aggressive.

People whose number is *two* have traditionally feminine qualities. They are quiet, tactful, lovers of peace and harmony.

If your number is *three*, you are brilliant, imaginative, versatile, energetic and probably artistic.

Four is the number of solid, practical people. Down-to-earth, calm and steady, they are the pillars of society.

Fives are adventurous, attractive people, lovers of travel and all things unusual. They make excellent salespeople.

Six is the number of harmony

and domesticity. Sixes tend to be loyal, conscientious, idealistic, and affectionate.

Seven is the number of the scholar and the philosopher. Dignified and serious, sevens have little patience with frivolity.

Eight stands for power and money. Eights have the capacity for massive material success, but also face the possibility of resounding failure.

Nine is the number of high mental and spiritual achievement. Nines are romantic people, with wide sympathies and great charm.

Some numerologists also stress the importance of the number found by adding up the figures of your birth date. For instance, if your were born on May 15, 1952:

$$M\ A\ Y\quad 1\ 5\quad 1\ 9\ 5\ 2$$
$$4+1+7\ +\ 1+5\ +\ 1+9+5+2$$

This adds to 35, which reduces to 8. This is your birth number. According to numerologists it is an indication of the stamp which the mysterious forces that move the universe impressed on your character and destiny at the moment you were born. If it does not harmonize with your name number, you may be torn by inner conflict and seem to be always struggling against fate.

The theory of numerology is of course much more complicated than this. Is there any truth in it? You may be surprised at how closely your friends seem to fit their numbers!

REVIEW AND PREVIEW TO CHAPTER 6

EXERCISE 1 *Function Notation*

1. If $f(x) = 2x + 3$, find:

(a) $f(1)$ (b) $f(2)$ (c) $f(0)$

(d) $f(-2)$ (e) $f(-4)$ (f) $f(9)$

2. If $g(x) = \frac{1}{2}x - 3$, find

(a) $g(2)$ (b) $g(8)$ (c) $g(-4)$

(d) $g(12)$ (e) $g(7)$ (f) $g(a)$

3. If $t(n) = n^2 + 4$, find:

(a) $t(1)$ (b) $t(2)$ (c) $t(-2)$

(d) $t(8)$ (e) $t(\frac{1}{2})$ (f) $t(x)$

4. If $f(x) = 2^x + 1$, find:

(a) $f(1)$ (b) $f(2)$ (c) $f(a)$

5. If $g(x) = 4(2)^x - 5$, find:

(a) $g(1)$ (b) $g(2)$ (c) $g(3)$

6. If $h(x) = -3x^2 + 2x - 4$, find:

(a) $h(-1)$ (b) $h(3)$ (c) $h(-2)$

(d) $h(m)$ (e) $h(0)$ (f) $h(1)$

EXERCISE 2 *Linear Systems*

1. Solve the following by elimination:

(a) $x + y = 7$ (b) $2x + y = 10$
     $x - y = 3$ $x + y = 4$

(c) $a + 3d = 11$ (d) $a + 5d = -17$
     $a + d = 3$ $a + 2d = 4$

(e) $a + 11d = -90$ (f) $2x + 3y = -13$
     $a + 3d = -10$ $3x + 2y = -12$

(g) $5x - 3y = 29$ (h) $5x - 6y = -45$
     $2x + 7y = -13$ $7x - 4y = -41$

FROM 0 TO 1

Complete the following tables; then match the equation with the appropriate curve on the graph.

1. $y = x^2$ **2.** $y = x^4$

x	y
0.00	
0.15	
0.30	
0.45	
0.50	
0.60	
0.75	
0.90	
1.00	

x	y
0.00	
0.15	
0.30	
0.45	
0.50	
0.60	
0.75	
0.90	
1.00	

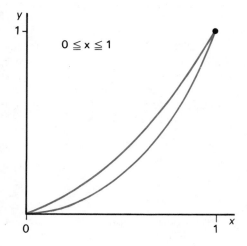

$0 \leqq x \leqq 1$

CHAPTER 6

Sequences and Series

6.1 SEQUENCES

The set of page numbers in this text, 1, 2, 3, 4, 5, . . . forms a sequence.

A sequence is a set of numbers which are written in a definite order. This particular sequence is a subset of the set of natural numbers N. This set has a definite number of elements corresponding to the number of pages in the book and is therefore a finite sequence. N, on the other hand, is an infinite sequence.

A student had a job after school and was offered payment of $1 for the first month, $2 the second month, $4 the third month . . . for one year. Complete the sequence and find how much the student was paid the 12th month.

Monthly wage = {$1, $2, $4, $8, $16, $32, $, $, $, $, $, $ }.

A sequence need not follow a predictable pattern. The sequence 6, 1, 2, 9, 8, 9, . . . was taken from a table of random numbers. Most sequences that mathematicians are interested in do follow a pattern, and the challenge is often in finding what it is. Study the pattern in each of the following sequences and determine a next term.

Find the next term

0, T, T, F, F, S, . . .

$$A = \{1, 5, 9, \ldots\}$$
$$B = \{3, 6, 12, \ldots\}$$
$$C = \{1, 4, 9, \ldots\}$$
$$D = \{1, 2, 6, 24, \ldots\}$$

Since sequences need not follow a particular pattern, your answer, whatever it is, is one of many possible correct answers. If we wish to define a specific sequence, this can be done by giving the general term $t(n)$, where $n \in N$.

In the above sequence A, $t(n) = 4n - 3$

$$t(1) = 4 - 3 = 1$$
$$t(2) = 8 - 3 = 5$$
$$t(3) = 12 - 3 = 9$$

Each member of a sequence is associated with a natural number.

In set A, $1 \rightarrow 1$
$2 \rightarrow 5$
$3 \rightarrow 9$
. .
. .

From this we see that a sequence can be considered a function in $N \times R$, where the domain is a subset of the natural numbers and the range is a subset of the real numbers. In this sense sequence A could have been written

$$\{(1, 1), (2, 5), (3, 9), \ldots (n, 4n - 3), \ldots\}$$

In sequence B, $t(n) = 3(2)^{n-1}$

$$t(1) = 3(2)^0 = 3$$
$$t(2) = 3(2)^1 = 6$$
$$t(3) = 3(2)^2 = 12$$

Sequence B could have been written

$$\{(1, 3), (2, 6), (3, 12), \ldots (n, 3(2)^{n-1}), \ldots\}$$

In sequence C, $t(n) = n^2$.
In sequence D, $t(n) = 1 \times 2 \times 3 \times \cdots \times n$.
$1 \times 2 \times 3 \times \cdots \times n$ is called factorial n and may be written $n!$ Thus:

$$t(1) = 1! = 1$$
$$t(2) = 2! = 1 \times 2 = 2$$
$$t(3) = 3! = 1 \times 2 \times 3 = 6$$

It is usual to refer to the nth term of a sequence as t_n (read "t sub n") rather than $t(n)$; $t(1)$ becomes t_1, $t(2)$ becomes t_2 and so on. We shall use this abbreviated notation in the remainder of the chapter.

Often valuable information can be derived from the graph of a sequence. Since we are dealing with a function in $N \times R$, the graph will be a discrete set of points. Compare the graphs of the preceding four examples. Which sequence has the most rapid rate of growth when $n \leqq 2$? when $n \leqq 4$?

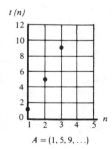

$A = (1, 5, 9, \ldots)$

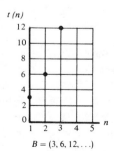

$B = (3, 6, 12, \ldots)$

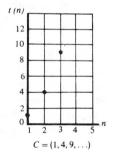

$C = (1, 4, 9, \ldots)$

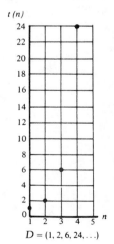

$D = (1, 2, 6, 24, \ldots)$

EXERCISE 6-1

B **1.** Determine the first 3 terms of each of the following sequences.

(a) $t_n = 2n + 1$ (b) $t_n = 4 + 6n$ (c) $t_n = 200 - 10n$

(d) $t_n = 3n - 6$ (e) $t_n = n(n + 2)$ (f) $t_n = 3^n$

(g) $t_n = 2^{n+1}$ (h) $t_n = 5(2^n)$ (i) $t_n = (n + 1)(n + 2)$

2. For each of the following sequences find a possible t_4 and t_5 and graph. $\{(1, t_1), (2, t_2), \ldots, (5, t_5)\}$

(a) $1, 4, 7, \ldots$ (b) $2, 7, 12, \ldots$ (c) $3, 6, 12, \ldots$

(d) $1, 4, 16, \ldots$ (e) $1, 4, 9, \ldots$ (f) $7, 4, 1, \ldots$

(g) $16, 8, 4, \ldots$ (h) $2, 6, 18, \ldots$ (i) $11, 9, 7, \ldots$

Find the next term

$1, 3, 6, 10, 15, 21, \ldots$

3. The Pythagoreans were a fraternity of mathematicians who studied under the leadership of the early Greek mathematician Pythagoras. They attributed mystical qualities to certain numbers. Odd numbers were masculine, even numbers feminine; the number 1 was the source of all numbers and represented reason. The Pythagoreans were particularly interested in the connection between numbers and geometry.

Some numbers were considered triangular:

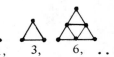

1,   3,   6,   . . .

Some square:

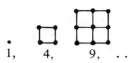

1,   4,   9,   . . .

Some pentagonal:

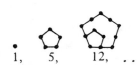

1,   5,   12,   . . .

(a) Continue each of the above sequences as far as t_6.

(b) For each of the sequences in (a) make a second sequence from the number of dots which must be added to get each succeeding term. What property has each of the sequences in common? Construct a sequence of hexagonal numbers to t_5. Does the property hold?

4. A prime number is an integer greater than one which is divisible only by itself and by one. Write the sequence of the first ten prime numbers.

Is this sequence predictable and can a general term be formed?

       applied mathematics for today: senior

> **Fibonacci Sequence**
>
> The sequence 1, 1, 2, 3, 5, 8, 13, . . . is called the Fibonacci sequence after Leonardo Fibonacci (1170–1250). The first two terms are both 1. Thereafter to find a term of the sequence you find the sum of the previous two terms.
>
> This sequence had its origin in the question of how many pairs of rabbits can be produced from a pair of rabbits in a year, if each pair produces a new pair each month and each new pair reproduces from the second month and no rabbit dies.
>
> This series has also been found to describe the spiral formation of leaves about a stalk and the seed formation in sunflowers.
>
> There is a Fibonacci society whose members have a special interest in finding new significance in this special set of numbers.

6.2 ARITHMETIC SEQUENCES

In Section 6.1 we investigated the sequence 1, 5, 9, 13, ... Notice that $5-1=4$, $9-5=4$, $13-9=4, \ldots$; that is, the difference between each succeeding pair of terms is a constant. Sequences of this form are called arithmetic sequences. This particular sequence could be written 1, $1+4$, $1+2(4)$, $1+3(4), \ldots$. The general arithmetic sequence is

$$a, a+d, a+2d, a+3d, \ldots$$

where a is the first term and d is the common difference.

$$t_1 = a$$
$$t_2 = a+d$$
$$t_3 = a+2d$$
.
.
.

$$\boxed{t_n = a + (n-1)d}$$

Put the numbers from 1 to 9 in the spaces to make the statements true:

$$\blacksquare \times \blacksquare + \blacksquare = 9$$
$$\blacksquare \times \blacksquare - \blacksquare = 9$$
$$\blacksquare \div \blacksquare + \blacksquare = 9$$

EXAMPLE 1. *Find t_7 and t_n for the arithmetic sequence 6, 10, 14, . . .*

Solution $a = 6$ and $d = 10 - 6 = 4$

$$
\begin{aligned}
t_7 &= a + 6d & t_n &= a + (n-1)d \\
&= 6 + 6(4) & &= 6 + (n-1)4 \\
&= 30 & &= 6 + 4n - 4 \\
& & &= 4n + 2
\end{aligned}
$$

$$t_7 = 30 \text{ and } t_n = 4n + 2$$

EXAMPLE 2. *How many terms are in the sequence 3, 5, 7, . . . 99?*

Solution The sequence is arithmetic: $a = 3$, $d = 2$

$$t_n = a + (n-1)d$$
$$99 = 3 + (n-1)2$$
$$99 = 3 + 2n - 2$$
$$98 = 2n$$
$$49 = n$$
$$99 = t_{49}$$

The sequence has 49 terms.

EXAMPLE 3. *In an arithmetic sequence $t_8 = 130$ and $t_{12} = 166$. Find t_1, t_2, and t_n.*

Solution

$$t_{12} = 166 \qquad a + 11d = 166$$
$$t_8 = 130 \qquad a + 7d = 130$$

By subtraction
$$4d = 36$$
$$d = 9$$

By substitution in t_8,

$$a + 7d = 130$$
$$a + 63 = 130$$
$$a = 67$$
$$t_1 = 67, \quad t_2 = 67 + 9 = 76$$

and
$$t_n = 67 + (n-1)9$$
$$= 67 + 9n - 9$$
$$= 9n + 58$$
$$t_1 = 67, \quad t_2 = 76 \text{ and } t_n = 9n + 58$$

EXERCISE 6-2

A **1.** Which of the following are successive terms of an arithmetic sequence? For those that are arithmetic sequences, state the value of d.

(a) 1, 6, 11, 16, . : .

(b) 25, 21, 17, 13, . . .

(c) 5, 7, 11, 17, . . .

(d) −4, −7, −10, −13, . . .

(e) 2, 6, 18, 54, . . .

(f) 16, 8, 4, 2, . . .

(g) 3, 3.5, 4, 4.5, . . .

(h) 8, −6, 4, −2, . . .

(i) $2x^2$, $3x^2$, $4x^2$, $5x^2$, . . .

(j) $3x^7$, $4x^8$, $5x^9$, $6x^{10}$, . . .

B **2.** Find the terms indicated for each of the following arithmetic sequences.

(a) t_{12} and t_{33} for 8, 10, 12, . . .

(b) t_{16} and t_{51} for 9, 13, 17, . . .

(c) t_{30} and t_n for 10, 17, 24, . . .

(d) t_{25} and t_n for -12, -8, -4, . . .

(e) t_{11} and t_k for 6, 0, -6, . . .

(f) t_{12} and t_{41} for a, $a+2b$, $a+4b$, . . .

(g) t_8 and t_{21} for $3x+y$, $3x+2y$, $3x+3y$, . . .

(h) t_9 and t_{16} for $4m-2k$, $4m-4k$, $4m-6k$, . . .

3. Find a, d and t_n for the following arithmetic sequences.

Find the next term

2, 2, 4, 6, 10, 16, . . .

(a) $t_4=16$, $t_7=25$　　　　(b) $t_{11}=52$, $t_{21}=102$

(c) $t_{50}=142$, $t_{70}=182$　　(d) $t_2=-12$, $t_5=9$

(e) $t_7=37$, $t_{10}=22$　　　　(f) $t_5=-20$, $t_{16}=-53$

(g) $t_{13}=-117$, $t_{22}=-207$　(h) $t_7=3+15k$, $t_{11}=3+23k$

4. How many terms are in the following arithmetic sequences?

(a) 3, 5, 7, . . . 99

(b) 5, 9, 11, . . . 165

(c) -29, -24, -19, . . . 26

(d) 51, 45, 39, . . . -9

(e) -6, -11, -16, . . . -156

(f) 5, $5\frac{1}{2}$, 6, . . . 35

(g) m, $m+3d$, $m+6d$, . . . $m+81d$

(h) $x+2$, $x+7$, $x+12$, . . . $x+242$

(i) multiples of 5 from 30 to 500 inclusive

(j) multiples of 7 from -56 to 560 inclusive

5. When money is lent at simple interest rates, the amounts required to pay off the loan at the end of each year are the terms of an arithmetic sequence.

Year	Now	1	2	3	4	$\cdots$	n
Amount	P	$P+Pi$	$P+2Pi$	$P+3Pi$	$P+4Pi$	$\cdots$	$P+nPi$

where P represents the principal and i the annual rate of interest.

If \$100 is lent at 5%/a simple interest, show the amount at the end of 1, 2, 3, 4, and n years. Find a and d for the sequence.

6. Repeat question 5 for \$800 lent at 7%/a. Find the amount required to repay the loan after 12 a.

C **7.** (a) Compare the equation $t_n=5n+4$ with the equation $y=mx+b$. Describe the graph of $t_n=5n+4$.

(b) Graph the sequence for $1 \leqq n \leqq 10$ and illustrate your answers to (a).

6.3 THE SUM OF A FINITE ARITHMETIC SERIES

When we indicate that the terms of a sequence should be added then the indicated sum is called a series:

sequence $\qquad 3, 5, 7, 9, \ldots$

series $\qquad 3+5+7+9+\ldots$

The sum of n terms is given by S_n:

$$S_n = 3+5+7+9+\cdots$$

$$S_4 = 3+5+7+9$$

For the general arithmetic series:

$$S_n = a + (a+d) + (a+2d) + \cdots + [a+(n-1)d]$$

Write an expression for 5 using four threes.

INVESTIGATION 6.3

Complete each of the following according to the instructions.

1. List the first 10 terms of the arithmetic series

$$S_{10} = 2+5+8+\ldots$$

2. List the terms again under the first starting with the last term

$$S_{10} = - + - + - + \ldots + 8 + 5 + 2.$$

3. Add the corresponding terms of the two series giving an expression of the form

$$2S_{10} = - + - + \ldots + - + - + -.$$

4. This might be rewritten in the form

$$2S_{10} = 10(\blacksquare)$$

$$S_{10} = 5(\blacksquare).$$

5. Note that the factor 5 is one-half the number of terms, and that the factor ($\blacksquare$) is the sum of the first and last terms.

6. Repeat steps 2, 3, and 4 for the series

$$S_n = a + (a+d) + (a+2d) + \ldots + (t_n - d) + t_n$$

Your result should be

$$\boxed{S_n = \frac{n}{2}(a + t_n)}$$

This formula gives us the sum of an arithmetic series when we know the number of terms n, the first term a, and the nth term t_n.

Substituting $\quad t_n = a + (n-1)d$

we have

$$S_n = \frac{n}{2}[a + a + (n-1)d]$$

$$\boxed{S_n = \frac{n}{2}[2a + (n-1)d]}$$

This formula gives us the sum of an arithmetic series when we know the number of terms n, the first term a, and the common difference d.

EXAMPLE 1. *Find the sum of the series* $12 + 8 + 4 + \ldots + (-28)$

Solution $a = 12$, $t_n = -28$, $d = -4$, $S_n = \frac{n}{2}(a + t_n)$

In order to find the sum we must evaluate n:

$$t_n = a + (n-1)d$$
$$= 12 + (n-1)(-4)$$
$$= 16 - 4n$$
$$\therefore \quad -28 = 16 - 4n$$
$$4n = 44$$
$$n = 11$$
$$S_{11} = \frac{11}{2}(12 - 28)$$
$$= \frac{11}{2}(-16)$$
$$= -88$$

∴ the sum of the series is −88.

Find the next term

$1, 1, 2, 4, 8, 16, \ldots$

EXAMPLE 2. *Find S_{15} for the the series* $10 + 13 + 16 + \ldots$

Solution $a = 10$, $d = 3$, $n = 15$

$$S_n = \frac{n}{2}[2a + (n-1)d]$$
$$S_{15} = \frac{15}{2}[20 + 14 \times 3]$$
$$= \frac{15}{2}[20 + 42]$$
$$= \frac{15}{2}(62)$$
$$= 465$$

∴ the sum of the series is 465.

EXERCISE 6-3

B **1.** Find the required sum for the following series.

(a) S_{12} of $5+9+13+\ldots$ (b) S_{20} of $40+45+50+\ldots$

(c) S_{14} of $-14-8-2+\ldots$ (d) S_{21} of $-2+6+14+\ldots$

(e) S_{50} of $50+48+46+\ldots$ (f) S_{11} of $20+15+10+\ldots$

(g) S_{100} of $-4-8-12-\ldots$ (h) S_{51} of $-50-60-70-\ldots$

(i) S_{50} of $\frac{1}{2}+\frac{3}{2}+\frac{5}{2}+\ldots$ (j) S_{21} of $\frac{1}{2}+\frac{3}{4}+1+\ldots$

2. Find the sum of the following series.

(a) $4+8+12+\ldots+400$ (b) $5+10+15+\ldots+265$

(c) $100+90+80+\ldots-50$ (d) $52+47+42+\ldots-48$

(e) $-17-10-3+\ldots+74$ (f) $2-5-12-\ldots-222$

(g) $\frac{5}{2}+\frac{11}{2}+\frac{17}{2}+\ldots+\frac{53}{2}$ (h) $\frac{1}{2}+\frac{1}{4}+0-\ldots-\frac{11}{2}$

3. A pile of logs is formed by first laying 12 logs side by side and piling others on top to form a prism. How many logs are there in the pile?

— 12 logs —

4. A student is offered the opportunity to earn \$3.25 the first day, \$3.50 the second day, \$3.75 the third day and so on for 20 working days, or accept \$120 for the whole job. Which offer pays more?

C **5.** (a) Find S_n for the series $1+2+3\ldots$. The answer to this can be used as a formula to give us the sum of n natural numbers.

(b) Find the sum of the natural numbers from 1 to 100, using the formula in (a).

(c) Find the sum of the natural numbers from 45 to 120 inclusive.

6. A set of boxes is stored in a warehouse. The pile is four boxes wide and 20 boxes long at the bottom. Each layer is one box shorter than the previous layer but the same width. How many boxes are there in the pile if the top layer is four boxes long?

6.4   THE GEOMETRIC SEQUENCE

Earlier we investigated the sequence 3, 6, 12, 24.... Notice that $6\div3=2$, $12\div6=2$, $24\div12=2,\ldots$; that is, the ratio of each succeeding pair of terms is a constant. Sequences of this form are called geometric sequences. This particular sequence could be written

$$3,\quad 3\times2,\quad 3\times2^2,\quad 3\times2^3,\ldots$$

The general geometric sequence is

$$a,\ ar,\ ar^2,\ ar^3,\ldots,$$

where a is the first term and r is the common ratio.

$$t_1=a$$

$$t_2=ar$$

$$t_3=ar^2$$

$$\cdot$$

$$\boxed{t_n=ar^{n-1}}$$

EXAMPLE 1. *Find t_5 and t_n for the geometric sequence 3, 6, 12, ...*

Solution $a = 3$ and $r = \frac{6}{3} = 2$

$$t_5 = ar^4 \qquad\qquad t_n = ar^{n-1}$$
$$= 3 \times 2^4 \qquad\qquad = 3(2)^{n-1}$$
$$= 48$$
$$t_5 = 48 \text{ and } t_n = 3(2)^{n-1}$$

EXAMPLE 2. *How many terms are in the sequence:*

$$2, 6, 18, \ldots, 486?$$

Solution The sequence is geometric: $a = 2$, $r = 3$

$$t_n = ar^{n-1}$$
$$486 = 2(3)^{n-1}$$
$$243 = 3^{n-1} \qquad\qquad \text{Dividing by 2}$$
$$3^5 = 3^{n-1}$$
$$n - 1 = 5$$
$$n = 6$$
$$486 = t_6$$

∴ the sequence has 6 terms.

EXAMPLE 3. *In a geometric sequence $t_8 = 10\,935$ and $t_6 = 1215$. Find t_1, t_2, and t_n.*

Solution
$$t_8 = 10\,935, \qquad \therefore ar^7 = 10\,935$$
$$t_6 = 1215, \qquad \therefore ar^5 = 1215$$

By division:

$$\frac{ar^7}{ar^5} = \frac{10\,935}{1215}$$
$$r^2 = 9$$
$$r = \pm 3$$

This indicates that there are two possible solutions:

(i) $r = 3$

(ii) $r = -3$

Substituting in t_6,

$a(3)^5 = 1215$

$243a = 1215$

$a = 5$

$t_1 = 5$, $t_2 = 15$, $t_n = 5(3)^{n-1}$

Substituting in t_6,

$a(-3)^5 = 1215$

$-243a = 1215$

$a = -5$

$t_1 = -5$, $t_2 = 15$, $t_n = -5(-3)^{n-1}$

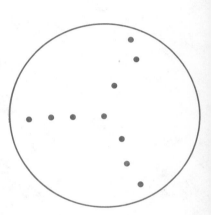

Separate the dots using 3 circles.

EXERCISE 6-4

A **1.** Which of the following are successive terms of a geometric sequence? For those that are geometric sequences, state the value of r.

(a) 1, 2, 4, 8, . . .   (b) 4, 12, 36, 108, . . .
(c) 6, 24, 48, 144, . . .   (d) 16, 8, 4, 2, . . .
(e) 1, 3, 9, 18, . . .   (f) 4, −8, 24, −48, . . .
(g) 27, −9, 3, −1, . . .   (h) x, x^3, x^5, x^7, . . .
(i) x^2, $2x^2$, $3x^2$, $4x^2$, . . .   (j) x^5, $−x^4$, x^3, $−x^2$, . . .

B **2.** Find the terms indicated for each of the following geometric sequences.

(a) t_6 and t_n for 1, 2, 4, . . .   (b) t_5 and t_n for 5, 15, 45, . . .
(c) t_7 and t_k for 3, 6, 12, . . .   (d) t_8 and t_k for 64, 32, 16, . . .
(e) t_5 and t_n for 4, −8, 16, . . .   (f) t_7 and t_n for 81, −27, +9, . . .
(g) t_{12} and t_{21} for $2x$, $2x^2$, $2x^3$, . . .
(h) t_{27} and t_{50} for $5x^{10}$, $−5x^9$, $5x^8$, . . .

Write an expression for 121 using four ones.

3. How many terms are in the following geometric sequences?

(a) 3, 6, 12, . . . , 384   (b) 4, 8, 16, . . . , 256
(c) 4, 12, 36, . . . , 972   (d) 625, 125, 25, . . . , $\frac{1}{25}$
(e) 2, −4, 8, . . . , −256   (f) 1458, 486, 162, . . . , 2
(g) $2x^2$, $2x^3$, $2x^4$, . . . , $2x^{15}$ (h) $5x^{27}$, $5x^{26}$, $5x^{24}$, . . . , $5x^3$

4. Find a, r, and t_n for the following geometric sequences.

(a) $t_3 = 36$, $t_4 = 108$ (b) $t_5 = 48$, $t_8 = 384$
(c) $t_2 = 28$, $t_4 = 448$ (d) $t_3 = 64$, $t_8 = 2$
(e) $t_4 = −9$, $t_5 = −3$ (f) $t_2 = 12$, $t_4 = 192$
(g) $t_3 = 5k^6$, $t_{10} = 5k^{20}$ (h) $t_4 = 8k^3$, $t_9 = 256k^8$

5. When money is lent and compound interest is charged, the amount required to repay the loan at the end of each year forms a geometric sequence.

Year	Now	1	2	3	4	. . .	n
Amount	P	$P(1+i)$	$P(1+i)^2$	$P(1+i)^3$	$P(1+i)^4$	. . .	$P(1+i)^n$

where P represents the principal and i the annual rate of interest.

If $100 is lent at 5%/a compounded annually, show the amount at the end of 1, 2, 3, 4, and n years. Show a and r for the sequence.

Compare the amounts in the above question to those found in Exercise 6-2, question 5, which uses simple interest.

6. Repeat question 5 for $500 invested at 8% compounded annually.

C **7.** (a) Graph the sequence $t_n = 3(2)^{n-1}$ for the domain defined by $1 \leqq n \leqq 5$.

(b) What type of growth is illustrated by the graph?

8. A virus reproduces by dividing into two, and after a period of growth by dividing again. How many virus will be in a system after division has taken place ten times?

applied mathematics for today: senior

6.5 THE SUM OF A FINITE GEOMETRIC SERIES

For the general geometric series,

$$S_n = a + ar + ar^2 + ar^3 + \ldots + ar^{n-1}$$

To develop a formula to give the sum of n terms of a geometric series with first term a and common ratio r:

$$S_n = a + ar + ar^2 + \ldots + ar^{n-1}$$

$$rS_n = \qquad ar + ar^2 + \ldots + ar^{n-1} + ar^n$$

Subtracting, $\quad S_n - rS_n = a \qquad\qquad\qquad - ar^n$

$$(1-r)S_n = a - ar^n$$

$$S_n = \frac{a(1-r^n)}{(1-r)} \quad \text{or} \quad \frac{a(r^n-1)}{(r-1)}$$

For $r > 1$, use

$$S_n = \frac{a(r^n-1)}{(r-1)}$$

$r < 1$, use

$$S_n = \frac{a(1-r^n)}{(1-r)}$$

EXAMPLE 1. *Find S_{10} for the series $1 + 2 + 4 + \ldots$.*

Solution

$a = 1, r = 2, \quad n = 10$

$$S_n = \frac{a(r^n-1)}{(r-1)}$$

$$S_{10} = \frac{1(2^{10}-1)}{2-1}$$

$$= \frac{1024-1}{1} = 1023$$

EXAMPLE 2. *Find the sum of the series $5 + 15 + 145 + \ldots + 10\,935$.*

Solution

$$S_n = \frac{a(r^n-1)}{r-1)},$$

where $a = 5$, $r = 3$, n is unknown.

$$t_n = ar^{n-1}$$

$$10\,935 = 5(3)^{n-1}$$

$$3^{n-1} = 2187$$

$$3^{n-1} = 3^7$$

$$n - 1 = 7$$

$$n = 8$$

$$S_8 = \frac{5(3^8-1)}{3-1}$$

$$= \frac{5(6561-1)}{2}$$

$$= \frac{5(6560)}{2} = 16\,400$$

EXERCISE 6-5

B **1.** Find the required sum for the following series.
(a) S_8 of $10+20+40+\ldots$ (b) S_5 of $2+6+18+\ldots$
(c) S_5 of $3+15+75+\ldots$ (d) S_7 of $2-6+18-\ldots$
(e) S_6 of $256+128+64+\ldots$ (f) S_6 of $486+162+54+\ldots$

2. Find the sum of the following series.
(a) $4+8+16+\ldots+256$ (b) $1+3+9+\ldots+729$
(c) $2-4+8-\ldots-256$ (d) $5-15+45-\ldots+3645$
(e) $81+27+9+\ldots+\frac{1}{27}$ (f) $3500+350+35+\ldots+0.0035$

3. Every person has two natural parents, four natural grandparents and so on into the ancestral past. What is the total number of direct ancestors in the previous six generations?

C **4.** At the beginning of each month an investor puts $100 into an account which pays 1%/mo. interest. At the end of one year the last deposit is worth $100(1.01), the second last is worth $100(1.01)², the third last is $100(1.01)³, and so on. Write an expression for the total value of his 12 deposits.*

5. A rubber ball is dropped from a height of 16 m. On each bounce it rebounds to $\frac{3}{4}$ of its previous height.
(a) How high does it bounce after hitting the ground (i) for the third time? (ii) for the fifth time?
(b) What is the total distance it has travelled when it hits the ground for the sixth time? (Refer to the diagram to determine which distances were travelled twice.)

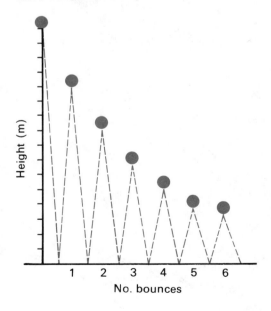

No. bounces

applied mathematics for today: senior

REVIEW EXERCISE

B   **1.** Identify each of the following sequences as arithmetic or geometric, and find t_n.

(a) $1, 10, 19, \ldots$

(b) $x, x+2y, x+4y, \ldots$

(c) $1, 10, 10^2, \ldots$

(d) $ab^6, a^2b^5, a^3b^4, \ldots$

(e) $\frac{1}{3}, \frac{1}{9}, \frac{1}{27}, \ldots$

(f) $2, -4, 8, \ldots$

(g) $56, 50, 44, \ldots$

(h) $2+3y, 4+4y, 6+5y, \ldots$

$1, 3, 4, 7, 11, 18, 29, 47, \ldots$

Find the next term.

2. Write the first three terms of each of the following series and find the sum of eight terms.

(a) $t_n = 3n + 4$

(b) $t_n = 5(3^{n-1})$

(c) $t_n = 2(n+1)$

(d) $t_n = 42 - 3n$

(e) $t_n = 3(2^n)$

(f) $t_n = 7(2^{-n})$

3. Find t_{40} and S_{100} for each of the following arithmetic sequences.

(a) $t_5 = 100, t_{10} = 130$

(b) $t_3 = 32, t_5 = 26$

4. Find t_6 and S_5 for each of the following geometric sequences.

(a) $t_2 = 15, t_3 = 75$

(b) $t_2 = 14, t_4 = 686, r > 0$

5. Find the number of terms in each of the following sequences.

(a) $7, 11, 15, \ldots, 99$

(b) $5, 10, 20, \ldots, 640$

6. A grandfather clock strikes the hours. How many times does the clock strike in 24 h?

7. In each year an automobile depreciates 20% of its value at the beginning of the year. If an automobile costs $4000 new, what is its value after 4 a?

8. If a town has a 10% population growth each year and its present population is 5000, what will its population be after 5 a?

9. Legend has it that the inventor of chess asked that his reward be one grain of wheat on the first square, two grains on the second square, four on the third and so on for all 64 squares of a chess board. Find an expression for the amount of wheat required to fulfill the request. (This figure is said to represent several times the world's annual crop of wheat!)

PERCENTAGES

EXERCISE 1

Complete the following calculations:

1. 6% of $45.65
2. 12% of $274.98
3. 43% of $154.70
4. 150% of $400.00
5. 95% of $214.75
6. 18% of $348.71
7. $5\frac{1}{2}$% of $5700.00
8. $2\frac{1}{2}$% of $974.63
9. $1\frac{1}{4}$% of $870.00
10. $24\frac{1}{2}$% of $700.00
11. $\frac{3}{4}$% of $58.93
12. $\frac{4}{5}$% of $8000.00

Express the first quantity as a percentage of the second:

13. $4.50 $4500.00
14. $85.00 $1700.00
15. $3.75 $7500.00
16. $43.00 $34 400.00
17. $74.00 $370.00
18. $6840.00 $57 000.00
19. $300.00 $12 000.00
20. $3.45 $460.00
21. $928.00 $5800.00
22. $0.81 $54.00
23. $4500.00 $3000.00
24. $387.00 $180.00

Simple Interest

Interest = Principal × Rate × Time

$$I = Prt$$

Amount = Principal + Interest

$$A = P + I$$
$$A = P + Prt$$
$$A = P(1 + rt)$$

Cover the one
you want to
find.

EXERCISE 2

Find the missing quantities:

	Interest	Principal	Rate	Time(a)	Amount
1.		$4500	12%	0.500	
2		$760	9.5%	0.750	
3.	$24.50		8%	0.250	
4.	$4.80		16%	0.125	
5.		$560		0.500	$610.40
6.		$1250		0.126	$1287.80
7.	$1179.50	$50 000	7%		
8.		$250	11%		$266.50
9.		$975	7%	0.663	
10.	$3.92			0.967	$54.62
11.	$2.87	$350	10%		
12.	$21.36		5.5%	0.411	
13.			12%	0.126	$24.97
14.			9%	0.751	$2028.42
15.			7.75%	0.600	$3558.10

Geometric Sequences and Series

$$t_n = ar^{n-1}$$

$$S_n = \frac{a(r^n - 1)}{(r - 1)}$$

Arithmetic sequences
2, 5, 8, 11, ...
5, 1, −3, −7, ...
Geometric sequences
2, 6, 18, 54, ...
5, −20, 80, −320, . . .

EXERCISE 3

1. Write the first five terms of the following geometric sequences.

(a) $a = 1$, $r = 2$

(b) $a = 32$, $r = \frac{1}{2}$

(c) $a = 27$, $r = \frac{2}{3}$

(d) $a = 4$, $r = -3$

(e) $\frac{1}{2}$, 1, —, —, —

(f) $\frac{5}{8}$, $\frac{5}{2}$, —, —, —

(g) $\frac{1}{9}$, $\frac{1}{3}$, —, —, —

(h) 1, −2, —, —, —

2. Find the required term for each of the following geometric sequences.

(a) $a = 2$, $r = 2$; t_7

(b) $a = -5$, $r = 3$; t_8

(c) $a = \frac{1}{4}$, $r = -2$; t_9

(d) $a = 9$, $r = \frac{2}{3}$; t_6

(e) $\frac{1}{8}$, $-\frac{1}{2}$, 2, . . . ; t_5

(f) -27, 9, -3, . . . ; t_8

(g) 1, $\frac{3}{2}$, $\frac{9}{4}$ . . . ; t_6

(h) $\frac{8}{81}$, $\frac{4}{27}$, $\frac{2}{9}$ . . . ; t_7

3. Find the required sum for the following geometric series.

(a) $a = 1$, $r = 2$; S_{10}

(b) $a = 2$, $r = 3$; S_8

(c) $a = 5$, $r = -2$; S_7

(d) $a = -9$, $r = \frac{1}{3}$; S_4

(e) $3 + 6 + 12 + . . .$; S_5

(f) $7 + 21 + 63 + . . .$; S_6

(g) $12 - 6 + 3 - . . .$; S_6

(h) $\frac{1}{3} + \frac{1}{9} + \frac{1}{27} + . . .$; S_4

n	2^n	3^n
1	2	3
2	4	9
3	8	27
4	16	81
5	32	243
6	64	729
7	128	2 187
8	256	6 561
9	512	19 683
10	1 024	59 049

Perform the following calculations:

$$1 = 1 = 1!$$
$$1 \times 2 = 2 = 2!$$
$$1 \times 2 \times 3 = 6 = 3!$$
$$\cdot \quad \cdot \quad \cdot \quad \cdot \quad \cdot$$
$$1 \times 2 \times 3 \times \cdots \times x = x!$$

1. $4!, 5!, 6!$

2. $\dfrac{1}{2!} + \dfrac{1}{3!} + \dfrac{1}{4!}$

3. $\dfrac{(5-3)!}{5! \times 3!}$

4. $\dfrac{(3.5)^4}{4!}$

5. $\dfrac{12!}{3! \times 4!}$

6. $\dfrac{7!}{3! + 4!}$

7. $(8! - 2!)(5! - 3!)$

8. $\dfrac{6! \times 5!}{11!}$

9. $\dfrac{4! \times 5! \times 6!}{4! + 5! + 6!}$

10. $\dfrac{5! + 6!}{6! - 5!}$

Annuities

7.1 COMPOUND INTEREST *Amount*

Compound interest is interest that is payable at regular intervals during the duration of the loan. The first payment falls due after an interval of time called the conversion period. If at the end of the first conversion period the interest is not actually paid, it is then added to the principal so that in the second conversion period interest is calculated on the interest from the first period, as well as on the original principal.

EXAMPLE 1. *If $100 is invested at 9%/a compounded annually, show how the amount grows over a term of n years.*

Solution

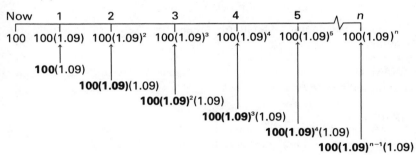

Time (a)

| Now | 1 | 2 | 3 | 4 | 5 | n |

$100 \quad 100(1.09) \quad 100(1.09)^2 \quad 100(1.09)^3 \quad 100(1.09)^4 \quad 100(1.09)^5 \quad 100(1.09)^n$

$100(1.09)$

$\mathbf{100(1.09)}(1.09)$

$\mathbf{100(1.09)^2}(1.09)$

$100(1.09)^3(1.09)$

$100(1.09)^4(1.09)$

$\mathbf{100(1.09)^{n-1}}(1.09)$

Notice that the amount at the end of each year forms the terms of geometric sequence where

$$a = \$100(1.09)$$

$$r = 1.09$$

and t_n is the nth term of the sequence.

The amount after n years:

$$t_n = ar^{n-1}$$
$$t_n = \$100(1.09)(1.09)^{n-1}$$
$$= \$100(1.09)^n$$

EXAMPLE 2. *If $100 is invested at 9%/a compounded semi-annually, show how the amount grows over a term of N years.*

"Pick up sticks" #1
Seven match sticks are placed in a row.

Two players each pick up 1 or 2 matches in turn. The player picking up the last match wins. Find a rule so that the player who picks first always wins.

9% compounded semi-annually gives 4.5% each conversion period.

Solution

Time (a)

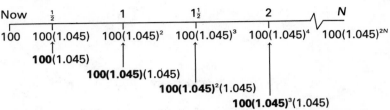

Now	$\frac{1}{2}$	1	$1\frac{1}{2}$	2	N
100	100(1.045)	100(1.045)²	100(1.045)³	100(1.045)⁴	100(1.045)²ᴺ

100(1.045)

100(1.045)(1.045)

100(1.045)²(1.045)

100(1.045)³(1.045)

N years gives 2*N* semi-annual conversion periods

The amount at the end of each half year forms the terms of a geometric sequence where $a = \$100(1.045)$ and $r = 1.045$. The amount after N years is the 2*N*th term of the sequence, $t_{2N} = 100(1.045)^{2N}$.

We may generalize from the above example to the relationship

$$A = P(1+i)^n$$

where A is the amount

        P is the principal invested

        i is the rate of interest per conversion period

        n is the total number of conversion periods.

To ease calculation a table of values for $(1+i)^n$ is given in the appendix.

EXAMPLE 3. *Find the amount of $5000 invested at 9%/a compounded semi-annually for 15/a.*

Solution
At 9% compounded semi-annually, $i = (0.5)(9\%) = 4.5\%$
For 15 a compounded semi-annually, $n = 15 \times 2$

$$= 30$$

$$\therefore A = P(1+i)^n$$

$$= \$5000(1+0.045)^{30}$$

$$\doteq \$5000(3.745\,32) \qquad \text{(from the tables)}$$

$$\doteq \$18\,726.60$$

The amount would be $18 726.60

EXERCISE 7-1

A   **1.** Complete the following.

      applied mathematics for today: senior

	Per annum rate	Term (a)	Conversion period	n	i
(a)	10%	20	semi-annual		
(b)	12%	10	quarterly		
(c)		5		10	4%
(d)	8%		semi-annual	30	
(e)			monthly	72	1.5%
(f)		2		24	0.75%
(g)	6%		annual	4	
(h)			quarterly	6	2%

B **2.** Find the amount of each of the following investments:

	Principal	Per annum rate	Conversion period	Term (a)
(a)	$4 500	12%	semi-annual	6
(b)	$750	6%	quarterly	1
(c)	$15 000	8%	annual	20
(d)	$3 250	6%	quarterly	$8\frac{1}{2}$
(e)	$730	12%	monthly	$2\frac{1}{3}$

3. What amount is required to pay off a loan of $4000 after 2 a if it has earned interest at the rate of 12%/a compounded semi-annually? How much of this amount is interest?

4. Find the amounts that $1000 invested at 12% for 3 a will grow to if the interest is compounded (a) semi-annually (b) quarterly (c) monthly.

5. How long must money be invested at 8% compounded semi-annually to double? (To the nearest 0.5 a)

6. Two loans of $500 each are taken out on Feb. 1, and Aug. 1, and repaid the following Aug. 1. If interest is charged at 11% compounded semi-annually, what total amount must be repaid?

7. (a) A savings account pays 1%/mo. on the minimum monthly balance with interest added every 3 mo. Find the interest paid for the period June 1—Sept. 1 given the following:
Balance: June 1 $465.00
Deposits: June 12 $250.00
             July 17 $175.00

"Pick up sticks" #2
Eleven match sticks are placed in a row.

Two players each pick up 1, 2, or 3 matches in turn. The player picking up the last match loses. Find a rule so the player who picks first always wins.

Aug. 20 $315.00

No withdrawals were made.

(b) If the only entry for September in the account from part (a) was a deposit of $85, on what amount would the interest for September be calculated?

8. Mr Collins noted that he could use collateral to borrow at 9% compounded semi-annually and invest in second mortgages at 16% compounded quarterly.

(a) If he borrowed and reinvested $20 000 under these terms for 5 a what profit did he make?

(b) What had Mr. Collins done to "earn" this money?

C   **9.** If money is borrowed at 8% compounded quarterly and reinvested at 12% compounded monthly what annual rate of return is being made? (Consider a principal of $1 invested at each rate for 1 a.)

10. Four years ago $10 000 was invested at 8% compounded semi-annually. If the principal and interest are now invested at 11% compounded semi-annually for 5 a, what will the investment be worth?

7.2   COMPOUND INTEREST *Present Value*

Present value refers to the amount of money that must be invested now, at a given rate of interest, to produce a desired amount at a later date.

EXAMPLE 1. *What principal invested now at 9% compounded annually will amount to $100 in n years? The principal to be invested is called the present value and is represented by PV.*

Solution

Time (a)						
Now	1	2	3		$n-1$	n
PV	$PV(1.09)$	$PV(1.09)^2$	$PV(1.09)^3$		$PV(1.09)^{n-1}$	$PV(1.09)^n$

The last term of the sequence $PV(1.09)^n$ represents the value of the investment after n years, which we know must be equal to $100 by the conditions of the question.

$$PV(1.09)^n = \$100$$

$$PV = \$100\,\frac{1}{1.09^n}$$

EXAMPLE 2. *What principal invested now at 9% compounded semi-annually will amount to $100 in n years?*

Solution If the interest had been compounded semi-annually, the number of conversion periods would have been $2n$ and the present value would have been reduced by a factor of $\frac{1}{1.045}$ for each period.

The above expression would become

$$PV = \$100 \, \frac{1}{1.045^{2n}}$$

From the above example we can generalize the relationship

$$PV = \frac{A}{(1+i)^n}$$

where PV is the present value

      A is the amount to be achieved
      i is the rate of interest per conversion period
      n is the total number of conversion periods.

To ease calculation a table of values for $\frac{1}{(1+i)^n}$ is given in the appendix.

EXAMPLE 3. *Ms Williams has decided to sell her house and move into an apartment, since her job requires that she move frequently. When she retires in 15 a, she wishes to have $75 000 for a retirement home. How much of the $40 000 cash that she received for her present house must she invest in guaranteed investment certificates at 10%/a compounded semi-annually to give her the $75 000 she desires in 15 a?*

Solution She must invest the present value of $75 000. At 10%/a compounded semi-annually, $i = (0.5)(10\%) = 5\%$. For 15 a compounding semi-annually,

$$n = 15 \times 2 = 30.$$

$$PV = \frac{75\,000}{(1.05)^{30}}$$

$$PV = \$75\,000(0.231\,38)$$

$$= \$17\,354.00$$

She must invest $17 354.

EXERCISE 7-2

B   **1.** Find the present value of each of the following amounts.

	Amount	Per annum rate	Conversion period	Term (a)
(a)	$1 500	10%	semi-annual	10
(b)	$350	12%	quarterly	4
(c)	$750	6%	annual	2
(d)	$1 250	8%	semi-annual	$5\frac{1}{2}$
(e)	$20 000	10%	quarterly	$8\frac{3}{4}$

2. How much money must be invested now at 7%/a compounded semi-annually to replace a $10 000 machine which is expected to wear out in 5 a?

3. Mr. Jones has a paid-up endowment policy that will pay him $20 000 on his 65th birthday. What is the present value of this policy on his 60th birthday if money is worth 9% compounded semi-annually?

4. Compare the present values of $1000 due in 3 a at 12% if the interest is compounded (a) semi-annually (b) quarterly (c) monthly.

5. You have signed a promissory note which requires you to pay $500 on Dec. 15. What is the value of the note on the June 15 before the due date if money is worth 9% compounded semi-annually?

6. Two debts of $500 come due in six months and one year respectively. If money is worth 11%/a compounded semi-annually, what amount paid now will discharge both debts?

C **7.** What principal invested for the next 5 a at 9% compounded semi-annually, and for the following 3 a at 7% compounded semi-annually will amount to $10 000?

8. Six years ago a sum of money was invested at 7%/a compounded semi-annually. If the principal and interest are now invested at 12% compounded semi-annually and in two years will amount to $1430.78, what was the principal originally invested?

7.3 THE AMOUNT OF AN ANNUITY

If a sum of money is paid as a series of regular equal payments, it is called an **annuity**. The name comes from the word annual or yearly. However, payments may be made monthly, quarterly, semi-annually, or at any other agreed-on interval. Unless otherwise stated, the payment is made at the end of the payment interval.

The **amount** of an annuity is the sum of the amounts of the individual payments invested at the stated interest rate from the time of payment until the end of the annuity when the last payment is made.

Want to be a millionaire for a day? How much would it cost to borrow $1 000 000 for 1 d at 12%/a?

To find the amount:

EXAMPLE 1. *Mr. Howard deposits $500 in the bank every Dec. 1 and June 1 for ten years. If interest is earned at 8% compounded semi-annually, how much will he have in the bank at the time of the last payment?*

Solution You are asked to find the amount of an annuity of 20 semi-annual payments of $500 at 8% compounded semi-annually.

$$\therefore i = (0.5)(8\%) = 4\%$$

The time diagram below illustrates the problem.

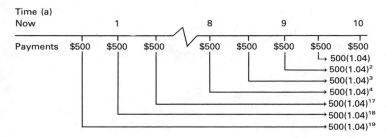

The amount of the annuity is given by the sum of the 20 compound amounts:

$$A = \$500 + \$500(1.04) + \$500(1.04)^2 + \ldots + \$500(1.04)^{19},$$

which is a geometric series with $a = 500$ $r = 1.04$ $n = 20$.

$$S_{20} = \frac{a(r^{20} - 1)}{(r - 1)}$$

$$= \frac{\$500(1.04^{20} - 1)}{(1.04 - 1)}$$

$$= \frac{\$500(2.191\,12 - 1)}{0.04} \qquad \text{(interest tables, amount at 4\% for 20 a)}$$

$$= \frac{\$500(1.191\,12)}{0.04} = \$14\,889 \qquad \left[\begin{array}{l}\text{Check for gross error:} \\ 20 \times 500 = 10\,000\end{array}\right]$$

The amount of the annuity is $14 889.00.

To find a general expression for the amount of an annuity (at the time of the last payment) we shall use a payment of $1 for n payments at rate i per payment interval. The amount of the annuity is given by the series

$$1 + 1(1 + i) + 1(1 + i)^2 + 1(1 + i)^3 + \ldots \text{ to } n \text{ terms.}$$

This quantity is represented by the symbol $S_{\overline{n}|i}$ and is evaluated in the table in the appendix for various values of i and n.

The regular annuity payment is called the periodic rent and is

$$S_n = \frac{a(r^n - 1)}{(r - 1)}$$

$$S_{\overline{n}|i} = \frac{1[(1 + i)^n - 1]}{(1 + i) - 1}$$

$$= \frac{(1 + i)^n - 1}{i}$$

$$RS_{\overline{n}|i} = \frac{R[(1 + i)^n - 1]}{i}$$

annuities   129

represented by R. If $S_{\overline{n}|i}$ represents the amount of an annuity of n payments of \$1 at i% per interval then $RS_{\overline{n}|i}$ represents the amount of an annuity of n payments of \$$R$ at i% per payment interval.

EXAMPLE 2. *Find the amount of an annuity of \$1000/a for 7 a. Interest is earned at 6% compounded annually.*

Solution

Now	1	2	3	4	5	6	7
	\$1000	\$1000	\$1000	\$1000	\$1000	\$1000	\$1000

Amount

$$R = \$1000 \qquad n = 7 \qquad i = 6\%$$

From the table for $S_{\overline{n}|i}$ in the 6% column, $n = 7$ row,

$$S_{\overline{7}|0.06} \doteq 8.393\,838$$

$$RS_{\overline{7}|0.06} = \$1000(8.393\,838) \qquad \begin{bmatrix} \text{Check for gross error:} \\ 1000 \times 7 = 7000 \end{bmatrix}$$

$$= 8393.838$$

The amount of the annuity is \$8393.84.

To find the rent:

Example 3. *How much money must I invest every half year at 9% compounded semi-annually in order for it to amount to \$25 000 after the 25th payment?*

Solution

For how many years have payments been made?

Now	1	2	3	4		23	24	25
	x	x	x	x		x	x	x

Amount
\$25 000

$$i = (0.5)(9\%) = 4.5\%$$

$$RS_{\overline{25}|0.045} = \$25\,000$$

$$\therefore \quad R = \frac{\$25\,000}{S_{\overline{25}|0.045}}$$

$$\doteq \frac{\$25\,000}{44.565\,210} \doteq \$560.975 \qquad \begin{bmatrix} \text{Check for gross error:} \\ \dfrac{25\,000}{25} = 1000 \end{bmatrix}$$

The semi-annual rent is \$560.98.

EXERCISE 7-3

B **1.** Find the missing quantities in the following using the S_n table.

	Amount	Periodic rent	Number of payments	Payment interval Conversion period	Interest rate per annum
(a)		$300	20	semi-annual	8%
(b)		$500	24	quarterly	12%
(c)		$100	36	monthly	12%
(d)		$4000	10	annual	6%
(e)	$20 000		40	semi-annual	8%
(f)	$6 000		24	quarterly	12%
(g)	$2 500		18	monthly	12%
(h)	$12 000		15	annual	6%

Find a and b if $\dfrac{1}{a}+\dfrac{1}{b}=\dfrac{1}{2}$ and $a, b \in N$, $a \neq b$.

2. Mr. Wilson bought a new taxi on June 30. He expects the car to last 2 a as a taxi, and then he will trade it in on a replacement. He estimates that he will require $3000 plus his old car for the new taxi. Starting July 30, how much must he invest monthly in an account paying 12% compounded monthly, to meet this expense in two years? This type of investment plan to meet a future expense is called a **sinking fund**.

3. Mrs. Brewer is self-employed and must make provision for her own pension. If she invests $500 every 6 mo., starting 6 mo. before her 35th birthday, in a fund which pays 8% compounded semi-annually, how much will she have after the last payment on her 55th birthday?

4. Acme Manufacturing Co. has a $150 000 custom-designed press which has a useful life expectancy of 15 a. How much should they invest semi-annually in a sinking fund at 9%/a compounded semi-annually to meet this expense in 15 a?

C **5.** Draw a time-payment diagram and use the formula $S_n = \dfrac{a(r^n - 1)}{(r - 1)}$ to find the amount of the following annuities after the last payment.
(a) 15 annual payments of $400 at 7% compounded annually.
(b) 24 quarterly payments of $600 at 12% compounded quarterly.
(c) 30 semi-annual payments of $1200 at 9% compounded semi-annually.
(d) 36 monthly payments of $50 at 18% compounded monthly.

6. Mr. Shapiro has just purchased a used car for $3300. In planning

for future transportation he makes the following assumptions:
(a) He will keep the present car for 4 a.
(b) In that time it will depreciate 66%.
(c) The cost of cars will increase by 36%.
(d) There will be a 7% sales tax on the difference between the trade-in and the new car.
e) He can invest money at 12% compounded quarterly.
Starting 3 mo. after the purchase date, how much should he invest each 3 mo. in a sinking fund to purchase his new car 4 a from now?

7. An investor deposited $200/mo. for 6 mo. in an account and then allowed the amount to remain for an additional 6 mo. If interest was paid at the rate of 1.5%/mo. what was the final amount?

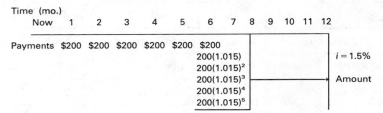

8. Ten semi-annual payments of $750 are paid into an annuity earning 9% compounded semi-annually. The amount is then invested for 4 a at 12% compounded quarterly. Construct a time diagram and find the final amount.

9. Use the formula and a time line to find the amount of 10 *annual* payments of $600 earning interest at 9% compounded semi-annually.

7.4 THE PRESENT VALUE OF AN ANNUITY

The present value of an annuity is the principal which must be invested now at a given rate of interest to provide the periodic rent. It is equal to the sum of the present values of the payments.
To find the present value

EXAMPLE 1. *How much money must be invested now at 8%/a compounded annually to provide an annuity of 5 annual payments of $600, the first payment being made in one year?*

Solution The problem can be illustrated by a time diagram as follows:

applied mathematics for today: senior

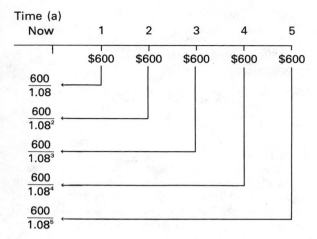

Time (a)

Now	1	2	3	4	5
	$600	$600	$600	$600	$600

$$\frac{600}{1.08}$$

$$\frac{600}{1.08^2}$$

$$\frac{600}{1.08^3}$$

$$\frac{600}{1.08^4}$$

$$\frac{600}{1.08^5}$$

The present value of the annuity is given by the sum of the five present values:

$$PV = \frac{\$600}{1.08} + \frac{\$600}{(1.08)^2} + \frac{\$600}{(1.08)^3} + \frac{\$600}{(1.08)^4} + \frac{\$600}{(1.08)^5}$$

Which is a geometric series where $a = \dfrac{\$600}{1.08}$, $r = \dfrac{1}{1.08}$, $n = 5$.

$$S_n = \frac{\$600}{1.08}\left(\frac{1 - \dfrac{1}{1.08^5}}{1 - \dfrac{1}{1.08}}\right)$$

$$\doteq \frac{\$600(1 - 0.680\,58)}{1.08(1 - 0.925\,93)} \qquad \text{(from tables for present values)}$$

$$= \frac{\$600(0.319\,42)}{1.08(0.074\,07)} \doteq \$2395.78 \qquad \begin{bmatrix}\text{Check for gross error:} \\ 5 \times 600 = 3000\end{bmatrix}$$

The present value of the annuity is $2395.78.

An expression for the present value of an annuity of $1 for n payment intervals at rate i per payment interval, at a time one payment interval before the first payment, is given by the series:

$$\frac{1}{1+i} + \frac{1}{(1+i)^2} + \frac{1}{(1+i)^3} + \ldots \text{ to } n \text{ terms.}$$

This quantity is represented by the symbol $a_{\overline{n}|i}$ and is evaluated in a table in the appendix for various values of i and n.

$Ra_{\overline{n}|i}$ represents the present value of an annuity of n payments of $R, at $i\%$ per interval.

EXAMPLE 2. *Find the price of an annuity of ten semi-annual payments of $750, the first payment to be made in 6 mo., if money is worth 7%/a compounded semi-annually.*

$$S_n = \frac{a(1 - r^n)}{(1 - r)}$$

$$a_{\overline{n}|i} = \frac{1\left(1 - \dfrac{1}{(1+i)^n}\right)}{1 - \dfrac{1}{(1+i)}}$$

$$Ra_{\overline{n}|i} = \frac{R\left(1 - \dfrac{1}{(1+i)^n}\right)}{1 - \dfrac{1}{(1+i)}}$$

Solution $r = \$750$ $n = 10$ $i = (0.5)(7\%) = 3.5\%$

From the table for $a_{\overline{n}|i}$ in the 3.5% column, $n = 10$ row:

$$a_{\overline{10}|0.035} = 8.316\,605$$

$$Ra_{\overline{10}|0.035} = \$750(8.316\,605)$$

$$= \$6237.453 \qquad \left[\begin{array}{l}\text{Check for gross error:}\\750 \times 10 = 7500\end{array}\right]$$

The price of the annuity is $6237.45.

To find the rent

Find a and b if $\dfrac{1}{a} + \dfrac{1}{b} = \dfrac{1}{3}$ and $a, b \in N$, $a \neq b$.

EXAMPLE 3. *Mrs. Rainey has an endowment insurance policy which pays her* $50 000 *at age 60, or she may leave the money invested with the insurance company at 6%/a compounded semi-annually and withdraw it in 30 equal semi-annual payments. The first payment is made 6 mo. after her 60th birthday. How large is each payment?*

Solution Let each payment in dollars be R.

Time (a)

$$\$50\,000 = Ra_{\overline{30}|0.03} \quad i = (0.5)(6\%) = 3\%$$

$$\therefore \quad R = \frac{\$50\,000}{a_{\overline{30}|0.03}}$$

$$= \frac{\$50\,000}{19.600\,441}$$

$$\doteq \$2550.96 \qquad \left[\begin{array}{l}\text{Check for gross error:}\\30 \times 2500 = 75\,000\end{array}\right]$$

Each semi-annual payment will be $2550.96.

EXERCISE 7-4

B **1.** Find the missing quantities in the following using the $a_{\overline{n}|i}$ table.

	Present value	Periodic rent	Number of payments	Payment interval Conversion period	Interest rate per annum
(a)		$300	20	semi-annual	8%
(b)		$500	24	quarterly	12%
(c)		$100	36	monthly	12%
(d)		$4000	10	annual	6%
(e)	$20 000		40	semi-annual	8%
(f)	$6 000		24	quarterly	12%
(g)	$2 500		18	monthly	12%
(h)	$12 000		15	annual	6%

Construct a time diagram for all problems.

2. Find the present value of an annuity of $100/mo. for 3 a beginning 1 mo. hence if interest is earned at 1.5%/mo.

3. John Fairchild has won $3000 to go to a community college for a three-year technician course. If he invests the money at 12%/a compounded monthly on Aug. 1, how much may he draw monthly for the next 3 a starting Sept. 1?

4. An insurance policy pays $30 000 cash at age 60 or it may be taken in 30 equal half-yearly payments with the endowment earning interest at 8%/a compounded semi-annually. If the first payment is made 6 mo. after the 60th birthday, how large is each payment?

5. Draw a time-payment diagram and use the formula $S_n = \dfrac{a(1-r^n)}{(1-r)}$ with tables for $(1+i)^{-n}$ to find the present value of the following annuities, first payment to be made after one period.
(a) 20 annual payments of $1000 at 8% compounded annually.
(b) 15 annual payments of $650 at 7% compounded annually.
(c) 36 monthly payments of $200 at 1.5%/mo.
(d) 4 quarterly payments of $500 at 18% compounded quarterly.

6. Mrs. Comtois won a $25 000 lottery prize. She invested the money in an annuity to receive payments over the next 10 a.
(a) How much will she receive every 3 mo. if the money is invested at 12%/a compounded quarterly?
(b) Consider your answer to (a) the *amount* of a three month annuity and approximate how much she could receive if she took payments monthly and the interest was paid at 1%/mo.
(c) When would she receive her first payment?

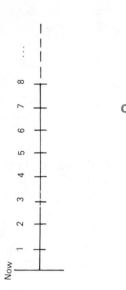

7. Mr. MacDonald owns an annuity which pays $4000 semi-annually for 8 a. What is the present value of the annuity if money is worth 11% compounded semi-annually and:
(a) The first payment is due in 6 mo.
(b) The first payment is due now.

C   **8.** Use the formula $S_n = \dfrac{a(1-r^n)}{(1-r)}$ and a time diagram to find the annual payment for a five year annuity with present value of $4000. Money is worth 8% compounded annually.

9. Use the formula and a time diagram to find the present value of an annuity of 10 *annual* payments of $750 if money is worth 9% compounded *semi-annually*. First payment due in one year.

7.5   ANNUITIES DUE

In section 7.3 it was mentioned that unless otherwise stated, the payment of an annuity is made at the end of the payment interval. When the payment is made at the beginning of the payment interval the annuity is referred to as an *annuity due*.

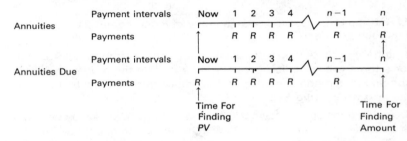

Find *a* and *b* if $\dfrac{1}{a} + \dfrac{1}{b} = \dfrac{1}{4}$
and *a*, *b* ∈ *N*, *a* ≠ *b*.

EXAMPLE 1. *Find the amount of an annuity due of 4 semi-annual payments of $500; interest is paid at 12% compounded semi-annually.*

Solution

$$i = (0.5)(12\%)$$
$$= 6\%$$

Note that the amount is calculated one payment interval after the last payment.

Time (a)   Now   1   2

$500 $500 $500 $500
500(1.06)
500(1.06)²
500(1.06)³
500(1.06)⁴

$$A = \$500(1.06) + \$500(1.06)^2 + \$500(1.06)^3 + \$500(1.06)^4$$
$$= \$500(1.06 + 1.06^2 + 1.06^3 + 1.06^4)$$
$$= \$500(1 + 1.06 + 1.06^2 + 1.06^3 + 1.06^4 - 1)$$

$$= \$500(S_{\overline{5}|0.06} - 1)$$
$$= \$500(5.637\,093 - 1)$$
$$= \$500(4.637\,093)$$
$$\doteq \$2318.55$$

$$\begin{bmatrix} \text{Check for gross error:} \\ \quad 500 \times 4 = 2000 \end{bmatrix}$$

The amount is \$2318.55.

$$S_{\overline{n}|i} = 1 + (1+i) + (1+i)^2 + \ldots$$

$$\longleftarrow n \text{ terms} \longrightarrow$$

> In general, the amount of an annuity due of n periodic payments of R at an interest rate of i per interval is $\mathbf{A}$
>
> $$\mathbf{A} = R(S_{\overline{n+1}|i} - 1)$$

EXAMPLE 2. *Mr. Nicols made 12 monthly deposits in an account paying 1.5%/mo. If he had \$992.76 in the account 1 mo. after the last deposit, how large was each deposit?*

Solution

This forms an annuity due where $i = 1.5\%$.

$$\mathbf{A} = R(S_{\overline{n+1}|i} - 1)$$

$$R = \frac{A}{S_{\overline{n+1}|i} - 1}$$

$$\begin{bmatrix} \text{Check for gross error:} \\ 12 \times 75 = 900 \end{bmatrix}$$

$$= \frac{\$992.76}{S_{\overline{13}|0.015} - 1}$$

$$\doteq \frac{\$992.76}{13.236\,830}$$

$$\doteq \$75.00$$

The monthly payment is \$75.00.

EXAMPLE 3. *Find the present value of an annuity due of five semi-annual payments of \$600. Interest is paid at the rate of 9% compounded semi-annually.*

Solution

$$i = (0.5)(9\%)$$
$$= 4.5\%$$

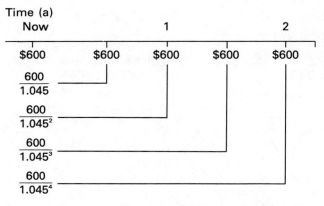

Time (a)

$$PV = \$600 + \frac{\$600}{1.045} + \frac{\$600}{1.045^2} + \frac{\$600}{1.045^3} + \frac{\$600}{1.045^4}$$

$$= \$600\left(1 + \frac{1}{1.045} + \frac{1}{1.045^2} + \frac{1}{1.045^3} + \frac{1}{1.045^4}\right)$$

$$= \$600(1 + a_{\overline{4}|0.04})$$

$$= \$600(1 + 3.587\ 526)$$

$$= \$600(4.587\ 526)$$

$$= \$2\ 752.52$$

$$a_{\overline{n}|} = \frac{1}{1+i} + \frac{1}{(1+i)^2} + \frac{1}{(1+i)^3} + \cdots$$
$$\longleftarrow\ n \text{ terms}\ \longrightarrow$$

The present value is $2752.52.

> In general, the present value of an annuity due of n periodic payments of R at an interest rate of i per interval is **PV**
>
> $$PV = R(1 + a_{\overline{n-1}|i})$$

EXAMPLE 4. *A color T.V. was purchased for $750.00 to be paid for in 30 equal monthly payments, the first payment due on delivery. If interest is charged at the rate of* 1.5%/mo., *how much is the monthly payment?*

Solution The repayment schedule takes the form of an annuity due of 30 payments, $i = 1.5\%$ and present value $750.00.

Time (mo.)

Delivery	1	2	3	4		28	29
R	R	R	R	R		R	R

(number months) $\neq$
(number payments)

$$PV = R(1 + a_{\overline{n-1}|0.015})$$

$$R = \frac{PV}{1 + a_{\overline{n-1}|0.015}}$$

$$= \frac{\$750}{1 + a_{\overline{29}\ 0.015}}$$

applied mathematics for today: senior

$$= \frac{\$750}{1+23.376\,076}$$

$$= \frac{\$750}{24.376\,076}$$

$$\doteq \$30.77$$

Each payment will be $30.77.

EXERCISE 7-5

A **1.** When an annuity becomes an *annuity due*, what is the effect on each of the following?
a) The time when each periodic payment is due.
b) The size of the amount of the annuity.
c) The time at which the amount is calculated.
d) The size of the present value of the annuity.
e) The time at which the present value is accumulated.

2. Find the amount of the following *annuities due* with periodic rent $1.

a)	7 payments	3% per interval
b)	20 payments	5% per interval
c)	40 payments	6% per interval
d)	7 payments	1.5% per interval
e)	15 payments	4.5% per interval

3. Find the present value of the following *annuities due* with periodic rent $1.

a)	12 payments	4% per interval
b)	18 payments	5.5% per interval
c)	8 payments	2% per interval
d)	24 payments	5% per interval
e)	48 payments	0.5% per interval

Find a and b if $\dfrac{1}{a}+\dfrac{1}{b}=\dfrac{1}{5}$ and $a,\, b \in N,\ a \neq b$.

4. Cathy Willis deposited $100/mo. for 3 a in an account paying 1%/mo. How much did she have on deposit 1 mo. after the last payment?

5. Find the amount of an annuity due of 12 quarterly payments of $700. Interest is charged at 8% compounded quarterly.

6. A debt of $5000 must be repaid in 4 a. How much must be invested in 8 equal semi-annual payments, if the initial payment is made now, to retire the debt in 4 a? Interest is earned at 11% compounded semi-annually.

7. Twenty annual payments accumulate to $23 395.64 one year after the last payment. If interest is earned at 6%/a, how large is each payment?

8. Find the present value of an annuity due of 48 quarterly payments of $300. Interest is paid at the rate of 10% compounded quarterly.

9. Mr. Parker has agreed to repay a debt by means of 30 monthly payments of $85. What single payment will retire the debt at the time of the first payment if money is worth 1%/mo.?

10. $25 000 is invested in an annuity to pay 50 equal quarterly instalments, the first one immediately. The money earns interest at 14% compounded quarterly. How much is received in each instalment?

11. Find the semi-annual rental required to repay a debt of $600 in 4 equal payments, the first payment due now, if money is worth 11% compounded semi-annually.

7.6 DEFERRED ANNUITIES

When the first payment of an annuity is not due for some time we say that the annuity is *deferred*.

EXAMPLE 1. *Find the present value of an annuity of ten quarterly payments of $500. Interest is earned at 10% compounded quarterly. The first payment is deferred one year.*

Solution

$$i = (0.25)(10\%)$$
$$= 2.5\%$$

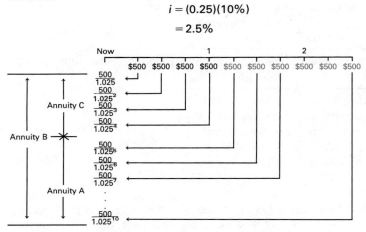

If the annuity had not been deferred the first payment would have been due one quarter from "Now". The deferment of one year makes the first payment due 5 quarters from "Now".

From the diagram it can be seen that:
Present value of the deferred annuity
$A = $ (Present value of Annuity B) $-$ (Present value of Annuity C)

applied mathematics for today: senior

$PV = \$500a_{\overline{10}|0.025} - \$500a_{\overline{4}|0.025}$

$= \$500(a_{\overline{10}|0.025} - a_{\overline{4}|0.025})$

$\doteq \$500(8.752\,064 - 3.761\,974)$

$\doteq \$2495.05$

$$\left[\begin{array}{l} \text{Check for gross error:} \\ 500 \times 6 = 3000 \end{array} \right]$$

The present value is \$2495.05.

In general, an annuity with n periodic payments of R, deferred m intervals, has a present value PV.

$$PV = R(a_{\overline{m+n}|i} - a_{\overline{m}|i})$$

EXAMPLE 2. *Find the amount of an annuity of 4 semi-annual payments of \$1200 if the repayment is deferred to 3 a after the last rent payment. Interest is paid at 8% compounded semi-annually.*

Solution

$$i = (0.5)(8\%)$$
$$= 4\%$$

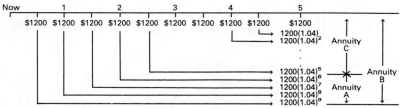

From the diagram it can be seen that:
Deferred amount of Annuity

$A = $ (Amount of Annuity B) $-$ (Amount of Annuity C)

$A = \$1200S_{\overline{10}|0.04} - \$1200S_{\overline{6}|0.04}$

$= \$1200(S_{\overline{10}|0.04} - S_{\overline{6}|0.04})$

$\doteq \$1200(12.006\,107 - 6.632\,975)$

$$\left[\begin{array}{l} \text{Check for gross error:} \\ 4 \times 1200 = 4800 \end{array} \right]$$

$\doteq \$6447.76$

The amount is \$6447.76.

In general, an annuity with n periodic payments of R, with repayment deferred m intervals, has an amount A

$$A = R(S_{\overline{m+n}|i} - S_{\overline{m}|i})$$

EXAMPLE 3. *Mrs. Wilson invested $10 000 at 12% compounded monthly. She wishes to withdraw the money in 24 equal monthly payments, the first payment deferred for one year. How much will she receive in each payment?*

Solution

$$i = \frac{1}{12}(12\%)$$

$$= 1\%$$

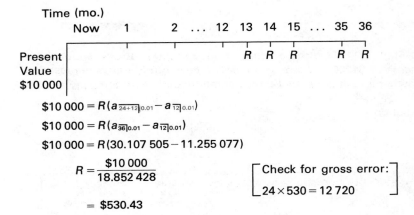

$$\$10\,000 = R(a_{\overline{24+12}|0.01} - a_{\overline{12}|0.01})$$

$$\$10\,000 = R(a_{\overline{36}|0.01} - a_{\overline{12}|0.01})$$

$$\$10\,000 = R(30.107\,505 - 11.255\,077)$$

$$R = \frac{\$10\,000}{18.852\,428}$$

$$\left[\begin{array}{l}\text{Check for gross error:} \\ 24 \times 530 = 12\,720\end{array}\right]$$

$$= \$530.43$$

Ms. Wilson receives $530.43 each month.

EXERCISE 7-6

A **1.** Describe what is meant by the following terms:
a) Annuity   b) Present value of an annuity
c) Amount of an annuity   d) Annuity due
e) Deferred annuity

2. A deferred annuity of 12 quarterly payments is purchased on November 1, 1978. If the annuity is deferred for 5 mo., when will the first payment be received?

3. (a) Will deferring an annuity increase or decrease its present value? Why?
b) When purchasing an annuity with a large sum, will deferring the annuity increase or decrease the rental payments?

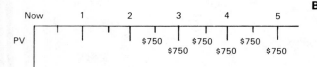

B **4.** An annuity of 6 semi-annual payments is deferred for 2 a. If the semi-annual rent is $750 and interest is paid at 12% compounded semi-annually, find the present value.

5. Find the present value of an annuity of $250/mo., the first payment is 6 mo. from now, and it is to continue for 12 payments. Interest is paid at a rate of 1.5%/mo.

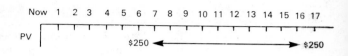

6. $5000 is invested at 12% compounded quarterly and withdrawn in 8 equal quarterly payments. If the first withdrawal is made 2 a after the investment date, how large is each payment?

7. A debt of $2500 is to be repaid by 24 equal monthly payments. The first monthly payment is due 3 mo. from the date of purchase. If interest is charged at 1.5%/mo., how large is each payment?

8. Find the present value of an annuity of 20 quarterly payments of $500, the first payment to be made in one year. The money is invested at 10% compounded quarterly.

9. An annuity of 30 semi-annual payments of $1000 is allowed to gather interest for an additional 2 a before being cashed in. If it has earned interest at 7% compounded semi-annually, how much is it worth?

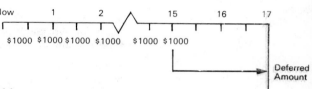

10. (a) Find the amount of an annuity of 36 monthly payments of $75 interest paid at 1%/mo.
(b) Find the amount of the same annuity if it is allowed to accumulate interest for an additional year.

C **11.** Mr. Kowalchuk wishes to invest while his earnings are high so that he and his wife can take a trip when he retires. He wants $10 000 when he is 65, and makes 20 equal semi-annual payments into an annuity with the last payment on his 55th birthday. If the investment earns 8% compounded semi-annually, how large must each payment be?

12. (a) Find the present value of an annuity of three annual payments of $500 which is deferred for 3 a, by finding the value at year 3 and then using compound interest tables to find the present value of this sum. Interest is paid at 6%/a.
(b) Repeat the solution using the method described in this section as a check.

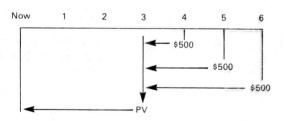

7.7 PROBLEMS SOLVED AS ANNUITIES.

The problems that follow all are related to annuities in some form. In finding their solution the following steps are helpful:

1. Draw a time payment diagram.

2. Determine whether you are given the periodic rent, the present value, or a deferred annuity.

3. Determine whether you are required to find a periodic rent payment, the present value, or the amount of the annuity.

4. Determine whether you are dealing with a simple annuity, an annuity due, or a deferred annuity.

5. Determine the correct formula.

6. Use the correct tables.

If

$$\frac{1}{2}=\frac{1}{3}+\frac{1}{6}, \quad \frac{1}{3}=\frac{1}{4}+\frac{1}{12},$$
$$\frac{1}{4}=\frac{1}{5}+\frac{1}{20}, \quad \frac{1}{5}=\frac{1}{6}+\frac{1}{30}, \ldots$$

Then

$$\frac{1}{99}=\frac{1}{\blacksquare}+\frac{1}{\blacksquare}, \ldots, \frac{1}{n}=\frac{1}{\blacksquare}+\frac{1}{\blacksquare}$$

When $n \in N$.

EXAMPLE 1. *Mr. Armstrong purchased a car for $4500. He paid $1000 down and financed the remainder at 1.5%/mo. on the unpaid balance over 3 a. What are the equal monthly payments?*

Solution Let each payment in dollars be R.
The amount financed is $4500 - $1000 = $3500 $i = 1.5\%$

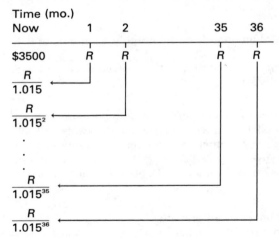

Time (mo.)

From the diagram we see that we are given the present value, are required to find the periodic rent, and are dealing with a simple annuity.

$$R = \frac{PV}{a_{\overline{n}|i}} \qquad \text{at 1.5\% where } n = 36$$

$$R = \frac{\$3500}{a_{\overline{36}|0.015}}$$

$$= \frac{\$3500}{27.660\,684} \qquad \text{Check for gross error:}$$

$$\doteq 126.53 \qquad 36 \times 120 = 4320$$

The monthly payment will be $126.53.

EXERCISE 7-7

B **1.** A stereophonic sound system costs $565 with no down payment. The account is paid in 18 equal monthly instalments with interest of 1.5/mo. on the unpaid balance. Interest starts immediately with payments due in one month. How large is each payment?

2. A new Bullroar 8 automobile costs $5500 with an allowance of $2200 on a trade-in as down payment. If the difference is paid in 36 equal monthly payments with interest at 1%/mo. on the unpaid balance, find the monthly payments. The first payment is due in one month.

3. A piano is advertised at $200 down and $30/mo. for 24 mo. If interest is being charged at 1.5%/mo., what is the cash price?

4. A small motorcycle is sold for $150 down and $20/mo. for 12 mo. If interest is being charged at 2%/mo., what is the cash price?

5. A fur coat costs $500. If a down payment of $50 is made and the remainder financed over 12 mo. at 1%/mo. service charge on the unpaid balance, what are the monthly payments?

6. A portable stereo cassette tape recorder costs $75 cash, or $10 down with interest on the unpaid balance at 2%/mo., financed over 10 mo. Find the monthly payment, the total amount paid, and the total interest charged.

7. Mr. Firth and Mr. Lasky both buy a new car every second year and pay an average of $1500 plus trade-in.
(a) Mr. Firth borrows the money for his car and pays the loan in 24 monthly payments, starting the month after the car is purchased. If the money is borrowed at 1%/mo. on the unpaid balance, what are his monthly payments?
(b) Mr. Lasky pays cash for his car and starts one month later to make monthly payments into an account paying 1%/mo. compounded monthly, so that in 24 mo. he will have $1500 for his new car. How much must he invest monthly?
(c) What is the difference in their total payments for the 2 a?

8. Mr. Borden bought a summer cottage for $5000 down followed by 10 half-yearly payments of $1000.
(a) If interest was charged at 8%/a compounded semi-annually, what was the cash price of the cottage?
(b) If the $5000 and the 10 half-yearly payments had been invested at the same interest rate, what would the value have been when the last payment was made? (Hint: Find the amounts of the down payment and the half-yearly payments separately.)

9. Acme Construction company replaces its power shovel every 5 a and invests in a sinking fund at 10% compounded quarterly. To provide the funds, the company expects to pay $25 000 plus trade and starts making quarterly deposits 3 mo. after the purchase of the latest shovel. If the last payment is made when the new shovel is bought, how large must each quarterly payment be?

10. A mortgage is repaid by payments of $1200, principal and interest, every 6 mo. Interest is being charged at 10% compounded semi-annually. If the mortgage has 20 a to run (40 payments) what sum of money will discharge the mortgage when the next payment is due?

(A mortgage that may be paid off at any time without penalty is called an *open mortgage*.)

Annuity due

11. Mrs. Samuels buys a new car for $2500 plus trade-in. She must also pay 7% sales tax plus $40 licence fee. This debt is to be repaid by 30 equal payments, the first due at the time of purchase. Interest is charged at the rate of 1.5%/mo. How large will each payment be?

Remember in calculating the deferment period, the regular annuity starts 6 mo. before the first payment.

12. (a) At age 45 Mr. McDermitt invests $20 000 to be repaid in 20 semi-annual payments starting on his 55th birthday. If the money is invested at 11% compounded semi-annually, how large will each payment be?
(b) How large are the payments if he waits until his 60th birthday?

REVIEW EXERCISE

In questions 1 to 5 find the missing quantities.

1.

	Principal	Per annum rate	Conversion period	Term (a)	Amount
(a)	$2500	6%	semi-annual	6	
(b)	$475	8%	quarterly	2	

2.

	Present value	Per annum rate	Conversion period	Term (a)	Amount
(a)		9%	semi-annual	16	$15 000
(b)		12%	quarterly	10	$20 000

3.

	Amount	Periodic rent	Number of payments	Payment interval/ Conversion period	Per annum rate
(a)		$150	30	monthly	18%
(b)		$250	20	semi-annual	12%
(c)	$8 500		16	quarterly	8%
(d)	$10 000		20	semi-annual	9%

4.	Present value	Periodic rent	Number of payments	Payment interval/ Conversion period	Per annum rate
(a)	$15 000		30	semi-annual	7%
(b)	$520		24	monthly	12%
(c)		$29	36	monthly	18%
(d)		$125	30	quarterly	10%

5.	Present value	Periodic rent	Number of payments	Deferral period	Payment interval	Interest per interval
(a)		$500	10	6 mo.	quarterly	3%
(b)		$4500	6	4 a	yearly	6%
(c)	$40 000		36	12 mo.	6 mo.	5.5%
(d)	$850		24	12 mo.	monthly	1.5%

6. A television set is sold for $25 down and $15/mo. for 24 mo. If interest is charged at 1.5%/mo. on the unpaid balance, find the cash price.

7. Mr. Morgan invested $500 every 6 mo. for 20 a in a retirement fund. If the fund earns 7%/a compounded semi-annually, how much will Mr. Morgan have when he retires? The last payment is deducted from his final pay cheque.

8. Mr. "Lucky" Lewis won $10 000 in the Oyster Oil Co. sweepstakes. If he uses his winnings to purchase an annuity of 30 semi-annual payments, how large will each payment be? His investment earns interest at 8%/a compounded semi-annually. He receives the first payment 6 mo. after investing.

9. Goman Delivery Service has found it economical to trade in their trucks every 3 a. If a new truck costs $2400 plus trade-in, how much money must be invested monthly in a sinking fund at 12% compounded monthly to replace a truck after 36 payments? The first payment is made 1 mo. after purchase.

10. Find the amount of an annuity due of 12 semi-annual payments of $500. Interest is earned at 10% compounded semi-annually.

11. A boat and outboard motor purchased for $1600 are paid for by 30 monthly payments, the first payment due at the time of purchase. If interest is charged at 1.5%/mo. how large are the monthly payments?

12. Starting on his daughter's *first birthday*, Mr. Pitman invested $25 each year in an account bearing annual interest of 8%. He did this up to and including her 18th birthday and the money was left in the

One year old

account until she was 25. Use a series calculation and compound interest tables to calculate the amount of the investment.

13. Joe Walsh received an inheritance which would pay him $1000 every 6 mo. for 4 a (8 payments) starting on his 21st birthday. If money is worth 11% compounded semi-annually, what is the value of the inheritance on his 18th birthday?

HOW LOUD IS LOUD?

Sound is measured by scientists in terms of how loud it is. The unit of measurement for 'the loudness of sounds' is called the *bel*, in honour of the inventor of the telephone, Alexander Graham Bell.

The rustle of the leaves of a tree has been agreed to represent the noise of 1 bel. A noise whose measure is 2 bels is 10 times stronger than 1 bel. A noise measuring 3 bels is 10 times stronger than 2 bels, therefore 100 times stronger than 1 bel. (In practice, the bel is much too large a unit to work with, so a smaller unit called a *decibel* is used. A decibel is one-tenth of a bel.)

The strength of a noise is its measure in bels, but the magnitudes of different sounds, when expressed in whole bels, form a sequence in which neighbouring members are in the same ratio, the common ratio in the sequence being 10. The relation can be set out as follows:

Strength (in bels):   1   2   3   4   5   6 . . .
Magnitude: 10 10^2 10^3 10^4 10^5 10^6 . . .

Thus the number of bels is the exponent of 10 when the magnitudes of the noises are expressed in powers of 10. In other words, the relation between the strength of noise and the magnitude of noise is a *logarithmic* one. When we have measured the strengths of two different noises in bels, we have the logarithms of the numbers that measure the respective magnitudes.

For example, the average conversation has been found to be 6.5 bels strong. This is 5.5 bels louder than the rustle of leaves. But how many times louder, in a simple number, is conversation than the rustle of leaves? We have

$$\frac{10^{6.5}}{10} = 10^{6.5-1} = 10^{5.5}.$$

Applying logarithms, we have

$$6.5 \log 10 - \log 10 = 6.5 - 1 = 5.5.$$

(log 10 to the base 10 is equal to 1)

The number whose logarithm is 5.5 is approximately 316 000. Conversation is therefore about

316 000 times louder than the rustle of leaves.

The roar of a lion has been measured at about 8.7 bels. The difference between the noise produced by an average conversation and that produced by a roaring lion is

$$8.7 \text{ bels} - 6.5 \text{ bels} = 2.2 \text{ bels}.$$

The number whose logarithm is 2.2 is approximately 158. Thus the roar of a lion is about 158 times louder than the average conversation. If an audience of 2000 people in a theatre were all talking at the same time, the noise of their conversation would be about equal to the noise produced by

$$\frac{2000}{158} = 13 \text{ lions}.$$

Niagara Falls makes a noise about 9 bels strong. The difference between this and an average conversation is

$$9 \text{ bels} - 6.5 \text{ bels} = 2.5 \text{ bels}.$$

The number whose logarithm is 2.5 is approximately 316. So the noise produced by Niagara Falls is about 316 times louder than that of an average conversation. This means that 316 people in one big room, all talking at the same time, would sound as loud as Niagara Falls! And our theatre audience of 2000 would be equal to

$$\frac{2000}{316} \doteq 6.5 \text{ Niagaras}.$$

The world around us is full of noises—passing trains, fire engines, airplanes, automobile horns, slamming doors, crying children, jack-hammers, etc. etc. Some of them are very hard on the ears. It has been found that a person can withstand a noise about 13 bels strong; any stronger noise is harmful. Some governments, indeed, are becoming very concerned about the noise levels in and around cities. (The British and French supersonic airliner Concorde, for instance, has been rigorously flight-tested in terms of the noise it produces at ground level.)

REVIEW AND PREVIEW TO CHAPTER 8

EXERCISE 1

Evaluate:

1. 2^3 **2.** 3^3 **3.** 3^2 **4.** 4^3 **5.** 3^4

6. $\left(\frac{2}{3}\right)^2$ **7.** $\left(\frac{3}{4}\right)^2$ **8.** $\left(\frac{3}{2}\right)^2$ **9.** $\left(\frac{5}{3}\right)^4$ **10.** $\left(1\frac{2}{7}\right)^2$

11. $(0.5)^2$ **12.** $(0.09)^3$ **13.** $(0.3)^6$ **14.** $(1.2)^2$ **15.** $(0.15)^2$

$$a^m \times a^n = a^{m+n}$$
$$a^m \div a^n = a^{m-n}$$

EXERCISE 2

$$2^4 = 2 \times 2 \times 2 \times 2$$
$$= 16$$

Evaluate:

1. $2^5 \times 2^2$ **2.** $3^2 \times 3^3$ **3.** 5×5^2 **4.** 3×3^3

5. $3^5 \div 3^2$ **6.** $7^5 \div 7^4$ **7.** $2^7 \div 2^4$ **8.** $4^3 \div 4^3$

9. $\dfrac{2^5 \times 2^4}{2^6}$ **10.** $\dfrac{3^4 \div 3}{3^2}$ **11.** $\dfrac{5^7 \times 5^4}{5^9}$ **12.** $\dfrac{4^2 \times 2^2}{4^4}$

13. $\dfrac{3+3}{3 \times 3}$ **14.** $\dfrac{2^2 + 2^2}{4^2}$ **15.** $\dfrac{4^2 \div 2^4}{2^3 - 2^2}$ **16.** $\dfrac{3^5 \div 3^4}{3(3^2 - 3)}$

$$(a^m)^n = a^{mn}$$

EXERCISE

Simplify:

1. $(3^2)^3$ **2.** $(a^3)^2$ **3.** $(a^4)^2$ **4.** $(b^3)^5$ **5.** $(c^3)^4$

6. $(ab^2)^3$ **7.** $(2a^2)^3$ **8.** $(3a^3)^2$ **9.** $2(a^2)^3$ **10.** $(5a^2)^3$

Graphs of Exponentials

EXERCISE 4

1. Complete the table and draw the graph for each of the following.

(a) $y = 2^x$

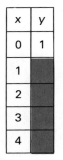

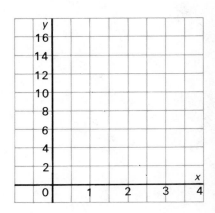

   applied mathematics for today: senior

(b) $y = 3^x$

x	y
0	1
1	
2	
3	
4	

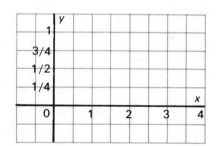

(c) $y = (\tfrac{1}{2})^x$

x	y
0	1
1	
2	
3	
4	

$$A = P(1 + i)^n \qquad P = A \times \frac{1}{(1 + i)^n}$$

Perform the following calculations:

1. $35\,520(1.0875)^{10}$

2. $2155(1.125)^3$

3. $83\,900(1.1075)^{10}$

4. $64\,900(1.0975)^{10}$

5. $3950(1.105)^3$

6. $6900 \times \dfrac{1}{(1.125)^3}$

7. $1525 \times \dfrac{1}{(1.375)^8}$

8. $9550 \times \dfrac{1}{(1.525)^4}$

9. $6525 \times \dfrac{1}{(1.0625)^6}$

10. $3510 \times \dfrac{1}{(1.1275)^8}$

radicals, exponents, and logarithms

CHAPTER 8

Radicals, Exponents, and Logarithms

8.1 REAL NUMBERS

Recall the development of our number system, and the following sets:

Natural numbers	$N = \{1, 2, 3, \ldots\}$
Whole numbers	$W = \{0, 1, 2, 3, \ldots\}$
Integers	$I = \{\ldots, -2, -1, 0, 1, 2, \ldots\}$
Rational numbers	$Q = \left\{ \dfrac{a}{b} \,\middle|\, a, b \in I, b \neq 0 \right\}$

Division by ZERO is not defined.

Rational numbers can also be expressed as decimals, by dividing the numerator by the denominator.

EXAMPLE 1. *Change the following rational numbers to their decimal equivalents:*

(a) $\frac{1}{8}$ (b) $\frac{3}{4}$ (c) $\frac{2}{3}$ (d) $\frac{1}{7}$

Solution

(a) $8\overline{)1.000}$ gives 0.125

(b) $4\overline{)3.00}$ gives 0.75

(c) $3\overline{)2.000\,000}$ gives $0.666\ldots$

(d) $7\overline{)1.000\,000\,000\,000\,000}$ gives $0.142\,857\,142\,857\ldots$ $\dfrac{1}{7} = 0.\dot{1}42\,85\dot{7}$

Rational numbers such as $\frac{1}{8} = 0.125$ and $\frac{3}{4} = 0.75$ reach a point of exact division and are called **terminating** decimals. Other rational numbers, such as $\frac{2}{3} = 0.\dot{6}$, and $\frac{1}{7} = 0.\dot{1}42\,85\dot{7}$, do not reach a point of exact division, but they do possess definite patterns that repeat, and they are called **repeating** decimals.

> Q | The set of RATIONAL NUMBERS is the set of all terminating and repeating decimals.

Rational numbers when written in decimal notation either terminate or repeat in a definite pattern and are referred to as **periodic decimals**. Not all decimal numbers are periodic. Although numbers such as

$$0.515\,115\,111\,5111\,1\ldots$$
$$0.232\,233\,222\,333\ldots$$

possess obvious patterns, they are not periodic because there is not a definite sequence of numbers that repeats. The value of π has been calculated to thousands of decimal places using computers, yet it shows no sign of terminating or repeating. Numbers such as $\sqrt{2}$, and $\sqrt{3}$, are also non-periodic, and non-terminating.

$\bar{Q}$	The set of IRRATIONAL NUMBERS is the set of all non-terminating and non-repeating decimals.

EXERCISE 8-1

A 1. Identify the following numbers as rational or irrational.
(a) $\frac{2}{3}$ (b) $\sqrt{5}$ (c) $\frac{1}{2}$ (d) π
(e) $\sqrt{16}$ (f) $\sqrt{27}$ (g) $5.2\dot{3}$ (h) $-\sqrt{3}$
(i) 4 (j) $1+\sqrt{2}$ (k) $5+\sqrt{4}$ (l) $0.2\dot{4}\dot{6}$

B 2. Express in decimal notation and state which are terminating and which are repeating.
(a) $\frac{7}{8}$ (b) $\frac{1}{3}$ (c) $\frac{1}{2}$ (d) $\frac{2}{11}$ (e) $\frac{3}{7}$
(f) $\frac{2}{7}$ (g) $\frac{5}{6}$ (h) $\frac{5}{7}$ (i) $\frac{5}{4}$ (j) $\frac{1}{9}$
(k) $\frac{2}{9}$ (l) $\frac{5}{9}$ (m) $\frac{3}{11}$ (n) $1\frac{1}{2}$ (o) $\frac{1}{6}$

3. Round off each of the following to (i) five decimal places, (ii) three decimal places, (iii) two decimal places.

Number	Approximations		
	5 decimal places	3 decimal places	2 decimal places
$\frac{1}{7} \doteq 0.142\,857\,14$			
$\sqrt{2} \doteq 1.414\,213\,6$			
$\sqrt{3} \doteq 1.732\,050\,8$			
$\pi \doteq 3.141\,592\,665$			

8.2 OPERATIONS WITH RADICALS

Numbers such as $\sqrt{2}$, $\sqrt{5}$, and $\sqrt{7}$ form an important subset of the irrational numbers called the RADICALS. The examples and the exercise which follow deal with the addition, subtraction, multiplication, and division of radicals.

$\sqrt{a} \times \sqrt{b} = \sqrt{ab}, \quad a, b > 0$
$\sqrt{a} \div \sqrt{b} = \dfrac{\sqrt{a}}{\sqrt{b}} = \sqrt{\dfrac{a}{b}}, \quad a, b > 0$
$a\sqrt{x} + b\sqrt{x} = (a+b)\sqrt{x}, \quad x > 0$

$3\sqrt{5}$, $2\sqrt{5}$ and $-4\sqrt{5}$ are LIKE RADICALS

radicals, exponents, and logarithms   153

EXAMPLE 1. *Simplify* (a) $4\sqrt{5}+7\sqrt{3}-3\sqrt{5}+\sqrt{3}$
(b) $\sqrt{45}-\sqrt{5}+\sqrt{20}$
(c) $3\sqrt{8}+2\sqrt{18}-4\sqrt{2}$

Solution

(a) $4\sqrt{5}+7\sqrt{3}-3\sqrt{5}+\sqrt{3}$

$= 4\sqrt{5}-3\sqrt{5}+7\sqrt{3}+\sqrt{3}$

$= (4-3)\sqrt{5}+(7+1)\sqrt{3}$

$= \sqrt{5}+8\sqrt{3}$

Entire Radical $\sqrt{12}$

$= \sqrt{4\times3}$

$= \sqrt{4}\times\sqrt{3}$

Mixed Radical $= 2\sqrt{3}$

(b) $\sqrt{45}-\sqrt{5}+\sqrt{20}$

$= 3\sqrt{5}-\sqrt{5}+2\sqrt{5}$

$= 4\sqrt{5}$

(c) $3\sqrt{8}+2\sqrt{18}-4\sqrt{2}$

$= 3(2\sqrt{2})+2(3\sqrt{2})-4\sqrt{2}$

$= 6\sqrt{2}+6\sqrt{2}-4\sqrt{2}$

$= 8\sqrt{2}$

Note that in Example 1 we added LIKE radicals. ($\sqrt{5}$ and $\sqrt{3}$ are not like radicals, hence we leave $\sqrt{5}+8\sqrt{3}$ as is.)

EXAMPLE 2. *Simplify* (a) $3\sqrt{2}(5\sqrt{3}+2\sqrt{5})$
(b) $(3\sqrt{2}+2\sqrt{3})(5\sqrt{2}-4\sqrt{3})$
(c) $(2\sqrt{5}-3)^2$
(d) $(3\sqrt{5}-2\sqrt{2})(3\sqrt{5}+2\sqrt{2})$

$\overparen{a(b+c)}$

$= ab+ac$

Solution

(a) $3\sqrt{2}(5\sqrt{3}+2\sqrt{5})=3\sqrt{2}\times5\sqrt{3}+3\sqrt{2}\times2\sqrt{5}$

$= 15\sqrt{6}+6\sqrt{10}$

(b) $(3\sqrt{2}+2\sqrt{3})(5\sqrt{2}-4\sqrt{3})$

$= 3\sqrt{2}\times5\sqrt{2}-3\sqrt{2}\times4\sqrt{3}+2\sqrt{3}\times5\sqrt{2}-2\sqrt{3}\times4\sqrt{3}$

$= 15\sqrt{4}-12\sqrt{6}+10\sqrt{6}-8\sqrt{9}$

$= 15(2)-2\sqrt{6}-8(3)$

$= 30-2\sqrt{6}-24$

$= 6-2\sqrt{6}$

F

O

$(a+b)$ $(C+d)$

I

L

(c) $(2\sqrt{5}-3)^2=(2\sqrt{5}-3)(2\sqrt{5}-3)$

$= 4(5)-6\sqrt{5}-6\sqrt{5}+9$

$= 20-12\sqrt{5}+9$

$= 29-12\sqrt{5}$

(d) $(3\sqrt{5}-2\sqrt{2})(3\sqrt{5}+2\sqrt{2})=9(5)+6\sqrt{10}-6\sqrt{10}-4(2)$

$= 45-8$

$= 37$

> Radicals such as $(\sqrt{a}+\sqrt{b})$ and $(\sqrt{a}-\sqrt{b})$ are called conjugate radicals.

EXAMPLE 3. *Simplify by first rationalizing the denominator.*

(a) $\dfrac{\sqrt{5}}{\sqrt{2}}$

(b) $\dfrac{4}{\sqrt{5}-\sqrt{2}}$

(c) $\dfrac{3\sqrt{2}}{3\sqrt{2}-5}$

Solution

(a) $\dfrac{\sqrt{5}}{\sqrt{2}} = \dfrac{\sqrt{5}}{\sqrt{2}} \times \dfrac{\sqrt{2}}{\sqrt{2}}$

$\quad = \dfrac{\sqrt{10}}{2}$

(b) $\dfrac{4}{\sqrt{5}-\sqrt{2}} = \dfrac{4}{\sqrt{5}-\sqrt{2}} \times \dfrac{\sqrt{5}+\sqrt{2}}{\sqrt{5}+\sqrt{2}}$

$\quad = \dfrac{4(\sqrt{5}+\sqrt{2})}{5-2}$

$\quad = \tfrac{4}{3}(\sqrt{5}+\sqrt{2})$

(c) $\dfrac{3\sqrt{2}}{3\sqrt{2}-5} = \dfrac{3\sqrt{2}}{3\sqrt{2}-5} \times \dfrac{3\sqrt{2}+5}{3\sqrt{2}+5}$

$\quad = \dfrac{3\sqrt{2}(3\sqrt{2}+5)}{9(2)-25}$

$\quad = \dfrac{18+15\sqrt{2}}{-7}$

$\quad = \dfrac{-18-15\sqrt{2}}{7}$

EXERCISE 8-2

A **1.** Express as entire radicals:

(a) $2\sqrt{3}$ (b) $3\sqrt{2}$ (c) $5\sqrt{2}$ (d) $3\sqrt{3}$ (e) $4\sqrt{2}$
(f) $4\sqrt{3}$ (g) $7\sqrt{2}$ (h) $5\sqrt{5}$ (i) $2\sqrt{5}$ (j) $3\sqrt{5}$

2. Express as mixed radicals:

(a) $\sqrt{12}$ (b) $\sqrt{48}$ (c) $\sqrt{18}$ (d) $\sqrt{288}$ (e) $\sqrt{24}$
(f) $\sqrt{125}$ (g) $\sqrt{45}$ (h) $\sqrt{63}$ (i) $\sqrt{98}$ (j) $\sqrt{60}$

3. Simplify:

(a) $3\sqrt{2} \times 2\sqrt{5}$ (b) $4\sqrt{3} \times 3\sqrt{2}$ (c) $5\sqrt{6} \times 2\sqrt{2}$
(d) $4\sqrt{3} \times 3\sqrt{2}$ (e) $3\sqrt{2} \times 4\sqrt{7}$ (f) $5\sqrt{3} \times 4\sqrt{2}$
(g) $3\sqrt{5} \times 5\sqrt{2}$ (h) $3\sqrt{2} \times \sqrt{8}$ (i) $\sqrt{2}(\sqrt{3}+\sqrt{5})$
(j) $\sqrt{3}(\sqrt{5}-\sqrt{2})$ (k) $2\sqrt{2}(\sqrt{7}-2)$ (l) $\sqrt{5}(3+\sqrt{2})$

4. Collect like radicals:

(a) $5\sqrt{3}+6\sqrt{3}-7\sqrt{3}$ (b) $4\sqrt{2}-\sqrt{2}+6\sqrt{2}$ (c) $3\sqrt{5}+2\sqrt{5}-5\sqrt{5}$
(d) $\sqrt{7}-3\sqrt{7}+4\sqrt{7}$ (e) $4\sqrt{3}-7\sqrt{3}+2\sqrt{3}$ (f) $6\sqrt{2}-9\sqrt{2}-2\sqrt{2}$

5. State the conjugate radical for each of the following:

(a) $\sqrt{3}+\sqrt{2}$ (b) $2\sqrt{5}+1$ (c) $4\sqrt{3}-2$
(d) $7\sqrt{2}+4\sqrt{3}$ (e) $3\sqrt{7}-2\sqrt{11}$ (f) $5\sqrt{2}+2\sqrt{7}$

B **6.** Simplify:

(a) $\sqrt{3} \times \sqrt{7}$ (b) $3\sqrt{2} \times \sqrt{5}$ (c) $5\sqrt{2} \times 3\sqrt{7}$
(d) $\sqrt{6} \times \sqrt{6}$ (e) $\sqrt{2} \times \sqrt{3} \times \sqrt{5}$ (f) $\sqrt{12} \times \sqrt{3}$
(g) $(\sqrt{7})^2$ (h) $\sqrt{15} \times 2\sqrt{2}$ (i) $(2\sqrt{5})^2$

Write an expression for 5 using four fours.

Put the numbers from 1 to 9 in the spaces to make the statements true:

▨ + ▨ − ▨ = 10

▨ ÷ ▨ + ▨ = 10

▨ − ▨ + ▨ = 10

radicals, exponents, and logarithms

(j) $3\sqrt{2}\times\sqrt{8}$ (k) $5\sqrt{7}\times4\sqrt{3}$ (l) $\sqrt{15}\times\sqrt{\tfrac{2}{5}}\times\sqrt{\tfrac{7}{3}}$

7. Simplify:

(a) $\dfrac{\sqrt{6}}{\sqrt{2}}$ (b) $\dfrac{\sqrt{12}}{\sqrt{3}}$ (c) $\dfrac{2\sqrt{21}}{\sqrt{7}}$

(d) $\dfrac{4\sqrt{14}}{2\sqrt{7}}$ (e) $\dfrac{3\sqrt{5}}{\sqrt{15}}$ (f) $\dfrac{\sqrt{2}\times\sqrt{8}}{2}$

(g) $\dfrac{3\sqrt{5}\times2\sqrt{3}}{\sqrt{15}}$ (h) $\dfrac{3\sqrt{6}}{\sqrt{2}\times\sqrt{3}}$ (i) $\dfrac{4\sqrt{7}\times\sqrt{2}}{3\sqrt{14}}$

8. Simplify by collecting like radicals:

(a) $3\sqrt{11}+5\sqrt{11}$ (b) $2\sqrt{7}+5\sqrt{7}-4\sqrt{7}$ (c) $5\sqrt{3}+7\sqrt{3}-6\sqrt{3}$

(d) $3\sqrt{2}+4\sqrt{2}+7\sqrt{3}-2\sqrt{3}$ (e) $5\sqrt{5}+4\sqrt{3}-2\sqrt{5}+\sqrt{3}$

(f) $3\sqrt{5}+5\sqrt{2}-\sqrt{5}+3\sqrt{2}$ (g) $\tfrac{1}{2}\sqrt{3}+\tfrac{3}{2}\sqrt{3}-\sqrt{3}$

9. Simplify by collecting like radicals:

(a) $2\sqrt{2}+\sqrt{8}+\sqrt{18}$ (b) $\sqrt{27}+\sqrt{12}-4\sqrt{3}$

(c) $\sqrt{32}+\sqrt{50}$ (d) $\sqrt{8}+\sqrt{98}+4\sqrt{2}$

(e) $\sqrt{50}+\sqrt{27}-\sqrt{8}-\sqrt{75}$ (f) $\sqrt{12}+\sqrt{18}-\sqrt{27}+\sqrt{32}$

(g) $\sqrt{125}+\sqrt{20}-\sqrt{28}$ (h) $\sqrt{28}+\sqrt{63}-\sqrt{12}+\sqrt{27}$

10. Simplify:

(a) $3\sqrt{8}+2\sqrt{18}$ (b) $5\sqrt{2}+2\sqrt{32}$

(c) $3\sqrt{27}+2\sqrt{12}$ (d) $2\sqrt{20}+\sqrt{125}-2\sqrt{5}$

(e) $2\sqrt{49}-5\sqrt{18}+3\sqrt{32}$ (f) $3\sqrt{18}-2\sqrt{12}+4\sqrt{27}$

(g) $7\sqrt{8}+4\sqrt{20}-5\sqrt{125}$ (h) $2\sqrt{50}+3\sqrt{75}-2\sqrt{18}+\sqrt{27}$

11. Simplify:

(a) $\sqrt{3}(\sqrt{5}+\sqrt{7})$ (b) $7\sqrt{5}(\sqrt{2}+\sqrt{3})$

(c) $2\sqrt{5}(\sqrt{2}-1)$ (d) $3\sqrt{2}(2\sqrt{5}-4\sqrt{3})$

(e) $(3\sqrt{2}+\sqrt{3})(5\sqrt{2}+\sqrt{3})$ (f) $(7\sqrt{5}-\sqrt{3})(3\sqrt{5}+\sqrt{3})$

(g) $(5\sqrt{7}+6\sqrt{3})(2\sqrt{7}+4\sqrt{3})$ (h) $(3\sqrt{7}-4\sqrt{6})(2\sqrt{7}+\sqrt{6})$

12. Simplify:

(a) $(\sqrt{7}-\sqrt{6})^2$ (b) $(5\sqrt{3}+2)^2$

(c) $(4\sqrt{3}-\sqrt{7})^2$ (d) $(3\sqrt{5}+2\sqrt{6})^2$

(e) $(3\sqrt{2}-5\sqrt{3})(3\sqrt{2}+5\sqrt{3})$ (f) $(\sqrt{5}+\sqrt{2})(\sqrt{5}-\sqrt{2})$

(g) $(8\sqrt{3}+7\sqrt{2})(8\sqrt{3}-7\sqrt{2})$ (h) $(3\sqrt{5}+2)(3\sqrt{5}-2)$

13. Simplify by first rationalizing the denominator:

(a) $\dfrac{1}{\sqrt{3}}$ (b) $\dfrac{2}{\sqrt{6}}$ (c) $\dfrac{\sqrt{2}}{\sqrt{5}}$ (d) $\dfrac{24\sqrt{21}}{\sqrt{2}}$

(e) $\dfrac{15\sqrt{7}}{2\sqrt{3}}$ (f) $\dfrac{7\sqrt{11}}{11\sqrt{7}}$ (g) $\dfrac{2\sqrt{5}}{\sqrt{10}}$ (h) $\dfrac{4}{3\sqrt{6}}$

14. (a) $\dfrac{\sqrt{3}+\sqrt{2}}{\sqrt{2}}$ (b) $\dfrac{1+2\sqrt{2}}{\sqrt{3}}$ (c) $\dfrac{2\sqrt{2}+\sqrt{5}}{\sqrt{6}}$

(d) $\dfrac{3\sqrt{3}-1}{2\sqrt{5}}$ (e) $\dfrac{\sqrt{3}+2\sqrt{5}}{\sqrt{15}}$ (f) $\dfrac{\sqrt{11}-2\sqrt{2}}{3\sqrt{6}}$

15. (a) $\dfrac{1}{\sqrt{3}-\sqrt{2}}$ (b) $\dfrac{12}{\sqrt{11}-\sqrt{3}}$ (c) $\dfrac{\sqrt{7}+\sqrt{5}}{\sqrt{7}-\sqrt{5}}$

How many license plates can you make using 3 letters followed by 3 numbers?

C A N . 0 0 1

(d) $\dfrac{3}{\sqrt{7}-\sqrt{2}}$ (e) $\dfrac{5+4\sqrt{3}}{5\sqrt{3}-3\sqrt{2}}$ (f) $\dfrac{\sqrt{7}+\sqrt{5}}{3\sqrt{2}+2\sqrt{3}}$

16. Find the value of each of the following to two decimal places by first rationalizing the denominator.

$$\sqrt{2} \doteq 1.414$$
$$\sqrt{3} \doteq 1.732$$
$$\sqrt{6} \doteq 2.449$$
$$\sqrt{10} \doteq 3.162$$

(a) $\dfrac{\sqrt{5}}{\sqrt{2}}$ (b) $\dfrac{\sqrt{3}}{\sqrt{2}}$ (c) $\dfrac{5}{\sqrt{3}+\sqrt{2}}$ (d) $\dfrac{8\sqrt{2}}{\sqrt{5}-\sqrt{3}}$

(e) $\dfrac{2\sqrt{2}}{\sqrt{5}+\sqrt{2}}$ (f) $\dfrac{3\sqrt{2}}{\sqrt{5}}$ (g) $\dfrac{2\sqrt{5}}{\sqrt{10}}$ (h) $\dfrac{\sqrt{3}+\sqrt{2}}{\sqrt{3}-\sqrt{2}}$

8.3 RADICAL EQUATIONS

Equations such as

$$\sqrt{x}+1=3$$
$$\sqrt{x-1}=5, \quad \text{and}$$
$$\sqrt{x+2}=\sqrt{2x-5}+\sqrt{x}$$

are called radical equations because the variable occurs under a radical sign.

We rationalize the radical variable before continuing to solve the equations.

EXAMPLE 1. *Solve* (a) $\sqrt{x}=2$
(b) $\sqrt{x}-3=0$
(c) $\sqrt{x}+1=0$

Solution

(a) $\sqrt{x}=2$
$(\sqrt{x})^2=(2)^2$
$x=4$

(b) $\sqrt{x}-3=0$
$\sqrt{x}=3$
$(\sqrt{x})^2=3^2$
$x=9$

(c) $\sqrt{x}+1=0$
$\sqrt{x}=-1$
$(\sqrt{x})^2=(-1)^2$
$x=1$

Write an expression for 486 using four twos.

Verification:
L.S. $=\sqrt{4}=2$
R.S. $=2$
∴ the root is 4.

Verification:
L.S. $=\sqrt{9}-3=3-3=0$
R.S. $=0$
∴ the root is 9.

Verification:
L.S. $=\sqrt{1}+1=1+1=2$
R.S. $=0 \Leftarrow$ note ↗
∴ there is no solution.

Examples 1(a) and 1(b) verified, and Example 1(c) did not. Since the value 1 did not verify in 1(c), and investigation shows that there are no mechanical errors, we conclude that *the equation has no roots.* We say the value 1 is *extraneous.*

Extraneous values occur because squaring both sides of an equation is not a reversible step.

The solutions to all radical equations must be verified.

EXAMPLE 2. *Solve:* (a) $\sqrt{x-1}=5$ (b) $\sqrt{x+2}=\sqrt{2x-5}$

Solution

(a) $\sqrt{x-1}=5$

$(\sqrt{x-1})^2 = 5^2$

$x-1=25$

$x=26$

Verification:

L.S. $=\sqrt{26-1}=\sqrt{25}=5$

R.S. $=5$

∴ the root is 26.

(b) $\sqrt{x+2}=\sqrt{2x-5}$

$(\sqrt{x+2})^2 = (\sqrt{2x-5})^2$

$x+2=2x-5$

$x=7$

Verification:

L.S. $=\sqrt{7+2}=\sqrt{9}=3$

R.S. $=\sqrt{14-5}=\sqrt{9}=3$

∴ the root is 7.

EXAMPLE 3. *Solve:* $\sqrt{x+7}-1=\sqrt{x}$

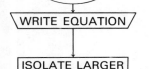

START

WRITE EQUATION

ISOLATE LARGER RADICAL ON ONE SIDE

SQUARE BOTH SIDES AND SIMPLIFY

ARE THERE ANY RADICALS LEFT? — YES

NO

CONTINUE SOLVING

VERIFY

CONCLUDE

STOP

Solution

$$\sqrt{x+7}-1=\sqrt{x}$$

$$\sqrt{x+7}=\sqrt{x}+1$$

$$(\sqrt{x+7})^2 = (\sqrt{x}+1)^2$$

$$x+7=x+2\sqrt{x}+1$$

$$6=2\sqrt{x}$$

$$3=\sqrt{x}$$

$$9=x$$

$$x=9$$

Verification:

L.S. $=\sqrt{9+7}-1=\sqrt{16}-1=4-1=3$

R.S. $=\sqrt{9}=3$

∴ the root is 9.

Unless otherwise stated all variables represent real numbers.

EXERCISE 8-3

B **1.** Solve:

(a) $\sqrt{x}=3$

(c) $\sqrt{x+1}=4$

(e) $\sqrt{x}=0$

(g) $\sqrt{2x-1}=1$

(b) $\sqrt{y}=1$

(d) $\sqrt{y-1}=1$

(f) $\sqrt{2x+1}=3$

(h) $\sqrt{3x+1}=2$

applied mathematics for today: senior

2. Solve:

(a) $\sqrt{x} - 1 = 3$ (b) $\sqrt{x} - 2 = 1$
(c) $\sqrt{x} + 3 - 5 = 0$ (d) $\sqrt{x} + 3 - 2 = 4$
(e) $\sqrt{3x} - 6 = 0$ (f) $\sqrt{2x} - 3 = 0$
(g) $\sqrt{x} + 2 = 5$ (h) $3 - \sqrt{x} = 5$

3. Solve:

(a) $\sqrt{5x - 1} = \sqrt{4x + 12}$ (b) $\sqrt{3x - 2} = \sqrt{3 - 2x}$
(c) $\sqrt{2x + 3} = \sqrt{3x}$ (d) $\sqrt{4x - 3} = \sqrt{2x}$

4. Solve:

(a) $\sqrt{3a + 2} - \sqrt{2a - 1} = 0$ (b) $\sqrt{x} + \sqrt{x - 9} = 1$
(c) $\sqrt{x - 3} = 3 - \sqrt{x}$ (d) $\sqrt{x} + \sqrt{x + 6} = 2$
(e) $\sqrt{x} + \sqrt{x + 5} = 1$ (f) $\sqrt{x - 4} = \sqrt{x + 11} - 3$

$\sqrt{1 + \sqrt{9}} = \blacksquare$

8.4 OPERATIONS WITH EXPONENTS

$$2^5 = 2 \times 2 \times 2 \times 2 \times 2 = 32, \quad \text{and}$$

$$a^n = a \times a \times a \times a \ldots \text{to } n \text{ factors.}$$

Exponent Laws:

$$a^m \times a^n = a^{m+n}$$
$$a^m \div a^n = a^{m-n}$$
$$(a^m)^n = a^{mn}$$
$$(ab)^n = a^n b^n$$
$$\left(\frac{a}{b}\right)^n = \frac{a^n}{b^n}$$
$$a^0 = 1, \qquad a^{-n} = \frac{1}{a^n}$$
$$a^{\frac{1}{2}} = \sqrt{a} \quad \text{and} \quad a^{\frac{1}{n}} = \sqrt[n]{a}$$

EXERCISE 8-4

1. Simplify:

(a) $x^4 \times x^7$ (b) $a^3 \times a^0$ (c) $2^2 \times 2^5$ (d) $a^4 \times a^{-2}$
(e) $2a^3 \times 3a^2$ (f) $2a^3 \times 7a$ (g) $15a^{12} \times 2a^5$ (h) $7a^7 \times 4a^4$

2. Simplify:

(a) $x^7 \div x^4$ (b) $c^{12} \div c^5$ (c) $m^{14} \div m^{11}$
(d) $m^{24} \div m^8$ (e) $8a^3 \div 2a^2$ (f) $24a^9 \div 8a^3$
(g) $50x^5 \div 2x^2$ (h) $343y^{15} \div 49y$

$2^{2^2} = \blacksquare$

3. Simplify:

(a) $(a^5)^3$ (b) $(x^{11})^4$ (c) $(m^5)^9$ (d) $(5a^2)^3$
(e) $3(a^2)^3$ (f) $(3a^2)^3$ (g) $(2x^4)^4$ (h) $5(2x^2)^4$
(i) $\left(\frac{5x^3}{6y^2}\right)^2$ (j) $\left(\frac{3x^2}{2y}\right)^3$ (k) $\left(\frac{x^3}{y^4}\right)^3$ (l) $\frac{2(x^3)^2}{(4x)^2}$

4. Simplify:

(a) $(a^3)^5 \div (a^2)^3$ (b) $(-1)^{10} \div (-1)^3$ (c) $(x^2y^3)^4$
(d) $a^2b^3 \div a^2b^3$ (e) $(3a^2)^0$ (f) $a^0 \times 3a^4$
(g) $4a^3b \div (2a)^2$ (h) $98x^4 \div (7x^2)^2$ (i) $81x^3 \div (3x)^3$

5. (a) Simplify $\dfrac{a^5}{a^8}$ so that the denominator is 1.

(b) Simplify $\dfrac{a^5}{a^8}$ so that the numerator is 1.

6. Evaluate:
(a) 7^0 (b) 5^{-2} (c) $(11^0)^{-3}$ (d) 568^0
(e) $3^{-4} \times 3^3$ (f) $(-2)^{-4}$ (g) $(-1)^{-1}$ (h) 2^{-5}
(i) $\dfrac{2^2 \times 2}{2^{-2}}$ (j) $\dfrac{2 \times 5^{-3}}{10^{-2}}$ (k) $\dfrac{5^2 \times 2^{-3}}{3^{-2}}$ (l) $\dfrac{3^2 \div 3^5}{3^{-2}}$

7. Expand:
(a) 9.87×10^3 (b) 9.87×10^2 (c) 9.87×10 (d) 9.87×10^0
(e) 9.87×10^{-1} (f) 9.87×10^{-2} (g) 9.87×10^5 (h) 9.87×10^{-5}

8. The numbers in question 7 are written in *scientific notation.* Write the following numbers in scientific notation:
(a) 645 (b) 0.654 (c) 65 400 (d) 65.4
(e) 0.0654 (f) 0.000 654 (g) 654 000 (h) 0.006 54

9. Simplify:
(a) $25^{\frac{1}{2}}$ (b) $36^{\frac{1}{2}}$ (c) $16^{\frac{1}{2}}$ (d) $121^{\frac{1}{2}}$ (e) $9^{0.5}$
(f) $100^{0.5}$ (g) $(3^{\frac{1}{2}})^2$ (h) $(4^{\frac{1}{2}})^3$ (i) 5^{-1} (j) $4^{-\frac{1}{2}}$
(k) $16^{-\frac{1}{2}}$ (l) $25^{\frac{3}{2}}$ (m) $(x^{\frac{1}{2}})^2$ (n) $x^2 \cdot x^{2.5}$ (o) $x \div x^{0.5}$

Since $\quad a^{\frac{3}{2}} = (a^3)^{\frac{1}{2}} = \sqrt{a^3}$

or $\quad a^{\frac{3}{2}} = (a^{\frac{1}{2}})^3 = (\sqrt{a})^3$, we can

generalize by writing:

$$\boxed{x^{\frac{p}{r}} = \sqrt[r]{x^p} \quad \text{or} \quad x^{\frac{p}{r}} = (\sqrt[r]{x})^p}$$

10. Evaluate:
(a) $8^{\frac{1}{3}}$ (b) $81^{-\frac{1}{4}}$ (c) $125^{\frac{2}{3}}$ (d) $27^{\frac{1}{3}}$
(e) $27^{0.3}$ (f) $16^{-1.5}$ (g) $625^{\frac{1}{4}}$ (h) $81^{\frac{3}{4}}$
(i) $64^{-\frac{1}{2}}$ (j) $64^{-\frac{1}{3}}$ (k) $25^{\frac{3}{2}}$ (l) $8^{-\frac{2}{3}}$

11. Write each of the following with rational coefficients.
(a) $\sqrt{x}$ (b) $(\sqrt{y})^3$ (c) $\sqrt[3]{m}$ (d) $\sqrt[3]{x^2}$

(e) $\sqrt[3]{p^9}$ (f) $\dfrac{1}{\sqrt{c}}$ (g) $\sqrt[3]{a^4}$ (h) $\dfrac{1}{\sqrt{a^3}}$

12. Evaluate:
(a) $32^{\frac{4}{5}}$ (b) $16^{\frac{3}{4}}$ (c) $8^{\frac{5}{3}}$ (d) $9^{-\frac{3}{2}}$
(e) $(\frac{25}{36})^{\frac{1}{2}}$ (f) $(\frac{36}{49})^{-\frac{1}{2}}$ (g) $(\frac{16}{9})^{\frac{3}{2}}$ (h) $(\frac{8}{27})^{-\frac{2}{3}}$
(I) $(8a^3)^{\frac{1}{3}}$ (j) $8(a^3)^{\frac{1}{3}}$ (k) $(a^4b^6)^{\frac{3}{2}}$ (l) $(64a^3b^6)^{\frac{1}{3}}$
(m) $10\,000\,000^{\frac{1}{7}}$ (n) $\sqrt[3]{64^2}$ (o) $(4^{-1})^{-\frac{1}{2}}$ (p) $100^{\frac{3}{2}}$
(q) $2^{\frac{1}{5}} \times 2^{\frac{4}{5}}$ (r) $2^{0.3} \times 2^{.25} \div 2^{\frac{1}{6}}$ (s) $(216^2)^{\frac{1}{3}} \div (32^{\frac{1}{5}})^2$
(t) $10^{0.6} \times 10^{0.3} \div 10^0$ (u) $32^{\frac{2}{5}} \times \dfrac{1}{81^{-\frac{1}{4}}}$ (v) $[(729^{0.5})^{\frac{1}{3}}]^6$

8.5 LOGARITHMS

Figure 8-1 is the graph defined by $y = 10^x$. If we interchange the x, and y in the equation we get a new equation

$$x = 10^y$$

This new equation can also be written

$$y = \log_{10} x$$

and is read

"y equals the logarithm of x to base 10"

This means that the logarithm to the base 10 of the number x is the exponent y such that $10^y = x$.

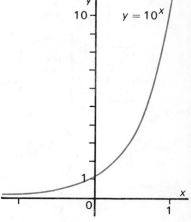

Figure 8-1

Exponential Form	Logarithmic Form
$x = 10^y$	$y = \log_{10} x$

In this chapter we will deal exclusively with base 10 and will omit the subscript and write simply $\log 100 = 2$ when we mean $\log_{10} 100 = 2$.

EXAMPLE 1. *Express in logarithmic form:*
(a) $10^3 = 1000$ (b) $0.01 = 10^{-2}$

Solution (a) $10^3 = 1000$ becomes $\log 1000 = 3$
(b) $0.01 = 10^{-2}$ becomes $\log 0.01 = -2$

EXAMPLE 2. *Express in exponential form:*
(a) $\log 100\,000 = 5$ (b) $\log 0.001 = -3$

Solution (a) $\log 100\,000 = 5$ becomes $10^5 = 100\,000$
(b) $\log 0.001 = -3$ becomes $10^{-3} = 0.001$

A table of logarithms for the values of $y = \log x$ for x-values from 1 to 10 is in the appendix, so that we can read values of logarithms for numbers other than powers of 10.

EXAMPLE 3. *Read from tables:*
(a) $\log 5.67$ (b) $\log 563$ (c) $\log 0.575$

Solution (a) Read down the left-hand column to 5.6.
Read across the 5.6 row to the 7 column.

Multiplication   *abcdef*
$$\frac{e}{f\ abcde}$$

radicals, exponents, and logarithms   161

$$\log 5.67 \doteq 0.7536$$

Logarithms

	0	1	2	3	4	5	6	7	8	9	1 2 3	4 5 6	7 8 9
												Differences	
5.5	.7404	.7412	.7419	.7427	.7435	.7443	.7451	.7459	.7466	.7474	1 2 2	3 4 5	5 6 7
5.6	.7482	.7490	.7497	.7505	.7513	.7520	.7528	.7536	.7543	.7551	1 2 2	3 4 5	5 6 7
5.7	.7559	.7566	.7574	.7582	.7589	.7597	.7604	.7612	.7619	.7627	1 2 2	3 4 5	5 6 7
5.8	.7634	.7642	.7649	.7657	.7664	.7672	.7679	.7686	.7694	.7701	1 1 2	3 4 4	5 6 7
5.9	.7709	.7716	.7723	.7731	.7738	.7745	.7752	.7760	.7767	.7774	1 1 2	3 4 4	5 6 7

row →

(b) $\log 563 = \log (10^2 \times 5.63)$
$\doteq 2 + 0.7505$

standard notation

(c) $\log 0.575 = \log (10^{-1} \times 5.75)$
$\doteq -1 + 0.7597$

Where a number has 4 significant digits, we use the mean differences columns in the tables.

EXAMPLE 4. *Read from tables*
(a) $\log 3.742$ (b) $\log 0.003\,568$

The mean difference 2 is an abbreviation for 0.0002.

Solution (a) $\log 3.74 \doteq 0.5729$
          2 (difference for 2)
$\log 3.742 \doteq 0.5731$

Logarithms

	0	1	2	3	4	5	6	7	8	9	1 2 3	4 5 6	7 8 9
												Differences	
3.5	.5441	.5453	.5465	.5478	.5490	.5502	.5514	.5527	.5539	.5551	1 2 4	5 6 7	9 10 11
3.6	.5563	.5575	.5587	.5599	.5611	.5623	.5635	.5647	.5658	.5670	1 2 4	5 6 7	8 10 11
3.7	.5682	.5694	.5705	.5717	.5729	.5740	.5752	.5763	.5775	.5786	1 2 3	5 6 7	8 9 10
3.8	.5798	.5809	.5821	.5832	.5843	.5855	.5866	.5877	.5888	.5899	1 2 3	5 6 7	8 9 10
3.9	.5911	.5922	.5933	.5944	.5955	.5966	.5977	.5988	.5999	.6010	1 2 3	4 5 7	8 9 10

(b) $\log 0.003\,568 = \log (10^{-3} \times 3.568)$
$\doteq -3 + .5524$

$\log 3.56 \doteq 0.5514$
(difference for 8)   10
$\log 3.568 \doteq 0.5524$

Examples 3 and 4 show that a logarithm consists of two parts: an integer called the **characteristic** and a positive decimal fraction called the **mantissa**.

$$\log (\text{number}) = \boxed{\text{characteristic}} + .\boxed{\text{mantissa}}$$

Note that the characteristic is always an integer and the mantissa is never negative.

Suppose we wish to perform the inverse operation. We may wish to find a number whose logarithm is given.

EXAMPLE 5. *Find x when*

(*a*) $\log x = 0.7543$

(*b*) $\log x = 1 + .7348$

(*c*) $\log x = -2 + .4324$

Solution (a) We first write $\log x = 0.7543$ in exponential form:

$$x = 10^{0.7543}$$

We obtain $10^{0.7543}$ from the table of exponentials in the appendix.

Addition

SEND
MORE
MONEY

$$\log x = 0.7543$$

$$x = 10^{0.7543}$$

$$10^{0.7540} \doteq 5.675$$

$$4 \quad \text{(difference of 3)}$$

$$10^{0.7543} \doteq 5.679$$

$$x \doteq 5.679$$

Values of the Exponential Function $y = 10^x$

	0	1	2	3	4	5	6	7	8	9	Differences								
											1	**2**	**3**	**4**	**5**	**6**	**7**	**8**	**9**
.72	5.248	5.260	5.272	5.284	5.297	5.309	5.321	5.333	5.346	5.358	1	2	4	5	6	7	9	10	11
.73	5.370	5.383	5.395	5.408	5.420	5.433	5.445	5.458	5.470	5.483	1	3	4	5	6	8	9	10	11
.74	5.495	5.508	5.521	5.534	5.546	5.559	5.572	5.585	5.598	5.610	1	3	4	5	6	8	9	10	12
.75	5.623	5.636	5.649	5.662	5.675	5.689	5.702	5.715	5.728	5.741	1	3	4	5	7	8	9	10	12
.76	5.754	5.768	5.781	5.794	5.808	5.821	5.834	5.848	5.861	5.875	1	3	4	5	7	8	9	11	12
.77	5.888	5.902	5.916	5.929	5.943	5.957	5.970	5.984	5.998	6.012	1	3	4	5	7	8	10	11	12
.78	6.026	6.039	6.053	6.067	6.081	6.095	6.109	6.124	6.138	6.152	1	3	4	6	7	8	10	11	13

(b) $\log x = 1 + .7348$

$$x = 10^{1+.7348}$$

$$\doteq 10^1 \times 10^{0.7348}$$

$$\doteq 10^1 \times 5.430$$

$$\doteq 54.30$$

$$10^{0.7340} \doteq 5.420$$

$$\text{(difference for 8)} \quad 10$$

$$10^{0.7348} \doteq 5.430$$

(c) $\log x = -2 + .4324$

$$x = 10^{-2+.4324}$$

$$= 10^{-2} \times 10^{0.4324}$$

$$\doteq 10^{-2} \times 2.707$$

$$\doteq 0.02707$$

$$10^{0.432} = 2.704$$

$$\text{(difference for 4)} \quad 3$$

$$10^{0.4324} \doteq 2.707$$

EXERCISE 8-5

A **1.** Express in logarithmic form.
(a) $10^2 = 100$ (b) $10^{-3} = 0.001$ (c) $10^0 = 1$ (d) $10^{-1} = 0.1$

2. Express in exponential form.
(a) $3 = \log 1000$ (b) $\log 0.001 = -3$
(c) $\log 1 = 0$ (d) $\log 10\,000 = 4$

3. State the characteristic of the logarithm of each of the following.
(a) 3.75   (b) 783   (c) 0.0255   (d) 68 300
(e) 5461   (f) 0.251   (g) 0.000 355   (h) 5.63

4. If $\log 2.00 \doteq 0.3010$, find:
(a) $\log 20$ (b) $\log 200$ (c) $\log 0.2$
(d) $\log 20\,000$ (e) $\log 0.002$ (f) $\log 2\,000\,000$

Solve for x. $2^{x+1} = 8$.

5. Read from tables.
(a) $\log 3.75$ (b) $\log 5.67$ (c) $\log 8.24$ (d) $\log 6.74$
(e) $\log 3.14$ (f) $\log 6.25$ (g) $\log 1.74$ (h) $\log 4.95$
(i) $\log 9.25$ (j) $\log 1.75$ (k) $\log 5.55$ (l) $\log 5.81$

6. Read from tables.
(a) $10^{0.625}$ (b) $10^{0.567}$ (c) $10^{0.301}$ (d) $10^{0.602}$
(e) $10^{0.903}$ (f) $10^{0.477}$ (g) $10^{0.125}$ (h) $10^{0.333}$
(i) $10^{0.666}$ (j) $10^{0.888}$ (k) $10^{0.444}$ (l) $10^{1.000}$

B **7.** If $\log 3.417 \doteq 0.5337$, evaluate:
(a) $\log 3417$ (b) $\log 0.3417$ (c) $\log 0.003\,417$
(d) $\log 3\,417\,000$ (e) $\log 34.17$ (f) $\log 0.000\,341\,7$

8. Read from tables.
(a) $\log 7.35$ (b) $\log 62.8$ (c) $\log 4750$
(d) $\log 3\,500\,000$ (e) $\log 0.275$ (f) $\log 4\,370\,000$
(g) $\log 0.005\,25$ (h) $\log 388$ (i) $\log 0.000\,671$

9. Read from tables.
(a) $\log 4.125$ (b) $\log 3.271$ (c) $\log 6.841$
(d) $\log 0.2472$ (e) $\log 0.035\,71$ (f) $\log 0.000\,487\,1$
(g) $\log 3541$ (h) $\log 65.82$ (i) $\log 3\,841\,000$

10. Read from tables.
(a) $10^{0.355}$ (b) $10^{0.425}$ (c) $10^{0.875}$
(d) $10^{4+.251}$ (e) $10^{-2+.503}$ (f) $10^{3+.301}$
(g) $10^{-2+.301}$ (h) $10^{4+.265}$ (i) $10^{0+.427}$

11. Read from tables.
(a) $10^{0+.4552}$ (b) $10^{1+.6021}$ (c) $10^{2+.4444}$
(d) $10^{2+.8888}$ (e) $10^{-2+.3571}$ (f) $10^{-3+.8911}$
(g) $10^{3+.4125}$ (h) $10^{-3+.3811}$ (i) $10^{5+.4257}$

8.6 MULTIPLICATION USING LOGARITHMS

By applying the laws of logarithms which follow, the operations of multiplication and division can be replaced by addition and subtraction.

$$\text{Let} \quad A = 10^x \quad \text{and} \quad B = 10^y$$
$$\log_{10} A = x \qquad \log_{10} B = y$$
$$\log_{10}(AB) = \log_{10}(10^x \times 10^y)$$
$$= \log_{10} 10^{x+y}$$
$$= x + y$$
$$= \log_{10} A + \log_{10} B$$

$$\boxed{\log_{10}(AB) = \log_{10} A + \log_{10} B}$$

$$\frac{1}{\dfrac{1}{1 + \frac{2}{3}}} = \blacksquare$$

In the logarithms which follow, we will write log A, when we mean $\log_{10} A$. When the base is not written, base 10 is understood.

EXAMPLE 1. *Use logarithms to evaluate*
(a) 568×58 \qquad (b) $673 \times 4.36 \times 0.004\,17$

Solution (a) Let $x = 568 \times 58$

$$\log x = \log(568 \times 58)$$
$$= \log 568 + \log 58$$
$$= \log(10^2 \times 5.68) + \log(10^1 \times 5.8)$$
$$\doteq (2 + 0.7543) + (1 + 0.7634)$$
$$\doteq 4 + .5177$$
$$x \doteq 10^{4 + .5177}$$
$$\doteq 10^4 \times 10^{0.5177}$$
$$\doteq 10^4 \times 3.294$$
$$\therefore \quad 568 \times 58 \doteq 3.294 \times 10^4$$

$$\begin{array}{r} 2 + .7543 \\ 1 + .7634 \\ \hline 4 + .5177 \end{array}$$

(b) Let $x = 673 \times 4.36 \times 0.004\,17$

$$\log x = \log 673 + \log 4.36 + \log 0.004\,17$$
$$= \log(10^2 \times 6.73) + \log(10^0 \times 4.36) + \log(10^{-3} \times 4.17)$$
$$\doteq (2 + .8280) + (0 + .6395) + (-3 + .6201)$$
$$\doteq 1 + .0876$$
$$x \doteq 10^{1 + .0876}$$
$$\doteq 10^1 \times 10^{0.0876}$$
$$\doteq 10^1 \times 1.224$$
$$\therefore \quad 673 \times 4.36 \times 0.004\,17 \doteq 1.224 \times 10^1$$

$$\begin{array}{r} 2 + .8280 \\ 0 + .6395 \\ -3 + .6201 \\ \hline 1 + .0876 \end{array}$$

EXERCISE 8-6

A **1.** Express as sums of logarithms:
(a) $\log(15 \times 20)$ \qquad (b) $\log(50 \times 33)$ \qquad (c) $\log(25 \times 11 \times 16)$

B **2.** Add the following logarithms:

(a) $\begin{array}{r} 1 + .5264 \\ 2 + .1427 \\ \hline \end{array}$ \qquad (b) $\begin{array}{r} 3 + .7416 \\ 1 + .5227 \\ \hline \end{array}$ \qquad (c) $\begin{array}{r} -3 + .2416 \\ 5 + .4126 \\ \hline \end{array}$ \qquad (d) $\begin{array}{r} -5 + .3056 \\ 2 + .8511 \\ \hline \end{array}$

radicals, exponents, and logarithms \qquad 165

3. Multiply using logarithms:

(a) 3.14×6.92 (b) 5.38×26.2 (c) 0.275×68.3

(d) $0.004\,35 \times 71.5$ (e) 0.0635×2.12 (f) 358×2.75

(g) 3.275×41.72 (h) $0.035\,54 \times 64.32$ (i) 3891×54.65

4. Evaluate using logarithms:

(a) $10.1 \times 14.1 \times 0.004\,34$ (b) $3.66 \times 5.27 \times 8.63$

(c) $2.734 \times 5.732 \times 0.5175$ (d) $18.76 \times 3.406 \times 0.6142$

(e) $5.271 \times 0.5833 \times 5.726$ (f) $0.4675 \times 4.935 \times 8.621$

Use logarithms to perform the calculations in the following problems:

5. Find the volume of a warehouse 42.7 m by 112 m and 4.25 m high.

6. The density, D, of a certain block of a light metal is 812.7 kg/m^3. Find the mass, m, of the block if its volume, V, is $0.000\,006\,594 \text{ m}^3$ ($m = DV$).

7. Find the volume of a cube with each side 0.7125 m.

8. If 0.2715 g of material are deposited at the anode in 1 s, how many grams are deposited in 7.875 s?

$2^{\log_2 2} = $ ▨

8.7 DIVISION USING LOGARITHMS

$$\text{Let} \quad A = 10^x \quad \text{and} \quad B = 10^y$$
$$\log_{10} A = x \qquad \log_{10} B = y$$
$$\log_{10} \frac{A}{B} = \log_{10} \frac{10^x}{10^y}$$
$$= \log_{10} 10^{x-y}$$
$$= x - y$$
$$= \log_{10} A - \log_{10} B$$

$$\boxed{\log_{10} \frac{A}{B} = \log_{10} A - \log_{10} B}$$

EXAMPLE 1. *Use logarithms to evaluate:*

(a) $518.7 \div 8.305$ (b) $0.007\,515 \div 0.000\,028\,54$

Solution (a) Let $x = 518.7 \div 8.305$

$$\log x = \log (518.7 \div 8.305)$$
$$= \log 518.7 - \log 8.305$$
$$= \log (10^2 \times 5.187) - \log (10^0 \times 8.305)$$
$$\doteq (2 + .7149) - (0 + .9194)$$
$$\doteq 1 + .7955$$
$$x \doteq 10^{1 + .7955}$$
$$\doteq 10^1 \times 6.243$$
$$\therefore \quad 518.7 \div 8.305 \doteq 6.243 \times 10^1$$

Subtracting

$2 + .7149$

$0 + .9194$

$\overline{1 + .7955}$

(b) Let $x = 0.007\,515 \div 0.000\,028\,54$

applied mathematics for today: senior

$$\log x = \log 0.007\,515 - \log 0.000\,028\,54$$
$$= \log\,(10^{-3} \times 7.515) - \log\,(10^{-5} \times 2.854)$$
$$\doteq (-3+.8759) - (-5+.4554)$$
$$\doteq 2+.4205$$
$$x \doteq 10^{2+.4205}$$
$$\doteq 10^2 \times 2.633$$
$$\therefore \quad 0.007\,515 \div 0.000\,028\,54 \doteq 2.633 \times 10^2$$

Subtracting

$$-3+.8759$$
$$\underline{-5+.4554}$$
$$2+.4205$$

EXAMPLE 2. *Evaluate* $\dfrac{35.75 \times 2.865}{14.63}$ *using logarithms.*

Solution Let $x = \dfrac{35.75 \times 2.865}{14.63}$

$$\log x = \log 35.75 + \log 2.865 - \log 14.63$$
$$= \log\,(10^1 \times 3.575) + \log\,(10^0 \times 2.865) - \log\,(10^1 \times 1.463)$$
$$\doteq (1+.5533) + (0+.4572) - (1+.1653)$$
$$\doteq 0+.8452$$
$$x \doteq 10^{0+.8452}$$
$$\doteq 10^0 \times 7.001$$

$$\therefore \quad \frac{35.75 \times 2.865}{14.63} \doteq 7.001$$

$$1+.5533$$
$$\underline{0+.4572}$$
$$2+.0105$$
$$\underline{1+.1653}$$
$$0+.8452$$

EXERCISE 8-7

A **1.** Express as differences of logarithms:
(a) $\log\,(26 \div 40)$ (b) $\log\,(7 \div 13)$ (c) $\log\,(0.72 \div 2.9)$

2 Express as sums and differences of logarithms:

(a) $\log \dfrac{35 \times 18}{112}$ (b) $\log \dfrac{30 \times 61}{71 \times 19}$ (c) $\log \dfrac{156}{21 \times 211}$

B **3.** Subtract the following logarithms:
(a) $5+.7124$ (b) $4+.6135$ (c) $-3+.5216$ (d) $-2+.5248$
    $\underline{2+.3317}$ $\underline{5+.2112}$ $\underline{4+.3114}$ $\underline{-1+.6848}$

4. Divide using logarithms:
(a) $32.5 \div 6.25$ (b) $5.86 \div 3.14$ (c) $318 \div 4.65$
(d) $37\,500 \div 0.179$ (e) $415 \div 31.6$ (f) $28.5 \div 3.14$
(g) $51.85 \div 2.125$ (h) $3.375 \div 5.866$ (i) $0.042\,75 \div 0.005\,166$
(j) $3856 \div 21.47$ (k) $0.7315 \div 6.275$ (l) $45.85 \div 0.3175$

5. Evaluate using logarithms:
(a) $5.26 \times 8.34 \div 5.92$ (b) $518 \times 804 \div 917$
(c) $0.375 \times 0.715 \div 3.25$ (d) $3.14 \times 6.25 \div 4.25$
(e) $66.2 \times 84.3 \div 114$

$$\log \frac{AB}{C}$$
$$= \log A + \log B - \log C$$

6. Evaluate using logarithms:
(a) $3.85 \div (2.14 \times 8.27)$ (b) $324 \div (211 \times 418)$
(c) $0.375 \div (5.16 \times 0.214)$ (d) $841 \div (24.5 \times 81.6)$
(e) $41.7 \div (21.3 \times 4.17)$

$$\log \frac{A}{BC}$$
$$= \log A - (\log B + \log C)$$

7. Evaluate using logarithms:

(a) $\dfrac{4.265 \times 47.45}{4.751}$ (b) $\dfrac{1}{3.142 \times 5.275}$ (c) $\dfrac{0.625}{3.125 \times 487.5}$

(d) $\dfrac{47.21 \times 5.866}{29.6 \times 345}$ (e) $\dfrac{81.25 \times 47.25}{86.41 \times 18.27}$ (f) $\dfrac{0.3621 \times 894.7}{0.052\,75 \times 65.23}$

8. Find the density, D, of 0.000 058 4 kg of a substance which occupies 0.000 000 361 m³, where $D = \dfrac{m}{V}$.

What is a GOOGOL?

8.8 POWERS AND ROOTS USING LOGARITHMS

$$A = 10^x \quad \text{and} \quad x = \log_{10} A$$

$$\log_{10} A^n = \log_{10} (10^x)^n$$

$$= \log_{10} 10^{nx}$$

$$= nx$$

$$= n \log_{10} A$$

$$\boxed{\log_{10} A^n = n \log_{10} A}$$

EXAMPLE 1. *Evaluate* $(1.07)^{18}$

Solution Let $x = (1.07)^{18}$

$$\log x = \log 1.07^{18}$$

$$= 18 \log 1.07$$

$$\doteq 18 (0 + .0294)$$

$$\doteq 0 + .5292$$

$$x \doteq 10^{0+.5292}$$

$$\doteq 3.383$$

$$\therefore \quad (1.07)^{18} \doteq 3.383.$$

EXAMPLE 2. *Evaluate* (a) $\sqrt{73.85}$ (b) $\sqrt[5]{0.052\,65}$

Solution (a) Let $x = \sqrt{73.85}$

$$= (73.85)^{\frac{1}{2}}$$

$$\log x = \log 73.85^{\frac{1}{2}}$$

$$= \tfrac{1}{2} \log 73.85$$

$$\doteq \tfrac{1}{2}(1 + .8684)$$

$$\doteq \tfrac{1}{2}(1.8684)$$

$$\doteq 0 + .9342$$

$$x \doteq 10^{0+.9342}$$

$$\doteq 8.594$$

$$\sqrt{73.85} \doteq 8.594$$

(b) Let $x = \sqrt[5]{0.052\,65}$

$$= (0.052\,65)^{\frac{1}{5}}$$

$$\log x = \log 0.052\,65^{\frac{1}{5}}$$

$$= \tfrac{1}{5} \log 0.052\,65$$

$$\doteq \tfrac{1}{5}(-2 + .7214)$$

$$\doteq \tfrac{1}{5}(-5 + 3.7214)$$

$$\doteq -1 + .7443$$

$$x \doteq 10^{-1+.7443}$$

$$\doteq 10^{-1} \times 5.550$$

$$\sqrt[5]{0.052\,65} \doteq 5.550 \times 10^{-1}$$

$$\doteq 0.555$$

$-2 + .7214$

$= -2 \; \boxed{-3 + 3} \; + .7214$

$= -5 + 3.7214$

The characteristic must remain an integer after multiplying by $\tfrac{1}{5}$.

applied mathematics for today: senior

EXAMPLE 3. *Evaluate* $\sqrt[3]{(38.75)^2}$

Solution Let $x = \sqrt[3]{(38.75)^2} = (38.75)^{\frac{2}{3}}$

$$\log x = \log 38.75^{\frac{2}{3}}$$
$$= \tfrac{2}{3} \log 38.75$$
$$\doteq \tfrac{2}{3}(1 + .5883)$$
$$\doteq \tfrac{1}{3}(2 + 1.1766)$$
$$\doteq \tfrac{1}{3}(3 + .1766)$$
$$\doteq 1 + .0589$$
$$x \doteq 10^{1 + .0589}$$
$$\doteq 10^1 \times 1.145$$
$$\sqrt[3]{(38.75)^2} \doteq 1.145 \times 10$$
$$\doteq 11.45$$

Addition: HOCUS
          POCUS
          PRESTO

EXERCISE 8-8

A   **1.** Apply the power law to the following.
   (a) $\log 3.7^2$ (b) $\log 5.25^3$ (c) $\log 318^4$
   (d) $\log \sqrt{318}$ (e) $\log \sqrt[4]{37.8}$ (f) $\log \sqrt[3]{0.275}$

B   **2.** Simplify:
   (a) $3(1 + .5712)$ (b) $2(-3 + .7214)$ (c) $3(-5 + .4120)$
   (d) $\tfrac{1}{2}(2 + .5274)$ (e) $\tfrac{1}{3}(1 + .5286)$ (f) $\tfrac{1}{2}(-2 + .4784)$
   (g) $\tfrac{1}{3}(-4 + .2581)$ (h) $\tfrac{1}{5}(-1 + .7285)$ (i) $\tfrac{1}{2}(-3 + .5612)$

   3. Evaluate using logarithms.
   (a) 144^3 (b) 3.65^4 (c) 5.62^5 (d) 3.14^2
   (e) 3.65^7 (f) 0.125^3 (g) 0.375^4 (h) 0.625^5

   4. Evaluate using logarithms.
   (a) $275^{\frac{1}{2}}$ (b) $1024^{\frac{1}{3}}$ (c) $3.14^{\frac{1}{2}}$ (d) $385.7^{\frac{1}{5}}$
   (e) $\sqrt{384}$ (f) $\sqrt{721}$ (g) $\sqrt[3]{32.1}$ (h) $\sqrt{58.65}$

   5. Evaluate using logarithms.
   (a) 25.35^3 (b) 1.125^2 (c) 4.375^4 (d) $\sqrt{688.4}$
   (e) $\sqrt[3]{125.7}$ (f) $0.052\,74^3$ (g) $\sqrt{0.7125}$ (h) $\sqrt[3]{0.047\,85}$

C   **6.** Evaluate using logarithms.
   (a) 3.14×5.25^2 (b) 7.25×5.25^2 (c) 3.14×48.3^2
   (d) 4.65×0.216^3 (e) 3.142×0.2875^2 (f) $57.65^2 \times 47.63$

   7. Calculate the area of a circle with radius 1.78 cm to two decimal places.

   8. Find the volume of a spherical ball bearing with radius 0.625 cm.

   9. The period, T, of a pendulum is given by $T = 2\pi\sqrt{\dfrac{l}{g}}$ where T is in seconds. Find T if $\pi = 3.142$, $l = 185.2$ cm and $g = 974.2$ cm/s².

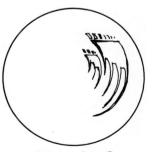

$$V = \tfrac{4}{3}\pi r^3$$

radicals, exponents, and logarithms   169

REVIEW EXERCISE

B **1.** Simplify:
(a) $3\sqrt{5}\times2\sqrt{6}$ (b) $5\sqrt{2}\times\sqrt{6}$ (c) $6\sqrt{3}\times2\sqrt{6}$
(d) $\sqrt{2}(\sqrt{3}+\sqrt{7})$ (e) $3\sqrt{5}(\sqrt{2}-2)$ (f) $2\sqrt{2}(\sqrt{6}+3\sqrt{2})$
(g) $4\sqrt{7}\times3\sqrt{21}$ (h) $2\sqrt{3}\times3\sqrt{2}$ (i) $4\sqrt{3}(\sqrt{3}-3)$

2. Simplify:
(a) $3\sqrt{6}+2\sqrt{6}$ (b) $\sqrt{8}+4\sqrt{2}$ (c) $\sqrt{27}+5\sqrt{3}$
(d) $\sqrt{12}+\sqrt{75}$ (e) $\sqrt{20}+\sqrt{45}$ (f) $\sqrt{8}+\sqrt{18}$
(g) $3\sqrt{12}+2\sqrt{27}$ (h) $7\sqrt{8}-\sqrt{32}$ (i) $2\sqrt{63}-3\sqrt{27}$
(j) $2\sqrt{18}-\sqrt{27}+\sqrt{32}-\sqrt{12}$ (k) $\sqrt{125}-\sqrt{28}+\sqrt{20}$

3. Simplify:
(a) $(\sqrt{3}+\sqrt{2})(3\sqrt{3}+4\sqrt{2})$ (b) $(5\sqrt{2}+1)(5\sqrt{2}-1)$
(c) $(3\sqrt{6}+\sqrt{2})(3\sqrt{6}-\sqrt{2})$ (d) $(\sqrt{5}+1)^2$
(e) $(3\sqrt{2}-4)^2$

4. Simplify by first rationalizing the denominator.

(a) $\dfrac{1}{\sqrt{5}}$ (b) $\dfrac{2}{\sqrt{2}}$ (c) $\dfrac{\sqrt{3}}{\sqrt{5}}$ (d) $\dfrac{3\sqrt{6}}{\sqrt{3}}$

(e) $\dfrac{1}{\sqrt{5}+\sqrt{2}}$ (f) $\dfrac{\sqrt{14}+1}{\sqrt{14}-1}$ (g) $\dfrac{3\sqrt{5}+2}{2\sqrt{5}-1}$

5. Solve.
(a) $\sqrt{x+1}=3$ (b) $\sqrt{x-1}=2$ (c) $\sqrt{2x+3}=\sqrt{3x}$
(d) $\sqrt{x-1}+2=0$ (e) $\sqrt{x-3}+\sqrt{x}=3$ (f) $\sqrt{3x+1}+\sqrt{x}=3$

Place the numbers from 1 to 23 in 3 groups so that no group contains a number which is the sum of two others in the same group.

6. Simplify:
(a) $x^5\cdot x^4$ (b) $24x^7\div8x^3$ (c) $3(a^2)^3$ (d) $(3a^2)^3$
(e) $\left(\dfrac{2x^4}{3y^3}\right)^3$ (f) $\dfrac{2(x^3)^3}{(3x)^2}$ (g) $3^{-2}\div3^{-3}$ (h) 3^{-2}
(i) $49^{\frac{1}{2}}$ (j) $64^{\frac{1}{2}}$ (k) $3^2\times4^{-1}$ (l) $(35xy)^0$

7. Evaluate:
(a) $144^{\frac{1}{2}}$ (b) $8^{\frac{2}{3}}$ (c) $8^{-\frac{2}{3}}$
(d) $64^{\frac{2}{3}}$ (e) $256^{\frac{1}{2}}$ (f) $256^{\frac{1}{4}}$
(g) $256^{\frac{3}{4}}$ (h) $16^{\frac{3}{2}}$ (i) $27^{-\frac{2}{3}}$

8. Evaluate using logarithms.
(a) 6.28×5.36 (b) 68.5×41.2 (c) 0.375×4.16
(d) $38.5\div2.75$ (e) $0.425\div2.17$ (f) $6.37\div0.0425$
(g) $\sqrt{58.6}$ (h) $\sqrt[3]{0.004\,265}$ (i) $\sqrt[5]{0.007\,265}$
(j) 3.14×5.65^2 (k) $\dfrac{6.375}{4.125\times5.875}$ (l) $\dfrac{4.175\times63.25}{115.2}$

C **9.** Evaluate using logarithms:

(a) $\dfrac{\sqrt{4.375}}{6.142\times41.85}$ (b) $\sqrt{\dfrac{42.55\times0.7125}{864.3}}$

(c) $\dfrac{(4.275)^2}{\sqrt{184.3}}$ (d) $\dfrac{65.78}{\sqrt{45.75\times127.3}}$

FOUCAULT'S PENDULUM

In 1851 the French physicist Leon
Foucault demonstrated a method to
illustrate the rotation of the earth. He
suspended a pendulum on a thin wire
from an 8 m ceiling, so the pendulum
could swing freely (with minimum
friction) in any vertical plane through
the suspension point. As the earth
rotated, so the floor of the room
appeared to move relative to the
pendulum, which kept swinging in the
same fixed plane in space. (The same
experiment will work in a high-ceilinged
classroom.)

At the north pole, the only significant
force acting on such a pendulum would
be the vertical pull of gravity. The earth
would rotate under the fixed plane of
the pendulum so as to make one
revolution in 24 h in an anticlockwise
direction (viewed from above). To an
observer in the room the plane of the
pendulum would appear to rotate in a
clockwise direction relative to the floor
at 360° in 24 h or 15°/h.

At the equator, on the other hand,
the plane of motion of the pendulum
would not change relative to the floor
of the room, since the meridian of
longitude passing through the room
would maintain a fixed direction in
space.

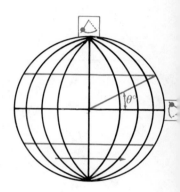

At other latitudes we would expect a
rate of change of the plane of swing
somewhere between the polar value
(15°/h) and the equatorial rate (0°/h). In
fact, at a latitude of $\theta°$, the plane of
swing moves relative to the floor at a
rate of 15 sin θ degrees per hour. In
Paris, where Foucault first used this
method, the latitude is 44.23°N, so the
pendulum plane changed relative to the
floor at 15 sin 44.23° = 10.5°/h.

It can be seen from the figure that
the meridians of longitude are parallel
to each other at the equator but not
elsewhere. The movement of the plane
of the swing of such a pendulum is
thus a direct consequence of the earth's
rotation.

If you performed this experiment in
your classroom, how far would you
expect the pendulum to appear to
rotate during the school day? You can
find the latitude of your school by
looking in an atlas.

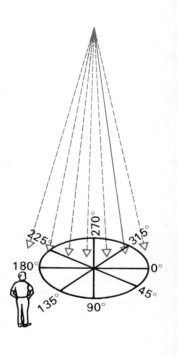

EXERCISE 1

Calculate the values of x and y.

1.

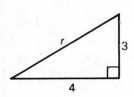

2.

3.

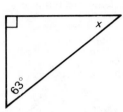

4.

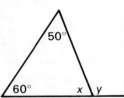

5.

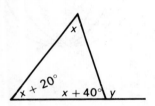

6.

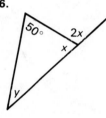

7.

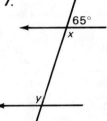

8.

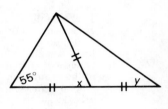

EXERCISE 2

Use the theorem of Pythagoras to find the values of the variables.

1.

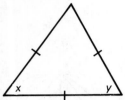

2.

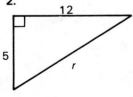

3.

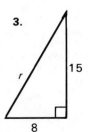

4.

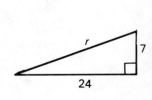

5.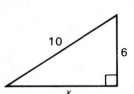

6.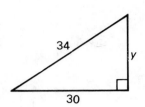

7.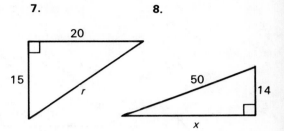

8.

EXERCISE 3

State the value of the trigonometric ratios for $\angle\theta$ in each of the following.

1.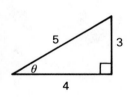

2.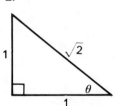

3.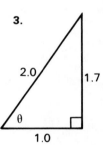

4.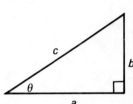

5.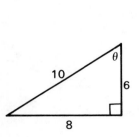

6.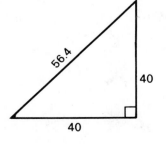

7.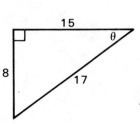

8.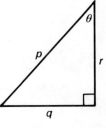

EXERCISE 4

Solve for x:

1. $\dfrac{x}{5} = \dfrac{9}{7}$ **2.** $\dfrac{x}{24} = \dfrac{11}{18}$ **3.** $\dfrac{x}{32} = \dfrac{47}{50}$ **4.** $\dfrac{x}{6.5} = \dfrac{3.7}{2.8}$

5.

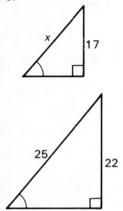

6. **7.** **8.**

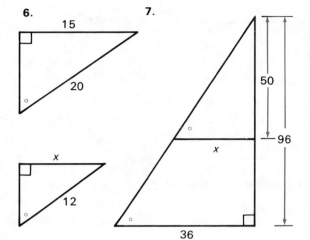

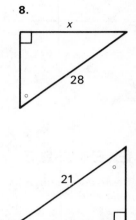

Evaluate the following;

1. $(1.225)^2$ **2.** $(0.037\ 51)^4$

3. $(62.35)^3$ **4.** $(2.375)^4 + (3.125)^3$

5. $(6.275)^2 + (6.125)^3$ **6.** $(3.125)^3(0.875)^2$

7. $\dfrac{(64.35)^2}{(4.125)^3}$ **8.** $\dfrac{6.375 \times (4.275)^3}{(2.375)^6}$

9. $\dfrac{(3.875)^3(4.125)^2}{(6.345)^4}$ **10.** $\dfrac{(8.625)^2(0.6755)^4}{(1.275)^3}$

Trigonometry

The word trigonometry means "measurement of triangles" and is derived from Greek. Today, trigonometry continues to grow in importance not only in the space program but also in the day-to-day work of skilled machinists, draftsmen, and other technologists. Trigonometry is also a valuable aid in the study of cycles such as those of the tides and of certain economic data.

9.1 SOLVING RIGHT TRIANGLES

Addition: MOON
          MEN
          CAN
          REACH

In Figure 9-1, θ is an acute angle of the right triangle.

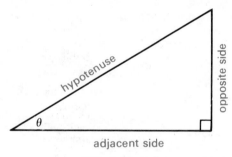

Figure 9-1

For θ in the right triangle, we can define the six trigonometric functions:

(i) The Primary Trigonometric Functions:

$$\text{sine of } \theta \dots \sin \theta = \frac{\text{opposite side}}{\text{hypotenuse}}$$

$$\text{cosine of } \theta \dots \cos \theta = \frac{\text{adjacent side}}{\text{hypotenuse}}$$

$$\text{tangent of } \theta \dots \tan \theta = \frac{\text{opposite side}}{\text{adjacent side}}$$

$$\frac{\text{opp}}{\text{hyp}}$$

$$\frac{\text{adj}}{\text{hyp}}$$

$$\frac{\text{opp}}{\text{adj}}$$

The values of these functions are determined by the indicated angle θ so that if we had another right triangle with the same acute angle θ, the triangles would be similar and the sides would be in the same proportion.

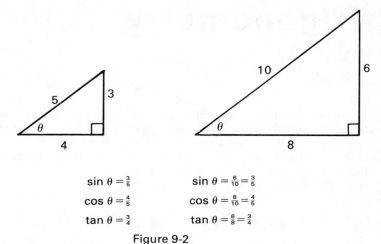

$$\sin \theta = \tfrac{3}{5}$$ $$\sin \theta = \tfrac{6}{10} = \tfrac{3}{5}$$

$$\cos \theta = \tfrac{4}{5}$$ $$\cos \theta = \tfrac{8}{10} = \tfrac{4}{5}$$

$$\tan \theta = \tfrac{3}{4}$$ $$\tan \theta = \tfrac{6}{8} = \tfrac{3}{4}$$

Figure 9-2

In Figure 9-2 we have two similar triangles demonstrating that the values of the primary functions are completely determined by the angles and are independent of the lengths of the sides.

By inverting the primary functions we get the remaining three trigonometric functions:

$\dfrac{\text{hyp}}{\text{opp}}$

$\dfrac{\text{hyp}}{\text{adj}}$

$\dfrac{\text{adj}}{\text{opp}}$

(ii) The Reciprocal Trigonometric Functions:

$$\text{cosecant of } \theta \ldots \csc \theta = \frac{\text{hypotenuse}}{\text{opposite side}}$$

$$\text{secant of } \theta \ldots \sec \theta = \frac{\text{hypotenuse}}{\text{adjacent side}}$$

$$\text{cotangent of } \theta \ldots \cot \theta = \frac{\text{adjacent side}}{\text{opposite side}}$$

In Figure 9-3, $\triangle ABC$ is a right triangle with $\angle C = 90°$. Notice that the side CB, whose length is a, is opposite the vertex A. Similarly, b is opposite the vertex B. A can represent the angle at vertex A if the meaning is clear.

Thus, in $\triangle ABC$:

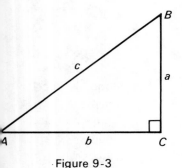

Figure 9-3

$\sin A = \dfrac{a}{c}$	$\cos A = \dfrac{b}{c}$	$\tan A = \dfrac{a}{b}$
$\sin B = \dfrac{b}{c}$	$\cos B = \dfrac{a}{c}$	$\tan B = \dfrac{b}{a}$
$\csc A = \dfrac{c}{a}$	$\sec A = \dfrac{c}{b}$	$\cot A = \dfrac{b}{a}$
$\csc B = \dfrac{c}{b}$	$\sec B = \dfrac{c}{a}$	$\cot B = \dfrac{a}{b}$
where $c = \sqrt{a^2 + b^2}$		

applied mathematics for today: senior

We say that a triangle is solved when we can state the lengths of the three sides and the measures of the three angles.

EXAMPLE 1. *In* $\triangle ABC$, *$\angle C = 90°$, $b = 2.5$ cm and $\angle A = 42°$. Solve the triangle by finding $\angle B$, a and c.*

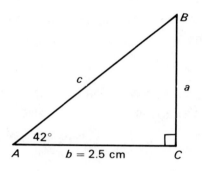

The birth certificates of John and Sally are correct and show that John was born earlier than Sally. Nevertheless, Sally is older. Explain.

Solution

(i) $\angle B = 90° - 42° = 48°$

(ii) $\dfrac{a}{2.5} = \tan 42°$

$$a = 2.5 \times \tan 42°$$
$$\doteq 2.5 \times 0.9004 \qquad \text{(from tables)}$$
$$\doteq 2.3$$

(iii) $c^2 = a^2 + b^2$ $\qquad\qquad \dfrac{c}{2.5} = \sec 42°$

$\quad = (2.3)^2 + (2.5)^2$

$\quad = 5.29 + 6.25 \qquad$ **OR** $\qquad c = 2.5 \times \sec 42°$

$\quad = 11.54 \qquad\qquad\qquad\quad \doteq 2.5 \times 1.3456$

$c \doteq 3.4 \qquad\qquad\qquad\qquad\quad \doteq 3.4$

$\therefore \angle B = 48°$, $a \doteq 2.3$ cm, and $c \doteq 3.4$ cm.

EXAMPLE 2. *In* $\triangle ABC$, *$\angle B = 90°$, $c = 3.2$ cm and $b = 5.3$ cm. Solve the triangle.*

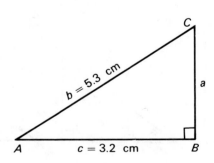

Solution

(i) $\sin C = \dfrac{3.2}{5.3}$

$\qquad \doteq 0.6038$

$\left.\begin{array}{l} \sin 37° \doteq 0.6018 \\ \sin 38° \doteq 0.6157 \end{array}\right\}$ from tables

$\angle C \doteq 37°$

$\angle A \doteq 90° - 37°$ $\qquad$ (to the nearest degree)

$\qquad \doteq 53°$

(ii) $\qquad \dfrac{a}{5.3} = \cos 37°$ $\qquad\qquad a^2 = b^2 - c^2$

$\qquad a = 5.3 \times \cos 37°$ $\qquad$ OR $\qquad = (5.3)^2 - (3.2)^2$

$\qquad \doteq 5.3 \times 0.7986$ $\qquad\qquad = 28.09 - 10.24$

$\qquad \doteq 4.2$ $\qquad\qquad\qquad = 17.85$

$\qquad\qquad\qquad\qquad\qquad a \doteq 4.2$

$\therefore \angle C \doteq 37°$, $\angle A \doteq 53$, and $a \doteq 4.2$ cm.

EXERCISE 9-1

A **1.** State the six trigonometric ratios for the angle labelled θ in the following triangles.

(a) $\qquad\qquad\qquad$ (b) $\qquad\qquad\qquad$ (c)

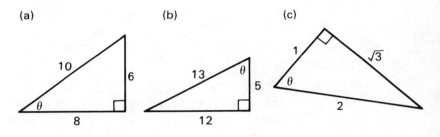

(d) $\qquad\qquad\qquad$ (e) $\qquad\qquad\qquad$ (f)

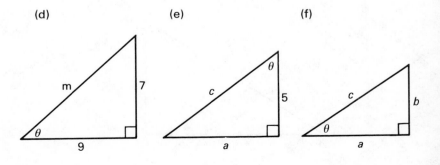

B **2.** Find the length of the side labelled x in each of the following.

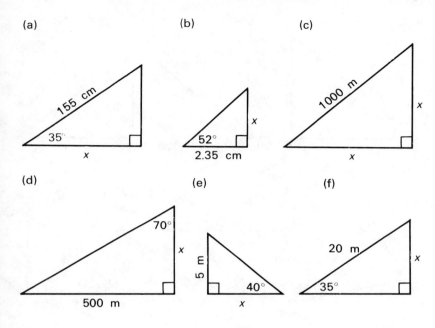

(a)

155 cm
35°
x

(b)

52°
2.35 cm
x

(c)

1000 m
x
x

(d)

70°
500 m
x

(e)

5 m
40°
x

(f)

20 m
35°
x

Continue the Table

1	1	1
2	2	2
3	4	4
4	8	7
5	15	11
6		16
7		

3. Find ∠θ to the nearest degree in each of the following.

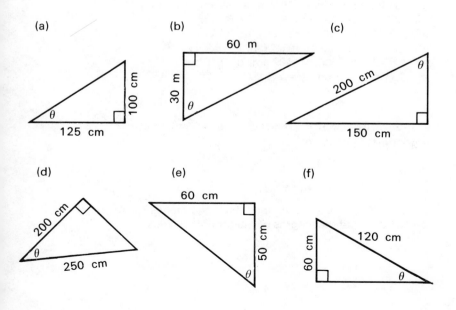

(a)

100 cm
θ
125 cm

(b)

60 m
30 m
θ

(c)

200 cm
θ
150 cm

(d)

200 cm
θ
250 cm

(e)

60 cm
50 cm
θ

(f)

120 cm
60 cm
θ

4. Solve the following triangles:

(a)

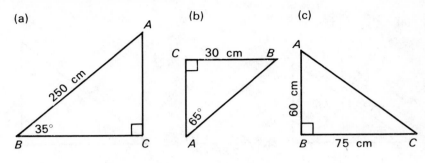

(b)

(c)

(d)

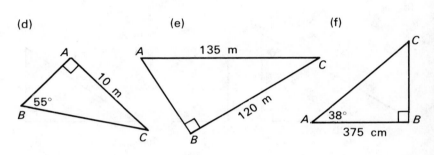

(e)

(f)

5. Make reasonably accurate diagrams, then solve the following triangles.
(a) $\triangle ABC$, $\angle B = 90°$, $c = 35$ cm, $a = 42$ cm
(b) $\triangle DEF$, $\angle E = 90°$, $f = 48$ cm, $e = 61$ cm
(c) $\triangle PQR$, $\angle P = 90°$, $r = 58$ cm, $p = 67$ cm
(d) $\triangle ABC$, $\angle A = 90°$, $c = 675$ cm, $a = 857$ cm
(e) $\triangle STU$, $\angle S = 90°$, $t = 487$ cm, $u = 518$ cm
(f) $\triangle XYZ$, $x = 70$ cm, $y = 240$ cm, $z = 250$ cm

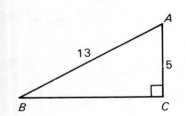

6. In $\triangle ABC$, $\sin B = \frac{5}{13}$ and $\angle C = 90°$. Find the trigonometric ratios of $\angle A$ and $\angle B$.

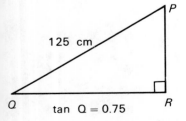

7. In $\triangle PQR$, $\tan Q = 0.75$ and the hypotenuse $r = 125$ cm. Find the lengths of the other two sides.

applied mathematics for today: senior

8. Solve the following triangles.

(a)

(b)

(c)

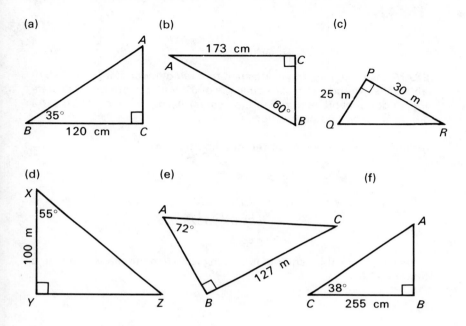

(d)

(e)

(f)

9. Find x in each of the following.

(a)

(b)

(c)

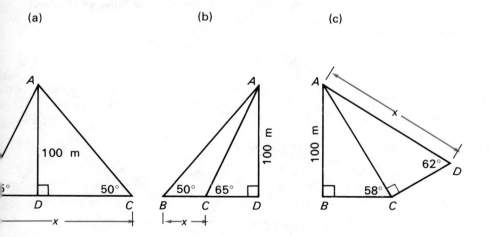

9.2 PROBLEMS INVOLVING RIGHT TRIANGLES

EXAMPLE 1. *A guy line is attached to a radio tower at a point 75.5 m above the ground and makes an angle of 62° with the ground. Calculate the length of cable required to the nearest 0.5 m, and include an extra 1.5 m for each end connection.*

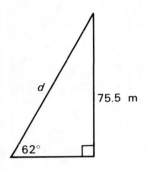

Solution   Let the length of the guy line be d m.

$$\frac{d}{75.5} = \csc 62°$$

$$d = 75.5 \times \csc 62°$$

$$\doteq 75.5 \times 1.1326$$

$$\doteq 85.5$$

∴ the length of cable required is 85.5 m plus 3.0 m for connections for a total of 88.5 m

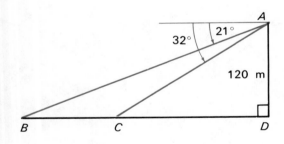

EXAMPLE 2.   *From the top of a 120 m cliff, two boats are observed in the same direction so that the angles of depression are 21° and 32° as shown in the diagram. Find the distance between the two boats.*

Solution

$$BC = BD - CD$$

In $\triangle ABD$, $\dfrac{BD}{120} = \cot 21°$ In $\triangle ACD$, $\dfrac{CD}{120} = \cot 32°$

$$BD = 120 \times \cot 21° \qquad\qquad CD = 120 \times \cot 32°$$

$$\doteq 120 \times 2.6051 \qquad\qquad\quad \doteq 120 \times 1.6003$$

$$\doteq 313 \qquad\qquad\qquad\qquad\quad \doteq 192$$

∴ $BC \doteq 313 - 192 \doteq 121$
The two boats are 121 m apart.

applied mathematics for today: senior

EXAMPLE 3. *A bridge 320 m long spans a valley. From the ends of the bridge, the angles of depression of an object on the ground below are 46° and 68°. Find the height of the bridge above the object.*

Solution We begin with a reasonably accurate diagram.

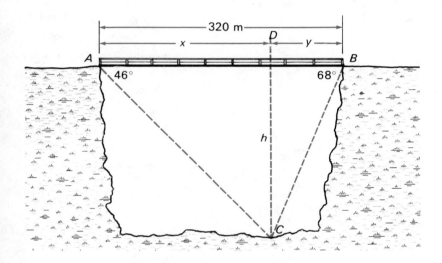

If a clock strikes 6 times in 5 s, how many times will it strike in 10 s?

Let the height of the bridge be *h* m and let us divide the bridge into sections *x* and *y* as in the diagram.

In $\triangle ADC$, $\dfrac{x}{h} = \cot 46°$ In $\triangle BDC$, $\dfrac{y}{h} = \cot 68°$

$$x = h \times \cot 46° \qquad\qquad y = h \times \cot 68°$$
$$\doteq h \times 0.9657 \qquad\qquad \doteq h \times 0.4040$$
$$\doteq 0.9657h \qquad\qquad\quad \doteq 0.4040h$$

Adding:
$$x + y \doteq 0.9657h + 0.4040h$$
$$\doteq 1.3697h$$

But $x + y = 320$
$$1.3697h = 320$$
$$h = \frac{320}{1.3697} \doteq 234$$

∴ the height of the bridge is 234 m.

Example 3 suggests the following derivation for a formula for the altitude of a triangle.

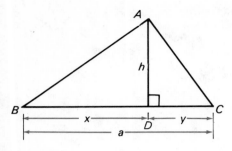

Figure 9-4

Referring to figure 9-4 in $\triangle ABD$,

$$\frac{x}{h} = \cot B \rightarrow x = h \cot B$$

In $\triangle ACD$,

$$\frac{y}{h} = \cot C \rightarrow y = h \cot C$$

Adding:

$$x + y = h \cot B + h \cot C$$
$$= h(\cot B + \cot C)$$
$$h(\cot B + \cot C) = x + y = a$$

$$\boxed{h = \frac{a}{\cot B + \cot C}}$$

The altitude from vertex A to the base BC

In some of the problems in the exercise the following terms will be used:

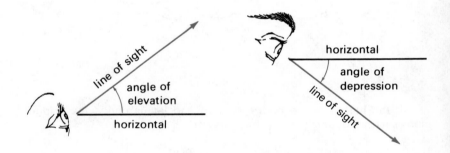

Addition: BEAVER
TIGER
RABBIT

The **angle of elevation** of an object which is above the observer is the angle which the line of sight makes with the horizontal. If the object is below the observer, then the angle which the line of sight makes with the horizontal is called the **angle of depression.**

EXERCISE 9-2

B **1.** The angle of elevation of the top of a building is 70° from a point 120 m from the foot of the building. Find the height of the building to the nearest metre.

2. From the top of a fire tower, the angle of depression of a cabin is observed to be 25°. Find the distance from the cabin to the foot of the tower if the tower is 200 m high.

3. A building casts a 57 m shadow when the elevation of the sun is 34°. Calculate to the nearest 0.5 m:
(a) the height of the building
(b) the length of the shadow when the elevation of the sun is 60°.

4. A 320 m guy wire makes an angle of 37° at the top of a communications tower. Calculate the height of the tower.

5. Find the length of cable required to secure a television tower 175 m high if the cable must make an angle of 28° at the top of the tower and 4 m are required for fastening.

6. From a point 120 m from the foot of a building, the angles of elevation of the top and bottom of the building's flagpole are 40° and 38° respectively. Calculate the height of
(a) the building
(b) the flagpole.

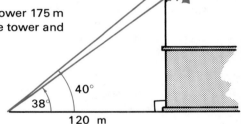

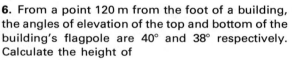

7. From the top of a cliff 110 m high the angles of depression of two small boats on the water are 9° and 15°. Calculate the distance
(a) from the foot of the cliff to the closer boat
(b) between the boats if they are sighted in the same direction.

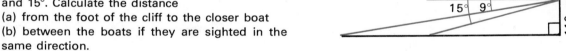

8. A ladder 15 m long is placed on level ground to reach a window 10 m above the ground.
(a) What angle does it make with the ground?
(b) How far is the foot of the ladder from the base of the building?

9. A ladder 15 m long is placed between two buildings in a driveway so that it reaches 12 m up on one building. If it is turned over, its foot being held in position, it will reach 8 m up on the other building. How wide is the driveway from building to building?

10. From an office window 30 m above level ground, a building 100 m tall at a distance of 200 m is observed across a courtyard. Find
(a) the angle of elevation of the top of the building.
(b) the angle of depression of its base.

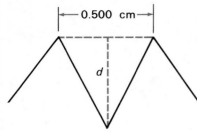

11. Calculate the depth of a sharp V-thread if the pitch of the thread is 5.00 mm.

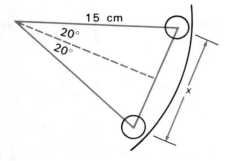

12. Calculate the distance between centres of two adjacent holes on a 300 mm bolt circle containing 9 holes.

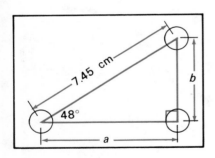

13. Three holes are to be located in a rectangular plate as shown. Find the dimensions a and b.

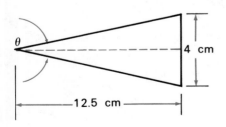

14. Find the indicated angle in the steel wedge as shown. Use a right triangle.

15. Calculations for tapers are similar to those for wedges. Calculate the angles marked *A* and *B* to the nearest degree for the conical taper to be turned on a lathe.

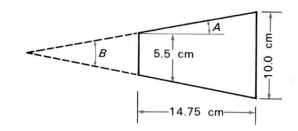

16. Calculate the length of the slot to be milled in the given plate.

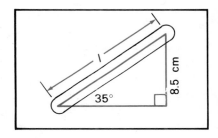

17. Calculate the chordal distance between centres of two adjacent holes on a five-hole bolt circle with diameter 340 mm.

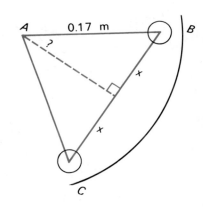

18. If the length of the hole *MN* is 50 mm and the hole is at an angle of 62°, calculate the thickness of the material *AC*.

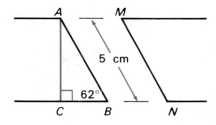

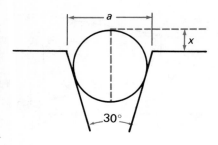

19. The diagram is a partial view of the Acme thread (or Worm). The diameter of the circle is 40.0 mm. If $a = 45.0$ mm, find the dimension x.

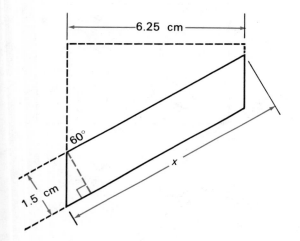

20. Calculate the dimension x in the given diagram.

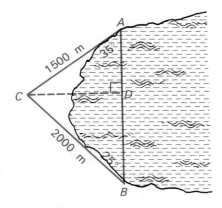

C **21.** From two points A and B on the opposite sides of a bay, the distances to a point C were measured and found to be 1500 m and 2000 m respectively. If $\angle A = 35°$ and $\angle B = 25°$, find the distance AB across the bay.

22. A surveyor wishes to find the height *BC* of an inaccessible cliff. To do this, he sets up his transit at *A*, and measures ∠*CAB* = 32°. He then lays off a base line *AD* so that ∠*BAD* = 90° and *AD* = 50 m. He measures ∠*ADB* = 58°. Calculate the height of the cliff.

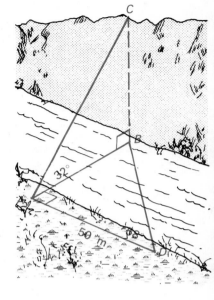

23. A cylindrical tank with a diameter of 3 m is rolled up a 15° incline. When the point of contact of the tank is 4 m from the start of the incline, what is the height of the centre of the tank from the base of the incline.

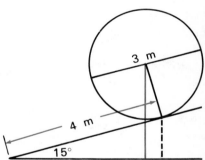

24. Find the height of a mountain if the angle of elevation of the summit from opposite ends of a 2.7 km tunnel are 48° and 62° (assume the tunnel is straight).

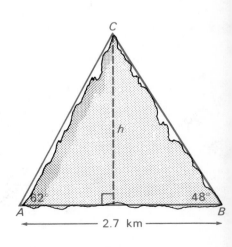

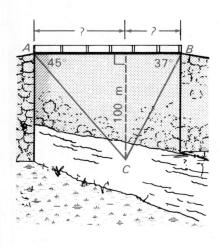

25. From the ends of a bridge the angles of depression of a marker buoy on the water are 45° and 37°. Find the length of the bridge if it is known that the bridge is 100 m above the water.

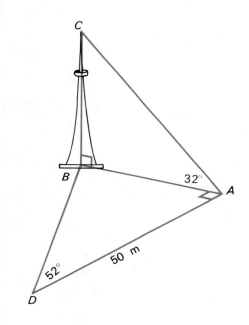

26. To determine the height of an inaccessible tower, readings as shown in the diagram were taken. △ABC is in the vertical plane and ∠A = 32°. △ABD is in the horizontal plane, with the baseline AD = 50 m, ∠ADB = 52° and ∠DAB = 90°. Calculate the height of the tower BC.

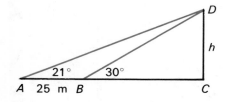

27. From two points A and B, in the same vertical plane as a tower, the angles of elevation are 21° and 30° respectively. Calculate CD, the height of the tower, if A and B are 25 m apart.

applied mathematics for today: senior

28. Two guy wires *AC* and *BC* secure a tower *CD*, making angles of 58° and 62° with the level ground. If *A* and *B* are 47 m apart, calculate the height of the tower.

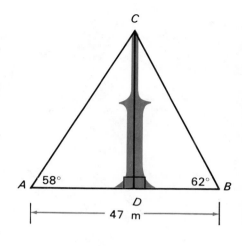

29. From a 100 m baseline *AB*, the angles of sight to a point *C* on the opposite shore of a river are 71° and 43° as shown in the diagram. Calculate the width of the river.

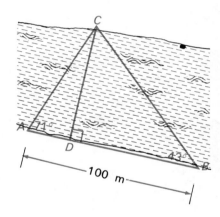

30. From the top of a lighthouse *CD*, the angles of depression of two small boats *A* and *B* in the same vertical plane are 15° and 21°. How far apart are the boats if the observer is 30 m above water level.

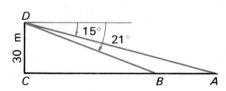

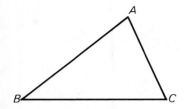

9.3 THE LAW OF SINES

Triangles that do not contain a right angle are called oblique triangles. In solving right triangles, three of the six parts (3 angles, 3 sides) of the triangle were given and the remaining three parts could be found using trigonometric ratios. In this section, we will solve oblique triangles using a general formula—the law of sines.

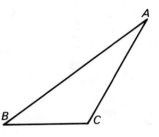

(i) Acute Triangle

(ii) Obtuse Triangle

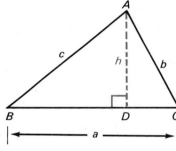

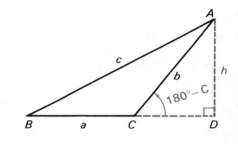

$\sin (180° - C)$
$= \sin C$

In $\triangle ACD$, $\dfrac{h}{b} = \sin C$

$h = b \sin C$

In $\triangle ABD$, $\dfrac{h}{c} = \sin B$

$h = c \sin B$

In $\triangle ACD$, $\dfrac{h}{b} = \sin (180° - C)$

$= \sin C$

$h = b \sin C$

In $\triangle ABD$, $\dfrac{h}{c} = \sin B$

$h = c \sin B$

For both the acute and obtuse triangles:

$$b \sin C = c \sin B$$

$$\frac{b}{\sin B} = \frac{c}{\sin C}$$

By drawing the altitude from C, we have

$$\frac{a}{\sin A} = \frac{b}{\sin B}$$

applied mathematics for today: senior

The results are the same for both the acute and obtuse triangles:

$$\frac{a}{\sin A} = \frac{b}{\sin B} = \frac{c}{\sin C} \quad \text{or} \quad \frac{\sin A}{a} = \frac{\sin B}{b} = \frac{\sin C}{c}$$

EXAMPLE 1. *In* $\triangle ABC$, $\angle A = 78°$, $\angle B = 68°$, *and* $a = 5.9$ cm. *Find* c.

Solution

$$\angle C = 180° - (78° + 68°)$$
$$= 34°$$
$$\frac{c}{\sin C} = \frac{a}{\sin A}$$
$$c = \frac{a \sin C}{\sin A}$$
$$\doteq \frac{5.9 \times 0.5592}{0.9782}$$
$$\doteq 3.4$$

The length of c is 3.4 cm.

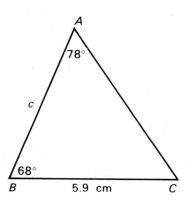

$$\frac{p}{q} = \frac{r}{s}$$
$$p = \frac{rq}{s}$$

EXAMPLE 2. *In* $\triangle ABC$, $c = 3.3$ cm, $\angle C = 36°$, *and* $a = 5.4$ cm. *Find* $\angle A$, *given that* $\triangle ABC$ *is acute*.

Solution

$$\frac{\sin A}{a} = \frac{\sin C}{c}$$
$$\sin A = \frac{a \sin C}{c}$$
$$\doteq \frac{5.4 \times 0.5878}{3.3}$$
$$\doteq 0.9619$$
$$A \doteq 74°$$

If example 2 had stated that the triangle was obtuse, then we would have used the $\sin (180° - \theta) = \sin \theta$ relationship, and

$$A \doteq 180° - 74°$$
$$\doteq 106°$$

EXAMPLE 3. *In* $\triangle ABC$, $\angle B = 28°$, $\angle C = 116°$, *and* $a = 31.2$ cm. *Find c.*

Solution

sin 116°
= sin (180°−116°)
= sin 64°

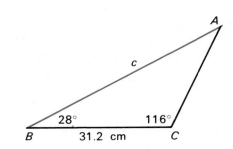

$$\frac{c}{\sin C} = \frac{a}{\sin A}$$

$$c = \frac{a \sin C}{\sin A}$$

$$\doteq \frac{31.2 \times 0.8988}{0.5878}$$

$$\doteq 47.7$$

The length of c is 47.7 cm.

EXERCISE 9-3

B **1.** Find the indicated side in each of the following:

(a)   (b)   (c)

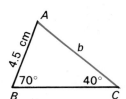
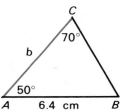
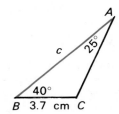

Starting with the word "hall" and changing 1 letter at a time, can you reach the word "feet" in 4 changes?

hall
1.
2.
3.
4. feet

2. In each of the following, make a reasonably accurate diagram and use the *law of sines* to find the required side.
(a) In $\triangle ABC$, $\angle A = 25°$, $\angle C = 85°$, $a = 15$ cm. Find b.
(b) In $\triangle ABC$, $\angle B = 40°$, $\angle C = 72°$, $b = 9.7$ cm. Find a.
(c) In $\triangle ABC$, $\angle B = 70°$, $\angle C = 75°$, $a = 53$ cm. Find b.
(d) In $\triangle ABC$, $\angle A = 105°$, $\angle B = 25°$, $a = 9.2$ cm. Find c.
(e) In $\triangle ABC$, $\angle A = 25°$, $\angle B = 20°$, $a = 25$ cm. Find b.

3. Solve the following triangles.
(a)   (b)   (c)

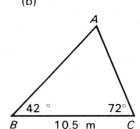
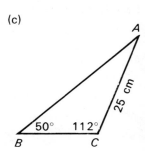

applied mathematics for today: senior

(d) $\triangle ABC$, $c = 40$ cm, $\angle B = 48°$, $\angle C = 63°$

(e) $\triangle ABC$, $a = 7.5$ cm, $\angle B = 32°$, $\angle C = 104°$

9.4 THE LAW OF COSINES

When an oblique triangle with two sides and the contained angle (*SAS*), or three sides (*SSS*), is given, we use the law of cosines.

(i) Acute Triangle   (ii) Obtuse Triangle

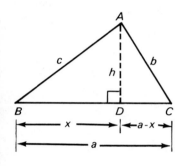

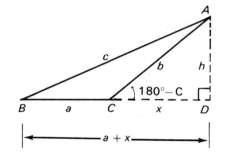

$\cos(180° - c)$
$= -\cos C$

In $\triangle ABD$, $\dfrac{x}{c} = \cos B$ In $\triangle ACD$, $\dfrac{x}{b} = \cos(180° - C)$

$x = c \cos B$ $x = b \cos(180° - C)$

and $c^2 = h^2 + x^2$ $= -b \cos C$

                            and $b^2 = h^2 + x^2$

In $\triangle ACD$, $b^2 = h^2 + (a - x)^2$ In $\triangle ABD$, $c^2 = h^2 + (a + x)^2$

$= h^2 + a^2 - 2ax + x^2$ $= h^2 + a^2 + 2ax + x^2$

$= a^2 + (h^2 + x^2) - 2ax$ $= a^2 + (h^2 + x^2) + 2ax$

                               $= a^2 + b^2 + 2a(-b \cos C)$

$\boxed{b^2 = a^2 + c^2 - 2ac \cos B}$ $\boxed{c^2 = a^2 + b^2 - 2ab \cos C}$

Similarly $\boxed{\begin{array}{l} c^2 = a^2 + b^2 - 2ab \cos C \\ a^2 = b^2 + c^2 - 2bc \cos A \end{array}}$ Similarly $\boxed{\begin{array}{l} a^2 = b^2 + c^2 - 2bc \cos A \\ b^2 = a^2 + c^2 - 2ac \cos B \end{array}}$

EXAMPLE 1. *In $\triangle ABC$, $a = 61.6$ cm, $\angle B = 36°$, and $c = 55.5$ cm. Find b.*

Solution

$b^2 = a^2 + c^2 - 2ac \cos B$

$b^2 \doteq (61.6)^2 + (55.5)^2 - 2(61.6)(55.5)(0.809)$

$\doteq 3795 + 3080 - 5532$

$\doteq 1343$

$b \doteq \sqrt{1343}$

$\doteq 36.6$

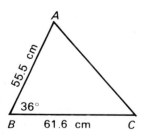

∴ the length of b is 36.6 cm.

EXAMPLE 2. *In* △*ABC*, *a* = 49.8 cm, *b* = 36.3 cm, *and* *c* = 72.4 cm. *Find* ∠*C*.

Solution

$$c^2 = a^2 + b^2 - 2ab \cos C$$
$$2ab \cos C = a^2 + b^2 - c^2$$
$$\cos C = \frac{a^2 + b^2 - c^2}{2ab}$$

$$\cos C = \frac{a^2 + b^2 - c^2}{2ab}$$

$$\cos C = \frac{(49.8)^2 + (36.3)^2 - (72.4)^2}{2(49.8)(36.3)}$$

$$\doteq \frac{2480 + 1318 - 5242}{2(49.8)(36.3)}$$

$$\doteq -0.3994$$

$$\cos 66 \doteq 0.4067 \text{ and } \cos 67° = 0.3907$$

$$\angle C \doteq 180° - 66°$$

$$\doteq 114°$$

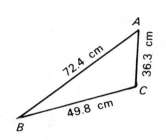

EXERCISE 9-4

B   **1.** Find the indicated side in the following:

(a)

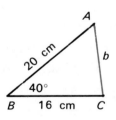

(b)

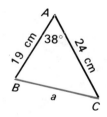

(c)

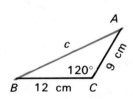

A 3 cm × 3 cm × 3 cm cube is painted red on all of its faces. It is then cut into 1 cm × 1 cm × 1 cm cubes. How many of these cubes will be red on
(i) 3 faces?
(ii) 2 faces?
(iii) 1 face?

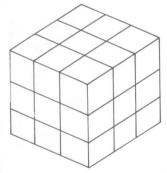

2. Find the indicated angle in the following:

(a)

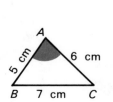

(b)

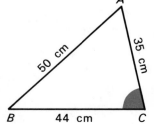

(c)

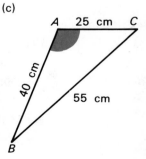

3. For each of the following, make a reasonably accurate diagram and use the law of cosines to find the required value.
(a) In $\triangle ABC$, $a = 55.5$ cm, $c = 50.5$ cm, and $\angle B = 43°$. Find b.
(b) In $\triangle ABC$, $a = 90$ cm, $c = 100$ cm, and $\angle B = 125°$. Find b.
(c) In $\triangle ABC$, $a = 65$ cm, $b = 45$ cm, $c = 55$ cm. Find $\angle A$.
(d) In $\triangle ABC$, $a = 500$ cm, $b = 460$ cm, $c = 810$ cm. Find $\angle C$.

9.5 PROBLEMS INVOLVING OBLIQUE TRIANGLES.

The six trigonometric ratios cannot be applied directly to oblique triangles because there is no right angle. Formulas that have been developed in previous sections, and the suggested approaches are summarized in the table below.

Given		Formula	You can calculate
ASA	Sine law	$\dfrac{a}{\sin A} = \dfrac{b}{\sin B} = \dfrac{c}{\sin C}$	Side
SAS	Cosine law	$a^2 = b^2 + c^2 - 2bc \cos A$ $b^2 = a^2 + c^2 - 2ac \cos B$ $c^2 = a^2 + b^2 - 2ab \cos C$	Side
SSS	Cosine law	$\cos A = \dfrac{b^2 + c^2 - a^2}{2bc}$ $\cos B = \dfrac{a^2 + c^2 - b^2}{2ac}$ $\cos C = \dfrac{a^2 + b^2 - c^2}{2ab}$	Angle
SSA	Sine law	$\dfrac{\sin A}{a} = \dfrac{\sin B}{b} = \dfrac{\sin C}{c}$	Angle *

* in the SSA case, additional information such as "the angle is acute" is often given where required to avoid having two solutions because $\sin(180° - \theta) = \sin \theta$. See example 2 in section 9.3.

EXERCISE 9-5

For each of the following problems complete a reasonably accurate diagram in your notebook marking on all given data, then find the required dimensions.

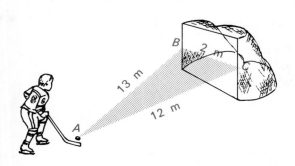

1. A hockey net is 2 m wide. A player shoots from a point where the puck is 13 m from one goal post and 12 m from the other. Within what angle must he make his shot to hit the net?

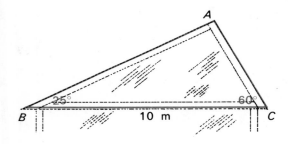

2. Football goal posts are measured and found to be 5.5 m apart. A player is to attempt a field goal from a point where the ball is 44 and 43 m from the ends of the goal posts. Within what angle must he kick the ball?

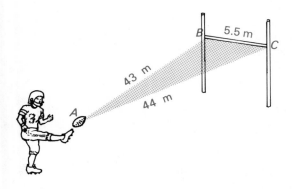

3. A greenhouse is 10 m wide and the rafters make angles of 25° and 60° with the joists. Make a diagram in your notebook and find the length of each type of rafter.

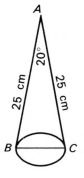

4. The vertical angle of a cone is 20°. Find the diameter of the cone at a point on the face 25 cm from the vertex.

5. Find the width of a small lake if from point B an angle of 61° is contained by the lengths 610 m and 560 m.

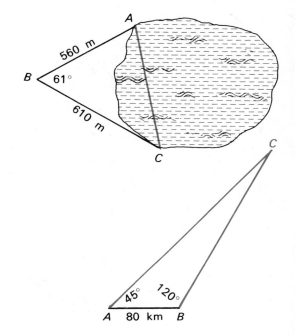

6. Town A is 80 km west of town B. The inclination of town C is 45° from A and 120° from B. Find the distances from A to C and B to C.

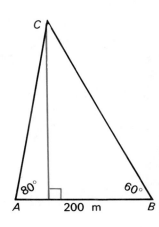

7. Along one bank of a river with parallel banks, a surveyor lays off a base line AB, 200 m long. From each end of the base line, he sights on an object C across the river. The lines of sight make angles of 60° and 80° with the base line. Find the width of the river.

8. Two highways diverge at 35° from point C. A third road, AB, is approximately 3.8 km long and joins the two highways as in the diagram, making an angle of 55° with one of the roads. How far are the A and B intersections from C?

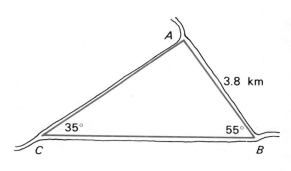

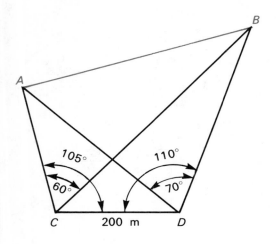

9. The perimeter of a triangle is 100 cm and the angles are in the ratio of 1:3:5. Find the length of each side.

10. In order to determine the distance between two inaccessible points A and B, a base line CD = 200 m was laid off. Angle measurements at C and D were made as follows: $\angle ACB = 60°$, $\angle ACD = 105°$, $\angle ADB = 70°$ and $\angle BDC = 110°$. Find the distance from A to B.

9.6   AREA OF A TRIANGLE

The area of a triangle has been calculated using the base and altitude (height) of the figure as

$$\triangle = \tfrac{1}{2}bh$$

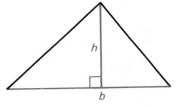

We can now develop formulas for the area of a triangle where the altitude h is not known.

(i) SAS (when two sides and the included angle are known)

In Figure 9-5, AD drawn perpendicular to BC or BC produced represents an altitude of $\triangle ABC$.

(a) Acute   (b) Obtuse

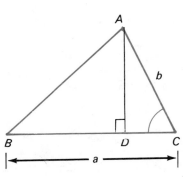

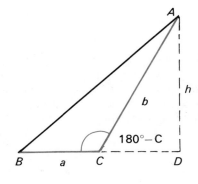

Figure 9-5

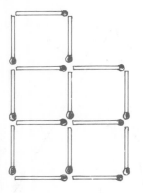

Remove 2 matches to leave 3 squares.

In △ACD,

(a) $\dfrac{h}{b}=\sin C$ (b) $\dfrac{h}{b}=\sin(180°-C)$

$\therefore\ h=b\sin C$ $h=b\sin(180°-C)$

$$= b\sin C$$

$$\sin(180°-C)$$
$$=\sin C$$

$$\triangle=\tfrac{1}{2}\times(\text{base})\times(\text{height})$$

$$\triangle ABC=\tfrac{1}{2}ah$$

$$=\tfrac{1}{2}ab\sin C$$

Thus the area of △ABC can be calculated using

$$\boxed{\begin{array}{l}\triangle=\tfrac{1}{2}ab\sin C \\ \triangle=\tfrac{1}{2}ac\sin B \\ \text{or }\ \triangle=\tfrac{1}{2}bc\sin A\end{array}}$$

depending on which pair of sides contain the given angle. Since $\sin(180°-C)=\sin C$, this formula holds for either acute or obtuse triangles.

EXAMPLE 1. *Find the area of △ABC, given that $\angle B=32°$, $AB=26.3$ m and $BC=31.5$ m.*

Solution

$$\triangle=\tfrac{1}{2}ac\sin B$$

$$\triangle ABC \doteqdot \tfrac{1}{2}\times31.5\times26.3\times0.5299$$

$$\doteqdot 219$$

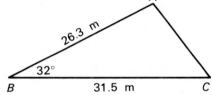

Therefore the area is 219 m².

(ii) AAS (when one side and any two angles are known)

(a) Acute   (b) Obtuse

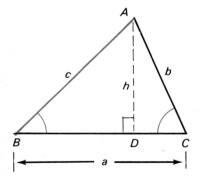 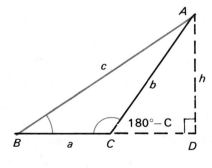

Figure 9-6

In Figure 9-6, AD represents an altitude of $\triangle ABC$.

In $\triangle ADC$

(a)

$$\frac{h}{b} = \sin C$$

$$\therefore \ h = b \sin C$$

In $\triangle ABD$,

$$\frac{h}{c} = \sin B$$

$$\therefore \ h = c \sin B$$

(b)

$$\frac{h}{b} = \sin(180° - C) = \sin C,$$

$$\therefore \ h = b \sin C$$

$$\frac{h}{c} = \sin B$$

$$\therefore \ h = c \sin B$$

$$b \sin C = c \sin B$$

$$b = \frac{c \sin B}{\sin C}$$

Using one of the SAS formulas,

$$\triangle = \tfrac{1}{2}bc \sin A$$

$$\triangle ABC = \tfrac{1}{2} \times \frac{c \sin B}{\sin C} \times c \sin A$$

$$\boxed{\triangle = \frac{c^2 \sin A \sin B}{2 \sin C}}$$

Similarly,

$$\boxed{\triangle = \frac{b^2 \sin A \sin C}{2 \sin B}}$$

$$\boxed{\triangle = \frac{a^2 \sin B \sin C}{2 \sin A}}$$

This formula can be used when you are given one side and any two angles, since the third angle can be found immediately.

EXAMPLE 2. Find the area of $\triangle ABC$, given that $\angle A = 28°$, $\angle B = 48°$, and $c = 125.7$ m.

Solution

$$\angle C = 180° - (\angle A + \angle B)$$

$$180° - (28° + 48°)$$

$$= 104°$$

$$\triangle = \frac{c^2 \sin A \sin B}{2 \sin C}$$

$$\triangle = \frac{(125.7)^2 \times \sin 28° \times \sin 48°}{2 \times \sin 104°}$$

$$\doteq \frac{(125.7)^2 \times 0.4695 \times 0.7431}{2 \times 0.9703}$$

$$\doteq 2841$$

Therefore the area of $\triangle ABC$ is 2841 m².

Starting with the words "four" and changing 1 letter at a time, can you reach "past" in 4 changes?

      four
1.
2.
3.
4. past

(iii) SSS (when three sides are known)

The area of a triangle whose three sides are known can be found using Heron's formula:

$$\triangle = \sqrt{s(s-a)(s-b)(s-c)}$$

where $s = \dfrac{a+b+c}{2}$

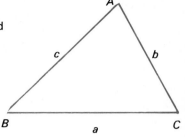

EXAMPLE 3. *Find the area of a triangle with sides 7.0 m, 8.0 m, and 9.0 m.*

Solution

$$a = 7.0, b = 8.0, c = 9.0 \qquad \triangle = \sqrt{s(s-a)(s-b)(s-c)}$$

$$s = \frac{a+b+c}{2}$$

$$\triangle = \sqrt{12(12-7)(12-8)(12-9)}$$

$$s = \frac{7.0+8.0+9.0}{2}$$

$$= \sqrt{12 \times 5 \times 4 \times 3}$$

$$= \frac{24.0}{2} = 12.0 \qquad\qquad = \sqrt{720} \doteq 27$$

Therefore the area of the triangle is 27 m².

HERON'S FORMULA

Heron (or Hero) of Alexandria, a Greek mathematician and natural philosopher, lived approximately 2000 years ago. He is credited with the invention of several machines, among which are "Hero's fountain" and a steam engine on a principle similar to that of a rotary lawn sprinkler. It is said that he was once presented with the problem of calculating the area of a triangular piece of land without entering the plot to make measurements—the only measurements he could make were the length of the three sides.

PROOF OF HERON'S FORMULA

In $\triangle ABD$ and $\triangle ADC$,

$$b^2 = h^2 + (a-x)^2 \qquad (1)$$

$$c^2 = h^2 + x^2 \qquad (2)$$

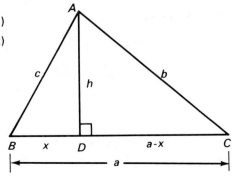

Subtracting,

$$b^2 - c^2 = (a - x)^2 - x^2$$

$$a^2 - 2ax$$

$$2ax = a^2 - b^2 + c^2$$

$$x = \frac{a^2 - b^2 + c^2}{2a} \qquad (3)$$

From (2), we have

$$h^2 = c^2 - x^2$$

$$= [c - x][c + x]. \qquad (4)$$

Substituting (3) in (4), we have

$$h^2 = \left[c - \frac{a^2 - b^2 + c^2}{2a} \right]\left[c + \frac{a^2 - b^2 + c^2}{2a} \right]$$

$$= \left[\frac{2ac - a^2 + b^2 - c^2}{2a} \right]\left[\frac{2ac + a^2 - b^2 + c^2}{2a} \right]$$

$$= \left[\frac{b^2 - (a - c)^2}{2a} \right]\left[\frac{(a + c)^2 - b^2}{2a} \right]$$

$$= \left[\frac{(a + b - c)(-a + b + c)}{2a} \right]\left[\frac{(a + b + c)(a - b + c)}{2a} \right]$$

Multiplying both sides by $\frac{1}{4}a^2$, we have

$$\tfrac{1}{4}a^2h^2 = \tfrac{1}{4}a^2\left[\frac{(a + b - c)(-a + b + c)}{2a} \right]\left[\frac{(a + b + c)(a - b + c)}{2a} \right]$$

$$= \frac{(a + b + c)}{2} \cdot \frac{(-a + b + c)}{2} \cdot \frac{(a - b + c)}{2} \cdot \frac{(a + b - c)}{2}$$

If we let $a + b + c = 2s$, then $s = \dfrac{a + b + c}{2}$,

and $\dfrac{-a + b + c}{2} = s - a, \ \dfrac{a - b + c}{2} = s - b, \ \dfrac{a + b - c}{2} = s - c$

$$\tfrac{1}{4}a^2h^2 = s(s - a)(s - b)(s - c)$$

$$\tfrac{1}{2}ah = \sqrt{s(s - a)(s - b)(s - c)}$$

But $\triangle = \frac{1}{2}ah$, therefore

$$\triangle = \sqrt{s(s - a)(s - b)(s - c)}, \text{ where } s = \frac{a + b + c}{2}$$

The results of this section are summarized below.

Area of a Triangle:

Case	Diagram	Formula
base-height		$\triangle = \frac{1}{2}bh$
SAS		$\triangle = \frac{1}{2}bc \sin A$
ASA		$\triangle = \dfrac{a^2 \sin B \sin C}{2 \sin A}$
SSS		$\triangle = \sqrt{s(s-a)(s-b)(s-c)}$ $s = \dfrac{a+b+c}{2}$

EXERCISE 9-6

Find the area of each of the following triangles.

A **1.** (a) (b)

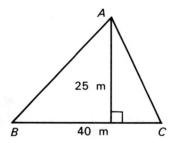

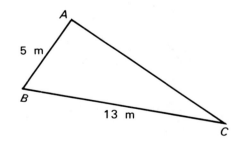

B **2.** (a)

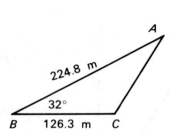

(b)

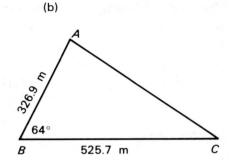

(c) △ABC, b = 32.80 m, c = 147.9 m, ∠A = 118°.
(d) △ABC, a = 3.125 m, ∠B = 72°, c = 2.375 m.
(e) △ABC, ∠A = 38°, b = 12.25 m, c = 14.50 m.

3. (a)

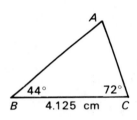

(b)

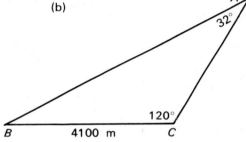

(c) △ABC, ∠A = 33°, ∠C = 76°, a = 5.530 m.
(d) △ABC, ∠A = 68°, b = 4500 m, ∠C = 45°.
(e) △ABC, a = 2000 m, ∠B = 119°, ∠C = 48°.

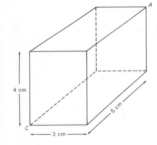

Find the distance from A
to C.

4. (a)

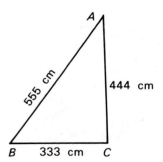

(b)

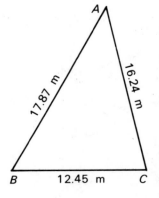

applied mathematics for today: senior

(c) △ABC, $a = 8.25$ m, $b = 12.75$ m, $c = 18.25$ m.
(d) △ABC, $a = 128.5$ cm, $b = 202.0$ cm, $c = 240.5$ m.
(e) △ABC, $a = 32.75$ m, $b = 46.25$ m, $c = 64.50$ m.

REVIEW EXERCISE

B   **1.** Find the length of the side labeled X in each of the following:

(a)

(b)

(c)

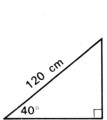

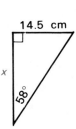

14.5 cm

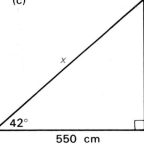

2. Find ∠θ to the nearest degree in each of the following:

(a)

(b)

(c)

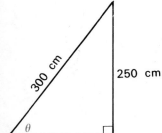

250 cm

100 cm

173 cm

100 cm

3. Make reasonably accurate diagrams, then solve the following triangles.
(a) △ABC, ∠A = 90°, $c = 45$ cm, $a = 55$ cm.
(b) △DEF, ∠D = 90°, $d = 65$ cm, $e = 48$ cm.
(c) △GHI, ∠I = 90°, ∠G = 52°, $i = 55$ cm.
(d) △JKL, ∠K = 90°, ∠L = 60°, $j = 200$ cm.

4. Find the area of each of the following triangles.
(a) △ABC, ∠A = 32°, $b = 175$ cm, $c = 145$ cm.
(b) △ABC, ∠A = 55°, ∠B = 75°, $c = 100$ cm.

5. Solve the following triangles:

(a)

(b)

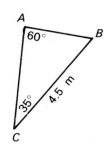

(c)

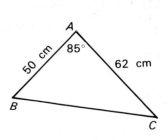

(d)

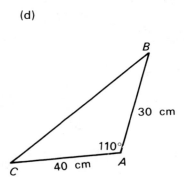

(e)

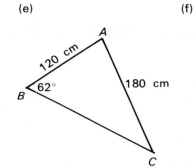

(f)

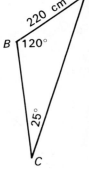

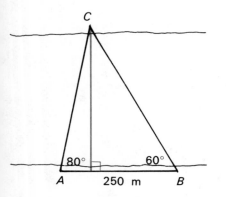

6. In order to find the distance across a river, two students measured a 250 m base line, *AB*, and the angles at *A* and *B* were found to be 80° and 60° respectively. Find the distance across the river.

7. A triangular plate has one side 45 cm and angles of 42° and 55° as in the diagram.
(a) Find the perimeter of the plate.
(b) Find the cost of grinding the edges at 8 cents for 3 cm.

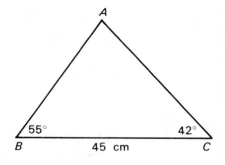

8. From two hilltops A and B, 5.7 km apart, a third hill C is sighted making angles of 63° and 78° at A and B as in the diagram. Find the distances from A to C and B to C.

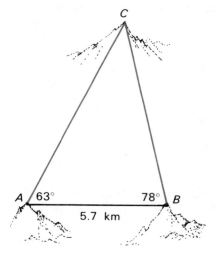

REVIEW AND PREVIEW TO CHAPTER 10

DEFINITIONS OF THE TRIGONOMETRIC FUNCTIONS

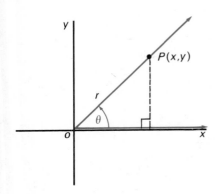

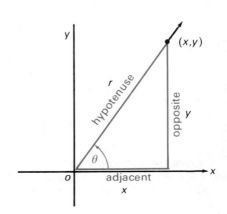

$$\sin \theta = \frac{y}{r}$$

$$\cos \theta = \frac{x}{r}$$

$$\tan \theta = \frac{y}{x}, \quad x \neq 0$$

$$\csc \theta = \frac{r}{y}, \quad y \neq 0$$

$$\sec \theta = \frac{r}{x}, \quad x \neq 0$$

$$\cot \theta = \frac{x}{y}, \quad y \neq 0$$

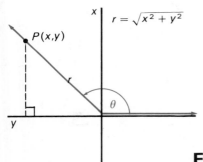

$$r = \sqrt{x^2 + y^2}$$

EXERCISE 1

Each point in the table below lies on the terminal arm of an angle θ in standard position. Make a diagram for each case, using $r = \sqrt{x^2 + y^2}$ to find r to three figures, and complete the table in your notebooks.

Point	(x, y)	(5, 12)	(−7, 24)	(−4, −4)	(3, −5)
r	$\sqrt{x^2 + y^2}$			5.66	
$\sin \theta$					−0.858
$\cos \theta$					
$\tan \theta$					
$\csc \theta$					
$\sec \theta$					
$\cot \theta$		0.417			

applied mathematics for today: senior

SPECIAL ANGLES

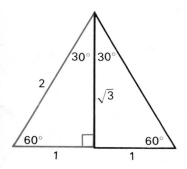

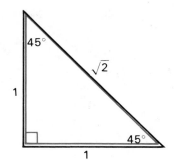

EXERCISE 2

1. Find the six trigonometric ratios for each of the following.

(a)

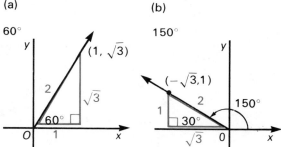

(b)

150°

(c)

45°

(d)

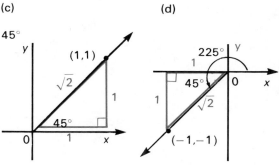

(e) 120°   (f) 30°   (g) 135°   (h) 315°   (i) 240°
Make your own diagrams for (e) to (i).

2. Find the six trigonometric ratios for each of the following.
(a)   (b)   (c)   (d)

0°

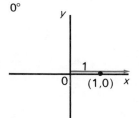

90°

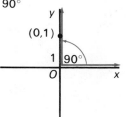

180°

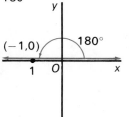

270°

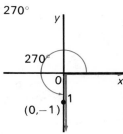

Solve for the indicated variables:

1. $\dfrac{x}{25.75} = \sin 47.5°$

2. $\dfrac{x}{28.35} = \tan 82.0°$

3. $\dfrac{x}{107.5} = \tan 53.5°$

4. $\dfrac{x}{0.5735} = \cos 8.5°$

5. $\dfrac{x}{2478} = \sin 81°$

6. $\sin \theta = \dfrac{1.271}{2.784}$

7. $\tan \theta = \dfrac{5.372}{2.712}$

8. $\cos \theta = \dfrac{54.95}{78.35}$

9. $\cos \theta = \dfrac{0.024\ 45}{0.087\ 54}$

10. $\tan \theta = \dfrac{38.57}{50.25}$

Trigonometric Functions

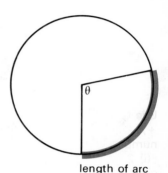

length of arc

Figure 10-1

10.1 RADIAN MEASURE

We have measured angles in degrees, where

$$1 \text{ revolution} = 360°$$

The measure of an angle can also be expressed in terms of the length of arc that subtends the angle at the centre of a circle as in Figure 10-1.

> An angle subtended at the centre of a circle by an arc equal in length to the radius has a measure of one radian.

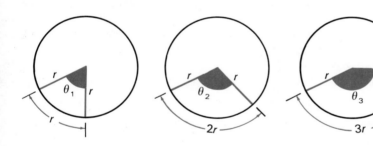

$\theta_1 = 1$ radian $\qquad\qquad$ $\theta_2 = 2$ radians $\qquad\qquad$ $\theta_3 = 3$ radians

Figure 10-2

The diagrams in Figure 10-2 suggest:

(a) $\theta_1 = \dfrac{r}{r} = 1$ $\qquad$ (b) $\theta_2 = \dfrac{2r}{r} = 2$ $\qquad$ (c) $\theta_3 = \dfrac{3r}{r} = 3$

This leads to the following generalization:

$$\theta = \frac{a}{r} \quad \text{or} \quad \text{Number of radians} = \frac{\text{arc length}}{\text{radius}}$$

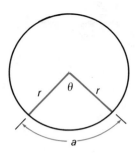

Since $\theta = \dfrac{a}{r}$, it follows that

$$a = r\theta, \qquad \theta > 0$$

Use the operations $\times$, $\div$, $+$, $-$ to form the following numbers:

(i) 24 using 3 identical digits.
(ii) 25 using 2 identical digits.
(iii) 100 using 5 identical digits.

where a, r, and θ are the measures of arc length, radius, and angle in radians respectively. Since the above expression for arc length holds for $\theta > 0$, this result can be generalized to

$$a = r|\theta|, \qquad \theta \in R$$

where $|\theta|$ is the absolute value or magnitude of θ.

It is often necessary to convert from degree measure to radian measure and vice versa. In order to do this we must establish the relation between degrees and radians. We have agreed that one revolution is 360° in degree measure. We now find the same angle in radian measure.

In Figure 10-3, the measure of θ is one revolution (360°), and the arc length a is the circumference of the circle: $2\pi r$. Hence the radian measure of θ is given by

$$\theta = \frac{a}{r} = \frac{2\pi r}{r} = 2\pi$$

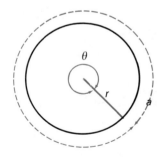

Figure 10-3

The relation between radian and degree measure is given by

$$2\pi \text{ radians} = 360°,$$

which simplifies to

$$\pi \text{ radians} = 180°$$

applied mathematics for today: senior

EXAMPLE 1. *Calculate degree measures of the angles whose radian measures are:*

(a) $\dfrac{\pi}{6}$ (b) $\dfrac{2\pi}{3}$

Rule of Three:
5 apples cost 60¢
1 apple costs 12¢
7 apples cost 84¢

Solution We use the Rule of Three.

(a) π radians $= 180°$

$\qquad 1$ radian $= \dfrac{180°}{\pi}$

$\qquad \dfrac{\pi}{6}$ radians $= \dfrac{\pi}{6} \times \dfrac{180°}{\pi}$

$\qquad\qquad = 30°$

(b) π radians $= 180°$

$\qquad 1$ radian $= \dfrac{180°}{\pi}$

$\qquad \dfrac{2\pi}{3}$ radians $= \dfrac{2\pi}{3} \times \dfrac{180°}{\pi}$

$\qquad\qquad = 120°$

EXAMPLE 2. *Calculate the radian measures of the following angles:*

(a) $210°$ (b) $315°$

Solution

(a) $180° = \pi$ radians

$\qquad 1° = \dfrac{\pi}{180}$ radians

$\qquad 210° = 210° \times \dfrac{\pi}{180°}$

$\qquad\qquad = \dfrac{7\pi}{6}$ radians

(b) $180° = \pi$ radians

$\qquad 1° = \dfrac{\pi}{180}$ radians

$\qquad 315° = 315° \times \dfrac{\pi}{180°}$

$\qquad\qquad = \dfrac{7\pi}{4}$ radians

EXAMPLE 3. *Calculate the number of degrees in 1 radian.*

Solution $\quad \pi$ radians $= 180°$

$\qquad 1$ radian $= \left(\dfrac{180}{\pi}\right)°$

$\qquad\qquad \doteq \left(\dfrac{180}{3.14159}\right)°$

$\qquad\qquad \doteq 57.2958°$

Twelve coins are identical in appearance, but 1 differs from the others in weight. How can you determine the odd coin using only a pan balance and 3 weighings?

EXERCISE 10-1

1. Convert the following radian measures to degree measure.

(a) 3π (b) $\dfrac{3\pi}{4}$ (c) $\dfrac{4\pi}{3}$ (d) $\dfrac{5\pi}{6}$ (e) $\dfrac{3\pi}{2}$

2. Convert the following degree measures to radian measure.

(a) $120°$ (b) $330°$ (c) $90°$ (d) $225°$ (e) $30°$

3. Calculate the radian measure of an angle whose measure is $1°$.

4. Convert the following radian measures to degree measure.

(a) 3   (b) 2.45   (c) 5.2

(d) 11.5   (e) 0.147   (f) 457

5. Convert the following degree measures to radian measure.

(a) $40°$ (b) $70°$ (c) $160°$ (d) $200°$ (e) $410°$ (f) $325°$

10.2 GRAPHING THE TRIGONOMETRIC FUNCTIONS

In this section we will draw the graphs of the functions defined by

$$y = \sin \theta \qquad y = \csc \theta$$
$$y = \cos \theta \qquad y = \sec \theta$$
$$y = \tan \theta \qquad y = \cot \theta$$

INVESTIGATION 10.2

1. THE UNIT CIRCLE

The circle in Figure 10-4 has a radius 1.0 unit, and centre at the origin of a pair of coordinate axes.

(a) Find the missing coordinates for points E to P.

$$\sin \theta = \frac{y}{r}$$

$$\cos \theta = \frac{x}{r}$$

$$\tan \theta = \frac{y}{x}, \quad x \neq 0$$

$$\csc \theta = \frac{r}{y}, \quad y \neq 0$$

$$\sec \theta = \frac{r}{x}, \quad x \neq 0$$

$$\cot \theta = \frac{x}{y}, \quad y \neq 0$$

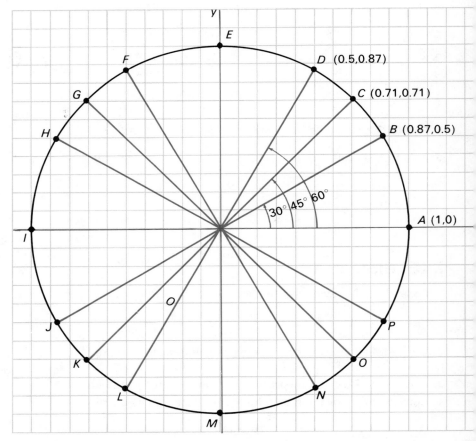

Figure 10-4

applied mathematics for today: senior

(b) Tabulate your results from part (a) and complete Table 10-5 in your notebook. A dash indicates that a value is undefined.

| θ | | $r=1$ | | Function values | | | | | |
Degrees	Radians	x	y	sin θ	cos θ	tan θ	csc θ	sec θ	cot θ
0°	0	1.00	0	0	1.00	0	—	1.00	—
30°	$\frac{\pi}{6}$	0.87	0.50					1.15	
45°	$\frac{\pi}{4}$	0.71	0.71				1.41		
60°	$\frac{\pi}{3}$	0.50	0.87			1.73			
90°	$\frac{\pi}{2}$	0	1.00		1.00	—		—	
	$\frac{2\pi}{3}$			0.87					−0.58
	$\frac{3\pi}{4}$		0.71					−1.41	
	$\frac{5\pi}{6}$	−0.87					2.00		
	π					0	—		—
210°	$\frac{7\pi}{6}$				−0.87				
	$\frac{5\pi}{4}$			−0.71					
	$\frac{4\pi}{3}$		−0.87						
	$\frac{3\pi}{2}$	0				—		—	0
	$\frac{5\pi}{3}$							2.00	
315°	$\frac{7\pi}{4}$						−1.41		
	$\frac{11\pi}{6}$					−0.58			
	2π				1.00		—		—

Table 10-5

2. THE GRAPH OF $y = \sin \theta$

(a) Using θ- and y-axes, plot the values of (θ, y) where $y = \sin \theta$, taking values from Table 10-5. Draw the curve of best fit. Draw your own axes like those in Figure 10-6.
(b) What is the maximum value of y?
(c) What is the minimum value of y?

Since every value of θ determines a unique value for $y = \sin \theta$, the graph of the ordered pairs (θ, y) is the graph of a function—the SINE FUNCTION.

3. THE GRAPH OF $y = \cos \theta$

(a) Using θ- and y-axes, plot the values of (θ, y) where $y = \cos \theta$, taking values from Table 10-5. Draw the curve of best fit. Draw your own axes like those in Figure 10-6.
(b) What is the maximum value of y?
(c) What is the minimum value of y?

Since every value of θ determines a unique value for $y = \cos \theta$, the graph of the ordered pairs (θ, y) is a graph of a function—the COSINE FUNCTION.

4. THE GRAPH OF $y = \tan \theta$

(a) On θ- and y-axes, as in Figure 10-7, draw dotted lines parallel to the y-axis at the values of θ for which $y = \tan \theta$ is not defined. Since $y = \tan \theta$ is not defined for these values of θ, no point on the graph of $y = \tan \theta$ can lie on these dotted lines.
(b) Plot the ordered pairs (θ, y) where $y = \tan \theta$, taking values from Table 10-5 and draw the curve of best fit.

Since every value of θ for which $y = \tan \theta$ is defined, determines a unique value for $y = \tan \theta$, the graph of the ordered pairs (θ, y) is the graph of a function—the TANGENT FUNCTION.

In questions 4, 5, and 6, draw dotted lines to serve as guides where undefined values occur.

5. THE GRAPH OF $y = \csc \theta$

Using values from Table 10-1 and axes as in Figure 10-6, plot the ordered pairs (θ, y) where $y = \csc \theta$ and draw the curve of best fit.

6. THE GRAPH OF $y = \sec \theta$

Using values from Table 10-1 and axes as in Figure 10-6, plot the ordered pairs (θ, y) where $y = \sec \theta$, and draw the curve of best fit.

7. THE GRAPH OF $y = \cot \theta$

Using values from Table 10-1 and axes as in Figure 10-6, plot the ordered pairs (θ, y) where $y = \cot \theta$, and draw the curve of best fit.

applied mathematics for today: senior

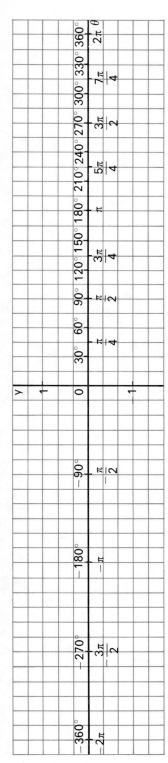

Figure 10-6

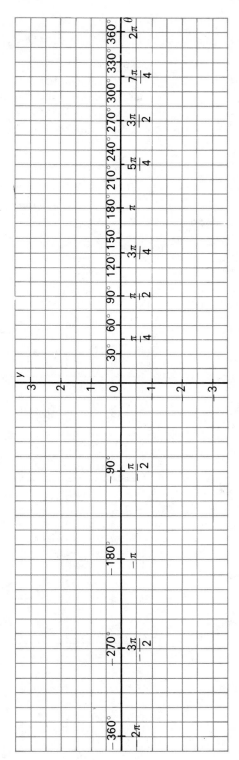

Figure 10-7

trigonometric functions 219

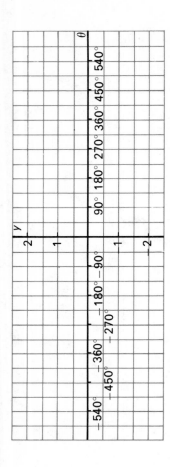

EXERCISE 10-2

Sketch the following for the indicated domains.

1. $y = \sin \theta, \; -180° \leqq \theta \leqq 540°$

2. $y = \cos \theta, \; -360° \leqq \theta \leqq 900°$

3. $y = \tan \theta, \; -360° \leqq \theta \leqq 360°$

4. $y = \cos \theta, \; -540° \leqq \theta \leqq 720°$

5. $y = \tan \theta, \quad -90° \leqq \theta \leqq 270°$

6. $y = \sin \theta, \quad 180° \leqq \theta \leqq 900°$

7. $y = \cos \theta, \quad -90° \leqq \theta \leqq 90°$

8. $y = \csc \theta, \; -180° \leqq \theta \leqq 180°$

9. $y = \sec \theta, \quad -90° \leqq \theta \leqq 90°$

10. $y = \cot \theta, \; -270° \leqq \theta \leqq 270°$

10.3 THE CAST RULE AND USING TRIGONOMETRIC TABLES

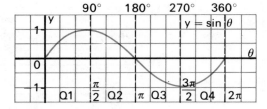

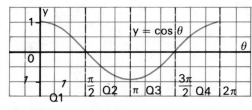

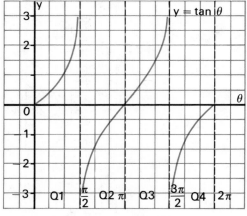

Figure 10-8

applied mathematics for today: senior

Trigonometric tables in the appendix are provided for angles from 0°
to 90° only. In Figure 10-8 we have the graphs of

$$y = \sin \theta$$
$$y = \cos \theta$$
$$y = \tan \theta \quad \text{for} \quad 0° \leq \theta \leq 360°.$$

If we designate the four quadrants as in the diagram below,

Q2 Second Quadrant	Q1 First Quadrant
Third Quadrant Q3	Fourth Quadrant Q4

we see that in the first quadrant, all ratios are positive; in the second
quadrant, the sine function has positive values; in the third quadrant,
the tangent is positive; in the fourth quadrant, the cosine is positive.
These results can be summarized in Figure 10-9.

Sine Positive	All Positive
Tangent Positive	Cosine Positive

This memory aid is called the
CAST RULE.

Figure 10-9

Insert plus and minus
signs to make

1▨2▨3▨4▨5▨6▨7▨8▨9 =
100 a true statement.

The trigonometric ratios of angles greater than 90° or less than 0°
are related to the ratios of acute angles as follows:

$$\frac{b}{c} = \sin \theta \qquad\qquad \frac{a}{c} = \cos \theta \qquad\qquad \frac{b}{a} = \tan \theta$$

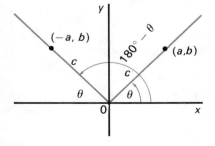

$$\sin(180° - \theta) = \frac{b}{c} = +\sin \theta$$

$$\cos(180° - \theta) = \frac{-a}{c} = -\cos \theta$$

$$\tan(180° - \theta) = \frac{b}{-a} = -\tan \theta$$

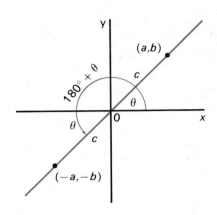

$$\sin (360° - \theta) = \frac{-b}{c} = -\sin \theta$$

$$\cos (360° - \theta) = \frac{a}{c} = +\cos \theta$$

$$\tan (360° - \theta) = \frac{-b}{a} = -\tan \theta$$

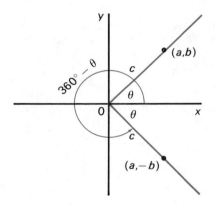

$$\sin (180° + \theta) = \frac{-b}{c} = -\sin \theta$$

$$\cos (180° + \theta) = \frac{-a}{c} = -\cos \theta$$

$$\tan (180° + \theta) = \frac{-b}{-a} = +\tan \theta$$

These diagrams are also used to derive the following relationships:

$\csc (180° - \theta) = \csc \theta$ $\csc (180° + \theta) = -\csc \theta$ $\csc (360° - \theta) = -\csc \theta$

$\sec (180° - \theta) = -\sec \theta$ $\sec (180° + \theta) = -\sec \theta$ $\sec (360° - \theta) = +\sec \theta$

$\cot (180° - \theta) = -\cot \theta$ $\cot (180° + 0) = +\cot \theta$ $\cot (360° - \theta) = -\cot \theta$

$\sin (180° - 140°)$
$= \sin 40°$

S	A
T	C

$\cot (360° - 330°)$
$= \cot 30°$

EXAMPLE 1.   *Find (a)* sin 140° *(b)* sec 215° *(c)* cot 330°

Solution

(a) $\sin 140° = \sin (180° - 40°)$
$= \sin 40°$
$\doteq 0.6428$ (from tables)

applied mathematics for today: senior

(b) $\sec 215° = \sec (180° + 35°)$

$\qquad = -\sec 35°$

$\qquad \doteq -1.2208$

(c) $\cot 330° = \cot (360° - 30°)$

$\qquad = -\cot 30°$

$\qquad \doteq -1.7321$

Eighteen years ago Bob was 3 times as old as Sally. Today he is twice as old. How old is Sally?

EXAMPLE 2. *Find 2 values for $\angle A$, given $\cos A = -0.8746$.*

Solution

$\qquad \angle A$ lies in the second or third quadrant.

From tables:

$$0.8746 = \cos 29°$$

(i) Second Quadrant $\qquad\qquad$ (ii) Third Quadrant

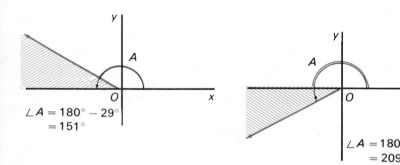

$\angle A = 180° - 29°$
$\quad = 151°$

$\angle A = 180° + 29°$
$\quad = 209°$

EXERCISE 10-3

A **1.** State the quadrant in which each angle lies:

(a) $\sin \theta$ and $\tan \theta$ are both positive.

(b) $\cos \theta$ and $\tan \theta$ are both negative.

(c) $\sin \theta$ is positive and $\cos \theta$ is negative.

(d) $\tan \theta$ is positive and $\sin \theta$ is negative.

(e) $\cos \theta$ is positive and $\tan \theta$ is negative.

S	A
T	C

2. State whether the following are positive or negative.

(a) $\sin 220°$ $\qquad$ (b) $\cos 315°$ $\qquad$ (c) $\tan 275°$ $\qquad$ (d) $\cos 350°$

(e) $\sin 75°$ $\qquad$ (f) $\sin 135°$ $\qquad$ (g) $\tan 175°$ $\qquad$ (h) $\cos 118°$

3. Insert $+$ or $-$ signs in the $\boxed{\text{blanks}}$ to make the following statements true.

(a) $\cos 220° = \blacksquare\cos 40°$ $\qquad\qquad$ (b) $\sin 137° = \blacksquare\sin 43°$

(c) $\sin 301° = \blacksquare\sin 59°$ $\qquad\qquad$ (d) $\tan 260° = \blacksquare\tan 80°$

(e) $\cos 100° = \blacksquare\cos 80°$ $\qquad\qquad$ (f) $\sin 350° = \blacksquare\sin 10°$

(g) $\tan 200° = \blacksquare\tan 20°$ $\qquad\qquad$ (h) $\tan 150° = \blacksquare\tan 30°$

(i) $\sin 270° = \blacksquare\sin 90°$ $\qquad\qquad$ (j) $\cos 180° = \blacksquare\cos 0°$

trigonometric functions $\qquad\qquad$ 223

4. Insert + or − signs in the blanks to make the following statements true.

(a) sec 140° = ▦ sec 40°   (b) csc 325° = ▦ csc 35°
(c) cot 220° = ▦ cot 40°   (d) csc 315° = ▦ csc 45°
(e) csc 240° = ▦ csc 60°   (f) sec 330° = ▦ sec 30°

B **5.** Using the tables, find:

(a) sin 225°   (b) cos 135°   (c) tan 125°
(d) sin 290°   (e) tan 205°   (f) cos 300°
(g) cos 325°   (h) sin 200°   (i) tan 215°
(j) tan 305°   (k) cos 160°   (l) sin 260°

6. Using the tables, find:

(a) csc 150°   (b) sec 300°   (c) csc 170°
(d) cot 220°   (e) csc 225°   (f) cot 150°
(g) cot 290°   (h) csc 320°   (i) sec 120°

7. Find two values (0° to 360°) for each of the indicated angles:

(a) sin A = +0.3746   (b) cos B = +0.6293   (c) tan C = +2.9042
(d) cos D = +0.3420   (e) sin E = +0.6820   (f) cos F = −0.7071
(g) cos G = −0.8910   (h) tan H = −0.3057   (i) sin J = −0.9569

10.4 THE PERIODIC NATURE OF THE TRIGONOMETRIC FUNCTIONS

π radians = 180°

Figure 10-10 represents a partial graph of y = tan θ. From the graph, we see that as θ increases from 0° to 180°, tan θ takes on all possible values. Hence we say that the period of y = tan θ is 180°, and the tangent function is called a periodic function.

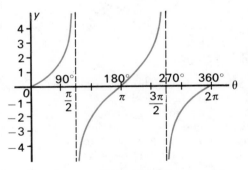

Figure 10-10

The smallest length measured along the θ-axis in which the function takes on all possible values is called the *period* of the function.

INVESTIGATION 10.4

1. State the period of the function defined by $y = \sin\theta$, by examining the partial graph of the function in Figure 10-11.

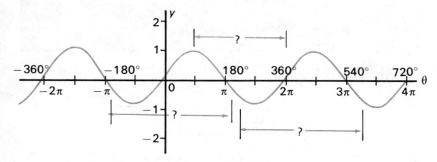

Figure 10-11

2. Sketch the graph of $y = \cos\theta$, $-360° \leq \theta \leq 720°$, then determine the period of the function.

3. Sketch graphs for each of the following and determine the period:
(a) $y = \csc\theta$, $-720° \leq \theta \leq 360°$
(b) $y = \sec\theta$, $-360° \leq \theta \leq 180°$
(c) $y = \cot\theta$, $-180° \leq \theta \leq 540°$

4. Complete the following Table 10-12 in your notebook as a summary of this investigation.

Function	Period
$y = \sin\theta$	
$y = \cos\theta$	
$y = \tan\theta$	180° or π rad
$y = \csc\theta$	
$y = \sec\theta$	
$y = \cot\theta$	

Table 10-12

How many minutes is it until 18:00 if 50 min ago it was four times as many minutes past 15:00?

10.5 AMPLITUDE

INVESTIGATION 10.5

1. (a) Complete the following table in your notebook.

trigonometric functions

θ	0°	45°	90°	135°	180°	225°	270°	315°	360°
$y = \sin\theta$	0	0.7	1.0	0.7	0	−0.7	−1	−0.7	0
$y = 2\sin\theta$		1.4							
$y = 3\sin\theta$				2.1					
$y = \frac{1}{2}\sin\theta$						−0.35			

(b) On the same set of axes, sketch the graphs of
(i) $y = \sin\theta$ (ii) $y = 2\sin\theta$
(iii) $y = 3\sin\theta$ (iv) $y = \frac{1}{2}\sin\theta$
These are the graphs defined by

$$\boxed{y = a\sin\theta}, \quad \text{for } a \in \{\tfrac{1}{2}, 1, 2, 3\}$$

(c) The a in $y = a\sin\theta$ is the *amplitude* of the function. Complete the following table in your notebook.

Defining sentence	Maximum value	Minimum value	Amplitude
$y = \sin\theta$			
$y = 2\sin\theta$	2		
$y = 3\sin\theta$		−3	
$y = \frac{1}{2}\sin\theta$			$\frac{1}{2}$
$y = a\sin\theta$			

)006

EXERCISE 10-5

A **1.** State the amplitude of the following curves:

(a)

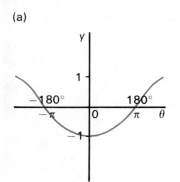

(b)

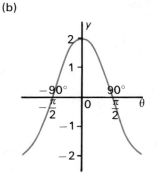

(c)

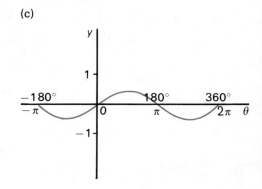

applied mathematics for today: senior

2. State the amplitude of the graph defined by each of the following:

(a) $y = 3 \sin \theta$ (b) $y = 7 \sin \theta$

(c) $y = 24 \sin \theta$ (d) $y = m \sin \theta, \quad m > 0$

(e) $y = -3 \sin \theta$ (f) $y = \frac{1}{3} \sin \theta$

B   **3.** Sketch the graphs defined by each of the following.

(a) $y = 2 \sin \theta, \qquad 0° \le \theta \le 720°$

(b) $y = 3 \sin \theta, \quad -180° \le \theta \le 540°$

(c) $y = \frac{1}{2} \sin \theta, \quad -360° \le \theta \le 180°$

(d) $y = 10 \sin \theta, \qquad 0° \le \theta \le 90°$

(e) $y = \frac{1}{4} \sin \theta, \qquad 0° \le \theta \le 540°$

C   **4.** Sketch the graphs defined by:

(a) $y = 3 \cos \theta, \qquad 0° \le \theta \le 360°$

(b) $y = 2 \cos \theta, \quad -180° \le \theta \le 360°$

(c) $y = \frac{1}{2} \cos \theta, \quad -360° \le \theta \le 180°$

10.6   PERIOD

INVESTIGATION 10.6

1. (a) Complete the following table in your notebook.

θ	0°	45°	90°	180°	270°	360°	Additional values if required				Period
$y = \sin \theta$	0	0.7	1.0	0	−1.0	0					360°
2θ	0°										
$y = \sin 2\theta$			0								
3θ	0°		270°								
$y = \sin 3\theta$											
$\frac{1}{2}\theta$	0°	22½°	45°								
$y = \sin \frac{1}{2}\theta$											

(b) On the same set of axes for each pair of equations, sketch the graphs of:

(i) $y = \sin \theta$ (ii) $y = \sin \theta$ (iii) $y = \sin \theta$

    $y = \sin 2\theta$ $y = \sin 3\theta$ $y = \sin \frac{1}{2}\theta$

These are the graphs defined by

$$\boxed{y = \sin k\theta} \text{ for } k \in \{\tfrac{1}{2}, 1, 2, 3\}$$

(c) The k in $y = \sin k\theta$ determines the period $\dfrac{360°}{k}$, of the function.

Complete the following table in your notebook.

Defining sentence	Value of k	Period
$y = \sin \theta$		
$y = \sin 2\theta$		
$y = \sin 3\theta$	3	
$y = \sin \frac{1}{2}\theta$		
$y = \sin k\theta, \quad k > 0$		$\dfrac{360°}{k}$

EXERCISE 10.6

A 1. State the period for each of the following:

(a)

(b)

(c)

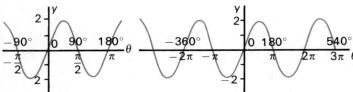

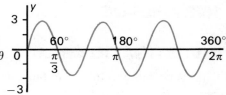

2. State the period for each of the following:

(a) $y = \sin \theta$ (b) $y = 2 \sin 3\theta$

(c) $y = 3 \sin 2\theta$ (d) $y = 5 \sin \frac{1}{2}\theta$

(e) $y = 3 \sin 4\theta$ (f) $y = \sin 2\theta$

B 3. Complete the following table in your notebook:

Amplitude	Period	Defining sentence $y = a \sin k\theta$
2	180°	
4	360°	
2	720°	
8	360°	
5	180°	

4. Sketch the graphs defined by each of the following:

(a) $y = \sin 2\theta,$ $0° \leqq \theta \leqq 540°$

(b) $y = \sin 4\theta,$ $0° \leqq \theta \leqq 540°$

(c) $y = \sin \frac{1}{2}\theta,$ $-360° \leqq \theta \leqq 720°$

(d) $y = \sin \frac{1}{4}\theta,$ $-360° \leqq \theta \leqq 720°$

(e) $y = \sin 3\theta,$ $-360° \leqq \theta \leqq 360°$

C **5.** Sketch the graphs defined by each of the following:
(a) $y = 3 \sin 2\theta$, $-180° \leqq \theta \leqq 180°$
(b) $y = \frac{1}{2} \sin 2\theta$, $-360° \leqq \theta \leqq 180°$
(c) $y = 2 \sin \frac{1}{2}\theta$, $-720° \leqq \theta \leqq 360°$
(d) $y = 2 \sin 3\theta$, $-360° \leqq \theta \leqq 360°$
(e) $y = \frac{1}{2} \sin \frac{1}{2}\theta$, $-720° \leqq \theta \leqq 720°$

6. Sketch the graphs defined by:
(a) $y = 2 \cos 2\theta$, $-180° \leqq \theta \leqq 180°$
(b) $y = 3 \cos \frac{1}{2}\theta$, $-360° \leqq \theta \leqq 360°$
(c) $y = \cos 3\theta$, $-180° \leqq \theta \leqq 360°$

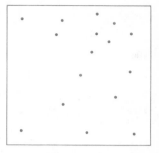

Separate the dots using 5 straight lines.

10.7 PHASE SHIFT

In sections 10-5 and 10-6 we saw that we were able to "stretch" and "compress" the graph of $y = a \sin k\theta$ in both the vertical and horizontal directions using appropriate values of a and k. In this section we will investigate the effect of adding to (or subtracting from) the angle θ.

INVESTIGATION 10.7

1. Complete the following tables in your notebook, and using the same axes for each pair of equations, graph:
(a) $y = \sin \theta$ and $y = \sin (\theta + 30°)$, for $-180° \leqq \theta \leqq 360°$.

θ	0°	30°	60°	90°	120°	150°	180°	210°	240°	270°	300°	330°	360°
$y = \sin \theta$													
$\theta + 30°$													
$y = \sin (\theta + 30°)$													

(b) $y = \sin \theta$ and $y = \sin (\theta + 45°)$, for $-180° \leqq \theta \leqq 360°$.

θ	0°	45°	90°	135°	180°	225°	270°	315°	360°
$y = \sin \theta$									
$\theta + 45°$									
$y = \sin (\theta + 45°)$									

(c) $y = \sin \theta$ and $y = \sin (\theta + 90°)$, for $-180° \leqq \theta \leqq 360°$

θ	0°	45°	90°	135°	180°	225°	270°	315°	360°
$y = \sin \theta$									
$\theta + 90°$									
$y = \sin (\theta + 90°)$									

(d) $y = \sin \theta$ and $y = \sin (\theta - 30°)$, for $-180° \leqq \theta \leqq 360°$.

θ	0°	30°	90°	120°	180°	210°	270°	300°	360°
$y = \sin \theta$									
$\theta - 30°$									
$y = \sin (\theta - 30°)$									

2. From observation of your graphs in question 1, you should have noticed that we were able to cause a shift to the left or right by adding to or subtracting from the variable. This is called a phase shift. Complete the following table in your notes, given that

$$y = \sin (\theta + \phi)$$

	Phase shift	Direction
$\phi > 0$		
$\phi < 0$		

EXERCISE 10-7

A **1.** State the phase shift of each of the following:
(a) $y = \sin \theta$ (b) $y = \sin (\theta + 30°)$
(c) $y = \sin (\theta - 90°)$ (d) $y = \sin (\theta + 360°)$

B **2.** Sketch the graph of each of the following:
(a) $y = \sin (\theta + 30°)$, $0° \leqq \theta \leqq 540°$
(b) $y = \sin (\theta + 45°)$, $-180° \leqq \theta \leqq 180°$
(c) $y = \sin (\theta - 90°)$, $-270° \leqq \theta \leqq 270°$
(d) $y = \sin (\theta + 180°)$, $-720° \leqq \theta \leqq 360°$
(e) $y = \sin (\theta - 180°)$, $-360° \leqq \theta \leqq 360°$

C **3.** Sketch the graph defined by:
(a) $y = \cos (\theta - 45°)$, $0° \leqq \theta \leqq 360°$
(b) $y = \cos (\theta + 45°)$, $-90° \leqq \theta \leqq 270°$
(c) $y = \cos (\theta - 90°)$, $-180° \leqq \theta \leqq 540°$
(d) $y = \tan (\theta + 90°)$, $0° \leqq \theta \leqq 360°$
(e) $y = \tan (\theta - 90°)$, $0° \leqq \theta \leqq 360°$
(f) $y = \tan (\theta + 30°)$, $-360° \leqq \theta \leqq 360°$

     applied mathematics for today: senior

10.8 THE GRAPH OF $y = a \sin k(\theta + \phi)$

In the three preceding sections, we investigated the amplitude, a, ($a > 0$), period $\frac{360°}{k}$, ($k > 0$), and phase shift, of sinusoids of the type

$$y = a \sin \theta$$
$$y = \sin k\theta$$
$$y = \sin (\theta + \phi)$$

The results of this section can be summarized as follows.

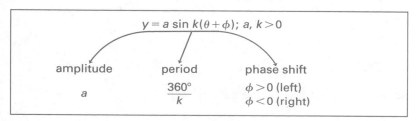

EXAMPLE 1. *Sketch the graph of* $y = 3 \sin 2\theta$, $-180° \leq \theta \leq 180°$.

Solution From the given equation, we have

amplitude: 3, period: $\frac{360°}{2} = 180°$, phase shift: 0°.

The graph is sketched as follows

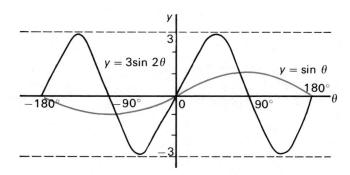

EXAMPLE 2. *Sketch the graph of* $y = 2 \sin \frac{1}{2}\theta$, $-180° \leq \theta \leq 360°$.

Solution From the equation, we have

amplitude: 2, period: $\frac{360°}{\frac{1}{2}} = 720°$, phase shift: 0°.

The graph is sketched as follows

Find the missing numbers in this multiplication.

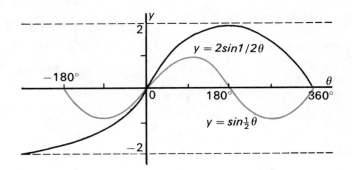

EXAMPLE 3. *Sketch the graph of* $y = \sin(2\theta + 60°)$, $-180° \leqq \theta \leqq 360°$.

Solution We first rewrite the defining sentence:

$$y = \sin(2\theta + 60°)$$
$$= \sin 2(\theta + 30°)$$

We now have:

amplitude: 1,   period: $\dfrac{360°}{2} = 180°$,   phase shift: $30°$ to the left.

The graph is sketched as follows:

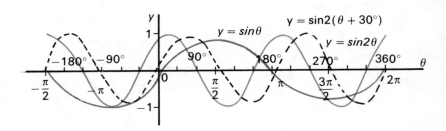

EXERCISE 10-8

B **1.** Complete the following table in your notebook.

Defining sentence	Amplitude	Period	Phase shift
$y = 2 \sin \theta$			
$y = 3 \sin 2\theta$			
(sine)	2	360°	0°
$y = 2 \cos (\theta + 45°)$			
(sine)	1	360°	90° left
$y = \sin (2\theta + 90°)$			
(sine)	3	180°	0°
(sine)	2	720°	0°
$y = 3 \sin \frac{1}{2}\theta$			
$y = a \sin k(\theta + \phi)$	a	$\dfrac{360°}{k}$	

Towns A and B are 60 km apart. Two motorcyclists leave at noon, one from A at 40 km/h, and the other from B at 50 km/h. Where will the cyclists meet?

2. Sketch the graph for the domains indicated in the following.
(a) $y = 3 \sin \theta$, $0° \le \theta \le 360°$
(b) $y = 2 \sin \theta$, $0° \le \theta \le 360°$
(c) $y = 2 \sin (\theta + 45°)$, $-90° \le \theta \le 180°$
(d) $y = 2 \sin (\theta - 45°)$, $-90° \le \theta \le 180°$
(e) $y = \sin 2\theta$, $0° \le \theta \le 180°$
(f) $y = \sin 3\theta$, $-360° \le \theta \le 360°$
(g) $y = 3 \sin \frac{1}{2}\theta$, $-180° \le \theta \le 360°$
(h) $y = \frac{1}{2} \sin \frac{1}{2}\theta$, $-360° \le \theta \le 720°$
(i) $y = \sin 2(\theta + 45°)$, $0° \le \theta \le 360°$
(j) $y = 2 \sin (\theta + 60°)$, $0° \le \theta \le 360°$

3. On the same set of axes, sketch the graphs of:
(a) $y = \sin \theta$,   (b) $y = 2 \sin \theta$,   (c) $y = \sin 2\theta$,
for $-360° \le \theta \le 360°$.

C   **4.** Sketch the graph for each of the following.
(a) $y = 3 \sin 2(\theta - 45°)$, $-180° \le \theta \le 180°$
(b) $y = 2 \sin \frac{1}{2}(\theta + 90°)$, $-720° \le \theta \le 360°$
(c) $y = 3 \sin (2\theta + 90°)$, $-360° \le \theta \le 360°$
(d) $y = \frac{1}{2} \sin \frac{1}{2}(\theta - 180°)$, $-180° \le \theta \le 360°$

10.9   TRIGONOMETRIC EQUATIONS

Equations such as $\sin \theta = \frac{1}{2}$, $0° \le \theta \le 360°$ are called trigonometric equations. To solve this equation we must find all measures of the angle θ within the stated domain for which $\sin \theta = \frac{1}{2}$.

EXAMPLE 1.   *Find all values of θ from 0° to 360° for $\sin \theta = \frac{1}{2}$.*

Solution We take the graph of $y = \sin \theta$, $0° \leqq \theta \leqq 360°$, and draw a horizontal line at $y = \frac{1}{2}$, as in the diagram.

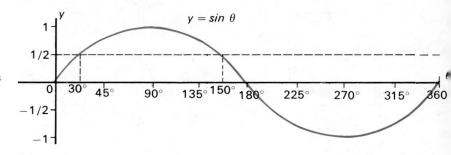

A 1ℓ-container has all dimensions doubled. What is the new volume?

From the graph, we see that the horizontal line cuts the graph of $y = \sin \theta$ at $\theta = 30°$ and again at $\theta = 150°$.

We say that the solution of $\sin \theta = \frac{1}{2}$, $0° \leqq \theta \leqq 360°$, is 30° and 150°.

Example 1 suggests a graphical method of solving trigonometric equations. Some equations, however, require solving algebraically before the graphical method can be used.

EXAMPLE 2. *Solve* $(\cos \theta - 0.5)(\cos \theta + 0.866) = 0$, *for* $0° \leqq \theta \leqq 360°$.

Solution $(\cos \theta - 0.5)(\cos \theta + 0.866) = 0$

$$\cos \theta - 0.5 = 0 \quad \text{or} \quad \cos \theta + 0.866 = 0$$
$$\cos \theta = 0.5 \qquad \cos \theta = -0.866$$

We take the graph of $y = \cos \theta$, $0° \leqq \theta \leqq 360°$, and draw two horizontal lines, one at $y = 0.5$ and another at $y = -0.866$, as in the diagram.

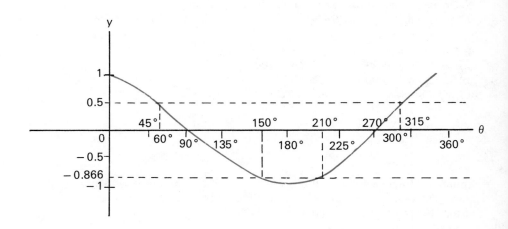

From the graph, the solution of the equation in the given range is 60°, 150°, 210°, 300°.

applied mathematics for today: senior

EXERCISE 10-9

Solve for $0° \leq \theta \leq 360°$.

B   **1.** $\sin \theta = 0.866$ **2.** $\cos \theta = 0.5$ **3.** $\sin \theta = -0.5$

4. $\tan \theta = 1$ **5.** $\tan \theta = -1$ **6.** $\sin \theta = 0$

7. $(\cos \theta + 0.5)(\cos \theta - 0.5) = 0$

8. $(\sin \theta - 0.5)(\sin \theta + 0.5) = 0$

9. $\sin \theta \ (\sin \theta + 1) = 0$

What relation is my father's sister's husband's daughter to me?

10.10   BASIC IDENTITIES

Algebraic sentences such as $x + 3 = 8$, $x \in R$, are true for only certain values of the variable (in this case $x = 5$). A sentence like $2x = x + x$ is true for all values of the variable. It is not always obvious that both sides of such an equation are equal, so proof is required. Since proof involves showing that the left side is *identical* to the right side, these sentences are called identities.

EXERCISE 10-10

The following examples and questions relate to a right triangle where r is the hypotenuse, y the opposite side, and x the adjacent side. [This can be extended to any angle θ in standard position.]

EXAMPLE 1. *Establish that* $\dfrac{1}{\csc \theta} = \sin \theta$.

Solution $\dfrac{1}{\csc \theta} = \dfrac{1}{\frac{r}{y}} = \dfrac{y}{r} = \sin \theta$, and $\csc \theta = \dfrac{1}{\sin \theta}$.

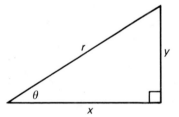

B   **1.** Establish that

(a) $\dfrac{1}{\sec \theta} = \cos \theta$, and $\sec \theta = \dfrac{1}{\cos \theta}$.

(b) $\dfrac{1}{\cot \theta} = \tan \theta$, and $\cot \theta = \dfrac{1}{\tan \theta}$.

EXAMPLE 2. *Establish that* $\dfrac{\sin \theta}{\cos \theta} = \tan \theta$.

Solution $\dfrac{\sin \theta}{\cos \theta} = \dfrac{\frac{y}{r}}{\frac{x}{r}} = \dfrac{y}{x} = \tan \theta$.

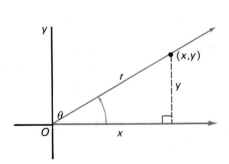

2. Establish that $\dfrac{\cos \theta}{\sin \theta} = \cot \theta$.

The results of questions 1 and 2 can be summarized by the following table.

trigonometric functions   235

Reciprocal identities		Quotient identities
$\csc \theta = \dfrac{1}{\sin \theta}$	$\sin \theta \cdot \csc \theta = 1$	
$\sec \theta = \dfrac{1}{\cos \theta}$	$\cos \theta \cdot \sec \theta = 1$	$\dfrac{\sin \theta}{\cos \theta} = \tan \theta \qquad \dfrac{\cos \theta}{\sin \theta} = \cot \theta$
$\cot \theta = \dfrac{1}{\tan \theta}$	$\tan \theta \cdot \cot \theta = 1$	

EXAMPLE 3. *Establish that* $\sin^2 \theta + \cos^2 \theta = 1$. [*Note that* $\sin^2 \theta$ *means* $(\sin \theta)^2$.]

Solution $\sin^2 \theta + \cos^2 \theta = \dfrac{y^2}{r^2} + \dfrac{x^2}{r^2}$

$$= \dfrac{x^2 + y^2}{r^2} = \dfrac{r^2}{r^2} = 1.$$

$r^2 = x^2 + y^2$

3. Establish that
(a) $1 + \tan^2 \theta = \sec^2 \theta$.
(b) $1 + \cot^2 \theta = \csc^2 \theta$.

Because these involve the Pythagorean relation $x^2 + y^2 = r^2$ in their proofs, they are called the Pythagorean identities. They are summarized in the following table.

Pythagorean identities
$\sin^2 \theta + \cos^2 \theta = 1$
$1 + \tan^2 \theta = \sec^2 \theta$
$1 + \cot^2 \theta = \csc^2 \theta$

The relationships presented in the above tables are called basic identities because their proofs involve the basic definitions in terms of x, y, and r. The basic identities are now used as formulas to prove more difficult identities. (Although the identities in the following examples can also be proved using the definitions in terms of x, y, and r, we prefer to use the basic identities because the "x, y, and r" method is limited and will not work for all formulas.)

EXAMPLE 4. *Prove that* $\sin \theta (1 + \cot \theta) = \sin \theta + \cos \theta$.

Solution

$$\text{L.S.} = \sin \theta (1 + \cot \theta) \qquad\qquad \text{R.S.} = \sin \theta + \cos \theta$$

$$= \sin \theta \left(1 + \frac{\cos \theta}{\sin \theta} \right)$$

$$= \sin \theta \left(\frac{\sin \theta + \cos \theta}{\sin \theta} \right)$$

$$= \sin \theta + \cos \theta, \qquad \sin \theta \neq 0$$
$$\text{L.S.} = \text{R.S.}$$

EXAMPLE 5. *Express each of the trigonometric ratios in terms of* $\sin \theta$.

Find a value of the variable that makes each of the following statements true.

Solution (i)   It is obvious that $\sin \theta = \sin \theta$.

(ii) $\cos \theta$: $\sin^2 \theta + \cos^2 \theta = 1$
$$\cos^2 \theta = 1 - \sin^2 \theta$$
$$\cos \theta = \pm\sqrt{1 - \sin^2 \theta}$$

$1^x = 1$

$0^a = 0$

$(-1)^b = -1$

$(-1)^c = 1$

(iii) $\tan \theta$: $\tan \theta = \dfrac{\sin \theta}{\cos \theta}$
$$= \frac{\sin \theta}{\pm\sqrt{1 - \sin^2 \theta}}$$

(iv) $\csc \theta$: $\csc \theta = \dfrac{1}{\sin \theta}$

(v) $\sec \theta$: $\sec \theta = \dfrac{1}{\cos \theta}$
$$= \frac{1}{\pm\sqrt{1 - \sin^2 \theta}}$$

(vi) $\cot \theta$: $\cot \theta = \dfrac{\cos \theta}{\sin \theta}$
$$= \pm\frac{\sqrt{1 - \sin^2 \theta}}{\sin \theta}$$

EXAMPLE 6.   *Prove that* $\sin^4 \theta - \cos^4 \theta = 1 - 2\cos^2 \theta$.

Solution

$$\text{L.S.} = \sin^4 \theta - \cos^4 \theta \qquad\qquad \text{R.S.} = 1 - 2\cos^2 \theta.$$
$$= (\sin^2 \theta + \cos^2 \theta)(\sin^2 \theta - \cos^2 \theta)$$
$$= 1(\sin^2 \theta - \cos^2 \theta)$$
$$= \sin^2 \theta - \cos^2 \theta$$
$$= 1 - \cos^2 \theta - \cos^2 \theta$$
$$= 1 - 2\cos^2 \theta.$$
$$\text{L.S.} = \text{R.S.}$$

Prove the following identities by the methods of Examples 4, 5, and 6.

4. $\sin \theta \cot \theta = \cos \theta$

5. $\dfrac{\tan \theta}{\cot \theta} = \dfrac{1 - \cos^2 \theta}{\cos^2 \theta}$

6. $\cot^2 \theta = \dfrac{1}{\sec^2 \theta - 1}$

7. $\dfrac{\sec \theta}{\csc \theta} = \tan \theta$

8. $\sin^2 \theta - \cos^2 \theta = 2 \sin^2 \theta - 1$

9. $(\sin \theta + \cos \theta)^2 = 1 + 2 \cos \theta \sin \theta$

10. $\dfrac{\tan \theta}{\cot \theta} = \dfrac{1 - \cos^2 \theta}{\cos^2 \theta}$

11. $\dfrac{1}{\sin^2 \theta} + \dfrac{1}{\cos^2 \theta} = \dfrac{1}{\sin^2 \theta \cos^2 \theta}$

12. $\sin^2 \theta + 2 \cos^2 \theta = 1 + \cos^2 \theta$

13. $\dfrac{\tan \theta}{\cot \theta} = \tan^2 \theta$

14. Express each of the trigonometric ratios in terms of $\cos \theta$, using the method in Example 5.

Determine which of the following are identities.

15. $\cot \theta + \cos \theta = \dfrac{\cos \theta (1 + \sin \theta)}{\sin \theta}$

16. $\cot \theta + \cos \theta = \dfrac{2 \cos \theta}{\sin \theta}$

17. $\cot \theta + \cos \theta = \tan \theta + \sin \theta$

REVIEW EXERCISE

B 1. Convert to radians.
(a) 225°   (b) 330°   (c) 540°   (d) −270°   (e) −495°

2. Convert the following radian measures to degrees.

(a) $\dfrac{5\pi}{6}$ (b) $\dfrac{5\pi}{2}$ (c) $\dfrac{3\pi}{4}$ (d) $-\dfrac{3\pi}{2}$ (e) $-\dfrac{11\pi}{6}$

3. Sketch the graphs of each of the following on separate axes.
(a) $y = 2 \sin 2\theta$, $-180° \leqq \theta \leqq 360°$
(b) $y = \sin (\theta - 30°)$, $0° \leqq \theta \leqq 540°$
(c) $y = 3 \sin 2\theta$, $-720° \leqq \theta \leqq 0°$
(d) $y = \sin 2(\theta + 45°)$, $-90° \leqq \theta \leqq 360°$
(e) $y = 2 \sin (\theta - 90°)$, $-90° \leqq \theta \leqq 450°$

4. Solve the following equations for $0° \leqq \theta \leqq 360°$.
(a) $\sin \theta = 0.5$
(b) $\sin \theta = -0.71$
(c) $\sin \theta (\sin \theta - 1) = 0$
(d) $\sin \theta (\sin \theta + 1) = 0$

5. Prove the following identities.

(a) $\tan \theta \sin \theta = \dfrac{1 - \cos^2 \theta}{\cos^2 \theta}$

(b) $(\sin \theta + \cos \theta)^2 = 1 + 2 \sin \theta \cos \theta$
(c) $\sin \theta \cos \theta \tan \theta = 1 - \cos^2 \theta$
(d) $\tan \theta + \sin \theta = \tan \theta (1 + \cos \theta)$

applied mathematics for today: senior

REVIEW AND PREVIEW TO CHAPTER 11

EXERCISE 1

Find the value of the variables in each of the following.

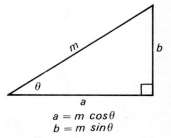

$a = m \cos\theta$
$b = m \sin\theta$

1.

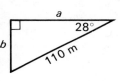

200 m 35° *b* *a*

2.

120 m 48° *b* *a*

3.

55 m 55° *b* *a*

4.

a 28° *b* 110 m

5.

a 62° 75 m *b*

6.

1414 m 45° *b* *a*

EXERCISE 2

1. How far will you travel in 3.5 h at 65 km/h?
2. How long will it take to travel 175 km at 70 km/h?
3. What was your average speed if you travel 200 km in 3.25 h?
4. How long will it take to run 10 km at 11 km/h?
5. What is the average speed of a car that travels 210 km in 2.15 h?
6. How far will you travel in 4.75 h at 71.5 km/h?

Solve for the variables:

1. $a^2 = (31.25)^2 + (84.63)^2 - 2(31.25)(84.63) \cos 40°$

2. $b^2 = (3.425)^2 + (4.835)^2 - 2(3.425)(4.835) \cos 68°$

3. $c^2 = (0.275)^2 + (0.894)^2 - 2(0.275)(0.894) \cos 57°$

4. $\cos A = \dfrac{(54.25)^2 + (21.65)^2 - (38.39)^2}{2(54.25)(21.65)}$

5. $\cos B = \dfrac{(0.2575)^2 + (0.5265)^2 - (0.4552)^2}{2(0.2575)(0.5265)}$

Vectors in Space

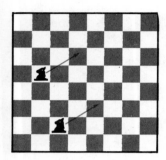

A quantity that has magnitude and direction is called a vector quantity. For example, a 300 km course N30°E or a move "two units to the right and up one" are both vector quantities since both have magnitude and direction.

11.1 VECTORS IN TWO DIMENSIONS

A vector representing a move "five units to the right and up two units" can be represented geometrically by a *directed* line segment, or algebraically using notation [5, 2] as in Figure 11-1. Note that while (a, b) represents a point and is an ordered pair, [a, b] represents a vector.

Figure 11-1

It is convenient to be able to take a vector in algebraic form [a, b] and determine the magnitude m, and the direction angle θ (measured counter-clockwise from the horizontal). We do this, using trigonometry, as follows:

Given [a, b]

$$m = \sqrt{a^2 + b^2}$$

$$\tan \theta = \frac{b}{a}$$

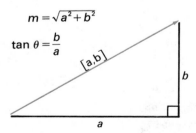

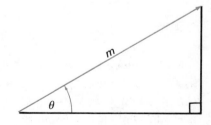

A car travels 20 km/h for the first half of a trip. How fast must it travel in the second half in order to average 40 km/h for the whole trip?

Given the magnitude m and the direction angle θ, it is also possible to express the vector in the form [a, b].

applied mathematics for today: senior

$$\cos \theta = \frac{a}{m} \qquad \text{and} \quad \sin \theta = \frac{b}{m}$$

$$a = m \cos \theta \quad \text{and} \qquad b = m \sin \theta$$

Hence the geometric vector with magnitude m and direction angle θ can be expressed algebraically as

$$[m \cos \theta, m \sin \theta]$$

Basic operations for vectors are required to plot courses in navigation, to calculate strengths and directions of electric fields, and also to solve problems involving forces.

EXAMPLE 1. *Find the missing terminal points of the vectors in the diagram if all the vectors are equal vectors.*

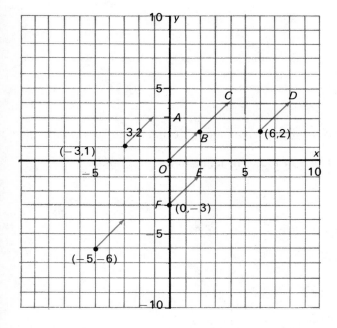

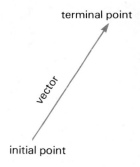

Solution The terminal points are $A(0, 3)$, $B(3, 2)$, $C(6, 4)$,

$$D(9, 4), \ E(3, -1), \ F(-2, -4).$$

Note: When vectors are related to a coordinate system, they need not have the initial point at the origin.

EXAMPLE 2. *State the magnitude and direction of the vector represented by* $[-5, 12]$.

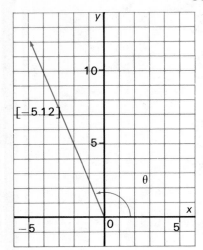

$$m = \sqrt{(-5)^2 + 12^2}$$
$$= \sqrt{169}$$
$$= 13$$
$$\tan \theta = \frac{12}{-5}$$

$$= -2.40 \text{ (and } \theta \text{ is in the 2nd quadrant)}$$
$$\theta = 180° - 67°$$
$$\theta = 113° \text{ (to the nearest degree).}$$

Note that the direction angle θ is measured counter-clockwise from the horizontal.

The magnitude and direction angle of [−5, 12] are 13 units and 113°.

EXAMPLE 3. *A vector has magnitude* 10 *units and direction angle* 255°.

Express the vector in the form [a, b] *to three-figure accuracy.*

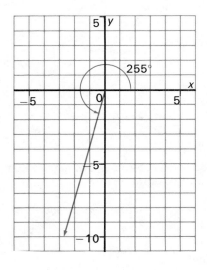

Solution Since $[a, b] = [m \cos \theta, m \sin \theta]$, and $m = 10$ units and $\theta = 255°$,

$$a = 10 \cos 255° \quad \text{and} \quad b = 10 \sin 255°$$
$$= 10(-\cos 75°) \qquad\qquad = 10(-\sin 75°)$$
$$\doteq 10(-0.259) \qquad\qquad \doteq 10(-0.966)$$
$$\doteq -2.59 \qquad\qquad\qquad \doteq -9.66$$

$[-2.59, -9.66]$ is the vector with magnitude 10 units and direction angle 255°.

EXERCISE 11-1

B **1.** Complete the following table in your notebook.

Initial point	Terminal point	Vector
(3, 2)	(7, 3)	[4, 1]
(2, 5)	▓	[6, −1]
▓	(3, 5)	[4, 2]
(2, 6)	(7, 11)	▓
(3, −2)	▓	[4, −3]
(−5, 7)	(−5, 7)	▓
(a, b)	(0, 0)	▓

Addition: STOP
DO
<u>STOP</u>
POPS

2. Equal vectors have the same magnitude and the same direction. Select equal vectors from the given diagrams.

(a)

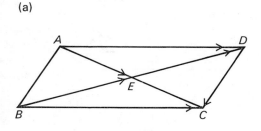

(b)

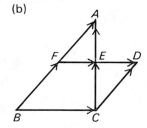

3. Given three points $A(-2, -2)$, $B(0, 3)$, $C(8, 5)$:
(a) find the coordinates of point D so that $\vec{AB} = \vec{DC}$.
(b) express $\vec{AB}$, $\vec{BC}$, $\vec{AD}$, and $\vec{DC}$ in the form $[a, b]$.
(c) identify figure $ABCD$.

vectors in space   243

4. Express the following vector quantities in the form [a, b].
(a) Magnitude 50 m, direction angle 90°.
(b) A course 40 m east.
(c) Magnitude 1.414 units with direction angle 45°.
(d) Magnitude 1.414 m with direction angle 225°.
(e) Magnitude 1 m with direction angle 49°.
(f) Magnitude m units with direction angle θ.

5. State the magnitude, to three figures, and the direction angle, to the nearest degree, of each of the following vectors.

(a) [3, 4]   (b) [−5, 12]   (c) [−9, −12]
(d) [7, −11]   (e) [−2, 2]   (f) [a, b]

11.2 ADDITION AND SUBTRACTION OF VECT

ADDITION

Algebraic   Geometric

$[a, b] + [c, d] = [a + c, b + d]$

$\overrightarrow{AB} + \overrightarrow{BC} = \overrightarrow{AC}$

SUBTRACTION

Algebraic   Geometric

$[a, b] - [c, d] = [a - c, b - d]$

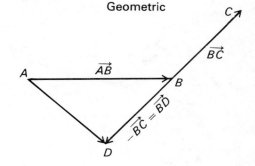

$$\overrightarrow{AB} - \overrightarrow{BC} = \overrightarrow{AB} + (-\overrightarrow{BC})$$
$$= \overrightarrow{AB} + \overrightarrow{BD}$$
$$= \overrightarrow{AD}$$

SCALAR MULTIPLICATION

Any real number not associated with direction is called a scalar quantity. If $\vec{v} = [a, b]$ and m is a scalar, then

$$m\vec{v} = m[a, b] = [ma, mb]$$

EXAMPLE 1. *Simplify* (*i*) $[3, 2] + [-5, 6]$
(*ii*) $[5, 3] - [4, 4]$
(*iii*) $4[2, -3]$
(*iv*) $2[-5, 7] + 3[2, -4]$

Solution

(i) $[3, 2] + [-5, 6]$
$= [3 - 5, 2 + 6]$
$= [-2, 8]$

(ii) $[5, 3] - [4, 4]$
$= [5 - 4, 3 - 4]$
$= [1, -1]$

(iii) $4[2, -3]$
$= [4(2), 4(-3)]$
$= [8, -12]$

(iv) $2[-5, 7] + 3[2, -4]$
$= [-10, 14] + [6, -12]$
$= [-4, 2]$

EXAMPLE 2. *An aircraft flying north with an air speed of* 200 kn *encounters a* 50 kn *east wind. Calculate the ground speed* (*to the nearest knot*) *and true direction of the flight (to the nearest degree).*

Solution Let m represent the ground speed in knots, and let θ represent the angle west of north. From the diagram,

$$m = \sqrt{50^2 + 200^2}$$

$$= \sqrt{2500 + 40\,000}$$

$$= \sqrt{42\,500}$$

$$\doteq 206$$

$$\tan \theta = \frac{50}{200} = 0.25$$

$$\theta \doteq 14°$$

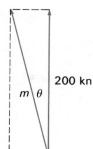

200 kn

50 kn

$\therefore$ the aircraft is travelling at 206 kn in a direction 14° west of north.

EXERCISE 11-2

1. Simplify:
(a) $[3, 5] + [2, 7] - [8, -2]$
(b) $3[2, -5] + [4, 8] - 2[2, 4]$
(c) $[5, 2] - [5, 2] - [2, 0]$
(d) $[5, 3] + [0, 0]$

magnitude of $[a, b]$ is
$\sqrt{a^2+b^2}$

2. The symbol $|\vec{x}|$ is read "the magnitude of $\vec{x}$." If $\vec{x} = [4, 3]$ and $\vec{y} = [-5, 12]$,
(a) Find (i) $|\vec{x}|$ (ii) $|\vec{y}|$ (iii) $|\vec{x} + \vec{y}|$
(b) Insert the correct sign ($<, =, >$) in

$$|\vec{x}| + |\vec{y}| \; \blacksquare \; |\vec{x} + \vec{y}|$$

3. If $\vec{s} = [3, 2]$ and $\vec{t} = [2, -4]$, find:

(a) $\vec{s} + \vec{t}$	(b) $3\vec{s}$	(c) $2\vec{s} + 3\vec{t}$
(d) $\vec{s} - \vec{t}$	(e) $\vec{t} - \vec{s}$	(f) $|\vec{s} + \vec{t}|$
(g) $|\vec{s}|$	(h) $|\vec{t}|$	(i) $|\vec{t} - \vec{s}|$

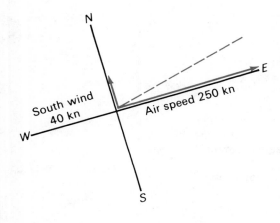

4. The navigator of an aircraft receives the wind speed and direction by radio from the control tower and draws the given diagram. Calculate the ground speed and direction of travel.

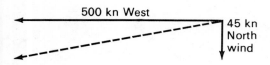

5. A pilot sets his course at 500 kn west relative to the ground. Find the true ground velocity and direction if the flight is affected by a 45 kn north wind.

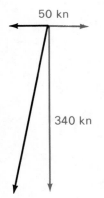

6. In what direction should a pilot set his course if he wants to fly south at 340 kn and there is a 50 kn west wind?

applied mathematics for today: senior

7. A pilot wishes to fly west at 425 kn while there is a 40 kn south wind. Find the course he must set, and the air speed.

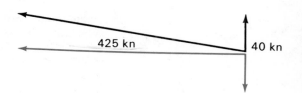

425 kn

40 kn

11.3 POINTS IN SPACE

In the preceding section, we studied vectors in the plane, which limited our study to only two dimensions, so that we could only describe what takes place on a flat surface. Although there are many applications of vectors in two dimensions, we must eventually study vectors in three dimensions.

Figure 11-2 shows the vector diagram of the forces acting on a football in flight with a wind blowing across the path of the ball.

$\vec{A}$ represents the force due to air resistance.

$\vec{W}$ represents the force due to the wind blowing perpendicular to the page.

$\vec{G}$ represents the gravitational force.

Figure 11-2

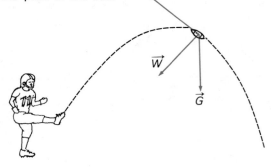

We can get a clearer picture of the *position* of the ball if we relate the situation to a set of *three-dimensional* axes. In Figure 11-3 we show the ball and its path related to a set of axes, so that the ball leaves the player's foot at the origin and continues in the *yz*-plane until acted upon by the wind. The position of the ball can be determined by an *ordered triple* (x, y, z).

Figure 11–3

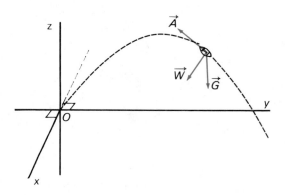

Note that in three dimensions, the y-axis is horizontal and the z-axis is vertical, with the x-axis perpendicular to the yz-plane.

EXAMPLE 1. *Locate the point P(2, 4, 7) on a set of three-dimensional axes.*

Solution

1. From the origin move +2 units along the positive x-axis.
2. Then move +4 units (4 units in a positive direction) parallel to the y-axis.
3. Then move +7 units parallel to the z-axis to the point P.

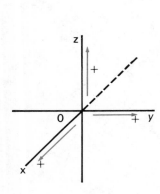

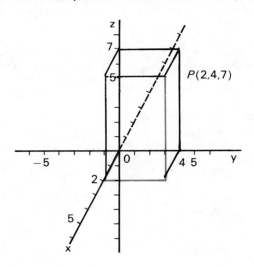

Note that the point P determines a rectangular box when the planes through P are combined with the planes determined by the axes.

EXAMPLE 2. *Plot the points Q(2, −5, 3), R(0, 4, 0) and S(0, 4, −4).*

Solution

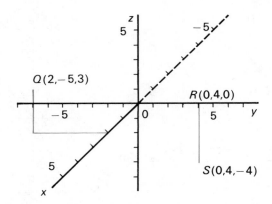

applied mathematics for today: senior

EXAMPLE 3. *Find the distance between $A(3, -5, 7)$ and $B(-2, 4, 4)$ given the distance formula $d = \sqrt{(x_2 - x_1)^2 + (y_2 - y_1)^2 + (z_2 - z_1)^2}$, where d is the distance from $P_1(x_1, y_1, z_1)$ to $P_2(x_2, y_2, z_2)$ as shown below.*

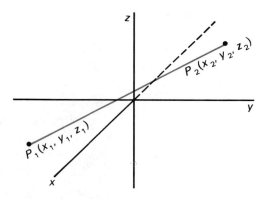

The boys outnumber the girls by 16. Seven times the number of boys exceeds 8 times the number of girls by 72. How many boys and girls are there?

Solution The formula $d = \sqrt{(x_2 - x_1)^2 + (y_2 - y_1)^2 + (z_2 - z_1)^2}$ is used when dealing with distances in space in the same manner as the formula

$d = \sqrt{(x_2 - x_1)^2 + (y_2 - y_1)^2}$ is used in two dimensions.

$d = \sqrt{(-2 - 3)^2 + (4 + 5)^2 + (4 - 7)^2}$

$ = \sqrt{(-5)^2 + (9)^2 + (-3)^2}$

$ = \sqrt{25 + 81 + 9}$

$ = \sqrt{115}$

$ \doteq 10.7$

The distance from A to B is approximately 10.7 units.

EXERCISE 11-3

Indicate the following points in space on a set of three-dimensional axes, using line segments to illustrate the coordinates.

B
1. $(4, 3, 2)$	**2.** $(2, 3, 6)$	**3.** $(4, 3, 5)$
4. $(-2, 1, 4)$	**5.** $(-2, -3, 5)$	**6.** $(3, -5, 7)$
7. $(6, 2, 8)$	**8.** $(-4, -3, -2)$	**9.** $(4, 7, -2)$
10. $(4, -3, -5)$	**11.** $(-2, 6, -7)$	**12.** $(0, 0, 0)$
13. $(1, 0, 0)$	**14.** $(0, 1, 0)$	**15.** $(0, 0, 1)$

Find the distance between the following pairs of points.

16. $A(3, 5, 7)$ to $B(4, 8, 10)$

17. $C(0, 0, 5)$ to $D(0, 12, 0)$

18. $E(-3, -5, 4)$ to $F(5, -7, 8)$

19. $G(0, 9, 12)$ to $H(8, 9, 12)$
20. $I(5, 5, 5)$ to $J(6, 7, 8)$
21. $K(3, -5, -4)$ to $L(4, -5, 4)$
22. $M(5, 0, -3)$ to $N(6, -5, 4)$

MODELS IN SPACE

EXAMPLE: *Calculate the lengths of the straws in this photograph, given the coordinates* $A(4, 2, 4)$, $B(8, 3, 4)$, $C(7, 9, 1)$, $D(2, 6, 2)$.

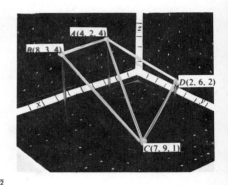

Solution:

$$d = \sqrt{(x_2 - x_1)^2 + (y_2 - y_1)^2 + (z_2 - z_1)^2}$$

$$AB = \sqrt{(8-4)^2 + (3-2)^2 + (4-4)^2}$$
$$= \sqrt{(4)^2 + (1)^2 + (0)^2}$$
$$= \sqrt{16+1} = \sqrt{17} \doteq 4.12.$$

$$BC = \sqrt{(7-8)^2 + (9-3)^2 + (1-4)^2}$$
$$= \sqrt{(-1)^2 + (6)^2 + (-3)^2}$$
$$= \sqrt{1+36+9} = \sqrt{46} \doteq 6.78.$$

$$CD = \sqrt{(2-7)^2 + (6-9)^2 + (2-1)^2}$$
$$= \sqrt{(-5)^2 + (-3)^2 + (1)^2}$$
$$= \sqrt{25+9+1} = \sqrt{35} \doteq 5.92.$$

$$AC = \sqrt{(7-4)^2 + (9-2)^2 + (1-4)^2}$$
$$= \sqrt{(3)^2 + (7)^2 + (-3)^2}$$
$$= \sqrt{9+49+9} = \sqrt{67} \doteq 8.18.$$

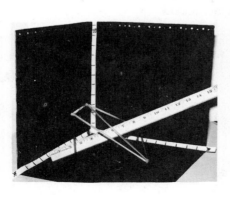

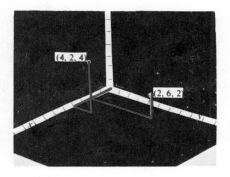

INVESTIGATION 11.3

1. Construct a model in space as shown in one of the previous photographs.

2. Locate the points given in Table 11-4 on your model as accurately as possible.

3. Test the distance formula

$$d = \sqrt{(x_2 - x_1)^2 + (y_2 - y_1)^2 + (z_2 - z_1)^2}$$

by (a) calculation using the formula.

(b) direct measurement of the model, where d is the distance from the first point to the second point; then complete the following table in your notebook.

First point	Second point	Distance by calculation $d = \sqrt{(x_2 - x_1)^2 + (y_2 - y_1)^2 + (z_2 - z_1)^2}$	Distance by measurement
$(0, 0, 0)$	$(4, 2, 4)$		
$(0, 0, 0)$	$(8, 4, 1)$		
$(4, 0, 3)$	$(0, 0, 0)$		
$(2, 3, 5)$	$(10, 7, 6)$		
$(0, 1, -5)$	$(4, 3, -1)$		
$(-3, 2, -5)$	$(1, 2, -2)$		
$(-3, 5, -2)$	$(2, 7, -4)$		
$(3, 7, -5)$	$(2, -5, 8)$		

Table 11-4

How many cubic centimetres of dirt are there in a hole that is 1 m deep, 2 m wide and 6 m long?

4. State whether the *x*-, *y*-, or *z*-coordinate is zero for each of the following.
(a) A point in the *xy*-plane.
(b) A point in the *xz*-plane.
(c) A point in the *yz*-plane.
(d) A point in the *xy*- and *yz*-planes.
(e) A point in the *yz*- and *xz*-planes.

11.4 VECTORS IN THREE DIMENSIONS

While a vector can be represented by an ordered pair with square brackets, [*a, b*], when dealing with two dimensions, we introduce a third component to represent a vector in three dimensions. Hence the vector [2, 4, 7] represents a vector two units in the direction of the positive *x*-axis, four units in the direction of the positive *y*-axis and seven units in the direction of the positive *z*-axis. The ordered triple [*a, b, c*] represents a vector in three dimensions.

EXAMPLE 1. *If A(−2, 3, 7) and B(4, 4, 3) are two points in space, find* $\overrightarrow{AB}$ *and illustrate with a diagram.*

Solution

$$\overrightarrow{AB} = [4-(-2), 4-3, 3-7]$$
$$= [6, 1, -4]$$

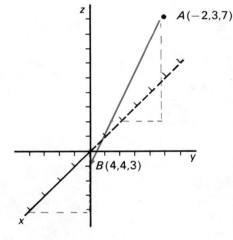

EXAMPLE 2. *Draw the given vectors with initial point at the origin:*

(a) $\vec{v} = [5, 7, 2]$ 　　　　　　(b) $\vec{w} = [3, -4, 5]$

Solution

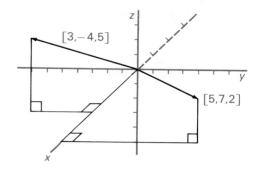

EXERCISE 11-4

B **1.** Plot the points $A(2, 4, 6)$, $B(7, 2, 5)$, $C(-3, -6, -5)$, $D(2, 4, 7)$ and find the algebraic vectors represented by $\overrightarrow{AB}$, $\overrightarrow{CD}$, $\overrightarrow{BA}$, $\overrightarrow{BC}$, $\overrightarrow{DC}$, $\overrightarrow{DA}$, $\overrightarrow{AD}$, $\overrightarrow{BD}$, $\overrightarrow{DB}$.

2. Given the points $P(-1, 3, 4)$, $Q(3, -5, 5)$, $R(8, 1, 5)$, $S(10, 9, 4)$,
(a) find $\overrightarrow{PQ}$, $\overrightarrow{QR}$, $\overrightarrow{SR}$, $\overrightarrow{PS}$.
(b) plot the points and identify figures $PQRS$.

3. Complete the following table in your notes.

Initial point	Terminal point	Vector
(3, 4, 7)	(2, 2, 11)	[−1, −2, 4]
(1, 1, 6)	(−5, 3, 2)	
(−2, −3, 7)	(7, 4, 11)	
(4, 2, −6)	(2, −5, 7)	
(3, 2, −6)		[4, 1, −3]
	(3, 2, 8)	[−3, −2, 8]
(4, −2, −7)		[5, 2, −7]
(3, −7, 5)	(−2, 7, 11)	
(6, 0, −2)		[0, 0, 0]
	(3, 5, −7)	[1, 0, 0]
(2, 1, 0)		[0, 1, 0]
	(7, −5, 7)	[0, 0, 1]
(3, 2, −1)		[2, −5, 7]
(4, 2, 7)	(4, 2, 7)	

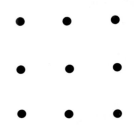

Draw four connected lines, without retracing your path, that pass through all the points.

EXAMPLE 3. *Find the length of the vector* $[4, 2, 4]$

Solution The magnitude of a vector expressed in the form $[a, b, c]$ can be found using $m = \sqrt{a^2 + b^2 + c^2}$

$$m = \sqrt{4^2 + 2^2 + 4^2}$$

$$= \sqrt{16 + 4 + 16}$$

$$= \sqrt{36}$$

$$= 6$$

The magnitude of $[4, 2, 4]$ is 6 units.

4. Use $m = \sqrt{a^2 + b^2 + c^2}$ to calculate the lengths of the following vectors.

(a) $[-4, -2, 4]$ (b) $[-4, 0, 3]$ (e) $[5, -2, 7]$
(d) $[-1, 4, 8]$ (e) $[3, -7, 5]$ (f) $[-5, 4, -6]$

11.5   EQUAL VECTORS

Vectors with the same magnitude and direction can be represented by the same ordered triple and are called equal vectors.

EXERCISE 11-5

B   **1.** (a) Complete the following table in your notes.

Find a quantity such that one quarter of its square is 36.

Initial point	Terminal point	Vector
$A(5, 2, -7)$	$B(3, 7, 5)$	$\overrightarrow{AB} = $ ▬▬▬
$C(0, 5, 1)$	$D(3, 5, -4)$	$\overrightarrow{CD} = $ ▬▬▬
$E(3, -2, -2)$	$F($ ▬▬▬ $)$	$\overrightarrow{EF} = [-2, 5, 12]$
$G($ ▬▬▬ $)$	$H(5, 2, 1)$	$\overrightarrow{GH} = [6, 7, -3]$
$I(0, 5, 7)$	$J(3, 5, 12)$	$\overrightarrow{IJ} = $ ▬▬▬
$K($ ▬▬▬ $)$	$L(3, 8, -1)$	$\overrightarrow{KL} = [6, 7, -3]$
$M(1, -2, -6)$	$N(-1, 3, 6)$	$\overrightarrow{MN} = $ ▬▬▬

(b) Name the vectors in (a) which are equal vectors.

2. If $A(-2, 5, 4)$, $B(3, 2, 4)$, and $C(1, 6, 4)$ are three points in space, make a diagram and find the coordinates of point D so that $\overrightarrow{AB} = \overrightarrow{CD}$.

3. Given points $A(2, 7, 4)$, $B(3, 1, 6)$, and $C(-2, 0, 2)$ find the following.
(a) The coordinates of point D so that $\overrightarrow{AB} = \overrightarrow{CD}$.
(b) The coordinates of point E so that $\overrightarrow{AC} = \overrightarrow{BE}$.

4. (a) Given points $A(-5, 5, 5)$, $B(9, 2, 5)$, and $C(4, -7, 5)$, find the coordinates of point D so that $ABCD$ is a parallelogram.

(b) Verify that *ABCD* is a parallelogram by showing that $\overrightarrow{AB} = \overrightarrow{DC}$, and also $\overrightarrow{AD} = \overrightarrow{BC}$.

5. (a) If $[3, -2, 5]$, $[3, -2, c]$, and $[a, -2, 5]$ are equal vectors, state the numerical values of *a* and *c*.
(b) If $[a, b, c] = [d, e, f]$, how are the numbers *a*, *b*, *c* and *d*, *e*, *f* related?
(c) If $a = d$, $b = e$ and $c = f$, how are $[a, b, c]$ and $[d, e, f]$ related?
In general:

> Two vectors $[a, b, c]$ and $[d, e, f]$ are equal if and only if $a = d$, $b = e$, and $c = f$.

11.6 ADDITION OF VECTORS

We can compare addition of vectors in three dimensions to addition of vectors in two dimensions.

> **Two Dimensions**
>
> $[2, 4] + [-5, 7] = [2-5, 4+7] = [-3, 11]$
>
> $[a, b] + [d, e] = [a+d, b+e]$
>
> **Three Dimensions**
>
> $[3, 1, 7] + [2, -5, -2] = [3+2, 1-5, 7-2] = [5, -4, 5]$
>
> $[a, b, c] + [d, e, f] = [a+d, b+e, c+f]$

EXERCISE 11-6

B **1.** Add the following vectors.
(a) $[3, 5, -2] + [4, 6, 0]$
(b) $[-2, 7, 5] + [6, 1, -7]$
(c) $[-3, -5, 2] + [4, 6, 5]$
(d) $[2, -6, 1] + [3, 1, 5]$
(e) $[2, 3, 1] + [-3, -4, -5]$
(f) $[2, 6, 5] + [-2, -6, -5]$
(g) $[-4, -7, 5] + [-4, -7, 5]$
(h) $[11, 1, 0] + [-1, -11, 0]$
(i) $[0, 0, 0] + [2, 5, -3]$
(j) $[2, 1, 3] + [6, -7, 4] + [-3, 5, -2]$

2. Find *x*, *y*, *z* for each of the following.
(a) $[x, y, z] + [3, -7, 2] = [0, 0, 0]$
(b) $[2, -6, -3] + [x, y, z] = [0, 0, 0]$
(c) $[3, 5, 7] + [-2, 6, -5] = [x, y, z]$
(d) $[x, y, z] + [x, y, z] = [6, 10, 8]$

In questions 3 and 4, simplify first the left side, then the right side, and insert the proper sign, $=$ or $\ne$.

3. (a) $[-3, 7, 2] + [2, -5, 7] \blacksquare [2, -5, 7] + [-3, 7, 2]$
(b) $[a, b, c] + [d, e, f] \blacksquare [d, e, f] + [a, b, c]$
(c) Name the property which has been demonstrated in (a) and (b).

4. (a) $([2, 4, 6] + [3, -2, 7]) + [-4, 8, 3] \blacksquare [2, 4, 6] + ([3, -2, 7] + [-4, 8, 3])$
(b) $([a, b, c] + [d, e, f]) + [g, h, i] \blacksquare [a, b, c] + ([d, e, f] + [g, h, i])$
(c) Name the property which has been demonstrated in (a) and (b).

Take a piece of paper 0.1 mm in thickness. Fold it in half. Fold it a second time at right angles to the first fold. If you continued folding until you had folded it 50 times, how thick would the paper be?

5. Find the sums indicated.

(i) $[4, 3, 2] + [0, 0, 0]$ (ii) $[0, 0, 0] + [-7, -2, 3]$

(iii) $[-4, -2, 5] + [0, 0, 0]$

(b) Find the values of x, y, and z, so that

$$[a, b, c] + [x, y, z] = [a, b, c]$$

and also $[x, y, z] + [a, b, c] = [a, b, c]$

(c) What is the identity or zero vector in three dimensions?

6. Find $[x, y, z]$ for parts (a) to (d).

(a) $[2, 3, 4] + [x, y, z] = [0, 0, 0]$

(b) $[x, y, z] + [4, 11, -7] = [0, 0, 0]$

(c) $[-4, 7, -3] + [x, y, z] = [0, 0, 0]$

(d) $[a, b, c] + [x, y, z] = [0, 0, 0]$

(e) What is the additive inverse, or negative, of $[a, b, c]$?

Note that in all examples of vector addition in Exercise 11-6, the result of adding two vectors in space was always another three-dimensional vector. Hence we say that the set of vectors of the form $[a, b, c]$ is closed under addition.

11.7 MULTIPLICATION OF A THREE-DIMENSIONAL VECTOR BY A SCALAR

We have represented vectors as directed line segments or as ordered triples $[a, b, c]$. When working with vectors, we can also use real numbers, which we call *scalars*, as we did when dealing with two-dimensional vectors. What is the effect of multiplying a vector in three dimensions by a scalar?

EXAMPLE 1. (*a*) *Simplify* $2[-4, 2, -4]$

(*b*) *Find the magnitudes of* (*i*) $[-4, 2, -4]$, (*ii*) $[-8, 4, -8]$

(*c*) *Compare* $2[-4, 2, -4]$ *to* $[-8, 4, -8]$

Solution (a) $2[-4, 2, -4] = [2(-4), 2(2), 2(-4)]$
$$= [-8, 4, -8]$$

(b) $m = \sqrt{a^2 + b^2 + c^2}$

(i) The magnitude of $[-4, 2, -4]$ is

$$\sqrt{(-4)^2 + (2)^2 + (-4)^2} = \sqrt{16 + 4 + 16}$$

$$= \sqrt{36}$$

$$= 6$$

(ii) The magnitude of $[-8, 4, -8]$ is

$$\sqrt{(-8)^2 + (4)^2 + (-8)^2} = \sqrt{64 + 16 + 64}$$

$$= \sqrt{144}$$

$$= 12$$

(c) Hence, $2[-4, 2, -4] = [-8, 4, -8]$

The cost of 3 is 27¢.
The cost of 35 is 54¢.
The cost of 356 is 81¢.
What am I buying?

EXAMPLE 2. (a) Simplify $\frac{1}{3}[1, -4, 8]$

(b) Compare the magnitudes of (i) $[1, -4, 8]$ and (ii) $[\frac{1}{3}, -\frac{4}{3}, \frac{8}{3}]$

Solution (a) $\frac{1}{3}[1, -4, 8] = [\frac{1}{3}, -\frac{4}{3}, \frac{8}{3}]$

(b) $m = \sqrt{a^2 + b^2 + c^2}$

(i) The magnitude of $[1, -4, 8]$ is

$$\sqrt{(1)^2 + (-4)^2 + (8)^2} = \sqrt{1 + 16 + 64}$$

$$= \sqrt{81}$$

$$= 9$$

(ii) The magnitude of $[\frac{1}{3}, -\frac{4}{3}, \frac{8}{3}]$ is

$$\sqrt{(\tfrac{1}{3})^2 + (-\tfrac{4}{3})^2 + (\tfrac{8}{3})^2} = \sqrt{\tfrac{1}{9} + \tfrac{16}{9} + \tfrac{64}{9}}$$

$$= \sqrt{\tfrac{81}{9}} = \sqrt{9} = 3$$

Hence, $\frac{1}{3}[1, -4, 8] = [\frac{1}{3}, -\frac{4}{3}, \frac{8}{3}]$

Examples 1 and 2 suggest that multiplying a three-dimensional vector by a scalar causes a "stretching" or "compression" in the same direction as the vector. This result may be generalized to

$$\boxed{m[a, b, c] = [ma, mb, mc]}$$

EXERCISE 11-7

A **1.** Express each of the following in the form $[a, b, c]$

(a) $2[4, 2, 7]$ (b) $3[6, -1, 5]$

(c) $\frac{1}{2}[4, 2, -8]$ (d) $(-3)[-2, -5, -1]$

(e) $\frac{2}{3}[-3, 0, 9]$ (f) $\frac{1}{2}[0, 0, 0]$

(g) $4[0, -2, 1]$ (h) $-\frac{1}{4}[4, -16, 12]$

B **2.** Express each of the following in the form $[a, b, c]$

(a) $3[4, 1, 2] + 2[3, 1, 5]$ (b) $2[-1, 5, 2] + [3, -2, 1]$

(c) $\frac{1}{2}[0, 4, -2] + 4[1, 0, 1]$ (d) $3[1, 1, 1] + (-2)[2, 2, 2]$

(e) $(-5)[2, 7, -1] + (-3)[7, -2, 1] + 4[2, -3, 1]$

(f) $3([4, 2, -1] + [4, -7, 3])$ (g) $4([3, 5, 2] + 2[-1, 2, 1])$

(h) $5([4, 2, -1] + (-2)[2, 1, 3])$

3. If $\vec{v} = [x, y, z]$ and $\vec{w} = [2x, -3y, 3z]$, find:

(a) $4\vec{v} + 2\vec{w}$ (b) $4(\vec{v} + \vec{w})$ (c) $-2(\vec{v} + \vec{w})$

(d) $2\vec{v} + 4\vec{w}$ (e) $0(\vec{v} + \vec{w})$ (f) $3(2\vec{v} + 3\vec{w})$

11.8 SUBTRACTION OF VECTORS

Subtraction of vectors has been defined as the addition of the negative (or additive inverse) of the given vector. To subtract $[3, -5, 2]$, simply add $[-3, 5, -2]$.

EXAMPLE 1. Simplify $[7, 5, 2] - [3, -5, 2]$

Solution

$$[7, 5, 2] - [3, -5, 2] = [7, 5, 2] + [-3, 5, -2]$$
$$= [4, 10, 0]$$

This result may be generalized to

$$\boxed{[a, b, c] - [p, q, r] = [a - p, b - q, c - r]}$$

EXERCISE 11-8

A **1.** Simplify and express your answer in the form $[a, b, c]$.
(a) $[3, 2, -2] - [2, 1, 5]$ (b) $[6, -5, 7] - [2, 4, -6]$
(c) $[-3, -2, 2] - [-7, -11, 5]$ (d) $[5, -7, 2] - [8, -5, 3]$
(e) $[3, 2, -5] - [3, 2, -5]$ (f) $[5, 12, 13] - [-5, -12, -13]$
(g) $[8, 15, 17] - [0, 0, 0]$ (h) $[2a, 5b, c] - [a, -b, -2c]$

B **2.** Simplify and express your answer in the form $[a, b, c]$.
(a) $3[5, -2, 1] - 2[1, -1, 1]$ (b) $4[6, -3, 2] - 2[5, 4, -1]$
(c) $\frac{1}{2}[-6, 4, -2] - \frac{1}{4}[-4, 8, 12]$ (d) $5[\frac{3}{5}, \frac{1}{5}, 0] - 4[6, -1, 0]$
(e) $-2[4, -1, 3] - 3[1, -2, 7]$ (f) $-5([6, -3, 2] - [-2, 5, 1])$
(g) $3(-2[1, 5, 2] - 4[-1, 0, -2])$

REVIEW EXERCISE

1. Find the terminal point determined by the vector $[4, -3, 5]$ if the initial point is:
(a) $(4, 0, 2)$ (b) $(-4, 3, -1)$ (c) $(0, 0, 0)$
(d) $(4, -3, 7)$ (e) $(5, 1, -2)$ (f) (x, y, z)

2. If $\vec{v} = [4, 2, -4]$ and $\vec{w} = [-1, 4, -8]$, find:
(a) $3\vec{v}$ (b) $\vec{v} + \vec{w}$ (c) $2\vec{v} + 3\vec{w}$
(d) $|\vec{v}|$, (the magnitude of $\vec{v}$)
(e) $|\vec{w}|$, (the magnitude of $\vec{w}$).

3. Given the points $A(4, 2, -3)$, $B(7, 3, -3)$, $C(-3, 0, -3)$ and $D(0, 1, -3)$, determine which of $\overline{AB}$, $\overline{CD}$, $\overline{BA}$, and $\overline{DC}$ are equal vectors.

4. Express the following in the form $[a, b, c]$:
(a) $[2, 3, -5] + [1, -2, 7] - [3, 5, -3]$
(b) $3[-2, 5, -2] - 2[-4, 6, 1]$

applied mathematics for today: senior

(c) $-2[3, -2, 0] + 2[-1, 0, 2]$ (d) $3([1, -2, 4] - [2, -1, 5])$

The following problems should be solved using vectors in the plane.

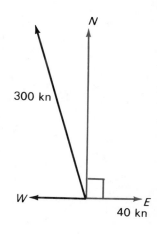

5. A ship sails 300 km north and 125 km east. Find the magnitude and direction of an alternative course equal to the resultant representing the ship's course.

6. What course must a pilot set to fly north if his air speed is 300 kn and there is a 40 kn west wind?

7. A pleasure craft is speeding across a river at 30 kn. Find the actual speed and direction if the current is 5 kn.

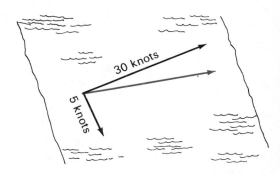

REVIEW AND PREVIEW TO CHAPTER 12

EXERCISE 1 *UNITS OF FORCE*

one newton = 1 N

$$F = ma$$

$$F = 1\,kg \times 1\,m/s^2$$
$$= 1\,kg{\cdot}m/s^2$$
$$= 1\,N$$

1. Find the force required to give a 10 kg mass an acceleration of 5 m/s².

2. Find the force exerted on a 90 kg man if acceleration due to gravity is 9.8 m/s².

3. What acceleration can a 100 N force impart to a 15 kg mass?

4. What acceleration can a 300 N force impart to a 20 kg mass?

5. Find the mass of an object that is given an acceleration of 18 m/s² by a 12 N force.

EXERCISE 2 *COPLANAR FORCES— RESULTANT*

State the magnitude and direction of the resultant, where

$$R^2 = P^2 + Q^2 + 2PQ \cos \theta$$

$\cos(180° - \theta)$
$= -\cos \theta$

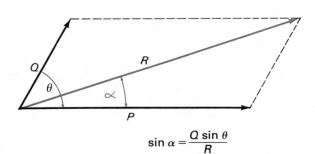

$$\sin \alpha = \frac{Q \sin \theta}{R}$$

1.

50 N   65°   60 N

2.

40 N   82°   65 N

3.

35 N   75°   60 N

applied mathematics for today: senior

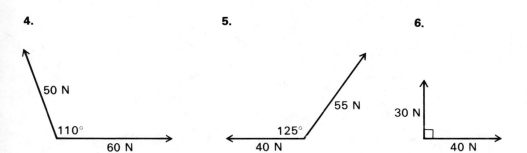

4. 50 N 110° 60 N

5. 55 N 125° 40 N

6. 30 N 40 N

EXERCISE 3 *RESOLUTION OF FORCES*

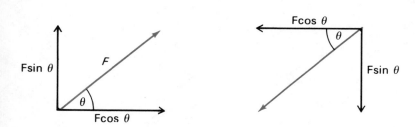

Resolve the following forces into horizontal and vertical components.

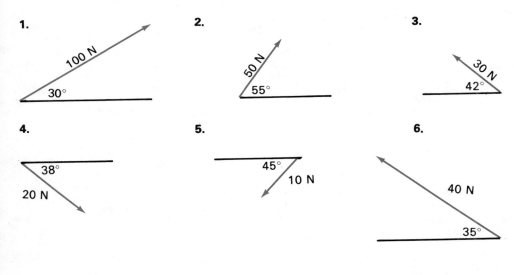

1. 100 N 30°

2. 50 N 55°

3. 30 N 42°

4. 38° 20 N

5. 45° 10 N

6. 40 N 35°

statics   261

Solve for x:

1. $\dfrac{x}{35.65} = \dfrac{42.83}{24.45}$

2. $\dfrac{x}{28.24} = \dfrac{34.72}{16.42}$

3. $\dfrac{x}{3.875} = \dfrac{72.83}{2.645}$

4. $\dfrac{284.7}{631.9} = \dfrac{x}{208.9}$

5. $\dfrac{58.75}{x} = \dfrac{72.65}{84.34}$

6. $\dfrac{2.194}{94.31} = \dfrac{5.785}{x}$

7. $\dfrac{x}{3.712} = \dfrac{3.712}{5.635}$

8. $\dfrac{0.027\ 51}{x} = \dfrac{34.47}{53.85}$

9. $\dfrac{3.288}{4.363} = \dfrac{x}{0.5452}$

10. $\dfrac{0.4216}{0.6974} = \dfrac{0.2455}{x}$

Statics

Statics is a branch of the physical sciences which deals with forces acting upon a body in a state of rest or equilibrium. For most practical purposes, we shall consider a force to be a push or pull that tends to produce or change the motion of a body.

12.1 ROTATIONAL EFFECT OF FORCES: MOMENTS

When a force is applied to a box sitting on the floor, as in Figure 12-1, any motion applied would be in a straight line. When a force is applied along the rim of a steering wheel, as in Figure 12-2, the effect is to turn the wheel. This turning effect of a force about a point is called the moment of the force (measured in newton metres), and is found by multiplying the magnitude of the force by the perpendicular distance from the point of rotation to the line of action of the force.

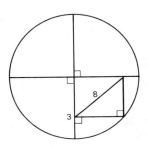

Find the radius of the circle.

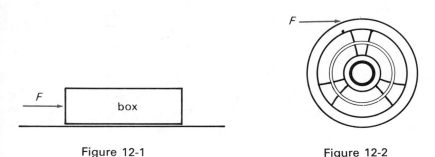

Figure 12-1   Figure 12-2

$$M = F \times d \text{ (newton metres)}$$

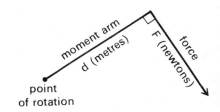

point
of rotation

EXAMPLE 1. *What is the moment produced by a* 10 N *force applied* 2 cm *from the point of rotation?*

Solution

2 cm = 0.02 m

  $M = F \times d$

  $M = 10\ \text{N} \times 0.02\ \text{m}$

    $= 0.2\ \text{N·m}$

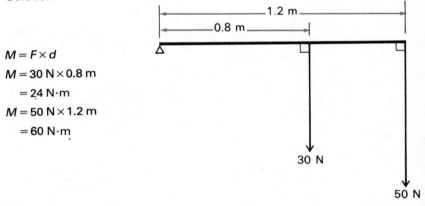

The moment is 0.2 N·m.

EXAMPLE 2. *What is the sum of the moments produced by forces of* 30 N *and* 50 N *applied* 0.8 m *and* 1.2 m *respectively from the point of rotation?*

Solution

$M = F \times d$

$M = 30\ \text{N} \times 0.8\ \text{m}$

  $= 24\ \text{N·m}$

$M = 50\ \text{N} \times 1.2\ \text{m}$

  $= 60\ \text{N·m}$

The sum of the moments is 24 N·m + 60 N·m = 84 N·m.

When two children sit on opposite ends of a seesaw, each produces a moment which tends to turn the system either clockwise or counterclockwise. How would you arrange the children in Figure 12-3 so that they just balance if child *A* is heavier than child *B*?

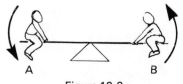

Figure 12-3

applied mathematics for today: senior

The **mass** of a body is the measure of the amount of matter present in the body and remains constant. The force of attraction between a mass and the earth (or any large mass such as the moon) is called the **weight**.

The weight of the mass on the surface of the earth can be found using the formula $F = ma$.

$$\text{weight in newtons} = \text{mass in kilograms} \times 9.8 \text{ m/s}^2$$

Because 9.8 gives awkward values, in this book we shall use 10 instead to simplify calculations so that a mass of 1 kg has an approximate weight of 10 N.

Gravity is the force of attraction that exists between any two masses.

The force of gravity between an object and the earth is commonly called the weight of the object on earth.

INVESTIGATION 12.1
LAW OF MOMENTS

1. (a) Suspend a metre stick so that it balances (near the centre) and is free to rotate about the point from which it is suspended.

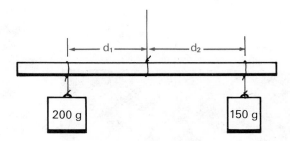

(b) Suspend masses of 200 g and 150 g on opposite sides of the point of rotation, adjusting the positions of the masses until equilibrium occurs.

(c) Record the distance from each mass to the point of rotation.

(d) Repeat the procedure four times, changing the positions of the masses and complete the following table in your notebook.

A mass of 100 g has an approximate weight of 1 N.

mass	weight
100 g	1 N
150 g	1.5 N
200 g	2 N
500 g	5 N

200 g mass		150 g mass	
d_1	$M \times Fd_1$	d_2	$M = F \times d_2$

(e) The 200 g mass produces a counterclockwise moment, while the 150 g mass produces a clockwise moment. Compare the clockwise moments to the counterclockwise moments when the system is in equilibrium.

2. (a) With the metre stick balanced near the centre, and using masses of 100 g, 50 g, and 200 g, set up five systems in equilibrium as in the diagram and complete the following table.

General Mack lived $\frac{1}{4}$ of his life as a boy, $\frac{1}{5}$ of his life as a young man, $\frac{1}{3}$ as a man with responsibilities, and 13 a in retirement. How long did he live?

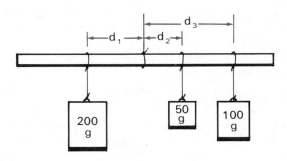

200 g mass		50 g mass		100 g mass		Sum
d_1	$M_1 = F \times d_1$	d_2	$M_2 = F \times d_2$	d_3	$M_3 = F \times d_3$	$M_2 + M_3$

(b) The 200 g mass produces a counterclockwise moment about the point of rotation while the 100 g and 50 g masses produce clockwise moments. Compare the clockwise moments and counterclockwise moments.

3. (a) Arrange four or five masses at various positions on a balanced metre stick to form a system in equilibrium.
(b) Complete the following table in your notebook.

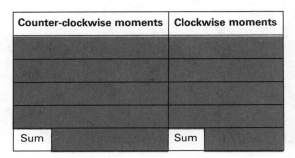

Counter-clockwise moments		Clockwise moments	
Sum		Sum	

applied mathematics for today: senior

(c) Compare the sum of the clockwise moments to the sum of the counterclockwise moments for a system in equilibrium.

> **LAW OF MOMENTS**
>
> When a system is in equilibrium, the sum of the clockwise moments about any point is equal to the sum of the counterclockwise moments about the same point.

EXAMPLE 3. *The system in the following diagram is in equilibrium. Calculate the value of x.*

A 300 g mass has an approximate weight of 3 N.

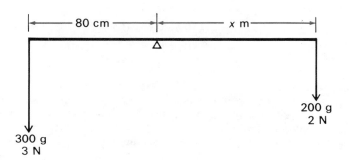

Solution

$$\text{Counterclockwise moment:} \quad 3\,N \times 0.8\,m = 2.4\,N \cdot m$$

$$\text{Clockwise moment:} \quad 2\,N \times x\,m = 2x\,N \cdot m$$

Since the system is in equilibrium,

$$2x \times N \cdot m = 2.4\,N \cdot m$$

$$x = 1.2\,m$$

Therefore $x = 1.2$ m.

The diagonal of a square is 10 cm. Find the length of a side.

EXAMPLE 4. *The system shown below is in equilibrium. Calculate the value of x.*

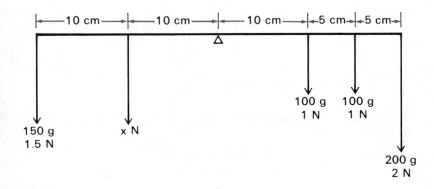

Solution

An object that weighs 3.5 N has a mass of approximately 350 g.

Counterclockwise moments:

$$1.5 \text{ N} \times 0.2 \text{ m} = 0.3 \quad \text{N·m}$$
$$x \text{ N} \times 0.1 \text{ m} = 0.1x \text{ N·m}$$

Total $\quad\quad\quad (0.3 + 0.1x) \text{ N·m}$

Clockwise moments:

$$1 \text{ N} \times 0.10 \text{ m} = 0.10 \text{ N·m}$$
$$1 \text{ N} \times 0.15 \text{ m} = 0.15 \text{ N·m}$$
$$2 \text{ N} \times 0.20 \text{ m} = 0.40 \text{ N·m}$$

Total $\quad\quad = 0.65 \text{ N·m}$

Since the system is in equilibrium,

$$0.30 + 0.10x = 0.65$$
$$0.10x = 0.65 - 0.30$$
$$0.10x = 0.35$$
$$x = 3.5$$

Therefore x is 3.5 N.

When the point of rotation is not at the centre of gravity of the metre stick, we must take into account the weight of the metre stick. The total weight of the metre stick is considered as a single force acting through the centre of gravity of the stick.

EXAMPLE 5. *A uniform 5 m plank has a mass of 20 kg. It is placed over a narrow bar 2 m from one end and two people sit on either end. If an 80 kg person sits on the short end, what is the mass of the other person if the system is in equilibrium?*

Solution We consider the 5 m plank to be a uniform rod with its entire mass acting through the centre as in the diagram.

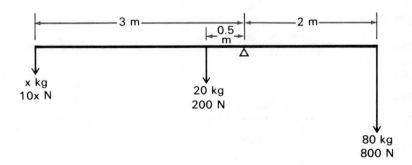

Since the system is in equilibrium, we equate the counterclockwise and clockwise moments.

$$(10x \times 3) + (200 \times 0.5) = (800 \times 2)$$
$$30x + 100 = 1600$$

$$30x = 1500$$
$$x = 50$$

A mass of 1 kg has an approximate weight of 10 N.

The other person has a mass of 50 kg.

EXERCISE 12-1

A **1.** Calculate the moment of each of the following:

(a)

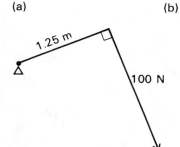

(b)

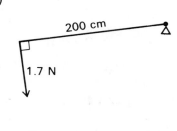

(c)

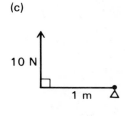

(d)

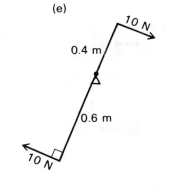

(e)

(f)

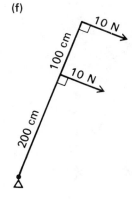

B Assume each system to be in equilibrium and calculate the value of *x* in each diagram for questions 2 to 11.

2.

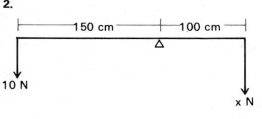

3.

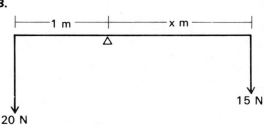

4.

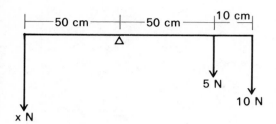

5.

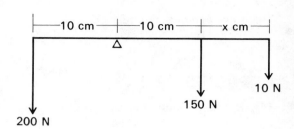

6.

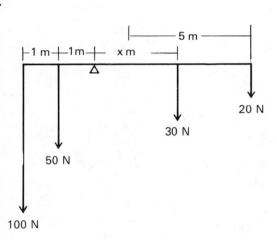

7.

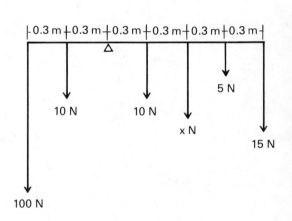

8.

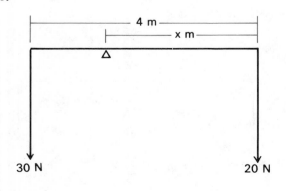

9.

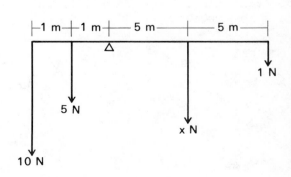

applied mathematics for today: senior

10.

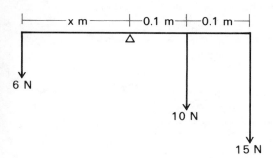

11.

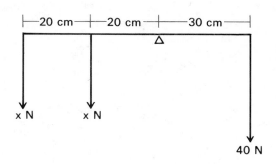

12. (a) Find the force of gravity in newtons exerted by the uniform rod in the following diagram if the system is in equilibrium.

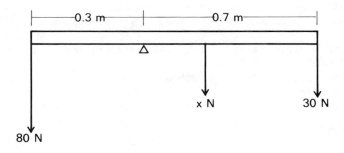

If 5 men pack 5 boxes of batteries in 5 min, how many men are required to pack 50 boxes in 50 min?

(b) Find the mass of the rod if an object that exerts a force of 10 N has a mass of approximately 1 kg.

13. A uniform rod 6 m long with a mass of 50 kg is placed on a pivot 2 m from one end. If a 100 kg mass is placed at the short end, what mass must be placed at the long end to keep the system in equilibrium?

14. A 10 m concrete utility pole has its centre of gravity 4 m from the larger end. The pole has a mass of 150 kg and is placed on a trailer so that it pivots about its midpoint. If a 300 kg mass is placed on the small end, what mass must be placed on the other end to form a system in equilibrium?

15. Find the force in the cable supporting the 10 m boom if the line of action in the cable is 4 m from the point of rotation and a force of 800 N is concentrated through the centre of the boom.

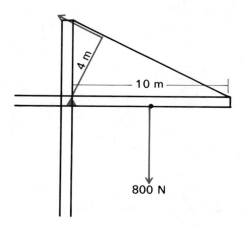

800 N

C **16.** A circular disc 1 m in diameter is pivoted about a horizontal axis through its centre and has a cord wrapped around its rim. A light rod 4 m long is fastened to the disc and an 85 N force is applied as in the diagram.

(a) Find the force that must be applied to the cord to form a system in equilibrium.

(b) What mass would you attach to the cord if a 1 kg mass weighs approximately 10 N?

Find a quantity such that the product of it and one eighth of it equals 10.

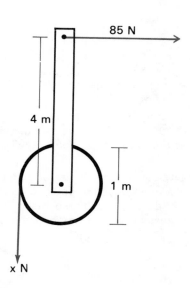

17. Find the tension in a cable if it makes an angle of 35° with a light rod at a position 5 m from the pivot and a force of 400 N is applied 6 m from the pivot as in the diagram.

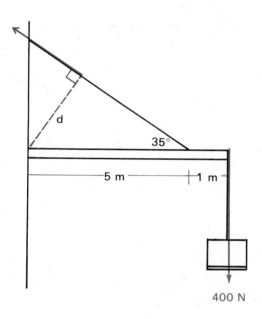

A crate is moved by rolling it over 3 cylindrical wooden rollers each having a diameter of 10 cm. How far will the crate advance when the rollers have made 1 revolution?

12.2 SIMPLE MACHINES: MECHANICAL ADVANTAGE

A machine is a device that can multiply a force. The purpose of a machine is not to convert one form of energy into another, but to exert a force on an object which is different from (usually greater than) the force which was applied to the machine. Simple machines such as the lever, the inclined plane, the jackscrew, the wheel and axle, and the pulley are studied in this section.

The force multiplication factor of a machine is called the mechanical advantage and is calculated by taking the ratio of the load (resistance to be overcome) to the effort (force applied to the machine to overcome the resistance).

Mechanical Advantage:

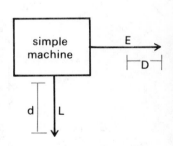

The applied force, E, acts through a distance, D, while the force, L, is exerted through a distance d.

M.A. $=\dfrac{L}{E}$	L : load
	E : effort

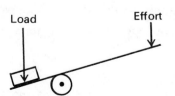

EXAMPLE 1. *Find the mechanical advantage of the system shown below:*

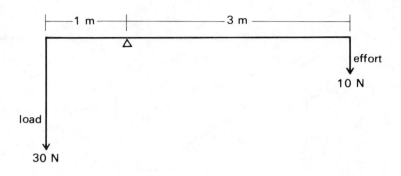

Solution

Equilibrium
$(M = M)$

$$M.A. = \frac{L}{E}$$

$$M.A. = \frac{30}{10} = 3$$

In this case every newton of force applied as effort results in 3 N being delivered to the load.

THE LEVER

There are three classes of levers, identified by the location of the fulcrum (*F*), effort (*E*), and load (*L*). See illustration opposite.

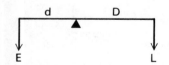

$$E \times d = L \times D$$

$$\frac{d}{D} = \frac{L}{E}$$

The mechanical advantage of the lever in Example 1 could also be calculated as follows:

$$M.A. = \frac{\text{length of effort arm}}{\text{length of load arm}} = \frac{d}{D}$$

In Example 1, the length of the effort arm is 3 m while the length of the load arm is 1 m.

$$M.A. = \frac{3}{1} = 3$$

This is the same result as was found using $\frac{L}{E}$. Note that this "length method" is used only for a single effort and a single load.

applied mathematics for today: senior

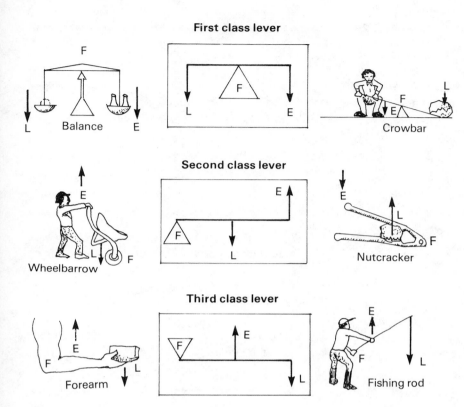

First class lever

Balance

L   E

Crowbar

Second class lever

Wheelbarrow

Nutcracker

Third class lever

Forearm

Fishing rod

THE INCLINED PLANE

When we wish to raise an object without exerting the required force vertically, we use an inclined plane. An inclined plane is often used to load trucks, and also in parking ramps to get from one level to another. If we neglect friction, the mechanical advantage is

$$\text{M.A.} = \frac{\text{length of plane}}{\text{height}} = \frac{l}{h}$$

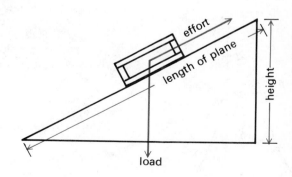

statics   275

EXAMPLE 2. *An inclined plane is* 4 m *long and* 1 m *high. Neglecting friction, find the effort required to slide a load exerting a force of* 1000 N *up the plane.*

Solution

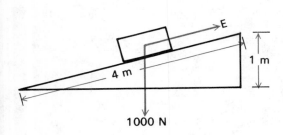

$$\text{M.A.} = \frac{l}{h} \quad \text{and} \quad \text{M.A.} = \frac{L}{E}$$

$$\text{M.A.} = \frac{4}{1} \quad \text{and} \quad \text{M.A.} = \frac{1000}{E}$$

$$\frac{4}{1} = \frac{1000}{E}$$

$$4E = 1000$$

$$E = 250$$

∴ an effort of 250 N is required to slide the load up the plane.

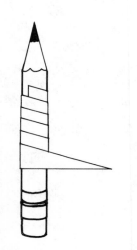

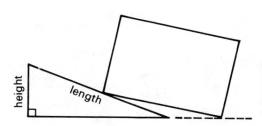

The *wedge* is considered to be an inclined plane. The applied force must overcome friction as well as raise the load up the slope.

THE JACKSCREW

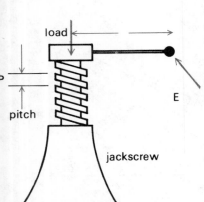

If we cut a piece of paper in the shape of a right triangle and wrap it around a pencil, we see that a screw is really an inclined plane wound around a cyclinder.

When great mechanical advantage is required to raise heavy objects, a jackscrew is used. One complete revolution of the lever arm causes one complete revolution of the screw, which moves the load a distance equal to the pitch of the screw. The mechanical advantage is

$$\boxed{\text{M.A.} = \frac{2\pi l}{P}}$$

where *l* is the length of the lever arm and *P* is the pitch of the screw.

EXAMPLE 3. *The lever of a jackscrew is* 1.5 m *long.*

(*a*) *If the screw has a pitch of 4 mm, find the mechanical advantage of this machine.*

(*b*) *If friction is neglected, find the force necessary to raise a mass of 5 t.*

tonne

$1 t = 10^3$ kg

Solution

(a) $P = 4$ mm $= 0.004$ m

$$M.A. = \frac{2\pi l}{P}$$

$$M.A. = \frac{2 \times 3.14 \times .5}{0.004}$$

$$= 2355$$

∴ the mechanical advantage of the screw is 2355

(b) $M.A. = \frac{L}{E}$, and the load $L = 5$ t $= 5000$ kg.

From part (a), M.A. $= 2355$

A mass of 5000 kg has an approximate weight of 50 000 N.

$$2355 = \frac{50\,000}{E}$$

$$E = \frac{50\,000}{2355}$$

$$\doteq 21.2$$

∴ an effort of 21.2 N is required to raise a 5 t mass using the given jackscrew.

THE PULLEY

A pulley is either fixed or movable. A pulley can be used to change the direction of a force or to gain mechanical advantage.

The mechanical advantage of a system of pulleys is found by counting the number of ropes pulling in a direction opposite to the load.

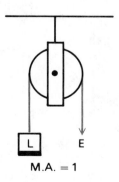

M.A. = 1

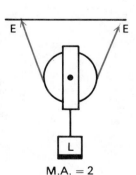

M.A. = 2

(a) (b)

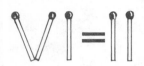

Make this statement true by
moving only 1 match.

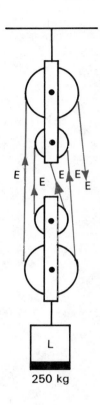

250 kg

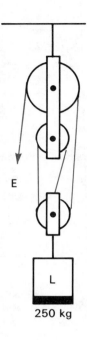

250 kg

Solution

(a) M.A. = 4   (b) M.A. = 3

$$M.A. = \frac{L}{E}$$

$4 = \dfrac{2500}{E}$ $3 = \dfrac{2500}{E}$

$4E = 2500$ $3E = 2500$

$E = 625$ $E = 833\frac{1}{3}$

∴ an effort of 625 N   ∴ an effort of $833\frac{1}{3}$ N
  is required.   is required.

THE WHEEL AND AXLE

This machine consists of a wheel which is rigidly attached to an axle so that they turn as a unit. Doorknobs, faucet handles, and the steering wheel of a car are examples of the wheel and axle.

If R is the radius of the wheel, and r is the radius of the axle, then

$$M.A. = \frac{R}{r}$$

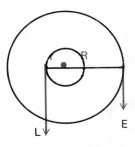

End view

$$L \times r = V \times R$$

$$\frac{L}{V} = \frac{R}{r}$$

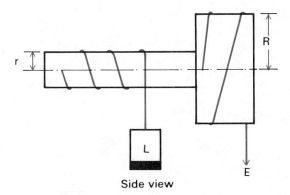

Side view

EXAMPLE 5. *A wheel having a diameter of 0.40 m is attached to an axle with a radius of 2 cm. If a load of 3000 N is applied to the axle, find the effort that must be applied to the wheel to balance the load.*

Solution

0.40 m diameter is equivalent to 0.20 m radius.

$$2\,cm = 0.02\,m$$

$$M.A. = \frac{R}{r}$$

$$M.A. = \frac{0.20}{0.02} = 10$$

$$M.A. = \frac{L}{E} \quad and \quad M.A. = 10$$

$$10 = \frac{3000}{E}$$

$$10E = 3000$$

$$E = 300$$

∴ an effort of 300 N must be applied to the wheel.

What 8 letter word contains only 1 vowel?

EXERCISE 12-2

B **1.** Identify the class of lever in the following systems and find the unknown quantity.

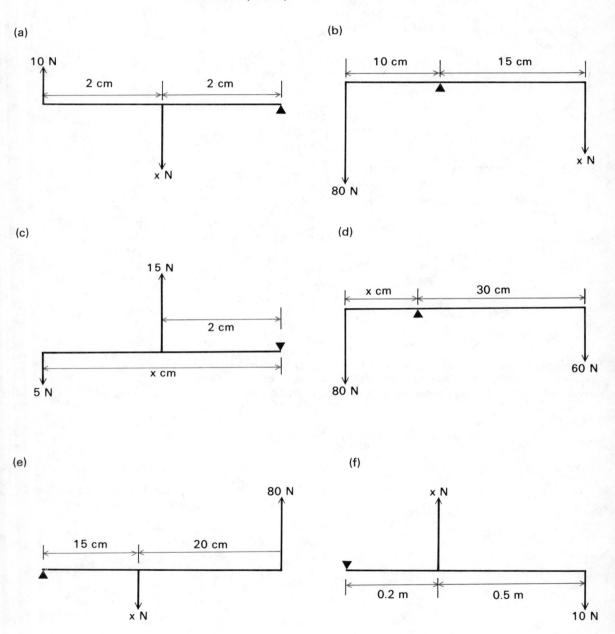

(a)

10 N

2 cm 2 cm

x N

(b)

10 cm 15 cm

80 N

x N

(c)

15 N

2 cm

x cm

5 N

(d)

x cm 30 cm

80 N

60 N

(e)

80 N

15 cm 20 cm

x N

(f)

x N

0.2 m 0.5 m

10 N

2. What effort must a person apply to lift the wheelbarrow? What is the mechanical advantage of the system?

A mass of 100 kg exerts an approximate force of 1000 N.

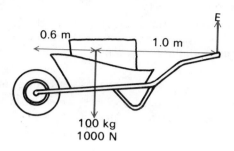

0.6 m
1.0 m
E

100 kg
1000 N

3. A fishing rod is 1.75 m long. If a person holds the rod 0.5 m from the end, what effort must be applied to raise a 1 kg fish?

4. A 5.0 m uniform lever having a mass of 50 kg rests on a fulcrum 1 m from one end. What is the least distance at 75 kg person can sit from the fulcrum to raise a mass of 300 kg on the short end? What is the mechanical advantage of this system?

5. A uniform rod used as a second class lever is pivoted at one end. The rod is 3 m long and has a mass of 5 kg. Masses of 2 kg and 10 kg are placed 1 m and 2 m from the pivot respectively. What effort must be applied to the end of the rod to balance it horizontally? What is the mechanical advantage of the system?

How can you plant 10 trees in 10 straight rows, with 3 trees in a row?

6. Calculate the load an effort of 30 N will balance in the given system. What is the mechanical advantage of the system?

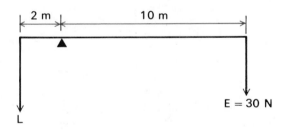

2 m
10 m
E = 30 N
L

7. A uniform rod acting as a third class lever is 3 m long and has a mass of 5 kg. The force applied is 200 N, 1 m from the fulcrum. What is the load that the lever can lift? What is the mechanical advantage of the system?

8. A burglar uses a crowbar to pry open a window. When he places the crowbar under the window, the fulcrum is 10 cm from the end. If the crowbar is 70 cm long, and the window offers a resistance of 1 kN, find the force the burgular must exert on the end of the bar to open the window. What is the mechanical advantage of the system?

9. An inclined plane has a length of 8 m and a height of 2 m. Neglecting friction, what will be the effort required to move a piano having a mass of 600 kg up the plane?

10. The load on an axle exerts a force of 200 N. If the radius of the wheel is 40 cm and the radius of the axle is 6 cm, what effort must be applied to the wheel to balance the load?

11. A jackscrew has a lever 1 m long. If the screw has a pitch of 10 mm, what is the effort required to balance a load of 500 N?

12. What is the mechanical advantage of the system in Figure 12-4? What effort is required to balance a load of 800 N?

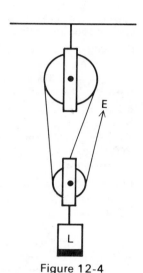

Figure 12-4

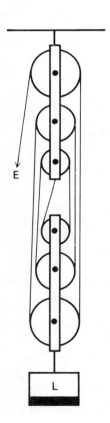

Figure 12-5

13. What is the mechanical advantage of the system in Figure 12-5? What effort is required to balance a load exerting a force of 800 N?

14. The diameters of a wheel and axle are 24 cm and 8 cm respectively. If a load of 700 N is attached to the axle, what effort must be applied to the wheel to balance the load?

15. An effort of 500 N is required to slide an object with a mass of 300 kg up an inclined plane. If the height of the plane is 2 m, what is the length of the plane?

16. The lever of a jackscrew is 1.2 m long and the pitch of the screw is 6 mm. What is the effort required to balance a load of 8 t?

17. Arrange the cable in each of the following systems to provide the required mechanical advantage.
(a) M.A. = 5 (b) M.A. = 4 (c) M.A. = 4

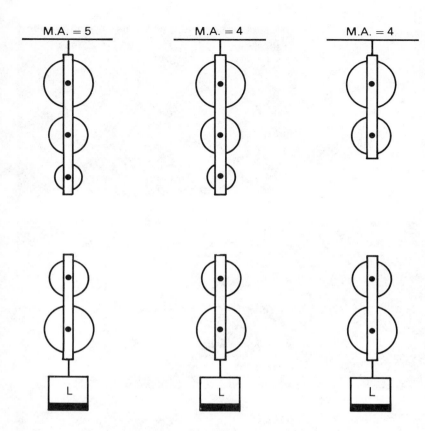

M.A. = 5   M.A. = 4   M.A. = 4

18. An inclined plane has the dimensions given in Figure 12-6. What is the effort required to slide an 800 kg mass up the plane?

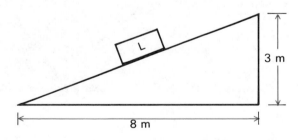

3 m

8 m

Figure 12-6

19. When an effort of 800 N is applied to a wheel, a load of 2000 N attached to the axle is balanced. Find the diameter of the wheel if the diameter of the axle is 3 cm.

20. When an effort of 150 N is applied to the lever of a jackscrew, a load exerting a force of 50 000 N is raised. If the pitch of the screw is 6 mm, what is the length of the lever arm?

These photographs show a fork, spoon, and toothpick balancing on the edge of a glass. The bottom photo was taken after both ends of the toothpick had been lit with a match; one end of the toothpick has burned away to the fork, the other to the edge of the glass, but the system has remained in equilibrium.

Can you explain it?

applied mathematics for today: senior

12.3 CENTRE OF GRAVITY

Although a body is made up of many small particles, each having its own mass, there is one point about which the body can be perfectly balanced. This "balance point" is called the **centre of gravity**.

INVESTIGATION 12.3

Find the square root of the nearest perfect square less than 6863.

1. (a) Cut out various irregular shapes from a piece of heavy cardboard. Hang each cardboard shape and a weighted string from a pin, as shown below.

(i)   (ii)   (iii)   (iv)

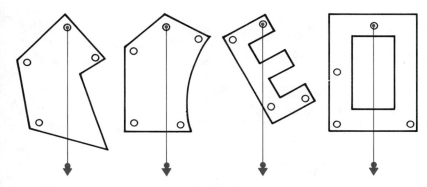

(b) Draw a line on each shape beside the string.

2. Suspend each shape from three other points, and draw a line beside the string each time.

3. Mark the point on each shape where the lines intersect. Test that this point is the centre of gravity by balancing the shape on your finger.

4. Find the centre of gravity for the following shapes:
(a) triangle   (b) rectangle   (c) square

EXAMPLE 1. *A uniform rod is* 3 m *long and has a mass of* 10 kg. *Masses of* 5 kg, *and* 7.5 kg *are suspended from the rod at* 1 m *and* 2 m *from one end. Find the centre of gravity of the system.*

Solution The mass of the rod acts through its midpoint. The total mass of the system may be considered to be concentrated at the centre of gravity.

The total force of gravity acting on the system is 225 N. We can suspend the system without rotation by applying a 225 N force at the centre of gravity.

A 1 kg mass has an approximate weight of 10 N.

Let the distance of the centre of gravity be *x* m from *A*.

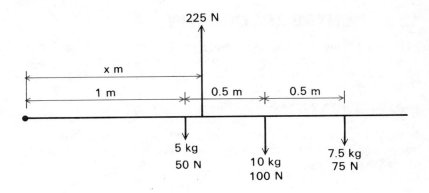

Taking moments about A:

$$225x = (50 \times 1) + (100 \times 1.5) + (75 \times 2)$$
$$225x = 50 + 150 + 150$$
$$225x = 350$$
$$x = \frac{350}{225}$$
$$= 1.6$$

Therefore the centre of gravity is 1.6 m from A.

Find a quantity such that the sum of it and one quarter of it equals 23.

EXAMPLE 2. *Two people carry a tapering pole, one at each end. One person exerts a force of* 250 N *and the other* 350 N. *If the length of the pole is* 6 m, *find the centre of gravity.*

Solution Let the distance of the centre of gravity from the smaller end, A, be x m.

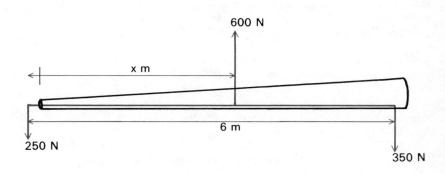

applied mathematics for today: senior

Taking moments about A,

$$600x = 350 \times 6$$
$$600x = 2100$$
$$x = 3.5$$

Therefore the centre of gravity is 3.5 m from the small end.

Note that the moment due to the 250 N force is 0. Why?

An object will not tip if the vertical line through its centre of gravity passes through its supporting base. When the vertical line does not pass through the supporting base the object will tip as in Figure 12-7.

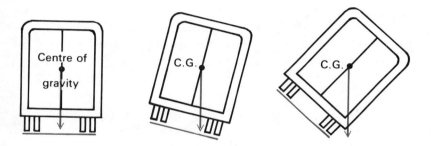

Figure 12-7

The angle between the base and the horizontal just before tipping occurs is called the critical angle. We can calculate the critical angle of an object using trigonometry if the dimensions of the object are known.

EXAMPLE 3. *A block has a base* 10 cm *by* 10 cm *and is* 25 cm *high. Calculate the critical angle of the block.*

Solution

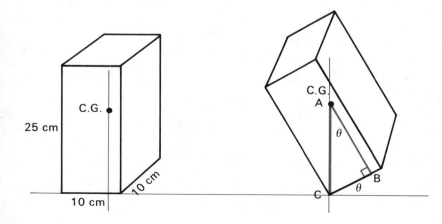

Tilt the object to form the critical angle, θ, as in the diagram.

In $\triangle ABC,$ $\angle BAC = \theta$

$AB = 12.5 \text{ cm}$

$BC = 5 \text{ cm}$

$\tan \theta = \dfrac{\text{opp.}}{\text{adj.}}$

and $\tan \theta = \dfrac{BC}{AB}$

$\tan \theta = \dfrac{5}{12.5}$

$= 0.4$

$\therefore \theta \doteq 22°$

Therefore the critical angle is 22°.

EXERCISE 12-3

B **1.** Determine the centre of gravity for each of the following systems of masses suspended from light uniform rods.

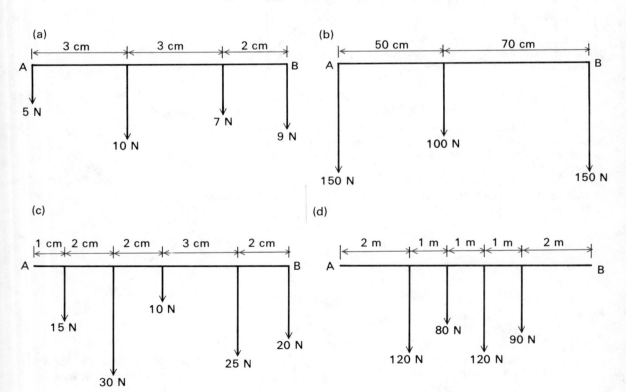

2. A light uniform rod has masses of 4 kg and 6 kg attached to each end. Locate the centre of gravity if the rod is 7 m long.

3. A uniform rod is 10 m long and has a mass of 15 kg. A 25 kg mass is hung 1 m from one end while a 20 kg mass is hung 1.5 m from the other end. Find the centre of gravity of the system.

4. A truck is 7 m long and has a mass of 2000 kg. Its centre of gravity is 3 m from the front. A 600 kg mass is placed on the truck with its centre of gravity 2.5 m from the rear. Make a diagram and find the centre of gravity of the loaded truck.

5. Two uniform rods both 3 m long are joined end to end. If one bar has a mass of 20 kg and the other a mass of 30 kg, find the centre of gravity of the 6 m rod.

6. Calculate the critical angle for each of the following objects:

(a)

(b)

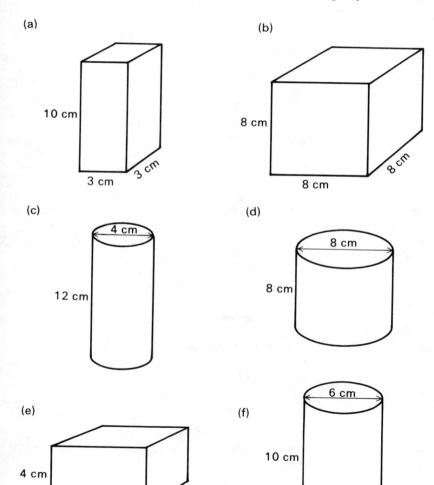

(c)

(d)

(e)

(f)

What is the maximum number of pieces that a block of cheese can be cut into using 5 cuts?

12.4 FRICTION

The force that resists a body when it slides or rolls over another body is called the force of friction. Because the surfaces in contact are so uneven, the simple laws of friction hold only approximately in an actual case.

The forces of friction provide advantages and disadvantages. Friction between brake pads and discs, tires and road surface is important when trying to stop an automobile (the greater the friction, the better the ability to stop). Friction between many parts in the same automobile is not desirable, and hence is reduced by using lubricants.

Name five advantages of friction.
Name five disadvantages of friction.

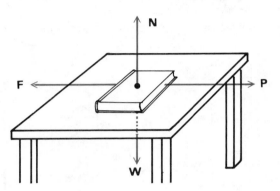

When a book rests on a table, the table exerts a force, **N**, on the book, equal in magnitude to the weight, **W**, of the book. This equal and opposite force is called the normal force, **N**. If you try to pull the book with a force, **P**, the force of friction, **F**, will oppose the motion caused by **P**. (**P** is just large enough to overcome friction).

μ is pronounced *mu*

The ratio $\dfrac{F}{N} = \mu$ is called the coefficient of starting friction

The coefficient of friction, μ, remains constant for two surfaces in contact. It does not change as the pressure between the two surfaces changes.

EXAMPLE 1. *A block has a mass of* 1.5 kg *(weight of* 15 N*) and rests on a table. A force of* 6 N *is sufficient to start the block moving. Find the coefficient of friction between the block and the table.*

Solution

$$W = N$$

$$\therefore \ N = 15 \text{ N}$$

$$P = F$$

$$\therefore \ F = 6 \text{ N}$$

$$\mu = \frac{F}{N}$$

$$\mu = \frac{6 \text{ N}}{15 \text{ N}}$$

$$= 0.40$$

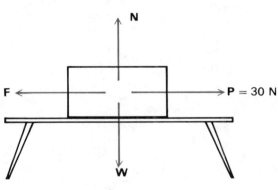

Therefore the coefficient of friction is 0.4

EXAMPLE 2. *A block of material rests on a table and just starts to move when a force of* 30 N *is applied. What is the weight of the block if the coefficient of friction is* 0.35?

Solution

$$F = P = 30 \text{ N}$$

$$\mu = 0.35$$

$$\mu = \frac{F}{N}$$

$$0.35 = \frac{30 \text{ N}}{N}$$

$$N \doteq 86 \text{ N}$$

$$W = N$$

$$W \doteq 86 \text{ N}$$

Therefore the weight of the block is 86 N (The mass is approximately 8.6 kg).

When a block rests on an inclined plane, the force of gravity **W**, on the block will still act vertically, while the normal force, **N**, is perpendicular to the plane. The force of friction, **F**, opposes the block's motion down the plane so it is directed up the plane. If θ is the angle of inclination at which the block just starts to slide, then

$$\boxed{\mu = \tan \theta}$$

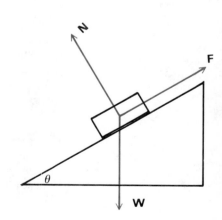

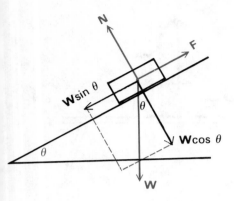

If θ is such that the block does not slide down the plane, then we apply a force, P, parallel to the plane so that the block just begins to slide down the plane; then

$$F = P + W \sin \theta$$

$$N = W \cos \theta$$

$$F = W \sin \theta$$

$$\mu = \frac{F}{N}$$

$$= \frac{W \sin \theta}{W \cos \theta} = \tan \theta$$

EXAMPLE 3. *A block weighing 10 N just starts to slide down a plane when a force of 3 N is applied parallel to the plane. If the angle of inclination is 15°, find the coefficient of friction, μ, between the block and the plane.*

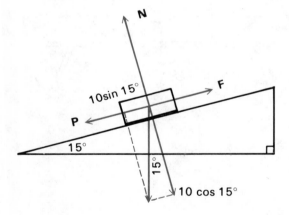

Solution

$$\mu = \frac{F}{N}$$

$$\mu = \frac{P + W \sin \theta}{N}$$

$$= \frac{3 + 10 \sin 15°}{10 \cos 15°}$$

$$\doteq \frac{3 + 10(0.2588)}{10(0.9659)}$$

$$\doteq 0.58$$

The coefficient of friction between the block and the plane is 0.58.

EXAMPLE 4. *A force of 20 N, parallel to the plane, is necessary to prevent a block with a mass of 6 kg (experiencing a gravitational force of approximately 60 N) from sliding down the plane. Determine the coefficient of friction between the block and the plane if the angle of inclination of the plane is 30°.*

Solution From the diagram,

$$N = W \cos 30° = 60 \cos 30°$$

$$F + P = W \sin 30° = 60 \sin 30°$$

$$F = 60 \sin 30° - 20$$

$$\mu = \frac{F}{N}$$

$$\mu = \frac{60 \sin 30° - 20}{60 \cos 30°}$$

$$\doteq \frac{10}{51.96}$$

$$\doteq 0.19$$

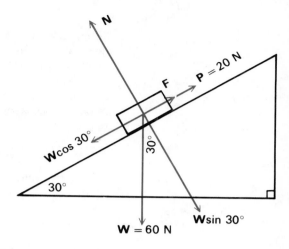

Therefore the coefficient of friction between the block and the plane is 0.19.

EXERCISE 12-4

B **1.** An object weighing 20 N rests on a table. A force of 7 N is enough to start the object moving. What is the coefficient of friction between the object and the table?

2. The coefficient of friction between a block and a table is 0.37. If a horizontal force of 15 N is necessary to start the block moving, what is the force of gravity on the block?

3. A man having a mass of 90 kg exerts a horizontal force of 600 N when he walks. What is the smallest value of the coefficient of friction between his shoes and the pavement that will allow him to do this?

4. A force of 30 N is necessary to slide a wooden box along the floor. The box weighs 100 N. What force would be necessary to slide the box if a 5 kg mass was placed inside the box?

5. A steel block experiencing a gravitational force of 2000 N rests on the floor. If the coefficient of friction between the block and the floor is 0.4, what horizontal force is necessary to start the block sliding along the floor? What force is necessary to slide the block if a 50 kg mass is placed on top of the block?

6. A block weighing 20 N starts to slide down a plane after a force of 5 N is applied parallel to the plane. If the angle of inclination is 10°, find μ between the block and the plane.

7. A force of 10 N is necessary to prevent an 8 kg block from sliding down a plane. If the angle of inclination of the plane is 25°, determine the coefficient of friction between the block and the plane.

8. The coefficient of friction between a block and a board is 0.75. Will the block slide down the board if the board is inclined at an angle of 44°?

A frog is 30 m down a slippery incline. It can jump 3 m at a time but then slides back 2 m. How many jumps does it take the frog to reach the top of the incline?

9. A block begins to slide down a board when the board is inclined at an angle of 30°. What force is necessary to prevent the block sliding down the board when the board is inclined at an angle of 40°? The block weighs 20 N.

10. A box begins to slide down a ramp when the ramp is inclined at an angle of 25°. If the box weighs 300 N, what force parallel to the ramp is necessary to start the box sliding down the ramp when the ramp is inclined at an angle of 15°?

REVIEW EXERCISE

1. Find the value of x in each of the following:

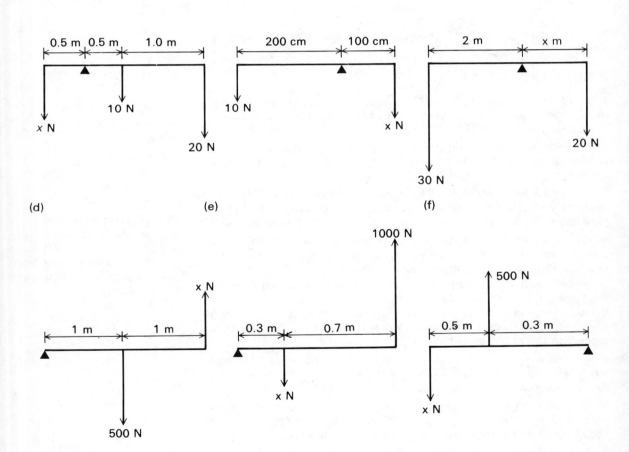

2. Find the mechanical advantage in each of the following:

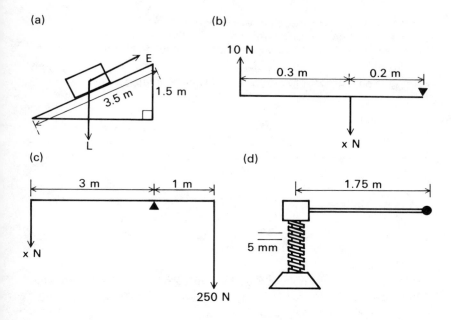

(a)

E

3.5 m

1.5 m

L

(b)

10 N

0.3 m   0.2 m

x N

(c)

3 m   1 m

x N

250 N

(d)

1.75 m

5 mm

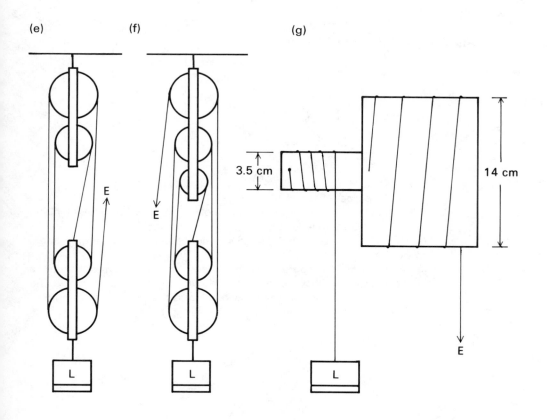

(e)

E

L

(f)

E

L

(g)

3.5 cm

14 cm

L

E

(h) An inclined plane 1.3 m high and 4 m long.

(i) A jackscrew with lever arm 2 m and pitch 5 mm.

(j) A wheel and axle with wheel diameter 0.80 m and axle diameter 0.03 m.

3. Find the centre of gravity in each of the following systems.

(a)

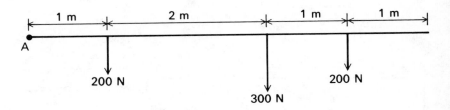

(b) A tapered utility pole carried by two men, one at each end. One man exerts a force of 400 N and the other 500 N. The pole is 9 m long.

4. Calculate the critical angle for tipping.

(a)   (b)

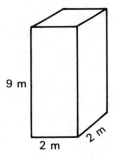 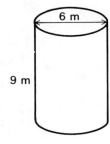

5. Find the coefficient of friction:

(a) A block with a weight of 40 N just slides on a horizontal plane when a force of 15 N is applied.

(b) A block just begins to slide down an inclined plane when the angle of inclination is 25°.

(c) A force of 10 N, parallel to the plane, is necessary to prevent a block weighing 100 N from sliding down the plane. Determine the coefficient of friction between the block and the plane if the angle of inclination of the plane is 25°.

REVIEW AND PREVIEW TO CHAPTER 13

EXERCISE 1 *THE PYTHAGOREAN THEOREM*

1. Calculate the value of x in each of the figures below correct to two decimal places.

(a)

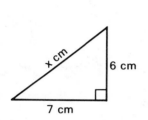

x cm

6 cm

7 cm

(b)

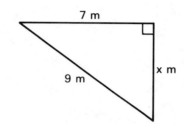

7 m

x m

9 m

(c)

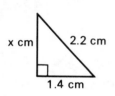

x cm   2.2 cm

1.4 cm

(d)

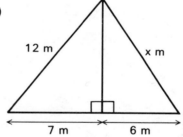

12 m

x m

7 m   6 m

a

c

b

$$a^2 = b^2 + c^2$$

(e)

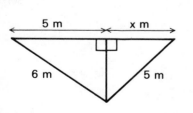

5 m   x m

6 m   5 m

(f)

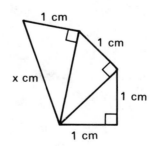

1 cm

1 cm

x cm

1 cm

1 cm

EXERCISE 2   *THE CIRCLE*

1. Calculate the perimeter and area of each of the following correct to two decimal places. (Use $\pi = 3.14$.)

(a)

$A = \pi r^2$
$C = 2\pi r$

(b)

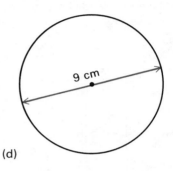

9 cm

4 cm

(c)

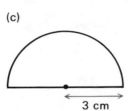

3 cm

(d)

2.5 cm

(e)

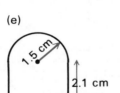

1.5 cm

2.1 cm

(f)

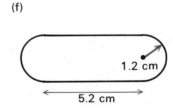

1.2 cm

5.2 cm

Evaluate the following:

1. $\sqrt{(31.65)^2 + (48.27)^2}$

2. $\sqrt{(3.675)^2 + (2.163)^2}$

3. $\sqrt{(0.0275)^2 + (0.0865)^2}$

4. $\sqrt{(54.75)^2 - (29.61)^2}$

5. $\sqrt{(3.025)^2 - (1.964)^2}$

6. $\sqrt{\dfrac{(32.75)(55.63)}{(284.5)}}$

7. $\sqrt{\dfrac{(39.65)^2}{(5.645)(21.85)}}$

8. $\sqrt{\dfrac{(5.675)^2 - (2.635)^2}{(4.285)}}$

9. $\sqrt{(54.65)^2 + (21.35)^2 - (42.65)^2}$

10. $\sqrt{\dfrac{(3.875)^2 + (2.643)^2}{(8.275)^2}}$

CONES AND CONIC SECTIONS

A *right circular cone*, which we will call simply a cone, is a funnel-shaped solid whose base is a circle and whose surface tapers up to a point called its *vertex*. More correctly, the cone should be thought of as two portions or *nappes* on both sides of the vertex.

When a plane intersects a cone, the boundary of the intersection forms curves which have been named *conic sections*.

If the plane has the same inclination as the edge of the cone, the boundary will form a *parabola*.

PARABOLA

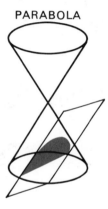

If both nappes of the cone are intersected, the boundary will form a *hyperbola*.

HYPERBOLA

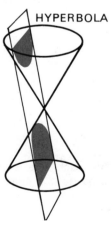

If the plane cuts the cone parallel to its base and does not pass through the vertex, the resulting curve is a *circle*.

CIRCLE

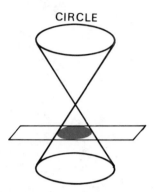

When the plane is not parallel to the base or a side and cuts only one nappe, the resulting curve is an *ellipse*.

ELLIPSE

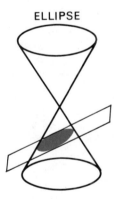

Each of the conic sections can be represented as a locus on a coordinate plane, and each has an identifying equation. Chapter 13 uses this algebraic approach to the study of conics.

The remarkable fact is that the parabola, ellipse, and hyperbola, created by the simple technique of cutting a cone with a plane, should have such diverse applications. Many of these applications have been in the forefront of the development of civilization.

CHAPTER 13

Conic Sections

The conic sections are the intersections of planes with a cone, as shown in the diagrams. Methods of constructing the conics will be considered first, followed by a study of their defining equations and some of their applications.

13.1 CONSTRUCTING THE PARABOLA

INVESTIGATION 13.1A *Using Ruler and Compasses*

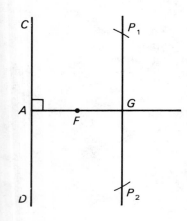

1. On a piece of graph paper draw line segment *CD*.

2. Select a point *F* not on *CD*.

3. Draw *FA* perpendicular to *CD*.

4. Select another point *G* on *AF* produced.

5. With centre *F* and radius *AG*, cut the line through *G* parallel to *CD* at P_1 and P_2.

6. Repeat steps 4 and 5 with four other points on *FA*.

7. Draw a smooth curve through the ten points so found.

8. What line appears to be the axis of symmetry?

The curve formed is called a parabola.

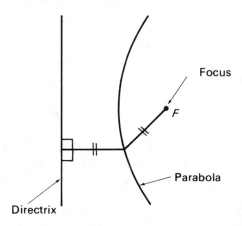

A parabola is a set of points such that each one is the same distance from a fixed point, the focus, as from a fixed line, the directrix.

INVESTIGATION 13.1B *Using String*

1. On a piece of paper draw line segment *CD*, point *F* (not in *CD*), and *FA* perpendicular to *CD*.

2. Fasten a piece of string of length *YZ* at *Z* on set square *XYZ*.

3. Fasten the other end of the string at *F* and keep it taut along *YZ* by using a pencil at *P*.

4. Slide the side *XY* of set square *XYZ* along *CD* allowing pencil *P* to draw a parabola.

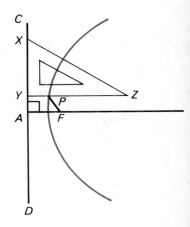

INVESTIGATION 13.1C *Drawing the Envelope*

1. Draw an acute angle on a piece of Bristol board or cardboard.

2. Make each arm of the angle 12 cm long and mark them off in 0.5 cm units.

3. Label the points along one arm 1, 2, 3, . . . , 24 from the vertex (but not including the vertex) and along the other arm *X, W, V, . . . , A* from the vertex (but not including the vertex).

4. Using a ruler and pencil join *A* to 1, *B* to 2, *C* to 3, . . . , *X* to 24.

5. Note that while a parabola appears to have been formed, we have actually drawn a number of straight lines. These lines are said to envelope the curve.

6. Repeat by varying the size of the angle.

7. Try making a design by using the four angles of a square or the four angles formed by two intersecting straight lines. You might even try to make an original curve stitching design. (This process is called curve stitching because it is often done using coloured thread instead of drawn lines.)

INVESTIGATION 13.1D *By Reflection*

1. Draw a line *d*.

2. Select point *F* not on the line.

3. Reflect point *F* onto the line and draw the reflecting line.

4. Repeat step 3 by reflecting *F* onto other points on the line.

5. The reflecting lines will envelop a parabola.

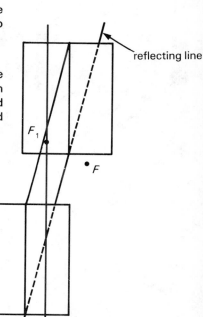

Some occurrences of the parabola:

1. A ball thrown, hit, or kicked through the air approximates a parabolic path as do projectiles, bullets and short-range missiles.

2. The cable of a steel suspension bridge will hang in a parabolic form if the weight is evenly distributed.

3. Supporting arches of bridges and of some modern buildings are often parabolic.

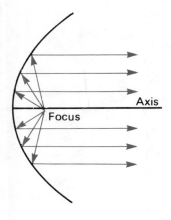

4. The reflecting property of a parabola makes its shape ideal for reflecting surfaces such as automobile headlights. If the source of light is placed at the focus of a parabolic mirror, rays of light falling on the reflector will leave as rays parallel to the axis and hence greatly increase efficiency. This property works in reverse also. Energy entering the parabola parallel to the axis will be reflected to the focus, as in reflecting telescopes, radio and television antennae, and solar furnaces.

5. Any geometric, physical, or electrical formula in which one quantity varies as the square of another will have a parabolic graph.

13.2   CONSTRUCTING THE ELLIPSE

INVESTIGATION 13.2A *Using Ruler and Compasses*

1. Mark two different points F_1 and F_2 on a sheet of paper.

2. Draw a line segment AC through F_1 and F_2 so that $AC > F_1F_2$.

3. Choose any point B_1 on AC.

4. With centre F_1 and radius AB_1 draw arcs above and below F_1F_2.

5. With centre F_2 and radius B_1C draw arcs to cut the former arcs at P_1 and P_2.

6. Repeat steps 3, 4, and 5 with four other points (B_2, B_3, B_4, B_5) on AC.

7. Draw a smooth curve through the ten points so found.

The curve formed is called an ellipse.

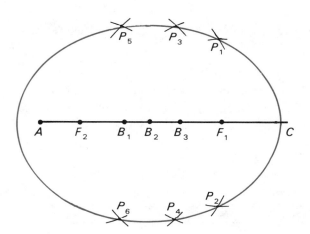

applied mathematics for today: senior

> An ellipse is a set of points such that the sum of the lengths of the line segments from each point to two fixed points, the foci, is a constant.

The line segments are called focal radii.

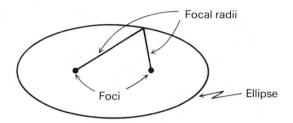

INVESTIGATION 13.2B *Using String*

1. Mark two different points F_1 and F_2 on a piece of paper and put a thumbtack at each of these points.

2. Tie a piece of string in a loop and place it around the tacks.

3. Place a pencil in the loop and move it about on the paper keeping the string taut, drawing an ellipse.

4. Draw all axes of symmetry.

5. What curve would be formed if F_1 and F_2 were the same point?

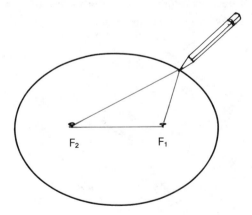

INVESTIGATION 13.2C *Drawing the Envelope*

1. Draw a circle and choose a point P (not the centre) inside the circle.

2. Draw at least 24 chords through point P.

3. Draw perpendiculars at the points of intersection of the circle and the chords.

4. These perpendiculars are lines which envelop an ellipse.

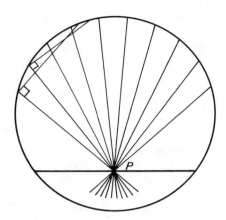

INVESTIGATION 13.2D *By Reflection*

1. Draw a circle.

2. Select point *F* inside the circle but not at the centre.

3. Reflect point *F* onto the circle and draw the reflecting line.

4. Repeat step 3 by reflecting *F* onto other points on the circle.

5. The reflecting lines will envelop an ellipse.

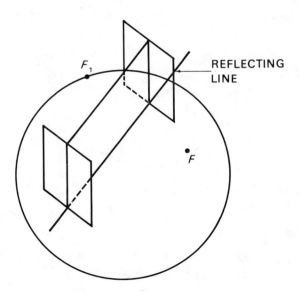

applied mathematics for today: senior

Some occurrences of the ellipse:

1. All planets travel in elliptical orbits with the sun at one focus. Spaceships travelling around the earth or the moon have followed elliptical paths.

2. Elliptical arches are sometimes used in bridges and in architecture, chiefly for beauty. The Coliseum in Rome is an elliptical structure.

3. Elliptical mirrors reflect to one focus the light or sound waves emitted from the other.

4. A spotlight on a stage gives an elliptical shadow on the floor. Can you explain why?

13.3   CONSTRUCTING THE HYPERBOLA

INVESTIGATION 13.3A *Using Ruler and Compasses*

1. Mark two different points F_1 and F_2 on graph paper.

2. On another piece of paper draw a line segment AC so that $AC < F_1F_2$.

3. Produce AC to a point B.

4. With centre F_1 and radius AB draw arcs above and below F_1F_2.

5. With centre F_2 and radius BC draw arcs to cut the former arcs at P_1 and P_2.

6. Repeat steps 4 and 5 by interchanging F_1 and F_2 in the instructions.

7. Repeat steps 3, 4, 5 and 6 with four other points on AC produced.

8. Draw a smooth curve through each of the sets of ten points.

The curve formed is called a hyperbola.

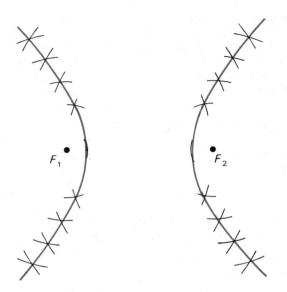

> A hyperbola is a set of points such that the difference of the lengths of the line segments from each point to two fixed foci is a constant.

INVESTIGATION 13.3B *Using String*

1. Choose two different points F_1 and F_2 on a piece of paper and put a thumbtack at each of these points.

2. Tie the centre of a piece of string to a pencil and put the ends around F_1 and F_2.

3. Hold the two ends of the string below F_2 together between your thumb and forefinger.

4. Move the pencil about on the paper keeping the string taut and letting out equal amounts of both ends of the string.

5. Repeat with the string held below F_1.
The curve formed is called a hyperbola.

6. Which line appears to be an axis of symmetry?

7. Is there another axis of symmetry?

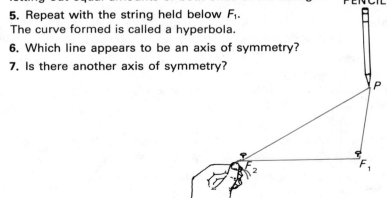

INVESTIGATION 13.3C *By Reflection*

1. Draw a circle.

2. Select point *F* outside the circle.

3. Reflect point *F* onto the circle and draw the reflecting line.

4. Repeat step 3 by reflecting *F* onto other points on the circle.

5. Place point *F* on the opposite side of the circle and repeat steps 3 and 4.

6. The reflecting lines will envelop a hyperbola.

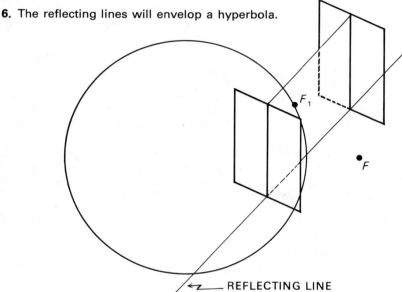

REFLECTING LINE

Some occurrences of the hyperbola:

1. Any physical or chemical formula in which one quantity varies as the reciprocal of another will have a hyperbolic graph. Example: "pressure varies inversely as volume."

$$p \propto \frac{1}{V}$$

2. The secondary mirror in a reflecting telescope is usually hyperbolic. The Cassegrain telescope contains a parabolic main mirror and a hyperbolic secondary mirror.

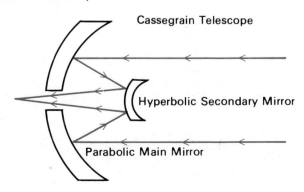

Cassegrain Telescope

Hyperbolic Secondary Mirror

Parabolic Main Mirror

3. The hyperbolic paraboloid roof is an attractive architectural feature of some modern buildings.

4. Sound ranging, used to locate enemy guns on land and submarines at sea, makes use of the properties of the hyperbola.

5. A hyperbola with transmitting stations at the foci can be used in navigation to locate ships on the hyperbola. If two hyperbolas are used, their point of intersection gives the exact location of the ship. This system is called LORAN (Long-Range Navigation).

13.4 EQUATION OF THE CIRCLE

A circle is a set of points such that each one is a constant distance, the *radius*, from a fixed point, the *centre*.

We saw that a circle could be obtained by cutting a right circular cone with a plane parallel to the base. A circle can also be constructed in the same way as the ellipse in Investigation 13.2B if F_1 and F_2 are the same point.

While a point is named by an ordered pair of numbers, a set of points is named by an equation. The straight line is named by the linear equation $y = mx + b$. To derive the equation of a circle with its centre at the origin, we use the distance formula.

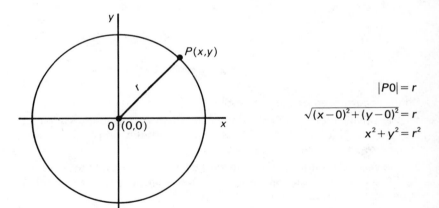

$$|PO| = r$$
$$\sqrt{(x-0)^2 + (y-0)^2} = r$$
$$x^2 + y^2 = r^2$$

The equation of a circle, centre the origin and radius r, is $x^2 + y^2 = r^2$

The same method is used to derive the equation of a circle with centre (h, k) and radius r. $P(x, y)$ is any point on the circle with centre (h, k) and radius r.

applied mathematics for today: senior

By definition $|PC| = r$

$$\sqrt{(x-h)^2+(y-k)^2} = r$$

$$\boxed{(x-h)^2+(y-k)^2 = r^2}$$

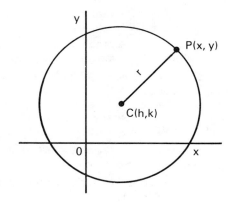

EXAMPLE 1. *State the radius and centre of each of the following circles.*
(a) $x^2+y^2 = 25$　　　　　(b) $(x-3)^2+(y+4)^2 = 36$

Solution
(a) $x^2+y^2 = r^2$
　　$x^2+y^2 = 25$
∴ radius is 5 and
centre $(0, 0)$

(b) $(x-h)^2+(y-k)^2 = r^2$
　　$(x-3)^2+(y+4)^2 = 36$
∴ radius is 6 and
centre $(3, -4)$

EXAMPLE 2. *State the equation of each of the following circles.*
(a) *Centre at the origin and radius* 11.
(b) *Centre* $(7, -4)$ *and radius* 2.

Solution
(a) The equation of the circle is

$$(x-0)^2+(y-0)^2 = 11^2$$
$$\therefore x^2+y^2 = 121$$

(b) The equation of the circle is

$$(x-7)^2+(y+4)^2 = 2^2$$
$$\therefore (x-7)^2+(y+4)^2 = 4$$

EXERCISE 13-4

A **1.** State the radius and centre of each of the following circles.
(a) $x^2+y^2 = 25$　　　　　(b) $x^2+y^2 = 36$
(c) $x^2+y^2 = 9$　　　　　(d) $x^2+y^2 = 1$
(e) $x^2+y^2 = 7$　　　　　(f) $(x-1)^2+(y-2)^2 = 16$
(g) $(x+3)^2+(y-4)^2 = 100$　　(h) $(x+7)^2+(y+3)^2 = 64$

B **2.** State the equation of the circle with:
(a) centre $(0, 0)$, radius 7
(b) centre $(0, 0)$, radius 9
(c) centre $(0, 0)$, radius $3\sqrt{2}$
(d) centre $(0, 0)$, radius $\frac{3}{2}$

How many axes of symmetry does a circle have?

(e) centre (3, 5), radius 5

(f) centre (2, −1), radius 4

(g) centre (−1, −1), radius $\sqrt{3}$

(h) centre (−2, 3), radius $2\sqrt{7}$

3. Sketch the graphs of the circles represented by each of the following equations.

(a) $x^2 + y^2 = 16$

(b) $4x^2 + 4y^2 = 25$

(c) $(x − 1)^2 + (y − 3)^2 = 9$

(d) $(x + 3)^2 + (y − 4)^2 = 4$

(e) $(x + 1)^2 + (y + 2)^2 = 25$

(f) $9(x − 2)^2 + 9(y + 3)^2 = 16$

C **4.** Find the equation of the circle with its centre at the origin and passing through the point (−5, 12).

5. Find the equation of the circle with its centre at (−3, 4) and passing through the point (1, 1).

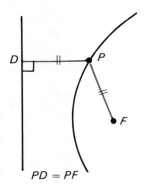

$PD = PF$

13.5 EQUATION OF THE PARABOLA

A parabola is a set of points P, such that each one is the same distance from a fixed point F, the focus, as from a fixed line, the directrix.

EXAMPLE 1. *Find the equation of the parabola with focus at* (3, 0) *and directrix* $x + 3 = 0$

Solution

$P(x, y)$ is any point on the parabola.

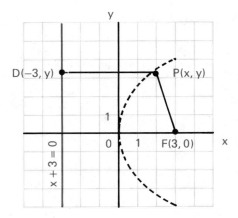

From the definition

$$|PF| = |PD|$$

$$\sqrt{(x − 3)^2 + (y − 0)^2} = x + 3$$

$$(x-3)^2 + (y-0)^2 = (x+3)^2$$
$$x^2 - 6x + 9 + y^2 = x^2 + 6x + 9$$
$$y^2 = 12x$$

∴ the equation of the parabola is $y^2 = 12x$

By the method of Example 1, we now derive the general formula for the equation of a parabola with focus $F(p, 0)$ and directrix $x + p = 0$. $P(x, y)$ is any point on the parabola. From the definition

$$|PF| = |PD|$$

$$\sqrt{(x-p)^2 + (y-0)^2} = x + p$$
$$(x-p)^2 + (y-0)^2 = (x+p)^2$$
$$x^2 - 2px + p^2 + y^2 = x^2 + 2px + p^2$$
$$y^2 = 4px$$

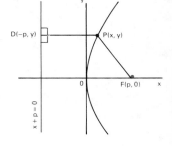

> The equation of a parabola with focus $F(p, 0)$ and directrix $x + p = 0$ is $y^2 = 4px$.

EXAMPLE 2. *Find the focus and directrix for the following parabolas.*
(a) $y^2 = 12x$ (b) $y^2 = -16x$ (c) $x^2 = -8y$

Solution

(a) $y^2 = 4px$
   $y^2 = 12x$
∴ $4p = 12$
   $p = 3$
The focus is at $(3, 0)$.
The directrix is $x + 3 = 0$.

(b) $y^2 = 4px$
   $y^2 = -16x$
∴ $4p = -16$
   $p = -4$
The focus is at $(-4, 0)$.
The directrix is $x - 4 = 0$.

(c) $x^2 = -8y$
In this case $4p = -8$
   $p = -2$
But the focus must be on the y axis.
The focus is at $(0, -2)$.
The directrix is $y - 2 = 0$

EXAMPLE 3. *For the parabola $y^2 = 16x$, state the coordinates of the vertex and the equation of the axis of symmetry. Find the coordinates of the points where the line through the focus and parallel to the directrix intersects the parabola. Use these two points together with the vertex to sketch the parabola. (This quick method of sketching parabolas is referred to as the "three-point method.")*

What year does MDCLXVI represent?

Solution

$$y^2 = 4px$$
$$y^2 = 16x$$
$$\therefore 4p = 16$$
$$p = 4$$

The focus is at (4, 0) and the directrix is $x + 4 = 0$. By definition the vertex must be the same distance from the focus as it is from the directrix. Therefore the vertex is (0, 0) and the axis of symmetry the x axis or $y = 0$. The equation of the line through the focus and parallel to the directrix is $x = 4$.

By substitution in $y^2 = 16x$ we have

$$y^2 = 16(4)$$

$$y^2 = 64$$

$$y = 8 \text{ or } -8$$

The points of intersection are (4, 8) and (4, −8).

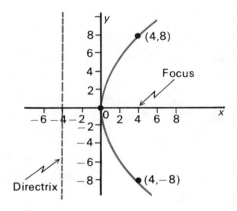

EXERCISE 13-5

B **1.** Find the focus and directrix for the following parabolas.

(a) $y^2 = 8x$ (b) $y^2 = 20x$

(c) $y^2 = 4x$ (d) $y^2 = -12x$

(e) $y^2 = -36x$ (f) $y^2 = 2x$

2. Use the "three-point method" to sketch the following parabolas.

(a) $y^2 = 12x$ (b) $y^2 = 4x$

(c) $y^2 = -4x$ (d) $y^2 = 20x$

(e) $y^2 = -24x$ (f) $y^2 = 28x$

(g) $y^2 = \dfrac{x}{2}$ (h) $y^2 = x$

3. For each of the following parabolas, state (i) the coordinates of the focus, (ii) the equation of the directrix, (iii) the x-coordinate of a point on the parabola with y-coordinate 3, (iv) the y-coordinates of points on the parabola with x-coordinate 9.

(a) $y^2 = 36x$ (b) $y^2 = x$

(c) $y^2 = 20x$ (d) $y^2 = -\frac{9}{2}x$.

4. State the equation of a parabola with:

(a) focus $(7, 0)$, directrix $x = -7$

(b) vertex $(0, 0)$, focus $(-10, 0)$

(c) vertex $(0, 0)$, directrix $x + 2 = 0$

(d) vertex the origin, directrix $2x + 3 = 0$.

5. Find the equation of a parabola having vertex the origin, focus on the positive x-axis and passing through the point $(4, -2)$.

6. What would the graph of $y^2 = ax$, $a = 0$, be? This is referred to as a *degenerate parabola*.

How far does the tip of the second hand of a clock travel in 18 s if the hand is 8 cm long?

7. Complete the following table

	$y^2 = 4x$	$y^2 = -4x$	$x^2 = 4y$	$x^2 = -4y$
Coordinates of vertex	$(0, 0)$			
Coordinates of focus		$(-1, 0)$		
Equation of directrix			$y = -1$	
x-intercept(s)				$0, 0$
y-intercept(s)				
Equation of axis of symmetry		$y = 0$		
Coordinates of ends of line segment through focus parallel to the directrix.	$(1, 2), (1, -2)$			

C **8.** For the parabola $y^2 = 4x + 4$,

(a) determine the intercepts

(b) state the coordinates of the vertex and the equation of the axis of symmetry

(c) sketch the graph.

9. By analogy with the graph of $y^2 = 4x$, which can be written $(y - 0)^2 = 4(x - 0)$, sketch the graph of $(y - 1)^2 = 4(x - 2)$.

13.6 APPLICATION OF PARABOLAS

EXAMPLE 1. (*a*) *Find an equation of the parabolic arch used to support a horizontal bridge across a stream. The width of the base of the arch is* 24 m *and the height of the vertex is* 9 m.

(*b*) *What would be the length of a horizontal beam* 4 m *below the vertex?*

(*c*) *What is the height of the arch* 4 m *from either end?*

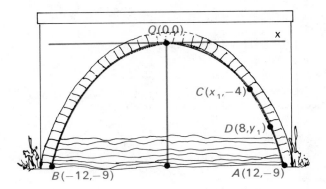

Solution (a) Let the equation of the arch be $x^2 = -4py$. Since A is on the arch,

$$12^2 = -4p(-9)$$
$$144 = 36p$$
$$p = 4$$

∴ the equation of the arch is $x^2 = -16y$.

(b) A point on the arch 4 m below the vertex could be $C(x_1, -4)$. Since C is on the arch,

$$x_1^2 = -16(-4)$$
$$x_1^2 = 64$$
$$x_1 = 8 \quad \text{or} \quad x_1 = -8$$

∴ the length of the beam would be 16 m.

(c) A point 4 m from either end could be $D(8, y_1)$. Since D is on the arch,

$$8^2 = 16y_1$$
$$y_1 = -4$$
$$9 - 4 = 5$$

∴ The arch is 5 m high, 4 m from either end.

EXERCISE 13-6

1. Find the equation of a parabola which opens downward, has its vertex at the origin, and passes through the point $A(6, -3)$.

2. (a) Find the point on $x^2 = -20y$ which has x-coordinate 4.
(b) Find the points on $x^2 = 16y$ which have y-coordinates 9.

3. (a) Find the equation of the parabolic arch used to support a horizontal bridge across a railway track. The width of the base of the arch is 60 m and the height of the vertex is 18 m.
(b) Find the length of a horizontal steel girder stretching across the arch 8 m below the vertex.

4. A ball is thrown horizontally from the top of a cliff 100 m high. It falls in a parabolic path and strikes the ground 150 m away (measured horizontally). Find the equation of parabolic flight.

5. The cross-section of a runway 40 m wide is a parabolic curve. The sides of the runway are 1 m lower than the crown which is in the middle.
(a) What is the equation of the parabolic cross-section?
(b) How much lower than the crown is a place on the runway 10 m from the middle?

6. A bridge is built with a parabolic arch which opens downward. A horizontal girder 80 m long is 20 m below the vertex. Find the equation of the parabola describing the shape of the bridge.

7. The cable of a suspension bridge hangs in the form of a parabola. Two supporting towers 50 m above the lowest point on the cable are 600 m apart.
(a) Find the equation of the parabola.
(b) Find the length of a vertical supporting cable from the parabolic cable to the bridge,
  (i) 60 m from the centre of the bridge,
  (ii) 60 m from the end of the bridge.

Write 1492 in Roman numerals.

13.7   EQUATION OF THE ELLIPSE

INVESTIGATION 13.7

Given the relation represented by $16x^2 + 25y^2 = 400$:

1. Solve the equation for y. (Note that there are two values for y for each value of x.)

2. Complete the following table of values in your notes.

x	0	±1	±2	±3	±4	±5
y						

3. Make a full-page graph, plotting the points and joining them with a smooth curve. The resulting figure is an ellipse.

4. What are the coordinates of the end points of the ellipse? These points are called vertices.

5. Plot the points $F_1(3, 0)$ and $F_2(-3, 0)$. Select any four points P_1, P_2, P_3, and P_4 on the curve. Set up a table of measures as follows:

$|F_1P_1| = $ ▧	$|F_1P_2| = $ ▧	$|F_1P_3| = $ ▧	$|F_1P_4| = $ ▧
$|F_2P_1| = $ ▧	$|F_2P_2| = $ ▧	$|F_2P_3| = $ ▧	$|F_2P_4| = $ ▧
Sum = ▧	Sum = ▧	Sum = ▧	Sum = ▧

F_1 and F_2 are each a focus of the ellipse. Each of the segments P_1F_1, P_1F_2, ... are focal radii (radius drawn from a focus). What do you notice about the sum of the two focal radii that can be drawn from any point on the curve?

6. The equation of this curve is:

$$16x^2 + 25y^2 = 400$$

$$\frac{16x^2}{400} + \frac{25y^2}{400} = \frac{400}{400}$$

$$\therefore \frac{x^2}{25} + \frac{y^2}{16} = 1. \quad \textcircled{1}$$

Compare $\textcircled{1}$ to $\frac{x^2}{a^2} + \frac{y^2}{b^2} = 1 (a, b > 0)$

From $\textcircled{1}$, $a^2 = $ ▨ $b^2 = $ ▨

$a = $ ▨ $b = $ ▨

$2a = $ ▨ $2b = $ ▨

If the foci are $(\pm c, 0)$, then $c = $ ▨

7. Find distances on your diagram which have length $2a$, $2b$, $2c$. Compare these figures to those in 5 and draw a conclusion about the sums of the focal radii for any ellipse represented by

$$\boxed{\frac{x^2}{a^2} + \frac{y^2}{b^2} = 1}$$

8. What relationship exists among the values for a^2, b^2, and c^2?

9. What are the equations of the axes of symmetry of the ellipse?

The relationships we have investigated for this particular ellipse hold for all ellipses and may be generalized as follows:

Equation of ellipse with centre at the origin, foci on x-axis: $\frac{x^2}{a^2} + \frac{y^2}{b^2} = 1.$

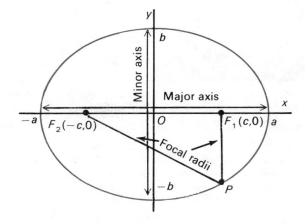

Semi-major axis ($\frac{1}{2}$ major axis) $= a$
Semi-minor axis $= b$
Foci $(\pm c, 0)$, vertices $(\pm a, 0)$

Sum of focal radii to any point on the ellipse = major axis = $2a$ (where $a^2 = b^2 + c^2$)

If the foci are placed on the y-axis, their coordinates become $(0, \pm c)$ and the equation becomes $\dfrac{x^2}{b^2} + \dfrac{y^2}{a^2} = 1$

> Note that the equation of the ellipse may be written
>
> $$\frac{x^2}{(x\text{-intercept})^2} + \frac{y^2}{(y\text{-intercept})^2} = 1$$

EXAMPLE 1. *State the equation of the ellipse with centre at the origin, foci on the x-axis, having a semi-major axis of length* 5 *and a semi-minor axis of length* 4.

Solution The equation is of the form $\dfrac{x^2}{a^2} + \dfrac{y^2}{b^2} = 1$, where $a = 5$, $b = 4$

$$\frac{x^2}{5^2} + \frac{y^2}{4^2} = 1$$

$$\frac{x^2}{25} + \frac{y^2}{16} = 1$$

If you see the face of a clock reflected in a mirror and the hands read 09:15, what is the real time on the clock?

EXAMPLE 2. *Determine the values of a, b, and c and state the coordinates of the foci for:*

(a) $\dfrac{x^2}{25} + \dfrac{y^2}{16} = 1$ 　　　　(b) $\dfrac{x^2}{25} + \dfrac{y^2}{36} = 1$

Solution (a) $\dfrac{x^2}{25} + \dfrac{y^2}{16} = 1$, $a^2 = 25$ and $b^2 = 16$

$\therefore a = 5$ $(a > 0)$ and $b = 4 (b > 0)$

But $a^2 = b^2 + c^2$

$\qquad c^2 = 25 - 16 = 9$

$\qquad c = 3 (c > 0)$

$\therefore$ the foci are $(3, 0)$ and $(-3, 0)$.

Solution (b) $\dfrac{x^2}{25} + \dfrac{y^2}{36} = 1$, $a^2 = 36$ and $b^2 = 25$

$$c^2 = 36 - 25 = 11$$

$$c = \pm\sqrt{11}$$

$\therefore$ the foci are $(0, \sqrt{11})$ and $(0, -\sqrt{11})$

EXERCISE 13-7

1. For each of the following ellipses, (i) determine the intercepts, (ii) state the lengths of the major and minor axes, (iii) state the coordinates of the vertices, (iv) state the equations of the axes of symmetry, (v) sketch the ellipse by plotting the two vertices and the ends of the minor axis.

(a) $16x^2 + 25y^2 = 400$

(b) $9x^2 + 5y^2 = 45$

(c) $x^2 + 2y^2 = 2$

(d) $4x^2 + 12y^2 = 48$

2. Write the equation of the ellipse with centre at the origin, foci on the x-axis, a semi-major axis of length 10 and semi-minor axis of length 6.

3. Write the equation of the ellipse centre $O(0, 0)$, foci on the x-axis, for which $a = 3$ and $b = 1$.

4. Write the equation of the ellipse with centre $O(0, 0)$, focus $F(4, 0)$ and vertex $A(5, 0)$.

5. Write the equation of the ellipse with centre $O(0, 0)$, x-intercepts 3 and -3, and y-intercepts 2 and -2.

6. For the ellipse with equation $\dfrac{x^2}{5} + \dfrac{y^2}{4} = 1$,

(a) find the values of a and b

(b) find the value of c and hence state the coordinates of the foci.

7. State the values of a, b, and c for the ellipse represented by each of the following equations.

(a) $\dfrac{x^2}{169} + \dfrac{y^2}{25} = 1$

(b) $\dfrac{x^2}{9} + \dfrac{y^2}{25} = 1$

What is the largest number you can write using the Roman numerals I, C, X, V, and L once each?

8. The foci of an ellipse with centre $O(0, 0)$ are 4 units apart and the sum of the focal radii is 8 units. Write the equation for the ellipse.

9. Find the equation of the ellipse having centre $O(0, 0)$, passing through the point $E(7, 4)$ and having a y-intercept of $4\sqrt{2}$.

10. An arch is in the form of a semi-ellipse with the major axis on the span.

(a) If the span is 100 m and the height is 30 m, find the equation for the ellipse.

(b) How high is the arch at a point 40 m from the centre line?

11. The earth's orbit around the sun is an ellipse with the sun at one focus, the semi-major axis is 150 000 000 km and the focus is 2 400 000 km from the centre. If the points on an ellipse nearest to and farthest from one focus are the vertices, find the least and greatest distances between the earth and the sun.

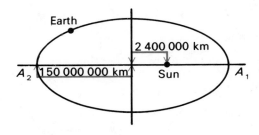

applied mathematics for today: senior

12. An elliptical flower bed has equation $\frac{x^2}{81}+\frac{y^2}{49}=1$. If the area of an ellipse is given by $A=\pi ab$, find the area of the flower bed.

13. Find the area of an ellipse with
(a) major axis 4, $c=\sqrt{3}$
(b) $a=b=r$

13.8 EQUATION OF THE HYPERBOLA

INVESTIGATION 13.8

Given the relation represented by $9x^2-16y^2=144$:

1. Solve the equation for y. (Note there are two values of y for each value of x.)

2. Complete the following table of values in your notes. Find square roots to one decimal place.

x	0	±2	±4	±5	±6	±8	±10	±12
y								

What is different about the values for y when $x=0$, ±2?

3. Make a full-page graph, plotting the points and joining them with a smooth curve. The resulting figure is a hyperbola.

4. What are the coordinates of the vertex?

5. Plot the points $F_1(5, 0)$, $F_2(-5, 0)$. Select any four points P_1, P_2, P_3, P_4 on the curve. Set up a table of measures as follows:

$|F_1P_1|=$▨	$|F_1P_2|=$▨	$|F_1P_3|=$▨	$|F_1P_4|=$▨
$|F_2P_1|=$▨	$|F_2P_2|=$▨	$|F_2P_3|=$▨	$|F_2P_4|=$▨
|Difference|=▨	|Difference|=▨	|Difference|=▨	|Difference|=▨

What are F_1 and F_2 called?
What are F_1P_1, F_2P_2, ... called?
What do you notice about the absolute value of the difference of the two focal radii that can be drawn from any point on the curve?

6. The equation of the curve is $9x^2-16y^2=144$

$$\frac{9x^2}{144}-\frac{16y^2}{144}=\frac{144}{144}$$

$$\frac{x^2}{16}-\frac{y^2}{9}=1 \quad \text{①}$$

Compare ① to $\frac{x^2}{a^2}-\frac{y^2}{b^2}=1$

From ① $a^2 = \blacksquare$ $\qquad b^2 = \blacksquare$

$\qquad\quad a = \blacksquare$ $\qquad\quad b = \blacksquare$

$\qquad 2a = \blacksquare$ $\qquad 2b = \blacksquare$

If the foci are $(\pm c, 0)$ then $c = \blacksquare$

7. Find distances on your diagram that have length $2a$, $2c$. Compare these figures to those in 5 and draw a conclusion concerning the differences of the focal radii for any hyperbola represented by

$$\frac{x^2}{a^2} - \frac{y^2}{b^2} = 1$$

8. What relationship exists among a^2, b^2 and c^2?

9. What are the equations of the axis of symmetry of the hyperbola?

10. Construct the lines $y = \pm\frac{3}{4}x$ on your diagram $\frac{x^2}{16} - \frac{y^2}{9} = 1$. Compare the direction of the lines to the direction of the hyperbola as $|x|$ gets large. These lines are called the asymptotes of the hyperbola.

By comparing the equations $\frac{x^2}{16} - \frac{y^2}{9} = 1$ and $y = \pm\frac{3}{4}x$, determine the equations of the asymptotes to $\frac{x^2}{a^2} - \frac{y^2}{b^2} = 1$.

11. Recall that the vertices of the hyperbola in your diagram are $(\pm 4, 0)$. On the same diagram sketch in with a broken line the hyperbola with vertices $(0, \pm 3)$ and the same asymptotes. This hyperbola is called the *conjugate hyperbola* to $\frac{x^2}{16} - \frac{y^2}{9} = 1$ and its equation is

$$\frac{x^2}{16} - \frac{y^2}{9} = -1$$

At what time between 11:00 and 12:00 will the two hands of a clock be in a straight line?

(Each is the conjugate of the other)

The line segment from $(-4, 0)$ to $(4, 0)$ is called the transverse axis of the hyperbola and the line from $(0, -3)$ to $(0, 3)$ is called the conjugate axis of the hyperbola (the transverse axis of the conjugate) even though it does not join points on the curve.

The relationships we have investigated for this particular hyperbola hold for all hyperbolas and can be generalized as follows:

Equation of hyperbola with centre at the origin, foci on x-axis: $\frac{x^2}{a^2} - \frac{y^2}{b^2} = 1$.

Semi-transverse axis $= a$

Semi-conjugate axis $= b$

Foci $(\pm c, 0)$, vertices $(\pm a, 0)$

$(|F_1P| - |F_2P|) = $ transverse axis $= 2a$ (where $a^2 = c^2 - b^2$). If the foci are placed on the y-axis, their coordinates become $(0, \pm c)$ and the equation becomes $\frac{x^2}{b^2} - \frac{y^2}{a^2} = -1$.

applied mathematics for today: senior

EXAMPLE 1. *Determine the values of a, b, and c and state the coordinates of the foci for*

(a) $\dfrac{x^2}{16}-\dfrac{y^2}{9}=1$ 　　　　　　　(b) $\dfrac{x^2}{16}-\dfrac{y^2}{9}=-1$

Solution

(a) $\dfrac{x^2}{16}-\dfrac{y^2}{9}=1,\ a^2=16$ and $b^2=9$

　　　　$a=4(a>0)$ and $b=3(b>0)$

　　But $c^2=a^2+b^2$

　　　　$c^2=16+9=25$

　　　　$c=5(c>0)$

$\therefore$ the foci are $(5,0)$ and $(-5,0)$

Solution

(b) $\dfrac{x^2}{16}-\dfrac{y^2}{9}=-1,\ a^2=9$ and $b^2=16$

　　　$\therefore a=3(a>0)$ and $b=4(b>0)$

　　But $c^2=a^2+b^2$

　　　　$c^2=9+16=25$

　　　　$c=5(c>0)$

$\therefore$ the foci are $(0,5)$ and $(0,-5)$.

EXAMPLE 2. *State the equation of the hyperbola with centre at the origin, foci on the y-axis, $a=5$, $b=4$.*

Solution The equation of the hyperbola is of the form $\dfrac{x^2}{b^2}-\dfrac{y^2}{a^2}=-1$

$$\dfrac{x^2}{4^2}-\dfrac{y^2}{5^2}=-1$$

$$\dfrac{x^2}{16}-\dfrac{y^2}{25}=-1$$

EXERCISE 13-8

B **1.** For each of the following hyperbolas, (i) determine the intercepts, (ii) state the lengths of the transverse and conjugate axes, (iii) state the coordinates of the vertices, (iv) state the axes of symmetry, (v) sketch the hyperbola by first plotting the two vertices and sketching the asymptotes.

(a) $16x^2-25y^2=400$ 　　　　(b) $x^2-4y^2=4$
(c) $9x^2-36y^2=324$ 　　　　(d) $4x^2-49y^2=196$

2. State the equation of a hyperbola with the centre at the origin and:
(a) foci on the x-axis, semi-transverse axis 5 and semi-conjugate axis 4.

Add the following without converting $CXVI + XIII + VI$.

(b) focus $F_1(10, 0)$, vertex $A_1(8, 0)$.

(c) foci on the y-axis, $a = 7$, $b = 9$.

(d) vertex $(0, 3)$, semi-conjugate axis 2.

3. Determine the values of a, b, and c for the hyperbolas represented by each of the following equations and hence state the coordinates of the foci.

(a) $\dfrac{x^2}{144} - \dfrac{y^2}{25} = 1$

(b) $\dfrac{x^2}{1} - \dfrac{y^2}{4} = 1$

(c) $\dfrac{x^2}{64} - \dfrac{y^2}{36} = 1$

(d) $\dfrac{x^2}{4} - \dfrac{y^2}{9} = 1$

4. The foci of a hyperbola are 20 units apart and the difference of the focal radii is 16 units. Write an equation for the hyperbola.

5. Find the equation of the hyperbola for which the length of the conjugate axis is 10 units and the foci are 26 units apart.

13.9 LINEAR-LINEAR SYSTEMS

Substitution is one algebraic method of solving a pair of linear equations.

EXAMPLE 1. *Solve*

$$y = 3x - 1 \qquad ①$$

$$5x + 3y = 11 \qquad ②$$

Solution

From ①, $y = 3x - 1$

Substituting in ② we have

$$5x + 3(3x - 1) = 11$$

removing brackets

$$5x + 9x - 3 = 11$$

simplifying

$$14x = 14$$

$$x = 1$$

Substitute in ① to find y

$$y = 3x - 1$$

$$= 3(1) - 1$$

$$= 2$$

$$(x, y) = (1, 2)$$

EXAMPLE 2. *Solve*

$$2x - 3y = -13 \qquad ①$$

$$4x + 5y = 7 \qquad ②$$

Solution

From ① $2x - 3y = -13$

$2x = 3y - 13$

$x = \dfrac{3y - 13}{2}$

Substituting in ②

$$4\left(\frac{3y - 13}{2}\right) + 5y = 7$$

$$2(3y - 13) + 5y = 7 \qquad\qquad \text{removing brackets}$$

$$6y - 26 + 5y = 7 \qquad\qquad \text{simplifying}$$

$$11y = 33$$

$$y = 3$$

Substituting to find x

$$x = \frac{3y - 13}{2}$$

$$= \frac{3(3) - 13}{2}$$

$$= -2$$

$$(x, y) = (-2, 3)$$

The graphical representation of a linear equation is a straight line. The solution of a pair of linear equations (if it exists) is the coordinates of the point of intersection of the graphs of the two lines.

EXAMPLE 3. *Solve graphically*

$$y = 2x + 1 \qquad ①$$

$$x + y = -5 \qquad ②$$

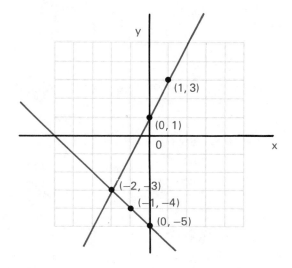

Solution $y = 2x + 1$ has slope 2 and y-intercept 1. We use these to plot the points $(0, 1)$ and $(1, 3)$ and hence draw $y = 2x + 1$. The equation $x + y = -5$ can be written as $y = -x - 5$ with slope -1 and y-intercept -5. Plot $(0, -5)$ and $(-1, -4)$ to draw $y = -x - 5$.

The point of intersection has coordinates $(x, y) = (-2, -3)$

EXERCISE 13-9

A **1.** For each of the following equations,
(i) state an expression for x (ii) an expression for y.
(a) $x + y = 13$ (b) $2x + y = 6$ (c) $2x + 3y = 7$
(d) $3x - y = 4$ (e) $2y - x = 9$ (f) $5x - 4y = 8$
(g) $3y - 2x = -2$ (h) $2x + 3y - 6 = 0$ (i) $2x = 4y + 5$

B **2.** Solve the following linear systems by substitution.
(a) $y = 3x + 1$ (b) $y = 2x - 3$
    $5x - 3y = -11$ $3x + y = 5$
(c) $3x + y = 4$ (d) $4x - y = 8$
    $2x - 3y = 43$ $3x - 2y = 6$

3. Solve by substitution:
(a) $4x - 7y = 18$ (b) $6x + 2y = 34$
    $x - 3y = 2$ $5x - 2y = -1$
(c) $5x + 4y = 0$ (d) $4x + 3y = 5$
    $4x + 5y = 9$ $12x + 6y = 13$

4. Solve the following linear systems graphically.
(a) $2x + y = 8$ (b) $x + 3y = 1$
    $x + y = 5$ $3x - y = -7$
(c) $5x - y = 8$ (d) $x + y = 11$
    $3x + 2y = 10$ $2x + 3y = 26$

Solve

$2317x + 5843y = 0$

$7684x - 2543y = 0$

13.10 LINEAR-QUADRATIC SYSTEMS

EXAMPLE 1. *Solve the linear-quadratic system*

$$x + y = 15 \qquad ①$$
$$x^2 + y^2 = 25 \qquad ②$$

and illustrate with a graph.

Solution From the linear equation ① $y = 15 - x$
Substituting in the quadratic equation ②

$$x^2 + (15 - x)^2 = 125$$
$$x^2 + 225 - 30x + x^2 = 125 \quad \text{simplifying}$$
$$2x^2 - 30x + 100 = 0$$
$$x^2 - 15x + 50 = 0$$
$$(x - 5)(x - 10) = 0 \qquad \text{factoring}$$
$$x - 5 = 0 \quad \text{or} \quad x - 10 = 0$$
$$x = 5 \quad \text{or} \quad x = 10$$

applied mathematics for today: senior

Substituting in the linear equation:

If $x = 5$,
$y = 15 - 5 = 10$,
$\therefore (x, y) = (5, 10)$

If $x = 10$
$y = 15 - 10 = 5$,
$\therefore (x, y) = (10, 5)$

Note that here there are two solutions.

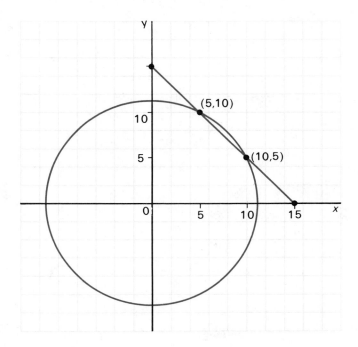

The equation $x + y = 15$ represents a straight line with slope -1 and y-intercept 15. The equation $x^2 + y^2 = 125$ represents a circle with centre the origin and radius $\sqrt{125}$ or $5\sqrt{5}$. The line intersects the circle at $(5, 10)$ and $(10, 5)$.

Steps in Solving a Linear-Quadratic System:
1. Express the linear equation in the form $y = mx + b$.
2. Substitute the expression $mx + b$ for y in the quadratic equation.
3. Solve the resulting quadratic equation in x by factoring or using the general formula (see Chapter 4).
4. Substitute both values of x in $y = mx + b$ to find all solutions.

EXAMPLE 2. *Determine the points of intersection of the line $x - y + 4 = 0$ and the parabola $y^2 = 18x$.*

Solution From $x - y + 4 = 0$, we get $y = x + 4$
Substituting in $y^2 = 18x$,

$$(x + 4)^2 = 18x$$

$$x^2 + 8x + 16 = 18x \qquad \text{simplifying}$$

$$x^2 - 10x + 16 = 0$$

$$(x - 8)(x - 2) = 0 \qquad \text{factoring}$$

$$x - 8 = 0 \quad \text{or} \quad x - 2 = 0$$

$$\therefore x = 8 \quad \text{or} \quad x = 2$$

If $x = 8$ \qquad\qquad If $x = 2$,
$y = 8 + 4 = 12$. \qquad $y = 2 + 4 = 6$

$\therefore$ the two points of intersection are $(8, 12)$ and $(2, 6)$

EXAMPLE 3. *Solve the system*

$$y^2 = 8x \qquad\qquad ①$$

$$x - y + 2 = 0 \qquad ②$$

and illustrate with a graph.

Solution From ② we get $y = x + 2$
Substituting in ①

$$(x + 2)^2 = 8x$$

$$x^2 + 4x + 4 = 8x \qquad \text{simplifying}$$

$$x^2 - 4x + 4 = 0$$

$$(x - 2)(x - 2) = 0 \qquad \text{factoring}$$

$$\therefore x = 2 \quad \text{or} \quad x = 2$$

If $x = 2$, $y = 2 + 2 = 4$
The two solutions are identical, namely $(2, 4)$ and $(2, 4)$.

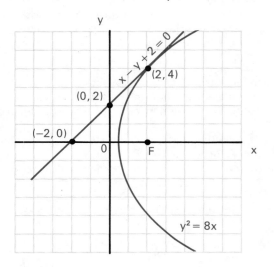

applied mathematics for today: senior

Graphically, $x - y + 2 = 0$ represents a line with slope 1, y-intercept 2. $y^2 = 8x$ represents a parabola, with vertex at the origin and focus on the positive x-axis. They intersect at one point only, the point $(2, 4)$.

When a straight line cuts a conic at only one distinct point, we say the line is a *tangent* to the conic. This line shows us the direction of the curve at that point.

The third possibility is that a line may not cut the curve at all. Algebraically this means there would be no real solution to such a linear quadratic system.

EXERCISE 13-10

B **1.** Solve the following linear-quadratic systems and illustrate your solutions with a graph.

(a) $x - y = -2$
$\quad y = x^2$

(b) $x - y = 0$
$\quad y^2 = 6x$

(c) $x + y = 5$
$\quad 2x^2 + 3y^2 = 35$

(d) $x + y = 2$
$\quad 3x^2 - y^2 = 2$

(e) $x + 2y = 2$
$\quad 9x^2 + 4y^2 = 36$

(f) $3x + y = 11$
$\quad x^2 - y^2 = 5$

2. (a) Solve each of the following systems.

(i) $4x + 3y = 0$
$\quad x^2 + y^2 = 25$

(ii) $4x + 3y = 25$
$\quad x^2 + y^2 = 25$

(iii) $4x + 3y = 30$
$\quad x^2 + y^2 = 25$

(b) Graph the systems to illustrate the number of solutions.

3. (a) Determine the points of intersection between each line and the corresponding conic in the following systems.

(i) $x - y + 3 = 0$
$\quad y^2 = 12x$

(ii) $9x - 8y = 25$
$\quad 9x^2 + 4y^2 = 25$

(b) What is the line $x - y + 3 = 0$ called with respect to the parabola $y^2 = 12x$?

4. (a) Determine the points of intersection in the following systems.

(i) $x - 2y = 0$
$\quad x^2 - 4y^2 = 4$

(ii) $2x - 3y = 6$
$\quad -x^2 + y^2 = 10$

(b) What is the line $x - 2y = 0$ called with respect to the hyperbola $x^2 - 4y^2 = 4$?

C **5.** The sum of two numbers is 9 and their product is 14. Find the numbers.

6. The perimeter of a rectangle is 28 m and its area is 45 m^2. Find its dimensions.

REVIEW EXERCISE

1. Identify each of the following curves by stating the name of the curve and two of its properties.

(a) $y^2 = 12x$

(b) $x^2 + y^2 = 9$

(c) $\dfrac{x^2}{16} + \dfrac{y^2}{9} = 1$

(d) $x^2 - y^2 = 9$

(e) $\dfrac{x^2}{25} - \dfrac{y^2}{9} = 1$

(f) $y = 12x + \frac{1}{3}$

2. State the values of a, b, and c for each conic defined by the following equations.

(a) $\dfrac{x^2}{16} + \dfrac{y^2}{25} = 1$

(b) $\dfrac{x^2}{64} - \dfrac{y^2}{36} = 1$

(c) $\dfrac{x^2}{9} - \dfrac{y^2}{4} = 1$

(d) $9x^2 + 4y^2 = 36$

3. Find the equation of the parabola with vertex at the origin and:

(a) focus $(5, 0)$

(b) focus on the x-axis and passing through $(2, -4)$

(c) directrix $y = 3$

4. Find the equation of the ellipse with centre at the origin and:

(a) foci on the x-axis, where $a = 7$ and $b = 5$

(b) vertices $(0, -8)$ and $(0, 8)$ and minor axis 10

(c) major axis 26 (along the x-axis) and $c = 5$

5. Find the equation of the hyperbola with centre at the origin and:

(a) foci on the y-axis, where $a = 5$ and $b = 6$

(b) vertex $(12, 0)$ and focus $(15, 0)$

(c) transverse axis (along the x-axis) and conjugate axis both 16.

6. Solve the following systems of equations.

(a) $2x + 3y = 10$
    $x^2 + y^2 = 25$

(b) $y = x + 3$
    $y^2 = 12x$

applied mathematics for today: senior

REVIEW AND PREVIEW TO CHAPTER 14

APPROXIMATE NUMBERS—THE PRECISION OF A MEASURE

The precision of a measure is determined by the implied unit of the measure. A measure of 57.36 m implies a unit of 0.01 m.

EXERCISE 1

	Measure	Bounds		Implied unit	Maximum error
		Upper limit	Lower limit		
(a)	27 cm	27.5 cm	26.5 cm	1 cm	±0.5 cm
(b)	47.3 g	—	—	0.1 g	±0.05 g
(c)	147 km	147.5 km	146.5 km	—	—
(d)	0.043 mm	—	—	—	—
(e)	63.81 kg	—	—	—	—
(f)	574 m	—	—	—	—
(g)	7.83×10^3 kg	7.835×10^3 kg	7.825×10^3 kg	10 kg	±5 kg
(h)	4.8×10^4 m	—	—	—	—
(i)	2.56×10^3 g	—	—	—	—
(j)	9.1×10^{-4} km	—	—	—	—
(k)	2.643×10^5 cm	—	—	—	—
(l)	5.03×10^{-2} mm	—	—	—	—

$$0.01 \times 10^3 = 10$$
$$\pm 0.005 \times 10^3 = \pm 5$$

When adding or subtracting approximate numbers:

1. Convert measures to the same unit.
If scientific notation is used convert to the same power of 10.

2. Round off measures to a precision of one more decimal place than the least precise measure.

3. Add or subtract as required.

4. Round off answer to the precision of the least precise measure.

EXAMPLE 1.

Add	4.6 cm	46 mm	*Least precise measure*
	32.64 mm	32.6 mm	
	0.5397 mm	0.5 mm	
	178.48 mm	178.5 mm	
		257.6 mm	*Total* 258 mm

A total can be no more precise than its least precise addend.

EXERCISE 2

1. Find the sum of the following quantities to the precision warranted by the data.

(a) 5.2 g
 27.95 g
 0.785 g

(b) 476 mm
 86.39 cm
 7482 mm
 57.0 cm

(c) 86.9 km
 568.0 km
 0.97 km
 46.812 km

(d) 87.34 g
 531.7 g
 50.357 kg
 1347 g

(e) 148.96 mm
 36.513 9 m
 57.0 m
 2.841 m

(f) 784.3 ml
 48.91 ml
 0.007 2ℓ
 1834 ml

(g) 4.786×10^3 cm
 5.12×10^2 cm
 8.043×10^2 cm
 1.19×10^3 cm

(h) 5.17×10 g
 7.3×10^2 g
 2.58×10^2 g
 0.849×10^3 g

(i) 2.15×10^{-1} m
 4.196×10^{-2} m
 8.31×10^{-1} m
 6.1×10^{-2} m

(j) 4.51×10^3 N
 2.6×10^2 N
 5.82×10^2 N
 8.000×10^3 N

2. Find the difference of the following measures to the precision warranted by the data.

(a) 57.49 cm
 31.5 cm

(b) 184.20 km
 84 km

(c) 734.01 g
 14 621 mg

(d) 76.43 mm
 1.849 7 cm

(e) 0.004 78 m
 0.000 815 9 m

(f) 2.46×10^2 cm
 1.52×10^2 cm

(g) 5.861×10^3 g
 $7.147\ 3 \times 10^2$ g

(h) 1.247×10^5 mm
 3.1×10^4 mm

(i) 2.51×10^5 mm
 6.41×10^3 cm

(j) 1.755×10^{-3} g
 5.13×10^{-4} g

3. For each of the following sets of measures find:
 (i) the sum
 (ii) the sum of the upper limits
 (iii) the sum of the lower limits
 each to the precision warranted by the data.

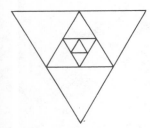

If the area of the large equilateral triangle is 320 mm² and each side is bisected, what is the area of the smallest triangle? What is the length of the side of the smallest triangle?

(iv) Find the average of the sum of the upper and lower limits and compare it to the sum in (i).

(a) 47.65 cm
     9.3 cm
   158.79 cm
_____

(b) 9587.4 kg
    742.87 kg
   4160 kg
_____

4. A group of students survey an orienteering trail. Find the total distance and the maximum and minimum distances. Give the final answer in the form: $d \pm e$, where d is the distance and e is the maximum error.

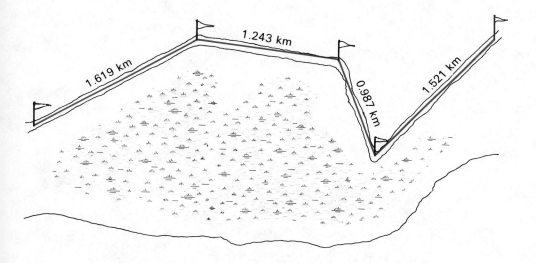

Evaluate:

1. $1\frac{1}{4}\%$ of $185 212.80

2. $5\frac{1}{2}\%$ of $74 900.00

3. $12\frac{1}{2}\%$ of $3709.40

4. $10\frac{3}{4}\%$ of $45 925.50

5. $16\frac{2}{3}\%$ of $7253.49

6. $2\frac{1}{2}\%$ of $202 493.18

7. $5\frac{1}{4}\%$ of $93 900.00

8. $7\frac{3}{8}\%$ of $32 427.50

9. $4\frac{1}{2}\%$ of $64 949.95

10. 17% of $4959.95

Investing in Stocks and Bonds

TORONTO STOCK EXCHANGE—Showing trading posts where the buying and selling of shares takes place.

applied mathematics for today: senior

14.1 TYPES OF INVESTMENT

"What am I bid for the use of my $1000?"

The government of Canada might pay you $40 every 6 mo. (8%/a, compounded semi-annually). In return for your money you would receive a $1000 bond.

Ourtown needs money to build a new pollution control centre. The town council, with the approval of the municipal board of the provincial government, has issued debentures at $8\frac{1}{2}$%/a and would be pleased to have the use of your money in return for one of these debentures.

King Corn Cannery Co. Ltd. is expanding its factory and must borrow $1 500 000. They have issued mortgage bonds and will pay $9\frac{3}{4}$%/a for the use of your money.

South-Western Trust can lend mortgage money at $11\frac{1}{2}$%/a. They will pay you 10% on a term savings certificate so that they may reinvest the money.

Perhaps you would like to buy part ownership in Speedy Cycle Corp. and share their profits. In that case you might buy stock in that company.

INVESTMENT IN SECURITIES

When we lend money to the government or to a company, we are investing in a debt security. We can do this by buying bonds or debentures. These are usually classified according to the security behind them.

Government bonds—secured by the ability of the government to raise money by taxation.

Mortgage bonds—secured by the property of the company. (If the company defaults, holders of these bonds will have first claim to the revenue from the sale of assets.)

Collateral trust bonds—secured by the money invested by the borrowing company in the bonds or securities of other companies.

Income bonds—bonds on which interest is paid only if the company makes a profit.

Debentures—secured by the general assets and earning power of the company or corporation.

When we buy part ownership of a company we are purchasing equity securities. In this case we are buying stock which is sold as shares in the company.

Common stock—A dividend will usually be declared at a rate per share if the company makes money. Also, holders of common stock have a voice in setting company policy at the annual stockholders meeting (one vote per share). These shares usually have no initial or par value; their price is set by what people are willing to pay on the open market.

Canada Packers Limited

Dividend Notice

A quarterly dividend of 22¢ per share on the Class C convertible common shares and a quarterly dividend payable out of tax-paid undistributed surplus on hand of 18.7¢ per share on the Class D convertible common shares have been declared. These dividends are payable on October 1, 1976 to shareholders of record at the close of business on September 10, 1976.

A. M. MacKenzie
Secretary

August 13, 1976

Canada Packers Limited

CARLING O'KEEFE LIMITED
DIVIDEND NOTICE

NOTICE is hereby given that the Board of Directors has declared the following dividends payable October 1, 1976 to shareholders of record at the close of business on September 3, 1976.
1. A quarterly dividend of 55 cents per share on the outstanding $2.20 Cumulative Preference Shares Series A with a par value of $50 each in the capital of the Company.
2. A quarterly dividend of 66¼ cents per share on the outstanding $2.65 Cumulative Preference Shares Series B with a par value of $50 each in the capital of the Company.
By Order of the Board

J W JAGO,
Secretary.

August 11, 1976

Carling O'Keefe Limited

Figure 14-1

Preferred stock—These shares have a par value and a fixed return set in dollars per share or as a percentage of the par value of the stock. The market value of the stock may vary considerably from the par value. (Figure 14-1.)

It is also possible that we might invest our money in some other way such as putting it in bank savings, buying mutual funds, buying life insurance, or buying real estate.

RATE OF RETURN ON AN INVESTMENT

What determines the rate of return on an investment?

One of the major factors is supply and demand. If money is readily avilable and many investors are looking for places to invest, then the rates will be lowered. If not many people have money to lend and there are many potential borrowers, the rates will go up.

Another important factor is risk. The most obvious risk is that we may lose our investment. If we invest in a high-risk venture such as the search for a mine or an oil well, we will expect a high return on our investment if the search is successful. If we are investing in a company with a long record of success in the business world, then it appears there will be little risk and the rates will therefore be lower.

A second risk which an investor takes is not so obvious. What will the value of my money be when it is returned? If I invest $1000 in a 20-year bond, what will my $1000 buy when I get it back? If the cost of living doubles approximately every 10 a, what will my $1000 be worth in 20 a?

Before a company can issue stocks it must receive a charter from the provincial government. The government requires that the company file a copy of its constitution and the names of the members of its board of directors, that it issue an audited annual financial statement and report to the stockholders, and that it hold an annual stockholders meeting for the election of the board of directors.

Since a company which is not fulfilling these obligations can lose its charter, there is a measure of protection for the wary investor.

To illustrate the relative risks in the securities named so far, it is worth noting the order of priority of the financial obligations the company incurs.

First—bond and debenture interest must be paid.
Second—if the company has made a profit, preferred shareholders will receive dividends.
Third—dividends will be paid to common shareholders from remaining profits as declared by the board of directors.

If the company finds that it is unable to meet its financial obligations and declares *bankruptcy*, the revenue from the sale of assets will be distributed in the same order with bond holders being paid off first, preferred shareholders next, and the residue, if any, being distributed among the common shareholders on the basis of the formula:

applied mathematics for today: senior

$$\frac{\text{residual assets}}{\text{total outstanding shares}} \times \text{number of shares held}$$

Since banks operate under strict government control, funds deposited with them are as secure as government bonds which are generally considered the safest of all investments.

EXERCISE 14-1

A **1.** Rank the following investments in order of relative security from most to least.

Common stock, Company mortgage bonds, Debentures, Government bonds, Preferred stock.

Remember that any form of investment is only as secure as the organization standing behind it.

2. (a) Which securities involve purchasing part ownership of a company?

(b) Which securities involve lending money to a company?

B **3.** If a company has a net worth of $5 000 000 and you own 100 shares out of a total of 100 000 shares, what is the value of your shares if the company is dissolved?

4. In winding up the affairs of a company which has gone out of business, there is $1 462 700 left after settling all debts. If there are 500 000 shares of common stock outstanding, how much will the owner of 1500 shares receive?

5. A company wishes to raise capital by selling a bond issue of $1 500 000 in $8\frac{1}{2}\%$ mortgage bonds. If the interest is paid semi-annually, how much money will the company pay in interest each half year?

6. A company has 800 000 shares in the hands of shareholders. The company declares a dividend of $1.35 per share.

(a) How much money will the company pay out in dividends?

(b) How much money will a shareholder with 2000 shares receive?

(c) If this is an annual dividend and the shares have a market value of $60, what rate of return is this on the investment?

7. A company declares $617 500 in dividends. There are 950 000 shares in the hands of shareholders.

(a) What is the dividend per share?

(b) What dividend will a shareholder with 500 shares receive?

(c) What annual rate of return does this represent if it is a semi-annual dividend from a stock with a market value of $25 per share?

C **8.** Determine the name and location of stockbrokers' offices (if any) in your community. A class representative should ask for a sample of investment literature and the print-out of a stock quotation.

9. From the financial section of a newspaper, find the names of three preferred stocks and three bond issues. Compare the income from each.

14.2 THE COST OF BUYING AND SELLING STOCK

Barbara Wilson decided to invest money in stocks. She wished to speculate on the probability that the price would increase, so she purchased common shares. In order to decide on an investment, she consulted the market page of the newspaper, read the comments of a market analyst, and decided to invest in Cygnus A.

Ms Wilson went to see her stockbroker, who obtained a quote on Cygnus from the teletype linking his office with the stock exchange where Cygnus was listed. (In Canada there are stock exchanges in Montreal, Toronto, Winnipeg, Calgary, and Vancouver.) The teletype was connected to a computer where all the latest information on the stock was stored.

```
CYG.A      4.10      4.30
4.30       180  DN  0.20
4.30       4.30      4.30
```

Figure 14-2

The first line (Figure 14-2) shows the abbreviated name for the stock: CYG. A, the bid price: $4.10, and the asked price: $4.30. The bid price is the highest price per share that a buyer is willing to pay, while the asked price is the lowest price per share that a shareholder is willing to sell for.

The second line shows the last sale was at $4.30 for 180 shares. This price was down $0.20 from the last sale. The last line tells us that the stock opened at $4.30 and the high and low for the day were both $4.30. This would indicate little trading in Cygnus A shares.

Ms Wilson decided to put in a purchase order for Cygnus A at $4.30. The next thing to be decided was how many shares she would buy. Most trading is done in "board lots." The number of shares in a board lot depends on the type of stock and the price per share (Figure 14-3).

The Stock Exchanges have uniformly ruled that the regular trading units of "board lots" are as follows:—

Selling under $0.10	1000 shares
Selling at $0.10 and under $1.00	500 shares
Selling under $0.10 (only applicable to mining, oil and gas shares on V.S.E.)	500 shares
Selling at $1.00 and under $100.00	100 shares
Selling at $100.00 and over	10 shares

Figure 14-3

Part lots are sold but they are more difficult to buy and sometimes hard to sell. The result of buying a part lot is that you buy above market price and usually sell below market price.

Ms Wilson had about $1000 to invest, so she decided to puchase two board lots of 200 shares at the asked price of $4.30. Ms Wilson's broker put in a purchase order to his representative at the exchange and the offer was given to a trader. The trader went to a "trading post" on the flcor of the exchange (Figure 14-4) where he offered to purchase the stock. There the trader met another trader representing an investor who wished to sell Cygnus A. If the price was agreeable a trade would be concluded.

```
CYG.A
2s                 4.30
```

Figure 14-5

Meanwhile, back at the broker's office, Ms Wilson watched the transactions of the exchange displayed on a board at the front. Soon she saw her purchase recorded on the board (Figure 14-5) and shortly after received confirmation from her broker that the purchase had been made.

The next step was to calculate the cost to Ms Wilson. For the services performed the broker charged a *commission*.

Courtesy Toronto Stock Exchange

Figure 14-4

For orders of value $20 000 or under, the following formulas determine commission for buying or selling shares.

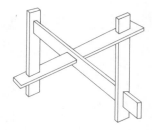

Conditions	Formula
	C = Commission ($) x = value of order ($), $x \leqq \$20\,000$ n = number of shares
Shares selling under $14.00: 2.50% of the value of the order	$C = 0.0250x$
Shares selling at $14.00 up to and including $30.00: 0.8875% of the value of the order plus 22.575¢ per share	$C = 0.008\,875x + \$0.225\,75n$
Shares selling over $30.00: 1.64% of the value of the order	$C = 0.0164x$

investing in stocks and bonds

EXAMPLE 1. *Find the cost to the purchaser of 200 shares of Cygnus A at $4.30 per share.*

Solution

$$\begin{aligned}
\text{Cost of shares} &= 200 \times \$4.30 \\
&= \$860.00 \\
\text{Commission} &= 0.0250 \times \$860.00 \\
&= \$21.50 \\
\text{Cost to purchaser} &= \$860.00 + \$21.50 \\
&= \$881.50
\end{aligned}$$

(share price under $14.00)

EXAMPLE 2. *Find the net proceeds to the seller of 500 shares of Pacific Petroleum at $16.50 per share.*

Solution

$$\begin{aligned}
\text{Proceeds} &= 500 \times \$16.50 \\
&= \$8250.00 \\
\text{Commission} &= 0.008\,875 \times \$8250 + \$0.225\,75 \times 500 \\
&= \$73.219 + \$112.875 \\
&= \$186.094 \\
\text{Net proceeds} &= \$8250.00 - \$186.09 \\
&= \$8063.91
\end{aligned}$$

$\$14 \leq \left(\dfrac{\text{share}}{\text{price}}\right) \leq \$30$

The commission is deducted from the proceeds.

Note that amounts are carried to the nearest $\frac{1}{10}¢$ until the final answer and then rounded down if less than one-half, rounded up if equal to, or over one-half.

EXAMPLE 3. *An investor buys 600 shares of International Nickel at $24.37 and sells at $25.25. Calculate his profit or loss.*

Solution

$$\begin{aligned}
\text{Cost of shares} &= 600 \times \$24.37 \\
&= \$14\,622.00 \\
\text{Commission} &= 0.008\,875 \times \$14\,622.00 + \$0.225\,75 \times 600 \\
&= \$129.770 + \$135.45 \\
&= \$265.22 \\
\text{Total cost} &= \$14\,622.00 + \$265.22 \\
&= \$14\,887.22
\end{aligned}$$

$$\begin{aligned}
\text{Proceeds} &= 600 \times \$25.25 \\
&= \$15\,150.00 \\
\text{Commission} &= 0.008\,875 \times \$15\,150 + \$0.225\,75 \times 600 \\
&= \$134.456 + \$135.45 \\
&= \$269.906 \\
\text{Net proceeds} &= \$15\,150 - \$269.91 \\
&= \$14\,880.09
\end{aligned}$$

Commission is deducted from proceeds.

$$\begin{aligned}
\text{Profit} &= \$14\,887.22 - \$14\,880.09 \\
&= \$7.13
\end{aligned}$$

EXERCISE 14-2

A **1.** Find the costs of the following purchases excluding the commission.

(a) Ashland, preferred   100 shares at $18.00
(b) Ashland, common   1000 shares at $6.00
(c) Baton B   300 shares at $3.75
(d) British American bank   100 shares at $13\frac{1}{2}$
(e) Jannock B   100 shares at $10\frac{1}{4}$
(f) Koffler, preferred   100 shares at $6\frac{3}{8}$
(g) Metropolitan Stores   2000 shares at $8\frac{5}{8}$
(h) Rothman   200 shares at $8\frac{3}{4}$
(i) Sunburst   7000 shares at $0.09
(j) Transair   2000 shares at $0.30

2. Calculate the commission on the following sales.

(a) Borex   5000 shares at $0.07\frac{1}{2}$
(b) B. C. Forest   300 shares at $8\frac{7}{8}$
(c) Copper Fields   1000 shares at $0.95
(d) Dustbane   200 shares at $5.00
(e) Petrofina   300 shares at $15\frac{3}{4}$
(f) Weston   750 shares at $22\frac{3}{8}$
(g) Canron   600 shares at $17.50
(h) Texaco   100 shares at $31\frac{5}{8}$
(i) Credit Foncier   150 shares at $78.00
(j) B. C. Telephone   200 shares at $48.50

3. Calculate the total cost of the following purchases.
(a) Calico Silver, 100 shares at $1.40
(b) Abitibi, 625 shares at $8\frac{3}{4}$
(c) Overland Express, 300 shares at $6.13
(d) Alcan, 200 shares at $25\frac{1}{2}$
(e) Penmans 6% pref., 50 shares at $97\frac{1}{2}$
(f) Numac, 300 shares at $7\frac{1}{8}$
(g) Imperial Life, 25 shares at $144.00
(h) Pamour, 1350 shares at $10\frac{1}{2}$

4. Calculate the net proceeds from the following sales.
(a) Cambridge Mines, 1500 shares at $0.40
(b) Consolidated Glass, 100 shares at $8\frac{3}{4}$
(c) Belltower Cottage Industries, 200 shares at $3\frac{1}{2}$
(d) Domtar, 110 shares at $19\frac{1}{4}$
(e) International Paper, 90 shares at $35.00
(f) Kamkotia, 1100 shares at $0.49\frac{1}{2}$
(g) Interplex, 700 shares at $0.60
(h) Voyageur, 100 shares at $3.15

5. Calculate the profit or loss resulting from each of the following sets of transactions.

Courtesy The Toronto Stock Exchange

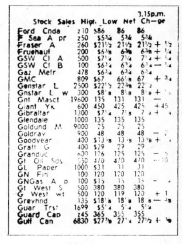

Figure 14-6

Stock sales are reported daily in the newspaper. A portion of a typical report is shown above.

Write as a decimal $99\frac{44}{100}$%.

			Bought at	Sold at
(a)	Economic Investment	300 shares	$18.00	10\frac{1}{2}$
(b)	Inland National Gas	500 shares	8\frac{1}{4}$	16\frac{3}{4}$
(c)	Guarantee Trust	200 shares	$11.87	$5.50
(d)	Donlee	1000 shares	$3.25	$4.60
(e)	I.A.C. Ltd.	600 shares	$13.20	$20.12
(f)	Intermetco	100 shares	$4.95	$3.50

14.3 RETURN ON STOCK INVESTMENTS

Individuals and organizations invest money in stocks in the hope of increasing their wealth. With stocks the increase may come in the form of a *dividend* or as a *capital gain*. In Exercise 14-2 we calculated capital gain (or loss) for various stocks—our profit or loss from buying at one price and selling at another, hopefully higher.

In this section we shall discuss dividends, which represent the return or yield on investments.

Common Stock

When a company makes a profit, the owners are entitled to share in the surplus income. The board of directors will decide how much of the profit should be used to expand or improve the company, often called "ploughing money back in," and how much should be distributed to the shareholders as dividends.

If a company has 500 000 shares of stock distributed among its stockholders and the directors wish to distribute $100 000 in earnings, they will declare a dividend of 20¢ per share. ($100 000 ÷ 500 000 shares.)

Figure 14-7 gives the dividend report as it might appear on the financial page of a daily newspaper.

Note that Livingston Industries Ltd. has declared a dividend of 8$\frac{1}{2}$¢ per share, payable on 10-31 to the shareholders on record as of 10-15. If a shareholder sold his shares of Livingston Industries Ltd. on 10-17, he would still receive the dividend of 10-31.

EXAMPLE 1. *A shareholder owns* 1500 *shares of Toronto Dominion Bank on* 09-26. *What dividend will he receive if a dividend is declared as shown in Figure* 14-7?

Solution Dividend declared 33¢ per share

Dividend received = 1500 × $0.33

= $495.00

Preferred Stock

Preferred stock has a par value, usually $100 per share, and a fixed rate of return, shown as a percentage of the par value. The stock may also be listed in terms of the annual return such as the Metroplitan Stores $1.30 preferred shares paying a semi-annual dividend of $0.65

Dividends

Corporation dividends, quarterly unless otherwise noted.

Canadian Hydrocarbons Ltd., 5$\frac{1}{2}$ percent pfd. series A 27$\frac{1}{2}$ cents, Sept 30, record Sept. 23.

Canadian International Power C Ltd., 32 cents, U.S.F., Sept. 30, record Sept. 24.

Cockfield Brown and Co. Ltd., 12$\frac{1}{2}$ cents, Sept. 30, record Sept. 18.

Dalex Co. Ltd., $1.75, Sept. 30, record Sept. 20.

Hawker Siddeley Canada Ltd., eight cents, Oct. 16, record Sept. 27; 5$\frac{3}{4}$-percent pfd., 1.43\frac{3}{4}$, Oct. 2, record Sept. 20.

Laurentide Financial Corp. Ltd., $1.25 pfd. 31$\frac{1}{8}$ cents, Dec. 1, record Nov. 8.

Livingston Industries Ltd., 8$\frac{1}{2}$ cents, Oct. 31, record Oct. 15.

Metropolitan Stores of Canada Ltd., 6$\frac{1}{2}$-pfd., 65 cents semi-annual; $1.30 pfd. 65 cents, semi-annual; both payable Nov. 1, record Sept. 30.

Niagara Structural Steel Co. Ltd., 6$\frac{1}{2}$-percent pfd., 97$\frac{1}{2}$ cents, interim. Sept. 30, record Sept. 20.

Reed Shaw Osler Ltd., class A, six cents, Dec. 13, record Nov. 29.

Toronto Dominion Bank, 33 cents, Nov. 1, record Sept. 26.

Figure 14-7

applied mathematics for today: senior

(Figure 14-7). If the company makes money these dividends must be paid before the dividends on common shares.

EXAMPLE 2. *A shareholder owns* 500 *shares of Hawker Siddeley Canada Ltd.* $5\frac{3}{4}$% *preferred and* 2500 *shares of Hawker Siddeley common as of the dates of record. How much dividend will he receive with a dividend declared as shown in Figure* 14-7?

Solution

Quarterly dividend declared.

Common shares = 8¢ per share

Dividend received = 2500 × $0.08

= $200.00

$5\frac{3}{4}$% Preferred shares = $1.43\frac{3}{4}$ per share

Dividend received = 500 × $1.4375

= $718.75

Total dividend received = $200.00 + $718.75

= $918.75

$$\frac{5\frac{3}{4}\% \times \$100 \text{ par value}}{4} = \$1.43\frac{3}{4}$$

Why must we divide by 4?

Yield

In order to compare two investments to determine which is the most profitable at the current prices and dividend rates, we may look at the yields.

$$\text{Yield} = \frac{\text{dividend rate}}{\text{price}} \times 100\%$$

The current value of an investment depends both on the dividend rate and the price. If two reliable stocks both paid $1.50 per share annually and one was priced at $35 per share and the other at $70 per share, which would you invest in? Compare returns on a $7000 investment.

EXAMPLE 3. *Find the yield from shares of Ford of Canada paying a dividend rate of* $4.65 *per share per year with a current price of* $63.50 *per share.*

Solution

$$\text{Yield} = \frac{\$4.65}{\$63.50} \times 100\%$$

$$\doteq 7.3\%$$

The yield is 7.3%/a.

Note the dividend is calculated on a yearly basis, a quarterly dividend would be multiplied by four.

EXAMPLE 4. *Reed Shaw Osler declared a quarterly dividend of* 6¢ *per share (Figure* 14-7). *If the stock is currently trading at* $6.00 *find the yield.*

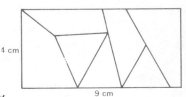

4 cm

9 cm

If the pieces can be arranged to form a square, what is its size?

Solution

$$\text{Annual dividend rate} = 4 \times \$0.06$$
$$= \$0.24 \text{ per share}$$
$$\text{Yield} = \frac{\$0.24}{\$6.00} \times 100\%$$
$$= 4.0\%$$

The yield is 4%/a.

Price/Earnings Ratio

If you are considering buying a stock, or if you own stock, you are naturally interested in whether your company is making money. The price/earnings ratio compares the price of the stock to the earnings per share of the company.

EXAMPLE 5. *Nebraska Fuels Inc. with* 100 000 *shares outstanding earned* $500 000 *last year. The current price is* $60 *per share. Find the price/earnings ratio.*

Solution Earnings per share $= \dfrac{\$500\ 000}{100\ 000} = \$5$

If the current market price of the shares is $60, then

$$\text{price/earnings ratio} = \tfrac{60}{5}$$
$$= 12.0$$

When the price/earnings ratio drops, it indicates that other investors do not have confidence in the stock even though it may be earning good dividends.

EXERCISE 14-3

A **1.** Match the following terms to the appropriate description.

(a) Common Share

(b) Preferred Share

(c) Capital Gain

(d) Dividend

(e) Yield

(i) A portion of company profits earned by shares.

(ii) An equity investment usually without par value, giving a variable return.

(iii) The ratio of dividend rate to price per share expressed as a percentage.

(iv) An equity investment giving a fixed return based on a par value.

(v) Profit made by buying at one price and selling at a higher price.

(f) Price/Earnings Ratio   (vi) The ratio of the price of a share to the earnings per share of the company.

2. What dividend per share should be paid in each of the following situations?

(a) Quarterly dividend on a $2.00 preferred share.

(b) Semi-annual dividend on a $1.50 preferred share.

(c) Quarterly dividend on an 8% preferred share, $100 par value.

(d) Semi-annual dividend on a 6% preferred share, $100 par value.

(e) The company directors declare $50 000 to be paid in dividends on 100 000 outstanding common shares.

(f) The company directors declare $250 000 to be paid in dividends on 1 000 000 outstanding shares.

B   **3.** What annual return should you expect on the following investments?

	Number of shares	Stock	Indicated dividend rate	Par value
(a)	500 shares	Maple Leaf Mills	$5\frac{1}{2}$% preferred	$100
(b)	700 shares	Power Corp.	$4\frac{3}{4}$% preferred	$ 50
(c)	100 shares	Rolland Paper	$4\frac{1}{4}$% preferred	$100
(d)	300 shares	United Corp.	5% preferred	$ 30
(e)	200 shares	Holdfast Corp.	$4\frac{1}{2}$% preferred	$100

4. Calculate the annual return and the yield from the following investments.

	Number of shares	Stock	Indicated dividend rate ($)	Current price ($)
(a)	200	Maher Shoes Ltd.	0.64	21.50
(b)	500	Walker-Good	1.45	41.21
(c)	150	Maclean-Hunter	0.36	11.25
(d)	1000	Phillips Cables	0.36	6.37
(e)	600	Reader's Digest	0.33	4.50

5. Find the par value of the following shares.

(a) Livingston Industries, 6% preferred *A*, dividend rate $3.00.

(b) Silknit, 5% preferred, dividend rate $2.00.

6. For each of the following stocks calculate the price/earnings (P/E) ratio.

	Stock	Closing price ($)	Earnings per share ($) (for fiscal year 19)
(a)	Rank Organization	2.95	0.53
(b)	Leon's Furniture	7.12	1.25
(c)	Macmillan Bloedel	23.50	3.90
(d)	Resource Service	1.65	0.35
(e)	United Trust	4.55	0.80

7. A.B.W. Construction Ltd. pays a quarterly dividend of $1.35 per share. If the shares have a market price of $129, find the yield.

8. Consolidated Corn Oil Co. Ltd. has annual earnings for the current year of $1 495 000, with 250 000 outstanding shares. If the current market price for the shares is $49.00 find the price/earning ratio.

9. Morrison Manufacturing Ltd. declared a semi-annual dividend of $3.40 per share. What is the yield if the shares have a market value of $84.50?

10. Lucky Find Iron Mines has current annual earnings of $4 500 000 with 500 000 shares outstanding. The market value is $45 per share. What is the price/earning ratio?

14.4 OBTAINING INFORMATION ABOUT THE MARKET

Who sets the price of a stock? The price is set by the people who are willing to trade it. Since the price depends on many different individual decisions, it is impossible to predict with certainty what the prices of stocks will do over any specified period of time. Unpredictable things can have a great effect for a short period of time. In 1962 the Cuban Missile Crisis, a confrontation between Russia and the United States over the placing of missiles in Cuba, caused a decline in prices on United States exchanges with repercussions felt on stock exchanges around the world. The long-term trend is for stock prices to increase, keeping pace with inflation in the economy.

To get an overall picture of what the market is doing we can consult the market indexes. An index reflects the average performance of a number of established stocks and indicates the general level of the market. If the selected index stocks are high, then the index average will be high. An index taken alone is not much help, but when we follow the index from day to day and month to month, we see the trend of prices. We can follow these trends by means of charts and graphs.

Since various sections of the market may differ in their sales appeal, the index samples different areas of the economy. For example the Toronto Stock Exchange Index covers industrials, gold, base metals (B.M.) and western oils (W.O.) separately. The number above each index indicates the number of stocks sampled.

One of the most frequently quoted indexes is the Dow-Jones Averages, which is the average of 3 indexes based on 30 industrials, 20 rail stocks and 15 utilities.

It is possible to compare the price/earnings ratio for any stock with the price/earnings ratio for the corresponding index. (See Figure 14-8.)

You might also compare the performance of your stock with respect to yield. Check the average stock yields. Is the market generally rising or falling? Compare the number of stocks rising to the number of those falling.

A general indication of the health of the market is the activity or volume of stock sales. If few investors are willing to buy, there may be a reason—the inexperienced buyer should seek expert advice.

Quick market facts

Price/earnings ratios for the major TSE indexes

Date	Industrial	Gold	Base Metal	Western Oil
Sept. 9, 1974	7.35	13.81	4.59	8.61
Week ago		H O L I D A Y		
Month ago	8.57	16.98	5.56	11.49
Year ago	13.79	17.79	12.65	27.15

Average stock yields

	Sept. 9, 1974 %	Week previous %	Month ago %	Year ago %
114 Average stock yields	6.92	6.66	5.90	4.51
6 Banks	5.38	5.31	4.58	3.68
18 Preferred	8.62	8.35	7.82	6.70
64 Common Industrial	6.10	5.90	5.20	3.92
26 Mining	8.11	7.67	6.60	4.63

(Compiled by Moss, Lawson & Co.)

Ups, downs

	Toronto						Montreal		
	Industrials			Mines & Oils			Combined		
Week Ended	Ups	Downs	No Change	Ups	Downs	No Change	Ups	Downs	No Change
Sept. 6	112	415	160	65	169	49	62	232	106
Aug. 30	87	477	154	52	188	50	54	270	99
Aug. 23	68	506	146	24	230	41	45	283	92
Aug. 16	99	409	169	55	187	47	69	225	109
Aug. 9	226	216	183	89	60	129	138	159	112

Volume of stock sales

	Montreal	Totonto	Alberta	Vancouver	N.Y.S.E.	American
Sept. 9	522 100	1 433 155	4 000	1 180 384	11 160 000	1 902 000
Sept. 6	531 100	1 492 334	13 400	1 825 949	15 130 000	1 444 000
Sept. 5	505 800	1 692 579	13 000	1 041 332	14 210 000	1 738 000
Sept. 4	790 800	1 924 805	17 200	1 084 225	16 930 000	2 098 000
Sept. 3	586 700	1 369 312	11 000	1 108 099	12 750 000	1 496 000

The Financial Post, 74-09-09.

Figure 14-8

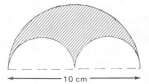

Find the area of the shaded region.

The quickest way to get an accurate picture of market trends is to examine a graph of the past performance of the market indexes.

A common form of graph shows a vertical line segment for each day giving the high and low of the index with a horizontal line segment to indicate the value at the close.

A high of 760, a low of 730, closing at 740 would be shown as in Figure 14-9.

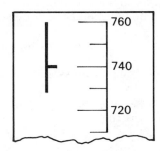

Figure 14-9

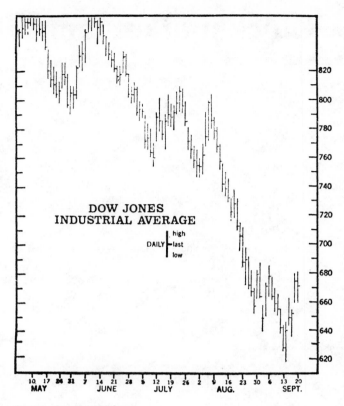

DOW JONES
INDUSTRIAL AVERAGE

DAILY — high
last

Figure 14-10

EXERCISE 14-4

A **1.** (a) Discuss the information contained in the graph in Figure 14-10.
(b) What was the high, low, and close for 09-17, the last entry on the graph?
(c) What periods had rising prices, as indicated by the Dow Jones index?
(d) What periods had falling prices as indicated by the Dow Jones index?

2. How does the information in Figure 14-11 tend to confirm the information in Figure 14-10?

applied mathematics for today: senior

NEW HIGHS

Brinco

NEW LOWS

Acme Gas	Coldstm	Frobex	Magnum	Norbaska	Scintrex
Am Larder	Coles B'k	Grey G	Majst Wil	Nordair	Seco Cem
Argosy	Cons Prof	Hambro C	Marcana	Nudlama	Silvmg
Auto El	C Zeirb A	Har Crp A	Martin	Oil Patch	Simpson S
Baton B	Dale R	Harlequin	MLW-Wor	P Dept S	Slat Walk
Bright A	D'Aragon	Holing'r A	Monenco	Pinacie P	Sogepet
Cam Chib	Decca R	Inv Gr 5p	Mt Wrig't	Precamb	Steetley
Campau A	East Mal	Koffler	N Hees	Que Sturg	Tr C Glas
Caron 6p	East Sull	Lajdl Bp	N Dimens	Rdpath A	Upp Can
Cassidy	Ego Mines	Lasitr KM	N Kelore	Rio Algom	
Celanese	Fields S	Lob Inc	Nfl Tel A	Riv Yarn	
Chib Kay	Fraser A	Madsen	Nick Rim	Rothman	

Figure 14-11

B **3.** (a) Use the type of graph illustrated in Figure 14-10 to illustrate the four Toronto Stock Exchange indexes. Use the 1976 high and low, and the Tues. close given in Figure 14-12.

(b) Repeat (a) for the Dow Jones, New York Stock Exchange, and Montreal averages.

4. Construct a graph from the following information.

TSE Industrial Index			
Date	High	Low	Close
08-02	184.2	182.6	182.8
06	182.6	181.8	182.6
07	184.4	183.8	184.0
08	185.6	184.0	185.6
09	186.6	186.0	186.2
12	186.4	184.8	185.6
13	186.0	184.6	184.6
14	184.6	183.8	183.8
15	183.0	180.8	180.8
16	179.6	179.0	179.0
19	179.0	178.2	178.6
20	178.0	176.0	176.4
21	177.4	176.0	176.8
23	177.0	175.4	175.4
26	175.0	172.2	172.8
27	172.8	170.4	170.4
28	170.2	168.4	170.0
29	169.2	167.8	168.0
30	168.0	167.2	167.6

Market indices

TORONTO EXCHANGE INDICES

	Indus.	Gold Metals		Oil
Change	+1.06	+6.61	−0.15	−0.63
Tues. close	189.14	234.04	90.28	225.20
Week ago	186.64	223.70	89.61	226.68
Month ago	188.65	232.40	91.77	228.44
Year ago	183.20	314.86	76.24	180.18
x1976 high	198.42	333.48	95.55	244.01
x1976 low	172.35	223.13	73.70	194.76

(Dow Jones)			
	Indust.	Rails	Utils.	Stocks
Change	+7.48	−0.12	+0.83	+1.73
Tues. close	996.59	220.28	95.35	311.86
x1976 high	1011.21	229.65	95.35	315.47
x1976 low	858.71	175.69	84.84	264.50

NYSE INDEX

	Comp.	Indus.	Trans	Fin.
Change	+0.39	+0.45	+0.08	+0.22
Tues. close	56.04	62.06	40.56	54.95
x1976 high	56.54	63.19	42.81	55.11
x1976 low	48.04	53.16	33.43	45.77

MONTREAL AVERAGES

	Indust.	Util.	Banks	Comp.
Change	+1.07	+0.53	+1.31	+0.98
Tues. close	191.66	148.68	254.94	190.08
x1976 high	211.83	148.15	262.51	202.96
x1976 low	176.62	125.06	230.36	173.67
x-Until previous close				

LONDON FINANCIAL TIMES

Tues.	357.6
S. African Mines	91.6

COMMODITY FUTURE INDEX

Tues.	347.78 5.78

Courtesy The Toronto Stock Exchange

Figure 14-12

14.5 BUYING ON MARGIN AND SHORT-SELLING

Mr Jones buys 100 shares at $10 per share on 60% margin. He pays $600. He owns $1000 worth of stock. His debt is $400. His equity is $600 or 60%. The stock drops to $5 per share. He now owns $500 worth of stock. His debt is still $400. His equity is now $100 or 20%. He must deposit an additional $200 to raise his equity to 60%.

Buying on Margin

An investor may feel certain that a stock is about to go up and wish to buy as much as he can. If the stock is selling at $4.50 and he can raise $900, the investor might purchase 200 shares. He can increase his purchasing power by borrowing money from the broker to buy additional shares. This is called buying on margin. It is said to give the purchaser "leverage," since he is buying more shares than he has cash to purchase, and he will make a greater profit and increase the rate of return on his investment.

Canadian law currently allows margin buying on stocks selling for more than $2 per share, and the purchaser must pay at least 60% of the cost of the shares. The broker, of course, will allow margin buying privileges only to good credit risks, and will charge interest. If it happens that the value of the shares goes down, the buyer has to pay out more money immediately in order to maintain the required margin percentage on his purchase.

EXAMPLE. *Mr. Ross purchased 1500 shares of Bombardier A at $2.75 on 75% margin. He sold 6 mo. later at $3.50. Calculate his profit if interest was charged at $8\frac{1}{2}\%/a$.*

Note that margin buying applies only to the cost of the shares; the brokerage charges must be paid in full.

Solution

$$\text{Cost of shares} = 1500 \times \$2.75$$
$$= \$4125.00$$
$$\text{Commission} = \$4125 \times 0.0250$$
$$= \$103.125$$
$$\text{Total cost} = \$4125.00 + \$103.13$$
$$= \underline{\$4228.13}$$
$$75\% \text{ margin} = 0.75 \times \$4125.00$$
$$= \$3093.75$$
$$\text{Payment} = \$3093.75 + \$103.13$$
$$= \underline{\$3196.88}$$
$$\text{Balance on account} = \$4228.13 - \$3196.88$$
$$= \$1031.25$$
$$\text{Interest} = \$1031.25 \times 0.085 \times 0.5$$
$$\doteq \$43.83$$

$$\text{Total amount} = \$1031.25 + \$43.83$$
$$\text{(On loan)} = \underline{\$1075.08}$$
$$\text{Proceeds from sale} = 1500 \times \$3.50$$
$$= \$5250.00$$
$$\text{Commission} = \$5250.00 \times 0.0250$$
$$= \$131.25$$
$$\text{Amount of loan} = \$1075.08$$
$$\text{Net proceeds} = \$5250.00 - (\$131.25 + \$1075.08)$$
$$= \underline{\$4043.67}$$
$$\text{Profit} = \text{Net proceeds} - \text{Original payment}$$
$$= \$4043.67 - \$3196.88$$
$$= \underline{\$846.79}$$

The profit on his transaction was $846.79.

Short-Selling

Short-selling is a method of making money while a stock's value is falling. It involves having your broker borrow shares which you sell at the current market price and then later buy back at what you hope will be a lower price. For example you might sell 500 shares of Defunct Mining Corp. at $1.00 by "selling-short." When the stock drops to $0.25, you buy 500 shares to replace what you sold. You have made a profit of $375 less commissions.

You must tell your broker when you are short-selling so that he can make provision for getting the shares. This is usually no problem, since when shares are bought on margin, the broker holds them for security and the purchaser usually signs a release giving the broker the authority to lend them for short-selling.

Since short-selling tends to depress the price of a stock (why?), you may only sell short at a price equal to or above the last sale price for a board lot and the stock exchange regularly publishes its position with regard to short-selling (Figure 14-13).

Short-selling is risky and you are subject to the same deposit regulations as buying on margin. When you buy stock in the normal fashion the most you can lose is what you invest and it is very seldom that an investment is a complete loss. In the above example, what would happen if Defunct Mining Corp. struck a hidden vein and jumped to $2.50 before you could buy?

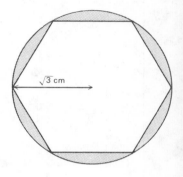

Find the shaded area.

THE TORONTO STOCK EXCHANGE

Semi-Monthly Report of Short Positions

AUGUST 19, 1976

THE SEMI-MONTHLY REPORT OF SHORT POSITIONS OF THE TORONTO STOCK EXCHANGE AS OF AUGUST 15,1976
SHOWED 690,991 SHARES OF 219 ISSUES COMPARED WITH 647,204 SHARES OF 212 ISSUES ON JULY 30,1976.

STOCK NAME	AUG. 15T	NET CHGE	STOCK NAME	AUG.15T	NET CHGE
ABBEY GLEN PROPERTY	600		DOMINION BRIDGE	200	200
ABBEY GLEN PPTY WT	300		DOMINION EXPLORERS	500	500
ABITIBI PAPER	6,445	2,345	DOW CHEMICAL	392	- 5
AFTON MINES LTD	1,000	- 200	E-L FINANCIAL WT	1,000	
AGNICO-EAGLE MINES	2,600	- 100	EGO MINES	3,000	- 2,500
AHED MUSIC CORP	1,000	400	EMCO	500	
ALBERTA NATURAL GAS	100	100	FALCONBRIDGE COPPER	600	
ALCAN ALUMINIUM	800		FALCONBRIDGE NICKEL	2,850	2,700
ALMINEX	1,200	1,200	FEDERAL PIONEER CL A	600	200
AMALG BONANZA PETE	7,500	3,900	FIELDS STORES LTD	846	246
ANGLO UNITED DEVEL	2,000		FOODCORP LIMITED	950	150
ASAMERA OIL	200	- 1,000	FOODEX SYSTEMS	2,900	2,116
ASHLAND OIL CAN	200	200	FOUR SEASONS WT	1,400	
BM-RT INVEST UNITS	200	- 1,800	FRASER CO CLASS A	100	
BP CANADA	1,400	- 200	FROBEX	12,000	
BANK OF NOVA SCOTIA	800	300	GSW LTD CL B	200	
BANKEND MINES	2,000	- 1,000	GENERAL MOTORS	100	
BELL CANADA WT	5,800	- 500	GENSTAR	500	- 100
BETHLEHEM COPPER A	100		GENSTAR WT	1,900	1,000
BOW VALLEY INDUSTRY	200		GIANT MASCOT MINE	18,400	- 5,700
BRAMEDA RESOURCES	3,600	- 1,900	GIANT YELLOWKNIFE	6,677	627
BRENDA MINES LTD	1,500	- 200	GOLDUND MINES LTD	2,500	2,500
BRIDGER PETROLEUM CO	300		GOZLAN BROTHERS LTD	1,600	
B.C. FOREST PRODUCTS	200	200	GT LAKES NICKEL LTD	4,000	
B.C. PACKERS CL B	100	- 100	GREAT LAKES PAPER	100	

Courtesy The Toronto Stock Exchange

Figure 14-13

EXERCISE 14-5

B **1.** Find (i) the total initial payment and (ii) the amount of the loan deducted from the proceeds at the time of sale. Interest is charged at $9\frac{1}{2}\%$/a.

(a) 200 shares at $72.50 bought on 75% margin for 300 d.

(b) 1000 shares at $12\frac{3}{4}$ bought on 70% margin for 240 d.

(c) 50 shares at $54\frac{1}{4}$ bought on 60% margin for 183 d.

(d) 500 shares at $17.35 bought on 60% margin for 30 d.

(e) 400 shares at $5.60 bought on 65% margin for 90 d.

2. Find the profit or loss resulting from the following short-selling.

(a) 200 shares sold at $3.20 and bought back at $2.50.

(b) 1000 shares sold at $7.80 and bought back at $4.20.

(c) 350 shares sold at $42.50 and bought back at $54.25.

(d) 60 shares sold at $84\frac{1}{2}$ and bought back at $61\frac{3}{8}$.

(e) 1000 shares sold at $1.15 and bought back at $0.65.

3. Suppose you have about $2000 to invest and are certain that MacBean Bag Co. stock will rise because of a large export order they are likely to receive. The stock is currently selling at $3.40 and in fact does rise to $4.60.

(a) You buy 600 shares outright at $3.40 and sell at $4.60. Calculate your profit. Include consideration of commissions.

(b) You buy 900 shares paying 60% margin plus commission at $3.40 and sell 90 d later at $4.60. The broker charges 9% interest. Calculate your profit.

(c) How much extra profit was made by buying on margin?

4. After consulting your broker you short-sell 500 shares of Consolidated Sled at $1.79.

(a) If the stock drops and you buy back at $0.65, what is your profit? Include broker's commission in your calculation.

(b) Suppose Consolidated introduces a new line of snowmobiles and the stock jumps to $3.90 per share before you buy. Calculate your loss.

14.6   MUTUAL FUNDS

If each member of your class put, say, $10 into a fund and you hired an investment counsellor to invest the money for you, you would have set up a small mutual fund.

There are advantages to mutual funds. You have the benefit of professional management of your money. You need not concern yourself with fluctuations in the market or with decision making. Because mutual funds are investing large amounts of money from many investors, they can sometimes buy at prices below those available to the individual investor. Also, because of the amount of capital involved, they can invest in a "balanced portfolio" of many different stocks, including some with a reasonably sure slow growth and others more speculative in nature. A failure in one investment then has a minor effect on the individual investor. Perhaps most significant is the opportunity it gives the small investor to invest small amounts of capital regularly, for instance on a monthly basis.

However, as with most things, you pay for what you get. Salesmen and administrators must be paid for their services. A loading fee or commission is charged when you invest. This fee varies from fund to fund but usually depends on the size of the investment. As the principal invested increases, the rate of commission is reduced. The table of rates shown below approximates the charges used by Canadian companies.

Size of transaction	Sales fee as a percentage of amount invested
Less than $25 000	8%
$25 000 but less than $50 000	6%
$50 000 but less than $100 000	4%
$100 000 but less than $200 000	3%
$200 000 but less than $500 000	2%

On a transaction where the aggregate purchase price is $500 000 and over, the sales fee is subject to negotiation.

investing in stocks and bonds

Figure 14-14 shows a typical mutual fund portfolio of investments.

INVESTMENT PORTFOLIO

As at June 30, 1976

Par Value or Number of Shares or Warrants		Market Value
	Long Term Bonds (1.78%)	
$ 150,000	Government of Canada 9 1/2% June 15, 1994	$ 146,250
		$ 146,250
	Preferred Stocks (4.95%)	
7,500	Anglo-Canadian Telephone Company $3.15	$ 240,000
7,000	Polysar Limited 8.40% cum. red 1st pfd. Series A	168,000
		$ 408,000
	Convertibles (16.01%)	
400	Canron Limited, 6%, cum, red, conv. pfd.	34,000
8,900	Four Seasons Hotels, 6% cum. red. conv. 1st pfd. "A"	52,243
250,000	Grafton Group Limited, 7-1/4% Conv. deb. June 30, 1979	270,000
10,000	Canada Trustco Mortgage Company 7-1/2% cum. conv. pfd., Series B	187,500
10,000	Oxford Development Group Ltd. 9% pfd.	112,500
100,000	Pacific Petroleum 5% conv. sub. deb. May 1, 1992	88,000
30,000	Reed Paper Ltd., $2.00 cum. red. conv. pfd.	345,000
15,000	Rothmans of Pall Mall Canada Limited 6-5/8%, 2nd conv. pfd.	250,625
		$ 1,319,868
	Common Stocks (75.96%)	
	Banks & Trust (7.40%)	
6,666	The Bank of Nova Scotia	259,974
20,000	The Toronto-Dominion Bank	350,000
		$ 609,974
	Construction (2.62%)	
10,000	Canron Limited	216,250
		$ 216,250
	Finance (2.05%)	
10,000	IAC Limited	168,750
		$ 168,750
	Insurance (5.46%)	
3,000	Crown Life Insurance Company	147,000
46,600	Reed Shaw Osler Limited	302,900
		$ 449,900
	Metals (13.25%)	
5,000	ASARCO Inc.*	81,726
8,000	Dome Mines Limited	316,000
8,000	The International Nickel Company of Canada, Limited	277,000
25,000	Kerr Addison Mines Limited	331,250
4,400	Sigma Mines (Quebec) Limited	85,800
		$ 1,091,776
	Office Equipment (4.73%)	
1,250	International Business Machines Corporation*	$ 335,377
1,400	Moore Corporation Limited	54,950
		$ 390,327
	Oils (6.39%)	
18,000	Husky Oil Ltd.	$ 373,500
9,000	Shell Canada Limited	153,000
		$ 526,500
	Oil and Gas Pipe Lines (10.77%)	
30,000	The Alberta Gas Trunk Line Company Limited	$ 360,000
5,500	Alberta Natural Gas Company Ltd.	144,375
13,300	Interprovincial Pipe Line Limited	186,200
19,500	Trans Mountain Pipe Line Company Ltd.	197,438
		$ 888,013
	Publishing and Communications (4.49%)	
20,000	Maclean-Hunter Limited 'A'	$ 170,000
25,000	Standard Broadcasting Corporation Limited	200,000
		$ 370,000
	Railroad (6.51%)	
30,000	Canadian Pacific Limited	$ 536,250
		$ 536,250
	Real Estate (1.73%)	
25,000	Monarch Investments Limited	$ 137,500
5,000	Monarch Investments Limited, Warrants	5,350
		$ 142,850
	Utilities (4.57%)	
8,000	Bell Canada	$ 377,000
		$ 377,000
	Merchandising (3.99%)	
3,000	Canadian Tire Corporation Limited, 'A'	$ 137,250
30,000	Simpsons, Limited	191,250
		$ 328,500
	Total Common Stocks	$ 6,096,090

SUMMARY OF NET ASSETS

Total Portfolio (96.70%)	$ 7,970,208
Cash and Other Current Assets (3.30%)	272,406
Total Net Assets**	$ 8,242,614
Net Asset Value per Share	$ 5.34

* Foreign Security
** Unaudited
Note: Percentages shown relate investments at market value to total net assets of the Fund.

Figure 14-14   *The AGF Companies, 50th Floor, Toronto-Dominion Tower, Toronto, Ontario*

When small amounts are invested regularly, the purchaser is said to purchase a contractual or accumulation plan. The total sales fees for a completed contractual plan are nearly equal to those for a single cash investment of the same size; however it is usual for the fees to be charged most heavily on the early payments. This is called "front-end loading." This serves to reimburse the company for the administrative costs of opening a new account, and also serves as a strong stimulus to the investor not to close the account before completion, since by doing so he will lose so much of the initial investment in fees.

As an example of typical charges, one such accumulation fund, involving a monthly investment of $100 for 10 a, carries sales fees of $46 on each of the first 13 payments, and only $3.30 on each of the remaining payments.

As well as the acquisition fee, there may be a management fee which will be taken from the dividends accumulated by the fund.

Although there are many types of funds, they all fall into two categories: open-ended and closed-ended. As an illustration let us return to the example of your class fund.

Suppose a new student joined your class and wanted to participate in the fund, so you totaled your assets and found that each student's share was now worth $15. For $15, which you added to your investment capital, you let the new student join. This would be an example of an open-ended fund.

If, when the new student asked to join the fund, the policy was that no new shares would be created but the new student could bid for existing shares and purchase them from classmates if anyone wished to sell, then you would be operating a closed-ended fund.

Most funds on the market today are open-ended. Within this group there is great variety catering to investors who want security with slow growth, or the possibility of fast growth with a greater measure of risk; funds which accept a large initial investment and pay out regular withdrawals, or funds which accept small regular investments. It is up to the investor to shop around for the best deal and one which satisfies his investment needs.

The *net asset value per share* for open ended-funds is listed regularly on the financial pages of the newspaper. (See Figure 14-15.)

EXAMPLE 1. *Figure* 14-14 *shows a typical investment portfolio with total net assets of* $8 242 614 *and with a net asset value per share of* $5.34. *How many outstanding shares has the fund?*

Solution:

$$\text{Net asset value per share} = \frac{\text{Total net assets}}{\text{Total outstanding shares}}$$

$$\therefore \text{Total outstanding shares} = \frac{\text{Total net assets}}{\text{Net asset value per share}}$$

$$= \frac{\$8\ 242\ 614}{\$5.34}$$

$$= 1\ 543\ 561 \text{ shares}$$

N.A.V.P.S.
Net asset value per share

$$\text{N.A.V.P.S.} = \frac{\text{Total net assets}}{\text{Total outstanding shares}}$$

Figure 14-15

The fund has 1 543 561 shares.

EXAMPLE 2. *Mrs. Carmichael invests $5000 in a mutual fund with N.A.V.P.S. of $3.40. The commission is 8% of the amount invested. How many shares did Mrs. Carmichael receive? (See "Sales fee as a percentage of amount invested.")*

Solution:

$$\text{Net amount invested} = 92\% \text{ of } \$5000$$
$$= 0.92 \times \$5000$$
$$= \$4600$$
$$\text{Number of shares} = \frac{\text{Net amount invested}}{\text{N.A.V.P.S.}}$$
$$= \frac{\$4600}{\$3.40}$$
$$= 1352.94 \text{ shares}$$

She received 1352.94 shares.

EXERCISE 14-6

B **1.** Find the missing quantities in the following table:

	Total net assets	Total number of outstanding shares	N.A.V.P.S.
(a)	$1 350 000	1 500 000	
(b)	$12 700 000	2 240 000	
(c)	$20 484 800	4 130 000	
(d)	$6 915 000		$9.22
(e)	$8 036 000		$2.05
(f)	$29 896 000		$11.84
(g)		1 470 000	$8.34
(h)		5 130 000	$10.18
(i)		875 000	$0.72

2. Calculate the sales fees and the actual principal invested for each of the following amounts. (Use the fee scale table.)
(a) $2 000   (b) $17 000   (c) $33 500
(d) $21 450   (e) $42 000   (f) $13 200

3. Determine the number of shares purchased in each of the following transactions.

	Amount invested	Commission (% of amount invested)	N.A.V.P.S.
(a)	$6 500	8%	$7.42
(b)	$75 000	4%	$3.87
(c)	$32 000	6%	$12.04
(d)	$125 000	3%	$2.18

Solar system —1
The solar system comprises 1 star (the sun), 9 large planets orbiting in the sun's gravitational field, and uncounted smaller planets. Earth, Mars, Jupiter, Saturn, Uranus, and Nepture all have their own satellites or moons. In studying the planets, scientists are interested in calculating their densities to give clues as to the elements of which they are composed.
Escape velocity is the speed at which a particle will have sufficient energy to escape the gravitational pull of the planet. Knowing the escape velocity and the surface temperature gives clues as to the elements in a planet's atmosphere.

4. Mr. Ablet invested in an accumulation fund with an objective of $150/mo. for 120 mo. Sales fees were $69.00 on each of the first 13 payments and $4.95 on each succeeding payment.

(a) What is the total amount (including fees) invested?

(b) What is the total sales fee charged?

(c) What is the actual principal invested in shares?

(d) What percentage sales fee has been charged on the total amount invested?

(e) What is the percentage sales fee on the net principal invested in shares?

(f) If the investor had discontinued the plan anytime during the first year, what percentage fee would have been charged:

 (i) on the total amount invested?

(ii) on the principal invested in shares?

14.7 BONDS

Bonds are a debt security. They represent a loan by the purchaser to the government or to the company who issues the bond. Recall the five types of debt security mentioned in Section 14.1 and the security that each represents.

Every bond displays four pieces of information: the amount or "face" of the bond, the interest rate or "bond rate," the maturity date, and the name of the issuing organization.

Bonds may be fully registered, in which case the name of the holder is recorded and interest payments are mailed out when due. On this type of bond certificate, nothing is lost if it is stolen. Alternatively, the bond may be registered as to principal only, in which case the certificate will contain dated interest coupons to be clipped and redeemed at a bank. Since the name of the bond holder is recorded, the principal is safe if the certificate is stolen, but the interest will probably be lost unless the theft is traced through the serial number of the bond. Bearer bonds, as the name implies, are valuable to whoever is holding them. If stolen, they are easily sold. For this reason they should be kept in a safety deposit box or some other safe place.

When a company wishes to raise money through a bond issue, it must file particulars and obtain permission from the government. The bonds will then be offered for sale to securities companies who will bid on large blocks of bonds and then sell them to individual investors at a profit. In many cases the announcement appears after all the bonds have been purchased by large investors and is a matter of record only.

EXAMPLE 1. *A $5000, $8\frac{1}{2}\%$ bond bears quarterly coupons. What is the value of each coupon when due? How much will the owner of the bond receive on the date of the last coupon?*

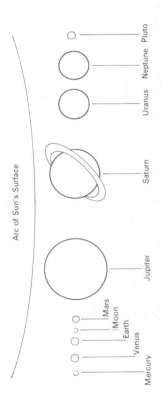

Solar system —2
Relative sizes of planets

Solution $I = Prt$

$$= \$5000 \times 0.085 \times 0.25$$
$$= \$106.25$$

Therefore each coupon is worth $106.25 when due, and on the date of the last coupon the owner will receive $5106.25.

The face value and bond rate are printed on the bond, so these quantities cannot change. But we have seen that the value of free investment capital changes as supply and demand vary. This change is reflected in the market value of the bond. These values are listed in the newspaper and brokerage offices (Figure 14-16) under a "bid" price (what people are offering to pay) and an "ask" price (what people want for their bonds). The amounts quoted are for $100 of face or par value. If current interest rates were 10%, and your bond carried $7\frac{1}{2}\%$, would investors pay more or less than par?

Figure 14-16

Corp. bonds

TORONTO (CP)—Selected bond quotes as of Oct. 11 provided to the investment Dealers Association of Canada by Richardson Securities Ltd. with yield on asking price:

CORPORATIONS

	Bid	Ask	Yield
Abitibi $9\frac{3}{4}$ 1 Apr 1990	89.00	91.00	10.97
Alt Gas $9\frac{1}{4}$ 15 Dec 90	86.00	88.00	10.84
Alq Stl $8\frac{3}{4}$ 31 Mar 91	83.50	85.50	10.63
Alcan $9\frac{3}{8}$ 2 Jan 91	89.00	91.00	10.54
Bell 8 1 Aug 1980	90.00	91.00	10.08
Bell $9\frac{3}{8}$ 1 Dec 1993	90.00	92.00	10.34
BC Sug $9\frac{1}{2}$ 15 Sep 87	88.00	90.00	10.97
BC Tel $8\frac{5}{8}$ 15 Oct 93	80.00	82.00	10.88
C Cem $8\frac{1}{4}$ 1 May 92	80.00	82.00	11.10
CPR $8\frac{7}{8}$ 1 Feb 1992	84.00	86.00	10.66
CPSL $9\frac{3}{8}$ 1 Oct 1990	86.00	88.00	10.98
Cominco $8\frac{1}{2}$ 15 Apr 91	80.00	82.00	10.87
Con Gas $8\frac{5}{8}$ 1 Feb 91	77.00	79.00	10.90
Con Gas $8\frac{5}{8}$ 15 Oct 93	80.00	82.00	10.88
Dofasco 9 1 Feb 1991	87.50	89.50	10.34
Eaton Ac 9 1 Sep 93	81.00	83.00	11.18
Falcbrq $7\frac{3}{4}$ 24 Feb 91	74.00	76.00	10.93
Glf Oil $8\frac{1}{2}$ 1 Dec 89	90.00	——	——
Gulf O $8\frac{5}{8}$ 15 Sep 75	97.00	——	——
HudB MS 9 15 Jun 91	83.00	85.00	10.98
Imp Oil $8\frac{1}{2}$ 15 Aug 89	86.00	88.00	10.07
Ind Acc $9\frac{1}{2}$ 15 Oct 92	91.00	93.00	10.83
Int Nick $9\frac{1}{4}$ 1 Oct 90	89.00	91.00	10.42
Labatt $9\frac{1}{4}$ 1 Sep 1990	89.50	91.50	10.35
McMil $8\frac{1}{2}$ 15 May 91	79.50	81.50	10.94
Noranda $9\frac{1}{4}$ 15 Oct 90	88.00	90.00	10.56
Nr Cen $9\frac{1}{2}$ 2 Jul 91	98.00	100.00	9.50
Royal Bk 7 15 Apr 91	93.25	93.75	9.87
Simpsns $9\frac{1}{2}$ 15 Dec 89	87.50	89.50	10.93
Traders $9\frac{1}{2}$ 15 Jun 91	93.50	95.50	12.55
Traders 9 15 Oct 93	74.50	76.50	12.20
TCPL 9 20 Mar 1991	84.00	86.00	10.84
TCPL $8\frac{5}{8}$ 20 Sep 92	82.50	84.50	10.85
Wstcst 7 8 15 May 91	78.00	80.00	10.58

From The Financial Post

CONVERTIBLES

Ackland $7\frac{1}{2}$ 15 Jun 88	84.00	88.00	9.04
Aqrain $6\frac{1}{2}$ 15 Mar 92	65.00	——	——
AltaGas $7\frac{1}{2}$ 1 Feb 90	108.00	112.00	6.27
Beav L $5\frac{1}{4}$ 1 May 89	70.00	——	——
Scur Rn $7\frac{1}{4}$ 1 May 88	68.00	72.00	11.34
SimSrs $4\frac{1}{2}$ 15 Oct 88	91.00	——	——
WstCst T $7\frac{1}{2}$ 1 Jan 91	82.00	84.00	9.45

Gov't bonds

CANADA AND GUARANTEED

$4\frac{1}{4}$	15 Dec 1974	99.28	99.32	8.23
$6\frac{1}{2}$	1 Apr 1975	98.86	98.91	8.91
$7\frac{1}{4}$	1 July 1975	99.20	99.30	8.27
$5\frac{1}{2}$	1 Oct 1975	97.00	97.10	8.68
$7\frac{1}{4}$	15 Dec 1975–85	98.50	98.60	8.53
$5\frac{1}{2}$	1 Apr 1976	95.90	96.00	8.45
$3\frac{1}{4}$	1 June 1976	92.40	92.60	8.16
$5\frac{3}{4}$	1 June 1976	95.75	95.95	8.45
7	1 July 1977	96.50	97.00	8.26
7	1 Sep 1977	96.30	96.30	8.27
$8\frac{3}{4}$	15 Jan 1978	86.75	87.25	8.29
8	1 Jul 1978	98.50	99.50	8.16
$6\frac{1}{2}$	1 Jun 1979	92.50	93.50	8.21
$3\frac{1}{4}$	1 Oct 1979	79.00	79.50	8.37
$5\frac{3}{4}$	15 Dec 1979	88.50	89.50	8.29
$6\frac{1}{4}$	1 Apr 1980	89.75	90.75	8.39
$5\frac{1}{2}$	1 Aug 1980	86.00	87.00	8.37
$4\frac{1}{2}$	1 Sep 1983	75.63	75.88	8.41
5	1 Jun 1988	65.00	67.00	9.32
$6\frac{3}{4}$	15 Feb 1989	77.00	79.00	9.45
$5\frac{1}{4}$	1 May 1990	65.00	67.00	9.30
$5\frac{1}{2}$	1 Sep 1992	67.00	69.00	9.35
$6\frac{1}{2}$	1 Oct 1995	71.50	73.50	9.42
$3\frac{3}{4}$	15 Mar 1998	49.00	52.00	8.51
3	Perps	33.50	35.50	8.45
CNR 5	15 May 1977	91.00	91.50	8.73
CNR 4	1 Feb 1981	76.00	77.00	8.83
CNR $5\frac{3}{4}$	1 Jan 1985	74.50	75.50	9.56

applied mathematics for today: senior

EXAMPLE 2. *What is the price of a $1000 bond sold at $89\frac{1}{2}$?*

Solution Price $= \dfrac{\$1000}{100} \times 89.5$

$\qquad\qquad = \$895.00$

No matter what the purchase price, the bond is worth its face value at the time of maturity.

Bonds are bought and sold through investment brokers and banks. They will arrange for the sale or purchase of your bonds on the bond market. The price arrived at will be a trading price somewhere between the bid and the ask. For handling your sale the broker will usually charge a commission of 0.5% of the purchase price, a minimum of $0.50 per $100 face value. Banks will handle Canada Savings Bonds without charging commission.

The seller of the bond will also receive from the purchaser the interest which has accrued from the date of the last coupon up to the time of purchase.

EXAMPLE 3. *Find the price of a $2000, 9% Government of Canada bond bought through a bank at the ask price of $84\frac{1}{2}$ on 09-15. The last coupon date was 06-15.*

Solution

Price $\left(\dfrac{\$2000}{100} \times 84.5 \right)$	$1690.00
Accrued interest ($2000 $\times 0.09 \times \frac{92}{365}$)	45.37
Total cost	$1735.37

EXAMPLE 4. *Find the proceeds from the sale of a $5000, $8\frac{1}{4}$% bond at $101\frac{1}{2}$ through a broker charging $\frac{1}{2}$% commission on the price of the bond (but not less than $0.50 per $100). The bond was sold 07-10. The last coupon date was 06-15.*

Solution

Price $\left(\dfrac{\$5000}{100} \times 101.5 \right)$	$5075.00
Accrued interest ($5000 $\times 0.0825 \times \frac{25}{365}$)	28.25
(25 d)	$5103.25
Less commission (0.005 $\times$ $5075)	25.38
Proceeds	$5077.87

EXERCISE 14-7

1. What are the advantages of a registered bond? Of a bearer bond?

investing in stocks and bonds

2. Would you expect a bond to bring a higher or lower return than preferred shares? Why?

3. Besides theft, what other sources of physical loss are securities liable to? How can they be guarded against?

B **4.** Calculate the coupon value for each of the following bonds bearing half-yearly coupons.
(a) $2000, Government of Canada $9\frac{1}{4}$%.
(b) $1000, Traders Group $7\frac{3}{4}$%.
(c) $5000, Canada Cement $8\frac{3}{4}$%.

5. Find the cost of the following bonds. (The minimum commission, if any, is $0.50 per $100 face value.)

	Face	Bond rate (%)	Price (%)	Commission	Last coupon date	Sale date
(a)	$1 000	8.75	81.00	—	09-15	10-15
(b)	$3 000	9.75	89.00	$\frac{1}{2}$%	03-01	05-01
(c)	$500	10.00	94.00	$\frac{1}{2}$%	12-15	01-30
(d)	$2 000	7.75	74.00	$\frac{1}{2}$%	10-01	10-25
(e)	$5 000	8.00	79.00	$\frac{1}{2}$%	02-01	04-15
(f)	$12 000	9.75	88.50	$\frac{1}{2}$%	12-15	01-03

6. Find the proceeds from the sale of the following bonds. (Minimum commission, if any, is $0.50 per $100 face value.)

	Face	Bond rate (%)	Price (%)	Commission	Last coupon date	Sale date
(a)	$1 000	10.00	92.00	—	06-01	07-15
(b)	$500	10.75	101.00	$\frac{1}{2}$%	09-15	09-30
(c)	$3 000	9.00	91.50	$\frac{1}{2}$%	02-15	02-20
(d)	$1 500	6.75	69.00	$\frac{1}{2}$%	06-01	06-28
(e)	$2 000	8.75	80.00	$\frac{1}{2}$%	07-15	08-12
(f)	$25 000	8.00	79.00	$\frac{1}{2}$%	01-03	01-18

7. A bank buys a $10 000 bond at a bid price of 85 and sells it at an ask price of 87. What profit is made in dollars and as a percentage of the bid price? No other commission is charged.

14.8 APPROXIMATE YIELD

To compare the relative value of bonds offered for sale at a premium (or discount) we should calculate the yield in each case.

When we were dealing with stocks we used the formula

$$\text{Yield} = \frac{\text{dividend rate}}{\text{price}} \times 100\%$$

A change in the price of the stock may change the yield but this is not predictable with any degree of certainty.

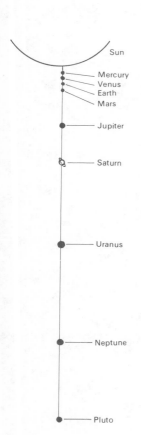

Solar system —3
Relative positions of the planets

Sun
Mercury
Venus
Earth
Mars
Jupiter
Saturn
Uranus
Neptune
Pluto

With bonds we can predict with certainty that, barring default, the value of the bond at maturity will be the face value. We make use of this fact in two ways.

1. We calculate the yield on an average investment principal:

$$\text{Average principal} = \frac{\text{face value} + \text{market value}}{2}$$

2. If a \$1000 bond selling at 90 matures in 5 a, then in addition to interest over the 5 a, you will make \$100 on the principal since you buy it for \$900 and redeem it for \$1000. We could approximate this amount as \$20 income per year. In general, for a bond maturing in n years:

Discounted bonds:

$$\text{Average income} = \text{interest} + \frac{\text{face value} - \text{market value}}{n}$$

Discounted bonds are bonds selling for less than their face value.

Premium bonds:

$$\text{Average income} = \text{interest} - \frac{\text{market value} - \text{face value}}{n}$$

$$\text{Approximate yield} = \frac{\text{average income}}{\text{average principal}} \times 100\%$$

Premium bonds are bonds selling for more than their face value.

EXAMPLE 1. *Find the approximate yield of a $9\frac{1}{2}\%$ bond selling at 90, maturing in 5 a. (Note that yield is a percentage and may be worked from 100 for any face value.)*

Solution

Average principal: $\dfrac{\$100 + \$90}{2} = \$95$

Average income: $\$9.50 + \dfrac{\$100 - \$90}{5} = \$9.50 + \$2$

$= \$11.50/\text{a}$

Approximate yield: $\dfrac{\$11.50}{\$95} \times 100\% \doteq 12.1\%$

EXAMPLE 2. *Find the approximate yield of a 12% bond selling at 101.5, maturing in $8\frac{1}{2}$ a.*

Solution

Average principal: $\dfrac{\$100 + \$101.5}{2} = \$100.75$

Average income: $\$12.00 - \dfrac{\$101.5 - \$100}{8.5} = \$12.00 - \$0.18$

$= \$11.82/\text{a}$

Approximate yield: $\dfrac{\$11.82}{\$100.75} \times 100\% = 11.7\%$

EXERCISE 14-8

B **1.** Find the approximate yield for each of the following bonds.

(a) $8\frac{1}{2}$% selling at 78.0, maturing in 10 a.

(b) $7\frac{3}{4}$% selling at 88.5, maturing in $3\frac{1}{2}$ a.

(c) 9% selling at 80.0, maturing in 9 a.

(d) 8% selling at 76.0, maturing in 17 a.

(e) $5\frac{1}{4}$% selling at 74.5 maturing in $8\frac{1}{2}$ a.

2. Find the approximate yield for each of the following bonds.

(a) 11% selling at 101.5, maturing in 12 a.

(b) $10\frac{3}{4}$% selling at 101.0, maturing in 8 a.

(c) $9\frac{1}{4}$% selling at 100.25, maturing in 2 a.

(d) 12% selling at 103.0, maturing in 6 a.

(e) $11\frac{3}{4}$% selling at 102.5, maturing in 9 a.

3. (a) Calculate the approximate yield for each bond and decide which gives the better return on the investment.

(i) 6% selling at 86.0, maturing in 3 a.

(ii) $9\frac{1}{4}$% selling at 87.0, maturing in 16 a.

(b) What other factor would you take into account when deciding which bond to invest in?

4. (a) Calculate the approximate yield on each bond.

(i) 9% selling at 95.0, maturing in 5 a.

(ii) 9% selling at 95.0, maturing in 15 a.

(iii) 12% selling at 102.0, maturing in 5 a.

(iv) 12% selling at 102.0, maturing in 15 a.

(b) For premium and discounted bonds what is the effect of the length of time to maturity on the yield?

Discount bond

Shorter term ⇒ greater yield

Premium bond

Shorter term ⇒ lower yield

14.9 THE PRESENT VALUE OF A BOND

How should we determine the price to pay for a bond so that we receive a desired rate of return? Suppose interest rates are currently at 10%; how much should we pay for a $1000, 7% bond? As we found in the last section; this will depend on the maturity date, but obviously it will be something less than $1000. There are two quantities to consider—the face value of the bond, and the interest payments.

> Price = (Present value of the face value)
>
> + (Present value of the annuity formed by the interest payments.)

Present value of an amount

$$PV = A(1+i)^{-n}$$

Present value of an annuity

$$PV = Ra_{\overline{n}|i}$$

Where no face value is given the price is calculated on a face value of 100.

EXAMPLE 1. *Find the price of a 7% bond, bearing semi-annual coupons, maturing in 15 a, if it is to yield 10% compounded semi-annually.*

Solution

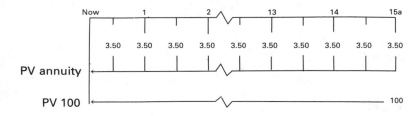

$$\text{Price} = (\text{PV of } 100) + (\text{PV of annuity})$$

PV of 100   where $A = 100$, $i = 0.05$, $n = 30$

PV of annuity   where $R = 3.50$, $i = 0.05$, $n = 30$

$$\text{Price} = 100(1.05)^{-30} + 3.50(a_{\overline{30}|0.05})$$
$$= 100(0.231\,38) + 3.50(15.372\,451)$$
$$= 23.138 + 53.804$$
$$= 76.942$$

The price would be 76.94

To find the price of a bond between coupon dates:

1. Find the price at the last previous coupon date.
2. Find the amount of the price invested at the desired yield rate from the previous coupon date to the date of sale.

EXAMPLE 2.   *Find the price of a $4000, 8% bond, bearing semi-annual coupons on 02-01 and 08-01 maturing on 1980-02-01. The bond is purchased on 1975-12-15, to yield 10% compounded semi-annually.*

Solution

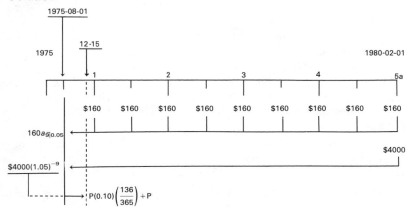

Solar system —4
The sun
Diameter 1.39×10^6 km
Mass 1.99×10^{30} kg
Find the volume. Find the density.
The total mass of the planets is about 0.1% of the mass of the sun. There are about 10^{22} stars in the observable universe. Are there other planetary systems? Other life forms?

$$\text{Price (1975-08-01)} = \$4000(1.05)^{-9} + \$160a_{\overline{9}|0.05}$$
$$= \$4000(0.644\ 61) + \$160(7.107\ 822)$$
$$= \$2578.44 + \$1137.25$$
$$= \$3715.69$$

08-01 to 12-15 is 136 d

$$\text{Price (1975-12-15)} = \$3715.69(0.10)(\tfrac{136}{365}) + \$3715.69$$
$$= \$138.45 + \$3715.69$$
$$= \$3854.14$$

EXERCISE 14-9

A **1.** Why is it not practical to adjust the yield of a bond by changing the coupon rate?

2. (a) If you buy a 7% bond when money is worth 10% on the market, would you pay more or less than face value?
(b) If you buy a 10% bond when money is worth 8% on the market, would you pay more or less than face value?

B **3.** Find the price of the following bonds.
(a) 6% bond bearing semi-annual coupons, maturing in 9 a, to yield 9%/a, compounded semi-annually.
(b) 9% bond bearing semi-annual coupons, maturing in 12 a to yield 11%/a, compounded semi-annually.
(c) $7\frac{1}{2}$% bond bearing semi-annual coupons, maturing in 8 a to yield 10%/a, compounded semi-annually.
(d) 8% bond bearing quarterly coupons, maturing in 6 a to yield 12%, compounded quarterly.
(e) $5\frac{1}{2}$% bond bearing semi-annual coupons, maturing in 10 a to yield 11%/a, compounded semi-annually.

4. Find the price of the following bonds.
(a) 12% bond bearing semi-annual coupons, maturing in 5 a to yield 9%/a, compounded semi-annually.
(b) 11% bond bearing semi-annual compounds, maturing in 8 a to yield 8%/a, compounded semi-annually.
(c) 12% bond bearing quarterly coupons, maturing in 4 a, to yield 10%/a, compounded quarterly.
(d) 9% bond bearing semi-annual coupons, maturing in $12\frac{1}{2}$ a to yield 8%/a, compounded semi-annually.
(e) 10% bond bearing semi-annual coupons, maturing in 6 a to yield 9%/a, compounded semi-annually.

5. Find the cost of a $500, $7\frac{1}{2}$% bond bearing semi-annual coupons, maturing in $10\frac{1}{2}$ a. It is to yield 11% compounded semi-annually. Include $\frac{1}{2}$% commission.

6. Find the cost of a $5000, 10% bond bearing semi-annual coupons. There are 25 coupons remaining and the bond is purchased 90 d after the last previous coupon date, to yield 8%/a, compounded semi-annually.

7. Find the cost of a $10 000, $7\frac{1}{2}$% bond bearing semi-annual coupons. 31 coupons remain and the bond is purchased 46 d after the last previous coupon date, to yield 11%/a, compounded semi-annually.

8. Find the price of a 12% bond bearing semi-annual coupons on

Solar system —5
Earth
Mean diameter 1.27×10^4 km
Mass 5.98×10^{24} kg
Mean distance to the sun 1.5×10^8 km
Period of solar orbit 365.26 d.
Escape velocity 11 km/s
Find the density of Earth and compare to that of the sun.
Find the mean speed of the earth about the sun.

applied mathematics for today: senior

01-15 and 07-15, maturing 1985-01-15. The bond is purchased on 1979-02-15 to yield 9%/a, compounded semi-annually.

REVIEW EXERCISE

A **1.** Explain the difference between debt securities and equity securities and classify each of the following: bonds, debentures, common stock, preferred stock.

2. A company has 100 000 shares of stock outstanding, trading at $10 per share.
(a) Approximately how much would it cost to buy control of the company at that price?
(b) If an investor starts buying large blocks of stock what is likely to happen to the price?

3. Why is it not profitable to buy and sell stocks frequently for small price increases?

4. (a) Give the formula for the yield of a stock.
(b) A stock selling for $10 has a quarterly dividend of 15¢ per share. What is the indicated yield?

5. What would you pay for a $5000 bond selling at 85, without consideration of interest or commission?

Control requires ownership of more than 50% of the shares.

B **6.** Find the cost including commission of these stock purchases.

(a) 500 shares at $21.30   (b) 2000 shares at $4.21

7. Find the proceeds from the following sales of stock. Include considerations of commission.
(a) 1000 shares at $0.75   (b) 25 shares at $32\frac{1}{8}$

8. Find the annual return and yield for each of these investments.

(a) 200 shares, $6\frac{1}{2}$% preferred stock, par value $100 with a market value of $56.
(b) 500 shares, $8\frac{1}{4}$% preferred stock, par value $50 with a market value of $30.

9. (a) 1000 shares of common stock were purchased at $10\frac{1}{2}$ on 60% margin. What payment was required at the time of purchase?
(b) The shares were sold 90 d later at $15. What were the proceeds from the sale if interest was charged at 8%?

10. 2000 shares are sold short at $2.50 and bought back at $1.25. What profit was made?

11. (a) Find the price of a $1000, $9\frac{1}{2}$% bond at 85, bought 30 d after the last previous coupon date. A commission of $\frac{1}{2}$% is charged (not less than $0.50 per $100 face value).
(b) Find the proceeds from a $500, $6\frac{3}{4}$% bond at 79, sold 20 d after the last previous coupon date. A commission of $\frac{1}{2}$% is charged (not less than $0.50 per $100 face value).

12. Calculate the yield for the bonds in question 11 if they each have 6 a to run.

13. An 8% bond bearing semi-annual coupons still has 15 coupons remaining. Find the price of this bond 30 d after the last previous coupon date if it is to yield 10%/a, compounded semi-annually.

Laser light, the fabulous light ray that can vaporize the hardest materials in a fraction of a second, is so intense it can bore holes in diamonds, yet when carefully controlled can be used to perform the most delicate eye surgery.

What is a laser? The word actually stands for *Light Amplification by Stimulated Emission of Radiation.*

Light is the small portion of the electromagnetic wave spectrum that is visible to the human eye. It can be thought of as the radiation we can see.

Amplification means a process by which something becomes expanded or increased. When we "amplify" the sound of a guitar, it becomes louder. When we amplify light, it becomes brighter or more intense.

To *stimulate* is to perform an action that will cause excitement. In the laser process, we stimulate the atoms in the laser material into an excited state of higher energy. The laser material, which may be a crystal, a gas, or a liquid, is like a sponge that soaks up energy.

Emission refers to the way the energy leaves the laser material. When the material has absorbed a certain amount of energy, it may be stimulated to emit a tremendous burst of energy in the form of light waves. (This is what happens in a *pulse* laser. A *continuous wave* laser emits a steady but less powerful beam.)

Radiation refers to the emission of light waves. (In fact, the laser light does not have to be visible. It may be invisible electromagnetic energy, either above or below the visible spectrum.)

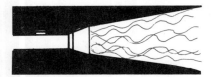

COHERENT LIGHT. In a flashlight beam (above), light moves out in all directions at different wavelengths; it is 'incoherent'. In the laser beam (below), the light is 'coherent'; that is, the light rays are all of the same wavelength moving in the same direction, and do not interfere with each other.

LASER LIGHT AND . . .

A light bulb is a familiar source of radiant energy. Electricity, a form of energy, heats the filament in the bulb, causing it in turn to give off energy in the form of heat and light. The laser depends on a similar process of energy exchange.

The basic requirements for the creation of a laser are simple enough. First of all we need a material that has the property of absorbing and releasing energy. Then we need an energy source for exciting this material, and we need a container to house and control the material producing the laser action.

In the lasing process, the laser material is placed inside the container, and then stimulated by means of an energy source into the emission of light waves. The laser beam itself is the result of channelling the energy of these waves into one particular direction. This is done by reflecting the light waves many times back and forth between mirrors at either end of the container. The bouncing light waves gather more and more energy from the excited atoms of the laser material, until finally they leave the container through one of the mirrors as an intense beam of light.

Laser light is not like sun rays, or like the light from a flashlight. We can't make a hole in a piece of steel with a flashlight, nor can we remove a skin tumour with a shaft of sunlight. The property of laser light that makes it different is called *coherence.*

Ordinary white light, like that from the sun or a flashlight, is actually a combination of all the colours in the spectrum. It contains all the different wavelengths and frequencies for each individual colour. These light waves are all jumbled up, travel in different directions, and so continuously interfere with each other.

Laser light is *monochromatic*, that is of one specific colour, with one specific wavelength. The light waves are all travelling in the same direction; there is no interference, they are 'in step' or 'in phase' with each other. This property of high coherence is what makes it possible to control the direction and confinement of the laser beam with great accuracy.

applied mathematics for today: senior

HOLOGRAPHY—3-D LENSLESS PHOTOGRAPHY

One dividend from laser research has been the development of *holography*. This is a process whereby 3-dimensional images are produced without using a camera or a lens. It was conceived by Denis Gabor, a British physicist, in 1948. (Gabor used a mercury lamp as a light source, but only with the use of coherent-light lasers have high quality holograms become possible.)

To make a hologram, an unexposed photographic film is set up facing the object. Part of a laser beam illuminates the object, and the rest of the beam is deflected to the film. The film receives the wave pattern of both the direct laser beam and the laser light reflected from the object. The result is an 'interference pattern' recorded on the film.

When the film is developed it looks no more like a picture than a record looks like music. But when the film is illuminated by a monochromatic light source, the interference pattern causes the original photographed object to become visible—in depth. When you move your head, you can even see 'around' the object.

The future possibilities of holography are almost limitless. Holograms would be useful in any learning situation in which a 3-dimensional image is important. Industrial training inspection of machined components and stereoscopic x-ray pictures are among the obvious uses of holography. Perhaps the most tempting aims are 3-dimensional movies and television.

A curious feature of holograms is that the holographic plate itself may be substantially damaged and yet produce a nearly perfect image. Each small area on the plate contains a complete set of information about the object photographed, so that a complete image may be reproduced with only a small broken corner of the plate.

One of the most exciting developments in recent years, and one that will inevitably lead to a more widespread use of holography by schools and individuals, is the 'sand-based' technique, invented in the United States by G. Pethick for Editions Inc.

Previously, research in holography was confined to expensive granite-based set-ups in scientific laboratories, because the slightest vibrations are enough to disturb the interference patterns from the laser beam. The sand-based technique, in which the optical components are mounted on aluminum or plastic tubes and simply inserted into a bed of fine deep sand, is simple and inexpensive and virtually eliminates vibration.

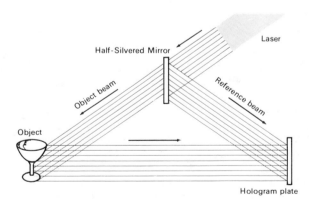

HOW A HOLOGRAM IS PRODUCED: A laser beam is split into two beams by a half-silvered mirror that allows only part of the light through. One beam is aimed at the object to be 'holographed', the other (the 'reference' beam) at a photographic plate or film. The interference between the direct reference beam and the reflection from the object produces the hologram pattern on the plate. The hologram plate is then developed as in the normal photographic process.

APPROXIMATE NUMBERS—THE ACCURACY OF A MEASURE

Solar system —6
Earth's Moon
Mean diameter 3.48×10^3 km
Mass 7.35×10^{22} kg
Mean distance to Earth
3.84×10^5 km
Period of orbit about Earth
27.32 d
Escape velocity 2.41 km/s
Find the moon's density
and compare to the earth's.
Find the mean speed of
the moon about the earth.

The accuracy of a measure is determined by the number of significant figures in the number.

All figures are significant *except:*

1. Leading zeros in a decimal fraction.

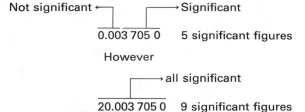

Not significant ←   → Significant

0.003 705 0   5 significant figures

However

          → all significant

20.003 705 0   9 significant figures

2. Trailing zeros in a whole number.

Significant ←   → Not significant

256 000   3 significant figures

However zeros between significant figures are significant.

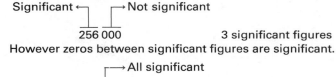

          → All significant

256 000.0   7 significant figures

EXERCISE 1

1. State the number of significant figures in each of the following measurements.

(a) 42.3 cm

(b) 503 000 kg

(c) 0.004 16 g

(d) 405.021

(e) 100.0 mm

(f) 0.0400 cm

(g) 58.23 km

(h) $500 000

(i) 521 384.650 g

(j) 4 000 021

(k) 6.54×10^2 km

(l) 4.50×10^{-3} g

(m) 9.6241×10^{15} m

(n) 1.000×10^8 ml

2. Complete the following table.

	Item	Measure	Implied unit	Number of implied units	Accuracy
(a)	Mass of a proton	1.67×10^{-27} kg	10^{-30} kg	167	3 significant figures
(b)	Speed of light	3.00×10^8 m/s			
(c)	Length of the year	365.2422 d	0.0001 d		
(d)	Radius of the sun	6.96×10^{10} cm			
(e)	1 pc	3.258 ly			
(f)	Radius of galaxy	15 000 pc			
(g)	Mean distance to moon	3.844×10^{10} cm			

pc is the short form for parsec, an astronomical unit of distance.

EXAMPLE 1. *Find the limits of the area of a rectangle* 4.6 cm × 3.2 cm.

Solution

ly is the short form for light year, the distance that light travels in one year.

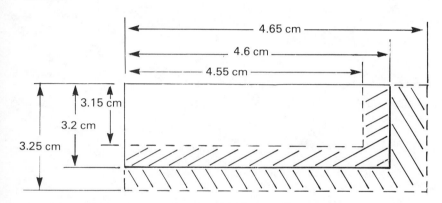

Area from upper limits
$A_{max} = 4.65$ cm × 3.25 cm
$= 15.1125$ cm^2

Area from given measure
$A = 4.6$ cm × 3.2 cm
$= 14.72$ cm^2

Area from lower limits
$A_{min} = 4.55$ cm × 3.15 cm
$= 14.3325$ cm^2

From this example we see that to represent the area as 14.72 cm^2 which implies a unit of 0.01 cm^2, is not realistic. The area can be between 15.1 cm^2 and 14.3 cm^2, a range of almost 1 cm^2. The accuracy of the answer is dependent on the number of significant figures in the data rather than the number of figures after the decimal.

When multiplying or dividing approximate numbers:
1. Check appropriateness of units.
2. Round off measures to a precision of one more significant figure than the least accurate measure.
3. Multiply or divide as required.
4. Round off answer to the accuracy of the least accurate measure.

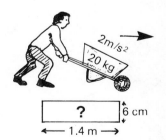

20 kg × 2 m/s^2 = 40 N but
1.4 m × 6.0 cm = 8.4?

Sometimes it makes sense to multiply quantities in different units, but often it does not.

s.f. = significant figures

EXAMPLE 2. *Find the area of a triangle with base* 94.2 cm *and altitude* 26.538 cm.

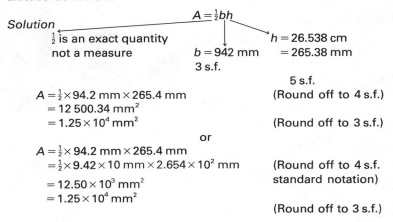

Solution

$A = \frac{1}{2}bh$

$\frac{1}{2}$ is an exact quantity not a measure

$h = 26.538$ cm $= 265.38$ mm

$b = 942$ mm 3 s.f.

5 s.f.

$A = \frac{1}{2} \times 94.2$ mm $\times 265.4$ mm   (Round off to 4 s.f.)

$= 12\,500.34$ mm^2

$= 1.25 \times 10^4$ mm^2 (Round off to 3 s.f.)

or

$A = \frac{1}{2} \times 94.2$ mm $\times 265.4$ mm

$= \frac{1}{2} \times 9.42 \times 10$ mm $\times 2.654 \times 10^2$ mm   (Round off to 4 s.f. standard notation)

$= 12.50 \times 10^3$ mm^2

$= 1.25 \times 10^4$ mm^2

(Round off to 3 s.f.)

EXERCISE 2

1. Simplify the following expressions. Consider all data given with units as approximate, other numbers as exact.

(a) 3.46 cm × 91.43 cm
(b) 184 kg × 9.0 m
(c) 43 000 m × 10.0 km
(d) 36 × 14.36 g
(e) 25.6 cm × 48.95 mm
(f) 47.83 m × 15.8 m
(g) 3.8×10^4 mm × 5.964×10^{-2} mm
(h) $256 \times 4.741 \times 10^3$ g
(i) 74.6 km/h × 3.29 h
(j) 3.75 kg × 5.8 m/s^2

2. Simplify the following expressions. Consider all data with units as approximate.

(a) $\frac{1}{2}$(3.9 cm)(146 cm)
(b) $\dfrac{59.0 \text{ N}}{45 \text{ cm}^2}$

(c) (94.31 km/h)(3.7 h)
(d) $\dfrac{5.91 \text{ kg}}{8.4719 \text{ m}}$

$\pi = 3.141\ 592\ 653\ 589$
$793\ 238\ 462\ 643\ 383\ 279$
$502\ 884\ 197\ 169\ 399$
$375 \ldots$

(e) $\dfrac{250.0 \text{ km}}{4.76 \text{ h}}$
(f) $\dfrac{7.63 \times 10^4 \text{ m}^2}{4.2 \times 10^{-1} \text{ m}}$

(g) $A = \pi (4.76 \times 10^5$ mm$)^2$
(h) $V = \frac{4}{3}\pi (7.21 \times 10^{-3}$ cm$)^3$
(i) $V = \pi (1.8 \times 10^3$ mm$)^2(8.47$ cm$)$
(j) $A = \pi (9.0$ cm$)^2(4.736$ cm$)$

3. Find the area of the trapezoid

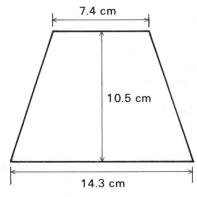

7.4 cm

10.5 cm

14.3 cm

applied mathematics for today: senior

4. $1\,C = 6.241\,96 \times 10^{18}$ electronic charges. Find the number of elec- tronic charges in $7.50 \times 10^3\,C$.

$1\,C =$ one coulomb

5. Find the area of the triangular parcel of land in hectares.

$$A = \sqrt{s(s-a)(s-b)(s-c)}$$

$$s = \frac{a+b+c}{2}$$

1 hectare $= 10^4\,m^2$ (exactly, by definition)

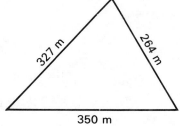

350 m

APPROXIMATE NUMBERS—RELATIVE ERROR

To compare the significance of the errors involved in various meas- ures, we can compare the relative errors.

EXAMPLE 1. *It is more significant to measure (a) the thickness of a sheet of metal as 0.050 cm (b) one leg of a survey as 476.4 m or (c) the mass of the sun as 1.99×10^{30} kg?*

Solution

$$\text{relative error} = \frac{\text{possible error}}{\text{measure}}$$

$$\text{Percentage error} = \frac{\text{possible error}}{\text{measure}} \times 100\%$$

(a) The thickness of the sheet metal is 0.050 ± 0.0005 cm

$$\text{Relative error} = \frac{0.0005}{0.050}$$

$$= 0.01$$

$$\text{Percentage error} = 0.01 \times 100\%$$

$$= 1\%$$

(b) The leg of the survey is 476.4 ± 0.05 m

$$\text{Relative error} = \frac{0.05}{476.4}$$

$$\doteq 0.0001$$

$$\text{Percentage error} = 0.0001 \times 100\%$$

$$= 0.01\%$$

(c) The mass of the sun is $(1.99 \pm 0.005) \times 10^{30}$ kg

$$\text{Relative error} = \frac{0.005}{1.99}$$

$$\doteq 0.0025$$

$$\text{Percentage error} = 0.0025 \times 100\%$$

$$= 0.25\%$$

Of the three measures the survey has the smallest relative error.

Why may the 10^{30} be omitted from both numerator and denominator?

EXERCISE 3

Find the relative errors and the percentage error in each of the following measures:

1. Velocity of light is 2.998×10^{10} cm/s.

2. Mass of the earth is 5.98×10^{27} g.

3. Mass of a hydrogen atom is 1.66×10^{-24} g.

4. Mean distance to the sun is 1.496×10^{13} cm.

5. The area of Canada is $9\,976\,000$ km^2.

6. The mass of a penny is 3.0197 g.

7. The thickness of a sheet of paper is 0.0713 mm.

8. The mass of a Boeing 747 is 322 t.

1 t = one tonne = 10^3 kg.

9. The specific heat of aluminum is 907.2 J/(kg · °C).

10. From St. John's, Newfoundland to Vancouver, British Columbia is 7025 km.

Evaluate:

1. $\dfrac{1200}{(1.0525)} + \dfrac{1300}{(1.0525)^2} + \dfrac{1500}{(1.0525)^3}$

2. $\dfrac{1000}{(1.0675)} + \dfrac{1200}{(1.0675)^2} + \dfrac{1400}{(1.0675)^3}$

3. $\dfrac{240}{(1.0875)} + \dfrac{250}{(1.0875)^2} + \dfrac{275}{(1.0875)^3}$

4. $\dfrac{125}{(1.095)} + \dfrac{150}{(1.095)^2} + \dfrac{200}{(1.095)^3}$

5. $\dfrac{1200}{(1.075)} + \dfrac{1500}{(1.075)^2} + \dfrac{1800}{(1.075)^3} + \dfrac{2000}{(1.075)^4}$

applied mathematics for today: senior

International Trade

15.1 FOREIGN EXCHANGE

Any international business transaction must take into account the currencies being used by the parties involved. If you wanted to buy a book advertised in the United States for $4.50 (U.S.), you could send a postal money order to pay for it. The postal clerk would check the current exchange rate and charge you the value in Canadian dollars, plus the charge for the money order. The rate of exchange is set in part by the demand for currencies in the foreign exchange banks. When a country imports more than it exports, it is said to have a negative balance of trade. The country requires foreign currencies to pay for the imports, but is not exporting to earn them. The result is that there is little demand for the currency on the foreign exchange market and the price drops.

To reduce fluctuations in the value of their currency, which would be harmful to trade, governments hold reserves of gold, U.S. dollars and other major foreign currencies to meet foreign exchange commitments (Figure 15-1).

The current value of foreign currencies in terms of Canadian dollars is shown daily in the financial section of the newspaper (Figure 15-2).

EXAMPLE 1. *How much must I pay for a $4.50 (U.S.) book in Canadian dollars if the exchange rate is as given in Figure 15-2.*

Solution

$$\$1 \text{ (U.S.)} = \$0.98 \text{ (Can.)}$$
$$\therefore \$4.50 \text{ (U.S.)} = 4.50 \times \$0.98 \text{ (Can.)}$$
$$= \$4.41 \text{ (Can.)}$$

Therefore the book costs $4.41 in Canadian funds.

EXAMPLE 2. *A vacationer travelling to France has $500 (Can.) to spend. How many francs can he buy? (Use the exchange rate given in Figure 15-2.)*

Solution

$$\$0.2075 \text{ (Can.)} = 1 \text{ Fr. (Fr.)}$$
$$\$1 = \frac{1}{0.2075} \text{ Fr.}$$
$$\$500 = \frac{1}{0.2075} \times 500$$

Currency

MONTREAL (CP) — U.S. dollar in terms of Canadian funds at noon today was unchanged at $0.97. 21-25. Pound sterling was down 14-25 at $2.26 7-25.

In New York, the Canadian dollar was unchanged at $1.02 21-200. Pound sterling was down 53-100 at $2.31 7-25.

MONTREAL (CP) — Thursday's foreign exchange selling rates supplied by the Bank of Montreal:

Australia dollar 1.4700
Austria schilling .0538
Bermuda dollar 1.01
Belgium convertible franc .0260
Brazil cruzeiro .1459
Bulgaria lev .9058
Czechoslovakia crown .1900
China renminbi .5100
Denmark kroner .1680
France franc .2075
Germany mark .3870
Hungary forint .0930
India rupee .1270
Italy lira .001545
Japan yen .003280
Mexico peso .0795
Netherlands guilder .3770
Norway kroner .1850
Poland zloty .04895
Romania leu .1631
Spain peseta .0175
Sweden kroner .2285
Switzerland franc .3325
United States dollar .9805
United Kingdom pound 2.3050
U.S.S.R. ruble 1.3021
Venezuela bolivar .4864
Yugoslavia dinar .0588
Quotations in Canadian funds.

Courtesy of the Canadian Press

Figure 15-2

Exchange rates change dramatically from year to year and even from day to day. Some currencies are now of very different values from these figures.

$$= 2409.64 \text{ Fr.}$$

Therefore he can buy 2410 Fr. for his vacation.

EXAMPLE 3. *Find the value of 250 Danish kroners in Hungarian forints.*

Solution

$$250 \text{ DKr.} = 250 \times \$0.1680 \text{ (Can.)}$$

$$= \frac{250 \times \$0.1680}{0.0930} \text{ Ft.}$$

$$= 451.6 \text{ Ft.}$$

Therefore 250 DKr. are worth 452 Ft.

When purchasing foreign currency, the financial institution you purchase the currency from will charge a commission. This commission varies and is usually hidden in the rate of exchange you are quoted. Check various institutions such as different banks, trust companies and travel agencies for the best rate.

Solar system —7
Mercury
Equatorial diameter 5×
10^3 km
Mass 0.04×the earth's
Mean distance to the sun
5.8×10^7 km
Period of solar orbit 0.24 a
Escape velocity 3.8 km/s
Find the density and compare to the earth's. Find the mean speed of Mercury about the sun.

EXERCISE 15-1

B **1.** Use Figure 15–2 to find the value of the following amounts in Canadian dollars, to the nearest cent.
(a) 5000 BF. (Belg.)
(b) 10 000 L. (It.)
(c) 2500 Kcs. (Czech.)
(d) 120 Zl. (Pol.)
(e) 75 NKr. (Norw.)
(f) 625 Dfl. (Netherlands)
(g) 75 DKr. (Den.)
(h) 45 DM. (Ger.)
(i) 850 Din. (Yugoslavia)
(j) £50 (U.K.)

2. Use Figure 15-2 to find the value of $100 (Can.) in each of the following currencies to the nearest unit.
(a) Australian dollars
(b) Norwegian kroner
(c) Austrian schillings
(d) Venezuelan bolivars
(e) Mexican pesos
(f) Netherlands guilders
(g) Spanish pesetas
(h) Belgian francs
(i) Roumanian leu
(j) French francs

3. Use figure 15-2 to find the following amounts.
(a) $5000 (Austl.) in Indian rupees
(b) 10 000 Zl. (Pol.) in U.S.S.R. rubles
(c) 50 000 ¥ (Jap.) in Chinese renminbi
(d) $750 (Mex.) in American dollars
(e) 6000 Ft. (Hun.) in Yugoslavian dinar

Canada and the United States are not the only two neighbours having currency with the same name but different values.

4. Use figure 15-2 to find the following amounts.
(a) 20 000 L. (It.) in German marks
(b) 2500 Cr $ (Braz.) in Venezuelan bolivars
(c) 850 Fr. (Fr.) in Swiss francs
(d) 25 000 SKr. (Swed.) in Norwegian kroner
(e) 14 000 BF. (Belg.) in French francs

applied mathematics for today: senior

5. Consult the financial page of a major newspaper and construct a double bar graph to show changes between current values for foreign currencies and those listed here. A separate scale will be required for small valued currencies such as the peseta or lira.

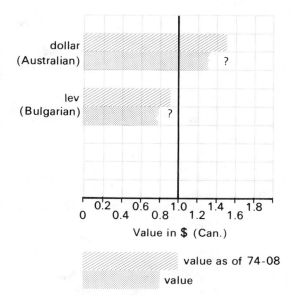

value as of 74-08

value

15.2 IMPORT DUTIES

Goods brought into Canada from a foreign country must pass through Canadian Customs and in most cases are subject to a tax called customs duty. Since producing goods in large number reduces the unit price, manufacturers in densely populated countries with large markets close at hand have an advantage.

Free trade, that is removing all duties, would lower prices of some goods in Canada but would force some Canadian manufacturers out of business; others might flourish because of expanded markets beyond our borders. This would cause a temporary displacement in the labour force. It could also mean that one country would become entirely dependent on another in a specific area of the economy. For example, suppose that due to free trade in clothing all cotton manufacturers in Canada were forced out of business, because cotton goods were made more economically in the United States. Apart from causing hardships for owners and employees in Canadian cotton mills and clothing industries, it would make Canada dependent on a foreign country for her needs in this area. In the event of an international dispute, we could be completely cut off from our supply of cotton.

In order to protect national industries, the government imposes a *duty* on most foreign goods entering the country. This raises their price to the equivalent of the same goods produced in Canada. The Canadian government can direct trade towards a country or group of countries by reducing the duties charged on goods imported from those countries.

A tariff is a schedule of duties. For tariff purposes countries fall into three main categories:

(a) *British Preferential Tariff.* This is the lowest of the tariffs and is an attempt to increase trade within the Commonwealth.

(b) *Most Favoured Nation Tariff.* This is the middle rate tariff and directs trade toward countries which allow similar reduced tariff rates on Canadian goods.

(c) *General Tariff.* This is the highest tariff rate and applies to all nations not covered by (a) or (b). In practice there are very few.

Duty may be charged as a percentage of the fair market price in which case it is an ad valorem duty.

Duty may also be charged at a given amount per unit quantity, for example cigars at $3.20/kg. This is a specific duty.

Some goods are subject to both ad valorem and specific duties.

Sometimes if a product is over-produced for the local market, rather than have the surplus force down the price in the country of manufacture, they will "dump" it at a much reduced price in a foreign country. Since the goods may be selling below manufacturer's cost, it is impossible for local industry to compete. To guard against this a special anti-dumping duty may be charged when the price for export is below the fair market price in the exporter's country.

The exporter's price plus the duty charged is called the duty paid value. It is calculated as follows:

1. Find the export price in Canadian dollars.
2. Add the ad valorem duty, if any, calculated on the price in Canadian dollars *to the nearest dollar.*
3. Add the specific duty, if any.
4. The sum is the duty paid value.

EXAMPLE 1. *Find the duty paid value of an English bicycle with an export price of £15, subject to an ad valorem duty of 20%.*

Solution
Referring to Figure 15-2. £1 = $2.3050

Export value (15 × $2.305)	$34.58
Ad valorem duty (0.20 × $35)	7.00
Duty paid value	$41.58

Therefore the duty paid value of the bicycle is $41.58.

EXAMPLE 2. *Find the duty paid value of 5000 cigars imported from Cuba. The import value is $500 (U.S.). Cigars are subject to a specific duty of $3.20/kg plus an ad valorem duty of 10%. The 5000 cigars have a mass of 115 kg.*

applied mathematics for today: senior

Solution

From Figure 15-2, $1 (U.S.) =	$0.9805 (Can.)
Export value (500 × $0.9805)	$490.25
Ad valorem duty (0.10 × $490.00)	49.00
Specific duty (115 × $3.20)	368.00
Duty paid value	$907.25

Therefore the duty paid value of the cigars is $907.25.

EXERCISE 15-2

A **1.** Name two kinds of duty and describe how they are assessed.

2. What is meant by (a) Fair market price?
(b) Dumping?

3. Name the three tariff classifications that countries may come under.

B **4.** Find the duty paid value for each tariff:

Goods	Value in $ (Can.)	British preferential tariff	Most favoured nation tariff	General tariff
(a) Canned beef	50 000	15%	20%	35%
(b) Glass tableware	6 000	10%	20%	$32\frac{1}{2}$%
(c) Guitar	150	$12\frac{1}{2}$%	20%	40%
(d) Steel bicycle rims	2 400	Free	$17\frac{1}{2}$%	35%
(e) Skis	1 800	20%	$22\frac{1}{2}$%	35%

Find the duty paid value in Canadian dollars for each of the following:

5. A book from France valued at 200 Fr. subject to $22\frac{1}{2}$% ad valorem duty.

6. Copper nails valued at $6450 (U.S.) subject to $17\frac{1}{2}$% ad valorem duty.

7. A German camera valued at 400 DM. subject to an ad valorem duty of 15%.

8. A French Renault automobile with import value of 10 500 Fr. subject to an ad valorem duty of 15%.

9. 500 English wool blankets valued at £1000. The blankets weigh 1.59 kg each. They are subject to an ad valorem duty of 20% and a specific duty of 11¢/kg.

10. An Italian sewing machine valued at 50 000 L. (It.) subject to 15% ad valorem duty.

11. A dining room suite in Danish modern design imported from Denmark, valued at 4500 DKr. subject to an ad valorem duty of 20%.

C **12.** Find the amount of duty paid on 1000 kl of crude petroleum subject to a specific duty of 0.11 ¢/ℓ.

Solar system —8
Venus
Equatorial diameter 1.24×
10^5 km
Mass 0.8×the earth's
Mean distance to the sun
1.08×10^6 km
Period of solar orbit 0.62 a
Escape velocity 10.1 km/s
Find the density and compare to the earth's. Find the mean speed of Venus about the sun.

15.3 EXCISE TAX, SALES TAX, AND EXCISE DUTIES

A federal sales tax of 12% is levied on most manufactured goods sold in Canada whether imported or not. Some exceptions are items used in education, farming, and fishing. It is the remission of this federal sales tax which is reflected in special farm prices on some catalogue items. (See Figure 15-3.) The federal sales tax on building supplies is 11%.

Figure 15-3

Prices for farmers, fishermen

Special prices, free of federal sales tax and/or duty, are available to bona fide farmers and commercial fishermen on items where the "farm price" is quoted. If you qualify, send a completed Tax Exemption Certificate with your order.

As seen in The Eaton Catalogue

An excise tax is applied to some luxury items such as tobacco, jewelry, wine, and playing cards. The rate of tax varies with the item and will be given in examples and exercises.

The excise tax is applied to the designated articles sold in Canada regardless of whether they are imported or domestic. It is not applied to goods manufactured for export.

Excise duty is an additional tax levied on spirits and tobacco manufactured in Canada. Similar items which are imported are subject to an equivalent import duty. These items are a major source of revenue for the federal government.

Where sales tax and excise tax both apply, they are calculated independently on the manufacturers selling price, or on the duty paid value if the goods are subject to customs or excise duties.

EXAMPLE 1. *Find the invoice price of a carton of* 10 *packs of* 20 *cigarettes with a manufacturer's price of $2.70 per carton. There is an excise duty of $4.00 per* 1000, *excise tax of 3ȼ per 5 and federal sales tax of 12%.*

Solution

Manufacturer's price	$2.70
Excise duty $\left(\$4.00 \times \dfrac{200}{1000}\right)$	0.80
Duty paid value	$3.50
Excise tax $\left(\dfrac{200}{5} \times \$0.03\right)$	1.20
Federal sales tax $(0.12 \times \$3.50)$	0.42
Invoice price	$5.12

EXAMPLE 2. *A television set is imported from Japan. The export price is 50 000 ¥ (1 ¥ = $0.003 28 Can.) The set is subject to an ad valorem duty of 15%, excise tax of 15%, and federal sales tax of 12%. (a) Find the invoice price to the retailer if the importer collects the tax and adds a mark-up of 20% of the tax paid price. (b) Find the cost to the consumer if the retailer adds a mark-up of 40% of his cost and then adds 7% provincial sales tax.*

1 ¥ = one yen

Solution

(a) Import price ($ Can.) (50 000 × $0.003 28)	$164.00
Ad valorem duty (0.15 × $164.00)	24.60
Duty paid value	$188.60
Excise tax (0.15 × $188.60)	28.29
Federal sales tax (0.12 × $188.60)	22.63
Tax paid price	$239.52
Mark-up (0.20 × $239.52)	47.90
Invoice price	$287.42
(b) Invoice price	$287.42
Retail mark-up (0.40 × $287.42)	114.97
Retail price	$402.39
Provincial sales tax (0.07 × $402.39)	28.17
Cost to consumer	$430.56

Note that the price of this television set in the shop is more than $2\frac{1}{2}$ times its original import price!

EXERCISE 15-3

A **1.** What type of items are subject to an excise tax?

2. Why are imported goods not subject to excise duty?

3. What tax are farmers and fishermen exempted from when the merchandise is used in their business?

B **4.** (a) Find the invoice price to the retailer of a wrist watch with a Canadian manufacturer's price of $60 subject to excise tax of 10% and federal sales tax of 12%.

(b) Find the cost to the consumer after the jeweller adds a mark-up of 50% of the invoice price plus Ontario sales tax of 7% of the retail price.

5. Find the cost to the retailer to import a Swedish automobile with export value at port of entry of 15 000 SKr. The price includes ad valorem duty of 15% and federal sales tax of 12%. (1 SKr = $0.2285.)

6. Find the invoice price of 50 cartons of Canadian cigarettes, 10 packs of 20 per carton, with a manufacturer's price of $2.90 per carton. They are subject to excise duty of $4.00 per 1000, excise tax of 3¢ per 5, and federal sales tax of 12%.

7. Find the cost to the importer of a chesterfield and chair set imported from the United States. Ad valorem duty is 20% and sales tax 12%. The manufacturer's price is $260 (U.S.). $1 (U.S.) = $0.9805 (Can.).

8. (a) Find the cost to the retailer to import a Japanese motorcycle with export price of 175 000 ¥, subject to an ad valorem duty of 20%, and federal sales tax of 12%.
(b) Find the retail price after a mark-up of 30% and the cost to the consumer including 7% Ontario sales tax. (1 yen = $0.003 28.)

9. (a) Find the cost to the retailer to import an Italian sewing machine with an export price of 80 000 L. (lt.), subject to an ad valorem duty of 15%, and federal sales tax of 12%.
(b) Find the retail price after a mark-up of $33\frac{1}{3}$% and the cost to consumer including 8% New Brunswick sales tax. (1 L. (lt.) = $0.001 545.)

10. A motorized fishing dory from Norway has an export price of 5480 NKr. It is subject to an import duty of 19%.
(a) Find the price to an Ontario commercial fisherman who must pay 7% provincial sales tax.
(b) Find the price to an Ontario pleasure fisherman who must pay 12% federal sales tax and 7% provincial sales tax on the retail price. Assume the boats were imported direct by the purchasers (1 NKr = $0.1850.)

11. An importer of jewelry imports silver bracelets from Mexico. Their export value is 250 Mex $ each. They are subject to excise tax of 10%, ad valorem duty of $37\frac{1}{2}$%, and federal sales tax of 12%. Find the cost to the retailer of 75 bracelets. (1 Mex $ = 0.0795.)

REVIEW EXERCISE

A **1.** Name 10 countries and their currencies.

2. What factor helps determine the value of one currency with respect to another?

3. Name the three tariff classifications countries come under.

4. What is the purpose of an anti-dumping duty?

5. Name four sources of federal revenue.

B **6.** An explorer takes $10 000 (Can.) on an expedition to Brazil. How many cruzeiros will he receive? (1 Cr $ = $0.1459.)

7. A traveller from Moscow to Budapest converts 600 R to forints. How many does he receive?

Solar system —9
Mars
Equatorial diameter 6.8×10^3 km
Mass $0.1 \times$ the earth's
Mean distance to the sun 2.28×10^8 km
Period of solar orbit 1.88 a
Escape velocity 5.0 km/s
Find the density and compare to the earth's. Find the mean speed of Mars about the sun.

8. Bathroom plumbing fixtures are subject to a duty of 20% under the most favoured nation tariff. Find the duty paid value of $14 560 (U.S.) worth of such fixtures in Canadian dollars. ($1 U.S. = $0.9805 Can.)

9. Wool stockings are subject to an ad valorem duty of 20% plus a specific duty of $0.30 per dozen pair under the British preferential tariff. Find the duty paid value of 100 dozen pair valued at 300£. (1£ = $2.305 Can.)

Duty is calculated on the price in Canadian dollars to the nearest dollar.

10. Acme Playing Card Co. sells playing cards at $4.80 per carton of 10 decks. The cards are subject to excise tax of 20¢ per pack and a federal sales tax of 12%.
(a) Find the price to the wholesaler of one carton of playing cards.
(b) The wholesaler marks his cost for the cards up $37\frac{1}{2}$%. Find the price to the retailer of one carton of playing cards.
(c) The retailer marks his cost up 50% and collects 7% provincial sales tax. Find the price to the consumer of one deck of playing cards.

11. A pair of skis is imported from Sweden at a price of 125 SKr. They are subject to an ad valorem duty of $22\frac{1}{2}$%.
(a) Find the duty paid price to the importer.
(b) The importer collects 12% federal sales tax and then adds a 60% mark-up. Find the price to the retailer.
(c) The retailer adds an 80% mark-up and collects 7% provincial sales tax. Find the price to the consumer. (1 SKr. = $0.2285.)

12. An importer can buy similar quality glass cream and sugar sets from either the United States or Great Britain.

n		Price	Duty
(a)	U.S.	$4.30 (U.S.)	20% (most favoured nation)
(b)	Great Britain	1.90£	10% (British preferential)

Calculate the duty paid price from each source, in Canadian dollars.

REVIEW AND PREVIEW TO CHAPTER 16

EXERCISE 1 *Percentages and Rates*

1. A real estate salesman receives a gross commission of 5% on his sales. In one year he made the following sales:

Month	Property value	Month	Property value
01	$45 000	07	
02	$37 500	08	$46 000
	$84 900		$25 000
03	$22 400	09	$73 000
	$57 800		$24 000
04		10	$58 000
05	$27 000	11	$84 000
	$73 500		
		12	
06	$48 200		

(a) Find his gross commission.
(b) The real estate company retains 2% of sales for advertising and office expenses. What is the salesman's net commission?

2. Alice McFadden works for Lakeshore Motors Ltd. as a salesperson. She receives a salary of $300/mo. plus 2% of sales. In the first quarter she had the following sales:

01 $46 500	02 $84 000	03 $31 200
$23 900		$57 600

How much did she earn each month?

3. A machinery salesperson receives a commission of 6% on sales in a month with a bonus of an additional $1\frac{1}{2}$% on sales over $25 000. What commission is received on monthly sales of:
(a) $14 000
(b) $31 000
(c) $2450
(d) $48 000

4. W. Atwood's bill for electrical power indicated that 4370 MJ of electrical power had been used over the previous 2 mo. The charges are as follows:
First 500 MJ @ 1¢/MJ
Next 2000 MJ @ 0.5¢/MJ
The remaining @ 0.25¢/MJ
Find the amount of W. Atwood's bill.

5. A hydro bill shows that 6778 MJ of power have been used over the summer at a cottage. The cost of hydro in the cottage area is considerably higher than in town, the charges being as follows:
First 200 MJ @ 1.4¢/MJ
Next 500 MJ @ 1¢/MJ
Next 2000 MJ @ 0.75¢/MJ

Next 4000 MJ @ 0.6¢/MJ
Remainder MJ @ 0.4¢/MJ
The bill is due on 09-30 but a 5% discount is given if the bill is paid before the due date. Calculate the amount of the bill if paid before 09-30, and if paid on or after 09-30.

6. A three-month bill dated 09-16 from Ontario Hydro indicates that 9698 MJ have been used by a householder, Grant McTavish. Mr. McTavish also rents an electric water heater at the rate of $1.75/mo. Retail sales tax of 7% is applicable on this total rental charge. A late payment charge of 5% of the total bill is added if the bill is not paid within 21 d. Find the total amount of the bill before 10-07 and after 10-07 if the following rates apply:
First 200 MJ/mo. @ 1.5¢/MJ
Next 500 MJ/mo. @ 0.7¢/MJ
Next 2000 MJ/mo. @ 0.5¢/MJ
Next 2000 MJ/mo. @ 0.4¢/MJ
Additional MJ/mo. @ 0.35¢/MJ

Evaluate:

1. $\sqrt{385.6}$

2. $\sqrt[4]{27.83}$

3. $\sqrt[8]{69.74}$

4. $\sqrt[4]{0.027\,43}$

5. $\sqrt[8]{0.4692}$

6. $(\sqrt{45.67})^3$

7. $(\sqrt[4]{27.25})^3$

8. $\sqrt{(48.75)^2}$

9. $\sqrt{(0.1495)^3}$

10. $\sqrt[4]{(27.65)^3}$

CHAPTER 16

Home Ownership and Municipal Taxation

16.1 CHOOSING A HOME

In today's modern cities people have several alternatives when selecting a home.

Apartments are available to be rented or purchased.

Town houses or row houses may be rented or purchased.

Houses may be purchased in either semi-detached or fully detached models. (Figures 16-1 to 16-3.)

Figure 16-1

Figure 16-2

Figure 16-3

applied mathematics for today: senior

Your choice of purchasing or renting accomodation will probably depend on the capital you have available and the type of life you wish to lead.

It is suggested by family financial counsellors that not more than 27% of the borrower's income should go to monthly mortage payments of principal, interest and taxes. If the wife is working also, up to half of her income may be included as part of the husband's in making the calculation.

EXAMPLE 1. *Bill Sampson has an annual income of $15 000, his wife earns $8000/a. What is the maximum monthly mortgage payment they should consider?*

Solution

$$\text{Husband's income} = \$15\,000$$
$$\tfrac{1}{2} \text{ of Wife's income} = \tfrac{1}{2}(\$8000)$$
$$= \$4000$$
$$\text{Total available income} = \$15\,000 + \$4000$$
$$= \$19\,000$$
$$\text{Maximum annual payment} = 27\% \times \$19\,000$$
$$= \$5130$$
$$\text{Maximum monthly payment} = \tfrac{1}{12}(\$5130)$$
$$\doteq \$427$$

The above calculation may also be used as a guide to amount of rent a family can afford to pay.

When purchasing or renting it is wise to have the advice of a lawyer. To ensure that the vendor really owns the property that he is selling, and that it is free from liens or other encumbrances, the lawyer will search the title. When renting an apartment or town house the landlord and the tenant are protected by a signed agreement called a lease. The lessor (owner) agrees to rent to the lessee (tenant) the accommodation for a stated rent, for a fixed number of months. (Figure 16-4 and 16-5) A lawyer will be able to advise the prospective tenant of any hidden obligations he may be assuming.

EXERCISE 16-1

A **1.** As though you were choosing accommodation, rank the following in order of importance:
(a) Is the dwelling situated in a community in which you would enjoy living?
(b) Is it close to the location of your leisure activities?
(c) Is it close to your place of work?
(d) Do you like the external design of the building and is it well maintained?
(e) Is there an outside area for living and recreation?
(f) Is there an outside area for children to play unsupervised?
(g) Will you have privacy from your neighbours?
(h) Are there street lights and sidewalks?

(i) Is there enough room for your furniture and needs?

(j) Are the working areas, kitchen, and laundry, well arranged?

(k) Is there adequate cupboard space?

(l) Is there adequate ventilation (windows or air conditioning)?

RULES AND REGULATIONS

OF THE

YOURTOWN   APARTMENTS

---

1. The sidewalks, halls, entry, passages and stairways shall not be obstructed by any of the tenants or used by them for any other purposes than for ingress and egress to and from their respective apartments.

2. The floors, skylights and windows that reflect or admit light into passage ways or into any place in the building shall not be covered or obstructed by any of the tenants; and no awning shall be put up over any window without the sanction of the Lessor. The water closets and other water apparatus shall not be used for any purpose other than those for which they were constructed and no sweepings, garbage, rubbish, rags, ashes or other substances shall be thrown therein. Any damage resulting to them from misuse or from unusual or unreasonable use shall be borne by the tenant who or whose family, guests, visitors, servants, clerks or agents shall cause it.

3. No sign, advertisement or notice shall be inscribed, painted or affixed on any part of the outside of the building whatever, or inside of the building unless and except a name plate bearing the name of the tenant and no other lettering, and of such color, size and style and in such places upon or in the building as shall be first designated by the Lessor and endorsed hereon.

4. All awnings or shades over and outside of the windows desired by tenants shall be erected at their own expense; they must be of such shade, color, material and make as may be prescribed by the Lessor and shall be put up under the direction of the Lessor or his agents.

5. All tenants must observe strict care not to allow their windows to remain open so as to admit rain or snow. For any injury caused to the property of other tenants, or to the property of the Lessor by such carelessness the tenants neglecting this rule will be held responsible.

6. No additional locks shall be placed upon any door of the building, without the written consent of the Lessor which shall be endorsed hereon.

7. No tenant shall do, or permit anything to be done in said premises or bring or keep anything therein which will in any way increase the risk of fire or the rate of fire insurance on the building, or on property kept therein, or obstruct or interfere with the rights of other tenants, or in any way injure or annoy them, or conflict with the laws relating to fires or with the regulations of the Fire Department or with any insurance policy upon the building or any part thereof, or conflict with any of the rules and ordinances of the Board of Health or with any statute or municipal By-law.

8. Nothing shall be placed on the outside of window sills or projections.

9. The water shall not be left running unless in actual use in the leased premises; spikes, hooks, screws or nails shall not be put into the walls or woodwork of the building.

10. The Lessor shall in all cases retain the power to prescribe the weight and proper position of iron safes; and all damage done to the building by taking in or putting out a safe or by a safe during the time it is in or on the premises, shall be made good and paid for by the tenant who has caused the safe to be taken in or put out.

11. All garbage is to be tightly wrapped in paper and tied and placed in chute or pail for purpose as directed by Caretaker.

12. Tenants, their families, guests, visitors and servants shall not make or permit any improper noise in the building or do anything that will annoy or disturb or interfere in any way with other tenants or those having business with them.

13. Nothing shall be thrown by the tenants, their families, guests, visitors, clerks or servants out of the windows or doors, or down passages or skylights of the buildings.

14. No animals shall be allowed upon or kept in or about the leased premises nor shall any parrot or other noisy bird be allowed therein.

15. If tenants desire telegraphic or telephone connections, the Lessor or his agents will direct the electricians as to where and how the wires are to be introduced and without such direction no boring or cutting for wires will be permitted. If tenants desire to install, add to or alter gas or electric light fittings for lighting their premises they must arrange with the Lessor for the necessary connections and no gas pipe or electric wire will be permitted which has not been authorized in writing by the Lessor or his agents.

16. No cooking shall be done upon the demised premises unless there is a kitchen in connection therewith provided by th Lessor.

17. No auction sale shall be held in the demised premises without the consent in writing of the Lessor.

18. No stores of coal or any combustible or offensive goods, provisions or materials shall be kept upon the

19   understood and agreed betwe   r and Lessee that   nt to changes
          spirit or letter shall   s made   ing
            his agents.

Figure 16-4

This Indenture

made in duplicate the 30th   day of   June   1977 .

IN PURSUANCE OF THE SHORT FORMS OF LEASES ACT.

Between   YOURTOWN APARTMENTS LIMITED

hereinafter called the Lessor, OF THE FIRST PART

and   MR.JOHN SMITH

hereinafter called the Lessee, OF THE SECOND PART

WITNESSETH that in consideration of the rents, covenants and agreements hereinafter reserved and contained on the part of the Lessee, his heirs, successors, executors, administrators and assigns, to be paid, observed and performed, the Lessor hath demised and leased and by these presents doth demise unto the Lessee, his heirs, successors, executors, administrators and assigns, for use and occupation as a residential flat unfurnished and for no other purpose, all those certain premises forming part of the YOURTOWN Apartments on the South side of Spruce St. in the town of Maplevale known and described as Suite 405 together with parking space on or in the apartment premises for one car, said car to be parked only in the space allotted to it from time to time by the Lessor. TO HAVE AND TO HOLD the said demised premises for and during the term of one year to be computed from the 1st. day of July 1977 and from thenceforth next ensuing and fully to be complete and ended.

YIELDING AND PAYING therefor during the said term hereby granted unto the said Lessor, his heirs, successors, executors, administrators and assigns, the sum of Two Thousand Four Hundred Dollars

to be payable on the following days and times, that is to say:— Two hundred dollars per month

payable on the first day of each month

In Witness Whereof the said parties hereto have hereunto set their hands and seals.

Signed, Sealed and Delivered
IN THE PRESENCE OF

David Wilson

John Smith
J. Smith

Paul Andrews
Attorney, Yourtown Apartments

The Lessee acknowledges receipt of a fully executed duplicate original of this lease on the 30th day of June 1977 .

Figure 16-5

home ownership and municipal taxation

Solar system —11
Saturn
Equatorial diameter 1.21×10^5 km
Mass $95 \times$ the earth's
Mean distance to the sun 1.43×10^9 km
Period of solar orbit 29.46 a
Escape velocity 36 km/s
Find the density and compare to the earth's. Find the mean speed of Saturn about the sun.

2. As though you were selecting an apartment or town house to rent, rank the following in order of importance:
(a) Is there a private entrance?
(b) Is there a garage or open-air parking?
(c) Is there an area for guest parking?
(d) Are halls and stairways well lighted?
(e) Are there adequate fire exits?
(f) Are garbage disposal facilities adequate?
(g) Is telephone included or extra?
(h) Is there a TV aerial?
(i) Are the major kitchen appliances included and in good condition?
(j) Is there air conditioning?
(k) Is the interior pleasingly decorated and well kept up?
(l) Is there a swimming pool for tenants' use?
(m) What are the terms of the lease?

3. As though you were considering buying a house, rank the following in order of importance:
(a) Is there an adequate water supply?
(b) Is the property serviced by public sewers?
(c) Can fuel deliveries and meter reading be done from outside?
(d) Is there adequate, safe, electrical wiring, including well-placed outlets?
(e) Are fuel costs reasonable?
(f) Is the basement area usable—dry, clean, high ceilings, well lighted?
(g) Are there adequate storm windows and screens?
(h) Are the plumbing and heating units in good condition?
(i) What down payment is required?
(j) What are the terms of the mortgage?

B **4.** A bachelor apartment is advertised for $210/mo., with a 12 mo. lease. What weekly income should a prospective tenant have if a guide of 27% for accommodation is used?

5. A condominium town house is for sale for $65 900. After the down payment the mortgage payment will be $368/mo. with taxes of $54/mo. and maintenance fees of $40/mo.
(a) What minimum annual income should a prospective purchaser have?
(b) If the wife is earning $8000/a., what income would the husband require?
(c) If the lawyer charges $1\frac{1}{4}\%$ of the total purchase price, what will his fee be?

6. A house is for sale for $85 000. A down payment of $25 000 leaves a mortgage with monthly payments of $540. The annual tax bill is $750, the gas company records show that last year's heating bill was $349.20 and electricity and phone average $38.40/mo. The house is insured for 80% of its estimated value of $60 000 (the land value is estimated to be $25 000), at an annual premium of $2.50 per $1000. Find the average monthly cost of running the house.

Why do developers put multiple units, such as the one shown above, on corner lots? How many similar models can you find in the picture below? Use driveways as a clue.

7. A house is purchased for $56 000 with a down payment of $15 000. Use the methods of Chapter 7 to calculate the half-yearly payment on a 20 a mortgage if interest is charged at 10% compounded semi-annually.

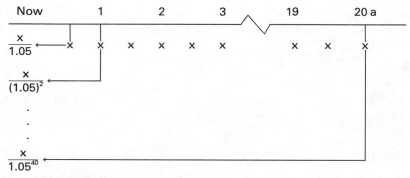

8. Use the classified section of your local newspaper or information obtained from a local real estate agent to complete Table 16-6

TYPICAL COST				
Buying	**Detached house**	**Semi-detached house**	**Town house**	**Apartment**
2 Bedrooms				
3 Bedrooms				
4 Bedrooms				

TYPICAL MONTHLY RENTAL		
Rental	**Apartment**	**Town house**
1 Bedroom		
2 Bedrooms		
3 Bedrooms		

Table 16-6

16.2 BUYING A HOUSE OR CONDOMINIUM

When buying a house, or condominium, purchasers must decide on the amount they can afford to pay monthly for principal, interest and taxes; they must decide the location, and the size of house desired. After these decisions have been made it is advisable to contact a reputable real estate agent and describe to him the type of house desired. He will show his prospective buyers a number of houses his firm has listed. This means that the real estate firm has signed an agreement with the home owner stating that if the firm can sell the house for a predetermined sum, the seller of the house will pay the real estate firm a fee, usually 5% to 8% of the sale price. For the higher fee the house will be put on M.L.S.: Multiple Listing Service, which allows any member real estate company to arrange a sale.

This means that the real estate agent is paid by the seller and his services are free to the house buyer.

When the desired house is located, the buyer signs an offer to purchase (Figure 16-7) in which he agrees to purchase the house for a stated sum of money and provides a deposit of a certain sum of money to show he is serious about the offer. If the seller accepts the offer before a specified time, called the expiry date, then he too will sign the offer to purchase. The offer to purchase also includes a closing date, at which time the final transactions are completed.

OFFER TO PURCHASE

I/WE, John Smith and Mary Smith, his wife
of the Town of Norton
(as purchaser), hereby agree to and with
William Brown
(as vendor), through Sunshine Realty Company Limited Agent
to purchase all and singular the premises situate on the South side of Alberta Ave.
in the City of Yourtown known as Municipal No. 23
being (herein called "the real property")
having frontage of about 50 feet more or less, by a depth of about 150 feet
being part of Lot No. 46 and 47 according to Plan No. 563B
Registered in the Registry Office London Ont.
at the price or sum of Sixty-five Thousand Dollars ($65 000)
as follows: Four Thousand Dollars ($4 000)
cash or certified cheque to the said Agent/Vendor on this date as a deposit, and covenant, promise and agree to pay

the sum of fifty-six thousand dollars in cash on closing, subject to adjustments, and to give back to the vendor a 10-year second mortgage on said property in the amout of five thousand dollars, repayable at $70.91 per month, which includes interest at 12% per annum, said payments to commence September 1st, 1977, and thereafter due on the 1st day of each succeeding month for a period of ten years from the date of issuance.

....u Fire Insu.. ...axes, Interc.. ...rtioned
and allowed to date ot c... .. of sale; Deed or Transte. ...n part o... ...y Mortgage
that by the terms of this instrument is to be assumed and preparec... ...expense of Vendor on ...the Purchaser's
solicitor and if a mortgage is to be given back, same to be prepared at the expense of the Purchaser c... ...acceptable to Vendor
and drawn pursuant to The Short Forms of Mortgages Act, Ontario.

Any tender of documents or money hereunder may be made upon the solicitor acting for the party on whom tender is desired and it shall be sufficient that a negotiable certified cheque may be tendered instead of cash.

Each party is to pay the costs for registration and taxes on his own documents.

Whenever the singular or masculine are used in this Offer, they shall mean and include the plural and feminine if the context or the parties hereto so require.

Dated at Yourtown this 16th day of July 19 77

SIGNED, SEALED AND DELIVERED
in the presence of David Wilson

IN WITNESS whereof we have hereunto set our hand and seal ,

John Smith
Purchaser
Mary Smith
Purchaser

I/WE, hereby accept the above offer and its terms, and covenant, promise and agree to and with the said above-named purchaser to duly carry out the same on the terms and conditions above mentioned, and I hereby accept the deposit of $ 4000 out of which the agent is hereby authorized to retain $3250 commission of 5 per cent of an amount equal to the above mentioned sale price; Provided that no commission shall be payable unless and until this transaction is completed.

Dated at Yourtown this 15th day of July 19 77

Signed, Sealed and Delivered
in the presence of

In Witness Whereof I have hereunto
set my hand and seal

William Brown
Vendor

David Wilson
Witness

Vendor

Figure 16-7

Since few people are able to pay cash for a house, it is often necessary to arrange a mortgage. This may be done through the seller, another individual, a credit union, or a commercial institution. The mortgage represents an agreement between the mortgagee (person buying the house) and the mortgagor (person lending the money). The mortgagee promises to pay the mortgagor a certain amount of money at regular intervals, usually every month, until the total mortgage is amortized or paid off.

Since a mortgage is usually paid by means of equal monthly payments, it is basically an annuity, and payments can be calculated by the methods covered in Chapter 7. However since mortgage calculations are very common, tables have been prepared giving the monthly payment per $1000 for various terms and interest rates. A sample table is given in Table 16-8.

EXAMPLE 1. *Find the equal monthly payment required to amortize a mortgage of $28 500 at $9\frac{1}{2}\%$ over 25 a.*

Solution

Payment per $1000	$8.6103	(From table: $9\frac{1}{2}\%$
Amount of loan in $1000	$\times 28.5$	row, 25 a 0 mo.
	$245.39	calculated.)

The monthly payment is $245.39.

EXAMPLE 2. *Use 27% as a guide to find the largest mortgage a person should assume if his annual income is $24 500.*
The mortgage is for 20 a at $9\frac{1}{2}\%$.
Solution

$$\text{Monthly income} = \frac{\$24\,500}{12}$$

$$\doteq \$2041$$

$$27\% \text{ of } \$2041 \doteq \$550$$

Monthly payment per $1000 at $9\frac{1}{2}\%$ for 20 a is $9.2023

$$\therefore \text{Maximum mortgage} = \frac{550}{9.2023} \times \$1000$$

$$= \$59\,768$$

The maximum mortgage would be $60 000.

Table 16-8
Partial Basic Monthly Payment Table For a Loan of $1000

Years	Months	Periods	8%	$8\frac{1}{2}$%	9%	$9\frac{1}{2}$%	10% .
10	0	120	12.0641	12.3202	12.5789	12.8399	13.1034
15	0	180	9.4815	9.7616	10.0452	10.3323	10.6227
20	0	240	8.2836	8.5856	8.8919	9.2023	9.5166
25	0	300	7.6321	7.9536	8.2798	8.6103	8.9449
30	0	360	7.2471	7.5854	7.9283	8.2755	8.6267
35	0	420	7.0083	7.3606	7.7174	8 0781	8.4423
40	0	480	6.8556	7.2195	7.5874	7.9587	8.3330

Years	Months	Periods	$10\frac{1}{2}$%	11%	$11\frac{1}{2}$%	12%	$12\frac{1}{2}$%
10	0	120	13.3629	13.6373	13.9077	14.1803	14.4550
15	0	180	10.9164	11.2133	11.5132	11.8161	12.1987
20	0	240	9.8347	10.1564	10.4815	10.8097	11.1411
25	0	300	9.2833	9.6253	9.9706	10.3190	10.6702
30	0	360	8.9814	9.3394	9.7003	10.0639	10.4298
35	0	420	8.8097	9.1797	9.5522	9.9268	10.3032
40	0	480	8.7098	9.0888	9.4696	9.8519	10.2355

Some mortgages are paid by making a regular monthly payment against the principal and a separate semi-annual interest payment. In these cases a schedule of payments must be prepared.

EXAMPLE 3. *A mortgage of $36 000 assumed on 1976-03-01 is repaid by payments of $150/mo. on the principal plus semi-annual interest payments. Interest is charged at 10% on the unpaid balance. Draw up a schedule of payments for the first 6 mo.*

Solution

Date	Principal (before payment)	Monthly interest	Payment			Principle (after payment)
			Principal	Interest	Total	
03-01	$36 000					
04-01	$36 000	$305.75	$150.00		$150.00	$35 850
05-01	$35 850	$294.66	$150.00		$150.00	$35 700
06-01	$35 700	$303.21	$150.00		$150.00	$35 550
07-01	$35 550	$292.19	$150.00		$150.00	$35 400
08-01	$35 400	$300.66	$150.00		$150.00	$35 250
	$35.250	$299.38	$150.00	$1795.85	$1945.85	$35 100
		$1795.85				

Interest Calculation

$\$36\,000 \times 0.10 \times \frac{31}{365}$
$\$35\,850 \times 0.10 \times \frac{30}{365}$
$\$35\,700 \times 0.10 \times \frac{31}{365}$

$\$35\,550 \times 0.10 \times \frac{31}{365}$

$\$35\,400 \times 0.10 \times \frac{31}{365}$
$\$35\,250 \times 0.10 \times \frac{31}{365}$

With a principal of $36 000 and monthly payments of $150, in how many months will the mortgage be paid off?

What equal monthly payment would amortize the mortgage at 10% over 240 mo. (Table 16-8)?

EXERCISE 16-2

A **1.** Why must a deposit accompany an offer to purchase for the protection of the vendor?

2. Why must an expiry date be shown on the offer to purchase for the protection of the purchaser?

3. When a vendor asks for terms of "Cash to mortgage," what is he requesting?

B **4.** Use table 16-8 to calculate the monthly payment for each of the following mortgages.

Full price	Down payment	Interest rate	Time
(a) $56 000	$20 000	$10\frac{1}{2}$%	20 a
(b) $75 000	$25 000	9%	15 a
(c) $32 500	$12 500	10%	30 a
(d) $48 600	$15 000	$9\frac{1}{2}$%	25 a
(e) $24 900	$4 500	12%	420 mo.
(f) $64 500	$24 500	10%	25 a

5. Using 27% of salary as a guide for payments and assuming a 25 a mortgage at 10%, determine to the nearest $1000 the largest mortgage a person with each of the following incomes should undertake.
(a) $550/mo.   (b) $1200/mo.
(c) $10 500/a   (d) $20 000/a

6. A mortgage for $27 000 is repaid by monthly payments of $100 against the principal with semi-annual interest payments. Interest is charged at $9\frac{1}{2}$% on the unpaid balance. If the mortgage is assumed on 1976-06-01, draw up a schedule of payments for the first 6 mo.

7. A mortgage for $40 500 is repaid by monthly payments of $175 against the principal with semi-annual interest payments. Interest is charged at $10\frac{1}{2}$% on the unpaid balance. If the mortgage is assumed on 1977-04-15 with payments on the 15th of each month, draw up a schedule of payments for the first half year.

Quite frequently when buying a house, the buyer does not have the full down payment available. The down payment is the difference between the mortgage amount and the sale price. It then becomes necessary to arrange a second mortgage to provide part of the down payment. The second mortgage is for a shorter period and has a greater risk, hence is at a higher rate of interest than the first mortgage.

8. On the purchase of a $75 000 house it was found necessary to take a second mortgage of $6500 from a Trust Company at 14% interest compounded quarterly. The terms of the mortgage were $450 quarterly for principal and interest for a three-year term.
(a) Prepare a schedule of payments as in the table.
(b) How much principal is still owing at the end of the 3 a?

Solar system —13
Neptune
Equatorial diameter 4.3×10^4 km
Mass 17×the earth's
Mean distance to the sun 4.50×10^9 km
Period of solar orbit 164.8 a
Escape velocity 25 km/s
Find the density and compare to the earth's. Find the mean speed of Neptune about the sun.

Payment	Interest	Principal	Amount outstanding
1			
2			
3			
.			
.			
.			
12			

HIGH DENSITY HOUSING

Can you estimate the number of apartments in each of the four apartment towers in the foreground of the above picture? Use the number of private balconies as a clue.

Give reasons for the selection of a "Y" design by the architect.

Any area accommodating a large number of people will require transportation routes, recreation facilities, schools, shopping facilities, park areas, and should contain a variety of housing modes from high to low density. How many of these items are in the area pictured?

DAY OF MONTH	JAN	FEB	MAR
1	1	32	60
2	2	33	61
3	3	34	62
4	4	35	63
5	5	36	64
6	6	37	65
7	7	38	66
8	8	39	67
9	9	40	68
10	10	41	69
11	11	42	70
12	12	43	71
13	13	44	72
14	14	45	73
15	15	46	74
16	16	47	75
17	17	48	76
18	18	49	77
19	19	50	78
20	20	51	79
21	21	52	80
22	22	53	81
23	23	54	82
24	24	55	83
25	25	56	84
26	26	57	85
27	27	58	86
28	28	59	87
29	29		88
30	30		89
31	31		90

DAY OF MONTH	APR	MAY	JUN
1	91	121	152
2	92	122	153
3	93	123	154
4	94	124	155
5	95	125	156
6	96	126	157
7	97	127	158
8	98	128	159
9	99	129	160
10	100	130	161
11	101	131	162
12	102	132	163
13	103	133	164
14	104	134	165
15	105	135	166
16	106	136	167
17	107	137	168
18	108	138	169
19	109	139	170
20	110	140	171
21	111	141	172
22	112	142	173
23	113	143	174
24	114	144	175
25	115	145	176
26	116	146	177
27	117	147	178
28	118	148	179
29	119	149	180
30	120	150	181
31		151	

16.3 ADJUSTMENTS TO THE SALE PRICE

When a house or condominium is sold the purchaser takes over all obligations relating to the property as of the date the sale is closed. The vendor is responsible for all obligations up to that point. It is highly unlikely that taxes and insurance will be paid up to exactly the date of sale. If some services are unpaid, the purchaser must be given credit; if some services are prepaid, the purchaser will be charged.

It is the responsibility of the lawyer for the vendor to prepare a "Statement of Adjustments". This document will set out the amounts which are allowed the purchaser and the amounts which are charged to the purchaser. It is arranged in the form of a balance sheet and will give the amount due to the vendor on closing.

EXAMPLE 1. *The closing date on a sale is* 1976-10-15. *Calculate the amount allowed in each of the following cases and to whom it is allowed.*
(*a*) *A* \$95 *insurance premium for 1 a, expiry date* 1977-03-30.
(*b*) *Annual taxes of* \$790, \$300 *paid to date.*

Solution (a): The purchaser is responsible for insurance from the date of purchase.

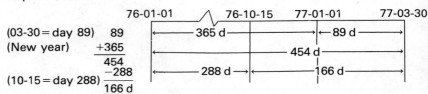

(03-30 = day 89)	89
(New year)	+365
	454
(10-15 = day 288)	−288
	166 d

The vendor is allowed $\frac{166}{365}$ of the premium.

$$\tfrac{166}{365} \times \$95 = \$43.21$$

Allow the vendor \$43.21.
(b) The vendor is responsible for taxes up to 10-15

$$10\text{-}15 = \text{day } 288.$$

The vendor must pay $\frac{288}{365}$ of the year's taxes.

$$\tfrac{288}{365} \times \$790 = \$623.34$$

The vendor has paid \$300.
\$623.34 − \$300 = \$323.34
Allow the purchaser \$323.34.

All companies and public utilities supplying services to the dwelling, such as electricity, gas, water, or phone, should be informed of the closing date. The vendor will ask to have meters read so that he is not responsible for charges due to the new tenants. The purchaser will make arrangements for the services to be continued. If he is moving into a community where he is not known, deposits may be required and should be allowed for when planning finances.

applied mathematics for today: senior

EXAMPLE 2. *Mr. R. Williams is selling his house, located at 15 Orange Cres., Newtown, Ontario, to Mr. and Mrs. B. Jones.*
 Particulars:
 Closing Date—1976-05-03
 Sale price—$46 500
 Deposit—$1600
 1976 taxes—$850
 First installment paid on taxes—$150
 Fire insurance—one-year premium—$130, expires 1976-10-15
 Mr. Williams will be paying off an open mortgage with some of the proceeds from the sale. Mr. and Mrs. Jones have arranged for a mortgage of $30 000 to finance their purchase. Draw up a statement of adjustments and calculate the balance due on closing.

Solution

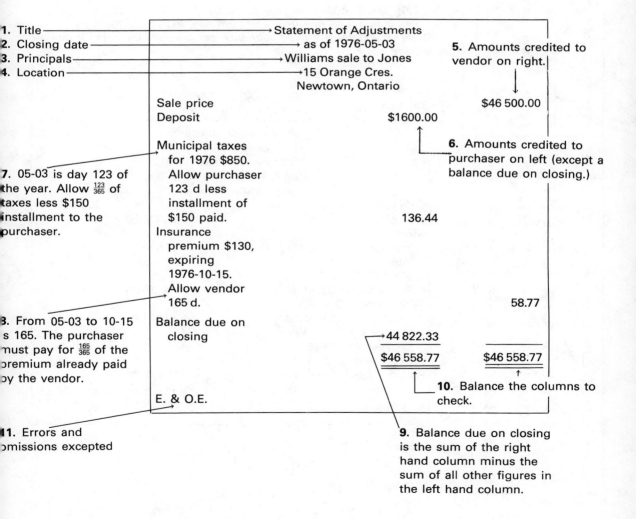

1. Title → Statement of Adjustments
2. Closing date → as of 1976-05-03
3. Principals → Williams sale to Jones
4. Location → 15 Orange Cres. Newtown, Ontario

5. Amounts credited to vendor on right.

6. Amounts credited to purchaser on left (except a balance due on closing.)

7. 05-03 is day 123 of the year. Allow $\frac{123}{365}$ of taxes less $150 installment to the purchaser.

8. From 05-03 to 10-15 is 165. The purchaser must pay for $\frac{165}{365}$ of the premium already paid by the vendor.

9. Balance due on closing is the sum of the right hand column minus the sum of all other figures in the left hand column.

10. Balance the columns to check.

11. Errors and omissions excepted

Sale price		$46 500.00
Deposit	$1600.00	
Municipal taxes for 1976 $850. Allow purchaser 123 d less installment of $150 paid.	136.44	
Insurance premium $130, expiring 1976-10-15. Allow vendor 165 d.		58.77
Balance due on closing	44 822.33	
	$46 558.77	$46 558.77

E. & O.E.

DAY OF MONTH	JUL	AUG	SEP
1	182	213	244
2	183	214	245
3	184	215	246
4	185	216	247
5	186	217	248
6	187	218	249
7	188	219	250
8	189	220	251
9	190	221	252
10	191	222	253
11	192	223	254
12	193	224	255
13	194	225	256
14	195	226	257
15	196	227	258
16	197	228	259
17	198	229	260
18	199	230	261
19	200	231	262
20	201	232	263
21	202	233	264
22	203	234	265
23	204	235	266
24	205	236	267
25	206	237	268
26	207	238	269
27	208	239	270
28	209	240	271
29	210	241	272
30	211	242	273
31	212	243	

DAY OF MONTH	OCT	NOV	DEC
1	274	305	335
2	275	306	336
3	276	307	337
4	277	308	338
5	278	309	339
6	279	310	340
7	280	311	341
8	281	312	342
9	282	313	343
10	283	314	344
11	284	315	345
12	285	316	346
13	286	317	347
14	287	318	348
15	288	319	349
16	289	320	350
17	290	321	351
18	291	322	352
19	292	323	353
20	293	324	354
21	294	325	355
22	295	326	356
23	296	327	357
24	297	328	358
25	298	329	359
26	299	330	360
27	300	331	361
28	301	332	362
29	302	333	363
30	303	334	364
31	304		365

When the vendor and the purchaser have made their mortgage arrangements independently of each other there is no mention of them in the statement of adjustments.

EXAMPLE 3. *Mr. and Mrs. G. Stanley are selling their condominium apartment, Unit 4, 16 Pleasant View Ave. Easton, Ontario, to Mr. and Mrs. F. McDonald.*

Particulars:

Closing date—1976-07-31

Sale price—$27 000

Deposit—$1000

Mortgage—McDonalds assume an existing mortgage. Last payment date—1976-06-30

Principal after last payment—$14 500

Interest rate—$9\frac{1}{2}$%/a.

1976 taxes—$375, not paid to date

Fire insurance—one-year premium $95, expires 1976-08-25.

Draw up a statement of adjustments and calculate the balance due on closing.

Solution

Statement of Adjustments
as of 1976-07-31
Stanley sale to McDonald
Unit 4, 16 Pleasant View Ave.
Easton, Ontario

Sale price		$27 000.00
Deposit	$1000.00	
Mortgage		
Principal	$14 500.00	
Interest		
$9\frac{1}{2}$% 06-30—07-31		
Allow to purchaser 31 d.	$116.99	
1976 taxes $375		
Allow purchaser 212 d.	$217.80	
Insurance premium $95.		
expires 1976-08-25.		
Allow vendor 25 d.		$6.51
Balance due on closing	$11 171.72	
	$27 006.51	$27 006.51

E. & O.E.

---

applied mathematics for today: senior

EXERCISE 16-3

A **1.** State whether each of the following items would be credited to the vendor or to the purchaser when a statement of adjustments is drawn up:

(a) Sale price   (b) Deposit

(c) The portion of a fire insurance policy premium covering future time.

(d) Unpaid municipal taxes.

(e) The value of furnace oil in the storage tank.

(f) Taxes prepaid by the vendor.

(g) Interest accrued since the last payment on a mortgage assumed by the purchaser.

2. Calculate the amount allowed in each of the following cases, and state to whom it is allowed.

(a) An insurance premium for 1 a in the amount of $170. Closing date 09-24, expiry date 12-30.

(b) An insurance premium for 3 a in the amount of $240. Closing date 1977-01-31, expiry date 1978-04-04.

(c) Municipal taxes of $643. Installment of $250 paid. Closing date 09-30.

(d) Municipal taxes of $759.30. Installment of $500.00 paid. Closing date 05-31.

(e) Mortgage assumed by the purchaser; principal at date of last payment, $46 250 as of 01-15. Closing date 01-30. Interest at $10\frac{1}{2}$%/a.

(f) Mortgage assumed by the purchaser; principal at date of last payment, $24 500 as of 05-05. Closing date 05-31. Interest accrued at 9%/a.

3. Miss J. Payne is selling her property to Mrs. W. Hanson.

Closing date   —1978-04-30
Location   —240 Sandford St.
                 Norton, Ontario
Sale price   —$38 500
Deposit   —$2000
Municipal taxes—$738, none paid this year.
Fire insurance —premium for 1 a, $176,
                  expiry date 07-10.

Draw up a statement of adjustments and calculate the balance due on closing.

4. Ms W. Morton is selling her cottage to Mr. I. Sorenson.

Closing date   —1976-02-28
Location   —Lot 45 Lakeside Rd.
                 Cowan Township, Ontario
Sale price   —$26 900
Deposit   —$600
First mortgage—Mr. Sorenson is to assume the existing
                 mortgage. The principal at the time of the
                 last payment was $18 450.
                 Interest is accrued at $10\frac{1}{2}$%/a from 01-31.

Solar system —14
Pluto
Equatorial diameter unknown
Mass unknown
Mean distance to the sun 5.91×10^9 km
Period of solar orbit 247.7 a
Escape velocity 3.0 km/s
Find the mean speed of Pluto about the sun.

Municipal taxes —$300 in arrears from previous year to be
assumed by the purchaser.
Taxes for this year $450.

Fire insurance —premium for 1 a, $96.50, expiry date 07-30.

Draw up a statement of adjustments and calculate the balance due on closing.

5. Miss V. Coleman is selling her condominium townhouse to Miss A. Walker.

Closing date —06-30

Location —Unit 3, 15 Sutherland Place
Saxton, B.C.

Sale price —$24 900

Deposit —$1300

First mortgage —Assumed by the purchaser, principal at the
time of last payment $10 200.
Unpaid interest accrued from 06-15, at 9%.

Second —$6000 taken back by the vendor
mortgage (allow to purchaser).

Municipal tax —$427, unpaid.

Fire insurance —premium for 1 a $83, expiry date 09-10.

Draw up a statement of adjustments and calculate the balance due on closing.

16.4 MUNICIPAL TAXATION

Since property owners pay a very large portion of all municipal taxes, we shall consider how the rates are arrived at.

The real property tax is levied in proportion to the value of the property, so it is necessary to set a value on each property in the community. The person appointed to carry out this task is called an assessor. The value set, called the assessment, is the going value of the property at the time of assessing. The assessors compile a list of all this data and enter it on an assessment roll.

Since property values are subject to change, each municipality revises its assessment roll periodically so that property owners will be taxed on an equitable basis.

The treasurer of the local municipality prepares a budget to cover the financial requirements of the municipality for the following year. Using the budget and the assessment role, he is able to set a tax rate.

EXAMPLE 1. *A municipality requires a budget of* $45 000 000 *to operate next year. Provincial and federal grants, fees and commercial taxes will cover* $25 000 000, *leaving* $20 000 000 *to be raised by a tax on residential assessments. Calculate the tax rate if the total assessed residential value for taxation purposes is* $500 000 000.

Solution

$$\text{Rate} = \frac{\text{tax revenue required from residential assessments}}{\text{current assessed value}}$$

$$= \frac{\$20\,000\,000}{\$500\,000\,000}$$

$$= 0.04$$

That is, for each dollar of assessed value on his residential property, each owner must pay 4¢.

Mill rate: The rate in property tax is usually expressed in mills per dollar where

$$1 \text{ mill} = 0.01|¢, \text{ or}$$

$$1¢ = 10 \text{ mills.}$$

Thus, in Example 1 the mill rate is $4 \times 10 = 40$

EXAMPLE 2. *For the municipality referred to in Example 1, find the tax on a building lot assessed as $5280.*

Solution The mill rate is 40 mills per dollar.

$$\text{Tax} = \frac{\text{Mill rate} \times \text{assessed value}}{1000}$$

$$= \frac{40 \times \$5280}{1000}$$

$$= \$211.20$$

The following three formulas will be useful in doing Exercise 16-4.

$$\text{Tax} = \frac{\text{mill rate} \times \text{assessment}}{1000}$$

$$\text{Mill rate} = \frac{\text{tax}}{\text{assessment}} \times 1000$$

$$\text{Assessment} = \frac{\text{tax}}{\text{mill rate}} \times 1000$$

TOWN OF STONEY CREEK

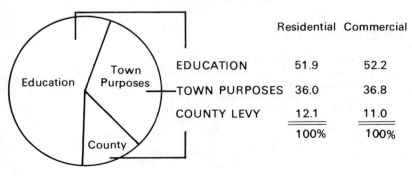

	Residential	Commercial
EDUCATION	51.9	52.2
TOWN PURPOSES	36.0	36.8
COUNTY LEVY	12.1	11.0
	100%	100%

The density of the project has been kept below the usual figure of other Toronto condominium developments being 12.79 units per acre.

This newspaper excerpt refers to the density of a housing development. Pictured here are areas ranging from high to low density housing.

EXERCISE 16-4

B **1.** Complete the following table.

	Assessment	Mill rate	Tax
(a)	$17 300	45	
(b)		30	$540.00
(c)	$8 500		$487.00
(d)	$16 550	42	
(e)	$28 900		$729.80

2. A suburban community has a total residential assessment of $61 300 000. The treasurer predicts that the taxes raised from this assessment should be $3 176 850. What should the mill rate be?

3. (a) Two people living in different communities build houses of the same design on lots of equal size. If the person in Smithville has his house and lot assessed at $50 000 with a mill rate of 20 mills, will his tax be more or less than the person in Brownsville with an assessment of $35 000 and a mill rate of 30 mills?
(b) Does it follow that in different communities the higher the assessed value the higher the tax?

4. A town has a total residential assessment of $97 500 000. The town treasurer has been advised that $6 252 500 must be raised by residential property taxation. In the meantime, city employees have negotiated a new wage scale requiring that $143 250 added expenditures be charged against residential property tax.
(a) What was the original mill rate?
(b) How many mills must be added to handle the unexpected expenditure?

5. A town has an assessed residential property value of $25 000 000. The town council must meet the following expenditures:
 (i) Education, $1 050 000
 (ii) General purposes, $200 000
(iii) Recreation, $25 000
(iv) Public works, $70 000
 (v) Police and fire protection, $85 000.
(a) If 80% of the expenditures is charged against residential real estate, calculate the total taxes needed from this source.
(b) What is the mill rate?
(c) What is the tax on a property assessed at $7500?

6. A town has a residential property assessment of $975 500 000. It is at first estimated that $45 567 000 must be raised through residential taxation to meet expenditures.
(a) What mill rate must be set?
(b) What is the tax on a property assessed at $25 000?

7. The town in question 6 finds that it underestimated building costs. An additional $2 000 000 must be raised.
(a) What is the increase in the mill rate?
(b) How much more must a person pay on property assessed at $25 000?

8. Obtain a copy of the municipal budget from the municipal clerk in your area for the current year. Use the data from the budget to draw a circle graph showing the relative percentages of expenditure directed to the following:
(a) Education
(b) Debts and interest on debts
(c) Local government
(d) Refuse collection and sanitation
(e) Fire
(f) Community services
(g) Police
(h) Roads
(i) Welfare and health
(j) Recreation

16.5 FAIR RENTAL VALUE

Many people use the rental of housing as a source of income. The operation can range from the building of multi-million-dollar apartment complexes to the rental of a small duplex or single room.

Money invested in stocks, bonds, or savings certificates earns income. It is reasonable therefore that a landlord with money invested in housing should expect an income from his investment as well. He will also expect that all expenses associated with the house will be paid from the rental income.

A landlord can expect:

1. A return on his investment comparable to the current return on other investment income, currently 7%–10%.

2. Sufficient income to pay—taxes

          —insurance (on building)

          —repairs and depreciation 2%–5%

          —water rates if billed to the owner on a flat rate.

Other expenses associated with a home such as electrical power, heating, insurance (on contents), metered water and telephone are usually paid by the tenant. It should be remembered however that the lease sets out the financial responsibilities of each party and can divide the costs any way that is mutually acceptable.

EXAMPLE 1. *Mr. McKnight has bought both halves of a semi-detached house; he lives in one half and rents the other. Calculate the fair rental value of the property given the following information:*

Investment value of the whole property	$95 000.00
Taxes for the whole property	835.00
Insurance for the whole property one-year premium	165.00
Value of the structure	$79 000.00
Investment income rate expected	$8\frac{1}{2}\%$
Allowance for depreciation and repair on the value of the structure	3%
Other expenses carried by the tenant.	

Solution

Annual investment income from rented half
$$\tfrac{1}{2}(\$95\ 000.00)(0.085) = \$4037.50$$

Expenses apportioned
to rented half

Taxes	$\tfrac{1}{2}(\$835.00) =$	417.50
Insurance	$\tfrac{1}{2}(\$165.00) =$	82.50

Depreciation and repairs
$$\tfrac{1}{2}(\$79\ 000)(0.03) = \underline{\ 1185.00}$$

Annual fair rental value $= \$5722.50$

Monthly rent charged $= \tfrac{1}{12}(\$5722.50)$
$$= \$476.88$$
$$\doteq \$475.00$$

applied mathematics for today: senior

If the rental value is too high for prospective tenants, Mr. McKnight may have to be satisfied with a smaller return on his investment.

EXERCISE 16-5

A **1.** Why is depreciation charged against the cost of the structure only?

2. Should the investment income be calculated on the purchase price or the current market value of the investment?

3. Which of the items taken into account in Example 1 would be affected by an increase in the market value of the land and which would be affected by an increase in the market value of the structure. (Assume the property is assessed at its market value).

B **4.** Find the annual fair rental value of the following property and the monthly rent to be charged.
Particulars:
Investment value—$35 000
Taxes—32.1 mills on an assessed value of $30 000
Insurance—one year premium $75
Value of Structure—$28 000
Investment income rate expected—8%
Allowance for repair and depreciation on the value of the structure—$2\frac{1}{2}$%

5. Miss Tamboso owns a duplex. She lives downstairs and rents out a smaller upstairs apartment. In calculating the fair rental value she assesses charges at a rate of 0.65 to her living area and 0.35 to the rental area. Heat is supplied to the apartment.
Particulars:
Investment value—$75 000
Taxes—24.9 mills on an assessment of $73 000
Insurance—three-year premium $225
Average water rate—$35/a
Value of structure—$63 700.
Heating cost—$350
Investment income rate expected—7%
Allowance for depreciation and repairs on the value of the structure—4%
Find the monthly rent Miss Tamboso will charge.

6. Consider the following property:
Particulars:
Investment value—$53 500
Taxes—32.1 mills on an assessment of $50 000
Value of the structure—$42 800
Insurance—one-year premium: 26¢ per $100 on 80% of the value of the structure.
Investment income rate expected—$7\frac{1}{2}$%
Allowance for depreciation and repair on the value of the structure—$3\frac{1}{2}$%
(a) Find the monthly fair rental value.
(b) Changing real estate values increase the total property value to

Mr. Smith, who has just purchased a new home, went to the hardware store to make a purchase for the house. He was told that 1 would cost 25¢, 5 would cost 25¢, 76 would cost 50¢, 187 would cost 75¢, and 1329 would cost $1. What was he buying?

$75 000. The structure is now worth $60 000 and the assessment is $70 000. Find the monthly fair rental value.

7. A duplex is completely rented out. The rental value is divided at the rate of 55% to the downstairs apartment and 45% to the upstairs apartment. Heat and electricity for the apartments is paid for by the tenants.
Particulars:
Investment value—$95 000
Taxes—18.9 mills on an assessed value of $70 000
Value of the structure—$80 750
Insurance—one-year premium: 30¢ per $100 on 80% of the value of the structure.
Water rates—$76/a average
Investment income rate expected—$8\frac{1}{2}$%
Allowance for depreciation and repairs on value of the structure—3%
(a) What should the gross annual return from the building be?
(b) What monthly rent should be charged for each apartment?
(c) The rent calculated is too high for the apartments to be rentable and the landlord decides to accept 7% on his investment and depreciate at $2\frac{1}{2}$. What are the new rents?

REVIEW EXERCISE

A **1.** (a) Give three advantages of living in a house.
(b) Give three advantages of apartment living.

2. Why is it wise to have a lawyer to protect your interests when purchasing a house?

3. What items are usually considered in calculating the fair rented value of a property?

4. What items are usually considered in the adjustment to the sale price of a dwelling?

B **5.** Mr. Collins is considering the purchase of a house. The purchase price is $42 000, requiring a down payment of $15 000. A first mortgage amortized over 25 a at $9\frac{1}{2}$% is available. Taxes are estimated at $900/a; heating, $250/a; electric power, water, and phone average $25/mo. Mr. Collins has saved $10 000 and can get a second mortgage for $5000 at 11% requiring payments of $75/mo.
(a) Calculate the total average monthly cost for accommodation.
(b) If 27% of his income is the maximum that Mr. Collins will allocate to accommodation, what should the family income be if they are to purchase this home?

6. A townhouse condominium is for sale for $30 000. The mortgage payments are $224.00/mo., taxes average $745/a. Electric power bills average $45/mo., which includes heating. Water and phone average $20/mo. and there is a $24/mo. maintenance charge. The insurance premium is $115 for 1 a. Calculate the monthly cost of occupancy if the prospective purchaser has the cash for a down payment.

7. (a) A mortgage for $57 000 is amortized over 30 a at $10\frac{1}{2}$%. What is the monthly payment?

(b) A second mortgage for $6000 is taken out to meet the down payment. This mortgage is amortized over 10 a at $12\frac{1}{2}$%. What is the total monthly cost for both first and second mortgages?

8. A mortgage for $15 000 is repaid by monthly payments of $100 on the principal and quarterly interest payment of 9% on the unpaid balance.

(a) Calculate the first two interest payments if the mortgage is taken out 03-01, and payments are due the first of every month.

(b) What is the total amount paid in the first 6 mo.?

9. Write up a statement of adjustments for the following sales and calculate the balance due on closing.

(a) Mr. and Mrs. O. Simpson are selling a house to Mr. and Mrs. P. Branson at 32 Plain Cres., Warwick, Ontario.

Closing date—08-15

Sale price—$64 500

Deposit—$2000

Taxes—$985, first installment of $350 paid.

Fire insurance, one-year premium—$117, expires 11-18.

(b) Mr. B. Wallace is selling a condominium townhouse to Miss W. Saxby at 12 Horton Place, Newtown, Ontario.

Closing date—02-13

Sale price—$35 000

Deposit—$900

Taxes—$745, none paid to date, none in arrears.

First mortgage—Assumed by the purchaser, principal at the time of last payment $21 430. Unpaid interest accrued from 01-25 at $9\frac{1}{2}$%.

Monthly maintenance charge—$27/mo. paid for February.

Fire insurance, one-year premium—$85, expires 04-01.

10. A municipality has a budget of $5 000 000 of which 29% is met from residential property tax. The residential assessment is $51 000 000.

(a) Calculate the mill rate.

(b What taxes are paid on a residence assessed at $27 000?

11. Mr. Thompson is being transferred out of the country for 2 a by his company. Since he will be returning he decides to rent his house for the time that he will be away. In establishing the rent he takes the following factors into consideration:

Investment value—$65 000

Taxes—25.6 mills on an assessed value of $48 000

Insurance—one-year premium—$134.50

Value of the structure—$59 000

Investment income rate expected—7%

Repair and depreciation allowance—3% on the value of the structure.

What monthly rent will Mr. Thompson charge?

Personal Income Tax

Because tax rates and allowable deductions vary, worked examples are not provided. Current tax forms are available at any branch of the Post Office or from the District Taxation Office. The following exercises provide data which will enable the student to complete an income tax form.

1. Terry Murphy was born on 1950-09-03. He is a bachelor whose address is 1104 King St., Apartment 1102, Toronto, Ontario. He is employed as a chemist by Dele Chemicals Ltd. He is also a part-time student at York University and his tuition fees were $400.00 this year. Below is a copy of Terry's T4 slip. Complete his income tax return.

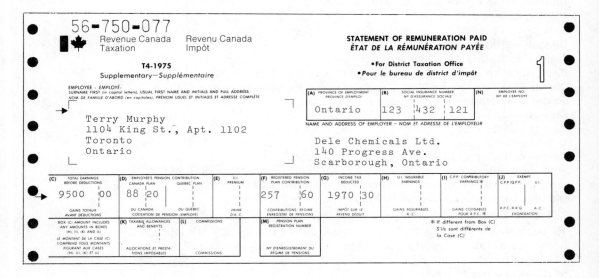

2. Janice Brown is employed as a research supervisor by the Komstock Co. Ltd. She shares an apartment with a girlfriend at 1307 Queen St., Apt. 1A, Oakville, Ontario. Her yearly union dues amount to $56.75. She was born 1951-10-07. Below is a copy of her T4 slip. Complete her income tax return.

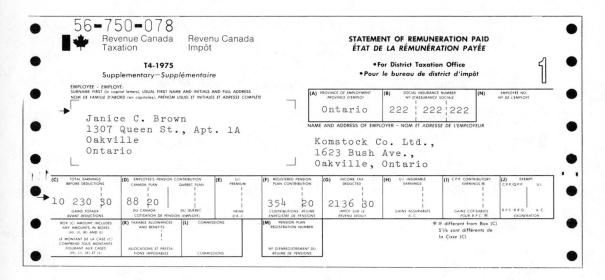

3. Marie Gagnon (born 1950-04-03) is a dietician and is employed by the Oshawa General Hospital. She lives in an apartment at 2156 Duke St., Oshawa, Ontario. As a part-time student at the University of Toronto, she paid tuition of $257.00. Her charitable donations amount to $137.50 and dues for the professional associations to which she belongs amount to $127.26/a. T5 slips from her bank and credit union show interest of $37.36 and $243.16 respectively. Below is a copy of her T4 slip. Complete her income tax return.

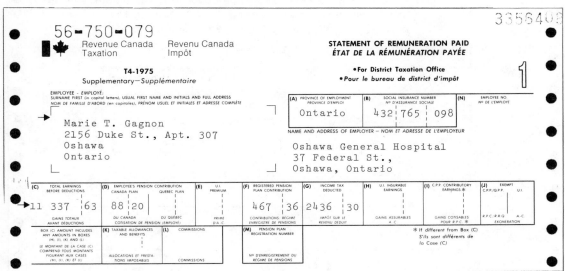

4. John Williams (born 1948-09-05) is married and lives with his wife at 105 Hunt St., Apt. 1102, Hamilton, Ontario. He is employed by Bell Telephone as an engineer. During the year his wife had a part time job and earned $200.00. His annual dues as a member of the Engineers Association are $152.50. Below is a copy of his T4 slip. Complete his income tax return.

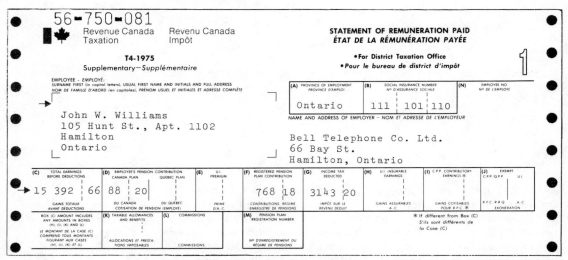

56-750-081

Revenue Canada Taxation — Revenu Canada Impôt

STATEMENT OF REMUNERATION PAID
ÉTAT DE LA RÉMUNÉRATION PAYÉE

• For District Taxation Office
• Pour le bureau de district d'impôt

1

T4-1975
Supplementary—Supplémentaire

EMPLOYEE - EMPLOYÉ:
SURNAME FIRST (in capital letters), USUAL FIRST NAME AND INITIALS AND FULL ADDRESS
NOM DE FAMILLE D'ABORD (en capitales), PRÉNOM USUEL ET INITIALES ET ADRESSE COMPLÈTE

John W. Williams
105 Hunt St., Apt. 1102
Hamilton
Ontario

(A) PROVINCE OF EMPLOYMENT PROVINCE D'EMPLOI	(B) SOCIAL INSURANCE NUMBER Nº D'ASSURANCE SOCIALE	(N) EMPLOYEE NO. Nº DE L'EMPLOYÉ
Ontario	111 101 110	

NAME AND ADDRESS OF EMPLOYER - NOM ET ADRESSE DE L'EMPLOYEUR

Bell Telephone Co. Ltd.
66 Bay St.
Hamilton, Ontario

(C) TOTAL EARNINGS BEFORE DEDUCTIONS GAINS TOTAUX AVANT DÉDUCTIONS	(D) EMPLOYEE'S PENSION CONTRIBUTION CANADA PLAN / QUEBEC PLAN DU CANADA / DU QUÉBEC COTISATION DE PENSION (EMPLOYÉ)	(E) U.I. PREMIUM PRIME D'A.-C.	(F) REGISTERED PENSION PLAN CONTRIBUTION CONTRIBUTIONS: RÉGIME ENREGISTRÉ DE PENSIONS	(G) INCOME TAX DEDUCTED IMPÔT SUR LE REVENU DÉDUIT	(H) U.I. INSURABLE EARNINGS GAINS ASSURABLES A.-C.	(I) C.P.P. CONTRIBUTORY EARNINGS * GAINS COTISABLES POUR R.P.C. *	(J) EXEMPT C.P.P./Q.P.P. / U.I. R.P.C. R.R.Q. / A.-C. EXONÉRATION
15 392 66	88 20		768 18	3143 20			

BOX (C) AMOUNT INCLUDES ANY AMOUNTS IN BOXES (H), (I), (K) AND (L) LE MONTANT DE LA CASE (C) COMPREND TOUS MONTANTS FIGURANT AUX CASES (H), (I), (K) ET (L)	(K) TAXABLE ALLOWANCES AND BENEFITS ALLOCATIONS ET PRESTA- TIONS IMPOSABLES	(L) COMMISSIONS COMMISSIONS	(M) PENSION PLAN REGISTRATION NUMBER Nº D'ENREGISTREMENT DU RÉGIME DE PENSIONS				

* If different from Box (C)
S'ils sont différents de la Case (C)

5. Phyllis Adams (born 1942-12-07) lives with her husband Mark and their 3 children in a rented house. David is 3 a old, Sally is 7 and Mark Jr. is 11. Phyllis works as a shoe buyer in Niagara Falls. Her husband had a part-time job and earned $1200.00 during the year. Below is a copy of Phyllis' T4 slip. Complete her tax return.

56-750-082

Revenue Canada Taxation — Revenu Canada Impôt

STATEMENT OF REMUNERATION PAID
ÉTAT DE LA RÉMUNÉRATION PAYÉE

• For District Taxation Office
• Pour le bureau de district d'impôt

1

T4-1975
Supplementary—Supplémentaire

EMPLOYEE - EMPLOYÉ:
SURNAME FIRST (in capital letters), USUAL FIRST NAME AND INITIALS AND FULL ADDRESS
NOM DE FAMILLE D'ABORD (en capitales), PRÉNOM USUEL ET INITIALES ET ADRESSE COMPLÈTE

Phyllis G. Adams
33 Pleasant Drive
Niagara Falls, Ontario

(A) PROVINCE OF EMPLOYMENT PROVINCE D'EMPLOI	(B) SOCIAL INSURANCE NUMBER Nº D'ASSURANCE SOCIALE	(N) EMPLOYEE NO. Nº DE L'EMPLOYÉ
Ontario	222 333 111	

NAME AND ADDRESS OF EMPLOYER - NOM ET ADRESSE DE L'EMPLOYEUR

Sally's Shoe Shops
121 Front St.
Niagara Falls, Ontario

(C) TOTAL EARNINGS BEFORE DEDUCTIONS GAINS TOTAUX AVANT DÉDUCTIONS	(D) EMPLOYEE'S PENSION CONTRIBUTION CANADA PLAN / QUEBEC PLAN DU CANADA / DU QUÉBEC COTISATION DE PENSION (EMPLOYÉ)	(E) U.I. PREMIUM PRIME D'A.-C.	(F) REGISTERED PENSION PLAN CONTRIBUTION CONTRIBUTIONS: RÉGIME ENREGISTRÉ DE PENSIONS	(G) INCOME TAX DEDUCTED IMPÔT SUR LE REVENU DÉDUIT	(H) U.I. INSURABLE EARNINGS GAINS ASSURABLES A.-C.	(I) C.P.P. CONTRIBUTORY EARNINGS * GAINS COTISABLES POUR R.P.C. *	(J) EXEMPT C.P.P./Q.P.P. / U.I. R.P.C. R.R.Q. / A.-C. EXONÉRATION
11 261 10	88 20		763 30	1375 88			

BOX (C) AMOUNT INCLUDES ANY AMOUNTS IN BOXES (H), (I), (K) AND (L) LE MONTANT DE LA CASE (C) COMPREND TOUS MONTANTS FIGURANT AUX CASES (H), (I), (K) ET (L)	(K) TAXABLE ALLOWANCES AND BENEFITS ALLOCATIONS ET PRESTA- TIONS IMPOSABLES	(L) COMMISSIONS COMMISSIONS	(M) PENSION PLAN REGISTRATION NUMBER Nº D'ENREGISTREMENT DU RÉGIME DE PENSIONS				

* If different from Box (C)
S'ils sont différents de la Case (C)

6. Robert Knight (born 1933-05-03) and his wife Jane live with their 4 children in Burnaby, British Columbia. Jane earned $900.00 on her job. The children are: Martha, 11 a old; Bill, 13; Peggy, 15; and Eric, 20. Eric is a full-time student at the University of British Columbia. His father paid his tuition fees amounting to $950.00. Eric earned $700.00 on a summer job. Robert's T5 slip from the bank shows interest of $72.20. Below is a copy of his T4 slip. Complete his income tax return.

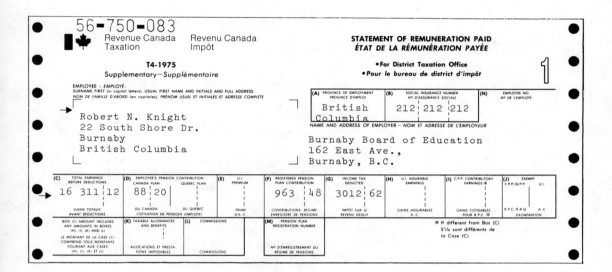

7. Mary Kowalski (born 1938-06-04), is a widow. She supports her two daughters who live at home with her. Theresa is 10 a old and Karen is 17. Mary works as a cost accountant for a large department store in Vancouver, B.C. Both her daughters attend school. Karen earned $1200.00 during the year as a part-time waitress. Mrs. Kowalski donated $200.00 to various charities. Her T5 Slip from the bank shows interest of $125.23. Below is a copy of her T4 slip. Complete her tax return.

56-750-084

Revenue Canada Taxation — **Revenu Canada** Impôt

STATEMENT OF REMUNERATION PAID
ÉTAT DE LA RÉMUNÉRATION PAYÉE

T4-1975
Supplementary—*Supplémentaire*

• For District Taxation Office
• *Pour le bureau de district d'impôt*

1

EMPLOYEE - *EMPLOYÉ:*
SURNAME FIRST (in capital letters), USUAL FIRST NAME AND INITIALS AND FULL ADDRESS
NOM DE FAMILLE D'ABORD (en capitales), PRÉNOM USUEL ET INITIALES ET ADRESSE COMPLÈTE

Mary K. Kowalski
2821 Parkview Rd.
Vancouver
British Columbia

(A) PROVINCE OF EMPLOYMENT *PROVINCE D'EMPLOI*	(B) SOCIAL INSURANCE NUMBER *N° D'ASSURANCE SOCIALE*	(N) EMPLOYEE NO. *N° DE L'EMPLOYÉ*
British Columbia	274 872 947	

NAME AND ADDRESS OF EMPLOYER – *NOM ET ADRESSE DE L'EMPLOYEUR*

Norton's Department Store,
889 Main St.
Vancouver, B.C.

(C) TOTAL EARNINGS BEFORE DEDUCTIONS	(D) EMPLOYEE'S PENSION CONTRIBUTION CANADA PLAN / QUEBEC PLAN	(E) U.I. PREMIUM	(F) REGISTERED PENSION PLAN CONTRIBUTION	(G) INCOME TAX DEDUCTED	(H) U.I. INSURABLE EARNINGS	(I) C.P.P. CONTRIBUTORY EARNINGS *	(J) EXEMPT C.P.P./Q.P.P. / U.I.
13 824 18	88 20		936 60	1924 20			

GAINS TOTAUX AVANT DÉDUCTIONS / *DU CANADA DU QUÉBEC COTISATION DE PENSION (EMPLOYÉ)* / *PRIME D'A.-C.* / *CONTRIBUTIONS: RÉGIME ENREGISTRÉ DE PENSIONS* / *IMPÔT SUR LE REVENU DÉDUIT* / *GAINS ASSURABLES A.-C.* / *GAINS COTISABLES POUR R.P.C.* / *R.P.C./R.R.Q. A.-C. EXONÉRATION*

* If different from Box (C) *S'ils sont différents de la Case (C)*

BOX (C) AMOUNT INCLUDES ANY AMOUNTS IN BOXES (H), (I), (K) AND (L) *LE MONTANT DE LA CASE (C) COMPREND TOUS MONTANTS FIGURANT AUX CASES (H), (I), (K) ET (L)*	(K) TAXABLE ALLOWANCES AND BENEFITS *ALLOCATIONS ET PRESTATIONS IMPOSABLES*	(L) COMMISSIONS *COMMISSIONS*	(M) PENSION PLAN REGISTRATION NUMBER *N° D'ENREGISTREMENT DU RÉGIME DE PENSIONS*

---

8. Fred Black (born 1949-08-17) is divorced and lives at 961 Swallow Cr., Edmonton, Alta. He is employed as a welder by the ABC Construction Co. Support payments to his ex-wife, who resides in Halifax, N.S., amounted to $1200.00. He received $315.00 worth of dividends from the White Company, Smith Falls, Ont. (a taxable Canadian Corporation). He has receipts to show charitable donations amounting to $233.50. His annual union dues amount to $257.60. Below is a copy of his T4 slip. Complete his income tax return.

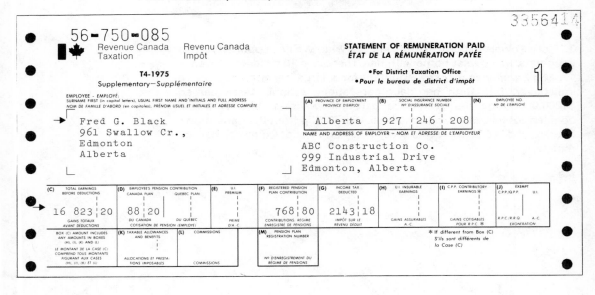

56-750-085

3356414

Revenue Canada Taxation — **Revenu Canada** Impôt

STATEMENT OF REMUNERATION PAID
ÉTAT DE LA RÉMUNÉRATION PAYÉE

T4-1975
Supplementary—*Supplémentaire*

• For District Taxation Office
• *Pour le bureau de district d'impôt*

1

EMPLOYEE - *EMPLOYÉ:*
SURNAME FIRST (in capital letters), USUAL FIRST NAME AND INITIALS AND FULL ADDRESS
NOM DE FAMILLE D'ABORD (en capitales), PRÉNOM USUEL ET INITIALES ET ADRESSE COMPLÈTE

Fred G. Black
961 Swallow Cr.,
Edmonton
Alberta

(A) PROVINCE OF EMPLOYMENT *PROVINCE D'EMPLOI*	(B) SOCIAL INSURANCE NUMBER *N° D'ASSURANCE SOCIALE*	(N) EMPLOYEE NO. *N° DE L'EMPLOYÉ*
Alberta	927 246 208	

NAME AND ADDRESS OF EMPLOYER – *NOM ET ADRESSE DE L'EMPLOYEUR*

ABC Construction Co.
999 Industrial Drive
Edmonton, Alberta

(C) TOTAL EARNINGS BEFORE DEDUCTIONS	(D) EMPLOYEE'S PENSION CONTRIBUTION CANADA PLAN / QUEBEC PLAN	(E) U.I. PREMIUM	(F) REGISTERED PENSION PLAN CONTRIBUTION	(G) INCOME TAX DEDUCTED	(H) U.I. INSURABLE EARNINGS	(I) C.P.P. CONTRIBUTORY EARNINGS *	(J) EXEMPT C.P.P./Q.P.P. / U.I.
16 823 20	88 20		768 80	2143 18			

GAINS TOTAUX AVANT DÉDUCTIONS / *DU CANADA DU QUÉBEC COTISATION DE PENSION (EMPLOYÉ)* / *PRIME D'A.-C.* / *CONTRIBUTIONS: RÉGIME ENREGISTRÉ DE PENSIONS* / *IMPÔT SUR LE REVENU DÉDUIT* / *GAINS ASSURABLES A.-C.* / *GAINS COTISABLES POUR R.P.C.* / *R.P.C./R.R.Q. A.-C. EXONÉRATION*

* If different from Box (C) *S'ils sont différents de la Case (C)*

BOX (C) AMOUNT INCLUDES ANY AMOUNTS IN BOXES (H), (I), (K) AND (L) *LE MONTANT DE LA CASE (C) COMPREND TOUS MONTANTS FIGURANT AUX CASES (H), (I), (K) ET (L)*	(K) TAXABLE ALLOWANCES AND BENEFITS *ALLOCATIONS ET PRESTATIONS IMPOSABLES*	(L) COMMISSIONS *COMMISSIONS*	(M) PENSION PLAN REGISTRATION NUMBER *N° D'ENREGISTREMENT DU RÉGIME DE PENSIONS*

9. Frank Levine (born 1950-07-04), lives with his wife Jane and their two children, Mary aged 4 and Sam aged 6, at 233 Smith Street, Gramston, New Brunswick. He is employed by the town as a policeman. His wife is a full-time student at the University of New Brunswick. Her tuition fees amounted to $1700 which Frank paid. Jane had a part-time job in the university bookstore where she earned $515.70. The Levines employed a housekeeper to look after the children while Jane was in school. These child care expenses amounted to $635. Frank's T5 slip from the bank shows interest of $63.25. His dues for professional associations amount to $135.27. Below is a copy of Frank's T4 slip. Complete his tax return.

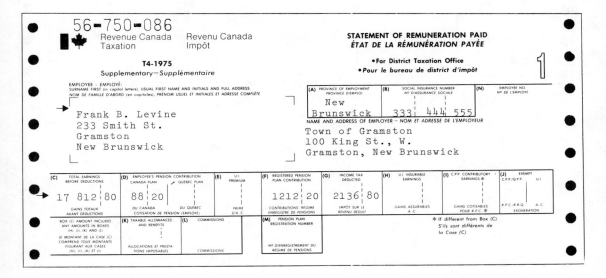

10. Glen Jones is a bachelor (born 1956-05-03). He lives with his mother at 237 Elm St., Halifax, Nova Scotia. He is employed as a bookkeeper by the Allied Steamship Lines of Halifax. Sandra, his mother, does not work and relies on Glen for support. She was recently ill and medical bills of $337.50 were paid by Glen on her behalf. His charitable donations amount to $157.60. Glen's T5 slip from the bank shows interest amounting to $357.30. His union dues for the year were $136.42. He received $123.50 in dividends from the Teltex Company, Halifax (a taxable Canadian Corporation). Glen paid $850 into a registered retirement savings plan. Below is a copy of his T4 slip. Complete his income tax return.

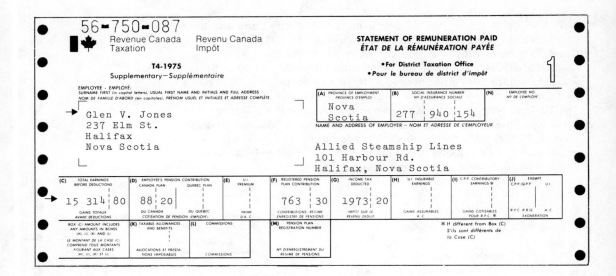

ANSWERS

REVIEW AND PREVIEW TO CHAPTER 1

Exercise 1

1. (a) 109.1   **(b)** 88.6   **(c)** 111.7   **(d)** 112.4
    (e) 123.4   **(f)** 545.2

2. (a) $\frac{11}{8}$ **(b)** $\frac{7}{6}$ **(c)** $\frac{10}{9}$ **(d)** $\frac{59}{56}$
    (e) $\frac{34}{33}$ **(f)** $\frac{41}{35}$ **(g)** $\frac{23}{24}$ **(h)** $\frac{38}{45}$
    (i) $\frac{7}{8}$ **(j)** $\frac{41}{28}$ **(k)** $\frac{11}{24}$ **(l)** $\frac{41}{39}$

3. (a) $\frac{2}{15}$ **(b)** $\frac{35}{72}$ **(c)** $\frac{5}{48}$ **(d)** $\frac{2}{3}$
    (e) $\frac{3}{25}$ **(f)** $\frac{3}{11}$ **(g)** $\frac{4}{15}$ **(h)** $\frac{5}{22}$
    (i) $\frac{32}{65}$ **(j)** $\frac{3}{8}$ **(k)** $\frac{5}{24}$ **(l)** $\frac{1}{5}$

4. (a) $\frac{3}{7}$ **(b)** $\frac{9}{11}$ **(c)** $\frac{17}{12}$ **(d)** $\frac{5}{8}$
    (e) $\frac{5}{3}$ **(f)** $\frac{1}{3}$ **(g)** $\frac{1}{3}$ **(h)** $\frac{19}{14}$
    (i) $\frac{5}{8}$ **(j)** $\frac{23}{24}$ **(k)** $\frac{8}{3}$ **(l)** $\frac{11}{20}$

5. (a) 58.9   **(b)** 553   **(c)** 0.162   **(d)** 2.06
    (e) 451   **(f)** 443   **(g)** 1160   **(h)** 83.0
    (i) 3.40   **(j)** 250

Display 1

1. 10.091   **2.** 1 024.917 769

3. 2.659 497 691   **4.** 20.935 267 86

5. 1211.27   **6.** 51.413 879 91

7. 1676.00   **8.** 12.0456

9. 1.104 311 872   **10.** 21.218 039 19

CHAPTER 1

Investigation

Exercise 1-1

1. (b) $\frac{1}{4}$ **2. (b)** $\frac{1}{6}$
3. (b) $\frac{1}{2}, \frac{1}{4}, \frac{1}{52}$.   **(c)** black card, ace of spades

Exercise 1-2

1. (a) 6   **(b)** 3   **(c)** $\frac{1}{2}$
2. (a) 7   **(b)** 3   **(c)** $\frac{3}{7}$
3. (a) $\frac{5}{9}$ **(b)** 3   **(c)** 6
4. (a) $\frac{1}{6}$ **(b)** $\frac{1}{6}$ **(c)** 0
5. (a) $\frac{1}{36}, \frac{2}{36}, \frac{3}{36}, \frac{4}{36}, \frac{5}{36}, \frac{6}{36}, \frac{5}{36}, \frac{4}{36}, \frac{3}{36}, \frac{2}{36}, \frac{1}{36}$.
    (b) Note the numerators.
6. (a) $\frac{1}{216}$ **(b)** $\frac{1}{36}$
7. (a) $\frac{1}{26}$ **(b)** $\frac{3}{13}$ **(c)** $\frac{1}{52}$ **(d)** $\frac{1}{13}$

8. (a) $\frac{3}{5}$ **(b)** $\frac{3}{10}$ **(c)** $\frac{1}{10}$ **(d)** $\frac{2}{5}$
(e) $\frac{7}{10}$ **(f)** $\frac{9}{10}$
9. $\frac{1}{2}$ **10.** $\frac{5}{12}$
11. (a) $\frac{1}{1000}$ **(b)** $\frac{1}{5000}$ **(c)** $\frac{1}{2500}$
12. (a) $\frac{1}{4}$ **(b)** $\frac{1}{2}$ **(c)** $\frac{1}{4}$
13. (a) $\frac{1}{2}$ **(b)** $\frac{1}{10}$ **(c)** $\frac{1}{5}$
14. (a) $\frac{1}{8}$ **(b)** $\frac{3}{8}$
15. $\frac{1}{8}$

Exercise 1-5

1. Mutually exclusive events are (a), (d), (g).
2. (a) $\frac{4}{5}$ **(b)** $\frac{1}{2}$ **(c)** $\frac{5}{7}$ **(d)** $\frac{5}{6}$
(e) $\frac{11}{18}$ **(f)** $\frac{3}{8}$ **(g)** $\frac{31}{50}$ **(h)** 1
3. (a) $\frac{1}{2}$ **(b)** $\frac{1}{10}$
4. $\frac{2}{13}$ **5.** $\frac{1}{6}, \frac{1}{18}, \frac{2}{9}$. **6.** $\frac{1}{9}$
7. (a) $\frac{3}{4}$ **(b)** $\frac{1}{4}$ **8.** $\frac{7}{10}$
9. $\frac{5}{18}, \frac{13}{18}$
10. (a) $\frac{5}{12}$ **(b)** $\frac{5}{12}$ **(c)** $\frac{5}{6}$
11. $\frac{2}{3}$
12. (a) $\frac{1}{64}$ **(b)** $\frac{3}{32}$ **(c)** $\frac{7}{64}$ **(d)** $\frac{11}{16}$
(e) $\frac{22}{64}$

Exercise 1-6

1. Independent events are (a), (c), (f).
2. (a) $\frac{1}{12}$ **(b)** $\frac{1}{10}$ **(c)** $\frac{1}{8}$ **(d)** $\frac{1}{90}$
(e) $\frac{1}{7}$ **(f)** $\frac{4}{21}$ **(g)** $\frac{1}{12}$ **(h)** $\frac{1}{1000}$
3. (a) No. **(b)** No. **4.** $\frac{1}{36}$ **5.** $\frac{1}{16}$
6. $\frac{1}{8}$ **7.** $\frac{8}{81}$ **8.** $\frac{1}{54\,872}$ **9.** $\frac{1}{48}$
10. 3 **11. (a)** 6 **(b)** 2 **(c)** 2
12. $\frac{1}{2\,400\,000}$ **13.** $\frac{1}{24}$ **14.** $\frac{12}{24}$ **15.** $\frac{21}{112}$

Review Exercise

1. (a) $\frac{1}{6}$ **(b)** $\frac{1}{36}$ **(c)** $\frac{1}{4}$ **(d)** $\frac{4}{11}$
2. (a) 1 **(b)** 0 **3.** $\frac{1}{2}$
4. (b) $\frac{3}{4}$ **5. (b)** $\frac{1}{12}$
6. (a) $\frac{1}{3}$ **(b)** $\frac{3}{4}$ **(c)** $\frac{7}{12}$ **(d)** $\frac{1}{11}$
(e) $\frac{1}{11}$ **(f)** $\frac{2}{11}$
7. (a) yes **(b)** $\frac{1}{6}, \frac{1}{6}$ **(c)** $\frac{1}{3}$ **(d)** 0
8. (a) yes **(b)** $\frac{1}{40}$
9. (a) $\frac{1}{2}$ **(b)** $\frac{1}{3}$ **(c)** 0
10. (a) $\frac{1}{16}$ **(b)** $\frac{1}{16}$ **(c)** $\frac{1}{8}$ **(d)** $\frac{3}{16}$
(e) $\frac{1}{4}$
11. (a) $\frac{1}{72}$ **(b)** $\frac{7}{18}$
12. $\frac{1}{6}, \frac{1}{3}, 0, \frac{1}{6}, \frac{1}{2}, \frac{1}{4}, \frac{1}{4}, \frac{1}{13}, \frac{1}{52}, \frac{3}{4}, \frac{1}{12}$ or $\frac{30}{365} = \frac{6}{73}, 0, \frac{5}{6}, \frac{1}{6}, \frac{1}{8}$.

REVIEW AND PREVIEW TO CHAPTER 2

1. 2.374 **2.** 9.182 **3.** 8.707 **4.** 11.38
5. 18.51 **6.** 27.54 **7.** 9.445 **8.** 6.879

9. 1.168   **10.** 2.095   **11.** 0.1204   **12.** 0.7662
13. 0.093 48   **14.** 0.029 00   **15.** 0.5849   **16.** 0.013 68
17. 2.171×10^2 **18.** 2.436×10^3 **19.** 3.379×10^3 **20.** 6.178×10^4
21. 2.392×10^{-1} **22.** 8.429×10^{-2} **23.** 9.430×10^{-3} **24.** 1.532×10^{-4}

Display 2

1. 6.480 446 927   **2.** 1.105 057 566
3. 0.037 201 101 9   **4.** 1.161 918 155
5. 0.909 467 648 7   **6.** 0.270 882 505 2
7. −1.656 274 98   **8.** 0.953 940 197 6
9. 2.097 039 474   **10.** −0.024 188 580 9

CHAPTER 2

Exercise 2-2

1. (a) 5.4   **(b)** 4.6   **(c)** 5.2   **(d)** 0.2   **(e)** 0.3
2. (a) 7   **(b)** 5.5   **(c)** 15   **(d)** 3   **(e)** 4
3. (a) 36   **(b)** 21   **(c)** 9   **(d)** 27   **(e)** −5, 0   **(f)** none
4. 24.7, 24, 24   **5.** 20.7 cm; bimodal 20 cm, 21 cm
6. 62.8 kg   **7. (a)** 1075.5   **(b)** 759   **8.** 162.2 cm

Exercise 2-3

2. (a) (i) 50th   (ii) 90th   (iii) 32.5th   **(b)** (i) 80th   (ii) 25th   (iii) 52nd
3. (a) (i) 20   (ii) 37   (iii) 6   **(b)** (i) 19th   (ii) 6th   (iii) 39th
4. (a) 94%, 80th   **(b)** 93%, 91st   **(c)** 47%, 40th   **(d)** 58%, 20th
     (e) 88%, 91st   **(f)** 88%, 88th
5. (a) 11th   **(b)** 67th   **(c)** 41st   **(d)** 116th
     (e) 44th   **(f)** 45th
6. (c) $M = 25.5$ **(d)** $P_{15} = 16.0$ $P_{95} = 43.2$
7. (b) $M = 161$ cm   **(c)** $P_{60} = 163.5$ $P_{80} = 168.3$
8. $Q_1 = 52.2$ kg $Q_z = M = 56.7$ kg $Q_3 = 61.4$ kg
9. $Q_1 = 156.1$ cm $Q_3 = 166.9$ cm

Exercise 2-4

1. (a) 6   **(b)** 5.9   **(c)** 10   **(d)** 7.0
     (e) 29.0   **(f)** 657
2. (a) 25 cm   **(b)** 48 kg   **(c)** 5°C   **(d)** 130 m
3. 2.2 m   **4.** 1.2   **5.** 16, 3.9
6. (a) 58.4 to 67.6   **(b)** 49.2 to 76.8
7. 7.8 cm
8. $A - 19, B - 147, C - 333, D - 333, E - 147, F - 19.$

Exercise 2-5

1. $12 673.80   **2.** 0.47 males   **3.** $268 536 (boys)
                             0.66 females $299 144 (girls)

Exercise 2-6

1. 0.5   **2. (a)** 0.1   **(b)** 0.9   **(c)** 0.77

3. (a) 5   **(b)** (i) $\frac{1}{2}$ (ii) $\frac{2}{9}$ (iii) $\frac{1}{42}$ (iv) $\frac{1}{252}$

5. $0.3n$, $0.9n$

Review Exercise

1. (a) 7   **(b)** 8   **(c)** 9   **(d)** 7

2. (a) 80th   **(b)** 225

4. $\bar{x} = 3.18$ g, $R = 0.31$ g, $S.D. = 0.07$ g

5. (a) 69.2   **(b)** 78.4

6. (a) $\frac{4}{5}$ **(b)** $\frac{1}{5}$

7. (a) $\frac{19}{30}$ **(b)** $\frac{11}{30}$

8. 4560

REVIEW AND PREVIEW TO CHAPTER 3

Exercise 1

1. (a) $2x - 6$ **(b)** $8a - 12b + 8c$ **(c)** $-3x + 9y$

     (d) $-10a + 15b + 5$ **(e)** $2x^2 + 6x$ **(f)** $-6m^2 + 4mn$

     (g) $-3x^3 + 6x^2 - 3x$ **(h)** $-6x^3y^2 + 9x^2y + 6x^2y^2$

2. (a) $x^2 - 5x + 6$ **(b)** $a^2 + 10a + 21$ **(c)** $4m^2 - 4m + 1$

     (d) $3x^2 + 19x + 20$ **(e)** $9x^2 - 4$ **(f)** $2a^2 + ab - 6b^2$

     (g) $12x^2 - 26xy + 10y^2$ **(h)** $6a^2 - 17ac - 14c^2$ **(i)** $x^2 - 14x + 49$

     (j) $4x^2 + 20x + 25$

3. (a) $2x^2 + 26x + 84$ **(b)** $3x^2 - 3x - 36$ **(c)** $-4a^2 + 10a + 6$

     (d) $4x^2 + 8xy - 12y^2$ **(e)** $2x^2 + 12x + 18$ **(f)** $-3x^2 + 24x - 48$

     (g) $-2x^2 - 8xy - 8y^2$ **(h)** $24a^2 - 68ab + 20b^2$

Exercise 2

1. (a) 240   **(b)** 160   **(c)** 60   **(d)** 58   **(e)** 2   **(f)** 2

2. (a) $l = \dfrac{V}{wh}$ **(b)** $T = \dfrac{D}{S}$ **(c)** $I = \dfrac{E}{R}$ **(d)** $l = \dfrac{P - 2w}{2}$

     (e) $a = \dfrac{2S - nl}{n}$ **(f)** $t = \dfrac{A - p}{pr}$ **(g)** $a = \dfrac{2(s - ut)}{t^2}$ **(h)** $x = \dfrac{2A - hy}{h}$

Display 3

1. 11.605 442 18   **2.** 0.090 781 592 4

3. 21.189 311 25   **4.** $-0.292\,888\,888\,9$

5. 5.506 793 113   **6.** 6.874 233 453

7. 2199.341 176   **8.** 0.044 776 258 9

9. $-0.673\,785\,449\,3$ **10.** $-3.569\,786\,535$

CHAPTER 3

Exercise 3-1

1. (a) $-2x - 26$
   (b) $-6a - 20b$
   (c) $4a - 16b + 21c$
   (d) $4x + 5y - 18$
   (e) $t^2 - 18t + 6$
   (f) 0
   (g) $3m^2 + 9mn$

2. (a) $2x^2 + 9x + 9$
   (b) $3x^2 + 7x + 2$
   (c) $5a^2 - 3a - 32$
   (d) $8b^2 - 25b + 2$
   (e) $-7x + 16$
   (f) $8m^2 - 12m - 12$
   (g) $-2x^2 + xy + y^2$
   (h) $3x^2 + 14x + 16$
   (i) $a^2 - 6ab + 11b^2$

3. (a) $x^3 + 2x^2 + 2x + 1$
   (b) $6x^3 - 13x^2 + 16x - 15$
   (c) $6a^3 - 8a^2 - 7a + 3$
   (d) $2x^3 - 13x^2 - x + 3$
   (e) $6b^4 - b^3 + 2b^2 - 6b - 4$
   (f) $x^4 - x^3 - 9x^2 - x + 2$

4. (a) $2x^2 + x$
   (b) $\frac{3}{2}a + \frac{3}{16}$
   (c) $2x^2 - 6x + \frac{17}{16}$
   (d) $-x^2 - \frac{3}{8}x + 1$

Exercise 3-2

1. (a) $3(x + 2)$
   (b) $x(3x + 5)$
   (c) $x(x^2 + 7)$
   (d) $x^2(x^2 + 7x + 5)$
   (e) $pm(pm - n)$
   (f) $3y(2y - 1)$
   (g) $6ab(4a - b)$
   (h) $5mnt(1 + 2m - 6mnt)$

2. (a) $(x + 3)(3x + 4)$
   (b) $(a - 7)(2a - 3)$
   (c) $(x - 1)(3x^2 - 4)$
   (d) $(a + 3)(5a + 1)$
   (e) $(t + 7)(6t + 5)$
   (f) $(x + 5)(2x - 1)$

3. (a) $(x + 2)(x + y)$
   (b) $(x + 5)(x + t)$
   (c) $(2x - 5)(x + y)$
   (d) $(5a + 4)(t + 1)$
   (e) $(x + 3)(x - y)$
   (f) $(3y - 2)(x - 1)$
   (g) $(2a - 3)(b - x)$
   (h) $(2x - 1)(2mx + 1)$

Exercise 3-3

1. (a) $(x + 4)(x + 3)$
   (b) $(x + 4)(x + 2)$
   (c) $(x - 3)(x - 2)$
   (d) $(x + 4)(x - 2)$
   (e) $(x - 5)(x + 2)$
   (f) $(x + 6)^2$
   (g) $(x - 2)(x + 1)$
   (h) $(x - 4)(x + 3)$
   (i) $(x + 4)(x - 3)$
   (j) $(x + 10)(x + 2)$

2. (a) $(x + 6)(x + 2)$
   (b) $(x - 9)(x - 4)$
   (c) $(x + 9)(x - 4)$
   (d) $(x + 8)(x + 2)$
   (e) $(x - 6)(x + 5)$
   (f) $(x + 9)(x - 3)$
   (g) $(x - 4)(x + 4)$
   (h) $(x - 3)(x + 3)$
   (i) $(x - 7)^2$
   (j) $(x - 5)(x + 5)$

3. (a) $(x + 4y)(x + 3y)$
   (b) $(x - 4y)(x + 3y)$
   (c) $(a - 4b)(a + b)$
   (d) $(p - 9q)(p + q)$
   (e) $(s + 2t)(s + t)$
   (f) $(c + 4d)(c - 3d)$
   (g) $(m - 3n)(m + 3n)$
   (h) $(ab - 1)^2$
   (i) $(x + 3y)(x + 6y)$
   (j) $(a - 5b)(a + 3b)$

4. (a) $4(a - 5)(a + 3)$
   (b) $3(b + 7)(b - 2)$
   (c) $6(c - 1)^2$
   (d) $5(d - 5)^2$
   (e) $2(e + 8)(e - 3)$
   (f) $x(1 - 3x)(1 - 2x)$
   (g) $4(a - 5)(a + 5)$
   (h) $2(x + 6)^2$
   (i) $7(a - 3)(a + 3)$
   (j) $a(x + 6)(x - 5)$

5. (a) $(x + \frac{1}{2})^2$
   (b) $(x - \frac{1}{2})^2$
   (c) $(x + \frac{1}{4})^2$
   (d) $(x - \frac{1}{2})(x + \frac{1}{4})$
   (e) $(x - \frac{1}{2})(x + \frac{1}{2})$
   (f) $(x - 1)(x + \frac{1}{6})$

Exercise 3-4

1. (a) $(2x + 5)(x + 1)$
   (b) $(3x + 1)(x + 2)$
   (c) $(2x + 5)(3x + 2)$
   (d) $(2x - 1)(x + 3)$
   (e) $(5x - 2)(x - 3)$
   (f) $(2x - 7)(x + 2)$
   (g) $(3x + 5)(2x + 3)$
   (h) $(2x + 3)(3x + 2)$
   (i) $(x - 1)(8x + 9)$
   (j) $(2x - 5)(5x + 2)$

2. (a) $(2x-1)(x+3)$ **(b)** $(5m-2)(m-3)$ **(c)** $(3x+1)(2x-5)$
   (d) $(3a-4b)(3a-2b)$ **(e)** $(5r-7)(3r-2)$ **(f)** $(2x+3y)(2x+y)$
   (g) $(7y-8x)(4y-x)$ **(h)** $(4x+y)(3x-2y)$ **(i)** $(3m+2n)(m-7n)$
   (j) $(5a+6b)(2a-5b)$

Exercise 3-5

1. (a) x^3 **(b)** x^2 **(c)** x **(d)** 1 **(e)** $3x^2$ **(f)** $6x^3$
   (g) $-6x$ **(h)** $-4x^2$ **(i)** $2x^2$ **(j)** -3 **(k)** x^2 **(l)** -2
2. (a) $(x+3)$ **(b)** $(x-6)$ **(c)** $(x-3)$
   (d) $(x+3)$ **(e)** $(x-2), R: -1$ **(f)** $(x-4), R: -3$
3. (a) $(3x-10), R: 13$ **(b)** $(x^2-2x-3), R: 12$ **(c)** $(3a-2)$
   (d) $(p^2-p+1), R: 1$ **(e)** $(3c^2-2c-5)$
4. (a) (y^2-14y) **(b)** (p^2-2p+1) **(c)** $(x^2+5x-13), R: -75$
   (d) $(a+2)$
5. $(a-2)(a+2)$
6. (a) x^2-3x+9 **(b)** 0 **(c)** $(x+3)(x^2-3x+9)$
7. $(y-4)(y^2+4y+16)$
8. (a) $(a+2)(a^2-2a+4)$ **(b)** $(a-2)(a^2+2a+4)$ **(c)** $(x+1)(x^2-x+1)$
   (d) $(x-1)(x^2+x+1)$ **(e)** $(b-5)(b^2+5b+25)$ **(f)** $(b+5)(b^2-5b+25)$
9. (a) Yes.   **(b)** No.   **(c)** Yes.   **(d)** No.

Exercise 3-6

1. (a) 0 **(b)** -5 **(c)** 0 **(d)** -1
   (e) $3, 4$ **(f)** $-1, -2$ **(g)** $\frac{1}{2}$ **(h)** 3
   (i) $4, -1$ **(j)** -7
2. (a) $\frac{12}{18}$ **(b)** $\frac{1}{5}$ **(c)** $\frac{20}{24}$
   (d) $\frac{18}{42}$ **(e)** $\dfrac{4a}{5a}$ **(f)** $\dfrac{4x^2}{5xy}$
   (g) $\dfrac{2(x+1)}{3(x+1)}$ **(h)** $\dfrac{2(x-3)}{5(x-3)}$ **(i)** $\dfrac{(x+3)(x-9)}{(x-7)(x-9)}$
3. (a) $\dfrac{1}{3a}$ **(b)** $2y$ **(c)** $4ab$ **(d)** $2x+3y$
   (e) $2b-3c$ **(f)** $\dfrac{x}{y-4t}$ **(g)** $\dfrac{x}{2y+3t}$ **(h)** 3
   (i) $\dfrac{a}{3}$ **(j)** $\dfrac{(x+2)}{(x^2-3)}$ **(k)** $\dfrac{1}{(x-2)}$ **(l)** $\dfrac{a}{(a-7)}$
4. (a) $\dfrac{(x+3)}{(x+2)}$ **(b)** $\dfrac{(x+3)}{(x+5)}$ **(c)** $\dfrac{(y+1)}{(y+3)}$ **(d)** $\dfrac{(x+2)}{(x-2)}$
   (e) $\dfrac{(m+3)}{m}$ **(f)** $\dfrac{(3k+4)}{(3k-4)}$ **(g)** $\dfrac{(3x+1)}{(2x-3)}$ **(h)** $\dfrac{(2m-1)}{(m-4)}$

Exercise 3-7

1. (a) $\frac{2}{5}$ **(b)** $\frac{5}{28}$ **(c)** $\frac{15}{7}$ **(d)** $-\frac{3}{8}$
   (e) $\frac{8}{15}$ **(f)** $\frac{3}{2}$ **(g)** $\frac{5}{4}$ **(h)** $\frac{8}{9}$
2. (a) $\dfrac{2b}{3}$ **(b)** $\frac{10}{3}$ **(c)** -1 **(d)** 2 **(e)** $\dfrac{2b}{3}$ **(f)** -1
3. (a) $\frac{1}{14}$ **(b)** $-\frac{1}{5}$ **(c)** $\dfrac{4x^3}{15y^2}$ **(d)** $(a+b)$
   (e) 1 **(f)** 1 **(g)** $\dfrac{(a+3)(a+2)}{a(a-3)}$

4. (a) $\frac{5}{4}$ **(b)** $\frac{5}{6y}$ **(c)** $\frac{3}{2}$ **(d)** $4b^2x$

(e) $\frac{2(x-2)}{(x+4)}$ **(f)** $\frac{(a-2)^2}{a(a+1)}$ **(g)** $\frac{(a-6)}{(a-3)}$ **(h)** $\frac{b(x-y)}{ax}$

5. (a) $\frac{x}{x-1}$ **(b)** $\frac{(x-2)(x-3)}{(x-4)(x-1)}$ **(c)** $\frac{(a+1)}{(a-2)}$

(d) 1 **(e)** $\frac{1}{2}$

Exercise 3-8

1. (a) $\frac{5}{7}$ **(b)** $\frac{3}{13}$ **(c)** $2x$ **(d)** $\frac{4}{x}$

(e) $\frac{5}{2a}$ **(f)** $\frac{10m}{3}$ **(g)** $\frac{6a}{5}$ **(h)** $\frac{6}{(y-1)}$

(i) $\frac{4}{(x+1)}$ **(j)** $\frac{10}{(a+3)}$ **(k)** $\frac{4}{(a+b)}$ **(l)** $\frac{(a-b)}{(x+y)}$

2. (a) $\frac{23x}{21}$ **(b)** $\frac{19a}{10}$ **(c)** m **(d)** $-\frac{13x}{24}$

(e) $\frac{13x}{30}$ **(f)** $\frac{4a-33b}{22}$ **(g)** $\frac{35d+6c}{14}$ **(h)** $\frac{9a+8b-10c}{12}$

3. (a) $\frac{3y+4x}{xy}$ **(b)** $\frac{5b+2a}{ab}$ **(c)** $\frac{7n-3m}{mn}$

(d) $\frac{4n+15m}{6mn}$ **(e)** $\frac{9b-20a}{12ab}$ **(f)** $\frac{x^2+y^2}{xy}$

(g) $\frac{az+bx}{xyz}$ **(h)** $\frac{bcx+acy-abz}{abc}$

4. (a) $\frac{7x+29}{12}$ **(b)** $\frac{7x+9}{10}$ **(c)** $\frac{2a-27}{15}$ **(d)** $\frac{-m+47}{30}$

(e) $-\frac{b}{6}$ **(f)** $\frac{22a+3}{20}$ **(g)** $\frac{-5x-30y}{18}$ **(h)** $\frac{9c-b}{6}$

5. (a) $\frac{7x+16}{(x+3)(x+2)}$ **(b)** $\frac{8a+1}{(a-1)(a+2)}$ **(c)** $\frac{m-13}{(m+3)(m-1)}$

(d) $\frac{3b-23}{(b+4)(b-3)}$ **(e)** $\frac{2x^2+x-5}{(x+1)(x-1)}$ **(f)** $\frac{2m^2-9m+7}{(m+1)(m-2)}$

(g) $\frac{6}{(x-2)(x-5)}$ **(h)** $\frac{12a-6}{(a-3)(a+3)}$

6. (a) $\frac{5x+5}{(x-4)(x-3)(x-2)}$ **(b)** $\frac{x-27}{(x+5)(x+2)(x-3)}$ **(c)** $\frac{3a+7}{(a+4)(a+3)(a+3)}$

(d) $\frac{-a^2+4a}{(a+2)(a-2)}$ **(e)** $\frac{2xy}{(x-y)(x+y)}$ **(f)** $\frac{-a^2+5a+2}{(a-1)(a+1)}$

(g) $\frac{x+5y+7}{(x-y)(x+y)}$ **(h)** $\frac{2a^2b}{a(a-b)(a+b)}$

7. $\frac{R_1R_2}{R_1+R_2}$

8. $\frac{R_1R_2R_3}{R_2R_3+R_1R_3+R_1R_2}$ **9.** $R(1+i)^2+R(1+i)+R$

Review Exercise

1. (a) $-x+26$ **(b)** $-a^2-11a-14$ **(c)** $-x^2+4x+13$

(d) $3a^2 - 16a - 12$ **(e)** $-x^2 - 8x + 26$ **(f)** $2x^3 + 5x^2 - 11x + 4$

(g) 8 **(h)** $2x^2 + \frac{7}{4}x - \frac{3}{2}$

2. (a) $3(x + 5)$ **(b)** $a(x + y - 1)$

   (c) $(x - 2)(x + 1)$ **(d)** $(x - y)(x + y)$

   (e) $(a - 4)(a - 3)$ **(f)** $(a - 4)(a + 3)$

   (g) $(x + 9)(x - 4)$ **(h)** $(x - 8)(x + 8)$

   (i) $(4p - 5q)(4p + 5q)$ **(j)** $2(x + 6)(x + 2)$

   (k) $x(x - 7)(x - 8)$ **(l)** $(p - 1)(p^2 + p + 1)$

   (m) $(a - 3)(a^2 + 3a + 9)$ **(n)** $(x + 2)(2x + 5)$

   (o) $(m + n)(m^2 - mn + n^2)$ **(p)** $(a + 4)(a^2 - 4a + 16)$

   (q) $(2a + 3b)(2a + b)$ **(r)** $(5x - 7)(3x - 2)$

   (s) $(x + 6y)(5x - 8y)$ **(t)** $(3m - 7)(3m - 2)$

3. (a) $6y$ **(b)** $4ab^2$ **(c)** $a - 2$

   (d) $\frac{4}{3}$ **(e)** $\frac{(x + 2)}{(x + 3)}$ **(f)** $\frac{(x + 3)}{(x - 3)}$

   (g) $\frac{x}{(x + 3)}$ **(h)** $\frac{(3x + 4)}{(3x - 4)}$ **(i)** $\frac{(4x + 1)}{(2x + 1)}$

4. (a) $\frac{a}{b}$ **(b)** $\frac{3x^3}{2y}$ **(c)** 2 **(d)** $\frac{(x - 4)}{(x + 5)}$

   (e) $\frac{(x - 4)}{(x + 2)}$ **(f)** 1 **(g)** $\frac{5(x + 5)}{(x + 1)(x - 2)}$

5. (a) $\frac{9x + 8y}{6}$ **(b)** $\frac{10a - 3b}{6}$ **(c)** $\frac{3n - 2m}{mn}$

   (d) $\frac{2bc + 3ac - 2ab}{abc}$ **(e)** $\frac{19x + 1}{6}$ **(f)** $\frac{13b}{12}$

   (g) $\frac{6x^2 + 22x + 18}{(x + 1)(x + 2)(x + 3)}$ **(h)** $\frac{(x - 4)}{(x - 1)(x - 2)}$ **(i)** $\frac{2x^2 + 8x + 7}{(x + 3)(x + 2)}$

   (j) $\frac{x - 12}{(x - 4)(x + 3)(x - 2)}$ **(k)** $\frac{-x^2 + 30}{(x - 5)^2}$ **(l)** $\frac{(x + 2)}{(x - 1)}$

REVIEW AND PREVIEW TO CHAPTER 4

Exercise 1

1. (a) 2 **(b)** -6 **(c)** 5 **(d)** 2

   (e) 6 **(f)** $\frac{21}{2}$ **(g)** $\frac{5}{2}$ **(h)** 6

2. (a) -6 **(b)** 12 **(c)** 12 **(d)** $\frac{19}{11}$ **(e)** -2

   (f) 15 **(g)** $-\frac{6}{13}$ **(h)** $-\frac{7}{3}$ **(i)** $\frac{13}{3}$ **(j)** $\frac{3}{2}$

3. (a) $-\frac{3}{4}$ **(b)** 8 **(c)** $\frac{2}{3}$ **(d)** $-\frac{5}{8}$

Exercise 2

1. (a) 21 **(b)** 9 **(c)** $\frac{24}{5}$ **(d)** $-\frac{70}{11}$ **(e)** 2

   (f) $-\frac{19}{27}$ **(g)** -17 **(h)** $\frac{23}{9}$ **(i)** $-\frac{2}{5}$ **(j)** $\frac{9}{13}$

2. (a) $-\frac{5}{2}$ **(b)** $-\frac{1}{8}$ **(c)** -1 **(d)** $-\frac{5}{6}$

   (e) $-\frac{2}{5}$ **(f)** 7 **(g)** $\frac{1}{2}$ **(h)** $\frac{7}{8}$

Display 4

1. $-0.331\,477\,235\,5$

2. $2.120\,743\,034$

3. $1.510\,003\,962$

4. $0.143\,673\,236\,2$

5. -0.475

6. $-16.406\,976\,74$

7. $-0.113\,838\,341\,1$

8. $3.000\,678\,541$

9. $0.546\,802\,900\,5$

10. $-0.629\,587\,803\,5$

CHAPTER 4

Exercise 4-1

1. (a) $2, -3$ (b) $-1, -2$ (c) $3, 4$ (d) $-5, 4$ (e) $0, -4$ (f) $0, 3$
2. (a) $3, 4$ (b) $3, -2$ (c) $-3, -1$ (d) $-5, 2$
   (e) $5, -3$ (f) $-3, -3$ (g) $5, 4$ (h) $4, 4$
   (i) $-7, 3$ (j) $-6, 5$ (k) $-3, -1$ (l) $-4, 2$
3. (a) $-2, 2$ (b) $-7, 7$ (c) $-5, 5$ (d) $-8, 8$
   (e) $-10, 10$ (f) $-9, 9$ (g) $-6, 6$ (h) $-3, 3$
4. (a) $7, 3$ (b) $4, -2$ (c) $\frac{7}{3}, -1$ (d) $-\frac{2}{3}, -\frac{1}{2}$
   (e) $\frac{1}{3}, -\frac{1}{3}$ (f) $0, \frac{5}{3}$ (g) $-2, 2$ (h) $0, 7$
   (i) $\frac{3}{2}, -\frac{3}{2}$ (j) $\frac{14}{3}, -1$ (k) $-\frac{5}{2}, -1$ (l) $\frac{2}{5}, 3$
   (m) $\frac{7}{2}, -2$ (n) $-\frac{2}{3}, -\frac{3}{2}$ (o) $-\frac{2}{5}, \frac{5}{2}$ (p) $\frac{7}{5}, \frac{2}{3}$
5. 7 cm
6. $3\sqrt{2}$ cm

Exercise 4-3

1. (a) $a = 2, b = 3, c = 4$ (b) $a = 3, b = -5, c = 2$ (c) $a = 1, b = 7, c = -1$
   (d) $a = 4, b = -1, c = -3$ (e) $a = 5, b = -3, c = 0$ (f) $a = 1, b = 0, c = -25$
   (g) $a = 1, b = 5, c = -16$ (h) $a = 2, b = -3, c = -4$ (i) $a = 2, b = -5, c = 3$
   (j) $a = 3, b = 0, c = 17$

2. (a) $3, 4$

   (b) $\dfrac{3+\sqrt{6}}{3}, \dfrac{3-\sqrt{6}}{3}$

   (c) $7, -1$

   (d) $11, -8$

   (e) $1, \frac{2}{3}$

   (f) $\dfrac{3+\sqrt{11}}{2}, \dfrac{3-\sqrt{11}}{2}$

   (g) $\dfrac{-3+\sqrt{15}}{3}, \dfrac{-3-\sqrt{15}}{3}$

   (h) $\dfrac{1+2\sqrt{2}}{7}, \dfrac{1-2\sqrt{2}}{7}$

   (i) $\dfrac{-5+\sqrt{17}}{4}, \dfrac{-5-\sqrt{17}}{4}$

   (j) $1, 1$

   (k) $\dfrac{+\sqrt{22}}{3}, \dfrac{-\sqrt{22}}{3}$

   (l) $7, \frac{11}{2}$

   (m) $3, -3$

   (n) $0, 5$

3. (a) $-2.62, -0.38$ (b) $4.19, -1.19$ (c) $4.79, 0.21$ (d) $2.35, -0.85$
   (e) $1.58, -1.58$ (f) $2.14, -0.47$ (g) $1.88, 0.32$ (h) $1, 0.17$
4. (a) $3, 2$ (b) $3, -1$

   (c) $1+\sqrt{3}, 1-\sqrt{3}$

   (d) $\dfrac{-1+\sqrt{1201}}{40}, \dfrac{-1-\sqrt{1201}}{40}$

   (e) $-\frac{3}{2}, 5$

   (f) $4, 7$

(g) $\dfrac{-3+\sqrt{39}}{3}, \dfrac{-3-\sqrt{39}}{3}$ **(h)** $\dfrac{1+\sqrt{2}}{2}, \dfrac{1-\sqrt{2}}{2}$

(i) $\dfrac{2+\sqrt{14}}{2}, \dfrac{2-\sqrt{14}}{2}$ **(j)** $\dfrac{15+3\sqrt{5}}{10}, \dfrac{15-3\sqrt{5}}{10}$

(k) $0, -\frac{7}{2}$ **(l)** $+\sqrt{5}, -\sqrt{5}$

(m) $-5, 2$ **(n)** $-2+\sqrt{3}, -2-\sqrt{3}$

5. (a) $2, -\frac{1}{2}$ **(b)** $-\frac{5}{2}, -\frac{1}{2}$

(c) $-1+\sqrt{10}, -1-\sqrt{10}$ **(d)** $\frac{1}{2}, -1$

Exercise 4-4

1. (a) 0; two equal real roots   **(b)** 12; two distinct real roots

(c) −8; two non-real roots   **(d)** 13; two distinct real roots

(e) −27; two non-real roots   **(f)** 0; two equal real roots

2. (a) 12; two distinct real roots   **(b)** −23; two non-real roots

(c) 0; two equal real roots   **(d)** −4; two non-real roots

(e) 196; two distinct real roots   **(f)** 0; two equal real roots

(g) 64; two distinct real roots   **(h)** 25; two distinct real roots

(i) −127; two non-real roots   **(j)** −24; two non-real roots

(k) 12; two distinct real roots   **(l)** 0; two equal real roots

3. (a) non-real roots   **(d)** non-real roots

Exercise 4-5

1. (a) $x+(x+1)+(x+2)$ **(b)** $x+x^2$ **(c)** x^2-2x

(d) $x^2+(x+1)^2$ **(e)** $2x^2$ **(f)** $(x+3)^2$

(g) $\dfrac{100}{x}$ **(h)** $3x$

2. 7, 8 and −7, −8   **3.** 9, 10, 11 and −9, −10, −11

4. 14, 15, 16, 17 and −14, −15, −16, −17

5. 3, 11 or −3, −11   **6.** 6, 7   **7.** 4, 13

8. 6 cm × 6 cm and 9 cm × 9 cm

9. 12 cm × 16 cm   **10.** 8 cm × 12 cm   **11.** 14 cm

12. 5.5 cm × 8 cm   **13.** 0.5 cm   **14.** 15 km/h, 20 km/h

15. 30 km/h, 40 km/h   **16.** 35 km/h, 50 km/h   **17.** 50 km/h, 55 km/h

Review Exercise

1. (a) −3, −4   **(b)** 7, −3   **(c)** 3, 3   **(d)** 9, −2

(e) 6, −6   **(f)** 7, −6   **(g)** $-\frac{1}{2}, 2$ **(h)** $-\frac{3}{2}, -4$

(i) $\frac{2}{3}, 1$ **(j)** $-\frac{4}{3}, \frac{1}{2}$ **(k)** $\frac{1}{5}, -\frac{3}{2}$ **(l)** $-6, -\frac{1}{6}$

2. (a) $\dfrac{-1+\sqrt{5}}{2}, \dfrac{-1-\sqrt{5}}{2}$ **(b)** $-\frac{1}{16}, 1$ **(c)** $2, -1$

(d) $-\frac{1}{2}, 1$ **(e)** $\dfrac{5+\sqrt{21}}{2}, \dfrac{5-\sqrt{21}}{2}$ **(f)** $\dfrac{3+\sqrt{69}}{5}, \dfrac{3-\sqrt{69}}{5}$

(g) $\dfrac{-1+\sqrt{11}}{10}, \dfrac{-1-\sqrt{11}}{10}$ **(h)** $-\frac{4}{9}, \frac{4}{3}$ **(i)** $\frac{1}{5}, -\frac{2}{3}$

(j) $\dfrac{+\sqrt{21}}{3}, \dfrac{-\sqrt{21}}{3}$ **(k)** 0, 4 **(l)** $\dfrac{3+\sqrt{37}}{2}, \dfrac{3-\sqrt{37}}{2}$

3. **(a)** -83; two non-real roots   **(b)** 0; two equal real roots
   (c) 400; two distinct real roots   **(d)** 0; two equal real roots
   (e) 65; two distinct real roots   **(f)** 53; two distinct real roots
4. 8, 9, 10 and $-8, -9, -10$ 5. 12, 7 and $-12, -7$
6. 16 cm $\times$ 11 cm   7. 8 cm $\times$ 8 cm and 9 cm $\times$ 9 cm
8. 50 km/h and 60 km/h   9. 10 km/h

REVIEW AND PREVIEW TO CHAPTER 5

1. **(a)** Yes.   **(b)** No.   **(c)** No.   **(d)** Yes.
   (e) No.   **(f)** No.   **(g)** Yes.   **(h)** No.
2. **(a)** Yes.   **(b)** No.   **(c)** No.   **(d)** Yes.
   (e) Yes.   **(f)** No.   **(g)** Yes.   **(h)** Yes.

Display 5

1. 0.192 471 512 7, 1.998 297 718

2. 0.691 616 469 2, -0.736 191 309 6

3. 0.910 579 990 9, -2.447 050 579

4. -0.157 134 894 1, -3.818 375 31

5. 0.297 832 477 7, -5.567 735 39

CHAPTER 5

Exercise 5-1

1. (a), (c), (e).   2. (b), (d), (f), (g).
3. **(a)** $a=2, b=3, c=7$ **(b)** $a=-3, b=-4, c=3$ **(c)** $a=1, b=0, c=5$
   (d) $a=-2, b=6, c=0$ **(e)** $a=1, b=3, c=-4$ **(f)** $a=2, b=10, c=0$
   (g) $a=2, b=6, c=-3$ **(h)** $a=1, b=-2, c=3$
4. **(a)** $k \in R, k \neq 0$ **(b)** $k \in R$ **(c)** $k=2$
   (d) $k=0, 1, 2$ **(e)** $k \in R, k \neq 3$ **(f)** $k \in R$

Exercise 5-5

1. **(a)** $(x+3)^2$ **(b)** $(x+2)^2$ **(c)** $(x+4)^2$ **(d)** $(x-2)^2$ **(e)** $(x-5)^2$
   (f) $(x+7)^2$ **(g)** $(x-3)^2$ **(h)** $(x-1)^2$ **(i)** $(x+\frac{1}{2})^2$
2. **(a)** 9   **(b)** 4   **(c)** 1   **(d)** 16   **(e)** 36
   (f) 25   **(g)** 100   **(h)** 81   **(i)** 64
3. **(a)** $\frac{25}{4}$ **(b)** $\frac{49}{4}$ **(c)** $\frac{9}{4}$ **(d)** $\frac{121}{4}$ **(e)** $\frac{1}{4}$ **(f)** $\frac{1}{4}$
   (g) $\frac{4}{25}$ **(h)** $\frac{1}{36}$ **(i)** $\frac{1}{16}$ **(j)** $\frac{9}{64}$ **(k)** $\frac{1}{49}$ **(l)** $\frac{25}{144}$

4. **(a)** $y = (x+3)^2 - 2$ **(b)** $y = (x-2)^2 - 1$ **(c)** $y = (x+4)^2 - 29$
   (d) $y = (x-5)^2 - 4$ **(e)** $y = (x+1)^2 + 2$ **(f)** $y = (x-6)^2 - 40$
   (g) $y = (x-7)^2 - 52$ **(h)** $y = (x+10)^2 - 100$
5. **(a)** $y = 2(x+1)^2 + 5$ **(b)** $y = 3(x-2)^2 - 14$ **(c)** $y = 2(x+4)^2 - 24$
   (d) $y = -2(x+2)^2 + 3$ **(e)** $y = -3(x-1)^2 + 2$ **(f)** $y = -4(x+2)^2 + 17$
6. **(a)** $y = 2(x+\frac{3}{2})^2 + \frac{5}{2}$ **(b)** $y = 3(x-\frac{5}{2})^2 - \frac{59}{4}$ **(c)** $y = -3(x+\frac{1}{3})^2 + \frac{22}{3}$
   (d) $y = 6(x-\frac{5}{12})^2 + \frac{23}{24}$ **(e)** $y = -4(x-\frac{5}{8})^2 + \frac{9}{16}$ **(f)** $y = 4(x-\frac{5}{4})^2 - \frac{13}{4}$
7. **(a)** $y = 2(x-\frac{7}{2}) - \frac{25}{2}$ **(b)** $x = \frac{7}{2}$
   (c) $(\frac{7}{2}, -\frac{25}{2})$ **(d)** minimum
8. **(a)** $y = -2(x-\frac{5}{4})^2 - \frac{7}{8}$ **(b)** $x = \frac{5}{4}, (\frac{5}{4}, -\frac{7}{8})$ **(c)** maximum
9. **(a)** $(-1, -3), x = -1$ **(b)** maximum

Exercise 5-6

1. **(a)** $3, 2$ **(b)** $3, -4$ **(c)** $3, -6$ **(d)** $4, 12$ **(e)** $2, 5$ **(f)** $5, 3$
2. **(a)** $-3, -4; 12$ **(b)** $-3, -2; 6$ **(c)** $-3, 4; -12$
   (d) $-5, 3; -15$ **(e)** $-5, -2; -10$ **(f)** $-2, 6; 12$
   (g) $2, 6; -12$ **(h)** $0, 7; 0$ **(i)** $-4, \frac{3}{2}; -12$
   (j) $-\frac{1}{2}, 2; -2$ **(k)** $-4+\sqrt{7}, -4-\sqrt{7}; 9$ **(l)** $-\frac{3}{4}, 2; -6$
3. **(a)** 1 **(b)** 2
4. **(a)** (i) $-1, -1$ (ii) $\frac{3}{2}, \frac{3}{2}$ **(b)** Two equal x-intercepts
5. **(a)** (i) $\dfrac{-1+\sqrt{-3}}{2}, \dfrac{-1-\sqrt{-3}}{2}$ (ii) $\dfrac{-5+\sqrt{-23}}{8}, \dfrac{-5-\sqrt{-23}}{8}$
   (b) No real intercepts.
6. **(a)** (i) vertex: $(-2, 0)$, y-int: 4, x-int: -2
   (ii) vertex: $(-2, -9)$, y-int: -5, x-int: $-5, 1$ (iii) vertex: $(-2, 3)$, y-int: 7
   (b) minimum value **(c)** (i) 0 (ii) -9 (iii) 3

Exercise 5-7

1. **(a)** minimum of 0 when $x = 0$ **(b)** maximum of 0 when $x = 0$
   (c) minimum of 2 when $x = 0$ **(d)** minimum of -4 when $x = 0$
   (e) maximum of 7 when $x = 0$ **(f)** maximum of -6 when $x = 0$
   (g) minimum of 11 when $x = 0$ **(h)** maximum of -5 when $x = 0$
2. **(a)** minimum of 3 when $x = 2$ **(b)** minimum of -4 when $x = -3$
   (c) maximum of -4 when $x = 3$ **(d)** maximum of 10 when $x = -1$
   (e) minimum of -18 when $x = -3$ **(f)** maximum of -2 when $x = 5$
   (g) minimum of 4 when $x = 1$ **(h)** maximum of -5 when $x = -2$
3. **(a)** minimum of -2 when $x = -3$ **(b)** minimum of -3 when $x = 2$
   (c) maximum of -2 when $x = -1$ **(d)** minimum of -13 when $x = -3$
   (e) maximum of -1 when $x = 1$ **(f)** minimum of $-\frac{25}{8}$ when $x = -\frac{3}{4}$
   (g) maximum of 18 when $x = \frac{5}{2}$ **(h)** minimum of $-\frac{4}{3}$ when $x = -\frac{2}{3}$

Exercise 5-8

1. **(a)** $x, 20-x$ **(b)** $x, 33-x$ **(c)** $x, 100-x$ **(d)** $x, 200-x$ **(e)** $x, 600-2x$
2. $7, 7$ 3. $7, 7$ 4. $100 \text{ m} \times 100 \text{ m}$ 5. 20 m
6. $200 \text{ m} \times 400 \text{ m}$ 7. 100 cm^2 8. 5 cm 9. $\frac{200}{3} \text{ m} \times 100 \text{ m}$

Exercise 5-9

1. **(b)** x-int: $-\frac{2}{3}$, y-int: 2 **(c)** No.
2. **(b)** x-ints: $2, -2$, y-int: -12 **(c)** minimum of -12 when $x = 0$
3. **(b)** x-ints: $-1, 1, 3$, y-int: 3 **(c)** 3

(d) $-1, 1, 3$ **(e)** no

5. (b) x-ints: $-2, 0, 2, 4$, y-int: 0 **(c)** 4

(d) $-2, 0, 2, 4$ **(e)** minimum of -15, when $x = -1$ or 3

Review Exercise

1. (b) $(0, 0)$, $x = 0$

(d) (i) $(0, 0)$, $x = 0$ (ii) $(0, 2)$, $x = 0$ (iii) $(-3, 0)$, $x = -3$ (iv) $(1, 5)$, $x = 1$

2. (a) $(0, 2)$, minimum   **(b)** $(-3, -4)$, minimum

(c) $(2, 5)$, maximum   **(d)** $(-5, -7)$, maximum

3. (a) $y = 2(x - \frac{3}{2})^2 + \frac{9}{2}$ **(b)** $y = -3(x - \frac{3}{2})^2 - \frac{1}{4}$ **(c)** $y = (x + 1)^2 + 7$

(d) $y = 2(x + 1)^2 + 2$ **(e)** $y = (x + 1)^2 - 7$ **(f)** $y = -\frac{1}{2}(x + 2)^2 + \frac{7}{3}$

4. (a) minimum of $\frac{9}{2}$ when $x = \frac{3}{2}$ **(b)** maximum of $-\frac{1}{4}$ when $x = \frac{3}{2}$

(c) minimum of 7 when $x = -1$ **(d)** minimum of 2 when $x = -1$

(e) minimum of -7 when $x = -1$ **(f)** maximum of $\frac{7}{3}$ when $x = -2$

6. $150 \text{ m} \times 150 \text{ m}$

7. (a) minimum of $-\frac{15}{2}$ **(b)** maximum of $\frac{57}{8}$

(c) maximum of 9 **(d)** minimum of $-\frac{25}{3}$

REVIEW AND PREVIEW TO CHAPTER 6

Exercise 1

1. (a) 5 **(b)** 7 **(c)** 3 **(d)** -1 **(e)** -5 **(f)** 21

2. (a) -2 **(b)** 1 **(c)** -5 **(d)** 3 **(e)** $\frac{1}{2}$ **(f)** $\frac{1}{2}a - 3$

3. (a) 5 **(b)** 8 **(c)** 8 **(d)** 68 **(e)** $\frac{17}{4}$ **(f)** $x^2 + 4$

4. (a) 3 **(b)** 5 **(c)** $2^a + 1$

5. (a) 3 **(b)** 11 **(c)** 27

6. (a) -9 **(b)** -25 **(c)** -20

(d) $-3m^2 + 2m - 4$ **(e)** -4 **(f)** -5

Exercise 2

1. (a) $x = 5, y = 2$ **(b)** $x = 6, y = -2$ **(c)** $a = -1, d = 4$

(d) $a = 18, d = -7$ **(e)** $a = 20, d = -10$ **(f)** $x = -2, y = -3$

(g) $x = 4, y = -3$ **(h)** $x = -3, y = 5$

Display 6

1. 0.0000
0.0225
0.0900
0.2025
0.2500
0.3600
0.5625
0.8100
1.0000

2. 0.0000
0.0005
0.0081
0.0410
0.0625
0.1296
0.3164
0.6561
1.0000

CHAPTER 6

Exercise 6-1

1. (a) 3, 5, 7   (b) 10, 16, 22   (c) 190, 180, 170   (d) $-3, 0, 3$
   (e) 3, 8, 15   (f) 3, 9, 27   (g) 4, 8, 16   (h) 10, 20, 40
   (i) 6, 12, 20
2. (a) $t_4 = 10, t_5 = 13$ (b) $t_4 = 17, t_5 = 22$ (c) $t_4 = 24, t_5 = 48$
   (d) $t_4 = 64, t_5 = 256$ (e) $t_4 = 16, t_5 = 25$ (f) $t_4 = -2, t_5 = -5$
   (g) $t_4 = 2, t_5 = 1$ (h) $t_4 = 54, t_5 = 162$ (i) $t_4 = 5, t_5 = 3$
3. (a) 1, 3, 6, 10, 15, 21; 1, 4, 9, 16, 25, 36; 1, 5, 12, 22, 35, 51.
   (b) 2, 3, 4, 5, 6; 3, 5, 7, 9, 11; 4, 7, 10, 13, 16
   Each sequence is formed by adding a constant to the previous term. Hexagonal numbers $= \{1, 6, 15, 28, 49\}$; set of differences $= \{5, 9, 13, 17\}$; the property holds.
4. 2, 3, 5, 7, 11, 13, 17, 19, 23, 29; NO.

Exercise 6-2

1. (a) $d = 5$ (b) $d = -4$ (d) $d = -3$ (g) $d = \frac{1}{2}$ (i) $d = x^2$
2. (a) $t_{12} = 30, t_{33} = 72$ (b) $t_{16} = 69, t_{51} = 209$
   (c) $t_{30} = 213, t_n = 7n + 3$ (d) $t_{25} = 84, t_n = 4n - 16$
   (e) $t_{11} = -54, t_k = 12 - 6k$ (f) $t_{12} = a + 22b, t_{41} = a + 80b$
   (g) $t_8 = 3x + 8y, t_{21} = 3x + 21y$ (h) $t_9 = 4m - 18k, t_{16} = 4m - 32k$
3. (a) $a = 7, d = 3, t_n = 3n + 4$ (b) $a = 2, d = 5, t_n = 5n - 3$
   (c) $a = 44, d = 2, t_n = 2n + 42$ (d) $a = -19, d = 7, t_n = 7n - 26$
   (e) $a = 67, d = -5, t_n = 72 - 5n$ (f) $a = -8, d = -3, t_n = -3n - 5$
   (g) $a = 3, d = -10, t_n = 13 - 10n$ (h) $a = 3 + 3k, d = 2k, t_n = 3 + k + 2kn$
4. (a) 49   (b) 41   (c) 12   (d) 11   (e) 31
   (f) 61   (g) 28   (h) 49   (i) 95   (j) 89
5. $105, $110, $115, $120, $(100 + 5n), a = $105, d = 5$
6. $856, $912, $968, $1024, $(800 + 56n), a = $856, d = $56, A = 1472
7. The points will lie on a straight line.

Exercise 6-3

1. (a) 324   (b) 1750   (c) 350   (d) 1638   (e) 50
   (f) -55 (g) $-20\,200$ (h) $-15\,300$ (i) 1250   (j) 63
2. (a) $20\,200$ (b) 7155   (c) 400   (d) 42
   (e) 399   (f) -3630 (g) $130\frac{1}{2}$ (h) -62.5
3. 78
4. The second by $7.50
5. (a) $\dfrac{n(n + 1)}{2}$ (b) 5050   (c) 6270
6. 816

Exercise 6-4

1. (a) $r = 2$ (b) $r = 3$ (d) $r = \frac{1}{2}$ (g) $r = -\frac{1}{3}$ (h) $r = x^2$ (j) $r = -\dfrac{1}{x}$
2. (a) $t_6 = 32, t_n = 2^{n-1}$ (b) $t_5 = 405, t_n = 5(3)^{n-1}$
   (c) $t_7 = 192, t_k = 3(2)^{k-1}$ (d) $t_8 = \frac{1}{2}, t_k = 64(\frac{1}{2})^{k-1}$
   (e) $t_5 = 64, t_n = 4(-2)^{n-1}$ (f) $t_7 = \frac{1}{9}, t_n = 81(-\frac{1}{3})^{n-1}$
   (g) $t_{12} = 2x^{12}, t_{21} = 2x^{21}$ (h) $t_{27} = \dfrac{5}{x^{16}}, t_{50} = -\dfrac{5}{x^{39}}$
3. (a) 8   (b) 7   (c) 6   (d) 7

(e) 8   (f) 7   (g) 14   (h) 25

4. (a) $a = 4$, $r = 3$, $t_n = 4(3)^{n-1}$ (b) $a = 3$, $r = 2$, $t_n = 3(2)^{n-1}$

  (c) (i) $a = 7$, $r = 4$, $t_n = 7(4)^{n-1}$ (ii) $a = -7$, $r = -4$, $t_n = -7(-4)^{n-1}$

  (d) $a = 256$, $r = \frac{1}{2}$, $t_n = 256(\frac{1}{2})^{n-1}$ (e) $a = -243$, $r = \frac{1}{3}$, $t_n = -243(\frac{1}{3})^{n-1}$

  (f) (i) $a = 3$, $r = 4$, $t_n = 3(4)^{n-1}$ (ii) $a = -3$, $r = -4$, $t_n = -3(-4)^{n-1}$

  (g) $a = 5k^2$, $r = k^2$, $t_n = 5k^2(k^2)^{n-1}$ (h) $a = 1$, $r = 2k$, $t_n = (2k)^{n-1}$

5. (a) \$105, \$110.25, \$115.76, \$121.55, $100(1.05)^n$

  (b) $a = \$105$, $r = 1.05$

6. (a) \$540, \$583.20, \$629.86, \$680.24, $500(1.08)^n$

  (b) $a = \$540$, $r = 1.08$

7. (b) Exponential

8. 1024

Exercise 6-5

1. (a) 2550   (b) 242   (c) 2343   (d) 1094   (e) 504   (f) 728

2. (a) 508   (b) 1093   (c) −170

  (d) 2735   (e) $121\frac{13}{27}$ (f) 3888.885

3. 126   4. $\dfrac{100(1.01)(1.01^{12} - 1)}{1.01 - 1}$

5. (a) (i) 6.75 m   (ii) approx. 3.8 m   (b) approx. 93.3 m

Review Exercise

1. (a) Arithmetic, $9n - 8$.   (b) Arithmetic, $x + (n - 1)2y$.

  (c) Geometric, 10^{n-1} (d) Geometric, $a^n b^{7-n}$,

  (e) Geometric, $\dfrac{1}{3^n}$ (f) Geometric, $2(-2)^{n-1}$

  (g) Arithmetic, $60 - 4n$ (h) Arithmetic, $2y + n(2 + y)$

2. (a) 7, 10, 13; 140   (b) 5, 15, 45; 16 400   (c) 4, 6, 8; 88

  (d) 39, 36, 33; 228   (e) 6, 12, 24; 1530   (f) $\frac{7}{2}, \frac{7}{4}, \frac{7}{8}; \frac{1785}{256}$

3. (a) 310, 37 300   (b) −79, −11 050

4. (a) 9375, 2343   (b) 33 614, 5602

5. (a) 24   (b) 8

6. 156   7. \$1638.40

8. 8100 (nearest 100 people)   9. $2^{64} - 1$

REVIEW AND PREVIEW TO CHAPTER 7

Exercise 1

1. \$2.74   2. \$33.00   3. \$66.52   4. \$600.00

5. \$204.01   6. \$62.77   7. \$313.50   8. \$24.37

9. \$10.88   10. \$171.50   11. \$0.44   12. \$64.00

13. 0.1%   14. 5%   15. 0.05%   16. 0.125%

17. 20%   18. 12%   19. 2.5%   20. 0.75%

21. 16%   22. 1.5%   23. 150%   24. 215%

Exercise 2

1. \$270, \$4770   2. \$54.15, \$814.15   3. \$1225, \$1249.50

4. \$240, \$244.80   5. \$50.40, 18%   6. \$37.80, 24%

7. 0.337 a, \$51 179.50   8. \$16.50, 0.600 a 9. \$45.25, \$1020.25

10. $50.70, 8%   11. 0.082 a, $352.87   12. $944.92, $966.28
13. $0.37, $24.60   14. $128.42, $1900   15. $158.10, $3400

Exercise 3

1. **(a)** 1, 2, 4, 8, 16   **(b)** 32, 16, 8, 4, 2
   (c) 27, 18, 12, 8, $\frac{16}{3}$ **(d)** 4, −12, 36, −108, 324
   (e) $\frac{1}{2}$, 1, 2, 4, 8   **(f)** $\frac{5}{8}$, $\frac{5}{2}$, 10, 40, 160
   (g) $\frac{1}{9}$, $\frac{1}{3}$, 1, 3, 9   **(h)** 1, −2, 4, −8, 16
2. **(a)** 128   **(b)** −10 935   **(c)** 64   **(d)** $\frac{32}{27}$
   (e) 32   **(f)** $\frac{1}{81}$ **(g)** $\frac{243}{32}$ **(h)** $\frac{9}{8}$
3. **(a)** 1023   **(b)** 6560   **(c)** 215   **(d)** $-\frac{40}{3}$
   (e) 189   **(f)** 2548   **(g)** $\frac{63}{8}$ **(h)** $\frac{40}{81}$

Display 7

1. 24, 120, 720   2. 0.708 333 33

3. 0.002 777 777 7   4. 6.252 604 167

5. 3 326 400   6. 168

7. 4 596 252   8. 0.002 164 502 1

9. 2400   10. 1.4

CHAPTER 7

Exercise 7-1

1. **(a)** 40, 5%   **(b)** 40, 3%   **(c)** 8%, semi-annual
   (d) 15 a, 4%   **(e)** 18%, 6 a   **(f)** 9% monthly
   (g) 4 a, 6%   **(h)** 8%, $1\frac{1}{2}$ a
2. **(a)** $9054.90   **(b)** $796.02   **(c)** $69 914.40   **(d)** $5391.75   **(e)** $964.54
3. $5049.92, $1049.92
4. **(a)** $1418.52   **(b)** $1425.76   **(c)** $1430.77
5. 9 a   6. $1143.63
7. **(a)** $20.70
   (b) $1225.70
8. **(a)** $12 763.00
   (b) assumed a risk
9. 4.44%   10. $23 377.09

Exercise 7-2

1. **(a)** $565.34   **(b)** $218.11   **(c)** $667.50   **(d)** $811.98   **(e)** $8427.40
2. $7089.20   3. $12 878.60
4. **(a)** $704.96   **(b)** $701.38   **(c)** $698.92
5. $478.48   6. $923.16   7. $5238.37   8. $750

Exercise 7-3

1. **(a)** $8933.42   **(b)** $17 213.24   **(c)** $4307.69   **(d)** $52 723.18
   (e) $210.47   **(f)** $174.28   **(g)** $127.46   **(h)** $515.55
2. $111.22   3. $47 512.76   4. $2458.73
5. **(a)** $10 051.60   **(b)** $20 655.80   **(c)** $73 208.53   **(d)** $2363.80
6. $178.68   7. $1362.33   8. $14 789.26   9. $9203.80

Exercise 7-4

1. (a) $4077.10   (b) $8467.77   (c) $3010.75   (d) $29 440.35
    (e) $1010.47   (f) $354.28   (g) $152.46   (h) $1235.55
2. $2766.07   3. $99.64   4. $1734.90
5. (a) $9818   (b) $5920   (c) $5532   (d) $1794
6. (a) $1081.56   (b) $367.75   (c) in one month
7. (a) $41 848.65   (b) $44 150.32   8. $1002   9. $4770.33

Exercise 7-5

2. (a) $7.89   (b) $34.72   (c) $164.05   (d) $7.43   (e) $21.72
3. (a) $9.76   (b) $11.86   (c) $7.47   (d) $14.49   (e) $42.79
4. $4350.76   5. $9576.23   6. $487.51   7. $600
8. $8540.24   9. $2215.59   10. $1029.80   11. $162.25

Exercise 7-6

2. May 1, 1980   3. (a) decrease   (b) increase   4. $2921.24
5. $2531.25   6. $876.02   7. $128.58   8. $7238.04
9. $59 238.21   10. (a) $3230.77   (b) $3640.52
11. $153.26   12. $1294.28

Exercise 7-7

1. $36.05   2. $109.61   3. $800.91   4. $361.51
5. $39.98   6. $7.24, $82.40, $7.40
7. (a) $70.61   (b) $55.61   (c) $360
8. (a) $13 110   (b) $19 407.31
9. $978.68   10. $21 620.45   11. $111.38
12. (a) $4628.55   (b) $7906.23

Review Exercise

1. (a) $3564.40   (b) $556.54   2. (a) $3667.50   (b) $6131.20
3. (a) $5630.80   (b) $9196.40   (c) $456.03   (d) $318.76
4. (a) $815.57   (b) $24.48   (c) $802.16   (d) $2616.29
5. (a) $4020.27   (b) $17 527.41   (c) $2865.65   (d) $50.74
6. $325.46   7. $42 275.14   8. $578.30   9. $55.71
10. $8356.49   11. $65.64   12. $1604.57   13. $4846.80

REVIEW AND PREVIEW TO CHAPTER 8

Exercise 1

1. 8   2. 27   3. 9   4. 64   5. 81
6. $\frac{4}{9}$ 7. $\frac{9}{16}$ 8. $\frac{9}{4}$ 9. $\frac{625}{81}$ 10. $\frac{81}{49}$
11. 0.25   12. 0.000 729   13. 0.000 729   14. 1.44   15. 0.0225

Exercise 2

1. 128   2. 243   3. 125   4. 81   5. 27   6. 343
7. 8   8. 1   9. 8   10. 3   11. 25   12. 1
13. $\frac{2}{3}$ 14. $\frac{1}{2}$ 15. $\frac{1}{4}$ 16. $\frac{1}{6}$

Exercise 3

1. 729   **2.** a^6 **3.** a^8 **4.** b^{15} **5.** c^{12}
6. a^3b^6 **7.** $8a^6$ **8.** $9a^6$ **9.** $2a^6$ **10.** $125a^6$

Exercise 4

1. (a)

x	y
0	1
1	2
2	4
3	8
4	16

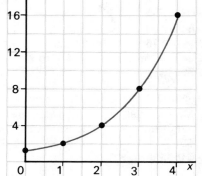

(b)

x	y
0	1
1	3
2	9
3	27
4	81

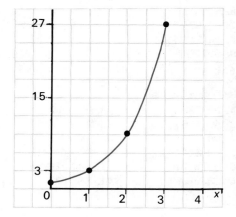

(c)

x	y
0	1
1	$\frac{1}{2}$
2	$\frac{1}{4}$
3	$\frac{1}{8}$
4	$\frac{1}{16}$

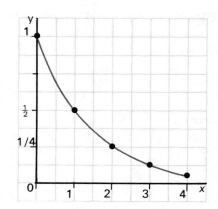

Display 8

1. 82 179.900 93

2. 3 068.349 609

3. 232 915.992 8

4. 164 547.006 5

5. 5 329.468 869

6. 4 846.090 535

7. 119.357 1

8. 1 765.728 785

9. 4 535.309 02

10. 1 343.924 007

CHAPTER 8

Exercise 8-1

1. **(a)** rat.　　**(b)** irr.　　　**(c)** rat.　　　**(d)** irr.　　　**(e)** rat.　　　**(f)** irr.
　　(g) rat.　　**(h)** irr.　　　**(i)** rat.　　　**(j)** irr.　　　**(k)** rat.　　　**(l)** rat.

2. **(a)** 0.875, ter.　**(b)** 0.$\dot{3}$, rep.　　**(c)** 0.5, ter.　　**(d)** 0.1$\dot{8}$, rep.
　　(e) 0.$\dot{4}$28 571, rep. **(f)** 0.$\dot{2}$85 714, rep. **(g)** 0.8$\dot{3}$, rep.　　**(h)** 0.$\dot{7}$14 28$\dot{5}$, rep.
　　(i) 1.25, ter.　　**(j)** 0.$\dot{1}$, rep.　　**(k)** 0.$\dot{2}$, rep.　　**(l)** 0.$\dot{5}$, rep.
　　(m) 0.2$\dot{7}$, rep.　**(n)** 1.5, ter.　　**(o)** 0.1$\dot{6}$, rep.

3.

5 d.p.	3 d.p.	2 d.p.
0.142 86	0.143	0.14
1.414 21	1.414	1.41
1.732 05	1.732	1.73
3.141 59	3.142	3.14

Exercise 8-2

1. **(a)** $\sqrt{12}$　　**(b)** $\sqrt{18}$　　**(c)** $\sqrt{50}$　　**(d)** $\sqrt{27}$　　**(e)** $\sqrt{32}$
　　(f) $\sqrt{48}$　　**(g)** $\sqrt{98}$　　**(h)** $\sqrt{125}$　**(i)** $\sqrt{20}$　　**(j)** $\sqrt{45}$
2. **(a)** $2\sqrt{3}$　　**(b)** $4\sqrt{3}$　　**(c)** $3\sqrt{2}$　　**(d)** $12\sqrt{2}$　**(e)** $2\sqrt{6}$
　　(f) $5\sqrt{5}$　　**(g)** $3\sqrt{5}$　　**(h)** $3\sqrt{7}$　　**(i)** $7\sqrt{2}$　　**(j)** $2\sqrt{15}$
3. **(a)** $6\sqrt{10}$　　**(b)** $12\sqrt{6}$　　　**(c)** $20\sqrt{3}$　　**(d)** $12\sqrt{6}$
　　(e) $12\sqrt{14}$　　**(f)** $20\sqrt{6}$　　　**(g)** $15\sqrt{10}$　　**(h)** 12
　　(i) $\sqrt{6}+\sqrt{10}$　**(j)** $\sqrt{15}-\sqrt{6}$　**(k)** $2\sqrt{14}-4\sqrt{2}$　**(l)** $3\sqrt{5}+\sqrt{10}$
4. **(a)** $4\sqrt{3}$　**(b)** $9\sqrt{2}$　　**(c)** 0　　**(d)** $2\sqrt{7}$　　**(e)** $-\sqrt{3}$　　**(f)** $-5\sqrt{2}$
5. **(a)** $\sqrt{3}-\sqrt{2}$　　　　**(b)** $2\sqrt{5}-1$　　　**(c)** $4\sqrt{3}+2$
　　(d) $7\sqrt{2}-4\sqrt{3}$　　　**(e)** $3\sqrt{7}+2\sqrt{11}$　　**(f)** $5\sqrt{2}-2\sqrt{7}$
6. **(a)** $\sqrt{21}$　**(b)** $3\sqrt{10}$　**(c)** $15\sqrt{14}$　**(d)** 6　　**(e)** $\sqrt{30}$　　**(f)** 6
　　(g) 7　　**(h)** $2\sqrt{30}$　**(i)** 20　　**(j)** 12　　**(k)** $20\sqrt{21}$　**(l)** $\sqrt{14}$
7. **(a)** $\sqrt{3}$　　　**(b)** 2　　　**(c)** $2\sqrt{3}$　　**(d)** $2\sqrt{2}$　　**(e)** $\sqrt{3}$
　　(f) 2　　　**(g)** 6　　　**(h)** 3　　　**(i)** $\frac{4}{3}$
8. **(a)** $8\sqrt{11}$　　　**(b)** $3\sqrt{7}$　　　**(c)** $6\sqrt{3}$　　　**(d)** $7\sqrt{2}+5\sqrt{3}$
　　(e) $3\sqrt{5}+5\sqrt{3}$　**(f)** $2\sqrt{5}+8\sqrt{2}$　**(g)** $\sqrt{3}$
9. **(a)** $7\sqrt{2}$　　　**(b)** $\sqrt{3}$　　　**(c)** $9\sqrt{2}$　　　**(d)** $13\sqrt{2}$
　　(e) $3\sqrt{2}-2\sqrt{3}$　**(f)** $-\sqrt{3}+7\sqrt{2}$　**(g)** $7\sqrt{5}-2\sqrt{7}$　**(h)** $5\sqrt{7}+\sqrt{3}$
10. **(a)** $12\sqrt{2}$　　　**(b)** $13\sqrt{2}$　　　**(c)** $13\sqrt{3}$　　　**(d)** $7\sqrt{5}$
　　(e) $14-3\sqrt{2}$　　**(f)** $9\sqrt{2}+8\sqrt{3}$　**(g)** $14\sqrt{2}-17\sqrt{5}$　**(h)** $4\sqrt{2}+18\sqrt{3}$
11. **(a)** $\sqrt{15}+\sqrt{21}$　　　**(b)** $7\sqrt{10}+7\sqrt{15}$　　　**(c)** $2\sqrt{10}-2\sqrt{5}$

(d) $6\sqrt{10}-12\sqrt{6}$ **(e)** $33+8\sqrt{6}$ **(f)** $102+4\sqrt{15}$

(g) $142+32\sqrt{21}$ **(h)** $18-5\sqrt{42}$

12. (a) $13-2\sqrt{42}$ **(b)** $79+20\sqrt{3}$ **(c)** $55-8\sqrt{21}$ **(d)** $69+12\sqrt{30}$
(e) -57 **(f)** 3 **(g)** 94 **(h)** 41

13. (a) $\frac{1}{3}\sqrt{3}$ **(b)** $\frac{\sqrt{6}}{3}$ **(c)** $\frac{\sqrt{10}}{5}$ **(d)** $12\sqrt{42}$

(e) $\frac{5\sqrt{21}}{2}$ **(f)** $\frac{\sqrt{77}}{11}$ **(g)** $\sqrt{2}$ **(h)** $\frac{2\sqrt{6}}{9}$

14. (a) $\frac{\sqrt{6}+2}{2}$ **(b)** $\frac{\sqrt{3}+2\sqrt{6}}{3}$ **(c)** $\frac{4\sqrt{3}+\sqrt{30}}{6}$

(d) $\frac{3\sqrt{15}-\sqrt{5}}{10}$ **(e)** $\frac{3\sqrt{5}+10\sqrt{3}}{15}$ **(f)** $\frac{\sqrt{66}-4\sqrt{3}}{18}$

15. (a) $\sqrt{3}+\sqrt{2}$ **(b)** $\frac{3(\sqrt{11}+\sqrt{3})}{2}$ **(c)** $6+\sqrt{35}$ **(d)** $\sqrt{7}+2$

(e) $\frac{25\sqrt{3}+60+15\sqrt{2}+12\sqrt{6}}{57}$ **(f)** $\frac{3\sqrt{14}+3\sqrt{10}-2\sqrt{21}-2\sqrt{15}}{6}$

16. (a) 1.58 **(b)** 1.22 **(c)** 1.60 **(d)** 22.44
(e) 0.77 **(f)** 1.90 **(g)** 1.41 **(h)** 9.90

Exercise 8-3

1. (a) 9 **(b)** 1 **(c)** 15 **(d)** 2
(e) 0 **(f)** 4 **(g)** 1 **(h)** 1
2. (a) 16 **(b)** 9 **(c)** 22 **(d)** 33
(e) 2 **(f)** $4\frac{1}{2}$ **(g)** 9 **(h)** no real roots
3. (a) 13 **(b)** 1 **(c)** 3 **(d)** $1\frac{1}{2}$
4. (a) no real roots **(b)** no real roots **(c)** 4
(d) no real roots **(e)** no real roots **(f)** 5

Exercise 8-4

1. (a) x^{11} **(b)** a^3 **(c)** 128 **(d)** a^2
(e) $6a^5$ **(f)** $14a^4$ **(g)** $30a^{17}$ **(h)** $28a^{11}$
2. (a) x^3 **(b)** c^7 **(c)** m^3 **(d)** m^{16}
(e) $4a$ **(f)** $3a^6$ **(g)** $25x^3$ **(h)** $7y^{14}$
3. (a) a^{15} **(b)** x^{44} **(c)** m^{45} **(d)** $125a^6$ **(e)** $3a^6$ **(f)** $27a^6$
(g) $16x^{16}$ **(h)** $80x^8$ **(i)** $\frac{25x^6}{36y^4}$ **(j)** $\frac{27x^6}{8y^3}$ **(k)** $\frac{x^9}{y^{12}}$ **(l)** $\frac{x^4}{8}$
4. (a) a^9 **(b)** -1 **(c)** x^8y^{12} **(d)** 1 **(e)** 1
(f) $3a^4$ **(g)** ab **(h)** 2 **(i)** 3
5. (a) a^{-3} **(b)** $\frac{1}{a^3}$
6. (a) 1 **(b)** $\frac{1}{25}$ **(c)** 1 **(d)** 1 **(e)** $\frac{1}{3}$ **(f)** $\frac{1}{16}$
(g) -1 **(h)** $\frac{1}{32}$ **(i)** 32 **(j)** $\frac{8}{5}$ **(k)** $\frac{225}{8}$ **(l)** $\frac{1}{3}$
7. (a) 9870 **(b)** 987 **(c)** 98.7 **(d)** 9.87
(e) 0.987 **(f)** 0.0987 **(g)** $987\,000$ **(h)** $0.000\,098\,7$
8. (a) 6.45×10^2 **(b)** 6.54×10^{-1} **(c)** 6.54×10^4 **(d)** 6.54×10^1
(e) 6.54×10^{-2} **(f)** 6.54×10^{-4} **(g)** 6.54×10^5 **(h)** 6.54×10^{-3}
9. (a) 5 **(b)** 6 **(c)** 4 **(d)** 11 **(e)** 3
(f) 10 **(g)** 3 **(h)** 8 **(i)** $\frac{1}{5}$ **(j)** $\frac{1}{2}$
(k) $\frac{1}{4}$ **(l)** 125 **(m)** x **(n)** $x^{4.5}$ **(o)** $x^{0.5}$

10. (a) 2 **(b)** $\frac{1}{3}$ **(c)** 25 **(d)** 3 **(e)** 3 **(f)** $\frac{1}{64}$
(g) 5 **(h)** 27 **(i)** $\frac{1}{8}$ **(j)** $\frac{1}{4}$ **(k)** 125 **(l)** $\frac{1}{4}$
11. (a) $x^{\frac{1}{2}}$ **(b)** $y^{\frac{3}{2}}$ **(c)** $m^{\frac{1}{3}}$ **(d)** $x^{\frac{2}{3}}$
(e) p^3 **(f)** $c^{-\frac{1}{2}}$ **(g)** $a^{\frac{4}{3}}$ **(h)** $a^{-\frac{3}{2}}$
12. (a) 16 **(b)** 8 **(c)** 32 **(d)** $\frac{1}{27}$ **(e)** $\frac{5}{6}$ **(f)** $\frac{7}{6}$
(g) $\frac{64}{27}$ **(h)** $\frac{9}{4}$ **(i)** $2a$ **(j)** $8a$ **(k)** a^6b^9 **(l)** $4ab^2$
(m) 10 **(n)** 16 **(o)** 2 **(p)** 1000 **(q)** 2 **(r)** $2^{\frac{5}{12}}$
(s) 9 **(t)** $10^{0.9}$ **(u)** 12 **(v)** 9

Exercise 8-5

1. (a) $\log 100 = 2$ **(b)** $\log 0.001 = -3$
(c) $\log 1 = 0$ **(d)** $\log 0.1 = -1$
2. (a) $1000 = 10^3$ **(b)** $0.001 = 10^{-3}$ **(c)** $1 = 10^0$ **(d)** $10\,000 = 10^4$
3. (a) 0 **(b)** 2 **(c)** -2 **(d)** 4
(e) 3 **(f)** -1 **(g)** -4 **(h)** 0
4. (a) $1 + .3010$ **(b)** $2 + .3010$ **(c)** $-1 + .3010$
(d) $4 + .3010$ **(e)** $-3 + .3010$ **(f)** $6 + .3010$
5. (a) $0 + .5740$ **(b)** $0 + .7536$ **(c)** $0 + .9159$ **(d)** $0 + .8287$
(e) $0 + .4969$ **(f)** $0 + .7959$ **(g)** $0 + .2405$ **(h)** $0 + .6946$
(i) $0 + .9661$ **(j)** $0 + .2430$ **(k)** $0 + .7443$ **(l)** $0 + .7642$
6. (a) 4.217 **(b)** 3.690 **(c)** 2.000 **(d)** 3.999 **(e)** 7.998 **(f)** 2.999
(g) 1.334 **(h)** 2.153 **(i)** 4.634 **(j)** 7.727 **(k)** 2.780 **(l)** 10
7. (a) $3 + .5337$ **(b)** $-1 + .5337$ **(c)** $-3 + .5337$
(d) $6 + .5337$ **(e)** $1 + .5337$ **(f)** $-4 + .5337$
8. (a) $0 + .8663$ **(b)** $1 + .7980$ **(c)** $3 + .6767$
(d) $6 + .5441$ **(e)** $-1 + .4393$ **(f)** $6 + .6405$
(g) $-3 + .7202$ **(h)** $2 + .5888$ **(i)** $-4 + .8267$
9. (a) $0 + .6154$ **(b)** $0 + .5146$ **(c)** $0 + .8352$
(d) $-1 + .3931$ **(e)** $-2 + .5528$ **(f)** $-4 + .6876$
(g) $3 + .5491$ **(h)** $1 + .8183$ **(i)** $6 + .5844$
10. (a) 2.265 **(b)** 2.661 **(c)** 7.499 **(d)** 17 820 **(e)** 0.031 84
(f) 2000 **(g)** 0.02 **(h)** 18 410 **(i)** 2.673
11. (a) 2.852 **(b)** 40.00 **(c)** 278.3 **(d)** 774.1 **(e)** 0.022 76
(f) 0.007 782 **(g)** 2585 **(h)** 0.002 405 **(i)** 266 500

Exercise 8-6

1. (a) $\log 15 + \log 20$ **(b)** $\log 50 + \log 33$
(c) $\log 25 + \log 11 + \log 16$
2. (a) $3 + .6691$ **(b)** $5 + .2643$ **(c)** $2 + .6542$ **(d)** $-2 + .1567$
3. (a) 21.73 **(b)** 140.9 **(c)** 18.78 **(d)** 0.3110 **(e)** 0.1346
(f) 984.5 **(g)** 136.6 **(h)** 2.286 **(i)** 212 600
4. (a) 0.6181 **(b)** 166.5 **(c)** 8.110 **(d)** 39.25 **(e)** 17.61 **(f)** 19.89
5. 20 330 m³ **6.** 0.005 359 kg **7.** 0.3617 m³ **8.** 2.138 g

Exercise 8-7

1. (a) $\log 26 - \log 40$ **(b)** $\log 7 - \log 13$ **(c)** $\log 0.72 - \log 2.9$
2. (a) $\log 35 + \log 18 - \log 112$ **(b)** $\log 30 + \log 61 - \log 71 - \log 19$
(c) $\log 156 - \log 21 - \log 211$
3. (a) $3 + .3807$ **(b)** $-1 + .4023$ **(c)** $-7 + .2102$ **(d)** $-2 + .8400$
4. (a) 5.200 **(b)** 1.866 **(c)** 68.39 **(d)** 209 500 **(e)** 13.13 **(f)** 9.076

(g) 24.40   **(h)** 0.5753   **(i)** 8.275   **(j)** 179.6   **(k)** 0.1166   **(l)** 144.4
5. (a) 7.410   **(b)** 454.2   **(c)** 0.082 50   **(d)** 4.618   **(e)** 48.95
6. (a) 0.2175   **(b)** 0.003 674   **(c)** 0.3396   **(d)** 0.4207   **(e)** 0.4694
7. (a) 42.60   **(b)** 0.060 34   **(c)** 0.000 410 2
    (d) 0.027 12   **(e)** 2.431   **(f)** 94.14
8. 161.8 kg/m^3

Exercise 8-8

1. (a) $2 \log 3.7$ **(b)** $3 \log 5.25$ **(c)** $4 \log 318$
    (d) $\frac{1}{2} \log 318$ **(e)** $\frac{1}{4} \log 37.8$ **(f)** $\frac{1}{3} \log 0.275$
2. (a) $4 + .7136$ **(b)** $-5 + .4428$ **(c)** $-14 + .2360$
    (d) $1 + .2637$ **(e)** $0 + .5095$ **(f)** $-1 + .2392$
    (g) $-2 + .7527$ **(h)** $-1 + .9457$ **(i)** $-2 + .7806$
3. (a) 2 986 000   **(b)** 177.5   **(c)** 5606   **(d)** 9.860
    (e) 8628   **(f)** 0.001 953   **(g)** 0.019 77   **(h)** 0.095 37
4. (a) 16.58   **(b)** 10.08   **(c)** 1.772   **(d)** 3.291
    (e) 19.59   **(f)** 26.85   **(g)** 3.178   **(h)** 7.659
5. (a) 16 290   **(b)** 1.266   **(c)** 366.4   **(d)** 26.24
    (e) 5.008   **(f)** 0.000 146 7   **(g)** 0.8441   **(h)** 0.3631
6. (a) 86.55   **(b)** 199.8   **(c)** 7325
    (d) 0.046 86   **(e)** 0.2597   **(f)** 158 300
7. 9.95 cm^2 **8.** 1.022 cm^3 **9.** 2.738 s

Review Exercise

1. (a) $6\sqrt{30}$ **(b)** $10\sqrt{3}$ **(c)** $36\sqrt{2}$
    (d) $\sqrt{6} + \sqrt{14}$ **(e)** $3\sqrt{10} - 6\sqrt{5}$ **(f)** $4\sqrt{3} + 12$
    (g) $84\sqrt{3}$ **(h)** $6\sqrt{6}$ **(i)** $12 - 12\sqrt{3}$
2. (a) $5\sqrt{6}$ **(b)** $6\sqrt{2}$ **(c)** $8\sqrt{3}$ **(d)** $7\sqrt{3}$
    (e) $5\sqrt{5}$ **(f)** $5\sqrt{2}$ **(g)** $12\sqrt{3}$ **(h)** $10\sqrt{2}$
    (i) $6\sqrt{7} - 9\sqrt{3}$ **(j)** $10\sqrt{2} - 5\sqrt{3}$ **(k)** $7\sqrt{5} - 2\sqrt{7}$
3. (a) $17 + 7\sqrt{6}$ **(b)** 49   **(c)** 52   **(d)** $6 + 2\sqrt{5}$ **(e)** $34 - 24\sqrt{2}$
4. (a) $\dfrac{\sqrt{5}}{5}$ **(b)** $\sqrt{2}$ **(c)** $\dfrac{\sqrt{15}}{5}$ **(d)** $3\sqrt{2}$

    (e) $\dfrac{\sqrt{5} - \sqrt{2}}{3}$ **(f)** $\dfrac{15 + 2\sqrt{14}}{13}$ **(g)** $\dfrac{32 + 7\sqrt{5}}{19}$
5. (a) 8   **(b)** 9   **(c)** 3   **(d)** no roots   **(e)** 4   **(f)** 1
6. (a) x^9 **(b)** $3x^4$ **(c)** $3a^6$ **(d)** $27a^6$ **(e)** $\dfrac{8x^{12}}{27y^9}$ **(f)** $\dfrac{2x^7}{9}$
    (g) 3   **(h)** $\frac{1}{9}$ **(i)** 7   **(j)** 8   **(k)** $\frac{9}{4}$ **(l)** 1
7. (a) 12   **(b)** 4   **(c)** $\frac{1}{4}$ **(d)** 16   **(e)** 16
    (f) 4   **(g)** 64   **(h)** 64   **(i)** $\frac{1}{9}$
8. (a) 33.66   **(b)** 2822   **(c)** 1.56   **(d)** 14.00   **(e)** 0.1959   **(f)** 149.9
    (g) 7.65   **(h)** 0.1622   **(i)** 0.3735   **(j)** 100.2   **(k)** 0.2630   **(l)** 2.292
9. (a) 0.008 140   **(b)** 0.1873   **(c)** 1.346   **(d)** 0.8619

REVIEW AND PREVIEW TO CHAPTER 9

Exercise 1

1. $x = y = 60°$
2. $x = y = 80°$
3. $27°$
4. $x = 70°, y = 110°$
5. $x = 40°, y = 100°$
6. $x = 60°, y = 70°$
7. $x = y = 115°$
8. $x = 70°, y = 35°$

Exercise 2

1. 5
2. 13
3. 17
4. 25
5. 8
6. 16
7. 25
8. 48

Exercise 3

	$\sin \theta$	$\cos \theta$	$\tan \theta$	$\csc \theta$	$\sec \theta$	$\cot \theta$
1.	$\frac{3}{5}$	$\frac{4}{5}$	$\frac{3}{4}$	$\frac{5}{3}$	$\frac{5}{4}$	$\frac{4}{3}$
2.	$\frac{1}{\sqrt{2}}$	$\frac{1}{\sqrt{2}}$	1	$\sqrt{2}$	$\sqrt{2}$	1
3.	$\frac{1.7}{2.0}$	$\frac{1.0}{2.0}$	1.7	$\frac{2.0}{1.7}$	2.0	$\frac{1.0}{1.7}$
4.	$\frac{b}{c}$	$\frac{a}{c}$	$\frac{b}{a}$	$\frac{c}{b}$	$\frac{c}{a}$	$\frac{a}{b}$
5.	$\frac{4}{5}$	$\frac{3}{5}$	$\frac{4}{3}$	$\frac{5}{4}$	$\frac{5}{3}$	$\frac{3}{4}$
6.	$\frac{4.0}{5.6}$	$\frac{4.0}{5.6}$	1	$\frac{5.6}{4.0}$	$\frac{5.6}{4.0}$	1
7.	$\frac{8}{17}$	$\frac{15}{17}$	$\frac{8}{15}$	$\frac{17}{8}$	$\frac{17}{15}$	$\frac{15}{8}$
8.	$\frac{q}{p}$	$\frac{r}{p}$	$\frac{q}{r}$	$\frac{p}{q}$	$\frac{p}{r}$	$\frac{r}{q}$

Exercise 4

1. $\frac{45}{7}$
2. $\frac{44}{3}$
3. $\frac{752}{25}$
4. 8.59
5. $19\frac{7}{22}$
6. 9
7. $18\frac{3}{4}$
8. $21\frac{1}{3}$

Display 9

1. 1.500 625
2. 0.000 001 979 6
3. 242 387.027 9
4. 62.334 228 52
5. 269.158 828 1
6. 23.365 020 75
7. 58.996 363 64
8. 2.775 280 362
9. 0.610 852 732
10. 7.472 898 209

CHAPTER 9

Exercise 9-1

1.

	$\sin \theta$	$\cos \theta$	$\tan \theta$	$\csc \theta$	$\sec \theta$	$\cot \theta$
(a)	$\frac{3}{5}$	$\frac{4}{5}$	$\frac{3}{4}$	$\frac{5}{3}$	$\frac{5}{4}$	$\frac{4}{3}$
(b)	$\frac{12}{13}$	$\frac{5}{13}$	$\frac{12}{5}$	$\frac{13}{12}$	$\frac{13}{5}$	$\frac{5}{12}$

(c)	$\dfrac{\sqrt{3}}{2}$	$\tfrac{1}{2}$	$\sqrt{3}$	$\dfrac{2}{\sqrt{3}}$	2	$\dfrac{1}{\sqrt{3}}$
(d)	$\dfrac{7}{m}$	$\dfrac{9}{m}$	$\tfrac{7}{9}$	$\dfrac{m}{7}$	$\dfrac{m}{9}$	$\tfrac{9}{7}$
(e)	$\dfrac{a}{c}$	$\dfrac{5}{c}$	$\dfrac{a}{5}$	$\dfrac{c}{a}$	$\dfrac{c}{5}$	$\dfrac{5}{a}$
(f)	$\dfrac{b}{c}$	$\dfrac{a}{c}$	$\dfrac{b}{a}$	$\dfrac{c}{b}$	$\dfrac{c}{a}$	$\dfrac{a}{b}$

2. (a) 88.9 cm   **(b)** 3.01 cm   **(c)** 707 m
   (d) 182 m   **(e)** 5.96 m   **(f)** 11.5 m

3. (a) 39°   **(b)** 63°   **(c)** 49°   **(d)** 53°   **(e)** 50°   **(f)** 30°

4. (a) $a = 205$ cm, $b = 143$ cm, $\angle A = 55°$ **(b)** $b = 14$ cm, $c = 33.1$ cm, $\angle B = 25°$
   (c) $b = 96$ cm, $\angle A = 51°$, $\angle C = 39°$ **(d)** $\angle A = 35°$, $a = 12$ m, $c = 7$ m
   (e) $\angle A = 63°$, $\angle C = 27°$, $c = 61.1$ m   **(f)** $\angle C = 52°$, $a = 231$ cm, $b = 480$ cm

5. (a) $\angle A = 50°$, $\angle C = 40°$, $b = 54$ cm   **(b)** $\angle D = 38°$, $\angle F = 52°$, $d = 38$ cm
   (c) $\angle R = 60°$, $\angle Q = 30°$, $q = 34$ cm   **(d)** $\angle B = 38°$, $\angle C = 52°$, $b = 528$ cm
   (e) $\angle T = 43°$, $\angle U = 47°$, $s = 711$ cm   **(f)** $\angle X = 16°$, $\angle Y = 74°$, $\angle Z = 90°$

6. $\sin A = \tfrac{12}{13}$, $\cos A = \tfrac{5}{13}$, $\tan A = \tfrac{12}{5}$, $\sin B = \tfrac{5}{13}$, $\cos B = \tfrac{12}{13}$, $\tan B = \tfrac{5}{12}$
   $\csc A = \tfrac{13}{12}$, $\sec A = \tfrac{13}{5}$, $\cot A = \tfrac{5}{12}$, $\csc B = \tfrac{13}{5}$, $\sec B = \tfrac{13}{12}$, $\cot B = \tfrac{12}{5}$

7. 75 cm and 100 cm

8. (a) $\angle A = 55°$, $b = 69$ cm, $c = 146$ cm   **(b)** $\angle A = 30°$, $a = 100$ cm, $c = 200$ cm
   (c) $\angle Q = 50°$, $\angle R = 40°$, $p = 45$ m   **(d)** $\angle Z = 35°$, $x = 143$ m, $y = 174$ m
   (e) $\angle C = 18°$, $b = 134$ m, $c = 41$ m   **(f)** $\angle A = 52°$, $c = 199$ cm, $b = 324$ cm

9. (a) 130 m   **(b)** 37 m   **(c)** 134 m

Exercise 9-2

  1. 330 m   **2.** 429 m   **3. (a)** 38.5 m   **(b)** 22.0 m
  4. 256 m   **5.** 202 m   **6. (a)** 93.8 m   **(b)** 6.9 m
  7. (a) 411 m   **(b)** 284 m   **8. (a)** 42°   **(b)** 11.1 m
  9. 21.7 m   **10. (a)** 19°   **(b)** 9°
 11. 4.33 mm   **12.** 102.6 mm   **13.** $a = 4.98$ cm, $b = 5.54$ cm
 14. 18°   **15.** $\angle A = 9°$, $\angle B = 18°$ **16.** 14.8 cm
 17. 200 mm   **18.** 44 mm   **19.** 13.3 mm   **20.** 8.08 cm   **21.** 3020 m
 22. 50 m   **23.** 2.54 m   **24.** 1.9 km   **25.** 232 m   **26.** 40 m
 27. 28.6 m   **28.** 40.6 m   **29.** 70.6 m   **30.** 33.8 m

Exercise 9-3

  1. (a) 6.6 cm   **(b)** 6.9 cm   **(c)** 7.9 cm
  2. (a) 33 cm   **(b)** 14.0 cm   **(c)** 87 cm   **(d)** 7.3 cm   **(e)** 20 cm
  3. (a) $\angle C = 62°$, $b \doteq 121$ cm, $c \doteq 115$ cm   **(b)** $\angle A = 66°$, $b \doteq 7.69$ cm, $c \doteq 10.9$ cm
   (c) $\angle A = 18°$, $a \doteq 10.1$ cm, $c \doteq 3.03$ cm   **(d)** $\angle A = 69°$, $a \doteq 42$ cm, $b \doteq 33$ cm
   (e) $\angle A = 44°$, $b \doteq 5.7$ cm, $c \doteq 11$ cm

Exercise 9-4

  1. (a) 12.9 cm   **(b)** 14.8 cm   **(c)** 18.3 cm
  2. (a) 78°   **(b)** 78°   **(c)** 114°
  3. (a) 39.4 cm   **(b)** 169 cm   **(c)** 80°   **(d)** 115°

Exercise 9-5

1. 8°   **2.** 7°   **3.** 8.7 m, 4.2 m   **4.** 8.7 cm

5. 595 m   **6.** 268 km, 219 km   **7.** 265 m   **8.** 6.6 km, 5.4 km

9. 44.9, 39.5, 15.6 cm   **10.** 385 m

Exercise 9-6

1. (a) 500 m²   (b) 32.5 m²

2. (a) 7520 m²   (b) 77 200 m²   (c) 2142 m²   (d) 3.53 m²   (e) 54.7 m²

3. (a) 6.25 m²   (b) 9 660 000 m²   (c) 25.8 m²

    (d) 7 210 000 m²   (e) 5 780 000 m²

4. (a) 73 900 cm²   (b) 98 m²   (c) 45.9 m²

    (d) 13 000 cm²   (e) 719 m²

Review Exercise

1. (a) 91.9 cm   (b) 9.06 cm   (c) 740 cm

2. (a) 57°   (b) 61°   (c) 55°

3. (a) $\angle B \doteq 35°, \angle C \doteq 55°, b \doteq 32$ cm   (b) $\angle E \doteq 48°, \angle F \doteq 42°, f \doteq 44$ cm

    (c) $\angle H \doteq 38°, g \doteq 43$ cm, $h \doteq 34$ cm   (d) $J \doteq 30°, k \doteq 400$ cm, $l \doteq 346$ cm

4. (a) 6720 cm²   (b) 5160 cm²

5. (a) $\angle A = 80°, a \doteq 41.9$ m, $b \doteq 21.2$ m   (b) $\angle B = 85°, b \doteq 5.12$ m, $c \doteq 2.98$ m

    (c) $a = 76.2$ cm, $\angle B \doteq 54°, \angle C \doteq 41°$ (d) $a \doteq 48.2$ cm, $\angle C \doteq 36°, \angle D \doteq 34°$

    (e) $\angle A \doteq 82°, \angle C \doteq 36°, a \doteq 202$ cm   (f) $\angle A \doteq 35°, a \doteq 299$ cm, $b = 451$ cm

6. 332 m   **7.** (a) 112 cm   (b) $3.00

8. 8.1 km and 8.9 km

REVIEW AND PREVIEW TO CHAPTER 10

Exercise 1

Point	(x, y)	$(5, 12)$	$(-7, 24)$	$(-4, -4)$	$(3, -5)$
r	$\sqrt{x^2 + y^2}$	13	25	5.66	5.83
$\sin \theta$	$\dfrac{y}{r}$	0.923	0.96	-0.707	-0.858
$\cos \theta$	$\dfrac{x}{r}$	0.385	-0.28	-0.707	0.515
$\tan \theta$	$\dfrac{y}{x}$	2.4	-3.43	1	-1.67
$\csc \theta$	$\dfrac{r}{y}$	1.08	1.04	-1.42	-1.17
$\sec \theta$	$\dfrac{r}{x}$	2.6	-3.57	-1.42	1.94
$\cot \theta$	$\dfrac{x}{y}$	0.417	-0.292	1	-0.6

Exercise 2

θ	60°	150°	45°	225°	120°	30°	135°	315°	240°
$\sin\theta$	$\dfrac{\sqrt{3}}{2}$	$\frac{1}{2}$	$\dfrac{1}{\sqrt{2}}$	$-\dfrac{1}{\sqrt{2}}$	$\dfrac{\sqrt{3}}{2}$	$\frac{1}{2}$	$\dfrac{1}{\sqrt{2}}$	$-\dfrac{1}{\sqrt{2}}$	$-\dfrac{\sqrt{3}}{2}$
$\cos\theta$	$\frac{1}{2}$	$-\dfrac{\sqrt{3}}{2}$	$\dfrac{1}{\sqrt{2}}$	$-\dfrac{1}{\sqrt{2}}$	$-\frac{1}{2}$	$\dfrac{\sqrt{3}}{2}$	$-\dfrac{1}{\sqrt{2}}$	$\dfrac{1}{\sqrt{2}}$	$-\frac{1}{2}$
$\tan\theta$	$\sqrt{3}$	$\dfrac{1}{\sqrt{3}}$	1	1	$-\sqrt{3}$	$\dfrac{1}{\sqrt{3}}$	-1	-1	$\sqrt{3}$
$\csc\theta$	$\dfrac{2}{\sqrt{3}}$	2	$\sqrt{2}$	$-\sqrt{2}$	$\dfrac{2}{\sqrt{3}}$	2	$\sqrt{2}$	$-\sqrt{2}$	$-\dfrac{2}{\sqrt{3}}$
$\sec\theta$	2	$-\dfrac{2}{\sqrt{3}}$	$\sqrt{2}$	$-\sqrt{2}$	-2	$\dfrac{2}{\sqrt{3}}$	$-\sqrt{2}$	$\sqrt{2}$	-2
$\cot\theta$	$\dfrac{1}{\sqrt{3}}$	$\sqrt{3}$	1	1	$-\dfrac{1}{\sqrt{3}}$	$\sqrt{3}$	-1	-1	$\dfrac{1}{\sqrt{3}}$

2.

θ	$\sin\theta$	$\cos\theta$	$\tan\theta$	$\csc\theta$	$\sec\theta$	$\cot\theta$
0°	0	1	0	und	1	und
90°	1	0	und	1	und	0
180°	0	−1	0	und	−1	und
270°	−1	0	und	−1	und	0

Display 10

1. 18.984 891 42
2. 201.720 731 6
3. 145.277 912 1
4. 0.567 200 597 6
5. 2 447.491 708
6. 27.163 894 14°
7. 63.213 533 42°
8. 45.465 377 22°
9. 73.781 515 86°
10. 37.508 480 98°

CHAPTER 10

Exercise 10-1

1. (a) 540°   (b) 135°   (c) 240°   (d) 150°   (e) 270°

2. (a) $\dfrac{2\pi}{3}$ (b) $\dfrac{11}{6}\pi$ (c) $\dfrac{\pi}{2}$ (d) $\dfrac{5\pi}{4}$ (e) $\dfrac{\pi}{6}$

3. 0.017 453 radians

4. (a) 172°   (b) 140°   (c) 298°   (d) 659°   (e) 8.42°   (f) 26 200°

5. (a) $\dfrac{2\pi}{9}$ (b) $\dfrac{7\pi}{18}$ (c) $\dfrac{8\pi}{9}$ (d) $\dfrac{10\pi}{9}$ (e) $\dfrac{41\pi}{18}$ (f) $\dfrac{65\pi}{36}$

Investigation 10-2

1. for the student

2.

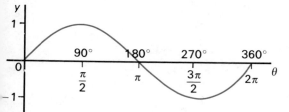
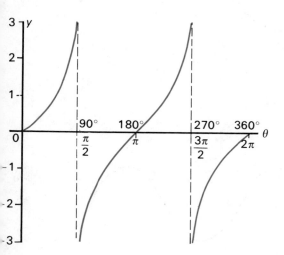

3.

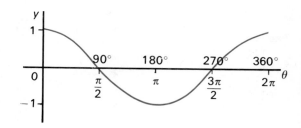
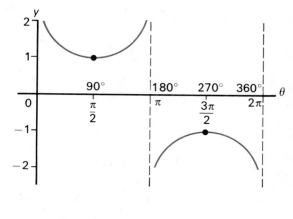

4.

5.

439

6.

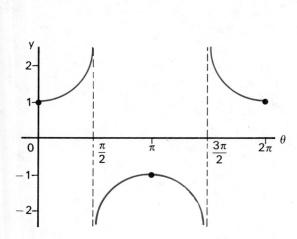

7.

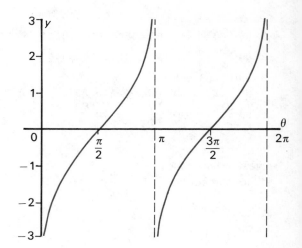

Exercise 10-2

1.

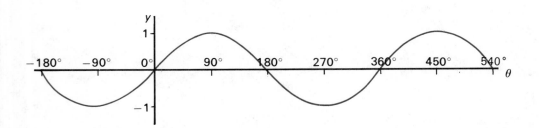

2.

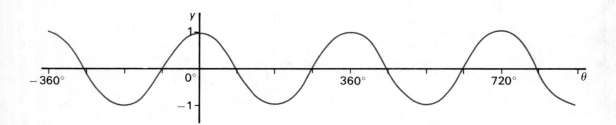

3.

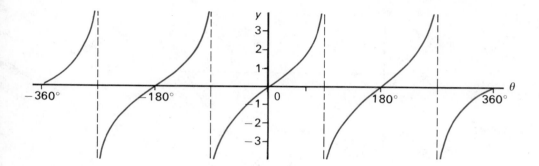

4.

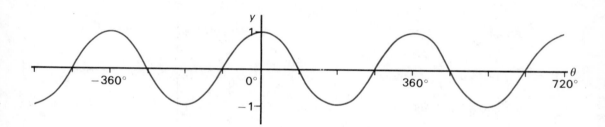

5.

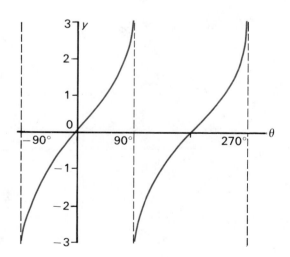

6.

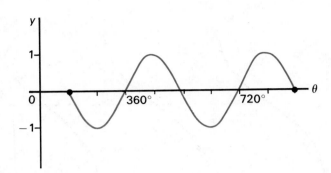

7.

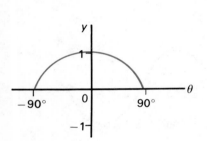

8.

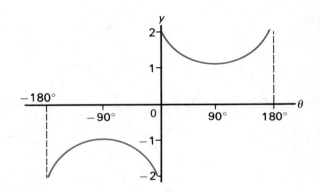

9.

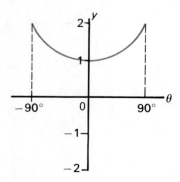

10.

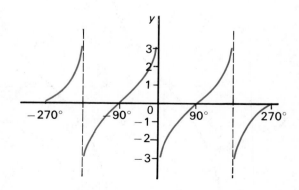

442

Exercise 10-3

1. **(a)** 1   **(b)** 2   **(c)** 2   **(d)** 3   **(e)** 4
2. **(a)** −   **(b)** +   **(c)** −   **(d)** +
   (e) +   **(f)** +   **(g)** −   **(h)** −
3. **(a)** −   **(b)** +   **(c)** −   **(d)** +   **(e)** −
   (f) −   **(g)** +   **(h)** −   **(i)** −   **(j)** −
4. **(a)** −   **(b)** −   **(c)** +   **(d)** −   **(e)** −   **(f)** +
5. **(a)** −0.7071   **(b)** −0.7071   **(c)** −1.4281   **(d)** −0.9397
   (e) 0.4663   **(f)** 0.5000   **(g)** 0.8192   **(h)** −0.3420
   (i) 0.7002   **(j)** −1.4281   **(k)** −0.9397   **(l)** −0.9848
6. **(a)** 2.0000   **(b)** 2.0000   **(c)** 5.7588   **(d)** 1.1918   **(e)** −1.4142
   (f) −1.7321   **(g)** −0.3640   **(h)** −1.5557   **(i)** −2.0000
7. **(a)** 22°, 158°   **(b)** 51°, 309°   **(c)** 71°, 251°
   (d) 70°, 290°   **(e)** 43°, 137°   **(f)** 135°, 225°
   (g) 207°, 153°   **(h)** 163°, 343°   **(i)** 253°, 287°

Exercise 10-5

1. **(a)** 1   **(b)** 2   **(c)** $\frac{1}{2}$
2. **(a)** 3   **(b)** 7   **(c)** 24   **(d)** m **(e)** 3   **(f)** $\frac{1}{3}$

3. **(a)**

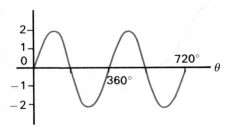

(b)

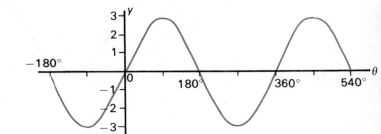

(c)

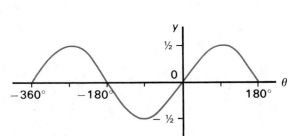

(d)

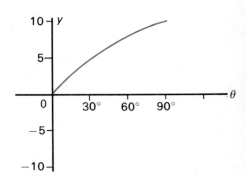

(e)

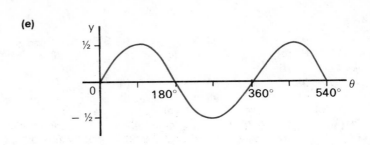

4. (a)

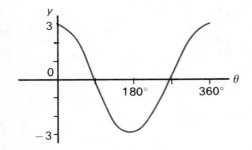

(b)

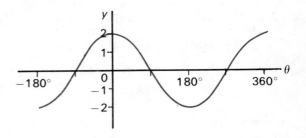

(c)

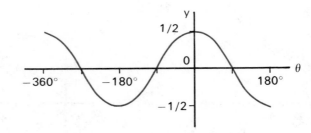

Exercise 10-6

1. (a) 180°   **(b)** 360°   **(c)** 120°

2. (a) 360° **(b)** 120° **(c)** 180° **(d)** 720° **(e)** 90° **(f)** 180°

3. $Y = 2 \sin 2\theta$
$Y = 4 \sin \theta$
$Y = 2 \sin \frac{1}{2}\theta$
$Y = 8 \sin \theta$
$Y = 5 \sin 2\theta$

4. (a)

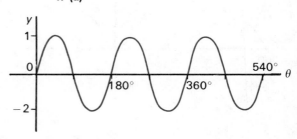

(b)

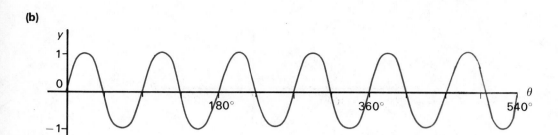

(c)

(d)

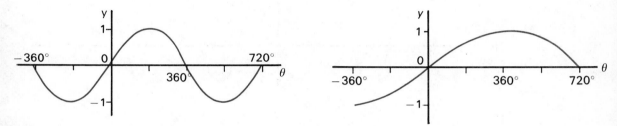

(e)

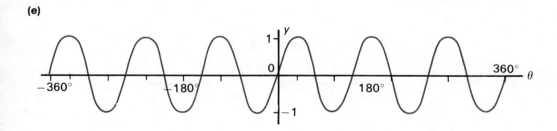

5. (a)

(b)

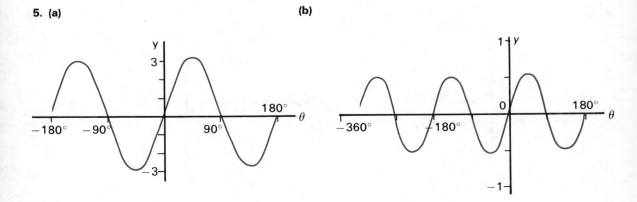

(c)

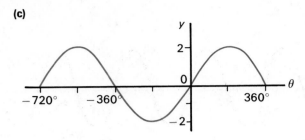

(d)

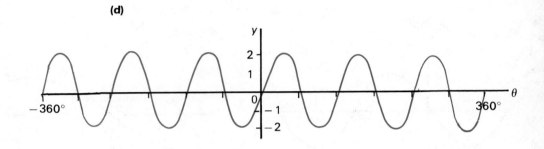

(e)

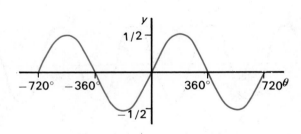

6. (a)

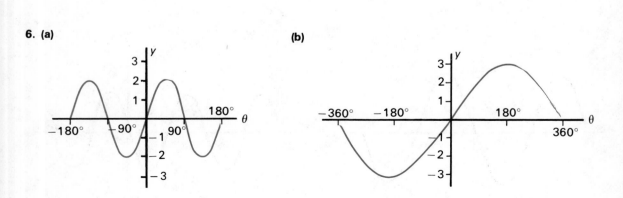

(b)

(c)

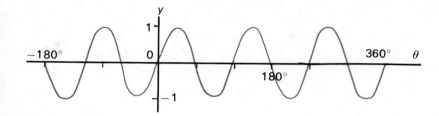

Exercise 10-7

1. **(a)** 0°   **(b)** 30° left   **(c)** 90° right   **(d)** 360° left
2. **(a)**

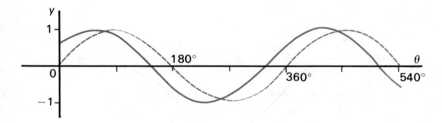

(b)

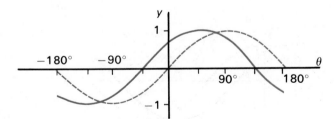

(c)

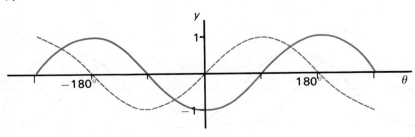

(d)

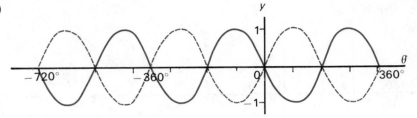

(e)

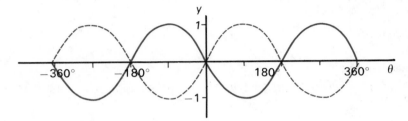

3. (a)

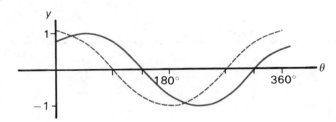

(b)

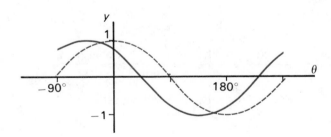

(c)

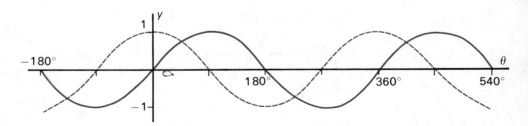

(d)

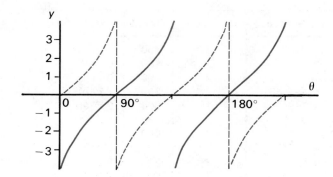

(e)

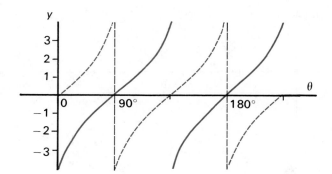

(f)

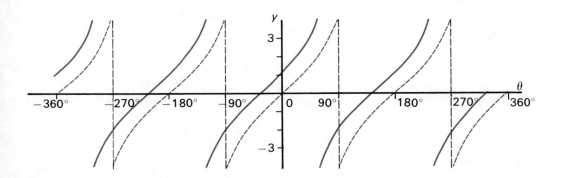

Exercise 10-8

1.

Defining Sentence	Amplitude	Period	Phase Shift
$Y = 2 \sin \theta$	2	360°	0°
$Y = 3 \sin 2\theta$	3	180°	0°
$Y = 2 \sin \theta$	2	360°	0°
$Y = 2 \cos (\theta + 45°)$	2	360°	45° left
$Y = \sin (\theta + 90°)$	1	360°	90° left
$Y = \sin (2\theta + 90°)$	1	180°	45° left
$Y = 3 \sin 2\theta$	3	180°	0°
$Y = 2 \sin \frac{1}{2}\theta$	2	720°	0°
$Y = 3 \sin \frac{1}{2}\theta$	3	720°	0°
$Y = a \sin k(\theta + \phi)$	a	$\dfrac{360°}{k}$	$\phi > 0$ left $\phi < 0$ right

2. (a)

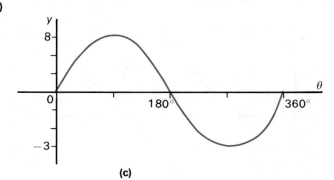

(b)

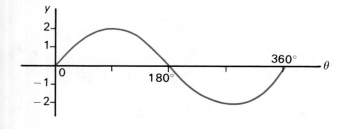

(c)

(d)

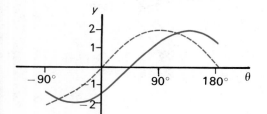

(e)

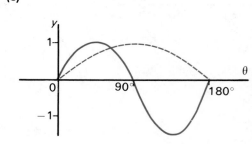

(f)

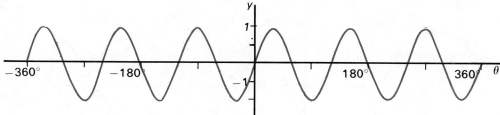

(g)

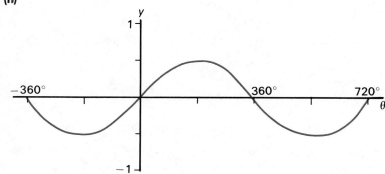

(h)

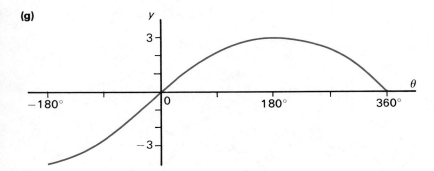

(i)

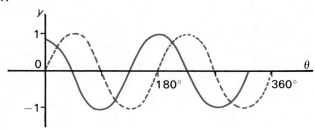

(j)

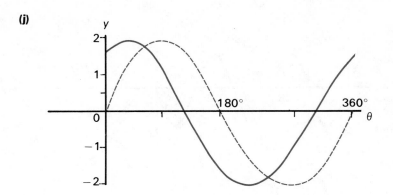

3.

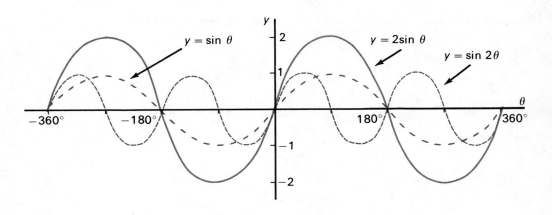

4. (a)

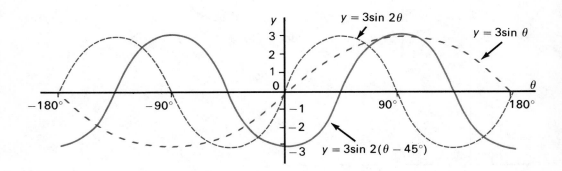

(b)

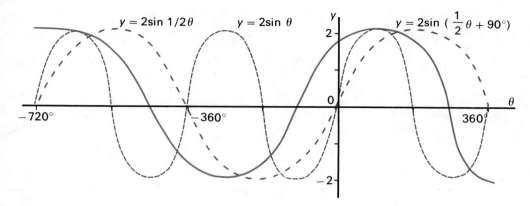

(c)

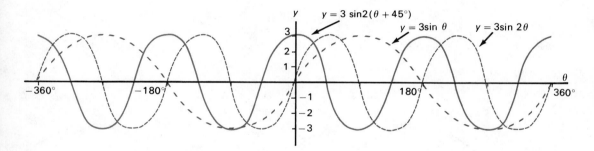

(d)

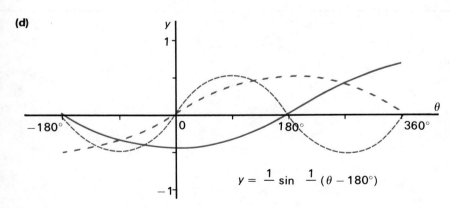

$$y = \frac{1}{2}\sin \ \frac{1}{2}(\theta - 180°)$$

Exercise 10-9

1. 60°, 120°	**2.** 60°, 300°	**3.** 210°, 330°
4. 45°, 225°	**5.** 135°, 315°	**6.** 0°, 180°, 360°
7. 60°, 120°, 240°, 300°	**8.** 30°, 150°, 210°, 330°	**9.** 0°, 180°, 270°, 360°

1. (a) $\dfrac{5\pi}{4}$ **(b)** $\dfrac{11\pi}{6}$ **(c)** 3π **(d)** $\dfrac{-3\pi}{2}$ **(e)** $-\frac{11}{4}\pi$

2. (a) $150°$ **(b)** $450°$ **(c)** $135°$ **(d)** $-270°$ **(e)** $-330°$

3. (a)

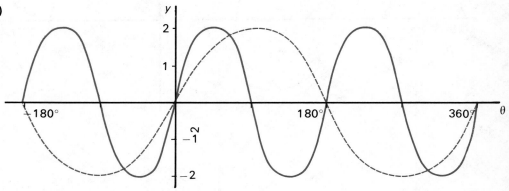

(b)

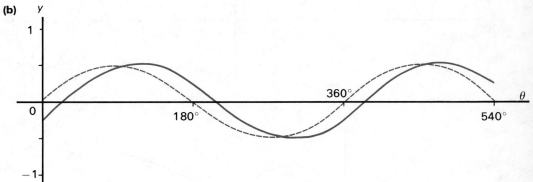

(c)

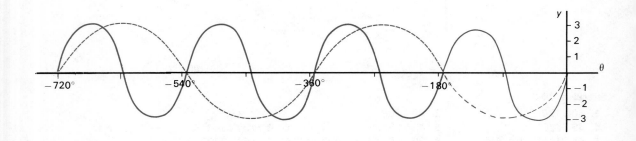

(d)

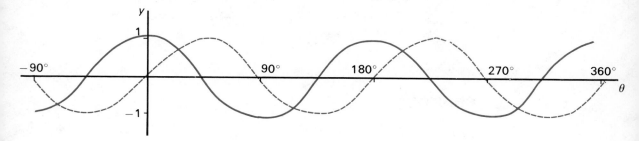

(e)

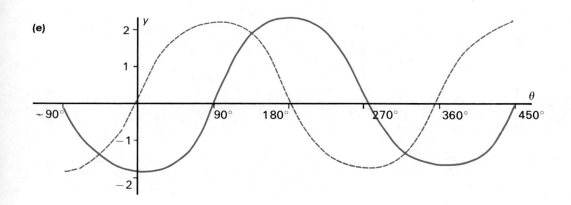

4. (a) 30°, 150°

(c) 0°, 90°, 180°, 360°

(b) 225°, 315°

(d) 0°, 180°, 270°, 360°

REVIEW AND PREVIEW TO CHAPTER 11

Exercise 1

1. 164 m, 115 m

4. 97.1 m, 51.6 m

2. 80.3 m, 89.2 m

5. 35.2 m, 66.2 m

3. 31.5 m, 45.1 m

6. 1000 m, 1000 m

Exercise 2

1. 227.5 km

4. 0.909 h

2. 2.5 h

5. 97.7 km/h

3. 61.5 km/h

6. 340 km

Display 11

1. 63.928 890 76

2. 4.764 553 838

3. 0.779 141 826 9

4. $\angle A \doteq 34.409\,468\,21°$

5. $\angle B \doteq 59.822\,280\,75°$

CHAPTER 11

Exercise 11-1

1.

Initial point	Terminal point	Vector
(3, 2)	(7, 3)	[4, 1]
(2, 5)	(8, 4)	[6, −1]
(−1, 3)	(3, 5)	[4, 2]
(2, 6)	(7, 11)	[5, 5]
(3, −2)	(7, −5)	[4, −3]
(−5, 7)	(−5, 7)	[0, 0]
(a, b)	(0, 0)	[−a, −b]

2. (a) $\overrightarrow{AE} = \overrightarrow{EC}$, $\overrightarrow{AD} = \overrightarrow{BC}$, $\overrightarrow{BE} = \overrightarrow{ED}$ **(b)** $\overrightarrow{fe} = \overrightarrow{ED}$, $\overrightarrow{BF} = \overrightarrow{FA} = \overrightarrow{CD}$, $\overrightarrow{CE} = \overrightarrow{EA}$

3. (a) D (6, 0)   **(b)** [2, 5], [8, 2], [8, 2], [2, 5]

     (c) parallelogram

4. (a) [0, 50]   **(b)** [40, 0]   **(c)** [1, 1]

     (d) [−1, −1]   **(e)** [0.656, 0.755]   **(f)** [$m \cos \theta, m \sin \theta$]

5. (a) 5, 53°   **(b)** 13, 113°   **(c)** 15, 233°

     (d) 13, 303°   **(e)** 2.82, 135°   **(f)** $\sqrt{a^2 + b^2}$, $\tan \theta = \dfrac{b}{a}$

Exercise 11-2

1. (a) [−3, 14]   **(b)** [6, −15]   **(c)** [−2, 0]   **(d)** [5, 3]

2. (a) 5, 13, 15   **(b)** >

3. (a) [5, −2]   **(b)** [9, 6]   **(c)** [12, −8]   **(d)** [1, 6]   **(e)** [−1, −6]

     (f) 5.39   **(g)** 3.61   **(h)** 4.47   **(i)** 6.08

4. 253 kn, N 81° E   **5.** 502 kn, S 85° W

6. S 8° W   **7.** 427 kn, S 85° W

Exercise 11-3

16. 4.36   **17.** 13   **18.** 15   **19.** 8

20. 3.74   **21.** 8.06   **22.** 8.66

Exercise 11-4

1. (a) $\overrightarrow{AB} = [5, -2, -1]$, $\overrightarrow{BA} = [5, 10, 12]$, $\overrightarrow{BC} = [-10, -8, -10]$, $\overrightarrow{DC} = [-5, -10, -12]$
$\overrightarrow{DA} = [0, 0, -1]$, $\overrightarrow{AD} = [0, 0, 1]$, $\overrightarrow{BD} = [-5, 2, 2]$, $\overrightarrow{DB} = [5, -2, -2]$

2. (a) $[-2, -8, 1]$, $[11, 6, 0]$, $[-2, -8, 1]$, $[11, 6, 0]$
(b) parallelogram

3.

Initial point	Terminal point	Vector
$(3, 4, 7)$	$(2, 2, 11)$	$[-1, -2, 4]$
$(1, 1, 6)$	$(-5, 3, 2)$	$[-6, 2, -4]$
$(-2, -3, 7)$	$(7, 4, 11)$	$[9, 7, 4]$
$(4, 2, -6)$	$(2, -5, 7)$	$[-2, -7, 13]$
$(3, 2, -6)$	$(7, 3, -9)$	$[4, 1, -3]$
$(6, 4, 0)$	$(3, 2, 8)$	$[-3, -2, 8]$
$(4, -2, -7)$	$(9, 0, -14)$	$[5, 2, -7]$
$(3, -7, 5)$	$(-2, 7, 11)$	$[-5, 14, 6]$
$(6, 0, -2)$	$(-6, 0, -2)$	$[0, 0, 0]$
$(2, 5, -7)$	$(3, 5, -7)$	$[1, 0, 0]$
$(2, 1, 0)$	$(2, 2, 0)$	$[0, 1, 0]$
$(7, -5, 6)$	$(7, -5, 7)$	$[0, 0, 1]$
$(3, 2, -1)$	$(5, -3, 6)$	$[2, -5, 7]$
$(4, 2, 7)$	$(4, 2, 7)$	$[0, 0, 0]$

4. (a) 6 **(b)** 5 **(c)** 8.83 **(d)** 9 **(e)** 9.11 **(f)** 8.78

Exercise 11-5

1. (a)

Initial point	Terminal point	Vector
$A(5, 2, -7)$	$B(3, 7, 5)$	$[-2, 5, 12]$
$C(0, 5, 1)$	$D(3, 5, -4)$	$[3, 0, -5]$
$E(3, -2, -2)$	$F(1, 3, 10)$	$[-2, 5, 12]$
$G(-1, -5, 4)$	$H(5, 2, 1)$	$[6, 7, -3]$
$I(0, 5, 7)$	$J(3, 5, 12)$	$[3, 0, 5]$
$K(-3, 1, 2)$	$L(3, 8, -1)$	$[6, 7, -3]$
$M(1, -2, -6)$	$N(-1, 3, 6)$	$[-2, 5, 12]$

(b) $\overrightarrow{AB} = \overrightarrow{EF} = \overrightarrow{MN}$, $\overrightarrow{GH} = \overrightarrow{KL}$
2. $D(6, 3, 4)$
3. (a) $D(-1, -6, 4)$ **(b)** $E(-1, -6, 4)$
4. (a) $D(-10, -4, 5)$
5. (a) $a = 3, c = 5$ **(b)** $a = d, b = e, c = f$ **(c)** equal

Exercise 11-6

1. (a) $[7, 11, -2]$ **(b)** $[4, 8, -2]$ **(c)** $[1, 1, 7]$ **(d)** $[5, -5, 6]$
(e) $[-1, -1, -4]$ **(f)** $[0, 0, 0]$ **(g)** $[-8, -14, 10]$ **(h)** $[10, -10, 0]$
(i) $[2, 5, -3]$ **(j)** $[5, -1, 5]$
2. (a) $[-3, 7, -2]$ **(b)** $[-2, 6, 3]$ **(c)** $[1, 11, 2]$ **(d)** $[3, 5, 4]$
3. $(a) = (b) = (c)$ commutative **4.** $(a) = (b) = (c)$ associative
5. (a) (i) $[4, 3, 2]$ (ii) $[-7, -2, 3]$ (iii) $[-4, -2, 5]$
(b) $[0, 0, 0]$ **(c)** $[0, 0, 0]$
6. (a) $[-2, -3, -4]$ **(b)** $[-4, -11, 7]$ **(c)** $[4, -7, 3]$
(d) $[-a, -b, -c]$ **(e)** $[-a, -b, -c]$

Exercise 11-7

1. (a) [8, 4, 14]　　(b) [18, −3, 15]　　(c) [2, 1, −4]　　(d) [6, 15, 3]
　 (e) [−2, 0, 6]　　(f) [0, 0, 0]　　(g) [0, −8, 4]　　(h) [−1, 4, −3]
2. (a) [18, 5, 16]　　(b) [1, 8, 5]　　(c) [4, 2, 3]　　(d) [−1, −1, −1]
　 (e) [−23, −41, 6]　(f) [24, −15, 6]　(g) [4, 36, 16]　(h) [0, 0, −35]
3. (a) $[8x, -2y, 10z]$　　(b) $[12x, -8y, 16z]$　　(c) $[-6x, 4y, -8z]$
　 (d) $[10x, -10y, 14z]$　(e) [0, 0, 0]　　(f) $[24x, -21y, 33z]$

Exercise 11-8

1. (a) [1, 1, −7]　　(b) [4, −9, 13]　　(c) [4, 9, −3]　　(d) [−3, −2, −1]
　 (e) [0, 0, 0]　　(f) [10, 24, 26]　　(g) [8, 15, 17]　　(h) $[a, 6b, 3c]$
2. (a) [13, −4, 1]　　(b) [14, −20, 10]　(c) [−2, 0, −4]　　(d) [−21, 5, 0]
　 (e) [−11, 8, −27]　(f) [−40, 40, −5]　(g) [6, −30, 12]

Review Exercise

1. (a) [8, −3, 7]　　　(b) [0, 0, 4]　　　(c) [4, −3, 5]
　 (d) [8, −6, 12]　　 (e) [9, −2, 3]　　 (f) $[x+4, y-3, z+5]$
2. (a) [12, 6, −12]　　(b) [3, 6, −12]　　(c) [5, 16, −32]
　 (d) 6　　　　　　　(e) 9
3. $\overrightarrow{AB} = \overrightarrow{CD}, \ \overrightarrow{BA} = \overrightarrow{DC}$
4. (a) [0, −4, 5]　　(b) [2, 3, −8]　　(c) [−8, 4, 4]　　(d) [−3, −3, −3]
5. 325 km, N 22° E　　　6. N 8° W　　　7. 30.4 kn, 9°

REVIEW AND PREVIEW TO CHAPTER 12

Exercise 1

1. 50 N　　　2. 882 N　　　3. 6.67 m/s²　　4. 15 m/s²　　5. 0.667 kg

Exercise 2

1. 92.9 N　　2. 78.7 N　　3. 73.3 N　　4. 71.2 N　　5. 58 N　　6. 50 N

Exercise 3

1. 86.6 N, 50 N　　　　2. 28.7 N, 41 N　　　　3. 22.3 N, 20.1 N
4. 15.8 N, 12.3 N　　　5. 7.07 N, 7.07 N　　　6. 32.8 N, 22.9 N

Display 12

1. 62.449 468 3　　　　　　2. 59.713 325 21
3. 106.698 015 1　　　　　4. 94.119 053 65
5. 68.203 372 33　　　　　6. 248.670 624 4
7. 2.445 242 946　　　　　8. 0.042 976 892 9
9. 0.410 868 118 3　　　　10. 0.406 099 857 7

CHAPTER 12

Exercise 12-1

1. **(a)** 125 N·m   **(b)** 3.4 N·m   **(c)** 10 N·m
   (d) 20 N·m   **(e)** 10 N·m   **(f)** 50 N·m
2. 15 N   **3.** 1.33 m   **4.** 17 N   **5.** 40 cm   **6.** 5 m
7. 12.5 N   **8.** 2.4 m   **9.** 3 N   **10.** 0.417 m   **11.** 20 N
12. 15 N, 1.5 kg   **13.** 37.5 kg   **14.** 270 kg   **15.** 1000 N
16. **(a)** 680 N   **(b)** 68 kg   **17.** 837 N

Exercise 12-2

1. **(a)** second, 20 N   **(b)** first, $53\frac{1}{3}$ N   **(c)** third, 6 cm   **(d)** first, 22.5 cm
2. **(a)** 375 N   **(b)** $\frac{8}{3}$ **3.** 35 N   **4.** 3 m, 4.6
5. $98\frac{1}{3}$ N, 1.73   **6.** 150 N, 5   **7.** $41\frac{2}{3}$ N, $\frac{5}{24}$ **8.** 167 N, 6
9. 1500 N   **10.** 30 N   **11.** 0.8 N   **12.** 2400 N
13. 6133 N   **14.** $233\frac{1}{3}$ N   **15.** 12 m   **16.** 64 N
17. **(a)**   **(b)**   **(c)**

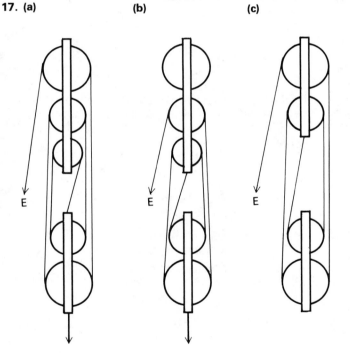

18. 3000 N   **19.** 0.075 m   **20.** 0.32 m

Exercise 12-3

1. **(a)** 5.5 cm from A **(b)** 57 cm from A
   (c) 5.6 cm from A **(d)** 3.4 m from A
2. 4.2 m from the 6 kg mass   **3.** 3.5 m from the 25 kg mass
4. 3.65 m from the rear   **5.** 0.3 m from the weld on the heavy bar
6. **(a)** 17°   **(b)** 45°   **(c)** 18°   **(d)** 45°   **(e)** 56°   **(f)** 31°

Exercise 12-4

1. 0.35   2. 40.5 N   3. 0.67   4. 45 N
5. 800 N, 1000 N   6. 0.43   7. 0.33   8. Yes.
9. 4 N   10. 58 N

Review Exercise

1. (a) 70 N   (b) 20 N   (c) 3.0 m
   (d) 250 N   (e) $3333\frac{1}{3}$ N   (f) 187.5 N
2. (a) 2.33   (b) 2.5   (c) 3   (d) 350   (e) 5
   (f) 5   (g) 4   (h) 3.08   (i) 2513   (j) 26.7
3. (a) 2.71 m from A (b) 4 m from the large end
4. (a) 13°   (b) 34°   5. (a) 0.38   (b) 0.47   (c) 0.36

REVIEW AND PREVIEW TO CHAPTER 13

Exercise 1

1. (a) 9.22 cm   (b) 5.66 m   (c) 1.70 cm
   (d) 11.45 m   (e) 3.74 m   (f) 2 cm

Exercise 2

1. (a) $c = 25.12$ cm; $A = 50.24$ cm²   (b) $C = 28.26$ cm; $A = 63.59$ cm²
   (c) $P = 15.42$ cm; $A = 14.13$ cm²   (d) $P = 8.93$ cm; $A = 4.91$ cm²
   (e) $P = 11.91$ cm; $A = 9.83$ cm²   (f) $P = 17.94$ cm; $A = 17$ cm²

Display 13

1. 57.721 013 5   2. 4.264 292 907
3. 0.090 766 183 1   4. 46.052 257 27
5. 2.300 723 582   6. 2.530 574 03
7. 3.570 142 063   8. 2.428 073 844
9. 40.291 717 51   10. 0.566 831 449 8

CHAPTER 13

Exercise 13-4

1. (a) $r = 5, (0, 0)$ (b) $r = 6, (0, 0)$ (c) $r = 3, (0, 0)$
   (d) $r = 1, (0, 0)$ (e) $r = \sqrt{7}, (0, 0)$ (f) $r = 4, (1, 2)$
   (g) $r = 10, (-3, 4)$ (h) $r = 8, (-7, -3)$
2. (a) $x^2 + y^2 = 49$ (b) $x^2 + y^2 = 81$
   (c) $x^2 + y^2 = 18$ (d) $4x^2 + 4y^2 = 9$
   (e) $(x-3)^2 + (y-5)^2 = 25$ (f) $(x-2)^2 + (y+1)^2 = 16$
   (g) $(x+1)^2 + (y+1)^2 = 3$ (h) $(x+2)^2 + (y-3)^2 = 28$
4. $x^2 + y^2 = 169$ 5. $(x+3)^2 + (y-4)^2 = 25$

Exercise 13-5

1. (a) $(2, 0)$, $x + 2 = 0$ **(b)** $(5, 0)$, $x + 5 = 0$ **(c)** $(1, 0)$, $x + 1 = 0$
(d) $(-3, 0)$, $x - 3 = 0$ **(e)** $(-9, 0)$, $x - 9 = 0$ **(f)** $(\frac{1}{2}, 0)$, $x + \frac{1}{2} = 0$
3. (a) $(9, 0)$, $x + 9 = 0$, $\frac{1}{4}$, 18, -18 **(b)** $(\frac{1}{4}, 0)$, $x + \frac{1}{4} = 0$, 9, 3, -3
(c) $(5, 0)$, $x + 5 = 0$, $\frac{9}{20}$, $6\sqrt{5}$, $-6\sqrt{5}$ **(d)** $(-\frac{9}{8}, 0)$, $x - \frac{9}{8} = 0$, -2, none
4. (a) $y^2 = 28x$ **(b)** $y^2 = -40x$ **(c)** $y^2 = -8x$ **(d)** $y^2 = 6x$
5. $y^2 = x$ **6.** $y = 0$, the equation of the x-axis

7.

	$y^2 = 4x$	$y^2 = -4x$	$x^2 = 4y$	$x^2 = -4y$
Vertex	$(0, 0)$	$(0, 0)$	$(0, 0)$	$(0, 0)$
Focus	$(1, 0)$	$(-1, 0)$	$(0, 1)$	$(0, -1)$
Directrix	$x + 1 = 0$	$x - 1 = 0$	$y + 1 = 0$	$y - 1 = 0$
x-intercept(s)	0	0	0	0
y-intercept(s)	0	0	0	0
Axis of symmetry	$y = 0$	$y = 0$	$x = 0$	$x = 0$
Ends of latus rectum	$(1, 2)$, $(1, -2)$	$(-1, 2)$, $(-1, -2)$	$(2, 1)$, $(-2, 1)$	$(2, -1)$, $(-2, -1)$

8. (a) x intercept -1, y intercepts 2, -2 **(b)** vertex $(-1, 0)$, axis of symmetry $y = 0$

Exercise 13-6

1. $x^2 = -12y$ **2. (a)** $(4, -\frac{4}{5})$ **(b)** $(12, 9)$, $(-12, 9)$
3. (a) $x^2 = -50y$ **(b)** 40 m   **4.** $x^2 = -225y$
5. (a) $x^2 = -400y$ **(b)** $\frac{1}{4}$ m   **6.** $x^2 = -80y$
7. (a) $x^2 = 1800y$ **(b)** (i) 2 m   (ii) 32 m

Exercise 13-7

1.

	(a)	(b)	(c)	(d)
x-intercepts	$5, -5$	$\sqrt{5}, -\sqrt{5}$	$\sqrt{2}, -\sqrt{2}$	$2\sqrt{3}, -2\sqrt{3}$
y-intercepts	$4, -4$	$3, -3$	$1, -1$	$2, -2$
Major axis	10	6	$2\sqrt{2}$	$4\sqrt{3}$
Minor axis	8	$2\sqrt{5}$	2	4
Vertices	$(5, 0)$, $(-5, 0)$	$(0, 3)$, $(0, -3)$	$(2, 0)$, $(-2, 0)$	$(2\sqrt{3}, 0)$, $(-2\sqrt{3}, 0)$
Axes of symmetry	$y = 0$(x axis), $x = 0$(y axis)			

2. $\dfrac{x^2}{100} + \dfrac{y^2}{36} = 1$ **3.** $\dfrac{x^2}{9} + \dfrac{y^2}{1} = 1$ **4.** $\dfrac{x^2}{25} + \dfrac{y^2}{9} = 1$

5. $\dfrac{x^2}{9}+\dfrac{y^2}{4}=1$ **6. (a)** $a=\sqrt{5},\,b=2$ **(b)** $c=1,\,(1,0),\,(-1,0)$

7. (a) $a=13,\,b=5,\,c=12$ **(b)** $a=3,\,b=5,\,c=4$

8. $\dfrac{x^2}{16}+\dfrac{y^2}{12}=1$ or $\dfrac{x^2}{12}+\dfrac{y^2}{16}=1$ **9.** $\dfrac{x^2}{98}+\dfrac{y^2}{32}=1$

10. (a) $\dfrac{x^2}{2500}+\dfrac{y^2}{900}=1$ **(b)** 18 m

11. (a) 147 600 000 km   **(b)** 152 400 000 km

12. 63π **13. (a)** 2π **(b)** πr^2

Exercise 13-8

1.

	(a)	(b)	(c)	(d)
x-intercepts	$5,-5$	$2,-2$	$6,-6$	$7,-7$
y-intercepts	no intercepts			
Transverse axis	10	4	12	14
Conjugate axis	8	2	6	4
Vertices	$(5,0),(-5,0)$	$(2,0),(-2,0)$	$(6,0),(-6,0)$	$(7,0),(-7,0)$
Axes of symmetry	x-axis and y-axis			

2. (a) $\dfrac{x^2}{25}-\dfrac{y^2}{16}=1$ **(b)** $\dfrac{x^2}{64}-\dfrac{y^2}{36}=1$ **(c)** $\dfrac{x^2}{81}-\dfrac{y^2}{49}=-1$ **(d)** $\dfrac{x^2}{9}-\dfrac{y^2}{4}=-1$

3. (a) $a=12,\,b=5,\,c=13;\,(13,0),\,(-13,0)$

     (b) $a=1,\,b=2,\,c=\sqrt{5};\,(\sqrt{5},0),\,(-\sqrt{5},0)$

     (c) $a=6,\,b=8,\,c=10;\,(0,10),\,(0,-10)$

     (d) $a=2,\,b=3,\,c=\sqrt{13};\,(\sqrt{13},0),\,(-\sqrt{13},0)$

4. $\dfrac{x^2}{64}-\dfrac{y^2}{36}=1$ or $-\dfrac{x^2}{36}+\dfrac{y^2}{64}=1$ **5.** $\dfrac{x^2}{144}-\dfrac{y^2}{25}=1$ or $-\dfrac{x^2}{25}+\dfrac{y^2}{144}=1$

Exercise 13-9

1. (a) $x=13-y,\,y=13-x$ **(b)** $x=\dfrac{6-y}{2},\,y=6-2x$ **(c)** $x=\dfrac{7-3y}{2},\,y=\dfrac{7-2x}{3}$

     (d) $x=\dfrac{y+4}{3},\,y=3x-4$ **(e)** $x=2y-9,\,y=\dfrac{x+9}{2}$ **(f)** $x=\dfrac{4y+8}{5},\,y=\dfrac{5x-8}{4}$

     (g) $x=\dfrac{3y+2}{2},\,y=\dfrac{2x-2}{3}$ **(h)** $x=\dfrac{6-3y}{2},\,y=\dfrac{6-2x}{3}$ **(i)** $x=\dfrac{4y+5}{2},\,y=\dfrac{2x-5}{4}$

2. (a) $(2,7)$ **(b)** $\left(\tfrac{8}{5},\tfrac{1}{5}\right)$ **(c)** $(5,-11)$ **(d)** $(2,0)$

3. (a) $(8,2)$ **(b)** $(3,8)$ **(c)** $(-4,5)$ **(d)** $\left(\tfrac{3}{4},\tfrac{2}{3}\right)$

4. (a) $(3,2)$ **(b)** $(-2,1)$ **(c)** $(2,2)$ **(d)** $(7,4)$

Exercise 13-10

1. **(a)** $(-1, 1), (2, 4)$ **(b)** $(0, 0), (6, 6)$ **(c)** $(2, 3), (4, 1)$
   (d) $(1, 1), (-3, 5)$ **(e)** $(2, 0), (-\frac{8}{5}, \frac{9}{5})$ **(f)** $(3, 2), (\frac{21}{4}, -\frac{19}{4})$
2. **(a)** (i) $(3, -4), (-3, 4)$ (ii) $(4, 3)$ (iii) no solution
3. **(a)** (i) $(3, 6)$ (ii) $(1, -2)$ **(b)** tangent
4. **(a)** (i) no solution   (ii) no solution   **(b)** asymptote
5. 2 and 7   6. 9 m by 5 m

Review Exercise

1. **(a)** Parabola, vertex $(0, 0)$, focus $(3, 0)$
   (b) Circle, centre $(0, 0)$, radius 3
   (c) Ellipse, major axis 8, minor axis 6
   (d) Hyperbola, transverse and conjugate axes 6
   (e) Hyperbola, transverse axis 10, conjugate axis 6
   (f) Line, slope 12, y-intercept $\frac{1}{3}$

2.

	a	b	c
(a)	5	4	3
(b)	8	6	10
(c)	3	2	$\sqrt{13}$
(d)	2	3	$\sqrt{13}$

3. **(a)** $y^2 = 20x$ **(b)** $y^2 = 8x$ **(c)** $x^2 = -12x$
4. **(a)** $\frac{x^2}{49} + \frac{y^2}{25} = 1$ **(b)** $\frac{x^2}{25} + \frac{y^2}{64} = 1$ **(c)** $\frac{x^2}{169} + \frac{y^2}{144} = 1$
5. **(a)** $\frac{x^2}{25} - \frac{y^2}{36} = -1$ **(b)** $\frac{x^2}{144} - \frac{y^2}{81} = 1$ **(c)** $x^2 - y^2 = 256$
6. **(a)** $(5, 0), (-\frac{25}{13}, \frac{60}{13})$ **(b)** $(3, 6)$

REVIEW AND PREVIEW TO CHAPTER 14

Exercise 1

1. **(b)** 47.35 g, 47.25 g   **(c)** 1 km, ± 0.5 km
   (d) 0.0435 mm, 0.0425 mm, 0.001 mm, ± 0.0005 mm
   (e) 63.815 kg, 63.805 kg, 0.01 kg, ± 0.005 kg
   (f) 574.5 m, 573.5 m, 1 m, ± 0.5 m
   (h) 4.85×10^4 m, 4.75×10^4 m, 1000 m, ± 500 m
   (i) 2.565×10^3 g, 2.555×10^3 g, 10 g, ± 5 g
   (j) 9.15×10^{-4} km, 9.05×10^{-4} km, 10^{-5} km, $\pm 5 \times 10^{-6}$ km
   (k) 2.6435×10^5 cm, 2.6425×10^5 cm, 10^2 cm, ± 50 cm
   (l) 5.035×10^{-2} mm, 5.025×10^{-2} mm, 10^{-4} mm, $\pm 5 \times 10^{-5}$ mm

Exercise 2

1. **(a)** 33.9 g   **(b)** 9392 mm   **(c)** 702.7 km   **(d)** 52 323 g
   (e) 4007.4 cm   **(f)** 2674 ml   **(g)** 7.29×10^3 cm   **(h)** 1.89×10^3 g

(i) 1.149 m   **(j)** 1.335×10^4 N
2. (a) 26.0 cm   **(b)** 1.00×10^2 km   **(c)** 719.39 g   **(d)** 57.93 mm
    (e) 0.003 96 m   **(f)** 9.4×10 cm   **(g)** 5.146×10^3 g   **(h)** 9.4×10^4 mm
    (i) 1.87×10^4 cm   **(j)** 1.242×10^{-3} g
3. (a) 215.7 cm, 215.80 cm, 215.68 cm   **(b)** 14 490 kg, 14 490.8 kg, 14 489.7 kg
4. 5.370, ±0.002 km

Display 14
1. $2315.16   **2.** $4119.50
3. $463.68   **4.** $4936.99
5. $1208.92   **6.** $5062.33
7. $4929.75   **8.** $2391.53
9. $2922.75   **10.** $843.19

CHAPTER 14

Exercise 14-1
3. $5000   **4.** $4388.10   **5.** $63 750
6. (a) $1 080 000   **(b)** $2700   **(c)** 2.25%
7. (a) $0.65   **(b)** $325   **(c)** 5.2%

Exercise 14-2
1. (a) $1800   **(b)** $6000   **(c)** $1125   **(d)** $1350   **(e)** $1025
    (f) $637.50   **(g)** $17 250   **(h)** $1750   **(i)** $630   **(j)** $600
2. (a) $9.38   **(b)** $66.56   **(c)** $23.75   **(d)** $25.00   **(e)** $109.66
    (f) $318.25   **(g)** $228.64   **(h)** $51.87   **(i)** $191.88   **(j)** $159.08
3. (a) $143.50   **(b)** $5605.47   **(c)** $1884.98   **(d)** $5190.41
    (e) $4954.95   **(f)** $2190.94   **(g)** $3659.04   **(h)** $14 529.38
4. (a) $585.00   **(b)** $853.13   **(c)** $682.50   **(d)** $2073.87
    (e) $3098.34   **(f)** $530.89   **(g)** $409.50   **(h)** $307.13
5. (a) $2444.40 loss   **(b)** $3959.67 gain   **(c)** $1360.85 loss
    (d) $1153.75 gain   **(e)** $3710.36 gain   **(f)** $166.13 loss

Exercise 14-3
1. (a) (ii)   **(b)** (iv)   **(c)** (v)   **(d)** (i)   **(e)** (iii)   **(f)** (vi)
2. (a) $0.50   **(b)** $0.75   **(c)** $2.00   **(d)** $3.00   **(e)** $0.50   **(f)** $0.25
3. (a) $2750   **(b)** $1662.50   **(c)** $425   **(d)** $450   **(e)** $900
4. (a) $128, 3.0%   **(b)** $725, 3.5%   **(c)** $54, 3.2%
    (d) $360, 5.7%   **(e)** $198, 7.3%
5. (a) $50   **(b)** $40
6. (a) 5.6   **(b)** 5.7   **(c)** 6.0   **(d)** 4.7   **(e)** 5.7
7. 4.2%   **8.** 8.2   **9.** 8%   **10.** 5

Exercise 14-5

1. (a) $11 112.80, $3908.05   (b) $9243.75, $4063.93
   (c) $1671.99, $1136.68   (d) $5395.74, $3497.09
   (e) $1512.00, $802.36
2. (a) $111.50 gain   (b) $3300 gain   (c) $4667.85 loss
   (d) $1243.96 gain   (e) $455 gain
3. (a) $600   (b) $872.84   (c) $272.84
4. (a) $539.51   (b) $1126.12

Exercise 14-6

1. (a) $0.90   (b) $5.67   (c) $4.96
   (d) 750 000   (e) 3 920 000   (f) 2 525 000
   (g) $12 259 800   (h) $52 223 400   (i) $630 000
2. (a) $160, $1840   (b) $1360, $15 640   (c) $2010, $31 490
   (d) $1716, $19 734   (e) $2520, $39 480   (f) $1056, $12 144
3. (a) 805.93   (b) 18 604.65   (c) 2498.34   (d) 55 619.27
4. (a) $18 000   (b) $1426.65   (c) $16 573.35
   (d) 7.9%   (e) 8.6%   (f) 46%, 85%

Exercise 14-7

4. (a) $92.50   (b) $38.75   (c) $218.75
5. (a) $817.19   (b) $2733.88   (c) $478.80
   (d) $1500.19   (e) $4055.00   (f) $10 740.90
6. (a) $932.05   (b) $504.68   (c) $2733.70
   (d) $1034.99   (e) $1603.42   (f) $19 707.19
7. $200, 2.35%

Exercise 14-8

1. (a) 12.0%   (b) 11.7%   (c) 12.5%   (d) 10.7%   (e) 9.5%
2. (a) 10.8%   (b) 10.6%   (c) 9.1%   (d) 11.3%   (e) 11.3%
3. (a) (i) 11.5%, (ii) 10.8%   (b) risk
4. (a) (i) 10.3%, (ii) 9.6%, (iii) 11.5%, (iv) 11.8%

Exercise 14-9

2. (a) less   (b) more
3. (a) 81.76   (b) 86.85   (c) 86.45   (d) 83.06   (e) 67.14
4. (a) 111.87   (b) 117.48   (c) 106.46   (d) 107.81   (e) 104.56
5. $395.10   6. $5895   7. $7526   8. 114.55

Review Exercise

2. (a) $500 000+   (b) rise   4. (b) 6%   5. $4250
6. (a) $10 857.40   (b) $8630.50   7. (a) $731.25   (b) $789.95
8. (a) $1300, 11.6%   (b) $2062.50, $13\frac{3}{4}$%
9. (a) $6562.50   (b) $10 358.28   10. $2312.50
11. (a) $8512.80   (b) $390.65   12. 13.0%, 11.5%   13. 90.36

REVIEW AND PREVIEW TO CHAPTER 15

Exercise 1

1. (a) 3 (b) 3 (c) 3 (d) 6 (e) 4
   (f) 3 (g) 4 (h) 1 (i) 9 (j) 7
   (k) 3 (l) 3 (m) 5 (n) 4
2. (b) 10^6 m/s, 300, 3 (c) 3 652 422, 7
   (d) 10^8 cm, 696, 3 (e) 0.001 light years, 3262, 4
   (f) 1000 parsec, 15, 2 (g) 10^7 cm, 3844, 4

Exercise 2

1. (a) 316 cm² (b) 1.7×10^3 kg·m (c) 4.3×10^2 km (d) 517.0 g
   (e) 1.25×10^4 mm² (f) 756 m² (g) 2.26×10^3 mm² (h) 1.214×10^6 g
   (i) 245 km (j) 22 kg·m/s²
2. (a) 2.8×10^2 cm² (b) 1.3 N/cm² (c) 3.5×10^2 km (d) 0.698 kg/m
   (e) 52.5 km/h (f) 1.8×10^5 m (g) 7.12×10^{11} mm² (h) 1.57×10^{-6} cm³
   (i) 8.6×10^8 mm³ (j) 1.2×10^3 cm³
3. 114 cm²   4. 4.68×10^{22} 5. 4.09 ha

Exercise 3

1. 0.000 17, 0.017%   2. 0.000 84, 0.084%
3. 0.003, 0.3%   4. 0.000 33, 0.033%
5. 0.000 05, 0.005%   6. 0.000 017, 0.0017%
7. 0.0007, 0.07%   8. 0.0016, 0.16%
9. 0.000 055, 0.0055%   10. 0.000 07, 0.007%

Display 15

1. 3 600.230 78   2. 3 140.674 635
3. 645.896 279 4   4. 391.587 666 4
5. 5 360.808 073

CHAPTER 15

Exercise 15-1

1. (a) $130 (b) $15.45 (c) $475 (d) $5.87 (e) $13.88
   (f) $235.63 (g) $12.60 (h) $17.42 (i) $49.98 (j) $115.25
2. (a) 68 (b) 541 (c) 1859 (d) 206 (e) 1258
   (f) 265 (g) 5714 (h) 3846 (i) 613 (j) 482
3. (a) 57 874 (b) 376 (c) 322 (d) 61 (e) 9490
4. (a) 80 (b) 750 (c) 530 (d) 30 878 (e) 1754

Exercise 15-2

4. (a) $57 500, $60 000, $67 500   (b) $6600, $7200, $7950
   (c) $168.75, $180.00, $210.00   (d) $2400, $2820, $3240
   (e) $2160, $2205, $2430
5. $50.95   6. $7430.93   7. $178.05   8. $2505.56
9. $2853.45   10. $88.80   11. $907.20   12. $1100

Exercise 15-3

1. Luxury goods   2. They are charged import duty
3. Federal sales tax
4. (a) $73.20   (b) $117.49   5. $4414.54   6. $267.20
7. $342.64   8. (a) $771.46   (b) $1073.10
9. (a) $159.26   (b) $212.35, $229.34
10. (a) $1290.91   (b) $1445.75   11. $2500.71

Review Exercise

1. See figure 15-2   2. Balance of trade
3. British preferential, most favoured nation, general
4. Prevent unfair competition
5. Sales tax, excise tax, excise duty, customs duty, income tax
6. 68 540 cruzieros   7. 8401 forints
8. $17 131.30   9. $859.70
10. (a) $7.38   (b) $10.14   (c) $1.63
11. (a) $35.09   (b) $62.88   (c) $121.11
12. (a) $5.06   (b) $4.82

REVIEW AND PREVIEW TO CHAPTER 16

Exercise 1

1. (a) $35 315   (b) $21 189   2. $1708, $1980, $2076
3. (a) $840   (b) $1950   (c) $147   (d) $3225
4. $19.68   5. $44.75, $47.11   6. $47.26, $49.62

Display 16
1. 19.636 700 33   2. 2.296 827 089
3. 1.699 946 458   4. 0.406 964 429 8
5. 0.909 745 153 1   6. 308.635 954 3
7. 11.926 825 91   8. 48.75
9. 0.057 804 518 6   10. 12.057 890 95

CHAPTER 16

Exercise 16-1

4. $194
   (c) $823.75

5. (a) $20 500
6. $679.70

(b) $16 500
7. $2389.40

Exercise 16-2

4. (a) $354.05 (b) $502.26 (c) $172.53 (d) $289.31 (e) $202.51 (f) $357.80
5. (a) $17 000   (b) $36 000   (c) $26 000   (d) $50 000   8. (b) $3251.07

Exercise 16-3

2. (a) $45.17, vendor
   (c) $230.93, purchaser
   (e) $46 449.57, purchaser
3. $36 291.61

(b) $93.80, vendor
(d) $185.88, vendor
(f) $24 657.07 to purchaser

4. $7368.84

5. $7166.88

Exercise 16-4

1. (a) $778.50   (b) $18 000   (c) 57.3   (d) $695.10   (e) 25.25
2. 51.8   3. (a) $1000, $1050   (b) No
4. (a) 64.1   (b) 1.5
5. (a) $1 144 000   (b) 45.8   (c) $343.50
6. (a) 46.7
7. (a) 2 mills   (b) $1167.50
                  (b) $50

Exercise 16-5

4. $4538, $380
6. (a) $600
7. (a) $12 090

5. $294.00
(b) $840
(b) $555, $455   (c) $470, $385

Review Exercise

5. (a) $428.31
7. (a) $511.94
8. (a) $338.01, $331.18
9. (a) $62 267.86
10. (a) 28.4

(b) $19 036/a   6. $384.66
(b) $598.67
(b) $1269.19
(b) $12 499.62
(b) $766.80   11. $640

APPENDIX

Days Expressed in Decimal Equivalents of a Year – 365 Day Basis

For Figuring Interest, Cancellation of Insurance Premiums, Etc.

Day of Month	January		February		March		April		May		June		July		August		September		October		November		December		Day of Month
	Day of Year	Decimal Equivalent	Day of Year	Decimal Equivalent	Day of Year	Decimal Equivalent	Day of Year	Decimal Equivalent	Day of Year	Decimal Equivalent	Day of Year	Decimal Equivalent	Day of Year	Decimal Equivalent	Day of Year	Decimal Equivalent	Day of Year	Decimal Equivalent	Day of Year	Decimal Equivalent	Day of Year	Decimal Equivalent	Day of Year	Decimal Equivalent	
1	1	0.0027	32	0.0877	60	0.1644	91	0.2493	121	0.3315	152	0.4164	182	0.4986	213	0.5836	244	0.6685	274	0.7507	305	0.8356	335	0.9178	1
2	2	0.0055	33	0.0904	61	0.1671	92	0.2521	122	0.3342	153	0.4192	183	0.5014	214	0.5863	245	0.6712	275	0.7534	306	0.8384	336	0.9205	2
3	3	0.0082	34	0.0932	62	0.1699	93	0.2548	123	0.3370	154	0.4219	184	0.5041	215	0.5890	246	0.6740	276	0.7562	307	0.8411	337	0.9233	3
4	4	0.0110	35	0.0959	63	0.1726	94	0.2575	124	0.3397	155	0.4247	185	0.5068	216	0.5918	247	0.6767	277	0.7589	308	0.8438	338	0.9260	4
5	5	0.0137	36	0.0986	64	0.1753	95	0.2603	125	0.3425	156	0.4274	186	0.5096	217	0.5945	248	0.6795	278	0.7616	309	0.8466	339	0.9288	5
6	6	0.0164	37	0.1014	65	0.1781	96	0.2630	126	0.3452	157	0.4301	187	0.5123	218	0.5973	249	0.6822	279	0.7644	310	0.8493	340	0.9315	6
7	7	0.0192	38	0.1041	66	0.1808	97	0.2658	127	0.3479	158	0.4329	188	0.5151	219	0.6000	250	0.6849	280	0.7671	311	0.8521	341	0.9342	7
8	8	0.0219	39	0.1068	67	0.1836	98	0.2685	128	0.3507	159	0.4356	189	0.5178	220	0.6027	251	0.6877	281	0.7699	312	0.8548	342	0.9370	8
9	9	0.0247	40	0.1096	68	0.1863	99	0.2712	129	0.3534	160	0.4384	190	0.5205	221	0.6055	252	0.6904	282	0.7726	313	0.8575	343	0.9397	9
10	10	0.0274	41	0.1123	69	0.1890	100	0.2740	130	0.3562	161	0.4411	191	0.5233	222	0.6082	253	0.6932	283	0.7753	314	0.8603	344	0.9425	10
11	11	0.0301	42	0.1151	70	0.1918	101	0.2767	131	0.3589	162	0.4438	192	0.5260	223	0.6110	254	0.6959	284	0.7781	315	0.8630	345	0.9452	11
12	12	0.0329	43	0.1178	71	0.1945	102	0.2795	132	0.3616	163	0.4466	193	0.5288	224	0.6137	255	0.6986	285	0.7808	316	0.8658	346	0.9479	12
13	13	0.0356	44	0.1205	72	0.1973	103	0.2822	133	0.3644	164	0.4493	194	0.5315	225	0.6164	256	0.7014	286	0.7836	317	0.8685	347	0.9507	13
14	14	0.0384	45	0.1233	73	0.2000	104	0.2849	134	0.3671	165	0.4521	195	0.5342	226	0.6192	257	0.7041	287	0.7863	318	0.8712	348	0.9534	14
15	15	0.0411	46	0.1260	74	0.2027	105	0.2877	135	0.3699	166	0.4548	196	0.5370	227	0.6219	258	0.7068	288	0.7890	319	0.8740	349	0.9562	15
16	16	0.0438	47	0.1288	75	0.2055	106	0.2904	136	0.3726	167	0.4575	197	0.5397	228	0.6247	259	0.7096	289	0.7918	320	0.8767	350	0.9589	16
17	17	0.0466	48	0.1315	76	0.2082	107	0.2932	137	0.3753	168	0.4603	198	0.5425	229	0.6274	260	0.7123	290	0.7945	321	0.8795	351	0.9616	17
18	18	0.0493	49	0.1342	77	0.2110	108	0.2959	138	0.3781	169	0.4630	199	0.5452	230	0.6301	261	0.7151	291	0.7973	322	0.8822	352	0.9644	18
19	19	0.0521	50	0.1370	78	0.2137	109	0.2986	139	0.3808	170	0.4658	200	0.5479	231	0.6329	262	0.7178	292	0.8000	323	0.8849	353	0.9671	19
20	20	0.0548	51	0.1397	79	0.2164	110	0.3014	140	0.3836	171	0.4685	201	0.5507	232	0.6356	263	0.7205	293	0.8027	324	0.8877	354	0.9699	20
21	21	0.0575	52	0.1425	80	0.2192	111	0.3041	141	0.3863	172	0.4712	202	0.5534	233	0.6384	264	0.7233	294	0.8055	325	0.8904	355	0.9726	21
22	22	0.0603	53	0.1452	81	0.2219	112	0.3068	142	0.3890	173	0.4740	203	0.5562	234	0.6411	265	0.7260	295	0.8082	326	0.8932	356	0.9753	22
23	23	0.0630	54	0.1479	82	0.2247	113	0.3096	143	0.3918	174	0.4767	204	0.5589	235	0.6438	266	0.7288	296	0.8110	327	0.8959	357	0.9781	23
24	24	0.0658	55	0.1507	83	0.2274	114	0.3123	144	0.3945	175	0.4795	205	0.5616	236	0.6466	267	0.7315	297	0.8137	328	0.8986	358	0.9808	24
25	25	0.0685	56	0.1534	84	0.2301	115	0.3151	145	0.3973	176	0.4822	206	0.5644	237	0.6493	268	0.7342	298	0.8164	329	0.9014	359	0.9836	25
26	26	0.0712	57	0.1562	85	0.2329	116	0.3178	146	0.4000	177	0.4849	207	0.5671	238	0.6521	269	0.7370	299	0.8192	330	0.9041	360	0.9863	26
27	27	0.0740	58	0.1589	86	0.2356	117	0.3205	147	0.4027	178	0.4877	208	0.5699	239	0.6548	270	0.7397	300	0.8219	331	0.9068	361	0.9890	27
28	28	0.0767	59	0.1616	87	0.2384	118	0.3233	148	0.4055	179	0.4904	209	0.5726	240	0.6575	271	0.7425	301	0.8247	332	0.9096	362	0.9918	28
29	29	0.0795			88	0.2411	119	0.3260	149	0.4082	180	0.4932	210	0.5753	241	0.6603	272	0.7452	302	0.8274	333	0.9123	363	0.9945	29
30	30	0.0822			89	0.2438	120	0.3288	150	0.4110	181	0.4959	211	0.5781	242	0.6630	273	0.7479	303	0.8301	334	0.9151	364	0.9973	30
31	31	0.0849			90	0.2466			151	0.4137			212	0.5808	243	0.6658			304	0.8329			365	1.0000	31

TRIGONOMETRIC RATIOS

$0°$	$\sin \theta$	$\cos \theta$	$\tan \theta$	$\cot \theta$	$\sec \theta$	$\csc \theta$
0	0.0000	1.0000	0.0000	—	1.0000	—
1	0.0175	0.9999	0.0175	57.290	1.0001	57.299
2	0.0349	0.9994	0.0349	28.636	1.0006	28.654
3	0.0523	0.9986	0.0524	19.081	1.0014	19.107
4	0.0698	0.9976	0.0699	14.301	1.0024	14.335
5	0.0872	0.9962	0.0875	11.430	1.0038	11.474
6	0.1045	0.9945	0.1051	9.5144	1.0055	9.5668
7	0.1219	0.9926	0.1228	8.1443	1.0075	8.2055
8	0.1392	0.9903	0.1405	7.1154	1.0098	7.1853
9	0.1564	0.9877	0.1584	6.3137	1.0125	6.3924
10	0.1737	0.9848	0.1763	5.6713	1.0154	5.7588
11	0.1908	0.9816	0.1944	5.1445	1.0187	5.2408
12	0.2079	0.9782	0.2126	4.7046	1.0223	4.8097
13	0.2250	0.9744	0.2309	4.3315	1.0263	4.4454
14	0.2419	0.9703	0.2493	4.0108	1.0306	4.1336
15	0.2588	0.9659	0.2680	3.7320	1.0353	3.8637
16	0.2756	0.9613	0.2867	3.4874	1.0403	3.6279
17	0.2924	0.9563	0.3057	3.2708	1.0457	3.4203
18	0.3090	0.9511	0.3249	3.0777	1.0515	3.2361
19	0.3256	0.9455	0.3443	2.9042	1.0576	3.0715
20	0.3420	0.9397	0.3640	2.7475	1.0642	2.9238
21	0.3584	0.9336	0.3839	2.6051	1.0711	2.7904
22	0.3746	0.9272	0.4040	2.4751	1.0785	2.6695
23	0.3907	0.9025	0.4245	2.3558	1.0864	2.5593
24	0.4067	0.9136	0.4452	2.2460	1.0946	2.4586
25	0.4226	0.9063	0.4663	2.1445	1.1034	2.3662
26	0.4384	0.8988	0.4877	2.0503	1.1126	2.2812
27	0.4540	0.8910	0.5095	1.9626	1.1223	2.2027
28	0.4695	0.8830	0.5317	1.8807	1.1326	2.1300
29	0.4848	0.8746	0.5543	1.8040	1.1433	2.0627
30	0.5000	0.8660	0.5774	1.7320	1.1547	2.0000
31	0.5150	0.8572	0.6009	1.6643	1.1666	1.9416
32	0.5299	0.8481	0.6249	1.6003	1.1792	1.8871
33	0.5446	0.8387	0.6494	1.5399	1.1924	1.8361
34	0.5592	0.8290	0.6745	1.4826	1.2062	1.7883
35	0.5736	0.8192	0.7002	1.4281	1.2208	1.7434
36	0.5878	0.8090	0.7265	1.3764	1.2361	1.7013
37	0.6018	0.7986	0.7536	1.3270	1.2521	1.6616
38	0.6157	0.7880	0.7813	1.2799	1.2690	1.6243
39	0.6293	0.7772	0.8098	1.2349	1.2867	1.5890
40	0.6428	0.7660	0.8391	1.1917	1.3054	1.5557
41	0.6561	0.7547	0.8693	1.1504	1.3250	1.5242
42	0.6691	0.7431	0.9004	1.1106	1.3456	1.4945
43	0.6820	0.7314	0.9325	1.0724	1.3673	1.4663
44	0.6947	0.7193	0.9657	1.0355	1.3902	1.4395
45	0.7071	0.7071	1.0000	1.0000	1.4142	1.4142

TRIGONOMETRIC RATIOS

θ°	sin θ	cos θ	tan θ	cot θ	sec θ	cosec θ
46	0.7193	0.6947	1.0355	0.9657	1.4395	1.3902
47	0.7314	0.6820	1.0724	0.9325	1.4663	1.3673
48	0.7431	0.6691	1.1106	0.9004	1.4945	1.3456
49	0.7547	0.6561	1.1504	0.8693	1.5242	1.3250
50	0.7660	0.6428	1.1917	0.8391	1.5557	1.3054
51	0.7772	0.6293	1.2349	0.8098	1.5890	1.2867
52	0.7880	0.6157	1.2799	0.7813	1.6243	1.2690
53	0.7986	0.6018	1.3270	0.7536	1.6616	1.2521
54	0.8090	0.5878	1.3764	0.7265	1.7013	1.2361
55	0.8192	0.5736	1.4281	0.7002	1.7434	1.2208
56	0.8290	0.5592	1.4826	0.6745	1.7883	1.2062
57	0.8387	0.5446	1.5399	0.6494	1.8361	1.1924
58	0.8481	0.5299	1.6003	0.6249	1.8871	1.1792
59	0.8572	0.5150	1.6643	0.6009	1.9416	1.1666
60	0.8660	0.5000	1.7320	0.5774	2.0000	1.1547
61	0.8746	0.4848	1.8040	0.5543	2.0627	1.1433
62	0.8830	0.4695	1.8807	0.5317	2.1300	1.1326
63	0.8910	0.4540	1.9626	0.5095	2.2027	1.1223
64	0.8988	0.4384	2.0503	0.4877	2.2812	1.1126
65	0.9063	0.4226	2.1445	0.4663	2.3662	1.1034
66	0.9136	0.4067	2.2460	0.4452	2.4586	1.0946
67	0.9205	0.3907	2.3558	0.4245	2.5593	1.0864
68	0.9272	0.3746	2.4751	0.4040	2.6695	1.0785
69	0.9336	0.3584	2.6051	0.3839	2.7904	1.0711
70	0.9397	0.3420	2.7475	0.3640	2.9238	1.0642
71	0.9455	0.3256	2.9042	0.3443	3.0715	1.0576
72	0.9511	0.3090	3.0777	0.3249	3.2361	1.0515
73	0.9563	0.2924	3.2708	0.3057	3.4203	1.0457
74	0.9613	0.2756	3.4874	0.2867	3.6279	1.0403
75	0.9659	0.2588	3.7320	0.2680	3.8637	1.0353
76	0.9703	0.2419	4.0108	0.2493	4.1336	1.0306
77	0.9744	0.2250	4.3315	0.2309	4.4454	1.0263
78	0.9782	0.2079	4.7046	0.2126	4.8097	1.0223
79	0.9816	0.1908	5.1445	0.1944	5.2408	1.0187
80	0.9848	0.1737	5.6713	0.1763	5.7588	1.0154
81	0.9877	0.1564	6.3137	0.1584	6.3924	1.0125
82	0.9903	0.1392	7.1154	0.1405	7.1853	1.0098
83	0.9926	0.1219	8.1443	0.1228	8.2005	1.0075
84	0.9945	0.1045	9.5144	0.1051	9.5668	1.0055
85	0.9962	0.0872	11.430	0.0875	11.474	1.0038
86	0.9976	0.0698	14.301	0.0699	14.335	1.0024
87	0.9986	0.0523	19.081	0.0524	19.107	1.0014
88	0.9994	0.0349	28.636	0.0349	28.654	1.0006
89	0.9999	0.0175	57.290	0.0175	57.299	1.0001
90	1.0000	0.0000	—	0.0000	—	1.0000

Logarithms

	0	1	2	3	4	5	6	7	8	9	Differences 1	2	3	4	5	6	7	8	9
1.0	.0000	.0043	.0086	.0128	.0170	.0212	.0253	.0294	.0334	.0374	4	8	12	17	21	25	29	33	37
1.1	.0414	.0453	.0492	.0531	.0569	.0607	.0645	.0682	.0719	.0755	4	8	11	15	19	23	26	30	34
1.2	.0792	.0828	.0864	.0899	.0934	.0969	.1004	.1038	.1072	.1106	3	7	10	14	17	21	24	28	31
1.3	.1139	.1173	.1206	.1239	.1271	.1303	.1335	.1367	.1399	.1430	3	6	10	13	16	19	23	26	29
1.4	.1461	.1492	.1523	.1553	.1584	.1614	.1644	.1673	.1703	.1732	3	6	9	12	15	18	21	24	27
1.5	.1761	.1790	.1818	.1847	.1875	.1903	.1931	.1959	.1987	.2014	3	6	8	11	14	17	20	22	25
1.6	.2041	.2068	.2095	.2122	.2148	.2175	.2201	.2227	.2253	.2279	3	5	8	11	13	16	18	21	24
1.7	.2304	.2330	.2355	.2380	.2405	.2430	.2455	.2480	.2504	.2529	2	5	7	10	12	15	17	20	22
1.8	.2553	.2577	.2601	.2625	.2648	.2672	.2695	.2718	.2742	.2765	2	5	7	9	12	14	16	19	21
1.9	.2788	.2810	.2833	.2856	.2878	.2900	.2923	.2945	.2967	.2989	2	4	7	9	11	13	16	18	20
2.0	.3010	.3032	.3054	.3075	.3096	.3118	.3139	.3160	.3181	.3201	2	4	6	8	11	13	15	17	19
2.1	.3222	.3243	.3263	.3284	.3304	.3324	.3345	.3365	.3385	.3404	2	4	6	8	10	12	14	16	18
2.2	.3424	.3444	.3464	.3483	.3502	.3522	.3541	.3560	.3579	.3598	2	4	6	8	10	12	14	15	17
2.3	.3617	.3636	.3655	.3674	.3692	.3711	.3729	.3747	.3766	.3784	2	4	6	7	9	11	13	15	17
2.4	.3802	.3820	.3838	.3856	.3874	.3892	.3909	.3927	.3945	.3962	2	4	5	7	9	11	12	14	16
2.5	.3979	.3997	.4014	.4031	.4048	.4065	.4082	.4099	.4116	.4133	2	3	5	7	9	10	12	14	15
2.6	.4150	.4166	.4183	.4200	.4216	.4232	.4249	.4265	.4281	.4298	2	3	5	7	8	10	11	13	15
2.7	.4314	.4330	.4346	.4362	.4378	.4393	.4409	.4425	.4440	.4456	2	3	5	6	8	9	11	13	14
2.8	.4472	.4487	.4502	.4518	.4533	.4548	.4564	.4579	.4594	.4609	2	3	5	6	8	9	11	12	14
2.9	.4624	.4639	.4654	.4669	.4683	.4698	.4713	.4728	.4742	.4757	1	3	4	6	7	9	10	12	13
3.0	.4771	.4786	.4800	.4814	.4829	.4843	.4857	.4871	.4886	.4900	1	3	4	6	7	9	10	11	13
3.1	.4914	.4928	.4942	.4955	.4969	.4983	.4997	.5011	.5024	.5038	1	3	4	6	7	8	10	11	12
3.2	.5051	.5065	.5079	.5092	.5105	.5119	.5132	.5145	.5159	.5172	1	3	4	5	7	8	9	11	12
3.3	.5185	.5198	.5211	.5224	.5237	.5250	.5263	.5276	.5289	.5302	1	3	4	5	6	8	9	10	12
3.4	.5315	.5328	.5340	.5353	.5366	.5378	.5391	.5403	.5416	.5428	1	3	4	5	6	8	9	10	11
3.5	.5441	.5453	.5465	.5478	.5490	.5502	.5514	.5527	.5539	.5551	1	2	4	5	6	7	9	10	11
3.6	.5563	.5575	.5587	.5599	.5611	.5623	.5635	.5647	.5658	.5670	1	2	4	5	6	7	8	10	11
3.7	.5682	.5694	.5705	.5717	.5729	.5740	.5752	.5763	.5775	.5786	1	2	3	5	6	7	8	9	10
3.8	.5798	.5809	.5821	.5832	.5843	.5855	.5866	.5877	.5888	.5899	1	2	3	5	6	7	8	9	10
3.9	.5911	.5922	.5933	.5944	.5955	.5966	.5977	.5988	.5999	.6010	1	2	3	4	5	7	8	9	10
4.0	.6021	.6031	.6042	.6053	.6064	.6075	.6085	.6096	.6107	.6117	1	2	3	4	5	6	8	9	10
4.1	.6128	.6138	.6149	.6160	.6170	.6180	.6191	.6201	.6212	.6222	1	2	3	4	5	6	7	8	9
4.2	.6232	.6243	.6253	.6263	.6274	.6284	.6294	.6304	.6314	.6325	1	2	3	4	5	6	7	8	9
4.3	.6335	.6345	.6355	.6365	.6375	.6385	.6395	.6405	.6415	.6425	1	2	3	4	5	6	7	8	9
4.4	.6435	.6444	.6454	.6464	.6474	.6484	.6493	.6503	.6513	.6522	1	2	3	4	5	6	7	8	9
4.5	.6532	.6542	.6551	.6561	.6571	.6580	.6590	.6599	.6609	.6618	1	2	3	4	5	6	7	8	9
4.6	.6628	.6637	.6646	.6656	.6665	.6675	.6684	.6693	.6702	.6712	1	2	3	4	5	6	7	7	8
4.7	.6721	.6730	.6739	.6749	.6758	.6767	.6776	.6785	.6794	.6803	1	2	3	4	5	5	6	7	8
4.8	.6812	.6821	.6830	.6839	.6848	.6457	.6866	.6875	.6884	.6893	1	2	3	4	4	5	6	7	8
4.9	.6902	.6911	.6920	.6928	.6937	.6946	.6955	.6964	.6972	.6981	1	2	3	4	4	5	6	7	8
5.0	.6990	.6998	.7007	.7016	.7024	.7033	.7042	.7050	.7059	.7067	1	2	3	3	4	5	6	7	8
5.1	.7076	.7084	.7093	.7101	.7110	.7118	.7126	.7135	.7143	.7152	1	2	3	3	4	5	6	7	8
5.2	.7160	.7168	.7177	.7185	.7193	.7202	.7210	.7218	.7226	.7235	1	2	2	3	4	5	6	7	7
5.3	.7243	.7251	.7259	.7267	.7275	.7284	.7292	.7300	.7308	.7316	1	2	2	3	4	5	6	6	7
5.4	.7324	.7332	.7340	.7348	.7356	.7364	.7372	.7380	.7388	.7396	1	2	2	3	4	5	6	6	7
	0	1	2	3	4	5	6	7	8	9	1	2	3	4	5	6	7	8	9

Logarithms

	0	1	2	3	4	5	6	7	8	9	Differences								
											1	2	3	4	5	6	7	8	9
5.5	.7404	.7412	.7419	.7427	.7435	.7443	.7451	.7459	.7466	.7474	1	2	2	3	4	5	5	6	7
5.6	.7482	.7490	.7497	.7505	.7513	.7520	.7528	.7536	.7543	.7551	1	2	2	3	4	5	5	6	7
5.7	.7559	.7566	.7574	.7582	.7589	.7597	.7604	.7612	.7619	.7627	1	2	2	3	4	5	5	6	7
5.8	.7634	.7642	.7649	.7657	.7664	.7672	.7679	.7686	.7694	.7701	1	1	2	3	4	4	5	6	7
5.9	.7709	.7716	.7723	.7731	.7738	.7745	.7752	.7760	.7767	.7774	1	1	2	3	4	4	5	6	7
6.0	.7782	.7789	.7796	.7803	.7810	.7818	.7825	.7832	.7839	.7846	1	1	2	3	4	4	5	6	6
6.1	.7853	.7860	.7868	.7875	.7882	.7889	.7896	.7903	.7910	.7917	1	1	2	3	4	4	5	6	6
6.2	.7924	.7931	.7938	.7945	.7952	.7959	.7966	.7973	.7980	.7987	1	1	2	3	3	4	5	6	6
6.3	.7993	.8000	.8007	.8014	.8021	.8028	.8035	.8041	.8048	.8055	1	1	2	3	3	4	5	5	6
6.4	.8062	.8069	.8075	.8082	.8089	.8096	.8102	.8109	.8116	.8122	1	1	2	3	3	4	5	5	6
6.5	.8129	.8135	.8142	.8149	.8156	.8162	.8169	.8176	.8182	.8189	1	1	2	3	3	4	5	5	6
6.6	.8195	.8202	.8209	.8215	.8222	.8228	.8235	.8241	.8248	.8254	1	1	2	3	3	4	5	5	6
6.7	.8261	.8267	.8274	.8280	.8287	.8293	.8299	.8306	.8312	.8319	1	1	2	3	3	4	5·	5	6
6.8	.8325	.8331	.8338	.8344	.8351	.8357	.8363	.8370	.8376	.8382	1	1	2	3	3	4	4	5	6
6.9	.8388	.8395	.8401	.8407	.8414	.8420	.8426	.8432	.8439	.8445	1	1	2	2	3	4	4	5	6
7.0	.8451	.8457	.8463	.8470	.8476	.8482	.8488	.8494	.8500	.8506	1	1	2	2	3	4	4	5	6
7.1	.8513	.8519	.8525	.8531	.8537	.8543	.8549	.8555	.8561	.8567	1	1	2	2	3	4	4	5	5
7.2	.8573	.8579	.8585	.8591	.8597	.8603	.8609	.8615	.8621	.8627	1	1	2	2	3	4	4	5	5
7.3	.8633	.8639	.8645	.8651	.8657	.8663	.8669	.8675	.8681	.8686	1	1	2	2	3	4	4	5	5
7.4	.8692	.8698	.8704	.8710	.8716	.8722	.8727	.8733	.8739	.8745	1	1	2	2	3	4	4	5	5
7.5	.8751	.8756	.8762	.8768	.8774	.8779	.8785	.8791	.8797	.8802	1	1	2	2	3	3	4	5	5
7.6	.8808	.8814	.8820	.8825	.8831	.8837	.8842	.8848	.8854	.8859	1	1	2	2	3	3	4	5	5
7.7	.8865	.8871	.8876	.8882	.8887	.8893	.8899	.8904	.8910	.8915	1	1	2	2	3	3	4	4	5
7.8	.8921	.8927	.8932	.8938	.8943	.8949	.8954	.8960	.8965	.8971	1	1	2	2	3	3	4	4	5
7.9	.8976	.8982	.8987	.8993	.8998	.9004	.9009	.9015	.9020	.9025	1	1	2	2	3	3	4	4	5
8.0	.9031	.9036	.9042	.9047	.9053	.9058	.9063	.9069	.9074	.9079	1	1	2	2	3	3	4	4	5
8.1	.9085	.9090	.9096	.9101	.9106	.9112	.9117	.9122	.9128	.9133	1	1	2	2	3	3	4	4	5
8.2	.9138	.9143	.9149	.9154	.9159	.9165	.9170	.9175	.9180	.9186	1	1	2	2	3	3	4	4	5
8.3	.9191	.9196	.9201	.9206	.9212	.9217	.9222	.9227	.9232	.9238	1	1	2	2	3	3	4	4	5
8.4	.9243	.9248	.9253	.9258	.9263	.9269	.9274	.9279	.9284	.9289	1	1	2	2	3	3	4	4	5
8.5	.9294	.9299	.9304	.9309	.9315	.9320	.9325	.9330	.9335	.9340	1	1	2	2	3	3	4	4	5
8.6	.9345	.9350	.9355	.9360	.9365	.9370	.9375	.9380	.9385	.9390	1	1	2	2	3	3	4	4	5
8.7	.9395	.9400	.9405	.9410	.9415	.9420	.9425	.9430	.9435	.9440	0	1	1	2	2	3	3	4	4
8.8	.9445	.9450	.9455	.9460	.9465	.9469	.9474	.9479	.9484	.9489	0	1	1	2	2	3	3	4	4
8.9	.9494	.9499	.9504	.9509	.9513	.9518	.9523	.9528	.9533	.9538	0	1	1	2	2	3	3	4	4
9.0	.9542	.9547	.9552	.9557	.9562	.9566	.9571	.9576	.9581	.9586	0	1	1	2	2	3	3	4	4
9.1	.9590	.9595	.9600	.9605	.9609	.9614	.9619	.9624	.9628	.9633	0	1	1	2	2	3	3	4	4
9.2	.9638	.9643	.9647	.9652	.9657	.9661	.9666	.9671	.9675	.9680	0	1	1	2	2	3	3	4	4
9.3	.9685	.9689	.9694	.9699	.9703	.9708	.9713	.9717	.9722	.9727	0	1	1	2	2	3	3	3	4
9.4	.9631	.9736	.9741	.9745	.9750	.9754	.9759	.9763	.9768	.9773	0	1	1	2	2	3	3	4	4
9.5	.9777	.9782	.9786	.9791	.9795	.9800	.9805	.9809	.9814	.9818	0	1	1	2	2	3	3	4	4
9.6	.9823	.9827	.9832	.9836	.9841	.9845	.9850	.9854	.9859	.9863	0	1	1	2	2	3	3	4	4
9.7	.9868	.9872	.9877	.9881	.9886	.9890	.9894	.9899	.9903	.9908	0	1	1	2	2	3	3	4	4
9.8	.9912	.9917	.9921	.9926	.9930	.9934	.9939	.9943	.9948	.9952	0	1	1	2	2	3	3	4	4
9.9	.9956	.9961	.9965	.9969	.9974	.9978	.9983	.9987	.9991	.9996	0	1	1	2	2	3	3	3	4
	0	1	2	3	4	5	6	7	8	9	1	2	3	4	5	6	7	8	9

VALUES OF THE EXPONENTIAL FUNCTION $y = 10^{x}$

	0	1	2	3	4	5	6	7	8	9	1 2 3	4 5 6	7 8 9
0.00	1.000	1.002	1.005	1.007	1.009	1.012	1.014	1.016	1.019	1.021	0 0 1	1 1 1	2 2 2
0.01	1.023	1.026	1.028	1.030	1.033	1.035	1.038	1.040	1.042	1.045	0 0 1	1 1 1	2 2 2
0.02	1.047	1.050	1.052	1.054	1.057	1.059	1.062	1.064	1.067	1.069	0 0 1	1 1 1	2 2 2
0.03	1.072	1.074	1.074	1.079	1.081	1.084	1.086	1.089	1.091	1.094	0 0 1	1 1 1	2 2 2
0.04	1.096	1.099	1.102	1.104	1.107	1.109	1.112	1.114	1.117	1.119	0 1 1	1 1 2	2 2 2
0.05	1.122	1.125	1.127	1.130	1.132	1.135	1.138	1.140	1.143	1.146	0 1 1	1 1 2	2 2 2
0.06	1.148	1.151	1.153	1.156	1.159	1.161	1.164	1.167	1.169	1.172	0 1 1	1 1 2	2 2 2
0.07	1.175	1.178	1.180	1.183	1.186	1.189	1.191	1.194	1.197	1.199	0 1 1	1 1 2	2 2 2
0.08	1.202	1.205	1.208	1.211	1.213	1.216	1.219	1.222	1.225	1.227	0 1 1	1 1 2	2 2 3
0.09	1.230	1.233	1.236	1.239	1.242	1.245	1.247	1.250	1.253	1.256	0 1 1	1 1 2	2 2 3
0.10	1.259	1.262	1.265	1.268	1.271	1.274	1.276	1.279	1.282	1.285	0 1 1	1 1 2	2 2 3
0.11	1.288	1.291	1.294	1.297	1.300	1.303	1.306	1.309	1.312	1.315	0 1 1	1 2 2	2 2 3
0.12	1.318	1.321	1.324	1.327	1.330	1.334	1.337	1.340	1.343	1.346	0 1 1	1 2 2	2 2 3
0.13	1.349	1.352	1.355	1.358	1.361	1.365	1.368	1.371	1.374	1.377	0 1 1	1 2 2	2 3 3
0.14	1.380	1.384	1.387	1.390	1.393	1.396	1.400	1.403	1.406	1.409	0 1 1	1 2 2	2 3 3
0.15	1.413	1.416	1.419	1.422	1.426	1.429	1.432	1.435	1.439	1.442	0 1 1	1 2 2	2 3 3
0.16	1.445	1.449	1.452	1.455	1.459	1.462	1.466	1.469	1.472	1.476	0 1 1	1 2 2	2 3 3
0.17	1.479	1.483	1.486	1.489	1.493	1.496	1.500	1.503	1.507	1.510	0 1 1	1 2 2	2 3 3
0.18	1.514	1.517	1.521	1.524	1.528	1.531	1.535	1.538	1.542	1.545	0 1 1	1 2 2	2 3 3
0.19	1.549	1.552	1.556	1.560	1.563	1.567	1.570	1.574	1.578	1.581	0 1 1	1 2 2	3 3 3
0.20	1.585	1.589	1.592	1.596	1.600	1.603	1.607	1.611	1.614	1.618	0 1 1	1 2 2	3 3 3
0.21	1.622	1.626	1.629	1.633	1.637	1.641	1.644	1.648	1.652	1.656	0 1 1	2 2 2	3 3 3
0.22	1.660	1.663	1.667	1.671	1.675	1.679	1.683	1.687	1.690	1.694	0 1 1	2 2 2	3 3 3
0.23	1.698	1.702	1.706	1.710	1.714	1.718	1.722	1.726	1.730	1.734	0 1 1	2 2 2	3 3 4
0.24	1.738	1.742	1.746	1.750	1.754	1.758	1.762	1.766	1.770	1.774	0 1 1	2 2 2	3 3 4
0.25	1.778	1.782	1.786	1.791	1.795	1.799	1.803	1.807	1.811	1.816	0 1 1	2 2 2	3 3 4
0.26	1.820	1.824	1.828	1.832	1.837	1.841	1.845	1.849	1.854	1.858	0 1 1	2 2 3	3 3 4
0.27	1.862	1.866	1.871	1.875	1.879	1.884	1.888	1.892	1.897	1.901	0 1 1	2 2 3	3 3 4
0.28	1.905	1.910	1.914	1.919	1.923	1.928	1.932	1.936	1.941	1.945	0 1 1	2 2 3	3 4 4
0.29	1.950	1.954	1.959	1.963	1.968	1.972	1.977	1.982	1.986	1.991	0 1 1	2 2 3	3 4 4
0.30	1.995	2.000	2.004	2.009	2.014	2.018	2.023	2.028	2.032	2.037	0 1 1	2 2 3	3 4 4
0.31	2.042	2.046	2.051	2.056	2.061	2.065	2.070	2.075	2.080	2.084	0 1 1	2 2 3	3 4 4
0.32	2.089	2.094	2.099	2.104	2.109	2.113	2.118	2.123	2.128	2.133	0 1 1	2 2 3.	3 4 4
0.33	2.138	2.143	2.148	2.153	2.158	2.163	2.168	2.173	2.178	2.183	0 1 1	2 2 3	3 4 4
0.34	2.188	2.193	2.198	2.203	2.208	2.213	2.218	2.223	2.228	2.234	1 1 2	2 3 3	4 4 5
0.35	2.239	2.244	2.249	2.254	2.259	2.265	2.270	2.275	2.280	2.286	1 1 2	2 3 3	4 4 5
0.36	2.291	2.296	2.301	2.307	2.312	2.317	2.323	2.328	2.333	2.339	1 1 2	2 3 3	4 4 5
0.37	2.344	2.350	2.355	2.360	2.366	2.371	2.377	2.382	2.388	2.393	1 1 2	2 3 3	4 4 5
0.38	2.399	2.404	2.410	2.415	2.421	2.427	2.432	2.438	2.443	2.449	1 1 2	2 3 3	4 4 5
0.39	2.455	2.460	2.466	2.472	2.477	2.483	2.489	2.495	2.500	2.506	1 1 2	2 3 3	4 5 5
0.40	2.512	2.518	2.524	2.529	2.535	2.541	2.547	2.553	2.559	2.564	1 1 2	2 3 4	4 5 5
0.41	2.570	2.576	2.582	2.588	2.594	2.600	2.606	2.612	2.618	2.624	1 1 2	2 3 4	4 5 5
0.42	2.630	2.636	2.642	2.649	2.655	2.661	2.667	2.673	2.679	2.685	1 1 2	2 3 4	4 5 6
0.43	2.692	2.698	2.704	2.710	2.716	2.723	2.729	2.735	2.742	2.748	1 1 2	3 3 4	4 5 6
0.44	2.754	2.761	2.767	2.773	2.780	2.786	2.793	2.799	2.805	2.812	1 1 2	3 3 4	4 5 6
0.45	2.818	2.825	2.831	2.838	2.844	2.851	2.858	2.864	2.871	2.877	1 1 2	3 3 4	5 5 6
0.46	2.884	2.891	2.897	2.904	2.911	2.917	2.924	2.931	2.938	2.944	1 1 2	3 3 4	5 5 6
0.47	2.951	2.958	2.965	2.972	2.979	2.985	2.992	2.999	3.006	3.013	1 1 2	3 3 4	5 5 6
0.48	3.020	3.027	3.034	3.041	3.048	3.055	3.062	3.069	3.076	3.083	1 1 2	3 4 4	5 6 6
0.49	3.090	3.097	3.105	3.112	3.119	3.126	3.133	3.141	3.148	3.155	1 1 2	3 4 4	5 6 6

VALUES OF THE EXPONENTIAL FUNCTION $y = 10^x$

	0	1	2	3	4	5	6	7	8	9	1	2	3	4	5	6	7	8	9
0.50	3.162	3.170	3.177	3.184	3.192	3.199	3.206	3.214	3.221	3.228	1	2	3	3	4	4	5	6	7
0.51	3.236	3.243	3.251	3.258	3.266	3.273	3.281	3.289	3.296	3.304	1	2	2	3	4	5	5	6	7
0.52	3.311	3.319	3.327	3.334	3.342	3.350	3.357	3.365	3.373	3.381	1	2	2	3	4	5	5	6	7
0.53	3.388	3.396	3.404	3.412	3.420	3.428	3.436	3.443	3.451	3.459	1	2	2	3	4	5	6	6	7
0.54	3.467	3.475	3.483	3.491	3.499	3.508	3.516	3.524	3.532	3.540	1	2	2	3	4	5	6	6	7
0.55	3.548	3.556	3.565	3.573	3.581	3.589	3.597	3.606	3.614	3.622	1	2	2	3	4	5	6	7	7
0.56	3.631	3.639	3.648	3.656	3.664	3.673	3.681	3.690	3.698	3.707	1	2	3	3	4	5	6	7	8
0.57	3.715	3.724	3.733	3.741	3.750	3.758	3.767	3.776	3.784	3.793	1	2	3	3	4	5	6	7	8
0.58	3.802	3.811	3.819	3.828	3.837	3.846	3.855	3.864	3.873	3.882	1	2	3	4	4	5	6	7	8
0.59	3.890	3.899	3.908	3.917	3.926	3.936	3.945	3.954	3.963	3.972	1	2	3	4	5	5	6	7	8
0.60	3.981	3.990	3.999	4.009	4.018	4.027	4.036	4.046	4.055	4.064	1	2	3	4	5	6	6	7	8
0.61	4.074	4.083	4.093	4.102	4.111	4.121	4.130	4.140	4.150	4.159	1	2	3	4	5	6	7	8	9
0.62	4.169	4.178	4.188	4.198	4.207	4.217	4.227	4.236	4.246	4.256	1	2	3	4	5	6	7	8	9
0.63	4.266	4.276	4.285	4.295	4.305	4.315	4.325	4.335	4.345	4.355	1	2	3	4	5	6	7	8	9
0.64	4.365	4.375	4.385	4.395	4.406	4.416	4.426	4.436	4.446	4.457	1	2	3	4	5	6	7	8	9
0.65	4.467	4.477	4.487	4.498	4.508	4.519	5.529	4.539	4.550	4.560	1	2	3	4	5	6	7	8	9
0.66	4.571	4.581	4.592	4.603	4.613	4.624	4.634	4.645	4.656	4.667	1	2	3	4	5	6	7	9	10
0.67	4.677	4.688	4.699	4.710	4.721	4.732	4.742	4.753	4.764	4.775	1	2	3	4	5	7	8	9	10
0.68	4.786	4.797	4.808	4.819	4.831	4.842	4.853	4.864	4.875	4.887	1	2	3	4	6	7	8	9	10
0.69	4.898	4.909	4.920	4.932	4.943	4.955	4.966	4.977	4.989	5.000	1	2	3	5	6	7	8	9	10
0.70	5.012	5.023	5.035	5.047	5.058	5.070	5.082	5.093	5.105	5.117	1	2	4	5	6	7	8	9	11
0.71	5.129	5.140	5.152	5.164	5.176	5.188	5.200	5.212	5.224	5.236	1	2	4	5	6	7	8	10	11
0.72	5.248	5.260	5.272	5.284	5.297	5.309	5.321	5.333	5.346	5.358	1	2	4	5	6	7	9	10	11
0.73	5.370	5.383	5.395	5.408	5.420	5.433	5.445	5.458	5.470	5.483	1	3	4	5	6	8	9	10	11
0.74	5.495	5.508	5.521	5.534	5.546	5.559	5.572	5.585	5.598	5.610	1	3	4	5	6	8	9	10	12
0.75	5.623	5.636	5.649	5.662	5.675	5.689	5.702	5.715	5.728	5.741	1	3	4	5	7	8	9	10	12
0.76	5.754	5.768	5.781	5.794	5.808	5.821	5.834	5.848	5.861	5.875	1	3	4	5	7	8	9	11	12
0.77	5.888	5.902	5.916	5.929	5.943	5.957	5.970	5.984	5.998	6.012	1	3	4	5	7	8	10	11	12
0.78	6.026	6.039	6.053	6.067	6.081	6.095	6.109	6.124	6.138	6.152	1	3	4	6	7	8	10	11	13
0.79	6.166	6.180	6.194	6.209	6.223	6.236	6.252	6.266	6.281	6.295	1	3	4	6	7	9	10	11	13
0.80	6.310	6.324	6.339	6.353	6.368	6.383	6.397	6.412	6.427	6.442	1	3	4	6	7	9	10	12	13
0.81	6.457	6.471	6.486	6.501	6.516	6.531	6.546	6.561	6.577	6.592	2	3	5	6	8	9	11	12	14
0.82	6.607	6.622	6.637	6.653	6.668	6.683	6.699	6.714	6.730	6.745	2	3	5	6	8	9	11	12	14
0.83	6.761	6.776	6.792	6.808	6.823	6.839	6.855	6.871	6.887	6.902	2	3	5	6	8	9	11	13	14
0.84	6.918	6.934	6.950	6.966	6.982	6.998	7.015	7.031	7.047	7.063	2	3	5	6	8	10	11	13	15
0.85	7.079	7.096	7.112	7.129	7.145	7.161	7.178	7.194	7.211	7.228	2	3	5	7	8	10	12	13	15
0.86	7.244	7.261	7.278	7.295	7.311	7.328	7.345	7.362	7.379	7.396	2	3	5	7	8	10	12	13	15
0.87	7.413	7.430	7.447	7.464	7.482	7.499	7.516	7.534	7.551	7.568	2	3	5	7	9	10	12	14	16
0.88	7.586	7.603	7.621	7.638	7.656	7.674	7.691	7.709	7.727	7.745	2	4	5	7	9	11	12	14	16
0.89	7.762	7.780	7.798	7.816	7.834	7.852	7.870	7.889	7.907	7.925	2	4	5	7	9	11	13	14	16
0.90	7.943	7.962	7.980	7.998	8.017	8.035	8.054	8.072	8.091	8.110	2	4	6	7	9	11	13	15	17
0.91	8.128	8.147	8.166	8.185	8.204	8.222	8.241	8.260	8.279	8.299	2	4	6	8	9	11	13	15	17
0.92	8.318	8.337	8.356	8.375	8.395	8.414	8.433	8.453	8.472	8.492	2	4	6	8	10	12	14	15	17
0.93	8.511	8.531	8.551	8.570	8.590	8.610	8.630	8.650	8.670	8.690	2	4	6	8	10	12	14	16	18
0.94	8.710	8.730	8.750	8.770	8.790	8.810	8.831	8.851	8.872	8.892	2	4	6	8	10	12	14	16	18
0.95	8.913	8.933	8.954	8.974	8.995	9.016	9.036	9.057	9.078	9.099	2	4	6	8	10	12	15	17	19
0.96	9.120	9.141	9.162	9.183	9.204	9.226	9.247	9.268	9.290	9.311	2	4	6	8	11	13	15	17	19
0.97	9.333	9.354	9.376	9.397	9.419	9.441	9.462	9.484	9.506	9.528	2	4	7	9	11	13	15	17	20
0.98	9.550	9.572	9.594	9.616	9.638	9.661	9.683	9.705	9.727	9.750	2	4	7	9	11	13	16	18	20
0.99	9.772	9.795	9.817	9.840	9.863	9.886	9.908	9.931	9.954	9.977	2	5	7	9	11	14	16	18	20

AMOUNT OF $1(1+i)^n$

i n	½%	1%	1½%	2%	2½%	3%	3½%	i n
1	1.005 00	1.010 00	1.015 00	1.020 00	1.025 00	1.030 00	1.035 00	1
2	1.010 03	1.020 10	1.030 23	1.040 40	1.050 63	1.060 90	1.071 23	2
3	1.015 08	1.030 30	1.045 68	1.061 21	1.076 89	1.092 73	1.108 72	3
4	1.020 15	1.040 60	1.061 36	1.082 43	1.103 81	1.125 51	1.147 52	4
5	1.025 25	1.051 01	1.077 28	1.104 08	1.131 41	1.159 27	1.187 69	5
6	1.030 38	1.061 52	1.093 44	1.126 16	1.159 69	1.194 05	1.229 26	6
7	1.035 53	1.072 14	1.109 84	1.148 69	1.188 69	1.229 87	1.272 28	7
8	1.040 71	1.082 86	1.126 49	1.171 66	1.218 40	1.266 77	1.316 81	8
9	1.045 91	1.093 69	1.143 39	1.195 09	1.248 86	1.304 77	1.362 90	9
10	1.051 14	1.104 62	1.160 54	1.218 99	1.280 08	1.343 92	1.410 60	10
11	1.056 40	1.115 67	1.179 95	1.243 37	1.312 09	1.384 23	1.459 97	11
12	1.061 68	1.126 83	1.195 62	1.268 24	1.344 89	1.425 76	1.511 07	12
13	1.066 99	1.138 09	1.213 55	1.293 61	1.378 51	1.468 53	1.563 96	13
14	1.072 32	1.149 47	1.231 76	1.319 48	1.412 97	1.512 59	1.618 69	14
15	1.077 68	1.160 97	1.250 23	1.345 87	1.448 30	1.557 97	1.675 35	15
16	1.083 07	1.172 58	1.268 99	1.372 79	1.484 51	1.604 71	1.733 99	16
17	1.088 49	1.184 30	1.288 02	1.400 24	1.521 62	1.652 85	1.794 68	17
18	1.093 93	1.196 15	1.307 34	1.428 25	1.559 66	1.702 43	1.857 49	18
19	1.099 40	1.208 11	1.326 95	1.456 81	1.598 65	1.753 51	1.922 50	19
20	1.104 90	1.220 19	1.346 86	1.485 95	1.638 62	1.806 11	1.989 79	20
21	1.110 42	1.232 39	1.367 06	1.515 67	1.679 58	1.860 29	2.059 43	21
22	1.115 97	1.244 72	1.387 56	1.545 98	1.721 57	1.916 10	2.131 51	22
23	1.121 55	1.257 16	1.408 38	1.576 90	1.764 61	1.973 59	2.206 11	23
24	1.127 16	1.269 73	1.429 50	1.608 44	1.808 73	2.032 79	2.283 33	24
25	1.132 80	1.282 43	1.450 95	1.640 61	1.853 94	2.093 78	2.363 24	25
26	1.138 46	1.295 26	1.472 71	1.673 42	1.900 29	2.156 59	2.445 96	26
27	1.144 15	1.308 21	1.494 80	1.706 89	1.947 80	2.221 29	2.531 57	27
28	1.149 87	1.321 29	1.517 22	1.741 02	1.997 50	2.287 93	2.620 17	28
29	1.155 62	1.334 50	1.539 98	1.775 84	2.046 41	2.356 57	2.711 88	29
30	1.161 40	1.347 85	1.563 08	1.811 36	2.097 57	2.427 26	2.806 79	30
31	1.167 21	1.361 33	1.586 53	1.847 59	2.150 01	2.500 08	2.905 03	31
32	1.173 04	1.374 94	1.610 32	1.884 54	2.203 76	2.575 08	3.006 71	32
33	1.178 91	1.388 69	1.634 48	1.922 23	2.258 85	2.652 34	3.111 94	33
34	1.184 80	1.402 58	1.659 00	1.906 68	2.315 32	2.731 91	3.220 86	34
35	1.190 73	1.416 60	1.683 88	1.999 89	2.373 21	2.813 86	3.333 59	35
36	1.196 68	1.430 77	1.709 14	2.039 89	2.432 54	2.898 28	3.450 27	36
37	1.202 66	1.445 08	1.734 78	2.080 69	2.493 35	2.985 23	3.571 03	37
38	1.208 68	1.459 53	1.760 80	2.122 30	2.555 68	3.074 78	3.696 01	38
39	1.214 72	1.474 12	1.787 21	2.164 74	2.619 57	3.167 03	3.825 37	39
40	1.220 79	1.488 86	1.814 02	2.208 04	2.685 06	3.264 04	3.959 26	40

AMOUNT OF $1(1 + i)^n$

i n	4%	4½%	5%	5½%	6%	7%	8%	i n
1	1.040 00	1.045 00	1.050 00	1.055 00	1.060 00	1.070 00	1.080 00	1
2	1.081 60	1.092 03	1.102 50	1.113 03	1.123 60	1.144 90	1.166 40	2
3	1.124 86	1.141 17	1.157 63	1.174 24	1.191 02	1.225 04	1.259 71	3
4	1.169 86	1.192 52	1.215 51	1.238 82	1.262 48	1.310 80	1.360 49	4
5	1.216 65	1.246 18	1.276 28	1.306 96	1.338 23	1.402 55	1.469 33	5
6	1.265 32	1.302 26	1.340 10	1.378 84	1.418 52	1.500 73	1.586 87	6
7	1.315 93	1.360 86	1.407 10	1.454 68	1.503 63	1.605 78	1.713 82	7
8	1.368 57	1.422 10	1.477 46	1.534 69	1.593 85	1.718 19	1.850 93	8
9	1.423 31	1.486 10	1.551 33	1.619 09	1.689 48	1.838 46	1.999 00	9
10	1.480 24	1.552 97	1.628 89	1.708 14	1.790 85	1.967 15	2.158 93	10
11	1.539 45	1.622 85	1.710 34	1.802 09	1.898 30	2.104 85	2.331 64	11
12	1.601 03	1.695 88	1.795 86	1.901 21	2.012 20	2.252 19	2.518 17	12
13	1.665 07	1.772 20	1.885 65	2.005 77	2.132 93	2.409 85	2.719 62	13
14	1.731 68	1.851 94	1.979 93	2.116 09	2.260 90	2.578 53	2.937 19	14
15	1.800 94	1.935 28	2.078 93	2.232 48	2.396 56	2.759 03	3.172 17	15
16	1.872 98	2.022 37	2.182 87	2.355 26	2.540 35	2.952 16	3.425 94	16
17	1.947 90	2.113 38	2.292 02	2.484 80	2.692 77	3.158 81	3.700 02	17
18	2.025 82	2.208 48	2.406 62	2.621 47	2.854 34	3.379 93	3.996 02	18
19	2.106 85	2.307 86	2.526 95	2.765 65	3.025 60	3.616 53	4.315 70	19
20	2.191 12	2.411 71	2.653 30	2.917 76	3.207 14	3.869 68	4.660 96	20
21	2.278 77	2.520 24	2.785 96	3.078 23	3.399 56	4.140 56	5.033 83	21
22	2.369 92	2.633 65	2.925 26	3.247 54	3.603 54	4.430 40	5.436 54	22
23	2.464 72	2.752 17	3.071 52	3.426 15	3.819 75	4.740 53	5.871 46	23
24	2.563 30	2.876 01	3.225 10	3.614 59	4.048 93	5.072 37	6.341 18	24
25	2.665 84	3.005 43	3.386 35	3.813 39	4.291 87	5.427 43	6.848 48	25
26	2.772 47	3.140 68	3.555 67	4.023 13	4.549 38	5.807 35	7.396 35	26
27	2.883 37	3.282 01	3.733 46	4.244 40	4.822 35	6.213 87	7.988 06	27
28	2.998 70	3.429 70	3.920 13	4.477 84	5.111 69	6.648 84	8.627 11	28
29	3.118 65	3.584 04	4.116 14	4.724 12	5.418 39	7.114 26	9.317 27	29
30	3.243 40	3.745 32	4.321 94	4.983 95	5.743 49	7.612 26	10.062 66	30
31	3.373 13	3.913 86	4.538 04	5.258 07	6.088 10	8.145 11	10.867 67	31
32	3.508 06	4.089 98	4.764 94	5.547 26	6.453 39	8.715 27	11.737 08	32
33	3.648 38	4.274 03	5.003 19	5.852 36	6.840 59	9.325 34	12.676 05	33
34	3.794 32	4.446 36	5.253 35	6.174 24	7.251 03	9.978 11	13.690 13	34
35	3.946 09	4.667 35	5.516 02	6.513 83	7.686 09	10.676 58	14.785 34	35
36	4.130 93	4.877 38	5.791 82	6.872 09	8.147 25	11.423 94	15.968 17	36
37	4.268 09	5.096 86	6.081 41	7.250 05	8.636 09	12.223 62	17.245 63	37
38	4.438 81	5.326 22	6.385 48	7.648 80	9.154 25	13.079 27	18.625 28	38
39	4.616 37	5.565 90	6.704 75	8.069 49	9.703 51	13.994 82	20.115 30	39
40	4.801 02	5.816 36	7.039 99	8.513 31	10.285 72	14.974 46	21.724 52	40

PRESENT VALUE OF I, $\dfrac{1}{(1+i)^n}$

i n	½%	1%	1½%	2%	2½%	3%	3½%	i n
1	0.995 02	0.990 10	0.985 22	0.980 39	0.975 61	0.970 87	0.966 18	1
2	0.990 07	0.980 30	0.970 66	0.961 17	0.951 81	0.942 60	0.933 51	2
3	0.985 15	0.970 59	0.956 32	0.942 32	0.928 60	0.915 14	0.901 94	3
4	0.980 25	0.960 98	0.942 18	0.923 85	0.905 95	0.888 49	0.871 44	4
5	0.975 37	0.951 47	0.928 26	0.905 73	0.883 85	0.862 61	0.841 97	5
6	0.970 52	0.942 05	0.914 54	0.887 97	0.862 30	0.837 48	0.813 50	6
7	0.965 69	0.932 72	0.901 03	0.870 56	0.841 27	0.813 09	0.785 99	7
8	0.960 89	0.923 48	0.887 71	0.853 49	0.820 75	0.789 41	0.759 41	8
9	0.956 10	0.914 34	0.874 59	0.836 76	0.800 73	0.766 42	0.733 73	9
10	0.951 35	0.905 29	0.861 67	0.820 35	0.781 20	0.744 09	0.708 92	10
11	0.946 61	0.896 32	0.848 93	0.804 26	0.762 14	0.722 42	0.684 95	11
12	0.941 91	0.887 45	0.836 39	0.788 49	0.743 56	0.701 38	0.661 78	12
13	0.937 22	0.878 66	0.824 03	0.773 03	0.725 42	0.680 95	0.639 40	13
14	0.932 56	0.869 96	0.811 85	0.757 88	0.707 73	0.661 12	0.617 78	14
15	0.927 92	0.861 35	0.799 85	0.743 01	0.690 47	0.641 86	0.596 89	15
16	0.923 30	0.852 82	0.788 03	0.728 45	0.673 62	0.623 17	0.576 71	16
17	0.918 71	0.844 38	0.776 39	0.714 16	0.657 20	0.605 02	0.557 20	17
18	0.914 14	0.836 02	0.764 91	0.700 16	0.641 17	0.587 39	0.538 36	18
19	0.909 59	0.827 74	0.753 61	0.686 43	0.625 53	0.570 29	0.520 16	19
20	0.905 06	0.819 54	0.742 47	0.672 97	0.610 27	0.553 68	0.502 57	20
21	0.900 56	0.811 43	0.731 50	0.659 78	0.595 39	0.527 55	0.485 57	21
22	0.896 08	0.803 40	0.720 69	0.646 84	0.580 86	0.521 89	0.469 15	22
23	0.891 62	0.795 44	0.710 04	0.634 16	0.566 70	0.506 69	0.453 29	23
24	0.887 19	0.787 57	0.699 54	0.621 72	0.552 88	0.491 93	0.437 96	24
25	0.882 77	0.779 77	0.689 21	0.609 53	0.539 39	0.477 61	0.423 15	25
26	0.878 38	0.772 05	0.679 02	0.597 58	0.526 23	0.463 69	0.408 84	26
27	0.874 01	0.764 40	0.668 99	0.585 86	0.513 40	0.450 19	0.395 01	27
28	0.869 66	0.756 84	0.659 10	0.574 37	0.500 88	0.437 08	0.381 65	28
29	0.865 33	0.749 34	0.649 36	0.563 11	0.488 66	0.424 35	0.368 75	29
30	0.861 03	0.741 92	0.639 76	0.552 07	0.476 74	0.411 99	0.356 28	30
31	0.856 75	0.734 58	0.630 31	0.541 25	0.465 11	0.399 99	0.344 23	31
32	0.852 48	0.727 30	0.620 99	0.530 63	0.453 77	0.388 34	0.332 59	32
33	0.848 24	0.720 10	0.611 82	0.520 23	0.442 70	0.377 03	0.321 34	33
34	0.844 02	0.712 97	0.602 77	0.510 03	0.431 91	0.366 04	0.310 48	34
35	0.839 82	0.705 91	0.593 87	0.500 03	0.421 37	0.355 38	0.299 98	35
36	0.835 64	0.698 92	0.585 09	0.490 22	0.411 09	0.345 03	0.289 83	36
37	0.831 49	0.692 00	0.576 44	0.480 61	0.401 07	0.334 98	0.280 03	37
38	0.827 35	0.685 15	0.567 92	0.471 19	0.391 28	0.325 23	0.270 56	38
39	0.823 23	0.678 37	0.559 53	0.461 95	0.381 74	0.315 75	0.261 41	39
40	0.819 14	0.671 65	0.551 26	0.452 89	0.372 43	0.306 56	0.252 57	40

PRESENT VALUE OF I, $\dfrac{1}{(1+i)^n}$

i n	4%	4½%	5%	5½%	6%	7%	8%	i n
1	0.961 54	0.956 94	0.952 38	0.947 87	0.943 40	0.934 58	0.925 93	1
2	0.924 56	0.915 73	0.907 03	0.898 45	0.890 00	0.873 44	0.857 34	2
3	0.889 00	0.876 30	0.863 84	0.851 61	0.839 62	0.816 30	0.793 83	3
4	0.854 80	0.838 56	0.822 70	0.807 22	0.792 09	0.762 90	0.735 03	4
5	0.821 93	0.802 45	0.783 53	0.765 13	0.747 26	0.712 99	0.680 58	5
6	0.790 31	0.767 90	0.746 22	0.725 25	0.704 96	0.666 34	0.630 17	6
7	0.759 92	0.734 83	0.710 68	0.687 44	0.665 06	0.622 75	0.583 49	7
8	0.730 69	0.703 19	0.676 84	0.651 60	0.627 41	0.582 01	0.540 27	8
9	0.702 59	0.672 90	0.644 61	0.617 63	0.591 90	0.543 93	0.500 25	9
10	0.675 56	0.643 93	0.613 91	0.585 43	0.558 39	0.508 35	0.463 19	10
11	0.649 58	0.616 20	0.584 68	0.554 91	0.526 79	0.475 09	0.428 88	11
12	0.624 60	0.589 66	0.556 84	0.525 98	0.496 97	0.444 01	0.397 11	12
13	0.600 57	0.564 27	0.530 32	0.498 56	0.468 84	0.414 96	0.367 70	13
14	0.577 48	0.539 97	0.505 07	0.472 57	0.442 30	0.387 82	0.340 46	14
15	0.555 26	0.516 72	0.481 02	0.447 93	0.417 27	0.362 45	0.315 24	15
16	0.533 91	0.494 47	0.458 11	0.424 58	0.393 65	0.338 73	0.291 89	16
17	0.513 37	0.473 18	0.436 30	0.402 45	0.371 36	0.316 57	0.270 27	17
18	0.493 63	0.452 80	0.415 52	0.381 47	0.350 34	0.295 86	0.250 25	18
19	0.474 64	0.433 30	0.395 73	0.361 58	0.330 51	0.276 51	0.231 71	19
20	0.456 39	0.414 64	0.376 89	0.342 73	0.311 80	0.258 42	0.214 55	20
21	0.438 83	0.396 79	0.358 94	0.324 86	0.294 16	0.241 51	0.198 66	21
22	0.421 96	0.379 70	0.341 85	0.307 93	0.277 51	0.225 71	0.183 94	22
23	0.405 73	0.363 35	0.325 57	0.291 87	0.261 80	0.210 95	0.170 32	23
24	0.390 12	0.347 70	0.310 07	0.276 66	0.246 98	0.197 15	0.157 70	24
25	0.375 12	0.332 73	0.295 30	0.262 23	0.233 00	0.184 25	0.146 02	25
26	0.360 69	0.318 40	0.281 24	0.248 56	0.219 81	0.172 20	0.135 20	26
27	0.346 82	0.304 69	0.267 85	0.235 60	0.207 37	0.160 93	0.125 19	27
28	0.333 48	0.291 57	0.255 09	0.223 32	0.195 63	0.150 40	0.115 91	28
29	0.320 65	0.279 02	0.242 95	0.211 68	0.184 56	0.140 56	0.107 33	29
30	0.308 32	0.267 00	0.231 38	0.200 64	0.174 11	0.131 37	0.099 38	30
31	0.296 46	0.255 50	0.220 36	0.190 18	0.164 25	0.122 77	0.092 02	31
32	0.285 06	0.244 50	0.209 87	0.180 27	0.154 96	0.114 74	0.085 20	32
33	0.274 09	0.233 97	0.199 87	0.170 87	0.146 19	0.107 23	0.078 89	33
34	0.263 55	0.223 90	0.190 35	0.161 96	0.137 91	0.100 22	0.073 05	34
35	0.253 42	0.214 25	0.181 29	0.153 52	0.130 11	0.093 66	0.067 63	35
36	0.243 67	0.205 03	0.172 66	0.145 52	0.122 74	0.087 54	0.062 62	36
37	0.234 30	0.196 20	0.164 44	0.137 93	0.115 79	0.081 81	0.057 99	37
38	0.225 29	0.187 75	0.156 61	0.130 74	0.109 24	0.076 46	0.053 69	38
39	0.216 62	0.179 67	0.149 15	0.123 92	0.103 06	0.071 46	0.049 71	39
40	0.208 29	0.171 93	0.142 05	0.117 46	0.097 22	0.066 78	0.046 03	40

Amount of an Annuity of 1 $S_{\overline{n}|}i$

n	$\frac{1}{2}\%$	1%	$1\frac{1}{2}\%$	2%	$2\frac{1}{2}\%$	3%
1	1.000 000	1.000 000	1.000 000	1.000 000	1.000 000	1.000 000
2	2.005 000	2.010 000	2.015 000	2.020 000	2.025 000	2.030 000
3	3.015 025	3.030 100	3.045 225	3.060 400	3.075 625	3.090 900
4	4.030 100	4.060 401	4.090 903	4.121 608	4.152 516	4.183 627
5	5.050 251	5.101 005	5.152 267	5.204 040	5.256 329	5.309 136
6	6.075 502	6.152 015	6.229 551	6.308 121	6.387 737	6.468 410
7	7.105 879	7.213 535	7.322 994	7.434 283	7.547 430	7.662 462
8	8.141 409	8.285 671	8.432 839	8.582 969	8.736 116	8.892 336
9	9.182 116	9.368 527	9.559 332	9.754 628	9.954 519	10.159 106
10	10.228 026	10.462 213	10.702 722	10.949 721	11.203 382	11.463 879
11	11.279 167	11.566 835	11.863 262	12.168 715	12.483 466	12.807 796
12	12.335 562	12.682 503	13.041 211	13.412 090	13.795 553	14.192 030
13	13.397 240	13.809 328	14.236 830	14.680 332	15.140 442	15.617 790
14	14.464 226	14.947 421	15.450 382	15.973 938	16.518 953	17.086 324
15	15.536 548	16.096 896	16.682 138	17.293 417	17.931 927	18.598 914
16	16.614 230	17.257 864	17.932 370	18.639 285	19.380 225	20.156 881
17	17.697 301	18.430 443	19.201 355	20.012 071	20.864 730	21.761 588
18	18.785 788	19.614 748	20.489 376	21.412 312	22.386 349	23.414 435
19	19.879 717	20.810 895	21.796 716	22.840 559	23.946 007	25.116 868
20	20.979 115	22.019 004	23.123 667	24.297 370	25.544 658	26.870 374
21	22.084 011	23.239 194	24.470 522	25.783 317	27.183 274	28.676 486
22	23.194 431	24.471 586	25.837 580	27.298 984	28.862 856	30.536 780
23	24.310 403	25.716 302	27.225 144	28.844 963	30.584 427	32.452 884
24	25.431 955	26.973 465	28.633 521	30.421 862	32.349 038	34.426 470
25	26.559 115	28.243 200	30.063 024	32.030 300	34.157 764	36.459 264
26	27.691 911	29.525 632	31.513 969	33.670 906	36.011 708	38.553 042
27	28.830 370	30.820 888	32.986 679	35.344 324	37.912 001	40.709 634
28	29.974 522	32.129 097	34.481 479	37.051 210	39.859 801	42.930 923
29	31.124 395	33.450 388	35.998 701	38.792 235	41.856 296	45.218 850
30	32.280 017	34.784 892	37.538 681	40.568 079	43.902 703	47.575 416
31	33.441 417	36.132 740	39.101 762	42.379 441	46.000 271	50.002 678
32	34.608 624	37.494 068	40.688 288	44.227 030	48.150 278	52.502 759
33	35.781 667	38.869 009	42.298 612	46.111 570	50.354 034	55.077 841
34	36.960 575	40.257 699	43.933 092	48.033 802	52.612 885	57.730 177
35	38.145 378	41.660 276	45.592 088	49.994 478	54.928 207	60.462 082
36	39.336 105	43.076 878	47.275 969	51.994 367	57.301 413	63.275 944
37	40.532 785	44.507 647	48.985 109	54.034 255	59.733 948	66.174 223
38	41.735 449	45.952 724	50.719 885	56.114 940	62.227 297	69.159 449
39	42.944 127	47.412 251	52.480 684	58.237 238	64.782 979	72.234 233
40	44.158 847	48.886 373	54.267 894	60.401 983	67.402 554	75.401 260
41	45.379 642	50.375 237	56.081 912	62.610 023	70.087 617	78.663 298
42	46.606 540	51.878 989	57.923 141	64.862 223	72.839 808	82.023 196
43	47.839 572	53.397 779	59.791 988	67.159 468	75.660 803	85.483 892
44	49.078 770	54.931 757	61.688 868	69.502 657	78.552 323	89.048 409
45	50.324 164	56.481 075	63.614 201	71.892 710	81.516 131	92.719 861
46	51.575 785	58.045 885	65.568 414	74.330 564	84.554 034	96.501 457
47	52.833 664	59.626 344	67.551 940	76.817 176	87.667 885	100.396 501
48	54.097 832	61.222 608	69.565 219	79.353 519	90.859 582	104.408 396
49	55.368 321	62.834 834	71.608 698	81.940 590	94.131 072	108.540 648
50	56.645 163	64.463 182	73.682 828	84.579 401	97.484 349	112.796 867

Amount of an Annuity of 1 $S_{\overline{n}|}i$

n	$3\frac{1}{2}\%$	4%	$4\frac{1}{2}\%$	5%	$5\frac{1}{2}\%$	6%
1	1.000 000	1.000 000	1.000 000	1.000 000	1.000 000	1.000 000
2	2.035 000	2.040 000	2.045 000	2.050 000	2.055 000	2.060 000
3	3.106 225	3.121 600	3.137 025	3.152 500	3.168 025	3.183 600
4	4.214 943	4.246 464	4.278 191	4.301 125	4.342 266	4.374 616
5	5.362 466	5.416 323	5.470 710	5.525 631	5.581 091	5.637 093
6	6.550 152	6.632 975	6.716 892	6.801 913	6.888 051	6.975 319
7	7.779 408	7.898 294	8.019 152	8.142 008	8.266 894	8.393 838
8	9.051 687	9.214 226	9.380 014	9.549 109	9.721 573	9.897 468
9	10.368 496	10.582 795	10.802 114	11.026 564	11.256 260	11.491 316
10	11.731 393	12.006 107	12.288 209	12.577 893	12.875 354	13.180 795
11	13.141 992	13.486 351	13.841 179	14.206 787	14.583 498	14.971 643
12	14.601 962	15.025 805	15.464 032	15.917 127	16.385 591	16.869 941
13	16.113 030	16.626 838	17.159 913	17.712 983	18.286 798	18.882 138
14	17.676 986	18.291 911	18.932 109	19.598 632	20.292 572	21.015 066
15	19.295 681	20.023 588	20.784 054	21.578 564	22.408 664	23.275 970
16	20.971 030	21.824 531	22.719 337	23.657 492	24.641 140	25.672 528
17	22.705 016	23.697 512	24.741 707	25.840 366	26.996 403	28.212 880
18	24.499 691	25.645 413	26.855 084	28.132 385	29.481 205	30.905 653
19	26.357 181	27.671 229	29.063 562	30.539 004	32.102 671	33.759 992
20	28.279 682	29.778 079	31.371 423	33.065 954	34.868 318	36.785 591
21	30.269 471	31.969 202	33.783 137	35.719 252	37.786 076	39.992 727
22	32.328 902	34.247 970	36.303 378	38.505 214	40.864 310	43.392 290
23	34.460 414	36.617 889	38.937 030	41.430 475	44.111 847	46.995 828
24	36.666 528	39.082 604	41.689 196	44.501 999	47.537 998	50.815 577
25	38.949 857	41.645 908	44.565 210	47.727 099	51.152 588	54.864 512
26	41.313 102	44.311 745	47.570 645	51.113 454	54.965 981	59.156 383
27	43.759 060	47.084 214	50.711 324	54.669 126	58.989 109	63.705 766
28	46.290 627	49.967 583	53.993 333	58.402 583	63.233 510	68.528 112
29	48.910 799	52.966 286	57.423 033	62.322 712	67.711 354	73.639 798
30	51.622 677	56.084 938	61.007 070	66.438 848	72.435 478	79.058 186
31	54.429 471	59.328 335	64.752 388	70.760 790	77.419 429	84.801 677
32	57.334 502	62.701 469	68.666 245	75.298 829	82.677 498	90.889 778
33	60.341 210	66.209 527	72.756 226	80.063 771	88.224 760	97.343 165
34	63.453 152	69.857 909	77.030 256	85.066 959	94.077 122	104.183 755
35	66.674 013	73.652 225	81.496 618	90.320 307	100.251 364	111.434 780
36	70.007 603	77.598 314	86.163 966	95.836 323	106.765 189	119.120 867
37	73.457 869	81.702 246	91.041 344	101.628 139	113.637 274	127.268 119
38	77.028 895	85.970 336	96.138 205	107.709 546	120.887 324	135.904 206
39	80.724 906	90.409 150	101.464 424	114.095 023	128.536 127	145.058 458
40	84.550 278	95.025 516	107.030 323	120.799 774	136.605 614	154.761 966
41	88.509 537	99.826 536	112.846 688	127.839 763	145.118 923	165.047 684
42	92.607 371	104.819 598	118.924 789	135.231 751	154.100 464	175.950 545
43	96.848 629	110.012 382	125.276 404	142.993 339	163.575 989	187.507 577
44	101.238 331	115.412 877	131.913 842	151.143 006	173.572 669	199.758 032
45	105.781 673	121.029 392	138.849 965	159.700 156	184.119 165	212.743 514
46	110.484 031	126.870 568	146.098 214	168.685 164	195.245 719	226.508 125
47	115.350 973	132.945 390	153.672 633	178.119 422	206.984 234	241.098 612
48	120.388 257	139.263 206	161.587 902	188.025 393	219.368 367	256.564 529
49	125.601 846	145.833 734	169.859 357	198.426 663	232.433 627	272.958 401
50	130.997 910	152.667 084	178.503 028	209.347 996	246.217 476	290.335 905

Present Value of an Annuity of 1 $a_{\overline{n}|}i$

n	$\frac{1}{2}\%$	1%	$1\frac{1}{2}\%$	2%	$2\frac{1}{2}\%$	3%
1	0.995 025	0.990 099	0.985 222	0.980 392	0.975 610	0.970 874
2	1.985 099	1.970 395	1.955 883	1.941 561	1.927 424	1.913 470
3	2.970 248	2.940 985	2.912 200	2.883 883	2.856 024	2.828 611
4	3.950 496	3.901 966	3.854 385	3.807 729	3.761 974	3.717 098
5	4.925 866	4.853 431	4.782 645	4.713 460	4.645 829	4.579 707
6	5.896 384	5.795 476	5.697 187	5.601 431	5.508 125	5.417 191
7	6.862 074	6.728 195	6.598 214	6.471 991	6.349 391	6.230 283
8	7.822 959	7.651 678	7.485 925	7.325 481	7.170 137	7.019 692
9	8.779 064	8.566 018	8.360 517	8.162 237	7.970 866	7.786 109
10	9.730 412	9.471 305	9.222 185	8.982 585	8.752 064	8.530 203
11	10.677 027	10.367 628	10.071 118	9.786 848	9.514 209	9.252 624
12	11.618 932	11.255 077	10.907 505	10.575 341	10.257 765	9.954 004
13	12.556 151	12.133 740	11.731 532	11.348 374	10.983 185	10.634 955
14	13.488 708	13.003 703	12.543 382	12.106 249	11.690 912	11.296 073
15	14.416 625	13.865 053	13.343 233	12.849 264	12.381 378	11.937 935
16	15.339 925	14.717 874	14.131 264	13.577 709	13.055 003	12.561 102
17	16.258 632	15.562 251	14.907 649	14.291 872	13.712 198	13.166 118
18	17.172 768	16.398 269	15.672 561	14.992 031	14.353 364	13.753 513
19	18.082 356	17.226 009	16.426 168	15.678 462	14.978 891	14.323 799
20	18.987 419	18.045 553	17.168 639	16.351 433	15.589 162	14.877 475
21	19.887 979	18.856 983	17.900 137	17.011 209	16.184 549	15.415 024
22	20.784 059	19.660 379	18.620 824	17.658 048	16.765 413	15.936 917
23	21.675 681	20.455 821	19.330 861	18.292 204	17.332 110	16.443 608
24	22.562 866	21.243 387	20.030 405	18.913 926	17.884 986	16.935 542
25	23.445 638	22.023 156	20.719 611	19.523 456	18.424 376	17.413 148
26	24.324 018	22.795 204	21.398 632	20.121 036	18.950 611	17.876 842
27	25.198 028	23.559 608	22.067 617	20.706 898	19.464 011	18.327 031
28	26.067 689	24.316 443	22.726 717	21.281 272	19.964 889	18.764 108
29	26.933 024	25.065 785	23.376 076	21.844 385	20.453 550	19.188 455
30	27.794 054	25.807 708	24.015 838	22.396 456	20.930 293	19.600 441
31	28.650 800	26.542 285	24.646 146	22.937 702	21.395 407	20.000 428
32	29.503 284	27.269 589	25.267 139	23.468 335	21.849 178	20.388 766
33	30.351 526	27.989 693	25.878 954	23.988 563	22.291 881	20.765 792
34	31.195 548	28.702 666	26.481 728	24.498 592	22.723 786	21.131 837
35	32.035 371	29.408 580	27.075 595	24.998 619	23.145 157	21.487 220
36	32.871 016	30.107 505	27.660 684	25.488 842	23.556 251	21.832 253
37	33.702 504	30.799 510	28.237 127	25.969 453	23.957 318	22.167 235
38	34.529 854	31.484 663	28.805 052	26.440 641	24.348 603	22.492 462
39	35.353 089	32.163 033	29.364 583	26.902 589	24.730 344	22.808 215
40	36.172 228	32.834 686	29.915 845	27.355 479	25.102 775	23.114 772
41	36.987 291	33.499 689	30.458 961	27.799 489	25.466 122	23.412 400
42	37.798 300	34.158 108	30.994 050	28.234 794	25.820 607	23.701 359
43	38.605 274	34.810 008	31.521 232	28.661 562	26.166 446	23.981 902
44	39.408 232	35.455 454	32.040 622	29.079 963	26.503 849	24.254 274
45	40.207 196	36.094 508	32.552 337	29.490 160	26.833 024	24.518 713
46	41.002 185	36.727 236	33.056 490	29.892 314	27.154 170	24.775 449
47	41.793 219	37.353 699	33.553 192	30.286 582	27.467 483	25.024 708
48	42.580 318	37.973 959	34.042 554	30.673 120	27.773 154	25.266 707
49	43.363 500	38.588 079	34.524 683	31.052 078	28.071 369	25.501 657
50	44.142 786	39.196 118	34.999 688	31.423 606	28.362 312	25.729 764

Present Value of an Annuity of 1 $a_{\overline{n}|i}$

n	$3\frac{1}{2}\%$	4%	$4\frac{1}{2}\%$	5%	$5\frac{1}{2}\%$	6%
1	0.966 184	0.961 538	0.956 938	0.952 381	0.947 867	0.943 396
2	1.899 694	1.886 095	1.872 668	1.859 410	1.846 320	1.833 393
3	2.801 637	2.775 091	2.748 964	2.723 248	2.697 933	2.673 012
4	3.673 079	3.629 895	3.587 526	3.545 951	3.505 150	3.465 106
5	4.515 052	4.451 822	4.389 977	4.329 477	4.270 284	4.212 364
6	5.328 553	5.242 137	5.157 872	5.075 692	4.995 530	4.917 324
7	6.114 544	6.002 055	5.892 701	5.786 373	5.682 967	5.582 381
8	6.873 955	6.732 745	6.595 886	6.463 213	6.334 566	6.209 794
9	7.607 687	7.435 332	7.268 791	7.107 822	6.952 195	6.801 692
10	8.316 605	8.110 896	7.912 718	7.721 735	7.537 626	7.360 087
11	9.001 551	8.760 477	8.528 917	8.306 414	8.092 536	7.886 875
12	9.663 334	9.385 074	9.118 581	8.863 252	8.618 518	8.383 844
13	10.302 738	9.985 648	9.682 852	9.393 573	9.117 079	8.852 683
14	10.920 520	10.563 123	10.222 825	9.898 641	9.589 648	9.294 984
15	11.517 411	11.118 387	10.739 546	10.379 658	10.037 581	9.712 249
16	12.094 117	11.652 296	11.234 015	10.837 770	10.462 162	10.105 895
17	12.651 321	12.165 669	11.707 191	11.274 066	10.864 609	10.477 260
18	13.189 682	12.659 297	12.159 992	11.689 587	11.246 074	10.827 603
19	13.709 837	13.133 939	12.593 294	12.085 321	11.607 654	11.158 116
20	14.212 403	13.590 326	13.007 936	12.462 210	11.950 382	11.469 921
21	14.697 974	14.029 160	13.404 724	12.821 153	12.275 244	11.764 077
22	15.167 125	14.451 115	13.784 425	13.163 003	12.583 170	12.041 582
23	15.620 410	14.856 842	14.147 775	13.488 574	12.875 042	12.303 379
24	16.058 368	15.246 963	14.495 478	13.798 642	13.151 699	12.550 358
25	16.481 515	15.622 080	14.828 209	14.093 945	13.413 933	12.783 356
26	16.890 352	15.982 769	15.146 611	14.375 185	13.662 495	13.003 166
27	17.285 365	16.329 586	15.451 303	14.643 034	13.898 100	13.210 534
28	17.667 019	16.663 063	15.742 874	14.898 127	14.121 422	13.406 164
29	18.035 767	16.983 715	16.021 889	15.141 074	14.333 101	13.590 721
30	18.392 045	17.292 033	16.288 889	15.372 451	14.533 745	13.764 831
31	18.736 276	17.588 494	16.544 391	15.592 811	14.723 929	13.929 086
32	19.068 865	17.873 552	16.788 891	15.802 677	14.904 198	14.084 043
33	19.390 208	18.147 646	17.022 862	16.002 549	15.075 069	14.230 230
34	19.700 684	18.411 198	17.246 758	16.192 904	15.237 033	14.368 141
35	20.000 661	18.664 613	17.461 012	16.374 194	15.390 552	14.498 246
36	20.290 494	18.908 282	17.666 041	16.546 852	15.536 068	14.620 987
37	20.570 525	19.142 579	17.862 240	16.711 287	15.673 999	14.736 780
38	20.841 087	19.367 864	18.049 990	16.867 893	15.804 738	14.846 019
39	21.102 500	19.584 485	18.229 656	17.017 041	15.928 662	14.949 075
40	21.355 072	19.792 774	18.401 584	17.159 086	16.046 125	15.046 297
41	21.599 104	19.993 052	18.566 109	17.294 368	16.157 464	15.138 016
42	21.834 883	20.185 627	18.723 550	17.423 208	16.262 999	15.224 543
43	22.062 689	20.370 795	18.874 210	17.545 912	16.363 032	15.306 173
44	22.282 791	20.548 841	19.018 383	17.662 773	16.457 851	15.381 182
45	22.495 450	20.720 040	19.156 347	17.774 070	16.547 726	15.455 832
46	22.700 918	20.884 654	19.288 371	17.880 067	16.632 915	15.524 370
47	22.899 438	21.042 936	19.414 709	17.981 016	16.713 664	15.589 028
48	23.091 244	21.195 131	19.535 607	18.077 158	16.790 203	15.650 027
49	23.276 565	21.341 472	19.651 298	18.168 722	16.862 751	15.707 572
50	23.455 618	21.482 185	19.762 008	18.255 925	16.931 518	15.761 861

Square Roots

n	$\sqrt{n}$	n	$\sqrt{n}$	n	$\sqrt{n}$	n	$\sqrt{n}$	n	$\sqrt{n}$
1	1.0000	41	6.4031	81	9.0000	121	11.0000	161	12.6886
2	1.4142	42	6.4807	82	9.0554	122	11.0454	162	12.7279
3	1.7321	43	6.5574	83	9.1104	123	11.0905	163	12.7671
4	2.0000	44	6.6333	84	9.1652	124	11.1355	164	12.8062
5	2.2361	45	6.7082	85	9.2195	125	11.1803	165	12.8452
6	2.4495	46	6.7823	86	9.2736	126	11.2250	166	12.8841
7	2.6458	47	6.8557	87	9.3274	127	11.2694	167	12.9228
8	2.8284	48	6.9282	88	9.3808	128	11.3137	168	12.9615
9	3.0000	49	7.0000	89	9.4340	129	11.3578	169	13.0000
10	3.1623	50	7.0711	90	9.4868	130	11.4018	170	13.0384
11	3.3166	51	7.1414	91	9.5394	131	11.4455	171	13.0767
12	3.4641	52	7.2111	92	9.5917	132	11.4891	172	13.1149
13	3.6056	53	7.2801	93	9.6437	133	11.5326	173	13.1529
14	3.7417	54	7.3485	94	9.6954	134	11.5758	174	13.1909
15	3.8730	55	7.4162	95	9.7468	135	11.6190	175	13.2288
16	4.0000	56	7.4833	96	9.7980	136	11.6619	176	13.2665
17	4.1231	57	7.5498	97	9.8489	137	11.7047	177	13.3041
18	4.2426	58	7.6158	98	9.8995	138	11.7473	178	13.3417
19	4.3589	59	7.6812	99	9.9499	139	11.7898	179	13.3791
20	4.4721	60	7.7460	100	10.0000	140	11.8322	180	13.4164
21	4.5826	61	7.8103	101	10.0499	141	11.8743	181	13.4536
22	4.6904	62	7.8740	102	10.0995	142	11.9164	182	13.4907
23	4.7958	63	7.9373	103	10.1489	143	11.9583	183	13.5277
24	4.8990	64	8.0000	104	10.1980	144	12.0000	184	13.5647
25	5.0000	65	8.0623	105	10.2470	145	12.0416	185	13.6015
26	5.0990	66	8.1240	106	10.2956	146	12.0830	186	13.6382
27	5.1962	67	8.1854	107	10.3441	147	12.1244	187	13.6748
28	5.2915	68	8.2462	108	10.3923	148	12.1655	188	13.7113
29	5.3852	69	8.3066	109	10.4403	149	12.2066	189	13.7477
30	5.4772	70	8.3666	110	10.4881	150	12.2474	190	13.7840
31	5.5678	71	8.4262	111	10.5357	151	12.2882	191	13.8203
32	5.6569	72	8.4853	112	10.5830	152	12.3288	192	13.8564
33	5.7446	73	8.5440	113	10.6301	153	12.3693	193	13.8924
34	5.8310	74	8.6023	114	10.6771	154	12.4097	194	13.9284
35	5.9161	75	8.6603	115	10.7238	155	12.4499	195	13.9642
36	6.0000	76	8.7178	116	10.7703	156	12.4900	196	14.0000
37	6.0828	77	8.7750	117	10.8167	157	12.5300	197	14.0357
38	6.1644	78	8.8318	118	10.8628	158	12.5698	198	14.0712
39	6.2450	79	8.8882	119	10.9087	159	12.6095	199	14.1067
40	6.3246	80	8.9443	120	10.9545	160	12.6491	200	14.1421

The Number of Each Day of the Year

DAY OF MONTH	JAN	FEB	MAR	APR	MAY	JUN	JUL	AUG	SEP	OCT	NOV	DEC	DAY OF MONTH
1	1	32	60	91	121	152	182	213	244	274	305	335	1
2	2	33	61	92	122	153	183	214	245	275	306	336	2
3	3	34	62	93	123	154	184	215	246	276	307	337	3
4	4	35	63	94	124	155	185	216	247	277	308	338	4
5	5	36	64	95	125	156	186	217	248	278	309	339	5
6	6	37	65	96	126	157	187	218	249	279	310	340	6
7	7	38	66	97	127	158	188	219	250	280	311	341	7
8	8	39	67	98	128	159	189	220	251	281	312	342	8
9	9	40	68	99	129	160	190	221	252	282	313	343	9
10	10	41	69	100	130	161	191	222	253	283	314	344	10
11	11	42	70	101	131	162	192	223	254	284	315	345	11
12	12	43	71	102	132	163	193	224	255	285	316	346	12
13	13	44	72	103	133	164	194	225	256	286	317	347	13
14	14	45	73	104	134	165	195	226	257	287	318	348	14
15	15	46	74	105	135	166	196	227	258	288	319	349	15
16	16	47	75	106	136	167	197	228	259	289	320	350	16
17	17	48	76	107	137	168	198	229	260	290	321	351	17
18	18	49	77	108	138	169	199	230	261	291	322	352	18
19	19	50	78	109	139	170	200	231	262	292	323	353	19
20	20	51	79	110	140	171	201	232	263	293	324	354	20
21	21	52	80	111	141	172	202	233	264	294	325	355	21
22	22	53	81	112	142	173	203	234	265	295	326	356	22
23	23	54	82	113	143	174	204	235	266	296	327	357	23
24	24	55	83	114	144	175	205	236	267	297	328	358	24
25	25	56	84	115	145	176	206	237	268	298	329	359	25
26	26	57	85	116	146	177	207	238	269	299	330	360	26
27	27	58	86	117	147	178	208	239	270	300	331	361	27
28	28	59	87	118	148	179	209	240	271	301	332	362	28
29	29		88	119	149	180	210	241	272	302	333	363	29
30	30		89	120	150	181	211	242	273	303	334	364	30
31	31		90		151		212	243		304		365	31

INDEX